Deconstructing Jack:

The Secret History of the Whitechapel Murders

Simon Daryl Wood

This book is for Susan, Miranda, Laura, Emma, Debra and Rik,

with love from the crazy old guy.

I also respectfully dedicate this book to

Aaron Kosminski

Montague John Druitt

Michael Ostrog

and everyone else

who has ever been accused

of being Jack the Ripper.

Requiescat in pace

CONTENTS

Introduction	1
Cloak and Truncheon	10
Bait and Switch	42
Grand Trunk Depot	53
Questions In The House	70
Passage To India	101
A Surfeit Of Suspects	106
Various Tall Tales	128
Notes In The Margin	174
Pandora's Box	185
Crimson Crimes	214
The Incident at Marble Arch	234
The Black Japanned Box	270
Chronicles Of Crime	275
The Wave of Terror	284
Secret Ceremony	292
The Malta Story	307
Blackmail	322
The Mad Snob	334
Rings On Her Fingers	374
Murder, Mystery and Madness	385
The Writing On The Wall	422
The Mysterious Inspector Soyle	435
Tales From The Vienna Woods	461
Jack And The Grapestalk	473
The Woman From Rotherhithe	493
Quatuor Coronati	513
The Woman Who Never Was	539
The Man Who Never Was	551
Index	

There is not an officer in the metropolitan force . . . who dares place on record a faithful account of the service to which he belongs. Consequently, the public are dependent for their information upon incomplete intelligence in the daily press, supplemented by casual magazine articles and spasmodic "revelations", all more or less garnished with fiction.

Charles Tempest Clarkson and J. Hall Richardson,

"Police!" 1889

"I wish to state emphatically that in recent years the Police have succeeded only by straining the law, or, in plain English, by doing utterly unlawful things . . ."

Metropolitan Police memo, Robert Anderson,

13th December 1898

HO45/10254/X36450, sub. 77.

We shall not cease from exploration. And the end of all our exploring will be to arrive where we started and know the place for the first time.

T. S. Eliot [1888 -1965]

ACKNOWLEDGMENTS

Writing is a solitary pursuit which is impossible to accomplish without lots of help and support.

Grateful thanks go to my wife, Susan—who has learned more about the Whitechapel murders than she ever imagined possible—for her love, encouragement and expert criticism.

I am also grateful to those pioneering authors who have trodden this path before, many of whom have shed a clear light on the subject. My thanks to the legendary Robin Odell, whose ear I bent until it almost fell off. To Don Rumbelow, Richard Whittington-Egan and the late Tom Cullen, all of whom gave me encouragement and unfailing support at a time when I truly was a stranger in a strange land. To Paul Emmett, a giant intellect and Professor of English at the University of Wisconsin, and Bill Veeder, Professor Emeritus at the Department of English, University of Chicago—thank you both for your insights into Millers Court and the mysterious cult of Dionysus. To writer, researcher and historian Stephen Butt who generously fact-checked my chapter on spiritualist Robert James Lees. To authors Bernard Porter, E. Thomas Wood and Owen McGee who over the years have been so generous with their specialist knowledge.

My thanks to the men and women I cannot mention by name but know who they are, for their insights into the political workings of the

Victorian secret world.

Others who have helped in my long search are Politiførstebetjent Glenryck Sardin of the "Politiets Sikkerhetstjeneste," Norway's MI5, photographer Alan Carter who opened my eyes to the beauty surrounding us, the Royal Archives in Madrid, the irrepressible Trevor Marriott, author and ex-Murder Squad detective who valiantly attempted to get the Special Branch ledgers into the public domain, and Sarah and Andrew Minney, two of the most indefatigable researchers in the business. My thanks are also due to Stephen Ryder and Howard Brown, whose respective websites, Casebook and JtRForums, are cornucopias of information, as is Adam Wood's e-magazine "Ripperologist" which has kindly published a few of my articles and one of whose editors, the long-suffering Eduardo Zinna, will always have a special place in my heart—*Asante, rafiki yangu*. To Wolf Vanderlinden for sharing his ground-breaking research on Inspector Walter Andrews' excursion to Canada. To Peter Kazmierczak and Michael Stead at Bournemouth Library for their generous help with ex-Chief Inspector Abberline. To Keith Chapman, now riding the range in New Zealand. To Alex Bartlett and his team of volunteers at the Germantown Historical Society for their help in identifying Bradford Mills. Josephine and Joe Chetcuti in San Francisco deserve a special mention, as does the very talented Tom Wescott in Oklahoma, and "Rippercast" host Jonathan Menges in Kansas [I'm still waiting]. Last but by no means least and impossible to ignore is the larger-than-life Tranter-packing writer and bon viveur A.P. Wolf who always asks the very best awkward questions.

My thanks to each and every one of you. You have helped make learning a joy and the world a better-informed place.

Any mistakes are purely of my own making.

INTRODUCTION

It was in the mid-1970s that I first took an interest in serial killing.

Stephen Knight's book *Jack the Ripper: The Final Solution* was being serialized in the London *Evening News,* and I read each day's installment with mounting incredulity. The story featured such a preposterous premise that, after buying the book, I decided to check out the facts for myself.

It took me less than three weeks to discover that Stephen Knight's compelling tale of a ruthless Masonic conspiracy to thwart a blackmail plot against Queen Victoria's grandson Prince Albert Victor—who secretly married a Catholic girl with whom he had fathered a child—was elaborate balderdash.

As no newspapers were interested in the truth, I duly sent the fruits of my research to Stephen Knight's agent, receiving in reply a polite letter of thanks, but, apart from a note in a subsequent edition of Knight's book to the effect that new information had come to light which warranted further investigation, that was an end to the matter. Facts were obviously an encumbrance to commercial success, for Knight's story involving Freemasons in high places and a royal surgeon prowling the East End of London at night in a horse-drawn carriage pressed all the right melodramatic buttons in the public imagination, making the book a runaway best-seller.

Through an old and dear friend, I met Donald Rumbelow, author of *The Complete Jack the Ripper*. Don generously offered his guidance during my research and later introduced me to such Ripper luminaries as Richard Whittington-Egan, Tom Cullen, Paul Begg, Martin Fido and Keith Skinner. A few years later, at a meeting of the Crime Writers' Association, Don introduced me to Stephen Knight, who was unrepentantly charming. It was not until years after his untimely death that I learned the extent of his spleen—

". . . I have been unable to do any more about the work of Mr. Simon D. Wood, other than throwing some poisoned meat to his dog and shooting his mother."

And—

"However, while taking this opportunity of thanking you for a delightful meeting, I am enclosing the only copy of Mr. Wood's article that I have. I point out that it is the only one in case, thinking it a duplicate, you either destroy it in disgust or frame it as a fine example of how to out-nasty a nasty."[1]

At around this time I firmly believed that if all us Ripperologists [I'm not absolutely certain if this particularly ugly descriptor was then in circulation][2] could spend a long weekend sitting around a conference table we could, based on an objective analysis of the available evidence, finally put a name to Jack the Ripper. Thirty-something years later I look back at what I can only describe as my naivety.

It has frequently been asserted that the mystery cannot be solved, that Jack the Ripper will never be identified. If true, then this has always been true, which begs the question of what has motivated people to buck the odds and try to fill the void of our unknowing. Today we are awash with theories. Most are ill-conceived sham and nonsense, whilst others with faint hints of merit require the glue and string of tortuous argument to stop them falling to pieces.

Over the years our imaginations have known no bounds. Amongst

---

[1]   From letters written by Stephen Knight, now in a private collection.

[2]   In an article entitled "A Life in Ripperology" the late Colin Wilson claimed invention of the term, first using it in a review for *Books and Bookmen*.

many other incarnations Jack has been a knuckle-dragging man-monster, a top-hatted surgeon, an insane Polish Jew, an effete London barrister, an American quack, a Russian secret agent and an impressionist painter. Luminaries such as Doctor Barnardo and Lewis Carroll have come under scrutiny. Jack has been a Liverpool cotton merchant considerate enough to leave behind a diary and the initials of his victims scratched inside a pocket watch. He has been a Jewish ritual slaughterman and a Malay seaman. She has been an East End abortionist midwife; also a Russian seamstress named Olga Tchkersoff. The list goes on . . . and on . . . and on.

Not one of these suspects has proved satisfactory. But this is not to suggest that a definitive solution would be welcome, for a vast majority of Ripperologists, whether consciously or unconsciously, want the mystery to remain unsolved. They don't want the delicious *frisson* of the hunt to end, which is why others with merely a passing interest in the subject regard it as nothing more than late Victorian history turned into an elaborate parlour game of Pin the Tail on the Ripper.

This is not to disparage the work of many dedicated researchers. As a result of their labours we are privy to all manner of police reports and Home Office files. Private letters have been unearthed and press archives scoured for contemporary references. We have maps, photographs and plans from the period. Families of suspects, policemen and witnesses have been traced through census records and birth, marriage and death registers. We have learned such pettifogging details as the speed limit for hansom cabs, the cost of pawn tickets and the dimensions of a Victorian police truncheon. In the true spirit of Shakespeare's Autolycus, more unconsidered trifles have been snapped-up than Charles Dickens could have ever hoped to cram into his Dictionary of London. But as individually fascinating as all these facts and details undoubtedly are, collectively they have not contributed one jot to our understanding. The core mystery remains just as impenetrable. To employ the essence of F.E. Smith's famous courtroom exchange, today we are much better informed about the 1888 Whitechapel murders but none the wiser.

Talk to any author, film-maker, lawyer, historian, FBI profiler, policeman, journalist, documentarian, criminologist, professor, sociologist, psychologist or one of the many authors who have written a book on the subject, and they will swear to you, hand upon heart, that Jack the Ripper was an actual but unknown person who—possessed of split-second timing, lightning-fast surgical skills, a mordant sense of humour and the Devil's own luck—murdered five East End prostitutes and outwitted the combined resources of two police forces to become the world's prototypical serial killer. Some also argue that with Jack's invention of serial-killing the police were dealing with a new kind of killer who was so far ahead of the game, so far beyond late Victorian period jurisprudence or criminological understanding that he was able to confuse and confound the top echelons of Scotland Yard to such an extent that for the next three decades they were unable to reach a consensus as to his identity.

Ten years ago I might have broadly agreed, but this was at a time before I came to realise that history had fallen for an elaborate hoax.

Many people ask if Jack the Ripper will ever be identified. The answer to this question is an emphatic "No", simply because he did not exist. There was no such person. The Whitechapel murders were about something very different.

The Oxford English Dictionary defines an urban legend as "an entertaining story or piece of information of uncertain origin that is circulated as though true."

Jack the Ripper is the ultimate urban legend. He has much in common with the Bogeyman, that formless creature of the imagination who, on nights when the wind howls, rattling the trees and making the house creak, still has the power to make the all-knowing children of the internet age shiver with fear in the belief that he is hiding in the wardrobe or lurking under the bed. And the reason they fear the Bogeyman is because we feared him when we were children, as did our forebears in the late nineteenth century.

East London Advertiser, 6th October 1888—

"So inexplicable and ghastly are the circumstances surrounding the

4

crimes that people are affected by them in the same way as children are by the recital of a weird and terrible story of the supernatural. It is so impossible to account, on any ordinary hypothesis, for these revolting acts of blood that the mind turns as it were instinctively to some theory of occult force, and the myths of the Dark Ages rise before the imagination. Ghouls, vampires, bloodsuckers, and all the ghastly array of fables which have been accumulated throughout the course of centuries take form, and seize hold of the excited fancy. Yet the most morbid imagination can conceive nothing worse than this terrible reality; for what can be more appalling than the thought that there is a being in human shape stealthily moving about a great city, burning with the thirst for human blood, and endowed with such diabolical astuteness, as to enable him to gratify his fiendish lust with absolute impunity?"

Even the usually starchy *Daily Telegraph* joined in, writing of "beings who look like men, but are rather demons, vampires, of whom society has the right to be quickly rid, without too much attention to the theories of mental experts."

Jack the Ripper was being promoted as the Bogeyman incarnate, and it is doubtful that the handful of police-named suspects—a simple-minded Polish Jew, an effete barrister/schoolteacher, a poisoner, or a man with an iron-clad alibi—could have ever fitted the bill and so successfully generated and stage-managed such hype and hysteria.

Today, amidst heated differences of opinion regarding his identity, otherwise rational people insist on believing in the fundamental existence of someone known as Jack the Ripper—witness the thousands of people from around the world who take guided pilgrimages through the streets of London's East End to catch a glimpse of his fast-disappearing murder sites whilst discussing where he might have lived, if he was married, a gentile or a Jew, and whether he had a day job.

Even the FBI joined in the speculation. In 1988 one of its Special Agents compiled an eight-page profile of the Whitechapel murderer[3] for

---

3   John E. Douglas's "criminal investigative analysis" of the Whitechapel murders also included a psychological profile of the "Unsub; aka Jack the Ripper."

a ponderous Jack the Ripper TV Special in which a panel of legal and criminological experts hosted by actor Peter Ustinov discussed the eligibility of five "suspects" who appear to have been plucked at random from a party hat.[4] The panel duly deliberated, finally concluding on the basis of absolutely no evidence whatsoever against any of the suspects that Aaron Kosminski, a Polish Jew committed to a lunatic asylum in 1891, was the best fit for Jack the Ripper.

"Good night, Ladies and Gentlemen," Peter Ustinov intoned gravely before walking off into swirls of dry ice, "and, oh, sleep well."

Centenary year was a busy time for the burgeoning Ripper industry. BBC2's *Timewatch* series ran "Shadow of the Ripper," an examination by Christopher Frayling into how the Whitechapel murders became legend and why we continue to be interested; ITV visited The Black Museum, and Michael Caine starred as a drunken Inspector Abberline in a big budget TV mini-series which defied logic by collaring Physician-in-Ordinary to Queen Victoria, Sir William Withey Gull.

Jack has been the subject of books, plays, movies, TV documentaries, operas, musicals, jigsaw puzzles, board games and comics. People cannot get enough of him, and for many he has developed into something of an obsession. So much so that, whenever in the past I have suggested Jack didn't exist and was an invention, the reaction is always the same mixture of indignant outrage, scorn and accusations of my being a conspiracy theorist who should stick with the facts.

I am not a hard or even soft-boiled conspiracy theorist. Their hall of mirrors universe of alternative history holds no appeal. But, having said that, I am realistic enough to grasp the fact that world history is littered with conspiracies, large and small, of which the most successful have undoubtedly been those about which we know nothing and suspect even less.

So, was Jack the Ripper and his five murdered Whitechapel[5] prostitutes a conspiracy—defined as *a group of people entering into a secret*

---

[4]   "The Secret Identity of Jack the Ripper," 1988, available on DVD.

[5]   In order, the murders took place in Bethnal Green, Spitalfields, Whitechapel, the City of London and Spitalfields.

agreement to achieve an illicit or harmful objective?

This might be pitching things too high, for it is difficult to imagine a conclave of beetle-browed conspirators sitting around a table plotting the Whitechapel murders from beginning to end in the desultory way they played out. But there was certainly a high-level cover-up involved, for there is much to suggest that, rather than a linear mystery, the Whitechapel murders were a series of discrete events, with a quasi-supernatural Jack the Ripper employed as an umbrella device to explain things away whilst whipping up a diversionary scare.

Whatever the prize—and there had to be a prize to make the exercise worth the candle—it is clear it could not have been won by wholly clandestine means. Whatever was going on during the autumn of 1888 required the diversion of a non-existent Jack the Ripper, which explains the epic failure of two police forces to catch him, the secrecy surrounding the murders and the fog of official obscurantism generated throughout the following years.

It also explains the most important aspect of the mystery: the matter of Jack the Ripper's identity; for if he was a myth, an official device upon which to—say—conduct extralegal activities, then once he had served his purpose he could never be identified. He had to vanish as mysteriously as he had first appeared.

Such a scenario provides a credible reason for the Whitechapel murders remaining a mystery. But it also poses the biggest question of all: what was the reason for Jack's creation? What exactly was the prize?

Could the perceived failure of the police to catch Jack the Ripper have been a demonstration of the consequences of the operational disputes current at Scotland Yard[6] remaining unresolved, a situation which ultimately led to the resignation of Sir Charles Warren,

---

[6]   I have used this name throughout for convenience. In 1888 Metropolitan Police headquarters occupied Nos. 3, 4, 5, 21 and 22 Whitehall Place, Nos. 8 and 9 Great Scotland Yard, Nos. 1, 2 and 3 Palace Place, plus various stables and outbuildings as well as a freestanding structure in the centre of the Yard which over the years held stores, the Public Carriage Office and the CID offices. In 1890 Metropolitan Police headquarters were moved into New Scotland Yard and, later, also Scotland House, the iconic Norman Shaw-designed buildings on Victoria Embankment.

Commissioner of the Metropolitan Police?

This is not a wholly new idea. In a September 1888 interview in the *Star* newspaper, US private detective William Pinkerton said of the Metropolitan Police, "I am greatly surprised at the futility of their efforts in connection with these murders. However, it is an ill wind that blows no good, and if the British public is at all like the American, the very failures in these cases will be the means of bringing about an undeniably necessary reorganisation of police methods in London."

Was there a political agenda behind the Whitechapel murders?

Could the prize have been connected with the Special Commission, a judicial inquiry at the Royal Courts of Justice into criminal allegations by *The Times* against Charles Stewart Parnell and the Irish Home Rule Party; an inquiry which led to a shooting, two suspected London murders, an alleged suicide in Madrid, illegal Scotland Yard activity in North America and the sudden resignation of a second Metropolitan Police Commissioner, James Monro?

There are other possible scenarios.

Following the death of coroner Wynne Baxter[7] the *Evening News*[8] stated that he attributed the Whitechapel murders to the Fenians. Apparently, "Dr. Baxter advanced his theory to the Home Office, who told him he was not alone in his opinion."

In 1956 author Douglas Gordon Browne, grandson of Charles Dickens' most famous illustrator "Phiz", published "The Rise of Scotland Yard: A History of the Metropolitan Police," in which he wrote—"A third head of the C.I.D., Sir Melville Macnaghten, appears to identify the Ripper with the leader of a plot to assassinate Mr. [Arthur] Balfour [Chief Secretary for Ireland] at the Irish Office" [author's brackets].

The Whitechapel murders did not take place on an otherwise empty stage. They are far more complex and intriguing than a century-and-a-quarter of over-exploited cliches involving freemasons, gaslight, fog, drabs and a top-hatted West End doctor or a local knuckle-dragging

---

[7] Coroner Wynne Edwin Baxter conducted inquests on three of the alleged five Ripper victims.

[8] 1st October 1920

lunatic—Gentile or Jew—running split-second rings around two hopelessly outmatched but nevertheless tenacious police forces sporting white hats.

As you will hopefully come to appreciate by the time you finish this book, for a wide variety of reasons everything we think we know about Jack the Ripper is just so much moonshine.

Dr. Alex Murray, Senior Lecturer at Exeter University[9]—

"Jack the Ripper never existed. The facts in the case of Jack the Ripper are contained within a certain moment in time and space: Whitechapel, East London in Autumn 1888. Everything outside of this co-ordinate is conjecture . . . The only thing to be revealed in the investigation of Jack the Ripper is ourselves . . ."

Heretical ideas which challenge over a century of belief and opinion tend to bring people up with a start. Is it too late for Jack to be set free from the darkest corners of our collective psyche? Can Ripperdom ever bring itself to shrug off old dogma, discard cherished beliefs and smile ruefully at having fallen for a three-card trick? Or will a challenge to orthodoxy be peremptorily dismissed as revisionist nonsense, allowing the game of Pin the Tail on the Ripper to continue unabated?

There was only one way to find out.

Simon Daryl Wood
Claremont, California
January 2016

---

[9]   "Jack the Ripper, "The Dialectic of Enlightenment and the Search for Spiritual Deliverance in White Chappell, Scarlet Tracings" Critical Survey 16.1, pp. 52-66.

1. CLOAK AND TRUNCHEON

Jack the Ripper being an invention is not a new idea.
Burlington Hawkeye [Iowa], 28th April 1891—

"There is probably not one person in ten thousand who reads of 'Jack the Ripper' knows the true origin of the term. Mr. [Arthur] Brisbane, who was a London journalist at the time of some of the atrocious Whitechapel murders, enlightened the reporter today.

"The story of the title, said he, and all of the Ripper literature is a curious tale of an Englishman's enterprise and has never been told. When the Whitechapel murders began the Central News and the Press Association were two rival London companies, bitterly fighting each other in the work of supplying news to English publications.

"The Press Association was much the older, more powerful and more widely known, until one fine morning a postal card came to the Central News written in blood, telling in free language what the Whitechapel fiend's future plans of slaughter were, and signed 'Jack the Ripper.' That afternoon the famous name 'Jack the Ripper' was in every one's mouth. The big Press Association was compelled humbly to get the 'Jack the Ripper' postal cards as fast as they came in from their young rival and to advertise everywhere the name of the Central News. The Central News advertisement was complete when the police authorities reproduced the Ripper postal cards, Central News address and all, on a gigantic scale and plastered the walls of all England with them. Somehow it did not seem strange to the English public that an ignorant Whitechapel murderer should write his communication to a news agency which he could not possibly know anything about, instead of to the Pinkun[10], or to whatever was his favorite publication.

"It was observed by some of the friends of Mr. John Moore, manager of the Central News, that 'Jack the Ripper's' postal cards did not seem to surprise him as they might have done, but only gratified him, and investigation revealed the interesting fact that 'Jack the Ripper,' though illiterate, wrote a hand marvellously like that of the refined Mr. Moore.

"Mr. Moore was no criminal, but he was 'Jack the Ripper'. This fact was not mentioned in London, as public feeling would not have endured being imposed upon to that extent nor have accepted business enterprise as an excuse."

A number of high-ranking police officers of the period later agreed.

Sir Robert Anderson, in his 1910 reminiscences, thought Jack "the creation of an enterprising London journalist . . . I am almost tempted to disclose the identity of . . . the pressman who wrote the letter . . .but no public benefit would result . . ."

In 1913 ex-Chief Inspector Littlechild had no such qualms. In a private letter to journalist George R. Sims he wrote, "With regard to the term 'Jack the Ripper' it was generally believed at the Yard that Tom Bullen of the Central News was the originator, but it is probable Moore, who was his chief, was the inventor."

In his 1914 memoirs Sir Melville Leslie Macnaghten felt that he could "discern the stained forefinger of the journalist—indeed, a year later, I had shrewd suspicions as to the actual author!"

If, as all this suggests, "Jack" was solely a press invention, then it succeeded beyond the wildest imaginings of its accountants and circulation managers, for an apparently gullible Metropolitan Police fell for the ruse and ordered Jack the Ripper's correspondence to be reproduced on posters for display outside police stations across London.

---

[10]   The *Financial Times, The Globe* and the *Sporting Times* were printed on pink paper.

Yet the Metropolitan Police was far from gullible. In the fifty nine years since its inception it had matured into a sophisticated, well-oiled law-and-order machine which, with no municipal oversight, was accountable only to its political masters of the day.[11]

Late-Victorian Scotland Yard was immensely powerful, a nascent amalgam of all future discrete police and security agencies. Aside from its day-to-day regulatory tasks, public order duties and detective work, it also operated from under its single metaphorical roof on a clandestine political level—intelligence-gathering, infiltrating anarchists groups, policing political dissent and countering the well-funded activities of extreme Irish nationalist organisations based in America—and in the process demarcation lines often became blurred, making it impossible to tell if the amiable Inspector Bucket was wearing his CID or Special Branch/Secret Service hat.

Professor Bernard Porter neatly summed up Britain's security apparatus during the 1880s[12]—

"We know when its distinctive agencies were founded, why, and by whom. What we cannot be sure about is exactly what they did: the methods they employed, how effective they were, and the extent to which they kept to 'the rules' . . . That is the nature of the animal in this cloak-and-truncheon world."

The police exchanged the usual niceties with the press, but there was also an undercurrent of professional friction, even outright competition, as reporters tried to outsmart the CID in solving crimes.

In a 19th September 1888 memo John Satterfield "Jack" Sandars, private secretary to Home Secretary Henry Matthews, and also the Home Office's liaison with the Irish Office, wrote that Sir Charles Warren, Commissioner of the Metropolitan Police, had remarked to him

---

[11]   On 22nd February 1889 James Rowland MP [Liberal, Finsbury East] introduced a Bill to transfer the powers, duties and responsibilities of the Metropolitan Police to the newly-formed London County Council. The Bill did not succeed. Until July 2000 the Metropolitan Police remained the only police force in England to be controlled directly by national government via the Home Office.

[12]   *Origins of the Vigilant State,* Bernard Porter. Weidenfeld and Nicolson, 1987.

very strongly "about the great hindrance, which is caused to the efforts of the Police, by the activity of agents of Press Associations & Newspapers. These 'touts' follow the detectives wherever they go in search of clues, and then having interviewed persons with whom the police have had conversation and from whom inquiries have been made, compile the paragraphs which fill the papers. This practice impedes the usefulness of detective investigation and moreover keeps alive the excitement in the district and elsewhere."[13]

Understandably perhaps, the *Star* newspaper took an opposite view—

"[The police] treat the reporters of the newspapers, who are simply news-gatherers for the great mass of the people, with a snobbery that would be beneath contempt were it not senseless to an almost criminal degree . . . some of the inspectors at the offices seemed to wilfully mislead them; they denied information which would have done no harm to make public, and the withholding of which only tended to increase the public uneasiness over the affair."

The police remained guarded, defensive of their reputation, and whenever necessary fell back on official strictures [14] laid down by Howard Vincent, the first Director of the CID—

"Police must not on any account give any information whatever to gentlemen connected with the press, relative to matters within police knowledge, or . . . communicate in any manner, either directly or indirectly, with editors, or reporters of newspapers, on any matter connected with the public service, without express and special authority . . ."

Howard Vincent also wrote—

"The Press is a power in the detection of crime which we must not omit to take into account. Occasionally, and I am afraid not infrequently, the competition for news leads to the premature publication of information fatal to the objects of the police, and proceedings are not

---

[13]   HO 144/221/A49301C/8
[14]   *A Police Code, and Manual of the Criminal Law, 1881*

unknown, such as dogging and following the officers engaged, and interviewing witnesses, which entail the greatest annoyance and entirely frustrate the performance of public duty. But, on the whole, the conductors of the Press are willing to give assistance, and when publicity is desirable their help is invaluable."[15]

Throughout the Whitechapel murders the Metropolitan Police maintained a stern silence. This constantly frustrated the press, giving rise to rumour and wild speculation. On the face of things it seemed the police were hamstrung by regulation, but their silence ran deeper than simply not divulging the latest details of its investigation.

During the latter months of 1888 "horrible murder" was delivered three or more times daily straight to the homes and hearths of Londoners. The press ruthlessly exploited and handsomely profited from "Leather Apron", the first manifestation of a widespread scare, and later Jack the Ripper, but the whole thing was not a purely press-driven phenomenon.

Such sustained levels of news coverage and public interest would have been impossible without Coroner Wynne Edwin Baxter's grandstanding inquests on three of the five alleged Jack the Ripper victims. These elaborate showcase events with their endless cavalcades of police, doctors and motley East End denizens had a circus-like air over which he presided like a ringmaster, allowing the proceedings to drag on and far exceed the remit of an inquest.

Judy, or the London Serio-Comic Journal [a *Punch* look-alike], 26th September 1888—

". . . what benefit can the continued prolongation of the inquest on the butchered Annie Chapman of Whitechapel do any human being? The duty of a coroner and his jury is simply to identify the body and determine the cause of death. This could have been done in an hour, and would have been had not the case excited extraordinary attention."

Wynne Baxter's three inquests ran for a total of fourteen days over a period of almost two months. This played straight into the hands of a

---

[15]   Address to the 27th Annual Congress of the National Association for the Promotion of Social Science, Huddersfield, October 1883.

hungry press, and by 10th October 1888 the *Star* was able to announce that for the first six days of the month circulation had reached 1,302,950.

"Hideous malice, deadly cunning, insatiable thirst for blood - all these are the marks of the mad homicide," screamed the *Star*. "The ghoul-like creature who stalks through the streets of London . . . is simply drunk with blood, and he will have more." This was the stuff of Gothic melodrama, spilled fresh everyday onto the streets of Whitechapel.

Here we should perhaps divest ourselves of the notion that everyone was standing around teary-eyed in Whitechapel bewailing the latest tragic loss of one of its sisterhood. Far from it. This was no time for silent reflection. The murders presented unparalleled opportunities for egregious commercial exploitation. Murder was good for business.

Daily News, 10th September 1888—

"Thousands of respectably dressed persons visited the scene, and occasionally the road became so crowded that the constables had to clear it by making a series of raids upon the spectators . . . half a dozen costermongers took up their stands and did a brisk business in fruit and refreshments . . ."

People paid a halfpenny or more to stare from windows overlooking the Hanbury Street backyard murder scene, whilst following the double event an entrepreneurial woman wandered up and down Berner Street peddling the latest in self-defense—

"Here you are, now," she cried. "Sixpence for a swordstick. That's the sort to do for 'em."[16]

Whilst the Victorian appetite for gruesome murder and mystery was being amply served, another agenda was coming slowly to the boil—

"The question is, what are the people of London to do? Whitechapel is garrisoned with police and stocked with plain-clothes men. Nothing comes of it. The police have not even a clue. They are in despair at their utter failure to get so much as a scent of the criminal."[17]

---

16   *Star*, 1st October 1888.
17   *Star*, 8th September 1888

This was tame in comparison to the savagery that would ensue. The radical press constantly berated the police for its bumbling incompetence, and as the body count climbed with no hope of a satisfactory outcome in sight Sir Charles Warren and Home Secretary Henry Matthews were repeatedly called on to resign. Yet until the moment came when the offering of a sacrificial lamb became unavoidable, they ignored all the brickbats. The Metropolitan Police and Home Office never raised a defensive glove. They took it all on the chin, stumbling blindly through ten weeks of low comedy and grand guignol horror without offering the public so much as a crumb of reassurance or a word in defense of its handling of the situation.

The first four "Ripper murders" [Nichols to Eddowes] took place within a political and operational vacuum.

Parliament had gone into summer recess on 13th August and would not reconvene until 6th November. On 31st August, the date of Polly Nichols' murder, James Monro, Assistant Commissioner CID, resigned due to irreconcilable differences with Sir Charles Warren over manpower levels and the autonomy of the detective department. Almost immediately afterwards his replacement, Dr. [later Sir [18]] Robert Anderson, travelled to Switzerland on sick leave. Superintendent Charles Cutbush of Scotland Yard's Executive Branch would not return from leave until 23rd September 1888. Chief Constable Adolphus Frederick Williamson, still exhausted after a long illness and a three-month convalescence, was barely operational, his position at Scotland Yard now little more than a sinecure.

The CID was headless. So, too, was H Division [Whitechapel], for on the weekend of Polly Nichols' murder two of its most senior officers, Superintendent Thomas Arnold and Local Inspector Edmund Reid, began their annual leave, which gives us a fairly good indication of the importance they attached to Nichols' murder [which took place in the adjacent J Division].

This was the operational situation which decided someone at

---

[18]   November 1901.

Scotland Yard to send Inspector Frederick George Abberline back to his old stamping ground of Whitechapel.[19]

Sir Charles Warren was isolated atop Scotland Yard. Primarily a soldier, he believed that prevention of crime was better than cure. He did not hold the CID in high regard, dismissing it as "a drop in the ocean for all the myriads of common-place offences which might develop readily into serious crime if not looked after by the uniform police and by citizens."[20] Warren further believed that the Metropolitan Police was best run along strict military lines.

And so it was to this wholly ill-equipped martinet that responsibility fell for heading the Whitechapel murders investigation. Failure was inevitable. If someone had been out to prove a point, here was a perfect storm of opportunity.

The *Pall Mall Gazette*,[21] 8th October 1888—

"Sir Charles Warren, with Colonel Pearson and his imposing staff of military commanders, is now acting as Chief of the Detective Department. Mr. Monro's place is nominally filled by a Dr. Anderson, who is said to be in Switzerland. In his absence the Criminal Investigation Department is delivered over to anarchy plus the incessant interference of Sir Charles Warren. Sir Charles Warren presiding over the Criminal Investigation Department is like a hen attempting to suckle kittens."

The crux of the disagreement between Scotland Yard's two top officers was the CID's manpower levels and independence. Monro would not tolerate Warren's constant interference with its running, and his concerns with what he regarded as a wholly untenable situation were expressed in a June 1888 memo to Charles Beilby Stuart-Wortley, Parliamentary Under-Secretary of State at the Home Department—

" . . . with the restrictions now attempted to be imposed upon my action as Head of Department, I must, in justice to myself disclaim all responsibility meanwhile for any unfavourable results, to which the

---

[19] Abberline had been with H Division between 1878 and 1887.

[20] Murray's Magazine, November 1888

[21] The *Pall Mall Gazette* took its name from a fictional newspaper in the novel "The History of Pendennis" by William Makepeace Thackeray.

system now initiated will lead."[22]

It is not clear what James Monro may have been suggesting.

Following a July 1888 meeting at the Home Office between Monro, Warren and Matthews, the *Belfast News Letter,* 5th September 1888, reported that "it was decided that Mr. Monro should take an immediate leave of absence with a view to his subsequent resignation."

Monro did take an immediate leave of absence, but allegedly on health grounds.

On 24th July 1888 he wrote to Sir Charles Warren—

"I came to town today being sent for by S of S [Secretary of State]. I had intended to return to office but was unable. I am unfit for work and shall be glad to have leave to the end of the week, after which I propose taking my [usual] leave for August."

Sir Charles Warren replied the same day—

"I am sorry to hear that you are ill. You can as you propose have leave till the end of August and I will arrange for your duties during that time to be carried out by another Assistant Commissioner."[23]

Sir Charles Warren had no idea he was about to be blindsided by James Monro and Henry Matthews.

The Link, the weekly journal of the Law and Liberty League, an association dedicated to fighting worker exploitation, abusive police practices, injustice and oppression, described what it saw as the fundamental difference between Monro and Warren—

Warren was "bitten by the military craze" and wanted to be the "head of an army of Gendarmes", whilst Monro "was bitten by the craze of being a political policeman, the head of an English third section.[24] Mr. Monro could think of nothing but dynamite and Invincibles.[25] Sir Charles Warren dreams of the threatened Revolution, and sends his horsemen to smash up political meetings. In the meanwhile the thief and the burglar flourish, and a series of horrid murders are perpetrated with impunity

---

[22]   HO 144/190/A4672B, sub. 18

[23]   MEPO 4/487.

[24]   The Tsarist secret police, replaced in 1880 by the Okhrana.

[25]   A radical splinter group of the Irish Republican Brotherhood.

and under the very noses of the police."[26]

Sir Charles Warren returned to Scotland Yard on 10th September.[27] At this time Anderson was in Switzerland, Monro had moved across Whitehall to the Home Office and Abberline was in Whitechapel. Internal communications were bad and had, it appears, been steadily going from bad to worse.

The Globe [London], 10th September 1888—

"It seems hardly credible, and yet it is perfectly true, that when the first of the three recent diabolical murders in Whitechapel occurred about a month ago, Mr. Superintendent[28] Williamson, though attending daily at Scotland Yard, in charge of the Detective Department, received no notice whatever for a whole week that any such crime had been committed, and that this happened not accidentally or through carelessness, but in accordance with a deliberate plan on the part of the Commissioner of Police."

The reason for this unsatisfactory situation was that Sir Charles Warren had issued a Police Order dated 9 February 1888—

"A special report, containing the fullest obtainable information and the steps taken by Police, with the names of officers engaged in the inquiry, is to be sent to the Executive Branch immediately on the occurrence of a Crime of such importance as to require the submission of special reports."[29]

Why Warren had decided that such reports were to bypass the CID and be sent to a primarily statistical and logistical department is uncertain.

Five days later Sir Charles Warren finally grasped the nettle, sending a memo on 15th September to Alexander Carmichael Bruce, Acting Assistant Commissioner [CID] in the temporary absence of Robert Anderson—

"I am convinced that the Whitechapel murder case is one which can

---

[26]   *The Link*, 8th September 1888

[27]   *Irish Times*, 11th September 1888

[28]   Williamson's rank was Chief Constable.

[29]   MEPO 7/50

be successfully grappled with if it is systematically taken in hand," he wrote, adding in a mixture of bluff and bluster, "I go so far as to say that I could myself in a few days unravel the mystery provided I could spare the time and give undivided attention to it . . ."

Sir Charles Warren clearly had more pressing demands on his time than the savage murders of four East End women.

". . . I feel therefore the utmost importance to be attached to putting the whole Central Office work in this case in the hands of one man who will have nothing else to concern himself with. Neither you or I or Mr. Williamson can do this . . ."

Somebody was about to draw the short straw.

". . . I therefore put it in the hands of Chief Inspector [Donald] Swanson who must be acquainted with every detail. I look upon him for the time being as the eyes and ears of the Commissioner in this particular case.

"He must have a room to himself, & every paper, every document, every report [and] every telegram must pass through his hands. He must be consulted on every subject. I would not send any directions anywhere on the subject of the murder without consulting him. I give him the whole responsibility. On the other hand, he should consult Mr. Williamson, you, or myself on every important particular before any action unless there is some extreme urgency."

Chief Inspector Donald Sutherland Swanson had been saddled with an enormous responsibility, but, as we shall subsequently learn, not necessarily *every* paper, document, report and telegram concerned with the Whitechapel murders passed across his desk.

The Whitechapel murders played out against a backdrop of social unrest and human misery. The victims were drabs, given to drink and forced to peddle their raddled charms in order to earn the price of a bed in an insanitary common lodging house. Nowhere was the gulf between the haves and have nots more visible than in Whitechapel, where the past met the future in a head-on collision between sweated labour, drink and vice in stinking labyrinths of crumbling rookeries versus a brave new world of wide gas-lit boulevards, electricity, telephones, department stores, mass-circulation newspapers and rapid public transport.

The murders also played out against an unfolding drama in which tales of political chicanery, forgery, suicide and murder would eventually emerge.

The drama began in 1887 when *The Times* published a series of anti-Irish Home Rule articles entitled "Parnellism and Crime". These included a letter purportedly signed by Charles Stewart Parnell, leader of the Irish Parliamentary Party, expressing tacit approval of the 1882 Phoenix Park murders of Lord Frederick Cavendish, Chief Secretary for Ireland, and Thomas Henry Burke, Permanent Under Secretary at the Irish Office. This damning letter appeared at a time when the Irish Home Rule movement had distanced itself from the earlier murder and dynamite tactics of the Fenian IRB [Irish Republican Brotherhood] and was seeking the democratic establishment of an Ireland freed from the yoke of British rule.

The letter was an obvious forgery, and after much political wrangling Parnell finally won his day in court. On 13th August 1888, the last day of the parliamentary season, the *Members of Parliament (Charges and Allegations) Bill* establishing a Special Commission to investigate the charges made against Parnell and the Home Rule party received its royal assent.

The Special Commission was an elaborate conjuring trick, a piece of political sleight of hand which would put the cause of Irish Home Rule on trial in a case prosecuted by *The Times* newspaper. Lord Salisbury's government was careful to avoid any direct involvement in the proceedings, but behind the scenes was placing its not inconsiderable police and intelligence resources at the disposal of *The Times*. By the late summer of 1888 the archives at Dublin Castle had been carefully sifted and weighty consignments of documents delivered to the Irish Office at 18 Great Queen Street, Westminster.

On 17th August 1888, four days after the Special Commission received its royal assent, James Monro tendered his resignation as Assistant Commissioner in protest against the "change of policy and system" which Sir Charles Warren was attempting to impose.[30]

With no formal announcement of his resignation or any mention of his earlier illness, James Monro was whisked across Whitehall to the Home Office, and in early September he was reported to be "head of the Secret Inquiry Department" or "head of the Detective Service"

Freeman's Journal [Dublin], 6th September 1888—

"The appointment of Mr. Monro to the position of head of the Secret Inquiry Department at the Home Office makes it clear that the Government are bent on driving Sir Charles Warren out of Scotland Yard. In his new position Mr. Monro will be Sir Charles Warren's rival, and friction between them is inevitable.

"Eventually, of course, the Government will make Mr. Monro the Chief Commissioner . . . On the whole, Mr. Monro's sensational business last year [the Jubilee Plot] is likely to turn out profitably for him."

The exact nature of Monro's new rôle was never made clear, and later in parliament Home Secretary Henry Matthews commented, "I can only say that I have made arrangements to enable me to have the benefit of Mr. Monro's advice in relation to crime when it may be desirable."

Monro remaining "Head of the Detective Service" whilst beyond the purview of Scotland Yard was an undoubted slight at Warren, but "Head of the Secret Inquiry Department" was closer to the mark. In November 1888 the *Star* informed its readers that Monro had been "employed by Mr. Matthews to get up the Times case" for the Special Commission.

The *Star* happened to be right, for a 1910 Home Office memo records that following his 1888 resignation Monro "came over to the Home Office and continued from there to direct the secret Irish work."[31]

James Monro's unpublished memoir also confirmed his new appointment— "Commissioner Sir C. Warren made life so intolerable for me that I resigned. What the Home Secretary thought of the matter at issue between us may be gathered from the fact that he retained me as Chief of the Secret Department."

---

[30]   HO 144/190/A46472C, sub. 1
[31]   HO A49962/7

James Monro was a seasoned Fenian-hunter who investigated the 1885 Tower of London bombing and also foiled the Jubilee Plot, an alleged 1887 attempt by Fenians to assassinate Queen Victoria at Westminster Abbey. Here was exactly the right man to be relieved of all extraneous duties in order to help "get up the Times case" for the Special Commission, and also, as events would attest, plan the future expansion of the CID.

Bearing in mind the political exigencies of the day and the time-frame of events—the diversionary tactic of Jack the Ripper, Monro's temporary sideways move to the Home Office and subsequent return to Scotland Yard as Commissioner—the timing of his resignation smacks more of contrivance than coincidence.

His resignation obviously came as no surprise to some, for no time was wasted in replacing him at Scotland Yard. Somebody was waiting in the wings. On 18th August 1888, the day after Monro's resignation, Home Secretary Matthews "with his humble duty to Your Majesty" recommended that "Robert Anderson Esq. be appointed to the post of Assistant Commissioner of the Metropolitan Police in the room of J. Monro Esq. C.B. Resigned." James Monro had nominated his own replacement, and Robert Anderson was officially appointed to the post by Royal Warrant on 25th August 1888.

Anderson was a fellow Fenian-hunter and close personal friend of Monro who, whilst Assistant Commissioner, had employed him as "a secret agent". An understanding of his new appointment as head of the CID was that if ever Monro desired "to return to Scotland Yard Mr. Anderson should resign that appointment and should return to his place at the Home Office which was to be kept vacant."[32]

Anderson was keeping Monro's seat warm. A door was being held open. Monro's return to Scotland Yard as Assistant Commissioner CID would make Anderson's term of office the most short-lived in Metropolitan Police history.

Anderson accepted the post in a letter to Sir Charles Warren, who

---

[32]   ibid

was on vacation in France, requesting that he first be allowed a period of sick leave. Warren was nothing if not accommodating. On 28th August 1888, in a letter from the Côtes du Nord, he wrote—

"I expect to return to London about 7 Sept. and I see no reason why you should not be able to go on leave a day or two after . . . If a month will be long enough to put your throat right I think we can manage it."

If Robert Anderson's self-aggrandising 1910 memoirs are to be believed the Commissioner must have thought his ship had finally come in; for, as Anderson took pains to inform his readers, "Sir Charles Warren had said more than once that 'if Anderson were at Scotland Yard all would go smoothly.'" He also wrote that, "During my official life I never failed to 'get on' with any man, no matter what his moods, if only he was honourable and straight . . . I always found him perfectly frank and open, and he treated me as a colleague, leaving me quite unfettered in the control of my department . . ."

Anderson worked alongside Sir Charles Warren for a total of ten weeks,[33] more than four of which were spent away from London— barely long enough to gauge the measure of a man—but "when his imperious temper could no longer brook the nagging Home Office ways of that period, and he decided to resign that office, I felt sincere regret at his going."

In other quarters Robert Anderson's appointment was deeply unpopular.

Earl Spencer had been Lord Lieutenant of Ireland whilst Robert Anderson was at Dublin Castle. During the same period Sir William Vernon Harcourt was Liberal Home Secretary.

In a letter to Spencer, 17 August 1888, Harcourt wrote—

"I agree with you as to Anderson's appointment [as Assistant Commissioner CID]. He was worse than useless & I should think in the UK it was impossible to find a more unfit man for the place in which [he] has been put—except perhaps the Chief under whom he will serve."[34]

---

[33]   Warren's office was cleared out on 12th November 1888.

[34]   *JSPS, Harcourt, correspondence, box 3* [cited in Bernard Porter's *Origins of the Vigilant State*, p. 229].

"Spymaster-General" Mr. [later Sir] Edward Jenkinson, displaced in 1887 by James Monro, wrote to his old patron Earl Spencer on 24th September 1888—

"It is quite true R. Anderson has been appointed to succeed Monro as head of the criminal inv[estigation] Dept at Scotland Yard. What an infamously bad appointment it is! Anderson is not the 19th part of a man, and if it were known what kind of a man he is, there would be a howl all over London!

"[Major Sir Nicholas] Gosselin [once Jenkinson's deputy] writes in the greatest disgust about it all. He says 'I have lived to see a great many things in my time but the acuteness shown in finding this man is worthy of all admiration.'

"Matthews is too lazy or too weak, or too indifferent to make any stand."[35]

Gosselin's enmity towards Anderson was no more evident than in a note he wrote in 1896—

"I hope Robert Anderson will live long and die happily but if he should die from some uncanny cause and I am alive I will certainly be present at the autopsy that I may see what size his heart is—he has me nearly demented."[36]

Thus far, no correspondence applauding Anderson's appointment has been located.

Monro handed over the office keys to Robert Anderson on 31st August 1888, the day of the first "Ripper" murder.

Further resignations were soon rumoured.

Star, 4th September 1888—

"The London correspondent of the Manchester Courier says:- In confirmation of the announcement made in your columns today, we learn that Sir Charles Warren has decided to resign the position of Chief Commissioner of the Metropolitan Police . . . It is exceedingly probable that the appointment will be offered to Mr. Malcolm Wood, the Chief

---

[35]   Spencer family. Althorp Papers KS 252.
[36]   Gosselin to John Satterfield "Jack" Sandars, at the time political secretary to Arthur J. Balfour, 16th September 1896. Balfour MSS (Whittinghame) 32.

Constable of Manchester."

Evening News, 5th September 1888—

"The Manchester Evening News says no official confirmation can be obtained as to the resignation of Sir Charles Warren. Amongst persons suggested in the clubs as his successor is Lieut.-Colonel Pearson, C.B."

Echo, 5th September 1888—

"The appointment of Mr. Monro to the office held lately by Colonel [Edward] Jenkinson has struck Scotland Yard with some surprise, and the report which we mentioned a fortnight ago to the effect that Sir Charles Warren contemplated resignation, again spread with much persistency. It is believed that, if he goes, he will succeed Sir Hercules Robinson at the Cape, and the Chief Constable of Manchester—a civilian—will succeed him."

The *Croydon Advertiser*, 8th September 1888, repeated the Sir Hercules Robinson succession rumour, adding— "Let's hope it may prove true."

Later, when it was clear that Warren was not going to resign, *The Natal Witness*, published in Pietermaritzburg and Durban, declared—

"Good News for South Africa—Sir Charles Warren denies any intention of resigning at present."

Sir Charles Warren, archaeologist, explorer and secret agent, was the Indiana Jones of his day. Having returned from the Middle East, in January 1886 he was put in command of the troops at Suakin, Sudan, with the rank of "Major General on the Staff" and "Governor-General of the Soudan Red Sea Littoral."

"After three months in this appointment, when he was beginning to find that there was nothing to do but to sit down and hold the place, he received a telegram from Mr. Childers, the Home Secretary, offering him the Chief Commissionership of the Metropolitan Police, at a time when there had been a considerable panic in London, and Sir Edmund Henderson had resigned the office. He accepted the offer, and left Suakin at the end of March 1886."[37]

---

[37]   "Sir Charles Warren and Spion Kop: A Vindication", by 'Defender' (pseudonym), 1902.

In "The Life of General Sir Charles Warren" published in 1941, Warren's grandson, Watkin Wynn Williams, wrote—

"He [Warren] had accepted the Chief Commissionership solely from a sense of duty, and for the special purpose of increasing the efficiency of the police and restoring order among the riotous elements in the Metropolis. He had had, right from the start, no intention of remaining in office once that purpose had been achieved. In March 1888 he began to discuss the question of his resignation with [Home Secretary] Matthews: in the late summer he resigned, but the outbreak of murders in Whitechapel made it undesirable that his resignation should be accepted at this time."

Despite all the rumour and speculation in September 1888, on returning from France Sir Charles Warren did not resign.

On Friday 7th September 1888, the day prior to Annie Chapman's murder and with the Leather Apron scare in full swing, Robert Anderson left the country.[38]

If Watkin Wynn Williams is correct, and sufficient importance was attached to the murder of Polly Nichols on 31st August 1888 to warrant the government reconsidering Warren's resignation, it more than follows that Annie Chapman's murder [allegedly by the same hand] on 8th September should have resulted in the speedy curtailment of Anderson's rest-cure in Switzerland.

But this did not happen.

Notwithstanding the Whitechapel murders, it was an inopportune moment for Anderson to be heading for the cheese fondue and bracing air of Switzerland. Aside from not knowing if events might prohibit a return to his new job, by leaving the country at this time the head of the CID was also turning his back on a potentially explosive situation.

Robert Anderson was heavily invested in the forthcoming Parnell Special Commission. Throughout his twenty-year career as a "secret agent" he had retained exclusive control of Thomas Miller Beach, a

---

[38]   *The Lighter Side Of My Official Life*, 1910. "[the murder] occurred the night of the day on which I left London."

highly-placed informant within the American Clan-na-Gael movement operating under the pseudonym Henri Le Caron. Via Anderson, he had offered his services to *The Times* at the Special Commission. He would give evidence to link Parnell's Irish Party with the terror tactics of the Clan. His appearance in the witness box was going to require some very careful handling.

As would become apparent in later years, there were deeper matters for Anderson to consider. Whilst employed in 1887 by James Monro he had authored a number of the anti-Parnell articles in *The Times* which had helped light the blue touch paper for the Special Commission. Proceedings were to open at the Royal Courts of Justice on 22nd October 1888.

Thus in early September Monro and Anderson had much to discuss; all of it far more pressing than the recent murders of two middle-aged East End prostitutes.

In writing of his trip to Switzerland[39], Robert Anderson left his readers in no doubt that his political masters thought him indispensable—

"The newspapers soon began to comment on my absence.[40] And letters from Whitehall decided me to spend the last week of my holiday in Paris, that I might be in touch with my office. On the night of my arrival in the French capital two more victims fell to the knife of the murder-fiend; and next day's post brought me an urgent appeal from Mr. Matthews to return to London; and of course I complied."

Having left England on the day before Annie Chapman's murder, the timing of Anderson's arrival in Paris from Switzerland on the weekend of Jack the Ripper's "double-event" was little short of impeccable. However, it seems that he did not see fit to immediately comply with the Home Secretary's "urgent appeal" to return to London. The Whitechapel murder fiend had just claimed his third and fourth victims, yet four days

---

[39] Ibid.

[40] The one mention of Anderson's absence was in the Pall Mall Gazette, 8th October 1888: "Mr. Monro's place is nominally filled by a Dr. Anderson, who is said to be in Switzerland."

later, on 5th October 1888 in a PS to a letter to Sir Charles Warren, Henry Matthews wrote—

"I shall be very glad to hear whether Mr. Anderson's health has permitted him to resume his duties."[41]

On 27th September 1888, whilst Robert Anderson was away from London, a mysterious letter arrived at the offices of the Central News Agency—

"September 25, 1888.

"Dear Boss,

"I keep on hearing the police have caught me but they wont fix me just yet. I have laughed when they look so clever and talk about being on the <u>right</u> track. That joke about Leather Apron gave me real fits. I am down on whores and I shant quit ripping them till I do get buckled. Grand work the last job was. I gave the lady no time to squeal. How can they catch me now. I love my work and want to start again. You will soon hear of me with my funny little games. I saved some of the proper <u>red</u> stuff in a ginger beer bottle over the last job to write with but it went thick like glue and I cant use it. Red ink is fit enough I hope <u>ha. ha.</u> The next job I do I shall clip the ladys ears off and send to the police officers just for jolly wouldn't you. Keep this letter back till I do a bit more work, then give it out straight. My knife's so nice and sharp I want to get to work right away if I get a chance. Good Luck.

"Yours truly

"Jack the Ripper

"Don't mind me giving the trade name.

"PS Wasn't good enough to post this before I got all the red ink off my hands curse it No luck yet. They say I'm a doctor now - <u>ha ha.</u>"

Originally treating the letter as a joke, two days later, on 29th

---

[41]   HO 144/221/A49301C.

September 1888, Central News forwarded the letter to Scotland Yard. What decided them to finally take it seriously is not known.

In the early hours of the following day, Sunday 30th September 1888, two murders took place a mile apart and within forty minutes of each other. The first, by dint of a simple cut throat, was in Berner Street, Whitechapel. The second, in Mitre Square, within the one-square-mile jurisdiction of the City of London Police, was very different—a savage attack not dissimilar to that on Annie Chapman, involving bodily mutilation and facial disfigurement.

It soon became apparent that the police thought both murders the work of the same person.

Lloyds Weekly Newspaper received news of this second murder within twenty-five minutes of its discovery. A reporter visited Mitre Square, and less than two hours later *Lloyds'* presses began to roll. By 6.30 am a quarter of a million copies were ready for distribution to the Sunday breakfast tables of London and the southern counties.[42]

"In comparison with the horrible mutilation of the Mitre Square victim, this [the Berner Street victim] was said to be 'an ordinary murder', though reasons exist for believing that the assassin was disturbed, and thus his savage intention unfulfilled."

How in such a short space of time the police arrived at such a definitive conclusion about two very different murders being a 'double-event' is not known.

On Monday 1st October the "Dear Boss" letter appeared in the *Daily Telegraph*. The Central News scoop also crossed the Atlantic. On the same day Jack the Ripper and his "funny little games" appeared in Texas and Kansas newspapers.

Later London editions on 1st October printed the text of a postcard, also received by Central News, bearing a "London E." postmark dated "Oc 1 88"—

"I was not codding dear old Boss when I gave you the tip, you'll hear about Saucy Jacky's work tomorrow double event this time number one

---

[42]   Thomas Catling [editor] Lloyds Weekly Newspaper, 7th October 1888.

squealed a bit couldn't finish straight off. had not the time to get ears for police. thanks for keeping last letter back till I got to work again. Jack the Ripper."

The postcard confirmed earlier police suspicions. Both murders were by the same hand, the work of someone styling himself Jack the Ripper, and in writing that he "couldn't finish straight off" with "number one" lent credibility to the earlier notion that the murderer "was disturbed, and thus his savage intention unfulfilled."

The *Star*, 1st October 1888, did not take the correspondence seriously—

"A practical joker, who signed himself 'Jack the Ripper,' wrote to the Central News last week, intimating with labored flippancy that he was going to commence operations again in Whitechapel shortly. He said he would cut the woman's ears off to send to the police. This morning the same agency received a postcard smeared apparently with dirty blood. It was written with red chalk."

However, the Metropolitan Police, perhaps not renowned for its sense of humour, took "Jack the Ripper" very seriously, ordering government security printers *M'Corquodale & Co. Limited* to produce crown-size posters of Jack's correspondence for distribution across London.

The *Macclesfield Courier and Herald*, 6th October 1888—

"Early in the morning the police posted up at all the [police] stations facsimile copies of the post card and letter which pretend to be written by the murderer, and these were eagerly read and discussed by large crowds."

The scare which gripped London and later the world would never have taken place had it not been for the Metropolitan Police taking the decision to splash this inflammatory correspondence across London. Many considered it a blunder, and the reasoning behind the decision is hard to discern. Less than a week after the posters had been published Sir Charles Warren believed the correspondence to be a hoax, as evidenced by a 10th October memo he sent to Godfrey Lushington, Permanent Under-Secretary at the Home Office—

"I do not know whether the P.O. [Post Office] can tell in what letter boxes the letter of Jack the Ripper is posted. At present I think the whole thing a hoax, but of course we are bound to try & ascertain the writer in any case."

It did not take long for life to start imitating art, for on 9th October 1888, ten days after the "double-event", the Ripper publicity machine ground into action with the *New York World* publishing "A Startling Theory", a story which originated in London—

"Is It 'Dr. Jekyll and Mr. Hyde' in Real Life?

"London, Oct. 9. —I am informed by a gentleman who stands in close relations at Scotland Yard, that several of the leading detectives have thrown over the clues and ideas heretofore taken up and are working on an entirely new and most remarkable theory."

The *New York World's* London correspondent was 29-year-old Cardiff-born Edwin Tracy Greaves, a former New York night editor, known as the hardest working American newspaper man in London.

Greaves' informant told him that "a well-known, prosperous resident of Grosvenor Square [was] the man thus under police surveillance. He moves in the best of society and is completely removed from derogatory suspicion among those who are his daily associates.

"This man, however, as I am assured, has been tracked and traced until it is absolutely established that he does lead a double life. This Dr. Jekyll lives for the eminently respectable world in which he moves . . .

"Great secrecy is maintained by the police in the matter, and only very remote references to it have been published here."[43]

This story certainly knocked Leather Apron out of the ring, but just how reliable, well-connected and in-the-know was Edwin Tracy Greaves, the London correspondent whose report of the arrest of Dr. Kumblety [sic] in connection with the Whitechapel murders appeared in the *New York World*, 19th November 1888?

It is impossible to be certain, but in 1892 he was sued for libel in

---

[43]   Plus ça change. Seventy-eight years later, Richard H. Popkin, a professor at the University of California, advanced the idea that there were two Lee Harvey Oswalds: one the ill-fated Oswald-Jekyll; the other the murderous Oswald-Hyde.

London by opera singer Geraldine Ulmar and her composer husband Ivan Caryll, [44] the libel being that Mrs Caryll had undertaken an adulterous relationship and that the couple were about to obtain a divorce.

Greaves lost the case, having to pay the [then] huge sum of £1000 [$5000], an amount he could not afford, and Joseph Pulitzer's powerful newspaper empire was not about to foot the bill. Greaves fled back to America, having first sold his personal effects. The *New York World* then auctioned off the furniture in his office at 82 Cockspur Street, near Trafalgar Square. [45]

Four days after the *New York World's* Jekyll and Hyde story, on 13th October 1888, the *East London Observer* ran a column-filler entitled "People Who Know the Murderer"—

"Some extraordinary stories are being told regarding people who allege that they could easily identify the murderer."

Amongst tales of foreigners blackmailing unfortunates and assignations with peculiar men in dark courts and alleys was the story of "a well-known medical man in East London [who] has communicated information regarding a former assistant of his, who, he is equally convinced, is the man needed. He spent all his money amongst loose women in Whitechapel, and eventually contracted a disease, which utterly ruined his prospects and sent him mad. Ever since that time he has cherished the most intense hatred of these women, and has repeatedly declared his intention of revenging himself upon them."

Years later these fanciful scenarios would provide the foundation for some of the most enduring stories about Jack the Ripper.

Sir Charles Warren's memo highlights a disconnect between thinking at Scotland Yard and that of the Metropolitan Police rank and file. For whilst he and the Home Office might have been treating the whole thing as a hoax, constables on the beat were being instructed to

---

[44] Ivan Caryll wrote the music for Harry Dam's 1894 two-act musical comedy *The Shop Girl*.

[45] Greaves died of kidney failure in the Harlem Hospital, New York, 17 July 1905. He was aged 46.

take Jack the Ripper very seriously.

The Times, 20th October 1888—

"Last night, when the policemen on night duty were drawn up in their respective station-yards, preparatory to going on their beats, the last letter sent by 'Jack the Ripper' was read over to them. It was pointed out that the writer intimated his intention of committing further murders last night, and the necessity for special vigilance was impressed upon the police."

In all subsequent reports, memos and correspondence the police studiously avoided using the name Jack the Ripper, except in anecdotal references. All official paperwork bore headings specific to individual murders and, in general, "East End Murders" or "Whitechapel Murders".

Jack the Ripper was the Whitechapel murderer's stage-name. It was strictly for the public, and the facsimile posters, which ensured the name became known even to those who could not afford the luxury of a newspaper, drove the ensuing scare. The name went viral, kept alive by the press and people—theorists, hoaxers, profiteers, scaremongers, false witnesses, false confessors and numerous women of slender virtue who told of having oh-so-narrowly missed the kiss of his knife—who inundated the police with letters, telegrams, postcards[46] and bogus stories. Everyone, it seemed, wanted a walk-on rôle in this live-action drama.

Following his dramatic debut on the Whitechapel stage Jack the Ripper immediately ceased operations for six weeks. His alleged final murder took place on 9th November 1888 in a squalid Spitalfields room, and the degree of mutilation and disfigurement far surpassed the Mitre Square murder or anything imaginable by the hand of a rational human being.

Three days later, on 12th November 1888, Sir Charles Warren's resignation was announced in the House of Commons. No blame was attached to him for the failure of the Metropolitan Police to apprehend

---

[46]   A wide selection of this correspondence has been collected into a handsomely-illustrated volume, *Letters From Hell*, by Stewart Evans and Keith Skinner, Sutton Publishing, 2001.

the Whitechapel murderer, as the Home Secretary announced that his resignation had been dated the day before the Millers Court murder.

The alleged reason for his resignation was that in writing an article for *Murray's Magazine* he had contravened an 1870s Home Office gagging order. But, as was pointed out in Parliament, two years beforehand Warren had taken it upon himself to write a similar article for the *Contemporary Review* yet this had not resulted in his being censured. Warren's transgression appears to have been a political nicety. Better for him to resign on a matter of principle, thus allowing a resumption of his military career,[47] rather than one of incompetent leadership.

The earlier-mentioned Malcolm Wood, Chief Constable of Manchester and a co-applicant at the time of Warren's 1886 appointment as Metropolitan Police Commissioner, was widely touted as his successor. A Justice of the Peace in Bombay, decorated for special anti-Fenian work whilst in Manchester and an occasional batsman for the MCC, on paper he looked the ideal candidate.

However, on 3rd December 1888, his secret Irish work at the Home Office now at an end, James Monro returned to Scotland Yard as Commissioner of the Metropolitan Police, with Robert Anderson retained as his Assistant Commissioner [CID].

Thus had one chain of events come full circle.

Chief Inspector Donald Swanson's eyes and ears role in the Whitechapel murders ended in December 1888. It appears to have coincided with Monro's appointment as Commissioner.

Departmental Committee Upon Metropolitan Police Superannuation, 1889—

"Mr. D. Swanson, 29th November 1889.

2157 "You are a Chief Inspector of the Metropolitan Police? —Yes.

2158 "In the Criminal Investigation Department? —Yes.

2251 "You were employed in the Whitechapel cases? —Yes.

---

[47]   Despite being described by historian Byron Farwell as "perhaps the worst" commander in the Second Boer War, Warren was promoted to General in 1904, and in 1908 became involved with Baden-Powell in the formation of the Boy Scout movement. He died in January 1927.

2252 "What were your hours then? —I had to be in the office at half-past 8 in the morning; then I had to read through all the papers that had come in, which took me to 11 pm, and sometime 1 and 2 in the morning; then I had to go to Whitechapel and see the officers— generally getting home between 2 and 3 am.

2253 "How long did that go on? —That went on from September to December."

The *Toronto Daily Mail* of 27th November 1888 noted that Queen Victoria might oppose Monro's appointment because his lameness caused by a horse-riding accident whilst a Judge in Bengal which prevented him from mounting a horse—

"It would be lamentable if London should be deprived of the services of the very best man in the kingdom for the vacant place merely because his physical condition prevents his dancing attendance upon a whimsical old woman."

Whilst many newspapers welcomed Monro's promotion, the *Star*, 28th November 1888, thought it "thoroughly bad . . ." The newspaper then levelled the extraordinary accusation that ". . . assistant commissioner [Monro] was constantly intriguing against his chief and is associated in a peculiar degree with the anti-Irish policy of this government. He has been at the bottom of half the dynamite scares which came so opportunely at the eve of elections."

James Monro's first day in office was uneventful. Whitehall was quiet, but three thousand miles away across the Atlantic the city of New York was in a state of high excitement. Amidst an unprecedented blaze of publicity Jack the Ripper had arrived by transatlantic liner.

Frederick News [Maryland] 4th December 1888—

"Dr. Francis Tumblety, the eccentric American who was arrested in London some weeks ago on suspicion of being Jack the Ripper, the Whitechapel murder fiend, jumped his bail and escaped the vigilance of the London police, and landed at New York yesterday. According to the detectives he arrived on the French steamship *La Bretagne*, from Havre, and although there were a dozen or more reporters on the pier when he landed, all failed to recognize him. Two of Inspector Byrnes' most trusted aides were on the pier, however, and as they had been sent there specially to keep an eye on the doctor, whom they suspected was a passenger on the steamer, they had no difficulty in dogging him to a boarding house on West Tenth street where he is now under surveillance."

Compare this story with another which appeared in the *Dundee* [Scotland] *Evening Telegraph* on the same date—

"The latest American papers of the 23rd ult [November] just received state [sic] that a mysterious man, who admits that he is travelling incognito, was arrested at Castle Garden [America's first immigration centre], New York, on the previous evening, after alighting from the Guion steamer *Wyoming* from Liverpool. The police were armed with a cablegram from the Chief of Police of Northallerton, England, asking them to take into custody a passenger who was registered as James Shaw . . . The American papers further say that Shaw fully answers the description of 'Jack the Ripper' and there was in his pockets a paper containing the illustrated account of the Whitechapel horror, and the rumour spread that the Whitechapel murderer was a prisoner in New York."

Dr. Francis Tumblety arrived in America ten days after James Shaw, having jumped his bail at the Old Bailey, London. He was also allegedly suspected in connection with the Whitechapel murders. Yet no cablegram from London's Metropolitan Police requesting his arrest was received by the New York Police.

Meanwhile, in London, the hunt for the Whitechapel murderer continued unabated. Four days after his appointment Commissioner James Monro informed the Home Secretary that "one inspector, 9 sergeants and 126 constables of the uniformed branch of the Force have been employed specially in plain clothes to patrol the neighbourhood of the murders with a view to prevent a repetition of the crimes." An allowance of £300 covered the extra expense involved.[48]

In June 1888 Monro had disclaimed responsibility for any "unfavourable results to which the system now initiated will lead." These

---

[48]   HO A49301/1

unfavourable results may reasonably be construed as the Whitechapel murders, occasioned by the numerical weakness of the CID and hierarchical meddling.

On 15th March 1889 James Monro once again wrote to the Home Secretary, informing him that the extra patrols "had now ceased"; that expenses totalled £351 and would Henry Matthews kindly sanction the £51 balance.[49]

Two and a half months later, on 1st June 1889, Melville Leslie Macnaghten was appointed Assistant Chief Constable of the Metropolitan Police. An old Etonian and indigo planter from Nischindapur, he was a friend of Monro who at the time was Inspector-General of the Bengal Police. Their first meeting in May 1881 "changed my whole life's work" Macnaghten wrote in his 1914 memoirs. The change must have been dramatic, for by 24th June 1883 Macnaghten was in London as part of a delegation in Whitehall lobbying to have the Indian Criminal Procedure [Ilbert] Bill withdrawn.[50] He also spent time visiting his old Alma mater to watch the two-day Eton v. Winchester cricket match. Following Macnaghten's visit to London, Monro returned to England where, on 9th July 1884, he was appointed as an "additional Assistant Commissioner of Police of the Metropolis."

Macnaghten's candidature, salary and conditions of employment had been agreed in early 1888, but his appointment was thwarted at the eleventh hour by Sir Charles Warren who had heard an unsettling story about his being "bested by Hindoos" whilst in Bengal.[51] Warren also expressed severe misgivings about Macnaghten's lack of "former official, military or police experience." Why Monro considered Macnaghten more suitable than "any of the officers who are already on the list as applicants" was something of a mystery to him.

By December 1888 Sir Charles Warren was safely out of the way, and in Police Orders dated 1st June 1889 Melville Macnaghten's

---

[49]   HO A49301/6/7/8/9

[50]   The Times, 25th June 1883

[51]   Macnaghten mentions the incident, which first brought him together with James Monro, in his memoir, *Days of My Years*, 1914.

appointment as Assistant Chief Constable [CID] was formally announced, with the stipulation that his position did not carry with it "the right of succession to the Chief Constableship when it falls vacant."[52]

James Monro now had two well-trusted placemen immediately under his command at Scotland Yard.

In June 1889 the extra Whitechapel patrols recommenced, now composed of CID officers from other divisions, and further augmented by 3 sergeants and 39 constables. Yet despite this renewed vigilance, in July 1889 a forty-year old prostitute, Alice McKenzie, was found murdered in Castle Alley, Whitechapel.

Two months later, on 11th September 1889, the day after a headless and legless female torso was found under a Whitechapel railway arch, Monro submitted a long report on this latest discovery to John Satterfield Sandars at the Home Office, in which he concluded, "Meanwhile I am inclined to the belief that, taking one thing with another, this is not the work of the Whitechapel murderer . . ."[53]

On the same day Monro wrote to the Home Secretary—

"Our experience in connection with the last Whitechapel Murder shows that notwithstanding every precaution the murderer has been enabled to slip through our patrols, and dispose of the body of his victim without being observed by police. All that I can do is to strengthen the force of police in the locality, and make it more difficult than before for these lamentable occurrences to take place. For this purpose I shall require 100 more men, both uniform and plain clothes."[54]

From this latter correspondence it is clear that James Monro had paid no heed whatsoever to Jack the Ripper's arrival in New York.

In an article by American journalist Richard Harding Davis in the *Pall Mall Gazette,* 4th November 1889, Robert Anderson touched upon the Whitechapel murders. Talking about London criminal "show places" he said, "You ought to see Whitechapel. Even if the murders had not taken place there it would still be the show part of the city for those who

---

[52]   E. Leigh Pemberton letter to Sir Charles Warren, 1st June 1889. HO A46472 D
[53]   HO144/221/A49301K
[54]   MEPO 2/222

take an interest in the dangerous classes." And, after dispelling what he perceived as a few stereotypical conceptions of life in England, said, "But I don't think you will be disappointed by the district. After a stranger has gone over it he takes a much more lenient view of our failure to find Jack the Ripper, as they call him, than he did before."

This was a far cry from his later pronouncement that the murderer had been caught and that his "hideous career was cut short by committal to an asylum."

On 9th December 1889 Chief Constable Adolphus Frederick Williamson died, aged 59. Melville Leslie Macnaghten would later be promoted to take his place.

It has not been discovered by this author whether James Monro got his extra 100 men, but by January 1890 he had reduced the Whitechapel patrols to 3 sergeants and 26 constables; and in February 1890 "Acting Commissioner" Alexander Carmichael Bruce effected another reduction, asking that just "2 sergeants and 11 constables be retained on patrol for a further month".

The hunt for the Whitechapel murderer appeared to be winding down.

On May 28th 1890 *Cassell's Saturday Journal* published an interview with Commissioner James Monro. It was a cosy armchair chat in which the journalist asked about the workings of the CID at Scotland Yard, and far from *The Link's* earlier depiction of Monro he was described as "not the counterpart of a Fouché [Napoleon's Minister of Police] or a Vidocq [founder of France's *Sûreté Nationale*] . . . but just a bright-faced, genial, precise, military-looking man, with the grey hair and moustache of middle age, and the eyes and countenance of early manhood."

Amongst other things, the journalist wanted to know about Scotland Yard's relationship with the press.

Monro replied that, "the press perhaps occasionally exceeds its proper limits, and argues and builds up theories from insufficient facts; and in its eagerness to be ahead of all rivals, a paper is often apt to get on a wrong scent; but we are by no means averse to accepting hints from that source."

"You doubtless find," ventured the journalist, "that harm is sometimes done by rash publicity?"

"Certainly; and that the police are often censured wrongly."

The journalist agreed. ". . . to take the notorious example of the Whitechapel murders; the police have been made the butt of much ill-natured criticism because they have not yet caught the culprit."

"You are right; the public are ingenious enough in working out imaginary plans of capture, but in the majority of instances they show a lamentable ignorance of even the first principles of criminal investigation."

"What are your own views," asked the journalist' "for I presume that you have framed some theory on this subject?"

"Decidedly, I have." Asked to elaborate, Monro added, "I can hardly take you so far into my confidence as that, but I may say this, when I do theorize it is from a practical standpoint, and not upon a more visionary foundation."

"Are you in possession of any clue at all?"

"Nothing positive. You see, crimes of this kind—when we consider the particular class of victims selected—are the most easy of all crimes to commit. The person entrapped is as anxious to secure secrecy as the murderer himself."

That was all Monro had to say on the matter, and all this amiable interview reveals about the Whitechapel murders investigation is that in May 1890 the police believed the perpetrator to be still at large; that the press was no substitute for professional detectives, and Monro had a theory but no clues to support it.

James Monro was portrayed as a mature, experienced, able and supremely confident police officer who was in complete control of Scotland Yard's intricate law-and-order machine. Yet just under two weeks later, on 10th June 1890, his resignation landed on the desk of Home Secretary Henry Matthews.

2 BAIT AND SWITCH

James Monro's resignation was due to differences with the Home Secretary regarding police pensions and superannuation.

This oft-repeated trope has always been something of a conundrum, for after Monro's resignation his demands in this regard on behalf of the Metropolitan Police were met almost in full.

There were other disagreements between Monro and Matthews.

During the first ten months of Monro's tenure the Acting Commissioner [when Monro was on leave etc.] was Assistant Commissioner Lieutenant-Colonel Richard Lyons Otway Pearson. In the autumn of 1889 Pearson fell ill and took himself off to the French Riviera and Aix-les-Bains for a rest cure. During his absence Assistant Commissioner Alexander Carmichael Bruce filled the breach whilst the matter of a permanent replacement was discussed.

James Monro did not have Robert Anderson in mind.

He wanted Chief Constable [London, No.2 Northern District] Andrew Charles Howard, whilst Home Secretary Henry Matthews had his eye on Evelyn John Ruggles Brise, who had served as principal private secretary to four Home Secretaries, including himself, but lacked any police experience.

Events moved apace during May and June 1890.

20th May 1890. Pearson returned to London from Aix-les-Bains.

22nd May 1890. Parliament entered a short recess.

28th May 1890. Henry Matthews note to Ruggles Brise—

"I should be very glad if, before I leave office, I could give you a permanent berth. In this matter again, Monro's recommendation does not accord with your wishes; but I shall settle nothing till I return to town."[55]

28th May 1890. *Cassell's Saturday Journal* interviewed Monro.

30th May 1890. Lieutenant-Colonel Pearson died, aged 59.

2nd June 1890. Parliament reconvened.

5th June 1890. Monro wrote to Matthews, stating that, as drafted, he was unable to accept the Police Pensions and Superannuation Bill.

9th June 1890. Monro met with Matthews at the Home Office.

10th June 1890. James Monro resigned by letter—

"The result of our interview yesterday has been to convince me that I can no longer with propriety continue to hold the appointment of Commissioner of Police. The views which I entertain as to the justice and reasonableness of the claims of the Metropolitan Police in connection with superannuation being unfortunately on vital points diametrically opposed to those of the Secretary of State, I cannot for reasons given in my Memorandum of the 5th inst., accept the Bill as adequately meeting such just and reasonable claims . . .

"My views as to police administration, unfortunately, differ in many important respects from those held by the Secretary of State, and I have received clear indications that the duties of the successor of Colonel Pearson are to be entrusted to a gentleman who, however estimable personally, has no police, military, or legal training. I have no wish whatever to trench on the authority and prerogative of the Secretary of State, and, under such circumstances, I feel it only right to place my resignation of the appointment which I have the honour to hold in your hands. I hereby do so, and shall be ready at once to make over charge to any officer who, on my resignation being accepted, may be appointed to succeed me."

---

[55] *Sir Evelyn Ruggles-Brise: A Memoir of the Founder of Borstal*, Shane Leslie, 1938.

In the House of Commons, Friday 12th June 1890, Matthews announced his acceptance of Monro's resignation.

House of Commons, Saturday 13th June—

Mr. James Stuart [Liberal, Shoreditch, Hoxton]—"I beg to ask the Secretary of State for the Home Department what are the points in which difference of opinion between himself and the Commissioner of the Metropolitan Police has led to the resignation of the latter?"

Mr. Edward Pickersgill [Liberal, Bethnal Green, S.W.]—"Before the right hon. Gentleman answers that question, perhaps he will state whether it is true that for the office of Assistant Commissioner, vacated by the death of Colonel Pearson, Mr. Monro submitted the name of Chief Constable Howard, a police officer of great experience, and that the right hon. gentleman nominated his own private secretary, Mr. Ruggles Brise, who has had no police, military, or legal experience at all."

In answer Home Secretary Henry Matthews read James Monro's letter of resignation to the House, after which he said—

"With regard to the question of patronage, I informed Mr. Monro that I could not regard that as a ground for his resignation, inasmuch as I had formed no decision on the subject, and had expressed none. As to differences of view in regard to police administration, I told him I should hope those were capable of being reasonably adjusted. But, looking at the attitude which Mr. Monro considered he was bound to take up with regard to my views on the subject of superannuation, and at the whole tenor of the letter I have read, I felt I had no alternative but to accept his resignation."

Matthews next played a surprise card—

"In answer to the question of the hon. Member for Bethnal Green, I have to inform him that I have not rejected the name of Chief Constable Howard. On the contrary, I propose to appoint him to the post."

The Times, 17th June 1890—

"The letter in which Mr. Monro learned that his resignation was accepted was the first intimation which he received of the fact that Mr. Ruggles Brise was not to be appointed Assistant Commissioner . . ."

James Monro should not have been surprised that the Police

Pensions and Superannuation Bill, as finally passed in parliament, met a good many, if not all, of his demands.

House of Commons, 16th June 1890—

Mr. Richard Causton [Liberal, Southwark West]— "I beg to ask the Home Secretary if he will state, for the convenience of hon. Members, whether the Police Bill, which has been circulated among Members to-day, is in the same form as when it was submitted to the Chief Commissioner of Police?"

Mr. Matthews— "I do not think it is right for the hon. Member to inquire into all the different stages through which a Bill has passed; and, therefore, the only reply I can make is to decline to answer his question . . . I do not think a question on this subject, put in a general form and without notice, ought to be answered."

Sir William Harcourt [Liberal, Derby (Home Secretary 1880-1885)]—

"I would submit to the Home Secretary that an answer to the question which has been put to him is due to Mr. Monro."

Mr. Matthews— "I hope I may, without committing an indiscretion, say that the Bill submitted to Mr. Monro was at least as favourable to the police as the Bill now on the Table of the House."

Matthews also addressed his change of heart regarding the appointment of a successor to Assistant Commissioner Pearson.

House of Commons, 20th June 1890—

"My reasons [for appointing Chief Constable Howard] are these, and I will be perfectly frank with the House: I felt the moment Mr. Monro's resignation was in my hands on June 10 that the want of experience in Mr. Ruggles Brise, which, under Mr. Monro's own guidance, would have been of comparatively small importance, now assumed, on the contrary, the gravest importance."

Monro appears to have been caught in a game of bait and switch. But something else was playing out in Whitehall. On the face of things Monro appeared to have more than sufficient grounds to press a case for some form of constructive dismissal, had such a procedure been in place at the time, but instead he obediently rolled over and, eighteen months later, sailed for India.

Various stories percolated throughout Whitehall that Monro had ignored all inducements to rescind his resignation; also that Prime Minister Lord Salisbury had personally interceded on his behalf.

In the House of Commons, 20th June 1890, Octavius Vaughan Morgan MP [Liberal, Battersea] asked the Home Secretary—

". . . whether it is true, as stated in yesterday's Standard, that there is reason to believe that through the action of Lord Salisbury the differences between Mr. Matthews and the Chief Commissioner of Police will be adjusted, and in that event Mr. Monro's resignation will be withdrawn?"

It was as if Henry Matthews had not heard the question—

"In answer to my hon. Friend, I have to say that Her Majesty has been graciously pleased to approve of the appointment of Sir Edward Bradford as Commissioner of Police, to the office just vacated by the resignation of Mr. Monro."

There was no way back for James Monro. This was not surprising given what Prime Minister Salisbury would later tell Queen Victoria.

She had written to Lord Salisbury, asking why James Monro had resigned and expressing her opinion that Henry Matthews should be moved out of the Home Office. This may have been because of the latter's political performance or, perhaps, because he was a Roman Catholic.

Salisbury replied on 20th July 1890—

"Mr. Monro . . . posed not as your Majesty's servant . . . but as if he had been captain of a band of allied troops taken into your service . . . It was owing to this contrivance that first Mr. [Edward] Jenkinson, afterwards Sir Charles Warren, were induced to resign."

He further informed Her Majesty that Henry Matthews' unpopularity was quite phenomenal, but believed that Mr. Monro's evil practises were responsible for a great portion of it."[56]

---

[56] The Letters of Queen Victoria, Third Series. Vol. I. 1886-1890. Edited by George Earle Buckle [Editor of *The Times* 1884 to 1911], Pub. 1930.

In papers written in 1903, but not discovered until the 1980s, James Monro wrote—

"There was but one course open which was consistent with right and honour—and that was the path of self-sacrifice for my men.

"Had I not done so I should have felt myself to be a coward. And I could never have looked my recruit in the face, and preached to him the duty of self-sacrifice, without condemning myself as one who had been called on to make such a sacrifice of self, and had refused to do so."

This strongly-principled man who liked to think of himself as discreet did not always hold his tongue. In 1883, whilst Commissioner of the Presidency Division in Bengal, he had in a Calcutta newspaper *Reis and Rayyet* [Prince and Peasant] criticized Viceroy of India Lord Ripon's "Ilbert Bill" which at a District level would have allowed Indian judges and magistrates to try cases involving British offenders. Although the Ilbert Bill was eventually withdrawn, the newspaper article led to Monro's resignation, a return to London in 1884 "on leave" and, remarkably under the circumstances, his appointment in July of that year as an "additional Assistant Commissioner of the Metropolitan Police".

Now in the wake of his 1890 resignation he was talking honour, obedience, duty and self-sacrifice. This was heady stuff. Coupled with his self-imposed exile in India, it was far too impassioned a reaction to what was apparently little more than a minor hiccup in the intricate machinery of government.

But Monro also wrote that he had "resigned not on account of any quarrel with the Home Secretary, but because he had refused to do what he considered to be *wrong,* and because, by government grace, he was able to sacrifice his own worldly interests on behalf of those of the men, which as their Commissioner he was bound to uphold, even at the sacrifice of his own."

Did grace, defined as "a favour rendered by one who need not do so—an indulgence", or "temporary immunity or exemption—a reprieve," have deeper implications?

By June 1890 the knives had been out for Commissioner James Monro for some time. In May 1889 his prosecution of aristocrats involved in illegal gambling at the Field Club, St. James's, had earned him powerful enemies, and in November of the same year the "West End Scandal," in which "more than eighty prominent persons" were identified as having visited a male brothel in Cleveland Street, [57] threatened to prompt his resignation.

On 18th October 1889 in a private waiting room at King's Cross Station Lord Salisbury, prior to taking his seven o'clock train to Hatfield, met with General Sir Dighton Probyn VC, secretary to the Prince of Wales and Comptroller and Treasurer of the Household.

According to MP Henry Labouchere, who was suspended from the House of Commons for a week for accusing the Prime Minister of "a criminal conspiracy to defeat the end of justice", Salisbury had allegedly warned Probyn that Lord Arthur Somerset, Extra Equerry to the Prince of Wales's eldest son, Prince Albert Victor, Duke of Clarence, was about to be arrested for gross indecency at a male brothel at 19 Cleveland Street. As a result of this brief encounter at King's Cross, on the very next day Somerset skipped the country to France.

Lord Salisbury countered that "while passing through London from France he saw Sir Dighton Probyn at the latter's request, the meeting taking place at King's Cross Station, and without any foreknowledge on his part of what was to be the subject of the interview . . . Probyn asked him whether there was any ground for certain charges which had been made in newspapers against sundry persons whom he named, and that he replied that so far as he knew there was no ground whatever, no vestige of evidence against anyone except one person, and against that person he understood the evidence was not thought to be sufficient in the judgment of those whose business it was to decide . . . he was quite certain he never said that a warrant was to be issued next day." [58]

On 13th November 1889 Liberal MP Henry Labouchere spelled out the situation in his newspaper, *Truth*—

"The talk tonight is that Police-Commissioner Monro threatens to

---

[57]   The brothel was originally reported to have been in Cavendish Street.

[58]   *Local Government Gazette*, 6th March 1890.

resign. Unless the warrants are allowed to be issued within ten days he will throw up his appointment. He is unable to issue the warrants himself. That should be done by the Home Office, which is keeping them back as long as possible to allow the fellows to get out of the country and as far away as possible."

James Monro had gone straight to the top.

Truth explained—

"Lord Salisbury has received a request from Mr. Monro, who asked to be allowed to issue the warrants. Lord Salisbury said he required 24 hours to consider the application before he could accede to the wish. In the meantime Lord Salisbury privately gave warning to the accused, who took the hint, packed their trunks and went to the Continent, where they are now. Lord Salisbury then wrote to Mr. Monro, saying that he thought it would be useless to issue the warrants, as the men wanted had fled the country."

Truth continued—

"If Commissioner Monro resigns the whole story must come out, as he will be obliged to tell his reasons for resigning. Mr. Monro says that if he is compelled to go he will publish the truth of the terrible scandal."

Bishop Stephen Neill [1900-1984] was the son of James Monro's daughter, Margaret Penelope. In his posthumously-published autobiography Neill wrote that there was more to his grandfather's resignation than met the eye, but confessed that he himself "never quite understood what occurred".

Bishop Neill explained—

"Apparently Grandfather had undertaken to get improved conditions for the men who served under him and for whom he had the greatest admiration (a feeling they reciprocated). This became a political matter, and an attempt was made to bribe him with a KCB to withdraw his opposition to government plans. Once again he felt compelled to resign rather than tarnish his honour. It has been alleged that he 'leaked' information, and therefore had to go, but this is inconceivable in a man of his integrity . . ."

Bishop Neill then added his personal interpretation of events.

" . . . I fancy that this was a smear circulated by the government to cover up their own shady actions, and to account for the disappearance of a popular figure."[59]

Bishop Neill's instincts appear sound.

Quincy [Illinois] *Daily Journal*, December 23, 1889—

"London, Dec. 23 – It is reported that Mr. Monro, the commissioner of police, has accepted a foreign appointment and that he will retire from his present office before parliament convenes [11th February 1890].

"No reason is assigned for this change either by Monro or the government, but nevertheless, every one seems to be aware of it. There is no doubt the West End scandal, the revelation of which has shocked the country, is primarily responsible for it. Monro had determined to arrest and prosecute the titled offenders, but he was held by the Home Secretary. In the meantime, the principal offenders escaped to the continent where they are now hiding from the public gaze.

"An exposure of the scandal is promised in parliament by Labouchere, who has been accumulating evidence regarding the criminals, and . . ."

According to this report Lord Salisbury's spin machine was pulling out all the stops to hush up a litany of malfeasance—

". . . the government has attempted to spike his guns by shifting the responsibility for the escape of the offenders from the shoulders of Home Secretary Matthews to those of the hapless Monro, who will then be out of the country . . ."

Next, it seems, some strong-arm tactics were employed to ensure Monro's compliance—

". . . and who, if he wishes to continue in the enjoyment of the sinecure provided for him, will not defend himself.

"Almost every day adds something to the popular knowledge of the distinguished personages involved in the blackest scandal with which London has had to deal for many years. Two men of high social standing

---

[59]   *God's Apprentice*, Bishop Stephen Neill, Hodder & Stoughton, 1991

were arrested by Inspector Abberline today in connection with the unspeakable scandal. They were not brought before the magistrate publicly, but as the inspector was seen in the private room of that official, it is thought the case was tried privately."

Needless to say, none of this appeared in the British press. During December 1889 the only news item concerning James Monro was a report in *The Times* about his attendance at a memorial service for the recently-deceased Chief Constable Frederick Adolphus Williamson.

James Monro is the only Commissioner in the history of the Metropolitan Police not to have received a knighthood; but his being offered a KCB to withdraw his opposition to a Pensions Bill or the Home Secretary's patronage, both of which finally met his demands, does not add up. And contrary to what *Truth* reported, James Monro never did "publish the truth of the terrible scandal."

Whitehall boasts a long memory. In 1925 Sir Charles Edward Troup, senior Home Office clerk during Monro's tenure as Commissioner, wrote—

"Sir Charles Warren's successor, Mr. James Monro, who had been head of the Criminal Investigation Department and hitherto a sound and level headed administrator, followed within two years the same course, defied the Home Secretary, supplied to newspapers materials for attacking his policy, and allowed the force with which he was popular to reach a stage of indiscipline bordering on mutiny. Like his predecessor he was not handled very tactfully and like his predecessor he had to resign."[60]

Here, perhaps, was the nidus for Bishop Stephen Neill's rumoured story that his grandfather had 'leaked' information.

It is hard to be certain about the truth of the matter, but police superannuation and political patronage were small beer compared to other rumours swirling around Whitehall at the time. James Monro remained in office until June 1890, by which time he had become embroiled in another scandal, one which threatened to eclipse events at

---

[60]   Troup, *The Home Office*, G.F. Putnam, April 1925

the Field Club and Cleveland Street.

The scandal had its origins in *The Times'* case against Charles Stewart Parnell at the Special Commission. It involved allegations of corruption and conspiracy surrounding the illegal activities of Scotland Yard detectives in North America.

It also involved the hunt for Jack the Ripper.

3. GRAND TRUNK DEPOT

Patrick Joseph Sheridan was a wanted man. Alive or dead.

A Land League[61] organizer, alleged "Invincible"[62] and conspirator in the 1882 Phoenix Park murders, Sheridan, now living in Colorado, was wanted alive by *The Times*. In exchange for his coming to London to give evidence against Parnell at the Special Commission the newspaper offered to purchase his Del Norte sheep ranch for £100,000, the money to be paid to Sheridan's wife so that "you will be able to state on the stand—[the American phrase for witness-box]—that you have received no money for giving evidence."[63] Negotiations were being handled by Joseph T. Kirby, a 60-year-old Montreal businessman hired as a detective by *The Times*.

Parnell, on the other hand, preferred that Sheridan did not reach London.[64]

In November 1888 Scotland Yard Inspector Frederick Jarvis arrived in New York. Armed with 44 warrants, he had come to extradite Thomas Barton, wanted in England for forging signatures on *London and*

---

61   An Irish political organization founded in 1879 with Parnell as its president which sought to abolish landlordism and allow tenant farmers to own the land which they worked.

62   A Fenian splinter group dedicated to revolutionary violence.

63   Thomas Sexton [Irish Parliamentary Party], House of Commons, 10th March 1890.

64   Memo, Michael Davitt Papers. Trinity College, Dublin.

Northwestern Railway Company stock certificates.

Shortly after 19th November 1888 Francis Tumblety, a quack doctor bailed in the sum of £300 [$1500] on four counts of gross indecency [homosexual practices], jumped his bail and fled London for France where, on 24th November at the port of Havre, under the name Frank Townsend, he boarded the steamship *La Bretagne*, bound for New York. Little about Tumblety's four offences or alleged arrest on suspicion of being the Whitechapel murderer appeared in the British press. The first the world knew about any of it was when a spate of articles, which could only have originated in London, appeared in the American press.

New York Times, 19th November 1888—

"The Dr. Tumblety who was arrested in London a few days ago on suspicion of complicity in the Whitechapel murders, and who when proved innocent of that charge was held for trial in the Central Criminal Court under the special law covering the offences disclosed in the late "Modern Babylon" scandal . . . He dropped out of sight some 10 years ago, and the first that has been heard of him since is the news of his arrest and imprisonment in London."

On the same day a cablegram from J.T. Kirby crossed the Atlantic—

"Pueblo, Colo., to Assert, London 65. Have been with Sheridan three days. He will give whole history of Land League that will convict if I buy his two ranches and 3,000 sheep, price £25,000 [$125,000]."

A second Scotland Yard detective was soon to arrive in North America.

New York Herald, 29th November 1888—

"Toronto, Ont., Nov 28—The Chief of Police has received a cablegram from the Commissioner of the Metropolitan Police of London stating that an official will leave for Canada tomorrow with Roland Gideon Israel Barnett to surrender him on the charge of being implicated in the wrecking of the Central Bank last winter."

The official was Inspector Walter Andrews. He and Barnett sailed from Liverpool aboard the *SS Sarnia* on 29th November 1888, bound for

---

65   Assert, London: the telegraphic address of Joseph Soames, solicitor for *The Times*.

Halifax, Nova Scotia.

New York Times, 4th December 1888—

"'Dr. Francis Tumblety, who left his bondsmen in London in the lurch, arrived by *La Bretagne* of the Transatlantic Line Sunday. Chief Inspector Byrnes had no charge whatever against him, but he had him followed so as to secure his temporary address, and will keep him in view as a matter of ordinary police precaution. Mr. Byrnes does not believe that he will have to interfere with Tumblety for anything he may have done in Europe, and laughs at the suggestion that he was the Whitechapel murderer or his abettor or accomplice."

Dr. Tumblety was keeping everyone guessing as to his whereabouts.

Philadelphia Times, 8th December 1888—

"Chicago, December 7. — Dr. Tumblety, who was gaining an unenviable notoriety by reason of a fancied connection with the Whitechapel murders, was expected to arrive in Chicago this morning on the Pennsylvania limited. He failed to appear, however, and a conversation with the Pullman conductor developed the fact that a man whose description answers to that of the physician with the odd name, rode from New York to Pittsburgh, but was transferred to the sleeper which went down to Cincinnati."

One New York City policeman did not buy a word of it. He believed Jack the Ripper was still in London.

Brooklyn Daily Eagle, 9th December 1888—

"Speaking of the Whitechapel murderer, a few nights ago, Detective Michael Powers, of the Eighth, said impressively, 'Mark my words, sir, we have not yet heard the last of this ultra-morbid misogynist, this demon incarnate, whose unholy delight is to dye his hands in the blood of his foully murdered victims . . . Soon will the death groan of another unfortunate punctuate the stillness of some Whitechapel purlieu, and next morning palsy-stricken London will cry, 'Where are the police?'"

On the same day the *SS Sarnia* berthed at Halifax, Nova Scotia, where Andrews delivered Barnett into the custody of Inspector William Stark, who in 1887 had been appointed head of Toronto's detective department. The three men then boarded a special mail train for the

1000-mile journey to Toronto, breaking their journey in Quebec the following morning to change trains. During this brief stopover Andrews and Stark took in the city sights, and with their prisoner boarded the 1.30 pm Canadian Pacific train for Toronto.[66]

Alerted to the impending arrival of Barnett a *Toronto Daily Mail* reporter contrived to intercept the train when it stopped to take on water at Myrtle, about forty miles north-east of Toronto.[67] Shown into a stateroom aboard the train, the reporter spoke to both Inspector Stark and Inspector Andrews about Barnett, who was described as a "Hebrew financier." There was no mention during this interview of Dr. Francis Tumblety or Jack the Ripper.

New York Times, 12th December 1888—

"Toronto, Dec. 11—Roland Gideon Israel Barnett, the crooked financial man of London, England, and New York, and the man who played a prominent part, as it is alleged, in wrecking the Central Bank of this city over a year ago, arrived in Toronto this morning, having been brought from England, whither he had escaped from New York, by a Scotland Yard detective."

On the same morning Barnett was arraigned before a magistrate, pleading not guilty to the charges. Later the same day Inspector Andrews was quizzed about the Whitechapel murders—

"[Andrews] said it was one of those things he did not like to talk about. He thought that the chances were that the perpetrator would never be caught unless he was caught in the act or dropped some clue, which he had not done so far. The reports published in the papers about the murders were very sensational. Only one of the bodies was badly mutilated, but the papers took it for granted that the rest were all served in a like manner. It was a great mystery."[68]

A third Scotland Yard detective was soon to arrive in America.

Chicago Daily Tribune, 16th December 1888—

"Scotland Yard Detectives Said To Be At Work In This Country.

---

[66]   *Quebec Daily Telegraph*, 11th December 1888.
[67]   *Toronto Daily Mail*, 12th December 1888.
[68]   *Toronto Daily Mail*, 12th December 1888.

"New York, Dec. 15—[Special.]—Several Scotland Yard detectives are in this country looking up evidence for *The Times* suit against Parnell. Fred Jarvis of Scotland Yard has been in this country and he is now at Kansas City. It was known in New York Friday last that Chief Inspector Shore, Superintendent of the Criminal Investigation Department of the Metropolitan Police, had arrived and proceeded without loss of time to Kansas City. There he was to meet with the representative of the Pinkerton's [detective agency] and with Fred Jarvis . . ."

The *New York Herald*, 16th December 1888, ran a similar story, adding that "Mr. Bangs[69] acknowledged that the Pinkertons are in the habit of doing business (Irish included) with Scotland Yard through the medium of Inspector Shore."

Three months earlier, in London, a reporter from the *Star* had caught up with one of the two Pinkerton brothers just before he caught a train to Liverpool for his return journey to New York aboard the steamship *City of Rome*.

A stipulation of the interview was that Pinkerton should not be named. The reporter complied, but dropped sufficient clues to remove all doubt about whom he was writing. He was a "superintendent of what is, perhaps, the most successfully managed private detective agency in the world" who had come to the UK "for a change of air and a glimpse of the highland home of his ancestors" [his father, Allan Pinkerton, founder of the agency, was born in Muirhead Street, Glasgow].

"I have been in Scotland for a month," said Pinkerton, "knocking about the highlands, and whenever I came to where I could get a newspaper I found it impossible to refrain from eagerly devouring all I could find about these Whitechapel murders."

Which of the Pinkerton brothers was in London during September 1888? Robert, who ran the New York office, or William, from the Chicago office?

It probably wasn't Robert, for on 28th August he was in New York

---

[69]   George Dennis Bangs, Pinkerton's New York manager, son of the late George Henry Bangs, general superintendent of Pinkerton's National Detective Agency.

talking to the *New York Times* and the Chicago *Daily Inter Ocean* about none other than his brother William.

On or about 18th August 1888 William Pinkerton travelled from Chicago to New York by train, and during the 20-hour journey contracted an eye infection from too much ventilation in the sleeping car. Shortly after his arrival in New York he booked himself into the New Amsterdam Eye and Ear Hospital at 212 W. 38th Street.

On 9th September a *Cincinnati Enquirer* report [datelined 4th September] in the Chicago *Daily Inter Ocean* stated that within a few days William Pinkerton's sight would be sufficiently restored so as to enable him to return to work. "For three weeks they have kept him close to his room, and the skill of the specialists has brought him through, and the doctor said tonight that before the end of the week he would discharge his patient."

The Anchor Line steamship *City of Rome* left Liverpool on 19th September, arriving at New York on 28th September. Author Tim Riordan[70] generously sent me a copy of the passenger manifest, but the name William Pinkerton was not listed. Nor was Pinkerton's oft-used alias "Mr. Dickinson."

At first glance all this might suggest that he was not aboard and that the person interviewed by the *Star* could not have been William Pinkerton. However, the *Star* reporter had prefaced his interview with an intriguing remark—

"Among the passengers by the City of Rome, from Liverpool to New York to-day, is a very quiet-looking man, whose name may appear on the ship's list as Smith, or possibly Brown . . ."

If William Pinkerton had travelled to London during September 1888 using an alias and the infected eye story and hospital stay as cover, it is possible he could have met with Superintendent John Shore.

The *Star* reporter made no mention of an eye infection, yet at William Pinkerton's next public appearance, in Milwaukee, 17th

---

[70]   *Prince of Quacks: The Notorious Life of Dr. Francis Tumblety, Charlatan and Jack the Ripper Suspect*, McFarland, 2009.

October 1888, in support of William Beck's candidacy for chief of police, he was reported to be wearing "smoked glass spectacles."

Meanwhile, back in Canada, his extradition duty done, Inspector Walter Andrews stayed in the country for a further week, during which time he was kept under twenty-four-hour surveillance by members of the Irish National League of the Dominion of Canada. This surveillance was in response to a message from England received by R.B. Teefy,[71] President of the Ontario branch of the League.

Boston Sunday Globe, 23rd December 1888—

". . . Inspector Andrews, who had done considerable and successful dirty work against the League in Ireland and England, would be given the task of bringing [Roland Gideon Israel] Barnett to this country.

"The fact that no Canadian officer was sent to England after a prisoner whom they wanted so badly, and that instead, an English officer was to bring him over, was in itself very suspicious. The communication further stated that Andrews accompanying Barnett hither was only a blind, and that it would not be injudicious if a watch were set upon the detective after he got to this country."

The Irish League's suspicions were understandable, but what they did not know was that Inspector Andrews' trip to Canada had almost not taken place.

Roland Gideon Israel Barnett originally appeared in court on 13th September 1888, charged with having obtained £45 from a butcher in Tooting, south London, with intent to defraud. Due to insufficient evidence Barnett was discharged, but on leaving the dock was rearrested by Inspector Andrews on an extradition warrant.

Later the same day Barnett appeared at Bow Street police court, charged with committing fraud in Toronto, Canada. The magistrate refused bail and in the first instance remanded Barnett in custody for a week.

---

[71] Robert Baldwin Teefy was also president of Branch 85 of the Catholic Mutual Benefit Society and an official of the Home Savings and Loan Company. In 1889 he moved to California, where he was to become a vice-president of the Bank of Italy, which later became Bank of America.

In order for Barnett to be returned to Toronto the Canadian authorities had to demonstrate that the charges were serious enough to warrant his extradition. This required the Toronto police providing detailed evidence of Barnett's guilt to the British authorities, but, due to the disappearance of witnesses, it was not until 4th October 1888 that they were able to do this.[72]

Barnett's extradition to Canada was finally ordered on 6th November 1888.

On 8th November 1888 Godfrey Lushington, Permanent Under-Secretary at the Home Office, wrote to Henry de Worms, Under Secretary of State at the Colonial Office, advising him that Barnett was in prison awaiting his surrender "in due course" to the Canadian authorities.

By 19th November 1888 no Canadian official had arrived to collect Barnett. This was because the Toronto police had not been informed of the outcome of his extradition hearing.[73]

It is not known whether up until this moment Robert Anderson had been looking for a surreptitious way to send another officer to North America, but if he had here was his perfect opportunity. In a letter of the same date he pointed out to the Home Office that if Barnett was not conveyed out of the United Kingdom within one month of the issuance of the extradition order [viz. by 6th December] the process would stall. He therefore suggested the Canadian authorities be advised that Scotland Yard would undertake to deliver Barnett to Canada if they would pay the costs involved, which he estimated to be £120.00.

On 23rd November 1888 Anderson was advised by Godfrey Lushington that his letter had been forwarded to the Colonial Office and a request to guarantee the expenses telegraphed to the Governor General of Canada. Anderson was sent a copy of this telegram on 24th November.

---

[72]   See Wolf Vanderlinden, "Inspector Andrews and the Secrets of His Office." Letter from Toronto Chief Constable Grasett to Robert Anderson.
[73]   Ibid. Letter from Toronto Chief Constable Grasett to John G. Meehan, a member of the U.S. Secret Service Bureau stationed in New York.

By this time the opportunity of returning Barnett to Canada aboard the *SS Peruvian* from Liverpool to Halifax on 27th November 1888 had apparently been lost, for on the same day a further letter from Robert Anderson was forwarded by the Home Office to the Under Secretary of State at the Colonial Office advising that "the vessel leaving for Canada on the 29th instant [*SS Sarnia*] is the last that will leave before the lapse of the statutory period during which the offender can be detained." Godfrey Lushington added that "it is consequently a matter of urgent necessity to leave [not wait for] the decision of the Colonial authorities as to his being sent to Canada."

The matter was now out of Robert Anderson's hands. Two Secretaries of State would decide whether to return Barnett to Toronto with no immediate financial guarantee from the Governor General of Canada or bear the added costs of keeping him in jail until such time as the extradition process could be repeated successfully.

A decision was soon reached. On 27th November 1888 Charles Murdoch, Assistant Under-Secretary at the Home Office, advised the Under Secretary of State at the Colonial Office that Home Secretary Henry Matthews had "issued warrants for the surrender of the fugitive who will be taken back under an escort of the Metropolitan Police by the vessel leaving on the 29th instant."

This letter was followed the same day by an "account of expenses incurred in connection with the arrest and reconveyance of the fugitive [Barnett] . . . I am to request that you will move Lord Knutsford[74] to cause application to be made to the Canadian Government for the payment of the amount (£128.5.7) for which purpose a Receivable Order is enclosed herewith."[75]

On the following day a cable was sent to Lieutenant-Colonel Henry James Grasett, Chief Constable of the Toronto Police—

"London, 28 Nov.

---

[74]   Secretary of State for the Colonies 1887 – 1892.

[75]   On 23rd July 1889 the Home Office was still pressing the Colonial Office for payment of the expenses by the Canadian Government. All correspondence except that otherwise acknowledged is from HO 134/10.

"Chief Constable — By Fugitive Offender's Act prisoner must be surrendered within thirty days after committal. Time expires 6th December. Officer must be sent from here. Will leave tomorrow.

"Commissioner Metropolitan Police."[76]

Extradition to Canada was a routine errand which could have been handled by a lowly Detective Sergeant, but from subsequent events it appears that Robert Anderson had extra-curricular activities in mind for a more senior officer. Thus did Inspector Andrews go to Canada at no expense to the CID and for reasons with no discernible connection to the Special Commission.

On 14th December Andrews returned from Niagara,[77] where at the "Prospect House [hotel] he was met by Jarvis and two other men—one of them undoubtedly an Irishman, the other an American in speech, style and manner. The latter carried a large valise which he never let out of his sight and reach."

After the three men parted company Inspector Andrews returned with the valise to Hamilton, Ontario. Here he was met by Superintendent Shore, who handed him a bundle of what looked like legal documents. Andrews put these into the valise, shook hands with Shore and returned to Toronto, where he met on the 17th and 18th December with a Scotland Yard detective resident in Toronto known as Mr. Sketchley.

Parts of the *Boston Sunday Globe's* chronology are clearly inaccurate, and much of the surveillance details melodramatic padding, but cross-checking other non-agency press reports suggests that the events described are fundamentally correct.[78]

We are on firmer ground as to Inspector Andrews' movements with a note sent to Robert Anderson by Toronto Chief Constable Grasett—

---

[76]   See Wolf Vanderlinden, *Ripper Notes* No. 24, p. 24-25.

[77]   *Toronto Daily Mail*, 15th December 1888.

[78]   The article appeared the same day in the *New York World*, alongside a story from Germany: Berlin. Dec. 22, —A man signing himself 'Jack the Ripper' wrote a letter to the police here this week stating his intention to slaughter fifteen Berlin women in the same manner as those murdered in Whitechapel, and to put to the test the vaunted ingenuity of the Prussian detectives, who are making strenuous efforts to discover the writer."

"Inspector Andrews left on 18th inst. *en route* for London".[79]

Prior to leaving Toronto Inspector Andrews spoke to a newspaper reporter.

Toronto Daily Mail, 19th December 1888—

". . . as I am leaving, I do not mind telling you that since I have been in Toronto I have obtained some important clues in the Parnell case— things that I never dreamt of before. But I can say no more, so don't press me."

The newspaper added, "Inspector Andrews is not the only officer of Scotland Yard in America at present on a similar mission. Inspector Fred Jarvis, a bosom friend of his, and also Chief Inspector Shore, of the same department, are in the United States hunting evidence. It is said that for over three years three of Pinkerton's most expert men have been at work on the Irish National Societies. One of these men is the celebrated McPharland [sic, *James McParland*], who broke up the Molly Maguires, and when Mr. Chamberlain was in Toronto last year two of the Pinkerton's men were his constant bodyguard. The question now is, who are they after? Time alone will tell."

It certainly wasn't Dr. Francis Tumblety.

Buffalo Morning Express, 20th December 1888—

"Toronto, Dec. 19—Inspector Andrews left last night for Europe."

Andrews next travelled three hundred miles north-east to Montreal. This made sense if he was *en route* for Halifax, Nova Scotia, for his return voyage to Liverpool. Due to freezing rain his train from Toronto, due in Montreal at 8.00 am, arrived at 9.15 am.[80]

Someone of alleged interest to Inspector Andrews had arrived in Montreal a few days beforehand.

New York Herald, 18th December 1888—

"Montreal, Dec. 17, 1888—Chief of Police Hughes received a big surprise when he opened his mail this morning. Among the letters, written on Windsor Hotel paper, and in an envelope bearing the same

---

[79]   Letter from Chief Constable Grasett to Dr. Robert Anderson, Assistant Commissioner, Scotland Yard. Toronto City Archives. Discovered by Canadian researcher Wolf Vanderlinden.
[80]   *Toronto Daily Mail*, 19th December 1888.

superscription, was this epistle: -

"Prefers Montreal to Whitechapel.

"Windsor Hotel, Dec. 16.

"Dear Boss—Owing to the annoyance and trouble the police and enraged citizens of Whitechapel have been to me of late, I determined to cross the water and, having heard so much of your beautiful city, made up my mind to come here. I wish to inform you that I have not finished the number I first decided upon to kill and that I am going to begin work in your city at once.

"This is to give you fair warning. I want no quarter and expect none.

"Yours truly, Jack the Ripper."

The author of the letter was 25-year-old John Langhorn M.D. [also reported as Laughon], a diminutive [four-foot-six] man with a London Cockney accent who had been arrested for assaulting Miss Florrie Newcomb. He "strutted around like a pouter pigeon" and claimed, "I am Jack the Ripper. All Whitechapel is looking for me. I came over in a cattle boat to Boston and have just arrived. I have come to give myself up . . ."

The *New York Herald* added—

"He will be held pending cable inquiries of Scotland Yard.

"He is probably a crank, though the police are very mysterious and say they believe there is more in his story than they would like to tell."

On 21st December 1888 the *New York World* reported a sudden change to Inspector Andrews' orders and itinerary—

"All The Way From Scotland Yard.

"An English Detective Coming Here in Search of Jack the Ripper.

"(Special To The World). Montreal, Dec. 20.

"Inspector Andrews, of Scotland Yard, arrived here today from Toronto and left tonight for New York. He tried to evade newspaper men, but incautiously revealed his identity at the Central Office, where he had an interview with Chief of Police Hughes. He refused to answer any questions regarding his mission, but said there were twenty-three detectives, two clerks and one inspector employed on the Whitechapel murder cases, and that the police were without a jot of evidence upon which to arrest anybody."

Galveston Daily News, 20th December 1888—

"The twenty-two English detectives hunting in the United States for the Whitechapel fiend expect to find him near an Irish brotherhood lodge, do ye naw?"

Two days later the same newspaper reported—

". . . It was announced at police headquarters today that Andrews has a commission in connection with two other Scotland Yard men to find the murderer in America. His inaction for so long a time, and the fact that a man suspected of knowing considerable [sic] about the murders left England for this side three weeks ago, makes the London police believe that Jack has left that country for this."

This was an unmistakable reference to Dr. Francis Tumblety.

Thus did the premise behind three Scotland Yard officers being in America suddenly undergo a change of complexion. However, it is worth recalling that at this particular time, three thousand miles away in London's East End, Metropolitan Police Commissioner James Monro was currently deploying "one inspector, 9 sergeants and 126 constables of the uniformed branch of the Force" in the hunt for the Whitechapel murderer.

The *Boston Sunday Globe*, 23rd December 1888, also reported Inspector Andrews' meeting with the newly-appointed Montreal Chief of Police, Lieutenant-Colonel George Edward Dumoulin Hughes.[81]

On afterwards being recognised by a reporter, Andrews gave him "reason to suspect that he had business here with the Whitechapel murders, and the reporter was satisfied with what he thought was a big piece of news."

A second reporter had other interests.

"It is generally understood, Mr. Andrews," he declared, "that your stay in this country has been lengthened by certain work you have been doing in connection with the Parnell Commission. Is there any truth in the rumour?"

"I had rather not answer that question," said Andrews.

---

[81]   Hughes was appointed Chief of Police for the City of Montreal on April 17th 1888.

"Will you deny that such was your mission or part of your mission here?"

"Why do you press me," asked Andrews. "You ought to know that I cannot divulge the secrets of my office."

"But won't you say yes or no?"

"No, I will not deny the statement."

After being pressed on Parnell, Andrews attempted to change the subject.

"Don't you want to know something about the Whitechapel murders?"

"No, thank you," replied the reporter, "I have got quite enough."

The *St. Louis Republic*, 22nd December 1888, added further details from the interview with Inspector Andrews—

"How many men have you working in America?"

"Half a dozen," he replied; then hesitating, continued: "American detective agencies have offered to find the murderer on salaries and payment of expenses. But we can do that ourselves, you know."

"Are you one of the half dozen?"

"No. Don't say anything about that. I meant detective agencies."

"But what are you here for?"

"I had rather not say just at present."

There are no reports of Inspector Andrews having interrogated John Langhorn M.D., the diminutive Jack the Ripper who had written to the Montreal police on stationery from the Windsor Hotel where the detective was now staying.

The story of Inspector Andrews leaving Montreal for New York City to hunt Jack the Ripper was completely bogus. The weather had closed in. Montreal was currently in the grip of the biggest blizzard of the season.

Sacramento Daily Union, 20th December 1888—

"Canada: The Worst Snowstorm For Years—A Train Snowed Under."

The *Coshocton Semi Weekly Age*, 21st December 1888—

"The Worst Storm of the Season Rages in Canada.

"Montreal—Train service in this province is greatly delayed."

While snowploughs cleared the railway tracks, Inspector Andrews had little choice but to stay in Montreal. He stayed for two nights at the Windsor Hotel on Dominion Square, Canada's first grand railway hotel, which in 1886 the editor of the *Western Gazette* described as "probably the finest hotel on the American continent." Robert Anderson was certainly not stinting on Inspector Andrews' *per diems,* but it is impossible to tell if these expenses had been factored into in the £128.5.7 being asked of the Canadian government or were being underwritten by *The Times* newspaper.

Tumblety disciples have long argued that Scotland Yard risking one of its officers to make such politically-sensitive inquiries in Canada when there was no shortage of private agents who could have done the same thing without attracting any publicity doesn't add up. Their contention was that Inspector Andrews was using Charles Stewart Parnell as a cover for his real agenda of inquiries about Dr. Francis Tumblety possibly having been Jack the Ripper.

This makes little sense.

J. T. Kirby, the 60-year-old Montreal businessman hired as a private detective by *The Times,* did not escape press attention in his attempts to bribe P.J. Sheridan to give evidence at the Special Commission. Nor the Pinkerton Detective Agency; nor ex-Superintendent James Thomson and his wife, hired by Robert Anderson to schmooze General F.F. Millen in New York. Nor Scotland Yard Inspector Fred Jarvis, doing business on behalf of *The Times* with Scotland Yard Superintendent John Shore at a time when he was reportedly arresting Thomas Barton, an absconder from British justice, in Philadelphia. They can't all have been chasing Jack the Ripper.

Boston Sunday Globe and *The World* [NY], 23rd December 1888—

"The evidence has all been put into shape; the documents, letters, affidavits and type-written memoranda, filling a large-sized valise that seriously taxed the strength of the Windsor Hotel's gigantic head porter when he carried it out yesterday morning and placed it on a sleigh with a tall, brown whiskered, fine looking man about 40 years old, whose sharp blue eyes were never off the valise from the time it left his room until it was safely deposited beside him in the sleigh. He was driven to the Grand Trunk depot, where he took the train for Halifax, his baggage, consisting of several large leather trunks, having preceded him. The man was Inspector of Scotland Yard detectives Andrews. He was going to Halifax to take a steamer on Monday for England . . ."

Due to the Montreal snowstorm Inspector Andrews missed his return voyage aboard the Dominion Line steamship *SS Sarnia* which sailed from Halifax on 23rd December 1888.

Inspector Andrews thus ". . . bought passage on the Allan Line steamer *Peruvian*, leaving Halifax on Monday evening [24th]."

At 7.55 am on Saturday 22nd December, Inspector Andrews' train with its parlor car and Pullman sleeper steamed out of Montreal's Grand Trunk Depot on Bonaventure Street on its 716-mile journey to Halifax, Nova Scotia, stopping five times along the way for food and refreshments and arriving during the evening of Sunday 23rd December. [82]

The *SS Peruvian* sailed from Halifax the next day, and in a story filed from Montreal the *New York World* reported that Inspector Andrews "left this country on December 24th for England with a satchel full of so-called evidence." [83]

Inspector Andrews' excursion in Canada was at an end. Having travelled over 2000 miles in three weeks, Robert Anderson's weary courier was on his way home, and the bulky contents of the valise he was bringing to London had nothing to do with Dr. Francis Tumblety or the identity of Jack the Ripper.

Christmas Day and New Year's Day were celebrated at sea.

On 2nd January 1889 the *SS Peruvian* docked at Queenstown, Ireland, just as a story appeared in the *Eastern Morning News* [Hull, UK]—

"Inspector Andrews, of Scotland Yard (the *Daily Telegraph's* correspondent says), has arrived in New York from Montreal. It is generally believed that he has received orders from England to commence his search in this city for the Whitechapel murderer."

---

[82]   This thirty-hour rail journey is described in *Faces and Places*, by Henry W. Lucy, 1892.

[83]   16th January 1889.

On 3rd January 1889, the *SS Peruvian* docked at Liverpool.

The contents of Inspector Andrews' valise are unknown. However, just over a month after his return to England, on 5th February 1889, Henri Le Caron [Thomas Billis Beach] entered the witness box at the Parnell Special Commission, having had sight of certain documents furnished by Robert Anderson.

Political storm clouds began to gather.

4. QUESTIONS IN THE HOUSE

House of Commons, 21st March 1889—

Mr. Timothy Healy [Irish Nationalist, Longford North] asked if Inspector Andrews, an officer from Scotland Yard, visited America since the passing of the Special Commission Act; and if his business there was connected with the charges and allegations made before the Royal Commission.

Mr. Henry Matthews—

"The answer to the first paragraph is in the affirmative . . ."

Had there been any truth to the story of Inspector Andrews pursuing Dr. Francis Tumblety in connection with the Whitechapel murders, now would have been an opportune moment to reveal it. But Matthews merely added— ". . . to the second in the negative."

Timothy Healy wasn't interested in Dr. Tumblety or Jack the Ripper. He was hunting bigger game.

Timothy Healy— "Will the right hon. Gentlemen state whether Inspector Andrews saw Le Caron?"

Mr. Henry Matthews— "I am not aware at all whether he did or not."

Henri Le Caron had an apartment at 177 La Salle Avenue, Chicago. Inspector Andrews secretly meeting with him there is an intriguing notion, but the two men could not have met.

In late 1888 Beach's father lay dying at the family home in Colchester, Essex, and on 8th December, the day before Andrews arrived with Roland Gideon Israel Barnett at Halifax, Nova Scotia, Beach sailed from New York aboard the *SS Umbria*, bound for Liverpool.[84]

The Times, 21st March 1889, published a letter from Robert Anderson explaining as best he could ["I could give a complete reply if I were relieved from the honourable obligations to reticence which now restrain me"] regarding the circumstances behind his putting certain documents at the disposal of Henri Le Caron prior to his witness appearance at the Special Commission. He closed by stating his readiness "to substantiate on oath the fact asserted by Mr. Matthews that neither the Assistant Commissioner of Police [himself] nor the department which he controls [his own] has given help to *The Times* in the presentation of its case before the Commission."

This was Robert Anderson at his mendacious best.

Michael Davitt, leading light of the Irish Home Rule movement and founder of the Land League, wrote of the Special Commission that Parnell was up against "the most powerful newspaper in the world and the government of England . . . All the resources of the secret service of the English Home Office, of Scotland Yard, and of Dublin Castle were at the disposal of The Times."[85]

RIC officer Samuel Waters, who at the time was "in charge of the Crime Special records in Dublin Castle," wrote—"I was required to go through these papers and to supply to the Counsel for the 'Times' all the information I could extract which might be of use."[86]

Many years later Sir Roger Casement wrote of the "infamy" surrounding the Special Commission. "The evidence is there, the debauchery of the 'public service' by the higher servants of the State is there: all for political ends against Ireland. It is an epitome of English dealing with Ireland and might walk straight out of the Calendar of State

---

[84] *New York Times*, 9th December 1888.

[85] *The Fall of Feudalism in Ireland*, 1904.

[86] *A Policeman's Ireland: Recollections of Samuel Waters, RIC,* Cork University Press, 1999.

Papers of Tudor days."[87]

The parliamentary questioning continued.

House of Commons, 22nd March 1889.

Timothy Healy—

"I beg to ask the right hon. Gentleman whether it was by his sanction that Mr. Anderson, as stated in his letter yesterday, furnished Mr. MacDonald, of the Times, with the name of a confidential person [Le Caron] to support the Times in what is called the American branch of the case; and, if not, on whose authority did Mr. Anderson proceed?

"I wish also to ask whether Inspector Andrews, whom he [Matthews] admits to have been sent out to America since the Act forming the Commission was passed, was the confidential person who helped *The Times* with the American part of the case at the suggestion of Mr Anderson."

Home Secretary Henry Matthews ducked the issue—

"The question with respect to Mr. Andrews does not in any way arise out of the question on the Paper. Perhaps the hon. Gentleman will put it down. With regard to the first part of the question, my answer is in the negative."

On 1st June 1889, the day of Melville Macnaghten's appointment as Assistant Chief Constable, it was announced that owing to ill-health Inspector Andrews was shortly to retire.[88]

Not all parliamentary questions were about Inspector Andrews. There was also the matter of his Scotland Yard colleagues he met at Niagara and Hamilton.

On 24th June 1889, Timothy Healy again rose in the House of Commons—

"I beg to ask the Secretary of State for the Home Department on what business was Constable[89] Jarvis in New York; and how long was he away from London?"

---

[87]   *The Prime Informer: A Suppressed Scandal*, Leon Ó Broin, Sidgwick & Jackson, 1971.
[88]   *Lloyds Weekly News*, 2nd June 1889. Ten years later, on 26 August 1899, Walter Simon Andrews committed suicide by hanging. He was 52 years old.
[89]   All Metropolitan Police officers were officially referred to as "Constable".

Mr. Matthews—"I am informed by the Assistant Commissioner of Police [Robert Anderson] that Jarvis went to New York in November 1888 . . ."

On 17th November 1888 Inspector Jarvis sailed from Liverpool on the Guion Line steamship *Arizona*, arriving in New York on 26th November 1888.

Jarvis arrived in America seven days before Tumblety, but—

" . . . His business was the extradition of Thomas Barton, whom he brought back to this country on 9th April 1889, and who was afterwards convicted at the Central Criminal Court of forging signatures on transfers of London and North Western Railway Stock."

Mr. Healy— "How was it [that] it took Jarvis four months to do this?"

Mr. Matthews— "I have given the Hon. Member all the information I have."

Henry Matthews had either been ill-informed about Inspector Jarvis's transatlantic adventures, or did not want it known by his parliamentary colleagues that Thomas Barton's extradition had been badly bungled, based as it had been on outmoded documents from an 1882 Act of Congress which Commissioner Henry R. Edmunds of Philadelphia held to be defective.[90] A new form of certificate had been agreed in 1883 between the United States and the Foreign Office in London and the extradition process stalled whilst the British government was given time to produce acceptable documentation.

Barton was held in a US jail[91] whilst hearings were held on January 29th and 31st; February 4th, 20th, 21st and 23rd; March 7th, 14th, 21st and 25th 1889, on which last date Thomas Barton was surrendered to Washington DC for extradition to England.

At New York on 9th April 1889 a handcuffed Barton was taken aboard the Guion Line steamship *Alaska*, arriving at Liverpool on 17th

---

[90]   Memo from Sir Julian Pauncefote, UK Ambassador to the US, 20th June 1889.
[91]   Possibly the Eastern State Penitentiary, Philadelphia. In 1897 Warden Michael J. Cassidy visited Scotland Yard. "I was kindly received by Mr. Jarvis, an officer in that service, whose acquaintance I made when he was in Philadelphia on business a short time ago."

April 1889. Two days later he appeared at Bow Street Magistrates Court, London.

Thomas Barton hightailed it to Canada in 1886. In March 1887 his wife, Jessy, and their two sons, George Edward [age 9] and Charles Frederick [age 3], emigrated to Canada, travelling aboard the Allan Line steamship *Parisian* to Halifax, Nova Scotia. The earliest reference to the family living in Canada was the 1891 Canadian Census, which recorded Jessy, George and Charles living together in "Manitoba, District No. 9 Selkirk, Sub District BB West Half Brandon City."

Inspector Frederick Jarvis's involvement in the arrest and extradition of Thomas Barton began in mid-January 1889, by which time he had been in the United States for approximately seven weeks. Jarvis did not personally know Barton. Nor did he have a photograph by which to recognize him. For the purposes of identification Inspector Jarvis took with him to America Barton's lifelong friend, "Edward Plant, of No. 64 Vincent Street, Macclesfield, England."[92]

As previously mentioned, Jarvis travelled to America aboard the Guion Line steamship *Arizona*. On the passenger manifest F.S. [Frederick Smith] Jarvis, a 'gentleman' from London, is listed, travelling in the company of Mrs F.S. [Fannie Sarah] Jarvis.

Nowhere on the *Arizona's* passenger manifest is there mention of an Edward Plant.

New York Times, 22nd January 1889—

"From Scotland Yard.

"St. Paul, Minn., Jan. 21. —The Scotland Yard detective, Jarvis, who was reported in a dispatch recently to be working up evidence in the London Times's case against Mr. Parnell, was in St. Paul a short time ago. His business in America has nothing to do with the London *Times* or Mr. Parnell. He was in this country looking for Thomas Barton . . . Six weeks ago the Pinkerton Agency was advised from Scotland Yard to look out for Barton, who was known to have crossed the Atlantic, and shortly after Chief Jarvis arrived in New York [26th November].

---

[92]   *New York Evening Telegram*, 23rd January 1889.

"As it was known that Barton had friends and connections in Manitoba, Jarvis started at once for the Northwest. He remained in Chicago one day and in St. Paul one day on his way to Winnipeg. While here he made himself known to Chief of Police [John] Clark and Chief of Detectives John O'Connor, and was entertained by them."

This press report is partly borne out by a memo[93] to Evelyn Ruggles Brise from Robert Anderson, stating that Jarvis "left for Canada on 7th December, stopping in Chicago for one day en route."

Jarvis should have been accompanied on this trip by the one person able to positively identify Barton. However, Edward Plant, if he ever did travel to America in the first instance, appears to have been co-opted by the Pinkertons, who also had no idea what Barton looked like.

The *New York Times* continued—

"While Jarvis was still in Winnipeg working on a false lead Barton was apprehended and arrested in Philadelphia by R.J. Linden, Superintendent of the Pinkerton Agency of Philadelphia."

Evening Telegram [New York], 23rd January 1889—

"[Edward Plant] recognised Barton as a man with whom he had played as a boy, and whom he had known intimately up to the time of his flight. Barton was formally remanded for his appearance before Judge Butler of the United States Court today, when preliminary steps will be instituted toward the extradition of the prisoner."

Thus was Inspector Fred Jarvis free to travel around, and press reports place him in the company of Inspector Andrews at the Prospect House Hotel, Niagara, on 14th December. Further press reports place Jarvis and his superior officer, Superintendent John Shore, over eight hundred miles west at Kansas City during the latter half of December 1888.

The *New York Times* had more—

"In returning from Winnipeg, Inspector Jarvis, knowing that Barton had been arrested, stopped over in St. Paul three days, being the guest

---

93   X27302 17th March 1890.

of the local police officials."[94]

However, on the following day there appeared to be no substance to Inspector Jarvis's three-day junket in St. Paul.

Atchison Daily Champion, Wednesday 23rd January 1889—

"Philadelphia, Jan. 22—Captain Linden, of Pinkerton's Detective Agency, with Frederick Jarvis, a detective inspector of Scotland Yard, London, England, arrested in this city last night Thos. Barton, of Macclesfield, England . . ."

This was confirmed by the *Philadelphia Enquirer*, Wednesday 23rd January 1889—

"Chased For Three Years

"An English Forger Arrested Here by a London Detective.

" . . . the man was arrested in this city late Monday night by Captain Linden of Pinkerton's Agency and Detective Inspector Frederick Jarvis of Scotland Yard, London, England, and was given a hearing yesterday before Magistrate Durham."

Press opinion indicated that in a cooperative hands-across-the-sea operation Inspector Frederick Jarvis of Scotland Yard, together with Superintendent R.J. Linden of the Pinkerton detective agency, had arrested Thomas Barton on Monday 21st January 1889.

The New York Times, 23rd January 1889, reported Barton's arrest as having taken place on the 22nd, adding the detail that, far from working on a false lead in Canada, Jarvis had located Barton's wife near Brandon City, Manitoba, which enabled him to arrest Barton Philadelphia.

There next followed an entirely gratuitous disclaimer—

"In speaking of Inspector Jarvis the Pinkerton officers here say: 'The published statements that he and Chief Inspector Shore of Scotland Yard were, with the assistance of Pinkerton's Agency, searching for evidence against Parnell in the interests of the London *Times* are not true. Chief Inspector Shore has not been in this country for a number of years. The Pinkerton Agency has never obtained a particle of evidence against

---

[94]   One of the Pinkerton Detective Agency's seven offices was in St. Paul, at 83-86 Union Block.

Parnell and has never been requested to hunt up such evidence by the London *Times* or the British Government.'"

But, as Little Buttercup observed in *HMS Pinafore*, "things are seldom what they seem," for Thomas Barton had been arrested at least eleven days earlier.

The Times [London], Monday 14th January 1889—

"Philadelphia, 12th January—Thomas Barton, alias Cave, of Macclesfield, England, has been arrested here . . . This arrest was effected through the skill of Inspector Jarvis, of Scotland Yard, who came out for the purpose. The prisoner is held in custody pending an application for his extradition."

From newspaper reports it is difficult to work out the actual sequence of events leading to Barton's arrest, but in the *Daily Telegraph*, 21st November 1897, the recently retired Inspector Jarvis recounted the incident which enabled him to arrest Thomas Barton.

"Barton was tracked by a trick. A detective, disguised as a letter carrier, called on Mrs Barton one day, and pulling from his pouch a horribly scrawled registered letter, asked if she was expecting a communication from America. On her claiming it she was asked what part of America, and replied Philadelphia. To make the arrest then was a comparatively easy task."

If we assume that the detective disguised as a letter carrier was Jarvis himself, then he had travelled from Philadelphia to Brandon City, Manitoba [a distance of 1738 miles], only to be informed that Barton was living in Philadelphia.

The New York *Evening Telegram*, 23rd January 1889, told its readers that Barton had been arrested in the Kensington[95] district of Philadelphia, where he had been living under the name of Henry Cave—

"Captain Linden, of Pinkerton's Detective Agency, found him a poorly clad, low spirited struggling weaver in Kensington, with the commonest of lodging houses as a place of abode."

---

[95]   Kensington was an industrial district, far removed from its elegant namesake in London.

Other newspapers reported him using the same alias but placed his capture at a boarding house known as the "Bradford Arms" in Germantown, about four miles north west of Kensington.

The Germantown Historical Society was contacted, but were unable to locate a "Bradford Arms" boarding house in 1888/89. However, they were able to confirm the existence of Bradford Mills, a huge textile concern. The 1881 UK Census lists Thomas Barton as a silk manufacturer, so it makes perfect sense if this was where he was working when apprehended.

Even allowing for Inspector Jarvis being present at Barton's arrest on 11th January 1889, from the time he set out for Canada on 7th December 1888 he had ample time to do what he was denying. But as Robert Anderson took care to point out in his memo to Ruggles-Brise— "At the date specified in the statement (20th—25th [December]) there was no English police officer within the United States."

One thing is certain about Inspector Jarvis's time in America: he did not spend one moment of it looking for "Ripper suspect" Dr. Tumblety.

The presence of Andrews, Jarvis and Shore in the United States came into sharp relief in a story which appeared in the *New York Herald*, 16th January 1889, under the headline "Devilish Schemes." The Scotland Yard detectives were said to be involved in a plot with "desperate Irishmen to blow up a British passenger steamer in New York harbor."

The newspaper's correspondent wrote—

"I have been told by well-informed Irishmen that most if not all the dynamite scares of the past few years were originated by special agents of the English government. From all I have learned in various quarters it is more than probable that the present scheme to blow up an English steamer in American waters is a plot to create a scare that will have the effect of damaging Mr. Parnell and his friends in their struggle with the London Times and the Tory government and of turning American sympathy away from the Irish cause. The promoters are known to be deadly enemies of Mr. Parnell.

"The Parnellites have not much to carry on the war against the English government's powerful Journal and depend a great deal upon

America for financial assistance. That is the reason, I was assured, that the London *Times* wanted some "outrage" committed in America to alienate the sympathies of Americans and Irish-Americans who do not believe in dynamite."

A *New York Herald* reporter interviewed Patrick Egan, President of the National League of America.

"Do you think this steamer business is a hoax," I asked.

"No," said Mr. Egan; "such a scheme has been hatching in Kansas City within the period during which the English detectives have been so busy in
America."

"Who are the conspirators?"

"For obvious reasons I must decline to mention the names. But I believe the object, and the only object, of such a scheme is to affect American public opinion and alienate American sympathy from the Irish movement. It would also have a very detrimental effect on the present Times investigation. There is another most important consideration in the case. As was brought out in the late campaign, the English government is extremely anxious to get an extradition treaty with this country by which it can lay hands at any time on any Irishman who is obnoxious to it politically. Don't you see that the blowing up of an English steamer in New York harbor would result in England forcing the hand of the American government and compelling the American Congress to pass the extradition treaty in the form that England desires?"

Egan's reasoning appeared sound; but, if the story was true, this proposed act of British state-sponsored terrorism, which also implicated the Pinkerton Agency, had been clumsily leaked and was now off the table. Or perhaps the story was simply an impromptu piece of Irish Nationalist propaganda whipped up to paint the British government as completely ruthless in the lengths to which it was willing to go to destroy any possibility of Home Rule for Ireland.75

The Parnell Special Commission sat for a total of 128 days, finally winding up on 22nd November 1889. *The Times* lost its case, the key evidence of the Parnell letters having been exposed as the work of forger

Richard Pigott.[96] Parnell brought a £100,000 libel action against *The Times*, but this was withdrawn on 3rd February 1890, the day the case was to be heard, after the newspaper offered him £5,000 in a personal out-of-court settlement, plus reimbursement of his legal costs.

In total, *The Times* paid out approximately £250,000 [$1.25 million] in legal expenses.

Although Charles Parnell had been vindicated it was a story which refused to lie down, and in March 1890 more parliamentary questions were tabled concerning the rôle of the Metropolitan Police in *The Times'* case.

Central to the story of Scotland Yard officers Andrews, Shore and Jarvis whipping up evidence on behalf of *The Times* was Patrick J. Sheridan, of Montevista, Del Norte, Colorado.

On 4th March 1890 the House of Commons debated the Special Commission and the body of charges made by *The Times* against Irish Members. Core to the debate was talk of a government conspiracy and an assertion that *The Times* knew before the proceedings that the Parnell letter was a forgery.

The government's position was neatly encapsulated by Colonel Edward Stock Hill [Conservative, Bristol South]—

"To suppose that the Government had anything to do with the letters, or that the Times published them otherwise than in perfect good faith, is against the presumption of common sense . . . I never heard of a conspiracy for which there was not some motive. What could have been the motive of the Times in publishing the articles other than the patriotic one of laying bare certain sayings and doings, which, in their opinion, seemed to be detrimental to the interests of the State?"

Timothy Harrington [Irish Parliamentary Party, Dublin Harbour] told the House—

"I propose to read to the House some statements which, I think, will startle hon. Members, and which, I think, will tell against the Government in the constituencies, and which will convince the people

---

[96]   Richard Pigott fled to Madrid, where he "committed suicide."

of England that if there was a foul conspiracy on foot it was against, and not among, the Irish Members. They will show that while we were accused of associating with dynamitards and murderers, our accusers were in constant association with dynamitards, and were trying to obtain the testimony, true or false, of alleged murderers and assassins . . ."

John Gordon Swift MacNeill [Irish Parliamentary Party, Donegal South][97]—

"It is the disclosure made by my hon. Friend (Mr. T. Harrington) of the close alliance which has existed between this Government and the Dynamite Party in America, and of the fact that even after the suicide of Pigott, through some influence or other, they sought to vamp up again that letter. It explains to me the language of Lord Salisbury, who, three or four days after Pigott's suicide, threw doubt upon the forgery, and said he believed it was a genuine document . . . In this foul conspiracy—for I cannot call it by any other name—it was the Times and the Government from beginning to end."

A week later, on 11th March 1890, Henry Labouchere [Liberal, Northampton] rose to speak—

"I will now call the attention of the House to the revelations which were made on Tuesday evening by the hon. Member for the Harbour Division of Dublin.

"Certain telegrams were read from Mr. Soames [solicitor for *The Times*] to his agent in America respecting a visit to Sheridan . . . I can explain to the House what was the connection of the Government with those telegrams."

Henry Labouchere continued—

". . . In the middle of December it happened to come to my knowledge that the Times were endeavouring to get hold of Sheridan. I had a little pardonable curiosity as to what was taking place, and, as I had the advantage of knowing a good many gentlemen in America, I telegraphed to one of them, in order to see whether he would be good enough to observe what was taking place. My friend immediately started

---

[97]   In December 1890 MacNeill changed allegiance and joined the anti-Parnellites.

for the West, and at Kansas City he came up with two of Pinkerton's men and a man named Jarvis, who was a constable employed by the British Government [which] employed Pinkerton's men to do some of their work. I gathered that there was an interview at Kansas between Jarvis and Shaw [Shore], another British constable who had been sent out to see Jarvis. Afterwards Jarvis went on and his friend followed him, running him down at Del Norte, which is within a few miles of Sheridan's ranch. I am prepared to prove by any amount of evidence that Jarvis, who was a British constable, did go to Del Norte on the 20th or 25th of December. What does this prove? It proves conclusively that the Government were aiding and abetting in this intrigue to get hold of Sheridan . . ."

According to Labouchere *The Times* had made it known that it would not be able to go on with its case unless the government came to its aid—

"The Government did thereupon agree to give them aid, or the thing would have broken down; and this was the reason why agents were sent to Ireland and detectives employed in America and elsewhere to do the dirty work of the Times."

House of Commons, 17th March 1890—

Mr. William Macartney [Irish Unionist, Antrim South]—"I beg to ask the Secretary of State for the Home Department whether there are two constables, named Jarvis and Shaw [Shore], in the employment of the British Government; and, if so, of what force are they members; whether it is the fact that they were employed by the Times for the purpose of procuring evidence or the attendance of Sheridan or other witnesses before the Special Commission; whether, if so employed, they were at Kansas City during the month of December, 1888; and whether they, or either of them, were at any time in communication with Sheridan?"

Mr. Matthews [Home Secretary]—"Jarvis and Shaw [Shore] are inspectors in the Metropolitan Police Force. It is not the fact that they were employed at any time, directly or indirectly, by or for The Times, in procuring evidence or the attendance of any witnesses. The answer to my Hon. Friend's remaining questions is in the negative."

Ten days later a letter in *The Times* sprang to the Home Secretary's defense—

> *The Times*, 20th March 1890—
>
> " . . . On the 11th inst., in the House of Commons, Mr. Labouchere made a speech in which he attempted to show that the Government were 'aiding and abetting' in an 'intrigue' with The Times 'to get hold of Sheridan' . . .
>
> "A pretty story, very circumstantial, and apparently, as Mr. Labouchere says, 'conclusive'. But there is a sequel. On Monday last the Home Secretary was questioned in the House. 83, and Shaw, he said, were inspectors in the Metropolitan police force, but 'it is not the fact that they were employed at any time, directly or indirectly, by or for The Times, in procuring evidence or the attendance of any witnesses'.
>
> "From all this it is clear that the entire story, including the presence of Jarvis at Kansas in December 1888 . . . is a fabrication, presumably on the part of Mr. Labouchere's 'friend' . . .
>
> "Your obedient servant,
>
> "CURIOUS
>
> "London, March 19"

"Curious" was Robert Anderson, who in 1906 would admit responsibility for smoking out Labouchere through letters to the press and also for sending Jarvis to America in November 1888.

House of Commons, 24th March 1890—

Henry Labouchere—"I beg to ask the Secretary of State for the Home Department whether Frederick Jarvis is now an Inspector in the employment of the Criminal Investigation Department, and is now in London; whether he was in the employment of the Department in December 1888; whether in that month of 1888 he was at Del Norte, Colorado, a town close by the ranch of P. J. Sheridan; and, if so, what was the object of his mission there; and whether, if he does not personally know if Jarvis was at Del Norte in December, 1888, and why he went there, he will cause inquiry to be made of Jarvis?"

Mr. Matthews— "The answer to the first two paragraphs is in the affirmative. I am informed that Inspector Jarvis was never at any time at or near Del Norte, Colorado."

Mr. Henry Labouchere— "Has the right hon. Gentleman caused inquiry to be made as to whether Inspector Jarvis is now in London, and was this information derived from him?"

Mr. Matthews— "I derived my information from the head of the Criminal Investigation Department [Robert Anderson], to whom I referred the Hon. Member's question this morning."

Happily for Henry Matthews nobody asked him to explain where Jarvis had been during his four months in North America. The story of a Scotland Yard Inspector trudging across the frozen wastes of Manitoba at a time when Barton had already been arrested by the Pinkerton Agency might have been a hard sell, as would the idea of him having assisted in the hunt for the Whitechapel murderer.

Inspector Frederick Jarvis would have been an ideal officer to send in search of alleged Jack the Ripper suspect Dr. Francis Tumblety. Although born in Devon, England, he knew the city of New York intimately, having lived there for a number of years.[98] His wife Fanny Sarah was a widow from Tarrytown, Westchester County, New York State, where in 1872 her son Walter was born. By 1881 Jarvis had returned with his family to England. They lived in Lambeth, south London, at which time he was an Inspector with the Metropolitan Police.[99]

While Thomas Barton was being held in custody pending extradition, Jarvis had plenty of time to hunt for Dr. Francis Tumblety,

---

[98]   Conflicting biographical details state that for seven years Jarvis worked as a private detective for the New York department store and mail-order magnate Alexander Stewart Turney; that he had been a member of the New York police force; and that he temporarily resigned from the CID at Scotland Yard for the period 1876 to 1878 to conduct secret service work in the United States.

[99]   1881 UK Census.

but no newspaper reported such activity on his part. However, he did find time whilst in New York to catch up with one of his "old customers."

In London, March 1886, Jarvis had arrested Prince George Eristoff de Gourie—who once challenged the Marquis de Leuville to a duel in London's Hyde Park over the favours of Miriam Leslie, widow of publisher Frank Leslie—charged on an extradition warrant with obtaining money under false pretenses.

On 19th February 1889 the Russian Prince found himself arraigned on similar charges at the Yorkville [New York's Upper East Side] Police Court, and Police Justice Charles Welde invited Jarvis to attend the hearing as his "expert guest".[100]

Also in New York at this time was ex-Superintendent [E Division, Holborn] James Thomson and his wife, Martha, who were staying at the Gilsey House on the corner of Broadway and 29th Street. Described in Moses King's 1893 *Handbook of New York City* as a hotel catering for "very wealthy and extremely particular" travellers, the Gilsey House boasted 300 rooms panelled with rosewood and walnut, fireplaces of the finest marble, and plastered ceilings from which hung bronze chandeliers.

Under the name Johnstone they had been there on expenses since November 1888, charged by Robert Anderson with the task of negotiating with double-agent General Francis Frederick Millen to give evidence before the Special Commission.

It is not known whether the expenses of Mr. and Mrs. Thomson at the Gilsey, those of Inspector Andrews at the Windsor, Montreal, and indeed the whole of the North American excursion by the Metropolitan Police were paid for out of police funds, and thus subject to political oversight, or being underwritten by *The Times*.

Thomson's conduit to Anderson and Monro[101] was the British Vice

---

[100]   *New York Herald,* 28th February 1889. On 4th December 1893 the New Orleans *Times-Picayune* reported from Nice in the South of France that the Prince had "put an end to his gay and varied, though not very useful, life, by blowing out his brains."

[101]   Report from Nicholas Gosselin to Home Secretary, Sir Matthew Ridley, 7th October 1896 — "At the time of my appointment, the year 1890, the [secret service] work was carried on openly by an agent, Mr. Monro, Commissioner of Police, in London, and in America by the Vice Consul in New York (Mr. Hoare), on both sides of the Atlantic."

Consul for New York, William Robert Hoare, whom Michael Davitt would later accuse, together with Inspector Jarvis, of putting an agent into the New York Post Office in 1883 for the purposes of illegally intercepting mail.[102]

Timothy Harrington, House of Commons, 4th March 1890—

"On December 13, 1888, while the Commission was sitting, an agent of The Times, named Thompson, thus telegraphed to Mr. Soames, addressed "Assert, London," which Mr. Soames swore was his telegraphic address. "The final decision of F.M. is that he is now ready to come over and give evidence on three days' notice, upon payment of £5,000 down and the remaining £5,000 to be paid to him after his evidence and cross-examination, and he is no longer required. I think him of the utmost importance. Cable reply in full.

"But when the House is informed who 'F. M.' was, I think they will be still more surprised. We have been accustomed in this House to violent denunciations of the Irish Americans, and during the course of these discussions one name has been prominently associated with the dynamite plots carried out in this country, and especially with the dynamite plot to blow up this House. That name was the name of General Millen [allegedly behind the Jubilee Plot to blow up Queen Victoria at Westminster Abbey], and that was the gentleman whose assistance the Attorney General was trying to obtain, in order to prove the charge against us.

"1st April, '89, London—To Johnstone, Gilsey House, New York—Hoare, British Consul, has authority to give you names of some informants like Major Le Caron. See him [Hoare]; get all particulars, and induce one or two men to come over. Assistance will be sent you for Millen."

The 53-year-old Millen did not appear before the Special Commission. On 10th April 1889 he was found dead from a heart attack in the study of his West 57th Street apartment and buried at New York's Woodlawn Cemetery. Six months later Thomas Clarke Luby, co-founder

---

102   *New York Sun*, 23rd October 1890.

of the Irish Revolutionary Brotherhood, wrote to John O'Leary, editor of *The Irish People*, telling him that Millen's body had been secretly disinterred and reburied by freemasons.

New York was a hot bed of intrigue in late 1888, but nobody was interested in whether or not Dr. Francis Tumblety was the Whitechapel murderer. Indeed, had Scotland Yard been remotely interested in his whereabouts, Jarvis or Thomson could have done no better than talk to the *New York World*, which on 29th January 1889 published an interview with Tumblety in which he castigated the London police for having charged him with "a series of the most horrible crimes ever recorded."

Questions about the activities of Inspector Jarvis continued to be tabled in parliament, and once again the "Curious" Robert Anderson sprang to his defense.

> *The Times* [Letters], 27th March 1890—
> "Mr. Labouchere and Inspector Jarvis.
> "Sir, —Mr. Labouchere has not made much progress with the proofs of his story about Inspector Jarvis . . . Permit me to recall the facts. On the 11th inst. Mr. Labouchere charged the Government and *The Times* with being concerned together in a discreditable intrigue to procure evidence in America incriminating the Irish members. He based this charge upon the presence of Inspector Jarvis of the Metropolitan Police in the neighbourhood of P. J. Sheridan's residence in Kansas at the end of the year 1888, and he described the officer's suspicious movements with great fullness of detail . . . and he was 'prepared to prove by any amount of evidence' that Jarvis was 'within a few miles of Sheridan's ranch' on the 20th or 25th December 1888.
> "Last night, for the second time, and in reply to Mr. Labouchere's own inquiry, the Home Secretary positively asserted that Inspector Jarvis 'was never at any time at or near' the spot to which Mr. Labouchere's friend had tracked him, and where his presence could be

proved by 'any amount of evidence.'

"Once more I ask, what is Mr. Labouchere going to do? I will not again dwell upon the singular characteristics of that inflexible conscience by which, as he explained to Parliament the other day, his political conduct is governed; I will only point out that, if he now allows the matter to drop, he will necessarily place himself in this inconvenient position, that in future no statement of his on political matters, however positive or circumstantial, need be regarded by plain, unsophisticated men as worthy of attention or requiring an answer.

"Your obedient servant,

"CURIOUS

"London, March 25th

Anderson made it clear that there was no going back for Henry Labouchere, but the Liberal politician had not yet finished.

House of Commons, 28th March 1890—

Mr. Henry Labouchere— "I beg to ask the Secretary of State for the Home Department whether he will cause Frederick Jarvis, now and in 1888 in the service of the Criminal Detective Department, to be asked whether he was, in November or December of 1888, at Kansas City with two persons named Pinkerton, who have a private detective agency in the United States . . ."

Robert Pinkerton, writing in an unpublished letter to the *New York Herald* [published in the *New York Tribune*, 26th January 1889], admitted to having been in Kansas City—

"I know of my own knowledge that Superintendent Shore has not been in this country for a number of years. Inspector Frederick Jarvis is here in connection with a criminal matter which has no relation whatever to Irish affairs, and neither he nor Mr. Shore has met any representatives of this agency in Kansas City. The recent visit of my brother Willie and myself to Kansas City and Denver was our yearly business trip to our offices in those cities. Inspector Andrews is unknown to us."

More Pinkerton denials followed.

The Press [New York], 8th February 1889—

"William A. Pinkerton most emphatically denies that his agency had ever been in the employ of the London *Times* on the Parnell case. During July 1887, he said, Maurice Moser, a Scotland Yard detective, called on Robert Pinkerton in New York, saying he was in search of evidence that would implicate Parnell and others in the Phoenix Park murders, and claimed that certain parties in this country had in their possession letters written by Parnell and others nearing on this case which he was anxious to get possession of. He solicited the help of the agency, and Robert Pinkerton told Moser the agency would not undertake such work.

"Moser then came to Chicago, called on William Pinkerton and made some proposals, which were again refused . . . He then returned to New York and fell in with one Roberts, an alleged detective who bled him out of considerable money . . . Roberts then sold his story to a New York newspaper, which exposed Moser thoroughly. Moser was given $50 by Pinkerton to return home, having been completely ruined."[103]

Henry Labouchere pressed on, wanting to know whether Jarvis "went with the two Pinkertons to Pueblo, Colorado, and whether he went himself to Del Norte, which is close to the ranch belonging to P. J. Sheridan; whether his presence in Del Norte was in any way connected with the vicinity of the ranch to that town; and whether the Pinkerton's agency is employed by Her Majesty's Government?"

The Home Secretary was not further pressed on the government having employed the Pinkerton Detective Agency, but the *New York World*, 23rd December 1888, revealed that Her Majesty's Government was paying Pinkerton agents $15 [£3][104] per day, plus expenses.

Henry Labouchere's allegations were protected by parliamentary privilege, allowing MPs to speak freely in the House of Commons without fear of legal action on the grounds of slander. The letters from "Curious" brought the subject out into the open, and on 3rd and 17th

---

[103] Moser had earlier retired from Scotland Yard's Irish Branch to establish the Anglo-Continental Enquiry Agency. At the time of this incident he was employed by *The Times*.

[104] The current exchange rate was £1 = $5.

April 1890 Labouchere responded in his weekly newspaper *Truth*.

No longer protected against slander by parliamentary privilege, Labouchere was now open to charges of libel.

The temperature in Whitehall rose rapidly. Scotland Yard was getting hot under the collar.

The Times [Letters], 19th April 1890—

"Truth and Falsehood.

"Sir, —My attention has been directed to a statement in this week's issue of *Truth*, which is a repetition of assertions made in the issue of the same periodical of the 3rd instant, to the effect that in November or December 1888, an officer of the Metropolitan Police—Inspector Jarvis—was at Kansas City, and at Del Norte, a village in the State of Colorado, United States of America, employed under the orders of Government in aiding *The Times* to procure the evidence of P. J. Sheridan.

"As Commissioner of Police of the Metropolis, responsible for and cognizant of the movements of the officers of the force under my orders, I think it right to give to the statements and assertions above referred to the most unqualified denial. Such statements and assertions are absolutely untrue. Since I became Assistant Commissioner of Police in 1884 until now, neither Inspector Jarvis nor any other officer of the Metropolitan Police has been at any time within many hundred miles of either Kansas or Colorado, nor has any officer of the force been in America assisting *The Times*, directly or indirectly, in connexion with their case before the Special Commission.

"I am, Sir, your obedient servant,

"J. Monro, the Commissioner of Police of the Metropolis

"4 Whitehall-place, SW., April 18.

A heavy fog of denial hung in the air. Quite naturally, the government was not eager for a public hearing, as borne out by Godfrey

Lushington, Permanent Under-Secretary at the Home Office, who warned in a 2nd May 1890 memo—

"It might be a public advantage if Mr. Labouchere was compelled to reveal his authority for the statements & the agency by which they were procured. On the other hand, if there have been any questionable proceedings on the part of the Government or Police Agents, these might come to light in the course of the trial with damaging consequences. At all events the matter is one which concerns the Government with reference to Fenian proceedings, and on which I think you would wish to consult Mr. Balfour."[105]

Echo, 21st May 1890—

"Inspector Jarvis declares, through Messrs. Wontner and Sons [solicitors to Scotland Yard], that 'he never saw or even sought to see Sheridan, and had no business in America, and conducted none, in reference to Sheridan or the Times,' and he positively declares 'that he never was at Kansas City or Del Norte in his life, or within hundreds of miles of those places.'

"'Unless,' says Messrs. Wontner, writing to Mr. Labouchere, 'we hear that you are willing to withdraw and apologise for these statements, we are instructed to take immediate action against you.'"

Jarvis's solicitors next hedged their bets—

"Messrs. Wontner point out that 'if what you [Labouchere] suggest be true, he [Jarvis] was doing business which was outside the scope of his authority, and spending time over matters which his superiors knew nothing about, and he never reported to them.'

"Mr. Labouchere, in his reply, definitely refuses to withdraw or to apologise 'for my statement that Inspector Jarvis was at Del Norte at or about the time that I stated he was there. I have the clearest evidence to show that either Inspector Jarvis was there, or that this is a strange and wonderful case of mistaken identity; if the latter, Inspector Jarvis is quite right to have the matter investigated in a Court of Law.'

"Declaring that his charge does not impugn the conduct of Inspector

---

[105]   HO144/478/X27302

Jarvis, Mr. Labouchere adds, 'Messrs. Lewis and Lewis will accept action on my behalf.'"

Wontner & Sons' message was unambiguous. Had Inspector Jarvis actually travelled to Del Norte to see Sheridan, it was of his own volition.

Scotland Yard absolving itself from any responsibility for a police officer's questionable actions was a tried and tested ploy. It had been used in June 1888 with regard to the alleged Irish-American dynamiter John Walsh. Following reports in the US press that English detectives had been tailing him, the following disclaimer was issued—

"Scotland Yard authorities . . . also state that if any detective followed him to Paris and thence to New York, he did so on his own responsibility and had no instructions from, or connection with, Scotland Yard."[106]

It was foolproof. Whatever the outcome of the libel action no blame would attach to Scotland Yard, the Home Office or Salisbury's government. Inspector Frederick Jarvis was out on his own.

Later in the month the unwanted public hearing appeared unavoidable.

Galveston Daily News, 26th May 1890—

"A Scotland Yard detective named Jarvis, well known in New York, has brought action against Mr. Labouchere for having refused to withdraw the allegation that Jarvis was engaged by the *Times* in the abortive negotiations with Sheridan at Del Norte."

The *Galveston Daily News* then delivered a fresh spin on affairs.

"There is no doubt that Jarvis was so employed. He was on leave, which was especially given him to undertake the work.

"The action has been brought at the instance of his superiors merely to intimidate Labouchere, but Labouchere intends to defend it, having irrefutable evidence. Spicy disclosures are anticipated."

And then the executioner's axe fell.

The Times, 13th June 1890—

"Resignation of Mr. Monro.

---

[106] St Paul [Minnesota] Daily Globe, 17th June 1888.

"It was announced yesterday in Parliament by the Home Secretary that Mr. James Monro CB has resigned the appointment of Commissioner of Police for the Metropolis, and that his resignation has been accepted."

Eight days later it was reported that Sir Edward Ridley Colbourne Bradford, K.C.S.I., K.C.B. was to be Commissioner of Police of the Metropolis.

Inspector Jarvis pressed on with his libel action.

Rocky Mountain News [Colorado], 17th July 1890—

"Special Cablegram to The News.

"London, July 16. —Papers will be served on Henry Labouchere in a couple of days in a suit for $10,000 brought against him by Inspector Jarvis of Scotland Yard . . . If the case comes to trial it will create a sensation in Irish circles on both sides of the Atlantic, and bring to light some hitherto undeveloped facts concerning the methods pursued by the *Times* to secure evidence, true or false, against Parnell and his associates."

Inspector Frederick Jarvis was represented by Wontner & Sons. Henry Labouchere, the son of a banker, was rich. Defending a legal action was well within his means. Justice is open to everybody in the same way as the Savoy Hotel, but what Labouchere wanted to know was how, on his Scotland Yard salary,[107] Jarvis could afford to sue him for libel.

House of Commons, 20th June 1890—

Mr. Henry Labouchere— "I want to know from the Home Secretary whether Jarvis is to pay for this or the police? I do not object to the police paying; but if I win my case, and Jarvis cannot pay, I want to know whether the Home Secretary, or someone in his Department, will pay the expenses. I know that the action may cost me £1,000 or £2,000, and I want to know, if I win my case, to whom I am to look for my expenses. If Jarvis is being supplied with funds by the police I think the Home Secretary will admit that if I win I ought to have my expenses

---

[107]   In 1878 the annual salary of a First Class Inspector was raised to £200 with annual increments of £5 to £250. *The Times*, 8th April 1878.

from those who are supplying him."

It soon became apparent that Inspector Jarvis had been given little choice in the matter of bringing a libel action against Henry Labouchere.

House of Commons, 20th June 1890—

Mr. Timothy Healy— "We have two grounds of complaint in the fact that Jarvis was detached in the service of the Times, and that Mr. Monro compelled this unfortunate man by a threat of dismissal to bring the libel action against the hon. Member for Northampton . . . Hitherto his life has been made miserable. He had to back up Mr. Monro and the Home Secretary, and was compelled to make a statement to the effect that he was never in America at all, or at all events, only in New York for a short time—these words having been put into the mouth of the Home Secretary by Mr. Monro . . ."

Timothy Healy piled on the pressure—

"The Home Secretary made his statement to the House, I presume, on the authority of Mr. Monro; but did he attempt to probe the statement to the bottom? I would suggest that he should get this new General whom he is placing in charge of the Police Force [Edward Bradford] to ask this question of Jarvis whether, as a matter of fact, he did make this journey to Del Norte? Mr. Monro now is in rather low water, but he has a following amongst a certain section of the police and the public, and I would point out to the Home Secretary that it would further discredit him to get his successor in office to question Jarvis and find out whether, as a matter of fact, he went further West than Mr. Monro informed the Home Secretary. In this way the right hon. Gentleman can go a long way in the direction of discrediting the general way in which Mr. Monro discharged his ordinary duties. Will the Home Secretary say distinctly whether Jarvis went to America on Scotland Yard business or for a holiday?"

Home Secretary— "I have over and over again stated to the House that Jarvis did not go to Del Norte, Colorado. What is the use of asking me what fund he was paid from?"

Timothy Healy— "Did he go to New York?"

Home Secretary— "He was not paid out of this fund, and he did not go to Colorado. I have given the hon. Member the best information I can . . ."

Henry Matthews was getting into an exasperated muddle. Here again was yet another opportunity to tell parliament about Dr. Francis Tumblety, the alleged Whitechapel murders suspect, having been in New York at the time. But the issue did not arise.

"I do not know why Jarvis went to New York," said the Home Secretary. "I should think he went on public business. The suggestion that he went on his holidays is a pure joke. It is as incorrect a statement as the rest of his version of this affair."

Inspector Jarvis's libel action did not reach court.

Too late to salvage the career of Metropolitan Police Commissioner James Monro, on 23rd October 1890, the day before the libel action was due to be heard, Henry Labouchere announced in his weekly journal *Truth* that he had "just ascertained beyond all doubt that Inspector Jarvis was, as a matter of fact, not at Del Norte, and that he consequently did not see Sheridan there, so that it was clearly 'a strange and wonderful case of mistaken identity.' I, therefore, take the earliest opportunity of giving this explanation, and I unreservedly withdraw my original statement and offer my apologies to Inspector Jarvis."

That at the eleventh hour Labouchere finally realised the error of his ways and decided to quietly settle out of court rather than face an embarrassing public climb-down is easy to believe, but doing so would be to ignore a hugely important political issue playing out at the time.

In December 1889 Captain William Henry O'Shea filed for divorce, citing his wife's long-standing affair with co-respondent Charles Stewart Parnell, considered in political circles to be the 'worst-kept secret in London.' As the matter rumbled on through 1890, with claims and counter-claims coming from either side, it became increasingly clear to politicians of all stripes that Parnell was not going to win the day and that the moral outrage and political fallout from his infidelity with Katherine O'Shea would bring about the downfall of the relationship between him, his Irish Parliamentary party and the Gladstonians.

Therefore, despite Labouchere's support for Irish Home Rule, an appearance in court at this time, which would have defended Parnell and again dredged up *The Times's* involvement with Scotland Yard in America, was politically undesirable.

As predicted, on 17th November 1890 the divorce court verdict was delivered in favour of Captain O'Shea. *The Times* took its revenge for its humiliating defeat over the forged Parnell letters, denouncing him as a lecherous family wrecker, and shortly afterwards William Gladstone announced in a speech that "I very soon found that the Liberal party in this country had made up its mind to draw a broad distinction between the national cause of Ireland and the person and the personal office of Mr. Parnell."

Described by historian Frank Callanan as a 'true utilitarian,' Labouchere, in the 20th November 1890 edition of *Truth*, endorsed Parnell, vilifying *The Times* in the process, but in the 27th November edition wrote, "it is evident that there are Liberals who are of the opinion that the triumph of Home Rule depends upon the withdrawal of Mr. Parnell from the Irish leadership." Winning the Home Rule battle outweighed "all advantage to the cause by his remaining Irish leader."

Amidst accusations that Liberal MPs Henry Labouchere, James Stuart [also a director of the *Star* newspaper] and Philip Stanhope, later Lord Weardale, were engaged in intrigues with anti-Parnellites, Parnell's political career soon drew to a close.[108]

On 20th December 1890 Robert Anderson wrote to the editor of *The Times*. In a letter signed "An Observer" he reiterated the Jarvis story, chastised Labouchere for not apologising in the House of Commons and wondered "whether truthfulness and honour and decency shall be required of men occupying prominent positions in political life."

Labouchere countered Anderson's letter on 23rd December 1890—

". . . My retraction was published in *Truth*, and it was copied in many newspapers . . . There was no reason, therefore, why I should repeat it in the House of Commons, and still less reason why I should apologise

---

[108]   Parnell married Katherine O'Shea in June 1891, dying in October 1891.

to Mr. Smith and Mr. Matthews, for, as I have said, much was done in America by English agents which was not reported to the Home Secretary, and, *a fortiori* [with greater reason], not to the First Lord of the Treasury."

There again was Labouchere's accusation.

Robert Anderson had the last word on the subject.

The Times, 25th December 1890—

"Mr. Labouchere evidently fails to understand the suggestion that anyone could be aggrieved by a charge of falsehood when he is the accuser. I presume the public must now be content to accept his own estimate of himself; and I hope they will bear it in mind hereafter when again he pledges his reputation, as he did in this case, 'to produce any amount of evidence' in support of some charge against political opponents."

Thus it is hard to discern if Henry Labouchere's allegations against Jarvis and Shore were false, or whether he was advised not to press the matter because of a greater political imperative.

Whatever the truth, for everyone except James Monro it was the perfect outcome. Scotland Yard and the Home Office were off the hook and Inspector Jarvis kept his job.

Here it is worth mentioning the huge amount of internal correspondence this question generated and which is preserved in the National Archives. Inspector Fred Jarvis and Superintendent John Shore co-signed a request to Monro for permission to take legal proceedings against Henry Labouchere. The Home Office wrote to Robert Anderson. The subject of who should pay Jarvis's legal fees was discussed. The Commissioner of Police wrote to the Home Office. Solicitors Wontner & Sons wrote to the Metropolitan Police. Around and around it went, everyone accepting everyone else's word that Jarvis had never been west of Chicago.

Labouchere's allegation should have been the easiest thing in the world for Scotland Yard to disprove, yet there is no record of anyone asking for, or offering, documentary evidence to the effect that Jarvis could not have been in Kansas City or Del Norte between 20th and 25th

December because on the dates in question he was somewhere in Manitoba, Canada.

Inspector Jarvis would soon return to America, arriving in New York aboard the Cunard steamship *Umbria* on 25th June 1892.

There is an apocryphal story about Dr. Thomas Neill Cream being Jack the Ripper. At his hanging for murder on 15th November 1892, as the trapdoor opened and he began his drop into eternity he is alleged by his hangman, James Billington, to have uttered the immortal words "I am Jack . . ." But as Cream was serving a prison sentence from 1881 to 1891 in Joliet, Illinois, his candidature for Ripperdom can be safely ignored.

This story is considered to be the sole "evidence" in support of Cream being Jack the Ripper. However, Inspector Fred Jarvis pre-dated it by five months.

The *San Francisco Morning Call*, 30th June 1892—

"Inspector Jarvis of the Scotland Yard detective force of London is in New York hunting for Thomas Neill, supposed to be Jack the Ripper."

Jack the Ripper aside, there was a legitimate purpose to Inspector Jarvis's interest in Neill Cream. Confusion had arisen between the identities of Thomas Neill and Dr. Cream and, hearing of the case, John Wilson McCulloch, a Canadian travelling salesman, wrote to the Montreal Chief of Police, Lieutenant-Colonel George Edward Dumoulin Hughes [who had earlier met with Inspector Andrews], saying he was able to positively state that they were one and the same person. At Thomas Neill's Old Bailey trial in October 1892, McCulloch told the court— ". . . a communication was made to me through Inspector Jarvis, who was out in America on this matter, and I was subpoenaed to come here and give evidence."

Still in New York in August 1892 Inspector Jarvis, acting upon a cable received from Superintendent John Shore at Scotland Yard, tracked down and arrested Ignatius Wieder, a jeweller with premises at No. 1 Piccadilly, who fled England having defrauded London wholesale jewellers out of almost $25,000 worth of diamonds and pearls.

Fred Jarvis retired in September 1897. He died in Brighton in 1908, aged 58, of a heart condition.

The final word on Inspector Jarvis came in 1906 with the publication of "Sidelights on the Home Rule Movement."

Fifteen years after the event—by which time the rest of the world had moved on—Sir Robert Anderson was still keen to vindicate himself.

". . . there are people still who credit Mr. Labouchere's statements that I sent police officers across the Atlantic to tout for evidence against the Parnellites. The allegation was unequivocally denied by the Secretary of State in Parliament, and by the Chief Commissioner of Police in a letter to the Times; but, giving the lie to both Mr. Matthews and Mr. Monro, Mr. Labouchere repeated it still more definitely in the House of Commons.

"I was naturally indignant, and I determined to bring him to book. But I could take no action on words spoken in Parliament. The course I adopted, therefore, was to give the facts to the editor of the *World*; and, as I expected, 'Edmund' [Yates] drew 'Henry' [Labouchere] in the 'par' [paragraph] columns of *Truth*.[109] Mr. Labouchere declared in his paper that he was fully prepared to prove that Inspector Jarvis of my department had been to a town named Del Norte to interview the Land Leaguer Sheridan in the interests of *The Times*.

"This was exactly what I wanted. Inspector Jarvis had, in fact, been in America at the time indicated [in his 17th March 1890 memo he had written "At the date specified in the statement (20th—25th [December]) there was no English police officer within the United States"]. But to have undertaken a mission outside the duty I had entrusted to him was a grave breach of discipline. So I directed his superintendent [John Shore] to bring him before me 'on the report'; and the charge having been preferred, I adjourned the case to give the incriminated officer an opportunity to clear himself . . ."

Anderson omitted to mention that John Shore had reportedly been with Jarvis in Colorado.

". . . In due time Mr. [St. John] Wontner called on me to say that, on

---

[109]   In 1874 Henry Labouchere helped Edmund Yates establish *The World*, a society journal.

Jarvis's instructions, he had commenced an action against Mr Labouchere, and that Messrs. *Lewis and Lewis* now wished to compromise it: would I be content if the defendant paid all costs, and allowed judgment to be entered against him? 'Certainly not,' I replied; 'the matter before me is the conduct of an officer of my department, and if the case is settled out of court, the settlement must be on terms that will veto all suspicion of collusion.' The matter ended by Mr. Labouchere paying the costs, plus £100 for damages, and inserting an apology in *Truth*.

"Apart from the Le Caron disclosures I had nothing to do with *The Times* case."

Anderson's 1910 revelations would give the lie to his closing remark.

According to Labouchere's apology and Anderson's version of events, the whole episode had been wildly misconstrued. If true, it makes James Monro's resignation at this critical moment difficult to comprehend.

In Monro's own words, he had resigned "because he had refused to do what he considered to be wrong, and, by government grace, was able to sacrifice his own worldly interests on behalf of those of the men, which as their Commissioner he was bound to uphold, even at the sacrifice of his own."

But if Henry Labouchere's story was true, Monro had done something wrong. In throwing a political lifeline to the Home Secretary, he had subverted justice and, by threatening the future career of one of his officers, imperiled the integrity of the Metropolitan Police—reason enough perhaps for him being allowed to resign "by government grace" on a matter of principle.

As "Chief of the Secret Department"[110] until his resignation in 1890, James Monro was privy to all manner of confidential information, and there is a family story that he was in possession of sensitive material regarding Jack the Ripper which he had kept secret, considering it a "hot potato."

---

[110] Monro papers, 1903

5. PASSAGE TO INDIA

The origins of the game Hot Potato are unclear, but may have connections with a game described by Sidney Oldall Addy in his 1888 "A Glossary of Words Used in the Neighbourhood of Sheffield, Volume 22"—

"Jack's Alive—a game.

"A number of people sit in a row, or in chairs round a parlour. A lighted wooden spill or taper is handed to the first, who says—

'Jack's alive, and likely to live; If he dies in your hand you've a forfeit to give.'

"The one in whose hand the light expires has to pay the forfeit. As the spill is getting burnt out, the lines are said very quickly, as everybody is anxious not to have to pay the forfeit."

Hot potato is an apt metaphor for various Scotland Yard officers not wanting to get their fingers burned.

In response to a 1973 BBC Television series "Jack the Ripper", in which the popular fictional TV detective duo Barlow and Watt investigated the Whitechapel murders, James Monro's grandson, Christopher Monro, wrote to the *Radio Times*—

"My grandfather had his own views on the identity of the Ripper, but came back into office too late to deal with the case as he would have wished. He bequeathed his notes on the affair to his eldest son who died in 1928, and it is possible that some cousins of mine may retain them to this day."

Martin Howells and Keith Skinner, co-authors of the 1987 book "The Ripper Legacy," contacted Christopher Monro, asking if he had "seen his grandfather's written opinion on the subject."

Christopher Monro replied—

". . . Whatever my grandfather knew, deduced or conjectured, he apparently set down in a highly private memoranda which at his death in 1920 passed intact to his eldest son. My uncle Charles Monro died in his early sixties about 1929, and a year or two before that he had a conversation with my father (1874-1958) which the latter related to me in India about ten years later. The gist of this was that James Monro's theory [about Jack the Ripper] was a very hot potato, that it had been kept secret even from his wife/widow, who survived until 1931, and that he was very doubtful whether or not to destroy the papers. He did not reveal the identity of the suspect(s?) to my father, who told me that he had made no attempt to ascertain them, and had just said 'Burn the stuff, Charlie, burn it and try to forget it!'"

Howells and Skinner wrote—

"He went on to tell us that these recollections went back nearly fifty years, and that not even his father had actually seen the papers, or could swear that they had ever existed, and we took his point. But this in itself only helped to convince us that Christopher Monro's recollections were essentially honest."

There is nothing to suggest Christopher Monro was being anything less than truthful. But he was relating a fifty-year-old story which, by his own account, originated in unseen documents whose very existence was uncertain.

It has been widely assumed that Monro's hot potato concerned the identity of Jack the Ripper, but this appealing idea is speculative at best. It cannot be tested, yet nevertheless has lent itself to all manner of inventive interpretations.

However, it is feasible that it referred to the exploitation by the Metropolitan Police and others of a non-existent Jack the Ripper mystery for political ends. This would most certainly have been a hot potato.

If true, such exploitation could only have been possible by keeping the situation closely monitored, news carefully managed, all possible eventualities calculated and as few people as possible in the know. This was a tried-and-tested strategy. Two and a half thousand years earlier in "The Art of War" the Chinese general and military strategist Sun Tzu wrote—

"All warfare is based on deception . . . Successfully deceiving the enemy also relies on not letting your subordinates know precisely what you're doing."

From June 1890, aged fifty-two, his career dashed, beyond mending, and without a Home Office or Metropolitan Police pension,[111] James Monro spent an uncertain eighteen months. Little was heard of him, save for an article about the Metropolitan Police written for the *North American Review* which also appeared in an Italian periodical, *Minerva Rassegna Internazionale*.

In his article James Monro addressed the inadvisability of arming the police. He also took care to stress that the Metropolitan Police only operated within the limits of the law, thus refuting any idea of it being an oppressive force—

"The police . . . are not the representatives of an arbitrary and despotic power, directed against the rights or obtrusively interfering with the pleasures of law-abiding citizens . . ."

Following his resignation James Monro approached the Church Missionary Society, offering to work in India on their behalf, but the CMS dragged its feet and Monro withdrew his offer.[112] Still determined to do God's work, in November 1891 he set out with his elder daughter to India, supporting them on his Indian Civil Service pension of £1000 a year, plus support from various friends, to establish the Dayabari [House of Mercy] Medical Mission at Ranaghat, Bengal.

---

[111]   Winston Churchill, House of Commons, 13th April 1910
[112]   *God's Apprentice*, Bishop Stephen Neill, p. 21.

Hackney Express and Shoreditch Observer, 1st August 1891—

"It has been decided, in accordance with the wishes and express desire of Mr. James Monro, C.B., the late Chief Commissioner, that the Metropolitan Police testimonial on his retirement, subscribed to by all ranks of the force, shall take the form of endowing a bed at the Brighton Convalescent Home for the use and comfort of members of the Metropolitan Police Force only, to be called the 'Monro Testimonial Bed'."

At a farewell meeting a few of Monro's old colleagues presented him and his daughter with bibles, and on 12th November 1891 Mr. and Miss Monro boarded the P&O steamer *Chusan*, bound for India. Here Monro would live and work until returning permanently to Britain in 1905.[113]

Controversy followed James Monro onto the high seas.

Lloyds Weekly Newspaper, Sunday 15th November 1891—

"What Has Become of the Monro Testimonial?

"Mr. James Monro left London on Thursday for India, where, it is understood, he will, with the assistance of his daughter, carry on a mission at his own expense in Bengal.

"In view of Mr. Monro's departure from our midst on such a philanthropic mission, it would be interesting to have a certain important question settled. That is, what has become of the testimonial subscribed by the officers and men of the Metropolitan Police force on the occasion of the retirement of Mr. Monro from the post of Chief Commissioner? A sum of about £330 was subscribed throughout the force and sent to Scotland Yard.

"When Mr. Monro was consulted on the subject of the testimonial he desired that it should take some charitable form, and suggested the endowment of a cot in one of the hospitals, to be called the 'Monro Cot.' This suggestion was made just after his retirement, but it does not appear to have taken a practical shape yet. But why? A very serious state of affairs in connection with the executive department of the police force was

---

[113]   James Monro returned to Britain for a brief period in 1893.

hinted at by a contemporary a short time ago. Can it be true that the allegations do not end with the testimonial fund? We refrain from further comment at present, but there is a growing feeling that the matter ought to be cleared up. If not, it will no doubt be brought before Parliament when the House meets."

This potential embarrassment was hastily cleared up by Scotland Yard. On Monday November 16, 1891, the *Echo* reported—

"The Monro Testimonial.

"Sir Edward Bradford has published to the Metropolitan Police Force a letter from James Monro, ex-Commissioner of the force in reply to the communication sent on the 17th [August] by members of the committee of the Monro Testimonial Fund. In making eulogistic reference to the members of the force, Mr. Monro gratefully acknowledged the receipt of £520, which has been raised by members of the force, 'as a token of their kindly feelings towards me as their late chief,' and announces that the money has been placed in the hands of the trustees of the Police Convalescent Home Fund for the establishment and maintenance of a bed at the Police Seaside Home, West Brighton, for the exclusive benefit of members of the Metropolitan Police."

Catherine Gurney [Hon. Sec., Christian Police Association] announced in *The Times*, 17th June 1893—

"When opened the home will be to a great extent still dependent on voluntary contributions, there being no endowment except the one Monro Memorial Bed."

The memorial stone for the new Police Seaside Home at Brighton was laid by Princess Christian on 29th October 1892, and the building was officially opened by the Countess of Chichester on 21st July 1893.

Almost one hundred years later a Seaside Home would play a rôle in the identification of Jack the Ripper.

6. A SURFEIT OF SUSPECTS

Sir Edward Bradford was the very model of Victorian aplomb.

The Times, 23rd June 1890—

"More than 20 years ago Sir Edward Bradford, then in command of one of the Central Horse Regiments, was shooting on foot in Central India in company with Colonel Curtis, of the Inniskillens. While the beaters were driving up in his direction Colonel Bradford, from his position behind a bush, saw a wounded tigress approach. He pulled the trigger, but a twig of the bush had got under the hammer—it was before the days of sporting breech-loaders—his rifle missed fire. He then made for a small tank [a pond, or tarn] close by; but the tigress felled him by a blow on the shoulder, and was about to seize him by the throat when her jaws closed upon the wrist of the arm which he raised to protect himself.

"It illustrates Sir E. Bradford's characteristic quality of nerve that he had the presence of mind to remain perfectly motionless while the tigress slowly chewed his arm nearly up to the shoulder."

On 23rd June 1890 Sir Edward Bradford, who for the past three years had been secretary at the Political and Secret Department of the India Office in London, took over from James Monro as Commissioner of the Metropolitan Police, with Robert Anderson retained as his Assistant Commissioner [CID] and Melville Macnaghten as his Chief Constable [CID].

Anyone hoping Bradford's leadership of the Metropolitan Police might bring about an elucidation of the Whitechapel murders was to be sorely disappointed, for over the next five years the question of the identity of Jack the Ripper began to mimic Newton's third law of motion— "For every theory there is an equal and opposite theory."

Aside from a smattering of anecdotal Jack the Ripper references in cases of common assault from San Francisco to Surabaya to Surbiton all fell silent until January 1891, when "Later Leaves", the second volume of reminiscences by the magistrate and barrister Montagu Williams Q.C. was published—

"As my readers are aware, the [Whitechapel] murderer has not been arrested; but a curious set of circumstances which tend, perhaps, to throw light upon the mystery came to my knowledge at the time . . .

"I was sitting alone one afternoon, on a day on which I was off duty, when a card was brought to me, and I was informed that the gentleman whose name it bore desired that I would see him.

"My visitor was at once shown in. He explained that he had called for the purpose of having a conversation with me with regard to the perpetrator, or perpetrators, of the East End murders. He had, he said, taken a very great interest in the matter, and had set on foot a number of inquiries that had yielded a result which, in his opinion, afforded an undoubted clue to the mystery, and indicated beyond any doubt the individual, or individuals, on whom this load of guilt rested . . .

"My visitor handed me a written statement in which his conclusions were clearly set forth, together with the facts and calculations on which they were based; and, I am bound to say, this theory—for theory it, of necessity, is—struck me as being remarkably ingenious and worthy of the closest attention.

"Besides the written statement, this gentleman showed me copies of a number of letters that he had received from various persons in response to the representations he had made. It appeared that he had communicated his ideas to the proper authorities, and that they had given them every attention.

"Of course, the theory set forth by my visitor may be a correct one or it may not. Nothing, however, has occurred to prove it fallacious during the many months that have elapsed since the last of this terrible series of crimes.

"As I have said, I cannot take the reader into my confidence over this matter, as, possibly, in doing so I might be hampering the future course of justice.

"One statement, however, I may make, and, inasmuch as it is calculated to allay public fears, I do so with great pleasure. The cessation of the East End murders dates from the time when certain action was taken as a result of the promulgation of these ideas."

The identity of Montagu Williams' visitor remained unknown to his Victorian readership[114], as did the nature of the information he disclosed, but it appeared that the implementation of his theory—known to the police—was responsible for bringing the murders to an end, although this did not result in an arrest. Montagu Williams was being circumspect, careful not to possibly hamper "the course of future justice", which implied that Jack the Ripper was still at large.

On 7th February 1891 Aaron Kosminski, a 26-year-old Polish Jewish immigrant, was admitted to Colney Hatch Lunatic Asylum on a committal order issued by Henry Chambers J.P. In 1894 he was transferred to Leavesden Asylum, where he died in 1919.

Four days later, on 11th February 1891, a Jack the Ripper story appeared in the *Pall Mall Gazette*—

"There is a West of England member who in private (writes the London correspondent of the Nottingham Guardian) declares that he has solved the mystery of Jack the Ripper. His theory, and he repeats it with so much emphasis that it might be called his doctrine, is that Jack the Ripper committed suicide on the night of the last murder. I cannot give

---

[114]   Montagu Williams' visitor was Edward Knight Larkins, an HM Customs clerk who had evolved a theory based on the dates of Portuguese cattlemen arriving by ship in London. Robert Anderson dismissed him as a "troublesome faddist". Larkins wrote to the Home Secretary in 1893 charging that Anderson had "deliberately connived at the escape of these men, [and] that he has deliberately thrown every obstacle in the way of their being brought to justice." HO144/221/A49301C, ff. 230-278

details, but the story is so circumstantial that a good many people believe it. He states that a man with bloodstained clothes committed suicide on the night of the last murder and he asserts that the man was the son of a father who suffered from homicidal mania. I do not know what the police think of the story, but I believe that before long a clean breast will be made and that the accusation will be sifted thoroughly."

The *Bristol Times and Mirror*, same date, published almost the same story under the heading "Our London Letter." The major difference between the two was that, whereas the *Pall Mall Gazette* identified the man as "the son of a father who suffered from homicidal mania, the *Bristol Times and Mirror* identified him as "the son of a surgeon, who suffered from homicidal mania." That comma makes all the difference. It wasn't clear exactly who was suffering from homicidal mania, so the *Bristol Times and Mirror* version also contained the following disclaimer— "I can't give details, for fear of a libel action."

Identifying the London correspondent in question is difficult, for it was normal practice for two or more provincial newspapers to use the same source. Before launching the *Star* in 1888, T.P. O'Connor was London correspondent for the *Liverpool Post*, the *Sheffield Independent* and the *Darlington Echo*. And Henry W. Lucy, "the best known Parliamentarian living," wrote a London letter for no less than eight provincial newspapers.

The British Almanac, 1876—

"A special feature in most provincial journals, both daily and weekly, is the letter from its London correspondent, in which every kind of metropolitan rumour and gossip is dished up for the edification of country readers."

Ripperologists favouring Montague John Druitt as the Ripper have seized on this report as confirmation of their belief. But it need not detain us here, for events soon proved that both Montagu Williams and "the West of England member" had got their wires crossed.

Two days later, on Friday 13th February 1891, the body of a woman was found in the idyllically-named Swallow Gardens, one of three dank arched passageways running through a Great Eastern Railway viaduct.

Old memories were immediately stirred, and many US newspapers used the murder to give new impetus to the Jill the Ripper theory first mooted in a letter to the *Echo* on 12th September 1888—

"Sir, It being everyone's duty to assist in any way possible the elucidation of the above dreadful tragedies, may I, through you, ask the police whether they have given a thought to the possibility of the crimes having been committed by a woman or a man disguised as such!

"Yours obediently, F. H. H. Sept. 11."[115]

San Francisco Chronicle, 14th February 1891—

"Inspector Swanson says that any ruffian might have cut the unfortunate woman's throat in the way that this was done, but when a second soft felt hat rolled from under the victim's arm, in addition to the one she wore, he felt that this must have been done by the 'Ripper.' The theory has long been that he [the Ripper] paraded in woman's attire, and Swanson thinks he [the Ripper] dropped the hat while struggling with his victim."

The truth was more prosaic. The victim's recently-purchased black crêpe hat was found beside her body, and later her old black hat was discovered partly hidden within the folds of her dress.

Lloyds Weekly London Newspaper, 15th February 1891—

"The body was first discovered at a quarter past two o'clock. At three a.m. the code message: 'Another murder in Whitechapel' was flashed all over London, putting each division on the alert. Five minutes later the intelligence was telegraphed: 'Woman found in Swallow Gardens, Whitechapel, with her throat slit. The supposed work of Jack the Ripper.'"

This victim was different to those who had gone before inasmuch as she was known to a number of local police officers, whereas at the time of discovery the canonical five were unknown. Some knew her by the nickname 'Carroty Nell', others as Frances Coleman or Frances Hawkins. Her actual name was Frances Coles. She was a thirty-two-year-old prostitute.

---

[115]   See Chapter Nineteen. Did Francis Hughes-Hallett pen this letter?

Lloyds Weekly London Newspaper continued—

"Shortly before five o'clock, Chief Inspector Swanson, of Scotland-yard, arrived, and with other inspectors made a searching examination of the spot where the body was found and the ground adjoining, as well as the walls of the railway arch and the wooden hoarding. In previous crimes of this nature, writings have been found on walls in the vicinity, but in the present case no marks of any kind were observed. By the direction of Mr. Swanson, the pool of blood in the roadway was washed away after a portion had been collected and preserved, probably for analysis. The archway was then open for traffic."

And on another page—

"About noon, yesterday, Serjeants Don and Gill arrested, at the Phoenix public-house, Upper East Smithfield, James Thomas Sadler, fireman on the *Fez* steamship, now lying in the St. Katharine's dock, on suspicion of the murder. He was conveyed to Leman Street police-station, and there identified as having been with the girl."

Lloyds Weekly London Newspaper continued—

"Was it Jack-The-Ripper?

"Sir Edward Bradford, Chief Commissioner of the Police, stated to a representative of the Press on Friday, that he felt convinced from evidence of previous murders in Whitechapel that the murdered woman found that morning was the victim of the same assassin who had previously struck terror in the East-end."

Lloyds Weekly London Newspaper next took the opportunity to run the West of England member's story under the sub-heading "Remarkable Fiction".

The *North Eastern Daily Gazette*, 18th February 1891, attempted to clarify matters—

"The Member of Parliament who recently declared that 'Jack the Ripper' had killed himself on the evening of the last murder, adheres to his opinion. Even assuming that the man Sadler is able to prove his innocence of the murder of Frances Coles, he [the MP] maintains that the latest crime cannot be the author of the previous series of atrocities . . ."

If the MP's story was true, this much was self-evident. No matter whether Sadler was guilty or innocent, the Frances Coles murder could not have been the work of the deceased Jack the Ripper.

The newspaper then confounded matters by adding that "this view of the matter is steadily growing among those who do not see that there is any good reason to suppose that 'Jack the Ripper' is dead."

No one in the Metropolitan Police was foolish enough to commit themselves, for any firm conclusion might have elicited a demand for evidence.

North Eastern Daily Gazette, 19th February 1891—

"It will not be for lack of effort on the part of the police if they fail to connect Sadler with the recent murders in Whitechapel, or even with others which have been said to be the work of the mythical Jack the Ripper . . ."

The Metropolitan Police confronted 53 year-old James Thomas Sadler with Joseph Lawende, the witness who in September 1888 had allegedly seen Catherine Eddowes, the Mitre Square victim, in the company of a man just minutes before she was found dead.[116]

Identification proved negative. Sadler also had an alibi. Between 27th July and 1st October 1888 he had been a crew member aboard the cargo ship *Winestead* which had sailed from London, bound for Fiume and Venice on the Adriatic.

On 1st March 1891 the *Weekly Dispatch* recycled Montagu Williams' story—

"I have at this moment before me all the details of the matter, and they are certainly curious; but, like the Worship Street magistrate, I have some scruple in publishing them to the world—first because I should not like to give the miscreant a useful hint; and secondly because I should rather not incur any liability to what might follow if I seemed to be pointing at a man who, after all, happened to be the wrong one. It is very startling to know, however, that I have before me the name and full

---

[116] This witness is generally presumed to have been Joseph Lawende, who gave evidence at Catherine Eddowes' inquest.

particulars of the man who is pointed at by various converging lines of evidence as the infamous Whitechapel murderer; that he is perfectly well known; that there is no secret at all about his present whereabouts, and that the London police actually did make an abortive attempt to catch him. It is very probable that more will be heard of this before long, and I hardly think the action of the London police will derive much credit from the affair."

This *I know but can't tell you in case I'm wrong* account and the *I can't give details for fear of a libel action* suicide story from the "West of England member" both failed to explain why the police had recently investigated James Sadler as Jack the Ripper, going so far as to confront him with the 1888 witness, Joseph Lawende.

On 3rd March 1891 the Treasury solicitor dropped the case against Sadler.

Nottingham Evening Post, 5th March 1891—

"The discharge of Sadler today ought really to force the West Country Member, who believes that he can point to the author of the Whitechapel murders, to put his evidence before the police authorities. The man he suspects is dead, but as the police authorities believe the last murder to be the work of Jack the Ripper it would be of immense advantage in tracking the real murderer to have all the facts before them."

Nothing more was heard from the West Country Member.

Almost a year later a new Ripper story appeared, this time in the *Rocky Mountain News* [Colorado], 17th January 1892. It was datelined "London, Jan 2."

After reporting that a Royal Commission was to "investigate the now almost forgotten Whitechapel murders", the newspaper continued—

"It is understood that the death of a Catholic priest in the east end of London has placed some important revelations in the hands of the police. There can be no doubt that the priest, under the seal of confession, died possessed of information that might have led to the arrest of the murderer or murderers of the wretched women known as Jack the Ripper's victims. That the priest had qualms of conscience regarding the sanctity of confession, even in connection with such atrocities, is evinced by the sealed packet he left behind him addressed to Sir Edward Bradford, chief of London's police department. On the package was inscribed, in the dead priest's handwriting, 'This is to be opened after my death - my lips must never reveal it.' Beyond the above, carelessly mentioned by a garrulous official who has since been severely reprimanded for his indiscretion, no further information can be obtained from the police."

The identity of the "garrulous official" is unknown, but here it should be noted that on 7th February 1892, Chief Inspector Frederick George Abberline, aged 49, lead investigator during the Whitechapel murders, retired from the Metropolitan Police.

Nothing more was heard of the Royal Commission, nor the mysterious packet delivered to Sir Edward Bradford, but it wasn't long before a story emanating from Scotland Yard appeared in the *Western Mail*, 26th February 1892.

Written by James Mackenzie Maclean, Conservative MP for Oldham, part- owner of the *Western Mail* and also the newspaper's London correspondent, it cast doubt upon all previous Jack the Ripper stories—

"Remarkable Statement By A Scotland Yard Detective," ran the headline. "The Chain of Evidence All But Complete.

"I am in a position to give, on the authority of a Scotland Yard detective, a somewhat remarkable piece of information respecting the hunt of the English police after the perpetrator of the terrible series of East End murders which convulsed the whole country with horror a while ago. We have heard nothing of 'Jack the Ripper' for some time past—over a year—and his murderous operations have not been renewed."

There followed official confirmation that Jack the Ripper had not committed suicide. He was very much alive and until recently been under surveillance.

"The reason of this is that the police have, for many months past, been perfectly certain that they have discovered the man. The chain of evidence has been completed with the exception of a single link. That link they have been making unavailing endeavours to supply. The suspected criminal, till within a month at any rate, has been shadowed night and day, awake and asleep, by Scotland Yard detectives. Everything points to the conclusion that he has himself been perfectly aware of this vigilance on the part of the police, and it is, no doubt, from this cause, and this alone, that the Whitechapel murders have ceased."

The *Western Mail* next identified the "West of England member" who had broken the 11th February 1891 Jack the Ripper suicide story.

"Mr. Farquharson, MP for West Dorset[117], was credited, I believe, some time since with having evolved a remarkable theory of his own in the matter. He believed that the author of the outrages destroyed himself. But if the police have been on the right track this theory is naturally exploded."

It was a big "but". An element of doubt had crept in, for if it proved that the police were on the wrong track then the murders had to have ceased for a different reason, perhaps putting the Jack the Ripper suicide story back in play. However, from what followed this seems unlikely. The police had a ready explanation for their inability to bring the suspect to justice. And if in the end he got away—well, there was a precedent for such an eventuality.

The *Western Mail* explained—

"There is, as a matter of fact, nothing improbable in the belief arrived at by the Scotland Yard detectives in this matter. It is quite common, indeed, for a criminal to get off in this manner . . . about two years ago the London police were on the track of a begging letter writer . . . They knew who the man was perfectly well, shadowed him persistently in the East End, knew his address, and several of his friends and accomplices. Yet they could not complete their chain of evidence. The man was never nailed, and he finally left London because his business was too much hampered by the police. But he has never to this day been arrested."

---

[117]   Henry Richard Farquharson MP was also Lord of the Manor and principal landowner at Tarrant Gunville in Dorset. He was a close neighbour of the Druitt family.

By now Victorian newspaper readers who were following the subject of the Whitechapel murders might have been forgiven for believing they had somehow wandered into a wilderness of mirrors.

Two weeks later, on 12th March 1892, in Southern Cross, near Perth, Western Australia, Frederick Bailey Deeming was arrested for murder. The details of his case need not detain us. The important aspect about Deeming is that the Australian press got it into its collective head to accuse him of being Jack the Ripper when the bodies of his first wife and four children were found with their throats slashed under the floor of a house he had rented on Merseyside. An account was published of his being seen in London on the night of the "double-event"; reports told of an acquaintanceship with Catherine Eddowes, and his handwriting was compared with certain "Ripper" letters.

On 28th March 1892 a story from Perth, Western Australia, appeared in *The Times*, reporting that Deeming had actually confessed to being the perpetrator of the "last two so-called Jack the Ripper murders in London."

Five days later, on 2nd April 1892, the *Hull and North Lincolnshire Times* published a story, again apparently emanating from Scotland Yard. Written by "A Belfast newspaper's London correspondent", it began—

"The Scotland Yard authorities did not believe the alleged confession of the Whitechapel murders by Deeming."

According to this report, Scotland Yard next took the unprecedented step of announcing a more likely candidate—

"The fact is they consider, rightly or wrongly, that they have the author of the Whitechapel tragedies now under lock and key at Portland prison undergoing a sentence of 20 years' penal servitude. He is a Belgian, tried and sentenced some six months ago for attempting to obtain money from ladies by threats of violence . . .

Once again there was that elusive "one link in the chain of evidence missing, [but] they expect, sooner or later, to be able to supply it."

The newspaper article then changed tack.

"This information reached me yesterday [1st April], and a few hours later, strange to say, another letter from an alleged Jack the Ripper was

116

received by Mr. Hopkins, stipendiary magistrate at Lambeth Police Court . . . The latest intimation is to the effect that 'Jack the Ripper' means to commence his tricks about Cable and Flower and Dean Streets, and he asks the magistrate to see if the bluecoats have their eyes open."

The Belgian in Portland prison may have been a Dane. Charles Le Grand, a blackmailer and erstwhile private detective who made a fleeting appearance during the investigation of "Ripper" victim Elizabeth Stride, was sentenced in November 1891 on charges of blackmail to twenty years' hard labour, plus another seven years for attempted fraud.

It has been suggested that the "Belgian" and the suspect in the *Western Mail* were one and the same, but at that time Le Grand had been in prison for only three months.

Also of interest is the letter "from an alleged Jack the Ripper" having been sent to the stipendiary magistrate at Lambeth Police Court, who had been the magistrate before whom Thomas Hayne Cutbush, a Jack the Ripper candidate, had first appeared in March of the previous year.

Two years passed.

Interest in the Whitechapel murders was resurrected on Tuesday 13th February 1894 by two newspaper stories; one in *The Morning Leader* which asserted that Jack the Ripper was in Dartmoor Prison Asylum, and a second in the *Sun*, stating that Jack the Ripper had been "sent forthwith to the living tomb of a lunatic asylum" but not at first naming the institution.

The Morning Leader had obtained its story from "a Scotland Yard officer", an Inspector in the Criminal Investigation Department who had been watching "the movements of this man for three years, and from the evidence in my possession I hope to be able to bring home to him the charges of the Whitechapel atrocities."

Meanwhile the *Sun* was ploughing its own Jack the Ripper furrow. Between Tuesday 13th and Monday 19th February 1894 it ran a six-part story, lavish in circumstantial detail and in places employing a narrative style worthy of Wilkie Collins or Arthur Conan Doyle.

The *Sun* story had its origins in a series of incidents which took place in 1891 at around the same time as the Frances Coles murder.

In the Brixton and Kennington districts of south London a number of women had been jabbed in the buttocks with a knife. Two young men were arrested. Despite pleas of mistaken identity, the first, 27 year-old John Edwin Colocott[118], was found guilty but, on the arrest of the second, released on two family sureties of £100.

The second young man did not fare so well. Lambeth magistrate Mr. Arthur Antwis Hopkins committed him for trial at the next Sessions.

Leopold John Manners De Michele, prosecuting for the Crown, argued whether the defendant was competent to plead, and Dr. Gilbert, the medical officer at Holloway prison, declared that although he was "not absolutely insane, he was sufficiently so not to understand the gravamen of the charge brought against him, and was quite incompetent to plead."

A jury at the London County Sessions agreed, and 26-year-old Thomas Hayne Cutbush was ordered to be detained "during her Majesty's pleasure".

Whilst much indignation was expressed at what was seen as a travesty of justice, there was a hint of deeper concern.

Lloyds Weekly Newspaper, 19th April 1891—

"What we plead for is inquiry, so that justice may be done, the innocent freed from suspicion, and the doubts of the public set at rest. For it is idle to deny that, in certain police circles, and among those who have had to inquire into the Brixton mystery, there is a growing feeling that it may in the end prove to be in some way connected with the darker and more tragic mysteries of the East-end."

Had Jack the Ripper finally been caught?

Without naming Cutbush, the *Sun* would polish this rough gem of a story into sparkling brilliance—

"Jack the Ripper . . . was first brought to imprisonment on the charge of being simply a dangerous lunatic. And the evidence of his lunacy - hopeless, abysmal and loathsome - was so palpable that he was

---

[118]   Age and name taken from the 1891 UK Census. In newspaper reports his age varied and his name was variously reported as Colocitt, Collicot and Collocott.

not permitted even to plead. In the brief of the counsel who prosecuted, in the instructions of the solicitor who defended, there was the same statement - that he was suspected of being Jack the Ripper. In the case of both the one and the other, the very mention of this or any other dark suspicion was precluded; for, unable to plead, the wretched creature in the dock was saved from all indictment; was spared the necessity of all defence. He was sent forthwith to the living tomb of a lunatic asylum, and there he might have passed to death without mention of his terrible secret if a chance clue had not put a representative of The Sun on the track. The clue thus accidentally obtained has been followed up by months of patient investigation, and has been thoroughly sifted. Today we lay before the world a story - consecutive, careful, and firmly knit - which we believe will offer the solution of the greatest murder mystery of the nineteenth century."

The *Sun* concluded—

"We understand that the attention of the highest police authorities has been called to our statements, and we confidently look forward to our story being subjected to the closest and most searching investigation."

The Metropolitan Police maintained its official silence, neither confirming nor denying matters in the London press, but a Canadian newspaper, *Qu'Appelle Progress*, later reported that, "The police who have been interested in the Whitechapel murder cases are not disposed to give much credit to the Sun's story, which is generally regarded as sensational, and open to grave suspicions as to its veracity."[119]

Lloyds Weekly Newspaper recognised the story as "an old narrative" from its own pages. "There is not a new feature in it, though the journalistic embellishments are as manifold as the assertion is daring. We asked for an inquiry into the strange case, and still expect that one will be held."

The *Sun's* editor was T.P. [Thomas Power] O'Connor, Irish Parliamentary Party MP for the Liverpool Scotland constituency. A supporter of Charles Parnell and Irish Home Rule, in January 1888 he

---

[119] 29th March 1894

launched the *Star,* the newspaper which in the energetic style of "new journalism" had almost single-handedly defined the Whitechapel murders.

Prior to publication of its story the *Sun* interviewed Henry Labouchere [120], whose comments appeared in the article's final installment—

"The Broadmoor lunatic may have been Jack, he may, for all that you know. Jack very probably was the same sort of man as the lunatic. But this, I should fancy, might be said of many inhabitants of the metropolis. But when you have to prove the commission of a murder by an individual, you must show, not that he might have committed it, but that there is no other hypothesis for an admitted effect but one. This you have not done."

Labouchere did not think the *Sun* had made its case.

He continued—

"I read through attentively all the proofs and suggestions of the *Sun,* for they interested me. The conclusion I arrived at was that the *Sun* had made out a fair case for public investigation."

"Then you would recommend public investigation?" asked the reporter.

"Yes," replied Labouchere; "if I were Mr. Asquith [Home Secretary] I should elect a clever officer to look into the matter. He would do so carefully, for I suppose that the reward still remains valid."

Other readers of the *Sun* agreed.

"A Liberal" wrote, "Surely some action by the Home Office is necessary. What have the Police authorities to say? It reflects no credit on Scotland Yard that the detection of this infamous scoundrel should be left to the enterprise of the *Sun.* If Scotland Yard still entertains a doubt, let Mr. Asquith appoint a committee of experts to examine into and sift the mass of evidence which you have gathered with so much labour."

"Pall Mall, W" wrote, "I have slowly come to the conclusion that you

---

[120] In 1887 Labouchere and O'Connor, plus mustard magnate Jeremiah Colman and a group of other wealthy Liberals, co-founded the *Star,* O'Connor's journalistic skills providing an opportunity to advance a Liberal agenda in the face of a predominantly Tory evening press.

have, at least, made out a very good case for official investigation."

The *Sun* story, normally the stuff of silly-season journalism, appeared at a critical time. In February 1894 Prime Minister William Gladstone, then 84 years old, frail and further afflicted by failing eyesight, had just returned from Biarritz to rumours of his resignation. There were also rumours of parliamentary dissolution, and *The Times* had earlier reported T.P. O'Connor as declaring that if an election were to take place under present circumstances the Liberals would undergo a crushing defeat; also that a big Tory majority would dash any future hopes of Irish Home Rule.

In the midst of such constitutional finagling the matter of Jack the Ripper would appear to have been of trifling interest. But there was a deeper purpose to the story. Using Cutbush as a stalking horse, the Sun was attempting to press for a full inquiry into the Whitechapel murders which had taken place during the previous Tory administration.

The *Morning Leader* story was published on the same day as the first installment of the serial in the *Sun*. The strange coincidence of two Jack the Ripper stories appearing in different newspapers on the same day was explained by T.P. O'Connor in the *Sun's* final installment.

"It was not our intention to have published the story for some weeks to come," he wrote, "but on Monday night I was called out to the Lobby of the House of Commons by two of my staff, to tell me that a portion of our information was to be offered to two morning papers. I am glad to say, for the credit of journalism, that *The Morning*, a Conservative contemporary, refused to have anything to do with a discovery the credit of which belonged to another office; in other quarters the taste and the honour were not so delicate as we had anticipated, and there was consequently nothing for it but to stop up all night and bring out the *Sun* as a morning paper at five o'clock instead of an evening paper at the usual hour."

That a portion of the *Sun's* exclusive story was being peddled amongst the competition doesn't add up, for although the two stories shared certain details—most notably that after the last Jack the Ripper murder, in 1891, the murderer had been removed to an asylum—they had many differences, the most obvious being *The Morning Leader's* substitution of Dartmoor for Broadmoor.

The *Sun's* elaborately-detailed 17,000-word story was intended to provoke an official inquiry into Scotland Yard's failure to catch Jack the Ripper. By contrast *The Morning Leader's* condensed 1000-word version was little more than the tale of a Scotland Yard Inspector who had a hunch about a lunatic in Dartmoor Asylum and claimed to have in his possession a "knife of Chinese manufacture with which the Whitechapel murders had been perpetrated".

"Do the Scotland Yard authorities believe in your story?" asked *The Morning Leader*.

"Well," said the Inspector, "they believe in my story to this extent, that they have allowed me a bonus for the information I have supplied."

However, not satisfied with financial reward and still wholly convinced of his case against the lunatic in Dartmoor Asylum, the anonymous Inspector, thwarted by red tape and also the victim of professional jealousy from within the Metropolitan Police at having solved the Whitechapel murders mystery, sought the aid of *The Morning Leader*.

"Only with the aid of the press can I hope to succeed, and you will do a public service by disclosing my story, and the statements so specifically made ought easily and readily to be either confirmed or contradicted."

Two days later *The Morning Leader* sought an opinion on its story from one of Scotland Yard's "head officials". By this time the *Sun* had published the second of its six-part Ripper series, and a sub-editor at *The Morning Leader,* suddenly aware that there was no lunatic asylum at Dartmoor, expeditiously moved Jack the Ripper to "the infirmary at Dartmoor Gaol."

"There is a large basis of truth in it," said the Scotland Yard official. "It's only defect is that it is about three years old . . . It's leading incidents are as familiar to me as the features of my 10-year-old child."[121]

---

[121] In February 1894, Donald Swanson's daughter, Ada Mary, was 10-years old.

Where did the "large basis of truth" lay in the Inspector's story? That Jack the Ripper was incarcerated in a non-existent lunatic asylum? If so, how could the Inspector have been watching "the movements of this man for three years . . ."? And which three year-old "leading incidents" were so familiar to the Scotland Yard official? The implication was the 1891 case of Thomas Hayne Cutbush. But there were no incidents in the Inspector's story; merely a litany of frustrated suspicions. What, then, could have been the truth? Was it, perhaps, that the Whitechapel murders had been perpetrated with the knife of Chinese manufacture?

The Scotland Yard official equivocated.

"I have seen the Chinese knife, and I have seen many other Chinese knives that have never see China."

The Morning Leader soon realized its story wasn't worth the candle.

"Even the original police-inspector who is said to be responsible for the story rejects the deduction which is sought to be drawn from it."

"I never said," the anonymous Inspector declared, now wildly back-pedalling, "that I had secured the Whitechapel murderer. All that I have endeavored to establish has been a carefully collected chain of circumstantial evidence, pointing almost entirely in one direction, yet at the same time capable, with added information and fresher facts, of being diverted into other possible channels."

The Morning Leader dropped its story, and the anonymous Inspector, still apparently believing in the truth of his story, walked off into history to the sound of his own footsteps.

Whilst there is not a hint of the anonymous Inspector and his Chinese knife in the *Sun* story, some modern theorists have posited that both newspaper stories were essentially the same and that their single source was Inspector William Nixon Race.

It was Inspector Race who, in 1891, had arrested Thomas Cutbush. Despite an excellent service record, in later years he was overlooked for promotion. Beset by ill health brought on by the untimely death of his son, in July 1898—a month short of eighteen years' service—he was invalided out of the Metropolitan Police on a reduced pension at the age of thirty nine.[122]

Theorists claim that Inspector Race being passed over for promotion was official payback from Scotland Yard for his dealings with the *Sun* newspaper and the embarrassment its revelations had caused.

The Morning Leader's anonymous Inspector having been William Race is a neat construct, but does not bear much scrutiny.

In *The Sun's* first installment T.P. O'Connor explained how the lunatic's "terrible secret" would have passed unnoticed had a "chance clue not put a representative of the *Sun* on the track. The clue thus accidentally obtained has been followed up by months of patient investigation, and has been thoroughly sifted."

In the final installment O'Connor again stressed how long his newspaper had been working on the story. "We had this information for months in our office; for months the representatives of the paper have been searching for witnesses, examining them, often finding them only after weeks of patient labour."

If this "chance clue" was William Race it implies that the Inspector took his story to the *Sun* "months" beforehand, during the latter quarter of 1893. By 13th February 1894 the investigation he apparently so eagerly sought was ready to go to print. Yet on the day before publication we are asked to believe he undermined the *Sun's* "weeks of patient labour" by seeking the assistance of a rival newspaper in a circumstantial story which was looked upon by his superiors with a wry smile.

There is also the matter of *The Morning Leader's* Inspector admitting that in going to the press his "statements so specifically made ought easily and readily to be either confirmed or contradicted." This didn't exactly speak volumes about his levels of confidence, so unless he had some sort of death wish it is unlikely in the extreme he might have risked his future career by breaking ranks and going to the press if there was the slightest possibility of his suspicions being groundless.

So what could have been the source and purpose of *The Morning Leader* story if it was not an act of self-immolation by Inspector Race, or,

---

[122] Lloyds Weekly Newspaper, 3rd July 1898

as T.P. O'Connor averred, a leaked portion of his own six-part series in the *Sun?*

The *Sun* and *The Morning Leader* were no ordinary rival newspapers.

In his 1928 volume of reminiscences *Memoirs of an Old Parliamentarian*, T.P. O'Connor, co-founder and first editor of the *Star*, recalled earlier days—

"I was recommended by Sir John Robinson, of the Daily News, to a young man named Ernest Parke, then working in the office of a City newspaper . . . He was, as he is, a singular mixture of shrewdness and ideals; an intense Radical, and at the same time a thoroughly practical journalist. He might be trusted to work up any sensational news of the day, and helped, with Jack the Ripper, to make gigantic circulations hitherto unparalleled in evening journalism."

Ernest Parke became chief sub-editor on the *Star*. He also edited his own obscure radical weekly, *The North London Press,* which in 1889 had named Henry Fitzroy, Earl of Euston, in "an indescribably loathsome scandal in Cleveland Street". Parke was sued for libel and in January 1890 sentenced to twelve months' imprisonment [he was released after twenty-five weeks on grounds of ill-health], during which time he lost a stone [14 pounds] in weight and the *Star* floundered.

On 27th May 1890 an unnamed London correspondent wrote in the New Zealand *West Coast Times*—

"Whether Mr. Ernest Parke did or did not keep the wheels of the Star running smoothly may be judged from the fact that though only a couple of months have elapsed since his departure, the editorial department of the paper is in a state of chaos . . . The 'Star' in fact, seems within an ace of collapse, and all for want of Parke's cool head, and infinite tact, and consummate knowledge of his comrades."

Later that year T.P. O'Connor parted acrimoniously from the *Star,* pocketing £15,000 compensation for his interest in the newspaper whilst giving a promise not to start a rival *daily* newspaper for three years. Henry Massingham continued as the *Star's* editor, resigning in January 1891 to be temporarily replaced by James Stuart MP, Chairman of the *Star's* board of directors, and, ultimately, Ernest Parke.

Adhering strictly to the terms of his promise, on Sunday 10th May 1891 T.P. O'Connor launched a new *weekly* newspaper, the *Sun*, whose immediate popularity soon killed off the weekly edition of the *Star*.

In the spring of 1892 the *Star* launched a rival to the new halfpenny daily newspaper, *The Morning,* a move which made Ernest Parke editor of both the *Star* and its new sister paper *The Morning Leader*.

In mid-July 1893, on the day following the expiration of his three-year promise, T.P. O'Connor launched his own evening daily, the *Sun*. Its first edition achieved a circulation of 277,540 copies as against the *Star's* same-day 142,600.[123]

And so it was that seven months later, in February 1894, T.P. O'Connor and Ernest Parke, the two pioneering journalists who whilst working together on the *Star* had almost defined the 1888 Whitechapel murders, found themselves at odds over a story concerning the identity of Jack the Ripper.

The Morning Leader, seemingly with the imprimatur of Scotland Yard, had run a spoiler story. Exactly who was behind it is anyone's guess, but it rendered T.P. O'Connor's lavish serial dead in the water.

Fate also proved to have been an accomplice in the demise of the *Sun* story.

On the afternoon of 15th February 1894, the third day of the *Sun's* Jack the Ripper serial, Greenwich Observatory was the object of an attempted bombing by a 26-year-old French anarchist, Martial Bourdin. He died shortly after the explosive device he was carrying accidentally detonated before he reached his target.[124]

Upon Bourdin's body was found a membership card for the Autonomie Club. The police wasted little time. On the following evening William Melville, Chief Inspector Littlechild's successor as head of Special Branch, led a highly-publicised raid on this "chief refuge of all Continental Anarchists arriving in London", located in Windmill Street, off Tottenham Court Road. Many of the arrestees were deported but

---

[123] *British Printer*, August 1893
[124] Joseph Conrad used the incident as the basis for his novel *The Secret Agent*.

with no charges made against them.

Bourdin's death was widely reported. Just days earlier in Paris a bomb had exploded in the crowded café of the Hôtel Terminus, close to the St Lazare railway station, and the Greenwich explosion caused many to fear that continental anarchist terrorism had once again crossed the Channel. Foreigners became regarded as suspicious with renewed vigour and questions were tabled in the House of Commons as to whether the government might consider reversing its immigration policy.

The *Western Mail,* 16th February 1894, reprinted *The Morning Leader's* story, noting that Scotland Yard had discredited it, before going on to condemn the *Sun's* version as "entirely uninteresting", intimating that it was an attempt to get mileage out of a rejected story by means of a different suspect. "It seems scarcely possible to imagine that there should be two men so closely associated with Whitechapel, and at the same time capable of such a succession of crimes all more or less alike."

Understandably, given the circumstances, there was no reaction to the *Sun's* call for an official inquiry into the 1888 Whitechapel murders, and no questions were raised in parliament.

However, unbeknownst to the public, press or parliament the *Sun* newspaper had touched a nerve at Scotland Yard.

The Jack the Ripper mystery was about to undergo its most defining moment.

7. VARIOUS TALL TALES

On Friday 23rd February 1894, four days after the *Sun's* final installment, Metropolitan Police Chief Constable Melville Leslie Macnaghten signed a confidential memorandum.

There are two versions of the "Macnaghten Memorandum," but before going into details it is useful to quote what Sir Basil Thomson[125] said about Macnaghten in his 1922 book "Queer People"—

"He had an astonishing memory both for faces and for names: he could tell you every detail about a ten-year-old crime, the names of the victim, the perpetrator, and every important witness, and, what was more useful, the official career of every one of his seven hundred men and his qualifications and ability."

Taken in chronological order of discovery, the first, an undated "draft version", came to light in 1959. Discovered amongst the papers of Macnaghten's daughter, Lady Christabel Aberconway, it was first revealed by journalist and investigative TV reporter Dan Farson.

The second version, dated 23rd February 1894, filed at the National Archives as the "Macnaghten Report"[126], was first seen in the mid-1960s by writer Robin Odell and reproduced in the *Mayflower* paperback

---

125 Basil Thomson was Macnaghten's successor at Scotland Yard.
126 MEPO 3/141, fols. 177-83

edition of his book *Jack the Ripper in Fact and Fiction*.

Although there are significant and insignificant differences between the two versions, the following is based on the signed and dated Macnaghten Report, which might reasonably be termed the definitive version.

The *Sun's* suspect had been unnamed, but Macnaghten immediately identified him as Thomas Cutbush, "nephew of the late [127] Supt. Executive" [Superintendent Charles Henry Cutbush, Executive Division, Scotland Yard].

Macnaghten identifying Thomas Cutbush as the nephew of Superintendent Charles Henry Cutbush is perplexing.

For Thomas Hayne Cutbush and Superintendent Charles Henry Cutbush to be nephew and uncle, the latter would have to have been the brother of Thomas Taylor Cutbush. But here we encounter yet another Macnaghten anomaly.

In a Cutbush "Pedigree" [family tree] drawn up for the 1891 case of *Cutbush v. Cutbush*128 he does not appear. Thomas Taylor Cutbush did not have a brother; only three sisters. The two men were born six months apart to quite separate and unrelated sets of parents—Charles in Ashford, Kent, January 1844; Thomas in Enfield, Middlesex, July 1844.

Before rejecting Cutbush as the Whitechapel murderer Macnaghten first countered the *Sun's* "terrible list" of *nine* Jack the Ripper murders which included Frances Coles as the final victim, by writing—

"Now the Whitechapel murderer had 5 victims -- & 5 victims only, -- his murders were . . . "(1) 31st August '88. Mary Ann Nichols . . . (2) 8th Sept. '88 Annie Chapman . . . (3) 30th Sept. '88. Elizabeth Stride & *on same date* Catherine Eddowes . . . 9th November. Mary Jane Kelly . . .

"No one ever saw the Whitechapel murderer; many homicidal maniacs were suspected, but no shadow of proof could be thrown on any one."

This prompts the question of just how many known homicidal

---

[127]   "Late" as in retired. Charles Cutbush died in 1896. This relationship was excised from the "Aberconway" version.

[128]   UK National Archives J86/270 & J68/853

maniacs were freely roaming the streets at the time.

Macnaghten continued—

"I may mention the cases of 3 men, any one of whom would have been more likely than Cutbush to have committed this series of murders:

"(1) A Mr. M. J. Druitt, said to be a doctor & of good family - who disappeared at the time of the Miller's Court murder, & whose body (which was said to have been upwards of a month in the water) was found in the Thames on 31st December - or about 7 weeks after that murder. He was sexually insane and from private inf[ormation] I have little doubt but that his own family believed him to have been the murderer.

"(2) Kosminski - a Polish Jew - & resident in Whitechapel. This man became insane owing to many years indulgence in solitary vices. He had a great hatred of women, specially of the prostitute class, & had strong homicidal tendencies: he was removed to a lunatic asylum about March 1889. There were many circumstances connected with this man which made him a strong 'suspect'.

"(3) Michael Ostrog, a Russian doctor, and a convict, who was subsequently detained in a lunatic asylum as a homicidal maniac. This man's antecedents were of the worst possible type, and his whereabouts at the time of the murders could never be ascertained."

As the Macnaghten Report bears no Scotland Yard or Home Office "date received" stamps it is widely believed to have been written as an informal briefing note for Metropolitan Police Commissioner Sir Edward Bradford or Home Secretary Herbert Asquith in the event of the *Sun* story turning septic. But whilst at a glance this might appear to be a plausible explanation, it is hard to believe that in the event of any searching questions being asked the Macnaghten Report could have ever hoped to obviate an official enquiry, for this hopelessly inaccurate and wildly misleading document would not have withstood a moment's close scrutiny.

Macnaghten stated quite categorically that the Whitechapel murderer had "5 victims -- & 5 victims only": that the killer ceased operations after Mary Jane Kelly, on 9th November 1888.

He next enumerated three suspects who, out of "many homicidal maniacs", were only "more likely" to have been the Whitechapel murderer.

The first was Mr. M.J. Druitt, "a doctor", whose body "was found in the Thames on 31st December 1888". He had been in the water for "upwards of a month".

A search of police, inquest and newspaper reports from January 1889 would have established that on 31st December 1888 the body of Montague John Druitt, *a barrister and schoolteacher,* was recovered from the River Thames. He appeared to have committed suicide following a troubling personal incident.

Whilst Macnaghten had got the name and date right, Druitt was not a doctor; nor did he disappear at the time of the Millers Court murder, and when discovered his body had been in the River Thames for slightly under a month. Nothing at his inquest offered any suggestion of a connection with the Whitechapel murders.

Druitt's candidature as a Ripper suspect may have been prompted by the suicide story from West of England MP Henry Farquharson, who claimed that Jack the Ripper had been the son of a surgeon.

Montague John Druitt's late father had been a surgeon, but aside from this fact there was nothing in the story to support the idea of the young barrister and teacher being the Whitechapel murderer. Quite the contrary. Far from Druitt committing suicide on the night of the last murder, 9th November 1888, reference to the *Law Journal* would have shown that, two-and-a-half weeks later, on 27th November 1888, he appeared as counsel in a case at the Court of Appeal. It was also revealed at his inquest that in a pocket was found a second-class return ticket from Hammersmith to Charing Cross dated 1st December, which established the earliest date on which he could have committed suicide.

The Druitt story purported to explain why the murders had ceased and why the murderer had not been caught. But this could not have been because Jack the Ripper drowned himself in the Thames in 1888, for the police had "watched and shadowed" Jack the Ripper until as late as January 1892. The killings stopped only because the suspect was aware of this surveillance. But for a want of evidence he would have been behind bars. There was also the matter of police suspicion regarding a Belgian in Portland prison.

With Druitt dead, who could the police have been shadowing in January 1892? Certainly neither of Macnaghten's other two "more likely than Cutbush" suspects for, as we shall see, at this crucial time both were in lunatic asylums.

Macnaghten's second suspect was a Polish Jew, "Kosminski", who "was removed to an asylum about March 1889".

This date was wildly off the mark, but at a casual glance a measure of cause and effect could be drawn from James Monro's 15th March 1889 report informing the Home Secretary that the extra Whitechapel patrols "had now ceased." But what Macnaghten neglected to explain was why, if Kosminski was the murderer and now in an asylum, four months later in a report to the Home Office dated 17th July 1889 Metropolitan Police Commissioner James Monro "was inclined to believe" that the murderer of Alice McKenzie was "identical with the notorious Jack the Ripper of last year."[129]

In February 1891 Sir Edward Bradford said exactly the same thing about the Frances Coles murder, so why two Commissioners of Police should have been so unaware that the Whitechapel murderer was either dead or had been removed to an asylum must remain a matter for conjecture.

Macnaghten would briefly address these inconsistencies in his 1914 memoirs. However, from an 1894 perspective there were other issues for him to resolve. And none more so than with his third suspect.

Michael Ostrog, a thief and confidence trickster, was described in the Police Gazette, 1873, as "a Russian Pole, evidently an educated man, and is said to speak seven different languages and [is] of plausible and pleasing manners."

Macnaghten wrote that Ostrog's "whereabouts at the time of the murders could never be ascertained"; also that he was "subsequently

---

[129]   HO144/221/A493011

detained in a lunatic asylum as a homicidal maniac."

The best lies contain an element of truth.

On 26th October 1888 a notice appeared in the *Police Gazette*—

"Convict Supervision Office . . . Michael Ostrog . . . On 10th March 1888 he was liberated from the Surrey County Lunatic Asylum, and failed to report. Warrant issued. Special attention is called to this dangerous man."

Michael Ostrog was rearrested in 1891, and on 18th April charged at Bow Street Magistrates Court for failing to report himself whilst under police supervision. It was also alleged at the time that he was in the habit of feigning insanity when in custody. On 7th May 1891 he was committed to Banstead Lunatic Asylum in Surrey, which received pauper lunatics from the county of Middlesex.

On the very same day Macnaghten wrote to the medical officer at Banstead—

"I shall feel obliged if you will cause immediate information to be sent to this office in the event of his discharge, as the Magistrate adjourned the case *sine die*[130] in order that he [Ostrog] might again be brought up and dealt with for failing to report himself if it is found that he is feigning insanity."[131]

Two years later, on 29th May 1893, Ostrog was discharged "recovered" from Banstead Lunatic Asylum. Whether or not Dr. T. Claye Shaw, Principal and Medical Superintendent, advised Macnaghten as requested is not known.

More details about Ostrog's earlier criminal career would later emerge.

In July 1894, five months after Macnaghten wrote his memorandum, Michael Ostrog appeared at Aylesbury Quarter Sessions charged on two counts of theft, one from a jeweller in Eton, Berkshire, on 13th May 1889. Ostrog pleaded his innocence, telling the court he had been in a French asylum until 1890, but the court did not believe his story and he

---

[130]   *sine die* (from the Latin "without day") means to adjourn "without assigning a day for a further meeting or hearing."
[131]   Greater London Record Office.

was sentenced to five years' penal servitude.

On 9th October 1894, just three months after Ostrog began his sentence, a letter arrived at HM Treasury from the Home Office[132] stating that, "Ostrog has established the fact that in 1889, when the offence was committed, he was in prison in France"; also, that "the Secretary of State has directed the Police to give him £10, taking his receipt as in full discharge of all claims."

Research by the late historian and author Philip Sugden [133] established that throughout the 1888 Whitechapel murders Michael Ostrog had been in a Parisian jail awaiting trial for the theft of a microscope, upon which charge he was sentenced on 14th November 1888 to two years' imprisonment and ordered to pay costs of almost 450 French francs.[134]

All government departments like to think themselves infallible, so this might have proved something of an embarrassment at the Home Office. And so, if at the time of Ostrog's release Herbert Asquith or one of his senior civil servants had recalled reading the Macnaghten Report, it is not unreasonable to suggest that questions might have been asked. Scotland Yard might also have wondered why £10 was being paid out of Metropolitan Police funds to a man who, eight months earlier, had been fingered as a possible Jack the Ripper suspect.

If Michael Ostrog's unknown 1888 whereabouts had suggested involvement in the Whitechapel murders, his arrest in 1891 would have been an ideal time to have him investigated and cleared of suspicion. But this did not happen, for in February 1894 Ostrog, the man with the iron-clad alibi, remained "more likely than Cutbush to have committed this series of murders." Even more telling, perhaps, is the fact that, on Scotland Yard having learned of Ostrog's circumstances in 1888, Macnaghten did not remove him from his list of suspects.

If at this time questions had also been asked about Kosminski's removal "to an asylum about March 1889", Macnaghten might have been

---

[132] A.56090/B

[133] *The Complete History of Jack the Ripper*, Carroll & Graff, 2002

[134] Approximately £18 or $90 in 1888.

asked to explain why the only person of that name to enter the asylum system did not do so until almost two years later, when on 7th February 1891 Aaron Kosminski, a Polish Jew, was committed to Colney Hatch Lunatic Asylum.

Even at this later date Kosminski's "removal to an asylum" could not have signalled an end to the Ripper's career, for, as previously mentioned, a week after his committal the police were investigating James Sadler as the Whitechapel murderer, and until January 1892 following a man they could not arrest because of a want of evidence.

In the year following the Macnaghten Report, on 7th May 1895, the *Pall Mall Gazette* reported the case of William Grant [aka Grainger].

In the early hours of Monday 11th February 1895, Grant had been "caught in the act of wounding a woman in the abdomen, in a street close by Buck's Row, the scene of the first in the real series of Whitechapel murders . . . Grainger's crime so much resembled the former outrages that infinite pains were taken to trace his antecedents. Nothing was found, however, to warrant placing him upon his trial for any previous outrage, and he was brought up at the Old Bailey, charged with feloniously wounding Alice Graham."

Mr. Horace Avory, prosecuting for the Treasury, was quoted in *The Times*, 28th March 1895—

"[He] said the crime bore a strange resemblance to the Jack the Ripper murders, and the police had turned their attention to the matter without result."

Earlier, the *New York Herald*, 12th February, had been less equivocal—

"The London police are of the opinion that at last they have got safely under lock and key the long-sought assassin known as Jack the Ripper . . . All the circumstances . . . so much resemble those which characterized the Whitechapel murders that the police believe Grant to be the perpetrator of the whole ghastly string of tragedies."

Most importantly, the *Pall Mall Gazette* noted that, ". . . there is one person whom the police believe to have actually seen the Whitechapel murderer with a woman a few minutes before that woman's dissected

135

body was found in the streets. That person is stated to have identified Grainger as the man he then saw . . ."

It appeared that Scotland Yard may have finally located the Whitechapel murderer. But, alas, it was not to be.

The *Pall Mall Gazette* continued—

". . . but identification after so cursory a glance and after the lapse of so long an interval could not be reliable, and the inquiries were at length pulled up in a cul-de-sac . . ."

This sounded uncannily like the Mitre Square witness who in 1891 failed to identify Thomas Sadler, but despite a now positive identification and the fact that after exhaustive inquiries Grant's whereabouts during the Whitechapel murders could not be established no further charges were pressed. On 25th March 1895 Grant was sentenced to ten years' penal servitude for feloniously wounding Alice Graham, the Recorder, Sir Charles Hall, expressing amazement that no indictment had been preferred for wounding with intent to murder, "as the facts would have amply justified a verdict of guilty for that offence."

Grant possibly having been the Whitechapel murderer need not detain us. The important point about this episode is its demonstration that in February and March 1895 the Metropolitan Police were seen to be of the belief that the Whitechapel murderer was still alive and at large, all despite the fact that in the same *Pall Mall Gazette* article Chief Inspector Donald Swanson was stated to be of the belief that the Whitechapel murders were "the work of a man who is now dead."

This comment was not necessarily contemporaneous with the *PMG* article. Swanson could have said it at any time after his 1891 investigation of Sadler, so it can only be construed as an implied rebuttal of Grant.

Swanson's involvement in Grant's investigation may have been slight. The Old Bailey trial evidence was deemed "unfit for publication", the case received scant newspaper coverage and no police documentation appears to have survived. But *The Illustrated Police News*, 9th March 1895, did report that Inspector Pitman was in charge of the case. Perhaps because Swanson had fallen ill.

The Times, 28th February 1895—

"The influenza epidemic has broken out with great severity among the members of the Metropolitan and City Police, and the sick returns of the latter show a great increase in the number of men on the sick-list as compared with this time last year."

Black and White, 2nd March 1895—

"The Public Prosecutor (the Hon. Hamilton Cuffe), Mr. Angus Lewis, and practically all the staff of the Criminal Department of the Treasury are down with the malady. Inspector Swanson and various other officers at Scotland Yard are also suffering from it, as are many men of the out-lying divisions."

If on 7th May 1895 Chief Inspector Swanson still believed the Whitechapel murders to be "the work of a man who is now dead," he would not have to wait long to be disabused of this idea by a superior officer.

In an article for the May 1895 edition of *Windsor Magazine* entitled "The Detective in Real Life," Alfred Aylmer [135] wrote: "Much dissatisfaction was vented upon Mr. Anderson at the utterly abortive efforts to discover the perpetrator of the Whitechapel murders. He has himself a perfectly plausible theory that Jack the Ripper was a homicidal maniac, temporarily at large, whose hideous career was cut short by committal to an asylum."

Why might Anderson contradict Swanson? Did the Assistant Commissioner know something he was unwilling to tell his Chief Inspector? And was he alluding to Cutbush, referencing Kosminski, or perhaps confirming the recent West End doctor story in the *People* newspaper? No matter. Whomever Anderson had in mind, almost seven years after the Millers Court murder the best he could offer was "a perfectly plausible theory".

Melville Macnaghten had not expressed a particular preference for any of his three "more likely" suspects. He had written, "A much more rational theory is that the murderer's brain gave way altogether after his

---

[135]   Pseudonym of Major Arthur Griffiths, author of *Mysteries of Police and Crime*, 1898.

awful glut in Miller's Court, and that he immediately committed suicide, or, as a possible alternative, was found to be so hopelessly mad by his relations, that he was by them confined in some asylum."

The "or, as a possible alternative" suggests the suspect may have been either Druitt or Kosminski. Yet in his supposed "draft version", which bears the reflective hallmarks of having been written at a later date, he wrote—

"I enumerate the cases of 3 men against whom Police held very reasonable suspicion. Personally, after much careful & deliberate consideration, I am inclined to exonerate the last 2 [Kosminski and Ostrog], but I have always held strong opinions regarding no. 1 [Druitt], and the more I think the matter over, the stronger do these suspicions become. The truth, however, will never be known, and did indeed, at one time lie at the bottom of the Thames if my conjections be correct" [Author's brackets].

Edmund Reid, Local Inspector [CID] H Division, retired in February 1896. In a later interview with a *News of the World* reporter, it became clear that he had formed little more than a general impression of the Whitechapel murderer, but he did observe that "The hand of the one madman could be traced through a series of nine murders," and concluded by stating his belief that Jack the Ripper was dead. "Most likely he died in a madhouse."

In later years details from the Macnaghten Report were "leaked", and in November 1898 the profiles, with the names redacted, of the three "more likely" suspects, appeared in the book "Mysteries of Police and Crime" by Major Arthur Griffiths.[136]

The book was reprinted in January 1899, just as a new Jack the Ripper story appeared, first in the *Yorkshire Post* and on the following day in the *Western Mail*. It was faintly reminiscent of the 1892 story of the Catholic priest.

---

[136] Griffiths, who died in 1908, had been a friend of Sir Robert Anderson. Also, in October 1893, he had sat with Macnaghten on the Troup Committee to inquire into the most effective methods for identifying habitual criminals. The committee presented its findings on 12th February 1894, eleven days prior to the Macnaghten Report.

Western Mail, 19th January 1899—

"Whitechapel Murders: Did 'Jack the Ripper' Make a Confession?

"We have received (says the Daily Mail) from a clergyman of the Church of England, now a North Country vicar, an interesting communication with reference to the great criminal mystery of our times - that enshrouding the perpetration of the series of crimes which have come to be known as the 'Jack the Ripper' murders. The identity of the murderer is as unsolved as it was while the blood of the victims was yet wet upon the pavements.

"Certainly Major Arthur Griffiths, in his new work on Mysteries of Police and Crime, suggests that the police believe the assassin to have been a doctor, bordering on insanity, whose body was found floating in the Thames soon after the last crime of the series; but as the Major also mentions that this man was one of three known homicidal lunatics against whom the police 'held very plausible and reasonable grounds of suspicion,' that conjectural explanation does not appear to count for much by itself.

"Our correspondent now writes: -

"I received information in professional confidence, with directions to publish the facts after ten years, and then with such alterations as might defeat identification.

"The murderer was a man of good position and otherwise unblemished character, who suffered from epileptic mania, and is long since deceased.

"I must ask you not to give my name, as it might lead to identification, meaning the identification of the perpetrator of the crimes.

"We thought at first the vicar was at fault in believing that ten years had passed yet since the last murder of the series, for there were other somewhat similar crimes in 1889.

"But, on referring again to Major Griffiths' book, we find he states that the last 'Jack the Ripper' murder was that in Miller's Court on November 9, 1888 - a confirmation of the vicar's sources of information. The vicar enclosed a narrative, which he called "The Whitechapel

Murders - Solution of a London Mystery." This he described as 'substantial truth under fictitious form.' 'Proof for obvious reasons impossible - under seal of confession,' he added in reply to an inquiry from us.

"Failing to see how any good purpose could be served by publishing substantial truth in fictitious form, we sent a representative North to see the vicar, to endeavour to ascertain which parts of the narrative were actual facts. But the vicar was not to be persuaded, and all that our reporter could learn was that the rev. gentleman appears to know with certainty the identity of the most terrible figure in the criminal annals of our times, and that the vicar does not intend to let anyone else into the secret.

"The murderer died, the vicar states, very shortly after committing the last murder. The vicar obtained his information from a brother clergyman, to whom a confession was made - by whom the vicar would not give even the most guarded hint. The only other item which a lengthy chat with the vicar could elicit was that the murderer was a man who at one time was engaged in rescue work among the depraved woman of the East End - eventually his victims; and that the assassin was at one time a surgeon."

With its two confirmatory references to Major Griffiths new book, the story sounds more like inventive publicity material. Certainly, the journalist and writer George R. Sims, a keen Ripper-watcher and friend of Melville Macnaghten,[137] did not believe a word of it.

Under the pseudonym Dagonet, Sims wrote in the *Sunday Referee*, 22nd January 1899—

"There are bound to be various revelations concerning Jack the Ripper as the years go on. This time it is a vicar who heard his dying confession. I have no doubt a great many lunatics have said they were

---

[137]   Sims wrote in his 1917 autobiography: "My friend of many long years, Sir Melville Macnaghten, late Chief of the CID at Scotland Yard, had the charming idea of giving little Corinthian dinners on Monday nights at his house, 32 Warwick Square. The little party usually consisted of Sir Melville, Colonel Vivian Majendie, Mr. B.J. Angle [a boxing referee], Mr. Tom Anderson, Mr. Charles Moore, an old friend of Sir Melville, and myself."

Jack the Ripper on their death-beds. It is a good exit, and when the dramatic instinct is strong in a man he always wants an exit line, especially when he isn't coming on in the little play of 'Life' any more."

Sims dismissed the north country vicar story, firmly convinced that Jack the Ripper drowned himself after the last murder.

"I don't want to interfere with this mild little Jack the Ripper boom which the newspapers are playing up in the absence of strawberries and butterflies and good exciting murders, but I don't quite see how the real Jack could have confessed, seeing that he committed suicide after the horrible mutilation of the woman in the house in Dorset-street, Spitalfields. The full details of that crime have never been published - they never could be. Jack, when he committed that crime, was in the last stage of the peculiar mania from which he suffered. He had become grotesque in his ideas as well as bloodthirsty. Almost immediately after this murder he drowned himself in the Thames. His name is perfectly well known to the police. If he hadn't committed suicide he would have been arrested."

Sims' championing of the drowned doctor suspect did not begin until after the reprint of Major Griffiths' book. Sims always sounded sure of his facts, whereas Griffiths, having profiled the three suspects, equivocated [as had Macnaghten in his 1894 report], writing, "It is at least a strong presumption that 'Jack the Ripper' *died or was put under restraint* after the Miller's Court affair, which ended this series of crimes" [author's emphasis].

Sims made no mention of the two other suspects. His mind was made up. He may, therefore, have talked privately on the matter with Melville Macnaghten.

Author Douglas G. Browne wrote in his 1956 book "The Rise of Scotland Yard, A History of the Metropolitan Police"—

"His [Jack the Ripper's] identity is unknown to this hour, though definite claims to the contrary have been made, and numberless theories propounded. Sir Robert Anderson, who succeeded Monro as Assistant Commissioner, C.I.D., just after the second Whitechapel murder, says that the murderer was a low-class Polish Jew. According to Sir Basil

Thomson,[138] 'in the belief of the police he was a man who committed suicide in the Thames at the end of 1888', and who 'had probably been at some time a medical student.'"

Most interestingly, Browne wrote— "A third head of the C.I.D., Sir Melville Macnaghten, appears to identify the Ripper with the leader of a plot to assassinate Mr. Balfour at the Irish Office."

Putting things together, Macnaghten appears to have been suggesting that M.J. Druitt, his drowned "doctor", was involved in an assassination plot.

Browne appears to have been allowed access to material which has not been made available to later researchers. His information may therefore have come from Special Branch files, of which those not closed in perpetuity have been rendered worthless by dint of heavy redaction.

Although no clues are available as to how Macnaghten [who did not join the Metropolitan Police until 1st June 1889], might have made this connection, there was an alleged assassination plot against Arthur Balfour.

Arthur Balfour became Irish Chief Secretary on 7th March 1887, the same day on which *The Times* began publication of its "Parnellism and Crime" articles which ultimately led to the 1888 Special Commission.

South Australian Weekly Chronicle, 31st March 1888—

"Plot to Murder Mr. Balfour.

"London, March 29. Some excitement has been occasioned by a statement which has been published to the effect that a plot has been discovered for the murder of Mr. Arthur Balfour, Chief secretary for Ireland. The police are reticent upon the subject, and no details have been ascertained nor are any arrests reported."

On 17th May 1888 James Monro informed the Home Secretary that there was a plot to murder Arthur Balfour, and that his would-be

---

[138] Sir Basil Thomson had no immediate knowledge of the Whitechapel murders. At the time he was on the staff of Sir William MacGregor who, on 4th September 1888, was appointed "Administrator of British New Guinea." The following year Thomson was invalided back to England, having contracted malaria. In 1890 he married, returned to Fiji and, later, Tonga.

assassins, John Walsh and Joseph Patrick McKenna, were currently in Paris.

New York Times, 5th June 1888—

"Walsh, the man suspected by the police of being implicated in a plot similar to that which led to the murder of Lord Frederick Cavendish and Under Secretary Burke in Phoenix Park, Dublin, finding himself dogged at every footstep, accorded an interview in Paris to an agent from Scotland Yard. He said that he had convinced himself that the police had discovered all the details of the matter in which he was interested, and that he had abandoned his mission . . . Joseph Patrick McKenna, a member of Lodge No. 96 of the Clan-na-Gael of Chicago, is said to have been assisting Walsh."

The two men sailed from Le Havre for New York aboard the *La Normandie* on Saturday 2nd June 1888.

News of a Balfour assassination plot travelled to the highest in the land.

Queen Victoria's Journal—"Osborne [House], 11th August 1888. A very hot night, but the day cooler than yesterday. Saw Lord Salisbury and talked with him of many things, of Germany, Russia, Ireland, but he was sorry to say the Government had notice from America of a plot to kill Mr. Balfour, which is terrible, and he has to be watched."

In "A Diary of the Home Rule Movement", 1896, Henry W. Lucy wrote—

"As far as is yet publicly known no design against the life of Mr. Balfour was plotted. Certainly no overt attack was made, even at a time when his iron hand held crime in Ireland with most relentless grip. This possibly may have been due to the fact that he was so carefully guarded."

The closest it is possible to place "Jack the Ripper" to Arthur Balfour is on Lord Mayor's Day, Friday 9th November 1888, when "Jack" was in Millers Court, Spitalfields, and later in the day Arthur Balfour was guest of honour at the Lord Mayor's Banquet at the Guildhall, City of London.

In the *Butte* [Montana] *Weekly Miner*, 2nd December 1897, a story appeared entitled "Skeletons in the Closet," written under the pseudonym Ex-Attaché, telling of the "Society of Reformers," a sort of self-help group for "gentlemen of birth and of breeding" who had fallen victim to blackmail. The article then went on to detail how certain noble families disposed of their embarrassing black sheep by having them consigned, often without trial, to Broadmoor asylum for the criminal insane, "there to be detained according to what is styled in official phraseology 'during Her Majesty's pleasure.'

"Behind the walls of [Broadmoor] are hidden many of the grandest names of the United Kingdom, and terrible secrets affecting old houses of the nobility, which are known to few save the officials of the home department in London, and perhaps to some of the superior officers of the London police."

Contained in the story was the following—

"Incidentally it may be mentioned that it was at Broadmoor that the blue-blooded perpetrator of the Whitechapel murders is now admitted by the authorities to have breathed his last . . ."

Which was immediately followed by—

" . . . and it is likewise to Broadmoor that will be consigned without trial the well-born and hitherto successful member of the bar whose homicidal mania has now been ascertained by the police to have led him to perpetrate the mysterious murder of Miss Camp, on the Suburban London railroad last spring,[139] and likewise to put to death in an equally unaccountable fashion a young woman whose body was found some six weeks later at Windsor.[140] It is probable that his true name will be kept from the public precisely in the same way as that of the author of the 'Jack the Ripper' series of murders."

That the Ripper may have been the black sheep of a well-to-do family was not a new idea. In 1889 the *Derby Mercury* picked up a story from the London correspondent of the *Dublin Express* who was musing

---

[139]   In February 1897 the body of 33-year-old Elizabeth Camp was found at Waterloo station underneath the seat of a second-class railway carriage. Officially her murder remains unsolved.

[140]   Emma Matilda Johnson, aged 20, murdered at Clewer, near Windsor, 15th September 1897. Charles Henry Russell, a gas worker aged 38, was charged with her murder but later cleared.

on various police theories currently doing the rounds.

Derby Mercury, 2nd January 1889—

". . . One of these theories, and, perhaps, the most remarkable, has come under my notice, and it is quite the latest, as to those Whitechapel crimes. Stated nakedly, the idea of those who have been so patiently watching for the murderer is that he has fallen under the strong suspicion of his near relatives, who, to avert a terrible family disgrace, may have placed him out of harm's way in safe keeping. As showing that there is a certain amount of credence attached to this theory, detectives have recently visited all the registered private lunatic asylums, and made full inquiries as to inmates recently admitted. It is needless to say that the various county asylums—particularly those in the neighbourhood of London—have been similarly visited."

This idea would feature in Melville Macnaghten's 1894 memorandum—

"A much more rational theory is that the murderer's brain gave way altogether after his awful glut in Miller's Court, and that he immediately committed suicide, or, as a possible alternative, was found to be so hopelessly mad by his relations, that he was by them confined in some asylum."

More would be heard from "Ex-Attaché" in the future.

In February 1901 Robert Anderson, then aged 59, retired, effective as of his 60th birthday in May. The official civil service retirement age was 65, and in his later volume of memoirs[141] he explained that—

"I retired when I did for the excellent reason that after forty busy years I felt a strong desire for a more restful life."

The truth was somewhat different.

Robert Anderson was asked to resign by Home Secretary Charles Ritchie "for the purpose of facilitating changes in the staff and organisation of the Metropolitan Police which . . . was required in the public interest . . . a fresh appointment should be made to the headship of the Criminal Investigation Department of a person who should serve

---

[141]   The Lighter Side Of My Official Life, 1910

for a considerable time under Sir Edward Bradford . . ."[142]

This appears to have come as an unwelcome surprise to Anderson, for he immediately wrote to the Home Secretary outlining "the hardship and serious pecuniary loss which he could sustain if he were not compensated to some extent for the loss of an office which he expected and had made arrangements to hold another five years in the ordinary course."[143]

Anderson [replaced by Edward Henry who, like Monro, was an appointee from Bengal], was given £1000 from the Police Fund and later the same year awarded a compensatory KCB in the King's birthday honours list.

Fate determined that the date of Anderson's knighthood was 9th November 1901, King Edward VII's 60th birthday and the thirteenth anniversary of the final "Jack the Ripper" murder in Millers Court.

Various biographical sketches of Sir Robert Anderson state—

"When he retired in 1901, he was made Knight Commander of the Order of the Bath. W. H. Smith, on the floor of the House of Commons, said Sir Robert "had discharged his duties with great ability and perfect faithfulness to the public."

W.H. Smith had been speaking twenty four years earlier, on 20th March 1877, in respect of Robert Anderson's rôle as Secretary to the Railway Accidents Commission.[144]

For the next twenty years the identity of Jack the Ripper, or the Whitechapel murderer, was a two-horse race between a drowned doctor and an insane Polish Jew, and during this time there was only one real moment of dissension.

On 23rd March 1903 the *Daily Chronicle* ran an article about the recently-convicted and soon-to-be-hanged poisoner George Chapman [Severin Klosowski].

---

[142]   Home Office B5005/8. Briefing memo from Sir Kenelm Edward Digby [Permanent Under Secretary of State at the Home Office] to Home Secretary Charles Ritchie, 22nd May 1901.
[143]   Ibid.
[144]   Hansard vol. 233 c. 196

"The police officers who have been engaged in tracing Klosowski's movements in connection with the three murders with which he is charged, are forming some rather startling theories as to the antecedent history of the criminal. These theories are connected with the Whitechapel murders which startled the world some fifteen years ago, and were attributed to 'Jack the Ripper.'"

What led the police to this conclusion was explained the following day in the *Manchester Courier*—

"The grounds for this curious theory are very slender, consisting mainly of the fact that at the time of the first two murders Klosowski occupied a lodging in George Yard, Whitechapel Road, and that he carried a black bag and wore a "P. and O." cap[145]. When the murders ceased in London similar crimes occurred in America at a time when Klosowski had opened a barber's shop in New Jersey City."

The *Manchester Courier*, 24th March 1903, reprinted a condensed version of an interview from the *Westminster Gazette* in which 'a gentleman well versed in the annals of crime' said, "The theory is reasonable enough, but I have every proof—of a circumstantial and private character, of course—in my possession that Klosowski and Jack the Ripper are not identical personages."

A full version of this contradictory interview later appeared in *The West Australian* [Perth], 19th May 1903, in which the 'gentleman well versed in the annals of crime' elaborated—

"The secret history of crime is, perhaps, the most fascinating of all studies, and many details in connection with the Whitechapel murder are on record which it would not be in the public interest to divulge. But it is quite certain that the heads of the Detective Department at Scotland Yard have not authorised or inspired this suggestion as to Klosowki's implication in the Whitechapel horrors. Some day the truth concerning these murders may be revealed. Meanwhile it is pretty safe to affirm that a report circulated at the time, that they were committed by a student of surgery suffering from a peculiar form of murder-mania, was the true

---

[145]   A peaked cap worn by P&O Shipping Line Commanders.

one. It has even been definitely reported that the student—long since dead—has been identified to the satisfaction of the police as the guilty man. But, all this apart, the series of crimes in the two cases are so distinct that I should scarcely suppose any student of criminology could accept the conclusion that with the capture of Klosowski the mystery of the Whitechapel murders has at last been solved."

The identity of the "gentleman well versed in the annals of crime" was not revealed, but if we assume that his proof of a "circumstantial and private character" about the long-dead "student of surgery suffering from a peculiar form of murder-mania" was a reference to the "sexually insane drowned doctor" [M.J. Druitt], our choice narrows to a short-list of one—Melville Macnaghten, whose promotion from Chief Constable to Assistant Commissioner [CID] had been announced in *The Times* just days earlier, on 16th March 1903.

Meanwhile the *Pall Mall Gazette* had sought out the opinion of retired Chief Inspector Frederick George Abberline.

Pall Mall Gazette, 24th March 1903—

"When a representative of the Pall Mall Gazette called on Mr. Abberline yesterday and asked for his views on the startling theory set up by one of the morning papers, the retired detective said: "What an extraordinary thing it is that you should just have called upon me now . . ."

Abberline liked the idea of George Chapman having been Jack the Ripper.

". . . I had just commenced, not knowing anything about the report in the newspaper, to write to the Assistant Commissioner of Police, Mr. Macnaghten, to say how strongly I was impressed with the opinion that 'Chapman' was also the author of the Whitechapel murders. Your appearance saves me the trouble. I intended to write on Friday, but a fall in the garden, injuring my hand and shoulder, prevented my doing so until today . . ."

This account of the chance arrival of a reporter from the *Pall Mall Gazette* may have been somewhat disingenuous.

At the time of the interview Abberline was living with his wife, Emma, at 313 Clapham Road, in south London. The 1901 Census records that, amongst others [including a consultant engineer (boarder) and a nine-year-old boy (visitor)], a John Philip Collins, described as a "boarder, age 30, author/newspaper editor" was also at this address, and at the time John Philip Collins, age 31,[146] was Literary Editor of the *Pall Mall Gazette*. It is therefore perfectly possible that he was still at this address in March 1903.

This is not to suggest anything underhand. Abberline affording an exclusive story to one of his boarders [lodgers] is perfectly understandable.

"I cannot help feeling," said Abberline, "that this is the man we struggled so hard to capture fifteen years ago . . . there are a score of things which make one believe that Chapman is the man; and you must understand that we have never believed all those stories about Jack the Ripper being dead, or that he was a lunatic, or anything of that kind."

This was the first time a Jack the Ripper "suspect" had been publicly named by a police officer closely connected with the case.

In discussing the merits of his Chapman theory Abberline flatly denounced the story of the 'young medical student who was found drowned in the Thames'. "I know all about that story. But what does it amount to? Simply this. Soon after the last murder in Whitechapel the body of a young doctor was found in the Thames, but there is absolutely nothing beyond the fact that he was found at that time to incriminate him. A report was made to the Home Office about the matter, but that it was 'considered final and conclusive' is going altogether beyond the truth."

Regretfully we shall never know if the retired Chief Inspector ever took up his pen, for Melville Macnaghten's response to being told by Abberline that his confidential 1894 memorandum was not worth the paper it was written on would have made interesting reading.

Journalist George R. Sims was having none of it. He was still peddling the drowned doctor theory fed to him via Major Griffiths by

---

[146]   John Philip Collins, b. 1870, d. 1954. See obituaries in *The Times*, 23rd January 1954, and *Catholic Herald*, 29th January 1954.

Melville Macnaghten.

Sunday Referee, 29th March 1903—

"I was rather surprised to find high-class newspapers suggesting Chapman as 'Jack the Ripper.'

"'Jack' was a homicidal maniac. Each crime that he committed was marked with greater ferocity during the progress of his insanity. How could a man in the mental condition of 'Jack' have suddenly settled down into a cool, calculating poisoner?

"'Jack the Ripper' committed suicide after his last murder - a murder so maniacal that it was accepted at once as the deed of a furious madman. It is perfectly well known at Scotland Yard who 'Jack' was, and the reasons for the police conclusions were given in the report to the Home Office, which was considered by the authorities to be final and conclusive.

"How the ex-Inspector can say 'We never believed Jack was dead or a lunatic' in face of the report made by the Commissioner of Police is a mystery to me. It is a curious coincidence, however, that for a long time a Russian Pole resident in Whitechapel was suspected at the Yard. But his name was not Klosowski! The genuine 'Jack' was a doctor. His body was found in the Thames on December 31, 1888."

In advancing their respective theories Abberline and Sims both cited a report sent to the Home Office. Major Griffiths did not mention such a report in his 1898 book; but as he, Abberline and Sims all repeated the "drowned doctor" error it becomes apparent that, one way or another, the source of their bogus information had been the Macnaghten memorandum.

On Detective Inspector Robert Sagar's retirement from the City of London Police, *The City Press*, 7th January 1905, wrote—

"His professional association with the terrible atrocities which were perpetrated some years ago in the East End by the so-styled 'Jack the Ripper' was a very close one. Indeed, Mr. Sagar knows as much about those crimes, which terrified the Metropolis, as any detective in London. He was deputed to represent the City police force in conference with the detective heads of the Metropolitan force nightly at Leman Street

Police Station during the period covered by those ghastly murders. Much has been said and written - and even more conjectured - upon the subject of the "Jack-the-Ripper" murders. It has been asserted that the murderer fled to the Continent, where he perpetrated similar hideous crimes; but that is not the case. The police realised, as also did the public, that the crimes were those of a madman, and suspicion fell upon a man, who, without a doubt, was the murderer. Identification being impossible, he could not be charged. He was, however, placed in a lunatic asylum, and the series of atrocities came to an end."

Sagar told the *Morning Leader*, 9th January 1905—

"We had good reason to suspect a certain man who worked in 'Butcher's Row,' Aldgate, and we watched him carefully. There was no doubt that this man was insane, and after a time his friends thought it advisable to have him removed to a private asylum. After he was removed there were no more Ripper atrocities."

The Mercury, 14th January 1905, told much the same story—

Sagar reportedly said, "Eventually we got him [Jack the Ripper] incarcerated in a lunatic asylum, and the series of murders came to an end."

In July 1906 another City of London detective retired. *Thomson's Weekly News* published Detective Inspector Henry Cox's memoirs in twenty-five weekly installments, the first of which appeared on 8th September 1906.

During the Ripper murders Cox[147] and Sagar[148] were Detective Constables in the City of London police. It is therefore not unreasonable to assume they knew of each other[149] at this time and may also have worked together on the Whitechapel murders. If so, it is also not unreasonable to expect their conclusions about Jack the Ripper to bear a certain similarity.

The installment of Henry Cox's memoirs entitled "The Truth About

---

[147] In 1893 Cox was promoted to Detective Sergeant.
[148] In December 1888 Sagar was promoted to Sergeant, and in June 1889 to Detective Sergeant.
[149] They worked together on a fraud case in November 1890.

the Whitechapel Mysteries" appeared on 1st December 1906 and opened in the arch manner of someone who appeared to know more than he was prepared to tell—

"It is only upon certain conditions that I have agreed to deal with the great Whitechapel crimes of fifteen years ago . . .

". . . There are those who claim that the perpetrator was well known to the police; that at the present moment he is incarcerated in one of His Majesty's penal settlements. Others hold that he was known to have jumped over London Bridge or Blackfriars Bridge; while a third party claims that he is the inmate of a private asylum. These theories I have no hesitation in dispelling at once."

This was a direct contradiction of Sagar, but anyone anticipating even a minor revelation was to be sorely disappointed, for after detailing the murders [the timing of which apparently suggested the murderer had a system and thus strengthened "the theory that the man was a sailor, and timed his murders so that he could board his vessel as it was on the point of sailing"], Henry Cox went on to describe an almost three-month surveillance operation on an unnamed Jewish suspect who "occupied several shops in the East End," who "was never arrested for the reason that not the slightest scrap of evidence could be found to connect him with the crimes."

Henry Cox concluded—

"The mystery is as much a mystery as it was fifteen years ago. It is all very well for amateur detectives to fix the crime upon this or that suspect, and advance theories in the public press to prove his guilt. They are working upon surmise, nothing more.

"The mystery can never be cleared up until someone comes forward and himself proves conclusively that he was the bloodthirsty demon who terrorised the country, or unless he returns to his crimes and is caught red-handed. He is still alive then? you ask. I do not know. For all I know he may be dead. I have personally no evidence either way."

Some believe Henry Cox's suspect and Robert Sagar's insane butcher were one and the same, but given the two detectives' diametrically opposed accounts it is impossible to put so implausible an idea to the test.

The *New York Times*, 13th December 1908, resurrected the earlier story of the "Society of Reformers." Written by "A Veteran Diplomat" it made no mention of Broadmoor, the Whitechapel murderer—aristocrat or commoner—or the member of the bar responsible for the murders of Elizabeth Camp and Emma Johnson.

In *Blackwood's* magazine, March 1910, it became clear that Sir Robert Anderson's 1895 reference to the homicidal maniac "whose hideous career was cut short by committal to an asylum" had nothing to do with Thomas Cutbush.

Anderson wrote that ". . . the conclusion we came to was that he and his people were low-class Jews, for it is a remarkable fact that people of that class in the East End will not give up one of their number to Gentile justice. And the result proved that our diagnosis was right on every point."

In a footnote Anderson explained the proof of "our diagnosis"—

When the "individual whom we suspected was caged in an asylum, the only person who had ever had a good view of the murderer at once identified him, but when he learned that the suspect was a fellow-Jew he declined to swear to him."

On 4th March 1910 Leopold Greenberg, the editor of the *Jewish Chronicle*, writing as 'Mentor', reacted angrily—

". . . A more wicked assertion to put into print, without the shadow of evidence, I have seldom seen . . . It is a matter of regret and surprise that so able a man as Sir Robert Anderson should, upon the wholly erroneous and ridiculous 'theory' that Jews should shield a raving murderer because he was a Jew, rather than yield him up to 'Gentile justice', build the series of statements he has made . . ."

Interviewed on 7th March 1910 by *The Globe*, a Conservative evening newspaper owned by Hildebrand Harmsworth, younger son of newspaper tycoon Lord Northcliffe, Sir Robert Anderson maintained that he "should be the last man in the world to say anything reflecting on the Jews as a community . . .

"When I stated that the murderer was a Jew, I was stating a simple

153

matter of fact. It is not a matter of theory . . . the man who identified the murderer was a Jew, but on learning that the criminal was a Jew he refused to proceed with his identification."

The following week Sir Robert Anderson poured oil on troubled waters.

Jewish Chronicle, 11th March 1910—

". . . will you allow me to express the severe distress I feel that my words should be construed as 'an aspersion upon Jews.' For much that I have written in my various books gives proof of my sympathy with, and interest in, 'the people of the Covenant'; and I am happy in reckoning members of the Jewish community in London among my personal friends."

Many insist that the religiously devout Robert Anderson, author of a number of theological and secular books as well as a staunch defender of Edwardian youth against the debilitating consequences of masturbation[150], was a pillar of moral rectitude who would never have lied in self-interest to a general readership. Thus, they argue, whatever Robert Anderson uttered about Jack the Ripper must have been the truth, or—falling back on that most fine of distinctions—what *he believed* to be the truth.

This view of a self-important man who, one senses from reading his memoir, never quite received the recognition he felt he so richly deserved, is hopelessly naive. Anderson was in the wrong profession to let truth be his guiding light.

Between 1888 and 1910 Anderson proffered a variety of inconsistent views on Jack the Ripper, making our present-day task of discovering which, if any, of them might be the truth an impossibility.[151]

In a 23rd October 1888 report he had mused on the fact that "five successive murders [for those who insist on being strictly canonical it was actually four at this time] should have been committed, without our having the slightest clue of any kind is extraordinary, if not unique, in the

---

[150]   Speech at a Purity Rally. *Alliance of Honour Record*, January 1911, pp. 2-3.

[151]   In *Jack the Ripper: Scotland Yard Investigates*, authors Stewart Evans and Donald Rumbelow came away empty-handed after an exhaustive discussion in Chapter Sixteen.

annals of crime."[152]

By August of 1889 Anderson, talking to a reporter about Whitechapel, said, "After a stranger has gone over it he takes a much more lenient view of our failure to find Jack the Ripper, as they call him, than he did before."

In June 1892 he told *Cassell's Saturday Journal*, "It is impossible to believe they were the acts of a sane man—they were those of a maniac revelling in blood."

Fifteen months after the Macnaghten Memorandum, in May 1895, Major Arthur Griffiths wrote that "Much dissatisfaction was vented upon Mr. Anderson at the utterly abortive efforts to discover the perpetrator of the Whitechapel murders. He has himself a perfectly plausible theory that Jack the Ripper was a homicidal maniac, temporarily at large, whose hideous career was cut short by committal to an asylum."

In February 1901, three months prior to his retirement, Anderson told the monthly literary magazine *The Nineteenth Century* with what appears to have been a degree of certainty that "the fiend . . . had been safely caged in an asylum."

Daily Chronicle, 1st September 1908—

In bemoaning the improper handling of crime scenes and the destruction of clues [which included erasure of the chalked message in Goulston Street]— "that might have very easily secured for us proof of the identity of the assassin"— Sir Robert Anderson said, "I told Sir William Harcourt, who was the Home Secretary, that I could not accept responsibility for non-detection of the author of the Ripper crimes, for the reasons, among others, that I have given you."

The memory of the retired 67-year-old Sir Robert Anderson appeared to be playing tricks. Henry Matthews was Home Secretary during the 1888 Whitechapel murders. Sir William Harcourt had been Home Secretary from April 1880 to June 1885.

Now, in March 1910, Anderson was being specific, telling the world that Jack the Ripper "and his people were low-class Jews."

---

[152]   HO 144/221/A49301C, f.117

He wrote in Blackwood's magazine, "the only person who ever had a good view of the murderer at once identified him, but when he learned that the suspect was a fellow-Jew he declined to swear to him."

In November 1910 Sir Robert Anderson's collected *Blackwood's* articles were published in a single volume, *The Lighter Side of My Official Life*. In Chapter Nine this reference underwent a subtle revision. The underlying premise remained the same, but the witness who refused to incriminate the suspect was now no longer necessarily a fellow-Jew—

"I will merely add that the only person who had ever had a good view of the murderer unhesitatingly identified the suspect the instant he was confronted with him; but he refused to give evidence against him."

Anderson then slipped in a new detail.

"In saying that he [the suspect] was a *Polish* Jew I am merely stating a definitely ascertained fact. And my words are meant to specify race, not religion. For it would outrage all religious sentiment to talk of the religion of a loathsome creature whose utterly unmentionable vices reduced him to a lower level than that of the brute."

Race is a genetic distinction, and Poland was racially diverse. The suspect's nationality was meaningless. Polish, German, Hungarian or Austrian: it made no difference. First and foremost, Anderson's "loathsome creature" was a Jew.

Writing as Dagonet in *The Referee*, 17th April 1910, George R. Sims took Anderson to task.

"The latest 'blazing indiscretion' of Sir Robert Anderson has raised the question of how far a pensioned public servant is justified in making use of information which came to him in the course of his employment in a confidential position. It was only the other day that the late esteemed head of the CID caused a storm of indignation among the King's Jewish subjects by stating that Jack the Ripper was a Jew, and that the Jews knew who he was and assisted him to evade capture. The statement went beyond ascertained facts.

"The mad Polish Jew, to whom Sir Robert refers, was only one of three persons who were each strongly suspected of being the genuine Jack. The final official record, which is in the archives of the Home

Office, leaves the matter in doubt between the Polish Jew, who was afterwards put in a lunatic asylum, a Russian doctor of vile character, and an English homicidal maniac, one Dr.—, who had been in a lunatic asylum. In these circumstances it was certainly indiscreet of Sir Robert to plump for the Polish Jew, and to imply that many of the Jewish community in the East End were accessories after the fact."

George R. Sims may have sounded to his readers as if he knew what he was talking about, whereas he was merely referencing the three unnamed suspects he first learned about from Major Griffiths' 1898 book "Mysteries of Crime and Police" and which, with hindsight, we know originated in the 1894 Macnaghten memorandum. Here again was the mistake about one of the suspects being a doctor, plus the mistake made in 1903 by both Sims and Abberline about all the details having been contained in an official Home Office report.

Sims evidently thought Sir Robert Anderson was referencing the same Home Office report, blissfully unaware that no such Home Office report existed and that he had been deliberately misled on the matter by his friend Melville Macnaghten who over the years fed him all manner of juicy tidbits for his "Crime Museum."[153]

As not one scintilla of incriminating evidence for the Whitechapel murders attaches to the 24-year-old Aaron Kosminski committed to Colney Hatch asylum on 7th February 1891, and there was no official Home Office report for Sir Robert Anderson to consult, from where else might he have found his Polish Jew?

Quite possibly he consulted the 1894 Macnaghten memorandum, taking the nationality and race of "Kosminski - a Polish Jew", the suspect its author was later "inclined to exonerate" in favour of Druitt, his "drowned doctor." Or perhaps, more mundanely and just like Sims, Anderson found his Polish Jew in the pages of Major Griffiths' book

---

[153]   In an article entitled "My Criminal Museum," *Lloyds Weekly Newspaper*, 22nd September 1907, Sims wrote, "I have in my museum some curious documents and gruesome photographs connected with the crime. Two of them are unprintable. The photograph of the scene in Miller's court is not one to be looked upon except by those who have in the exercise of their calling to study all phases of human perversion."

"Mysteries of Crime and Police."

There have been suggestions of Anderson playing the anti-Semitic card in accusing a Polish Jew of being the Whitechapel murderer. Apropos of this idea is a footnote spanning pages 279 and 280 of *The Lighter Side of My Official Life* which, as we so often find ourselves on factually thin ice with Robert Anderson, warrants closer examination.

The footnote follows on from a story of how Robert Anderson had brightened Queen Victoria's day by planting a real kiss on her hand "instead of the purely ceremonial touch" on the occasion of his receiving a C.B. at Windsor in July 1896.

Footnote, Page 279—

"In the following year I was offered another honour, which I declined for somewhat quixotic reasons which I need not mention here; and I have ever since regretted that I did so. On the 20th of September 1897, I had a visit from M. Goremykine (Russian Minister of the Interior) and M. Ratchkoysky, to express anew the Tsar's appreciation of the Police arrangements for his safety during his visit. And on the following . . ."

Footnote, Page 280—

". . . day M. Ratchkosky called again to offer me the insignia of the Order of St. Anne. I afterwards received a personal token of His Majesty's approval."

It is difficult to discern exactly what he was telling his readers, for you don't so much read Robert Anderson as try to decode him, and the facts at the heart of this footnote are darker and more complex than the story of a foreign potentate wishing to bestow a decoration upon him for a job well done.

Note the different spellings—Ratchkoysky and Ratchkosky—both incorrect.

The fiercely anti-Semitic Pyotr Ivanovich Rachkovsky [Tsar Nicholas II's personal emissary in secret matters and, from 1884-1902, head of the Okhrana's agentura in Paris] and Ivan Logginovitch Goremykin [Russian Minister of the Interior and, later, Prime Minister] were the two men most heavily involved in the creation and promulgation of *The Protocols of the Elders of Zion*, the faked manifesto purporting to detail a massive Jewish world-conspiracy which has since become anti-Semitism's sacred text.

The Protocols were rumoured to be based upon a plagiarised[154] pamphlet by the political journalist Elie De Cyon [Ilya Tsion] stolen by Rachkovsky in 1897. This timing is interesting, for Anderson's alleged September 20th 1897 meeting with the two Russians took place just three weeks after the close of the First Zionist Congress, held in Basle, Switzerland.[155] Could Anderson, noted theologian and lay preacher, have been hinting at a personal involvement in the biggest anti-Semitic conspiracy of all time?

Robert Anderson had been most specific about the date of his meeting,[156] but a trawl through British, American and European archives fails to reveal an 1897 visit to London by Ivan Goremykin. However, during the late 1890s Sergei Witte was the Russian Minister of Finance, and the original text of his memoirs, held at Columbia University's Bakhmeteff Archive of Russian and East European History and Culture, records the following—

"Before leaving the subject of Goremykin I want to say something about Rachkovsky, the head of our secret police in Paris, and his trip to England with Goremykin in the summer of 1899."[157]

Prior to this trip Rachkovsky had received the Order of St. Anne— the insignia he was allegedly offering Anderson—in belated recognition of fifteen years of accomplished security work.[158]

Antisemitism aside, Robert Anderson citing the Tsar wishing to express anew his appreciation of the Police arrangements for his safety during his visit could only have been a reference to a state visit [by September 1897 his only visit to Britain as the newly-crowned Tsar]

---

154   See *The Times*, 16th – 18th August 1921.
155   The "protocols" purport to refer to the recorded minutes of a series of meetings at this Basle Congress which took place among the innermost circle of Zion elders.
156   Coincidentally, the day following the retirement of Inspector Fred Jarvis.
157   See also *The Times*, 2nd November 1899.
158   *Fontanka 16*, Ruud and Stepanov, McGill-Queen's University Press 1999.

Nicholas II made to Balmoral, in Scotland, between 22nd September and 5th October 1896 to celebrate Queen Victoria becoming Britain's longest-reigning monarch.[159]

Another visitor to Balmoral during this period was British Prime Minister, Lord Salisbury, who held talks with the Tsar on the 27th and 29th September.

Security was understandably tight.

The Chicago Sunday Tribune, 20th September 1896—

"Several members of the Russian secret police have been in England for a week past, and they will be reinforced by a squad of the most famous of the Czar's Nihilist detectives."

Other reports added that the Russians would be augmented "by a picked squad of Scotland Yard detectives who will remain attached to the Czar and Czarina's party until they leave Great Britain."

Prior to the Tsar's arrival, Chief Inspector William Melville, who in 1893 had taken over as head of Special Branch from the retired Chief Inspector John George Littlechild, allegedly uncovered a plot by Irish nationalists to kill both Nicholas II and Queen Victoria. The aim was to spark an international crisis.

The ring-leader was Patrick Tynan, an Irish-American suspected of being the Invincibles "No. 1," who was already wanted in connection with the 1882 Phoenix Park Murders in Dublin. Tynan was quickly apprehended by British detectives in France. He was allegedly carrying a forged letter to the effect that he was a special envoy of Queen Victoria, and authorised to personally deliver a letter to the Tsar. One of his accomplices, Edward Bell, alias Edward J. Ivory, who had travelled from America, was arrested at Glasgow's Victoria Hotel.

The New York police disavowed any knowledge of the dynamite conspiracy having originated in their city and denied they had given any information to the British police that would have led to the arrest of Tynan and his fellow-plotters.[160]

---

[159]   In her journal for 23rd September 1896 Queen Victoria wrote, "Today is the day on which I have reigned longer, by a day, than any English sovereign."
[160]   New York Times, 18th September 1896.

The truth was that the conspirators were being closely watched by private detective Charles Heidelberg, an ex-NYPD officer from the staff of Superintendent Thomas Byrnes.

The Times, 15th September 1896—

"Four weeks ago an agent of Scotland Yard in America telegraphed home news of the departure for the Continent of several American members of the dynamite party . . . From the moment of landing these men were never lost sight of by British detectives who followed them like their shadows."

The dynamitards split up, some going to London, others to Antwerp.

The Times continued—

"Dr. Anderson, Chief of the Criminal Investigation Department in London, came himself to Antwerp, accompanied by five of his subordinates who at once organised a service of surveillance in Brussels, Ostend, Spa and Antwerp." At a house in Berchem, a suburb south of Antwerp, a bomb factory was discovered, and the two men who lived and worked there were later arrested in Rotterdam.

Also in Antwerp at the time was the New York private detective Charles Heidelberg. After the arrests he went to London, from where it was reported that he had exposed the dynamite conspiracy to the British police; but on returning to New York he denied any such involvement, claiming he had been in Antwerp for six weeks on the trail of Julius Freudenthal, President of the Columbia Typewriter Company, who in June 1896 fled America owing his creditors $500,000.

Due to the political nature of the charges laid against Tynan, France refused to extradite him to Britain. On 15th October 1896 he was released from custody and three days later sailed from Cherbourg aboard the North German Lloyd steamship *Saale* bound for New York.

Tynan later told an Associated Press reporter—

"All the statements made as to my desire to have the Czar of Russia blown up are villainous and infamous . . . As to all the stories published about me I can only say that they are Scotland Yard 'fakes', got up for the purpose of injuring me. I think their object has failed."[161]

Edward Bell did not fare so well. After a series of appearances on remand at Bow Street magistrates court he was finally committed for trial, and in January 1897 appeared at the Old Bailey charged with "conspiring . . . to cause by an explosive substance an explosion, in the United Kingdom, of a nature likely to endanger life, and likely to cause serious injury to property."

The case against Edward Bell soon collapsed.

Joseph McKenna, "The Irish-American Dynamite Campaign: A History, 1881 to 1896"—

"By the end of the first day of the trial a disquieting rumour had circulated through the court that an agent provocateur had been used. Bell's legal advisor saw Anderson and warned him that if the case continued the defense would be that his client was the victim of an agent provocateur. On the second day of the trial Bell's advisor announced that his client wished to withdraw his plea of not guilty for one of guilty. The solicitor general, who had learned that 'the prize ring rules had been violated,' as Anderson quaintly put it, [162] rose and announced the withdrawal of the prosecution. Bell was acknowledged by the prosecution as a victim of an agent provocateur. He was released."

The spy and agent provocateur was Meyrick Shaw Copeland Jones. Born in County Cavan and by turns a Liverpool petroleum worker and a Kent groundsman, he had been on the British secret service payroll since August 1890, operating first in Manchester and subsequently in New York City.

On 17th September 1896 Jones left New York for Montreal, from where he sailed for Liverpool, arriving 30th September aboard the Dominion Line steamship *Scotsman*.

In early October 1896 he made a long statement [it reads more like a debrief] detailing his involvement with a secret organisation known as the Irish Nationalists, in which Edward Bell was a member of "Camp 98",

---

[161] Ann Arbor Argus, 30th October 1896.
[162] See Sir Robert Anderson, *Sidelights on the Home Rule Movement*, p. 128. 1906.

and in the course of which he stated that Patrick Tynan had admitted to being No. 1 and to have given the handkerchief signal for the murders of Lord Cavendish and Thomas Burke in Phoenix Park.

Marginal notes dated 7th and 23rd October 1896 confirm that the statement was seen by Kenelm Digby, Permanent Under Secretary of State at the Home Office, and Hamilton Cuffe, Director of Public Prosecutions, after which the document went missing for 42 years.

Meyrick Jones's statement resurfaced in July 1938 following the death earlier that year of Sir Harry Gloster Armstrong, former British Consul General in New York. Found amongst his papers, which also included documents relating to Patrick Tynan and the Phoenix Park murders, it was handed to Vernon Kell, co-founder and first director of the Security Service, who passed it to Sir Alexander Maxwell, Permanent Secretary at the Home Office, who returned it to Registry together with a note of explanation.[163]

How the 23-page typewritten statement came into the possession of Sir Harry Gloster Armstrong is uncertain. However, an obituary in *The Times* and the New York *Post*, 7th February 1938, reports Sir Harry as first coming "to the United States in 1891," where he "became associated with the Manchester Ship Canal Company." Of possible interest, therefore, is that at this time one of the directors of the Manchester Ship Canal Company was Sir Edward Jenkinson, Britain's so-called "spymaster-general" up until January 1887, when he was fired by Henry Matthews and supplanted by James Monro.

After Bell's trial two Dublin newspapers accused Jones of inciting dynamite outrages and, later, Bell's barrister, John F. Taylor, charged him with conspiring to blow up the British Embassy in Washington DC.

Scribner's Magazine, October 1896—

"It is well known that many well-informed members of the Clan-na-Gael are in the pay of Scotland Yard, and those who remember the astonishing disclosures of Major le Caron [at the Special Commission] will not find it incredible that an innocuous dynamite conspiracy may be

---

[163]   HO144/98/A16380C.

hatched for the money there is in it. The Saturday Review, then, thinks it not at all impossible that the professional informers of England projected this dynamite scare *ab ovo* [from the beginning], paying Tynan handsomely for his trouble, and receiving from the Government a sum which still left them a handsome profit over this preliminary disbursement!"

In an unsuccessful attempt to reduce Secret Service funding by £1000 Tynan, Bell and Scotland Yard's involvement in dynamite plots against the Queen and Tsar surfaced in a heated parliamentary debate on 26th March 1897 [six months prior to Anderson's alleged meeting with Goremykin and Rachkovsky], and in her 1938 autobiography "A Servant of the Queen," Irish revolutionary Maud Gonne[164] put matters into a nutshell—

The 1897 Edward Bell case "had broken down because England dared not risk the exposure of how Scotland Yard had engineered a bogus plot on the Czar in order to discover it, a bogus plot grafted onto a real Irish plot shepherded by an agent provocateur."

The one person above all others who would have immediately seen through this state-sponsored attempt at Irish entrapment was Pyotr Rachkovsky, whose hand-picked detectives formed the Tsar's personal protection detail whilst in Scotland. Head of the Russian secret police in Paris, a skilled propagandist and master of perception management, Rachkovsky was doing to Russian dissidents what Scotland Yard was doing to Irish separatists. Given that details of the bogus assassination plot were in the public domain long before September 1897 it is hardly likely that Tsar Nicholas II dispatched the Russian Minister of the Interior and Pyotr Rachkovsky to London to "express anew" his appreciation to Robert Anderson for the "Police arrangements for his safety during his visit" to Scotland and present him with the insignia of

---

[164] Maud Gonne fought for Irish independence and the release of political prisoners. In 1900 she founded the Daughters of Ireland, which provided a home for Irish nationalist women. The Queen of the title was Caitlin Ní Houlihan, an Irish Queen of old. An ironic title, bearing in mind Maude Gonne's Irish beliefs and her repudiation of the British monarchy.

the Order of St. Anne.

Robert Anderson being offered the Order of St. Anne was not referenced in A.P. Moore-Anderson's biography of his father, although the book does lend weight to Anderson's final footnote remark that he afterwards received a personal token of His Majesty's approval—

"The detectives deputed to guard foreign royalties received many personal gifts. Occasionally their Chief was also remembered in this way, twice by the ill-fated Nicholas II of Russia, the first time when he was Czarevitch, the gift being a Russian salt-cellar. The second present was a diamond ring of such dimensions that it might fit a super-size thumb. The diamonds with the Imperial monogram made a fine brooch for my mother. The gold ring, reduced to normal size, with the Russian N, II and crown reproduced, I am wearing to-day."

The scale upon which the Romanovs dispensed largesse was immense.

New York Times, 3rd November 1889—

"The Czar left £500 for the poor of Berlin, and he gave a very handsome present to his Alexander Regiment and numerous diamond snuff boxes and a shower of decorations were distributed; but his veils appear insignificant when compared with those of his grandfather, the Emperor Nicholas I. When he visited England for a week in 1844 he gave £2000 to the servants at Windsor Castle, £1000 to the housekeeper and £4000 to various charities; twelve gold snuff boxes, with his cipher in diamonds, among the equerries and grooms in waiting; and literally a sackful of brooches, watches, rings and pins, which were distributed among the small fry who had been useful to him or in some way concerned with his visit."

Aside from his dealings with the Russians there are other curious anecdotes in Sir Robert Anderson's memoir.

He wrote that "after living for a brief interval in the Westminster Palace Hotel as a member of the 'Crown Club'—the acorn from which grew the oak of the St. Stephen's, now palatially housed opposite the clock tower at Westminster—I decided to return to lodgings."

There was no historical connection between the two institutions.

The Crown Club opened in May 1869 with a 'member ballot' and offered to waive the entrance fee for the first 150 applicants. A strictly commercial enterprise which sub-let various accommodations and facilities from the Westminster Palace Hotel, members paid a three guinea [£3.3s] entrance fee and an annual subscription of two guineas [£2.2s].[165]

The St. Stephen's Club was founded in 1870 under the patronage of Prime Minister Benjamin Disraeli for "those who profess and maintain Constitutional and Conservative principles." Purpose-built by architect John Whichcord, the club occupied the corner of Bridge Street and Victoria Embankment and was connected to the colonnade of the House of Commons and Westminster underground railway station by subterranean passages which, in the early 20th Century, MPs found especially useful for evading umbrella-wielding suffragettes. The St. Stephen's Club opened in January 1875. It levied a thirty guinea [£31.10s.] entrance fee and an annual subscription of ten guineas [£10.10s.].[166]

After leaving the Crown Club to take rooms in Park Lane Anderson lodged in a house at Albert Gate,[167] which novelist and dramatist Charles Reade[168] leased in mid-summer 1869 and shared with his platonic companion Mrs. Laura Seymour until her death in 1879.

A story about Anderson's time with Reade at this house earlier appeared in the *New York Times*, 29th December 1901.[169] In an article titled "The Punishment of Habitual Criminals" the newly-knighted Sir Robert Anderson was discussing the differences between the hunt for a burglar and an assassin.

"Here is a pretty escapade of Sir Robert's which he tells in good style," declared the *New York Times* columnist, "and it is interesting to

---

[165] *The Times*, 7th May 1869.

[166] *Dickens's Dictionary of London*, 1879.

[167] In 1869 the address of Reade's house was 2 Albert Terrace. In 1877 the address became 19 Albert Gate, and later 70 Knightsbridge.

[168] 8th June 1814 – 11th April 1884.

[169] The story also appeared in *The Twentieth Century* and *The Nineteenth Century and After*, 1901, *Criminals and Crime*, 1907, and *The Strand Magazine*, 1909.

know that the amateur burglar was the friend of Charles Reade."

Sir Robert Anderson's story, which did not appear in his collected 1910 memoir, ran thus—

"On arriving home one night after midnight I found I had forgotten my latchkey, and, being unable to arouse the inmates, I decided to enter burglariously. My experience of criminal courts had given me a theoretical knowledge of the business, and it was with a light heart that I dropped into the area and attacked the kitchen window . . . such was the effect on my nerves on spending twenty minutes in that area that the sound of a constable's tread in the garden made me retreat into the coal cellar. I felt then that my case was desperate. As there were no steps to the area, escape was impracticable, and a new bolt on the window baffled me. So at last I was driven to break the glass. It is extraordinary what a noise it makes to smash a pane of glass when one does it deliberately, and the passers-by were attracted by the sound. But they, of course, had no bull's-eye lantern to flash into the area, and as I had again taken refuge in the cellar they could see nothing to account for the noise. As soon as they were gone, it was an easy task to shoot the bolt, open the window and scramble into the house . . .

"The police were sent for next morning, and detectives investigated the crime. The broken glass and the marks both inside and outside gave proof of a felonious entry, but, mirable dictu, nothing was disturbed; nothing was stolen. The case was most mysterious, and it passed into the statistics as an undetected burglary. And those who knew Charles Reade will believe me when I add that when I afterward told him the facts his delight was unbounded."

The sheer unlikeliness of this story may be attested to by the fact that Charles Reade's house, built in 1778, did not have a front [or rear] basement area with access to coal cellars. All extant photographs, drawings and plans show the house set back from the street behind a small front garden with a path leading to the front door. At the back of the house a garden stretched to the wall of Hyde Park. Charles Reade developed part of this space, extending the house by adding a "'palatial apartment' opening on to the garden, which served in turn throughout the day as breakfast-room, study, reception room, dining-room and drawing-room."[170]

American journalist Edward Howard House was a close friend of Charles Reade.

"Personal Characteristics of Charles Reade," E.H. House, *The Atlantic Monthly*, August 1887—

"It was the fortune of the writer of this paper to reside with Reade and Mrs. Seymour at various times, from 1863 to 1873, often for months together, in each of the houses which they successively occupied, in Mayfair and at Knightsbridge."[171]

Nowhere is there a mention of the impossible-to-ignore Robert Anderson, for it appears that Charles Reade did not take in paying lodgers. He had more lucrative interests: the refurbishing and sub-letting of entire properties.

"Anecdotes of Charles Reade," E.H. House, *The Atlantic Monthly*, October 1887—

"No. 6 Bolton Row was much too large for his needs, if not for his inclinations. He removed successively to Curzon Street, to St. George's Road, and to Albert Terrace, Knightsbridge, and was dissatisfied with every change. His migratory habit would have been inconveniently expensive but for the speculative use to which he turned it. Finding himself burdened with long leases of houses not to his taste, he conceived the idea of altering and refitting them upon novel plans, making them attractive in ways which the original designers never dreamed of, and sub-letting them at a profit. The experiment was so successful that he presently enlarged the sphere of his operations, and rented houses in Mayfair, Knightsbridge, and Belgravia with the express purpose of putting a fresh face upon them, and disposing of them to desirable tenants."

By 4th March 1873, the date of his marriage to Agnes Alexandrina Moore, Robert Anderson was living at 7 Kensington Gore,[172] which

---

[170] British History On-Line.
[171] See also E.H. House's obituary, *New York Times*, 25 January 1902.
[172] Anderson's address on their marriage certificate.

remained the family home until in 1877 they moved to 39 Linden Gardens, Notting Hill Gate.

On 21st April 1910 Home Secretary Winston Churchill told the House of Commons—

"I have looked through [Anderson's] articles and they seem to me to be written in a spirit of gross boastfulness. They are written, if I may say so, in the style of 'How Bill Adams Won the Battle of Waterloo.'[173] The writer has been so anxious to show how important he was, how invariably he was right, and how much more he could tell if only his mouth was not what he was pleased to call closed."

Unbeknownst to UK magazine readers of the period there was a coda to Anderson's Ripper story. It appeared in the *New York Times*, 20th March 1910, at around the same time as the UK publication of his *Blackwood's* article. Complete with a flattering portrait of Sir Robert Anderson by American painter William George Krieghoff, the full-page article entitled "The Truth At Last About Jack the Ripper" discussed legal difficulties in dealing with the criminally insane.

The *New York Times* article was written by "A Veteran Diplomat", a pseudonym of Frederick Philip Lewis Cunliffe-Owen, the eldest son of exhibition-organiser Sir Philip Cunliffe-Owen and Jenny von Reitzenstein, daughter of Baron Fritz von Reitzenstein of the Prussian Royal Guard.

A former British diplomat in Europe and Egypt, Frederick Cunliffe-Owen had an encyclopaedic knowledge of European aristocracy, society and politics. In the late 1880s he and his second wife undertook a secret diplomatic mission to America. Details are scant, but they later suffered a financial collapse and to earn a living started writing for newspapers and magazines.

He wrote for *Munsey's Magazine* under his own name and the pseudonym 'Ex-Attaché', and for the New Orleans *Daily Picayune* and Chicago *Daily Tribune* under the name 'Marquis de Fontenoy'. His second

---

[173] Bill Adams, the self-proclaimed hero of a music hall monologue, was a garrulous braggart who placed himself at the centre of this great historical event.

wife, Marguerite de Godart, Comtesse Du Planty et de Sourdis, styled herself 'Marquise de Fontenoy' and proved to be quite the Kitty Kelly of her day, 'solving' the Mayerling incident and generally dishing the dirt on European aristocracy in a number of hugely-successful page-turners.[174]

New York Times, 20th March 1910—

"Sir Robert Anderson, for more than thirty years Chief of the Criminal Investigation Department of the British Government, and head of the Detective Bureau at Scotland Yard, has at length raised the veil of mystery which for nearly two decades has enveloped the identity of the perpetrator of those atrocious crimes known as the Whitechapel murders."

"Veteran Diplomat" first cleared the ground by disposing of a story which in 1897 he himself had written under the pseudonym "Ex-Attaché," namely—

". . . it may be mentioned that it was at Broadmoor that the blue-blooded perpetrator of the Whitechapel murders is now admitted by the authorities to have breathed his last . . .

"Sir Robert's revelations, in an article over his signature in one of the leading London reviews for the current month [Blackwood's], and supplemented by a letter from him printed in The London Times,[175] effectually disposes of the popular stories ascribing the outrages to a peer, now dead, who despite his great wealth had rendered himself an outcast by his vices and eccentricities . . ."

Veteran Diplomat also disposed of a story which fitted the popular notion of the Ripper being a society doctor—

". . . a man, untitled, but of birth and breeding, who after manifesting unmistakable signs of mental disorder had suddenly vanished from his accustomed haunts in London, eventually to die in a madhouse . . .

---

[174] It was only after Marguerite de Godart's death in 1927 that she was revealed to have been 'Marquise de Fontenoy.'

[175] No letter from Sir Robert Anderson appeared in *The Times* between 1st January and 31st March 1910.

" . . . Sir Robert establishes the fact that the infamous 'Jack the Ripper' . . . at whose hands no less than fourteen women of the unfortunate class[176] successively lost their lives . . . was an alien of the lower, though educated class, hailing from Poland, and a maniac of the most virulent and homicidal type . . ."

'Jack the Ripper' was Polish, but now no longer necessarily a Jew. Gone, too, was the witness who "refused to give evidence against him."

The *New York Times* continued—

"But the most important point of all made by Sir Robert is the fact that once the Criminal Investigation Department was sure that it had in its hands the real perpetrator of the Whitechapel Murders, it procured from the Secretary of State for the Home Department a warrant committing the man for detention "during the King's pleasure" to the great asylum for the criminal insane at Broadmoor five or six years ago."

It was in February 1901, a month after the death of Queen Victoria, when Anderson first positively asserted that "the fiend . . . had been safely caged in an asylum," which put the murderer's incarceration at some time prior to this date. Yet here was Anderson in 1910 being reported in the *New York Times* as saying the Ripper was committed to Broadmoor during the King's pleasure "five or six years ago", putting the date of incarceration in 1904 or 1905, three or four years after he had left the Metropolitan Police.

The *New York Times* story did not remotely correspond with what Anderson had written in *Blackwood*'s. Nor would any of these revised details appear in the collected edition of *The Lighter Side of My Official Life*, published in November 1910, or the American edition, published in April 1911.

Many who trust in what Anderson wrote in Blackwood's magazine about the Ripper being a Polish Jew [whom many also believe to have been Kosminski, the exonerated Polish Jew in Macnaghten's revised memorandum] dismiss the *New York Times* article. They contend that Anderson had somehow become an unwitting dupe who had nothing to

---

[176] A 270% increase in the Ripper's tally Anderson had reported in Blackwood's.

do with the article; that Frederick Cunliffe-Owen was an unprincipled hack who cobbled the story together from a variety of unreliable sources and that basically his article wasn't fit to line the bottom of a parrot cage.

Anderson having been the unwitting dupe of a story which contradicted much of what over the years he had told reporters and writers about the Ripper is hard to swallow. A subscriber to a press cuttings agency, Anderson maintained a shrewd watchfulness over his image in the press, making it unlikely that a full-page article could have appeared in a Sunday edition of one of New York's leading newspapers without the prior consent or subsequent opprobrium of this most cautious of men.

In the event of feeling misunderstood Anderson was never shy in dashing off a letter to a newspaper editor, but in the wake of this article no such correspondence is to be found in the archived letter columns of the *New York Times*. Nor in those of the *Washington Post* which ran the story the following day; nor the Chicago *Daily Inter-Ocean*, which a week later referenced Sir Robert Anderson in a substantially different version of the story under an illustration worthy of a dime detective novel bearing the headline— "Jack the Ripper in Insane Asylum: Former Chief of Scotland Yard Tells Truth At Last About Famous Whitechapel Murderer."

On 6th April 1910 Sir Robert Anderson told the *Daily News*, — "I disclaim any connection with any move in a political game," and in the appendix of *The Lighter Side of My Official Life*, published later that year, he further justified his actions with a fustian account of April's events. What he failed to reveal, however, was how he felt about the political hubbub he had caused.

Asked this question by the *New York Daily Tribune,* 10th April 1910, Sir Robert Anderson replied— "It has made me feel ten years younger."

Those who insist Sir Robert Anderson would have never lied in self-interest to a general readership forget that in *The Lighter Side of My Official Life* the reason he gave for his 1901 'retirement' was a blatant lie, which begs the question of why anyone should unreservedly accept his word that Jack the Ripper was a Polish Jew.

There is no accurate way to determine which, if any, of Robert

Anderson's many autobiographical anecdotes may have been true, so until such time as we are in receipt of more reliable and impartial corroborative evidence to support any one of them the wisest thing we can do is dismiss them all.

8. NOTES IN THE MARGIN

That Jack the Ripper was a Polish Jew depends solely upon the word of Sir Robert Anderson, who has been shown to be less than reliable, so when someone appears to agree with him all sorts of alarm bells start ringing.

At some time after November 1910 retired Superintendent Donald Sutherland Swanson was given a copy of Sir Robert Anderson's "The Lighter Side of My Official Life."

According to Sir Robert Anderson's son, Arthur Ponsonby Moore-Anderson, Swanson and Anderson enjoyed a close relationship which continued long after his 1901 retirement.

In November 1901, on the occasion of Anderson's knighthood, Swanson wrote to him, saying, "It was with real pleasure that I read this morning that my old master was the recipient of an honour from HM the King. Everybody I have spoken to here is pleased."

Moore-Anderson added that "every Christmas thereafter brought greetings from Mr. Swanson; in 1917 he wrote, 'My best wishes to Lady Agnes and you my dear former master. I often think of you and your kindnesses to me which are remembered with pleasure and are impossible to forget.'"

Considering their seemingly lengthy relationship, Sir Robert Anderson sent Swanson a reply which reads more like a collective note of thanks sent to his old department—

"I was greatly gratified by your remembrance of me. My very pleasant memories of my service at 'the Yard' are mainly associated with the Staff of the department, and very specially with my senior officers. I don't believe there was one of you who had an unkind thought about me . . . Very heartily do I wish you all good during the year about to begin. 'Tis a sad and a solemn time we are living in. As for me, its sadness would overwhelm me were it not for the Faith and the Hope which become more real and more gladdening as the days go by."

Following Sir Robert Anderson's death [15th November 1918] Swanson replied to a request from A.P. Moore-Anderson—

"Yes, certainly you have my willing permission to publish any letter to me from my dear respected master, if it will help you to portray his character as I found him during the many years I was under him . . . He was able, just, firm, good and kind. We never knew an unpleasantness, though we differed sometimes, but very seldom and then over very trivial matters. I am conscious that I owe him very much and shall always feel grateful. Under him were spent the happiest of my thirty-five years' service."[177]

It is not known how esteemed Swanson imagined himself to be in Anderson's mind, but if he was hoping to read a few kind words about himself in Moore-Anderson's biography he was to be sorely disappointed. His Christmas 1917 message of goodwill [together with Anderson's reply] was the only Swanson correspondence that A.P. Moore-Anderson reproduced in "Sir Robert Anderson: A Tribute and Memoir," published in 1919 by Morgan & Scott. This was the first iteration of his more ambitious "Robert Anderson and Lady Agnes Anderson," published in London, 1947, by Marshall, Morgan & Scott.

Swanson's copy is inscribed, "Mr. Donald S. Swanson with the sincere regards of A.P. Moore-Anderson, Nov 1919."

Robert Anderson had sent Swanson a copy of "Daniel in the Critic's Den." It was inscribed "For Donald S. Swanson with the author's good

---

[177] Sir Robert Anderson and Lady Agnes. A.P. Moore-Anderson, 1947.

wishes. Christmas 1903." And on New Year's Day 1908 he received a copy of "Criminals and Crime", inscribed "for Donald S. Swanson with my good wishes, R. Anderson."

Anderson's largesse did not extend to sending Swanson a copy of his 1910 book "The Lighter Side Of My Official Life." Swanson's copy was a gift from someone signing himself Fred.

"To Donald with every good wish from Fred," reads the inscription.

"The Lighter Side of My Official Life" is a collected volume of articles which first appeared in Blackwood's magazine in 1909 and 1910.

In the March 1910 edition Anderson wrote—

"During my absence abroad the Police had made a house-to-house search for him, investigating the case of every man in the district whose circumstances were such that he could go and come and get rid of his blood-stains in secret. And the conclusion we came to was that he and his people were low-class Jews [in the book "low-class Jews" was changed to "low-class Polish Jews"], for it is a remarkable fact that people of that class in the East End will not give up one of their number to Gentile justice . . . Scotland Yard can boast that not even the subordinate officers of the department will tell tales out of school, and it would ill become me to violate the unwritten rule of the service.

"The subject will come up again, and I will only add here that the 'Jack-the-Ripper' letter which is preserved in the Police Museum at New Scotland Yard is the creation of an enterprising London journalist."

There followed a footnote—

"Having regard to the interest attaching to this case, I should almost be tempted to disclose the identity of the murderer and of the pressman who wrote the letter above referred to . . . But no public benefit would result from such a course, and the traditions of my old department would suffer. I will only add that when the individual whom we suspected was caged in an asylum, the only person who had ever had a good view of the murderer at once identified him, but when he learned that the suspect was a fellow-Jew he declined to swear to him."

In the book this footnote became part of the main text, albeit with an amendment to the last sentence—

"I will merely add that when the individual whom we suspected was caged in an asylum, the only person who had ever had a good view of the murderer unhesitatingly identified the subject the instant he was confronted with him; but he refused to give evidence against him."

The suspect and witness were now no longer necessarily Jewish.

Following this paragraph at the bottom of page 138, Swanson made an annotation with a purplish pencil which explained in essence what Anderson had originally written—

"because the suspect was also a Jew and also because his evidence would convict the suspect, and witness would be the means of murderer being hanged which he did not wish to be left on his mind. D.S.S."

Anderson continued—

"In saying that he was a Polish Jew I am merely stating a definitely ascertained fact."

Using a blacker pencil Swanson wrote in the left margin of page 138— *"& after this identification which suspect knew, no other murder of this kind took place in London,"* which was an adaptation of what Anderson had written on page 136—

"However the fact may be explained, it is a fact that no other street murder occurred in the 'Jack-the-Ripper' series. The last and most horrible of that maniac's crimes was committed in a house in Miller's Court on the 9th November."

Here the reader was directed to a footnote—

"I am here assuming that the murder of Alice M'Kenzie on 17th July 1889 was by another hand. I was absent from London when it occurred, but the Chief Commissioner [James Monro] investigated the case on the spot. It was an ordinary murder, and not the work of a sexual maniac."

Robert Anderson was placing his Polish Jew incident at some point between Millers Court [9th November 1888] and the murder of Alice Mackenzie [17th July 1889], which tallies with what Macnaghten had written in his February 1894 memorandum—

". . . he [Kosminski] was removed to a lunatic asylum about March 1889."

But we know this to be not true.

To make his reasoning work Anderson had to lead his readers to believe that the Alice Mackenzie murder was "an ordinary murder, and not the work of a sexual maniac," whereas in a 17th July 1889 memo sent to the under Secretary of State at the Home Office, Commissioner James Monro expressed his opinion that the murderer was "identical with the notorious Jack the Ripper of last year."[178]

A glance at what is known about Aaron Kosminski [the only Kosminski in the asylum system at the time] suggests that Anderson, Macnaghten and Swanson were talking out of the backs of their hats.

Aaron Kosminski was born in 1864 or 1865. He came to England in 1882. In 1888 he was aged 23 or 24 years. He was unmarried. Occupation, hairdresser.

In December 1889, five months after the murder of Alice Mackenzie, he was fined for walking an unmuzzled dog in Cheapside.

LloydsWeekly Newspaper, 15th December 1889—

"City Summons Court.

"Fines for Unmuzzled Dogs.

"Aaron Kosminski was summoned for a similar offence. Police Constable Borer said he saw the defendant with an unmuzzled dog, and when asked his name gave that of Aaron Kosminski, which his brother said was wrong, as his name was Abrahams.

"Defendant said that the dog was not his, and his brother said it was found more convenient here to go by the name of Abrahams, but his name was Kosminski.

"Sir Polydore de Keyser imposed a fine of 10 shillings and costs which the defendant would not pay, as it was not right to pay money on Sunday. He was given till Monday to pay."

Kosminski's first mental breakdown took place in 1890 at the age of 25 or 26. He was admitted to Mile End Old Town Workhouse, 12th July 1890, from 3 Sion Square[179]. Deemed able-bodied but insane, three days later he was discharged into the care of an unnamed brother living

---

[178] A493011/1
[179] The 1891 census records the Abrahams family at 3 Sion Square, Mile End Old Town

at 16 Greenfield Street.

Seven months later, on Wednesday 4th February 1891, Aaron Kosminski was re-admitted to the workhouse from 16 Greenfield Street, Whitechapel. Two days later he was examined by Dr. Edmund King Houchin of 23 High Street, Stepney—

"In the matter of Aaron Kozminski of 16 Greenfield St, Mile End, E. in the county of London, Hair Dresser, an alleged lunatic.

"1. I, the undersigned Edmund King Houchin do hereby certify as follows . . .

"2. On the 6th day of February 1891 at the Mile End Old Town Workhouse in the county of London I personally examined the said Aaron Kozminski and came to the conclusion that he is a person of unsound mind and a proper person to be taken charge of and detained under care and treatment.

"3. I formed this conclusion on the following grounds, viz.:-

"(a) Facts indicating insanity observed by myself at the time of examination, viz.: -

"He declares that he is guided & his movements altogether controlled by an instinct that informs his mind; he says that he knows the movements of all mankind; he refuses food from others because he is told to do so and eats out of the gutter for the same reason.

"(b) Facts communicated by others, viz.: -

"Jacob Cohen, 51 Carter Lane, St Paul's, City of London, says that he goes about the streets and picks up bits of bread out of the gutter & eats them, he drinks water from the tap & he refuses food at the hands of others. He took up a knife & threatened the life of his sister. He says that he is ill and his cure consists in refusing food. He is melancholic, practises self-abuse. He is very dirty and will not be washed. He has not attempted any kind of work for years.

"4. The said Aaron Kozminski appeared to me to be in a fit condition of bodily health to be removed to an asylum, hospital or licensed house . . ."

On the same day Henry Chambers J.P. issued a committal order to that effect, and on Saturday 7th February 1891 Aaron Kozminski was admitted to the County Lunatic Asylum at Colney Hatch.

And that was that.

A week later, on Friday 13th February 1891, the body of Frances Coles was found in Swallow Gardens, and the Metropolitan Police resumed its hunt for Jack the Ripper.

Lloyds Weekly London Newspaper, 15th February 1891—

"Shortly before five o'clock, Chief Inspector Swanson, of Scotland-yard, arrived [at Swallow Gardens]."

San Francisco Chronicle, 14th February 1891—

"Inspector Swanson says that any ruffian might have cut the unfortunate woman's throat in the way it was done, but when a second soft felt hat rolled from under the victim's arm, in addition to the one she wore, he felt that this must have been done by the 'Ripper.' The theory has long been that he paraded in woman's attire, and Swanson thinks he dropped the hat while struggling with his victim."

The Times, 16th February 1891—

James Sadler "was at once taken before Chief Inspector Swanson, who, having cautioned him that he was not bound to answer any question, subjected him to a searching examination."

Swanson's memory had betrayed him.

"*& after this identification which suspect knew, no other murder of this kind took place in London.*"

His comment makes no more sense if you attempt to shift the Kosminski scenario back to March 1889—the date Macnaghten wrote that Kosminski had been removed to a lunatic asylum—for the murder of Alice McKenzie in July 1889 was thought by James Monro to be the Ripper's handiwork. Pushing it forward to May 1895 and the case of William Grant [aka Grainger], suspected of being the Ripper, doesn't work either, for almost a year earlier, on 19th April 1894, Aaron Kosminski, having been in Colney Hatch Asylum for three years, was moved to the Metropolitan Asylum for Chronic Imbeciles at Leavesden, where he died, aged 54 or 55, on 24th March 1919.

Thus far there is no way to square real life events with those advanced by Anderson, Macnaghten or Swanson. Fortunately, however,

Swanson elaborated on his scenario.

Using the blacker pencil, he wrote on the book's endpaper—

"Continuing from page 138. After the suspect had been identified at the Seaside Home where he had been sent by us with difficulty, in order to subject him to identification, and he knew he was identified. On suspects return to his brother's house in Whitechapel he was watched by police (City CID) by day & night. In a very short time the suspect with his hands tied behind his back, he was sent to Stepney Workhouse and then to Colney Hatch and died shortly afterwards – Kosminski was the suspect – DSS."

This rigmarole had proceeded despite Anderson knowing from experience that "it is a remarkable fact that people of that class in the East End will not give up one of their number to Gentile justice."

Anderson wrote—

"I will merely add that when the individual whom we suspected was caged in an asylum, the only person who had ever had a good view of the murderer unhesitatingly identified the subject the instant he was confronted with him; but he refused to give evidence against him."

Anderson was implying that the suspect had been committed to an asylum prior to the identification, whereas Swanson was putting the identification at a date prior to the asylum committal.

They can't both have been right.

Another question is why the witness had not already realised the suspect was Jewish? Why had this revelation come as such a late surprise? And who was "the only person who had ever had a good view of the murderer"?

In both versions of his memorandum Macnaghten wrote, "No-one ever saw the Whitechapel murderer," adding in the subsequent Aberconway version, "unless possibly it was the City PC who was [on] a beat near Mitre Square."

This ties in with the City CID watching the house of Kosminski's brother and would suggest the witness was either PC Watkins or PC Harvey, neither of whom claimed at Catherine Eddowes' inquest to have seen the perpetrator.

We can take this a stage further.

If "the only person who had ever had a good view of the murderer" was a City policeman, he was also Jewish and at the time of Kosminski's identification, recuperating in a Seaside Home, for the suspect was "sent" to see the witness.

You could drive yourself insane trying to identify the Seaside Home in question, for at the time there were sixty-nine such establishments in the British Isles.[180] But one particular Seaside Home has proved popular with Ripperologists.

In March 1890 the Police Convalescent Home opened at 51 Clarendon Villas, Hove, Brighton, Sussex. It was also the Southern Counties Police Orphanage, with accommodation for sixteen. This was the institution which in 1891 James Monro endowed a bed "for the use and comfort of members of the Metropolitan Police Force only, to be called the 'Monro Testimonial Bed.'"[181]

On 5th April 1891, seven weeks after Aaron Kosminski's incarceration at Colney Hatch the UK Census was taken, and at 51 Clarendon Villas the following people were recorded—

Mary M.P. Griffin, Head, Lives by Own Means, 33, Born Portsea, Hampshire.

Fanny March, Widow, 57, Born Ssx [Sussex] Biddlecombe.

James H. Archer, Visitor, Scholar, 10, Born Brighton.

James H. Cousens, Visitor, Scholar, 6, Born Leic[ester].

Lettice Roper, Servant, 41, Weeks, Ryde, Isle of Wight.

Eliza Inman, Servant, 14, London, Bow.

James M. Hay, Boarder, 42, Police Inspector, Kent.

Henry R. Hatch, Boarder, 47, Police Constable, Mdx [Middlesex] Southall.

Frederic Child, Boarder, Police Constable, 20 (?), Bucks, Beaconsfield.

Since the Home's opening a year earlier a similar mix of people

---

[180]   The Charities Register and Digest, third edition, 1890.
[181]   The Hackney Express and Shoreditch Observer, 1st August 1891.

would have been in residence, making it difficult to imagine the Metropolitan Police sending history's most infamous murderer to a small detached house in Hove partly tenanted by women and children.

Some argue that Macnaghten made an error in identifying "the only person who had ever had a good view of the murderer" as a City PC; that it was, in fact, Joseph Lawende, a Jewish tobacconist and commercial traveller who allegedly saw Catherine Eddowes in the company of her killer on the morning of the double-event and gave evidence at her inquest. But if he was the Jewish witness, what was he was doing in a Metropolitan Police convalescent home?

To resolve this conundrum someone had the idea that Swanson, by then heading towards his dotage [62 in 1910], had conflated Kosminski and the Seaside Home with James Sadler and the Seaman's Home at Well Street, Whitechapel, where the Ripper suspect de jour had been staying. Indeed, so convinced was the Metropolitan Police that they had caught their man that they confronted Sadler with Joseph Lawende.

At Eddowes' inquest Lawende was asked by the Coroner, "Would you know him again?" To which he replied, "I doubt it."

But almost thirty months later hope sprang eternal.

Daily Telegraph, 18th February 1891—

"Probably the only trustworthy description of the assassin was that given by a gentleman who, on the night of the Mitre Square murder, noticed in Duke Street, Aldgate, a couple standing under the lamp at the corner of the passage leading to Mitre Square. The woman was identified as one victim of that night, Sept. 30, the other having been killed an hour previously in Berner Street . . . The witness has confronted Sadler and has failed to identify him."

Lawende's suspect was around 30 years of age. James Sadler was 53, with ears that stuck out like a London black cab with its doors open. It is the sort of physical detail Joseph Lawende might have remembered.

Some of the pieces fit. There is a Ripper suspect, a Jewish witness, a Seaman's Home and an unsuccessful identification. Unhappily, though, James Sadler was not Jewish.

Donald Sutherland Swanson died in November 1924.

There is a body of Ripperological opinion which holds that sections of the marginalia—most specifically the last line, "Kosminski was the suspect" —were added after Swanson's death.

In 2006, prior to being put on display in Scotland Yard's crime museum, the marginalia was sent for scientific examination.[182]

In January 2007 a Forensic Science Service press release reported the findings of Dr. Christopher Davies, one of its senior document examiners. He had concluded that—" . . . [the marginalia] had been annotated twice in two different pencils at different times, which does raise the question of how reliable the second set of notes were as they were made some years later."

Dr. Davies felt that any differences in the writing could be attributed to the [human] ageing process.

"It is most likely to be Swanson, but I'm sure the report will be cause for lively debate amongst those interested in the case."

Hardly conclusive.

In August 2012 Dr. Davies was asked to revisit his report. Recently-discovered letters had become available for handwriting comparison. On 24th September 2012 he concluded that—

" . . . there is very strong support for the view that the notes toward the bottom of page 138 in Donald Swanson's copy of The Lighter Side of My Official Life [purplish pencil] and the notes on the last leaf in this book [blacker pencil] were written by Donald Swanson.

"I have concluded that there is no evidence to support the view that the final line on the last leaf of the book was added much later to a pre-existing text."

He then added, quite gratuitously—

"I have also found no evidence to support the view that this line was written by Jim Swanson."[183]

The jury is still out on the Swanson marginalia.

---

[182]   See Ripperologist No. 128, October 2012.
[183]   Donald Swanson's son, born 1912, died 2001.

9. PANDORA'S BOX

Sir Robert Anderson's Jack the Ripper revelation was a flash in the pan.

House of Commons, 19th April 1910—

"Mr. Jeremiah Macveagh [Irish Parliamentary Party, South Down] asked the Secretary of State for the Home Department whether his attention has been called to the revelations published by Sir Robert Anderson with regard to what are generally known as the Jack the Ripper murders; whether he obtained the sanction of the Home Office or Scotland Yard authorities to such publication; and, if not, whether any and, if so, what steps can be taken in regard to it?"

Winston Churchill, Home Secretary—

"Sir Robert Anderson neither asked for nor received any sanction to the publication, but the matter appears to me of minor importance in comparison with others that arise in connection with the same series of articles."

Winston Churchill was right: Jack the Ripper was quickly overshadowed by darker events, about which Sir Robert Anderson and James Monro would soon lock horns.

In April 1910 Sir Robert Anderson became enmeshed in a controversy of his own making when quite out of the blue he revealed in *Blackwood's* magazine—

"To the present hour I do not know whether the Home Secretary was then aware of my authorship of 'The Times' articles of 1887 on 'Parnellism and Crime', for in relation to this matter I acted with strict propriety in dealing with Mr. Monro and not with the Secretary of State."

Parliament was in uproar. Anderson's pension became at risk as the lid of a Pandora's Box threatened to be prised open—Henri Le Caron, the Special Commission, forged Parnell letters, Anderson's rôle at the Home Office, the resignations of Sir Charles Warren and James Monro, Secret Service funding, Scotland Yard officers in America . . . the list of apparent evils seemed endless.

Sir Robert Anderson conducted his defense via the press, denying that *The Times* had received any direct or indirect assistance from the CID and stating that his "Parnellism and Crime" articles had been written after he ceased to be political adviser to the Home Office[184] and without its knowledge; but with the full knowledge and sanction of James Monro, Assistant Commissioner of the Metropolitan Police at the time, who was also in charge of secret service work.

Two series of articles had been published in *The Times*. The first, 'Parnellism and Crime', implicated Charles Parnell in the terrorist activities of the Fenians/IRB. The second was entitled "Behind the Scenes in America."

At the Special Commission Joseph Soames, solicitor for The Times, stated that the author of 'Parnellism and Crime' was John Woulfe Flanagan, a barrister at Lincoln's Inn and for forty years a member of the editorial staff of *The Times*.

It was this series of articles which included the letter purporting to suggest that Charles Parnell supported the Phoenix Park murders. It was revealed under cross-examination to have been forged by Richard Pigott. Whilst under twenty-four hour surveillance by two officers from the Royal Irish Constabulary, he fled to Madrid where, in the Hotel Des Embazadores, booked in under the name Roland Ponsonby, he shot

---

[184]   ". . . he never held any post which could be described as 'Political Adviser to the Home Office'." Extract from Sir Robert Anderson's 'official history', 8th April 1910. HO A49.962/7

himself in the head with a pistol as two detectives arrived from Scotland Yard[185] to arrest him.

On pages 213-214 of *Sidelights on the Home Rule Movement*, 1907, Robert Anderson muddied the forgery waters. Whereas Lord Salisbury believed the letter to be genuine, Anderson wrote, "Pigott, I repeat, had no part in writing the letter, and he believed it to be genuine. The hand that wrote it was that of Arthur O'Keefe, assistant sub-editor of Mr. William O'Brien's paper, United Ireland, who was arrested under Forster's Act, on December 15, 1881, and imprisoned with Parnell in Kilmainham."

Twenty years later journalist George R. Sims challenged the story of Pigott's suicide, suggesting he had been murdered and further stating he had in his personal Criminal Museum "a photograph of the body taken in the room immediately after the tragedy was discovered."[186] Sims always talked a good game, but how much he actually knew is debatable. For instance, he named ex-Superintendent Thompson [sic] as being employed by *The Times* in connection with the matter, whereas at the time of Richard Pigott's Madrid suicide in March 1889 Thomson was in New York schmoozing Millen right up until the General's timely heart attack.

Anderson claimed to have only written the three subsequent "Behind the Scenes in America" articles which appeared under the "Parnellism and Crime" banner in May and June 1887. Any confusion was due to a typing error he had failed to spot in his *Blackwood's* manuscript. He originally put "May 1887", thus pinpointing the three articles he had written, whereas his typist had left out the all-important "May".

If Anderson was telling the truth, the author of the original Parnellism and Crime articles had to have been John Woulfe Flanagan.

However, twenty years earlier, on 10th March 1890, during an adjournment debate on the Special Commission, Thomas Sexton,

---

[185] Inspector [later Sir] Patrick Quinn and Sergeant Richard Owen. *The Times*, 12th March 1889.

[186] *The Referee*, 17th April 1910.

Nationalist MP for Belfast West, told the House of Commons—

". . . That infamous libeller, Mr. Woulfe Flanagan, the son of an Irish Judge, presented himself the other day for admission to the Athenaeum Club, but the number of black balls deposited against him was the largest ever known against any person seeking admission, although his patron, Mr. Buckle [George Earle Buckle, editor of *The Times*], pleaded piteously on his behalf that he had not written all the articles in The Times, but only three of them, and those not by any means the worst."

Further details appeared in overseas newspapers.

The Queenslander [Australia], 3rd May 1890—

"An extraordinary effort was made to save [Mr. Flanagan], Mr. Buckle, editor of The Times, arguing somewhat naively that he hadn't written "the worst parts", and Mr. Benjamin Jowett, the master of Balliol, spending a little fortune in telegrams, exhorting all the sons of Balliol who were members of the club to go up and vote for him. But 440 supporters would have been necessary to counteract the forty-four blackballs of the Gladstonians, and only 272 men came up in Mr. Flanagan's support."

The three articles "not by any means the worst" would appear to have been the "Behind the Scenes in America" articles, which gave the first intimation of the Jubilee Plot. So who wrote what? Anderson and Flanagan could not "have written" and "have not written" the same three articles.

The National Library of Ireland lists amongst its holdings "*Parnellism and Crime, reprinted from The Times*—1887. Main author, John Woulfe Flanagan," whilst the British Library lists Robert Anderson as author of the original 7th, 10th and 14th March 1887 *Parnellism and Crime* articles.

In reporting the death in November 1929 of John Woulfe Flanagan, the Catholic weekly *The Tablet* wrote—

". . . it is mentioned that he was the author of the series of articles on 'Parnellism and Crime'. But though Woulfe Flanagan wrote the articles, he had nothing to do, The Times makes clear, with accepting and printing the alleged 'Parnell Letters,' the outcome of which was the Parnell Commission and the vindication of the Irish leader in the historic libel action."

Anderson's 1910 comments were being avidly read, and in an office at New Scotland Yard an article was clipped from the *Westminster Gazette* of 7th April 1910, slipped into an envelope and mailed to an address in Scotland.

Two days later, James Monro, back in Britain since 1905 from the Dayabari Mission in Bengal, India, and now aged seventy-two, replied to his correspondent from No. 12 Rubislaw Terrace, Aberdeen—

"My dear Macnaghten,

"Thanks for [the newspaper] cutting. The alleged statement of Anderson to an interviewer that it was arranged between him and me that he should write the letters and that they should be offered to The Times as the best medium for their publication is absolutely incorrect . . ."

Monro went on to refute other comments by Anderson which had appeared in the *Aberdeen Free Press* "(copy enclosed)".

"I am willing," he continued, "to place myself at the disposal of the Home Office and give the fullest explanation of my action in the matter. And <u>you have my authority to inform the Commissioner of Police and the Home Office to this effect</u>."

More was to come.

"Anderson's statement as to his being political adviser to the Home Office at any time when I was at Scotland Yard is so far as I am aware unfounded. My principle throughout has ever been that in <u>police</u>, <u>politics</u> have no place—and this principle I followed during the whole time I was at Scotland Yard, under four different Secretaries of State. Appointed by Sir W. Harcourt, I served under Sir Richard Cross, Mr. Childers and Mr. Matthews—and the policy of Scotland Yard remained the same, whether the Govt. was Liberal or Conservative."[187]

Sir Melville Macnaghten[188] passed on the letter from his old Bengal friend to Sir Charles Edward Troup CB, KCB, Assistant Under-Secretary at the Home Office.

---

[187] Monro letter. HO A49962/35
[188] He was knighted in 1907.

On the same day David Littlejohn, James Monro's brother-in-law, sent a typewritten letter denying any truth in Anderson's comments to Eugene Wason[189] at the House of Commons.

Littlejohn wrote that James Monro's health was "completely broken but his powerful intellect and remarkable memory are unimpaired . . . he is desirous that the Home Office should be made aware that if they should desire to 'interview' him, any account which he might be able to give of certain past events, (and which might not agree with some things which have appeared) is at their disposal. Mr. Monro could not travel without danger: but he is quite able to receive callers . . .

"If you can at once communicate what I have written to the office to which I have referred I shall be obliged. There is a question down for Monday I think."

House of Commons, 13th April 1910—

Winston Churchill [Home Secretary]— "I have communicated with Mr. Monro, who resides in Scotland, and whose state of health prevents his attendance in London. I have not yet had his reply, and can only say at present that he certainly does not admit the accuracy of the statements made by or attributed to Sir Robert Anderson."

A week passed.

House of Commons, 21st April 1910—

Winston Churchill— "I have received the following statement from Mr. Monro—

"In 1887 I was Assistant Commissioner, Metropolitan Police, under the Home Office, in charge of secret work. Mr. Anderson was an agent of mine (as were others), chiefly as being a channel of information received from a man in America, who corresponded directly with him, and whose name I did not know. When 'The Times' earlier articles appeared they certainly caused a sensation in London, and everybody was talking about them. I have no doubt that Mr. Anderson and I talked about them, and I can quite imagine that I may have welcomed public interest being directed to the existence of a dangerous conspiracy. But

---

189   Liberal MP for Clackmannanshire and Kinross-shire.

such an expression of opinion was a very different thing from authorising an agent of mine to give information to the public. Such a course would have been opposed to all my training in a service where communication on the part of officials with the Press was carefully limited. As a matter of fact, no such authority was asked by Mr. Anderson, and none was given to him by me. When subsequently articles appeared in 'The Times,' I was unaware of the name of the author, and naturally I made no report on the subject to the Home Office. A long time afterwards Mr. Anderson informed me that he had written one or more of the articles, and I felt much annoyed. However, the evil, if such it was, was done, and nothing was to be gained by saying anything on the subject. I therefore observed silence. I may have mentioned the matter at the Home Office in confidential talk, but as the incident had passed many months previously, and there was no object in reopening the question, I did not report it officially."

Mr. Macveagh— "In view of that reply, I take it that the statement of Sir Robert Anderson that he had the permission of his official superior to write these articles for 'The Times' may be treated as another of 'Anderson's Fairy Tales'."

The House of Commons erupted into unbridled laughter.

A deep rift between the two men was revealed in *The Times*, 30th April 1910, when Sir Robert Anderson wrote of "a most painful incident which, on the eve of his resigning the Chief Commissionership of Police, broke up a close friendship of several years."

Monro and Anderson were joined at the Unionist and Millenarist hip, so a political or religious schism is unlikely to have broken up their friendship, and it is equally unlikely that the matter of police pensions and superannuation was the cause. Anderson sounded as if he was the aggrieved party, but author J.A. Cole suggests the rift was the result of Anderson revealing to Monro at this time his authorship of the 1887 articles in *The Times*.[190]

This makes perfect sense. Anderson's revelation would most

---

[190]   *Prince of Spies: Henri Le Caron*. J.A. Cole. Faber & Faber, April 1984.

certainly have put James Monro on the spot, especially coming amidst the political furor then going on in parliament regarding Scotland Yard's adventures in North America on behalf of the Special Commission, the political show trial for which *The Times* articles of 1887 had lit the blue touchpaper.

It was one man's word against another, and as J.A. Cole further suggested, Monro's response may simply have been an instinctive "dive for cover at the prospect of a controversy."

Despite the fact that Monro had resigned for reasons not unconnected with the situation under discussion, his explanation of events proved more palatable to Parliament than Anderson's exculpatory letters in *The Times*.

In deciding if it was his duty to deprive Sir Robert Anderson of his pension, Winston Churchill laid out the charges against him, of which "two lie in the past, and are charges of gravity [and] . . . one lies in the present . . ."

Churchill summed up—

"The authorship of the letters on 'Parnellism and Crime' occurred twenty-three years ago, and their authorship has only now been revealed by the garrulous inaccuracies and indiscretions of advancing years. The charge of helping The Times newspaper in preparing its case occurred twenty-one years ago. It is strenuously denied, and not merely is there the great lapse of time which even in serious criminal processes might be held to interpose some barrier of limitation, but there is also the difficulty of proving matters from which we are separated by almost a quarter of a century.

"So I put aside altogether, for the purposes of any action which I could take at the present time, both those charges which relate to the distant past, though I have expressed my opinion very clearly upon them.

"There only remains, therefore, the minor revelations contained in the Blackwood's articles. I have read the Blackwood's articles. It was my duty to do so—I do not think I should otherwise have been drawn into their perusal—but it was my duty to do so for the purpose of the case which has come under my notice. I have looked through these articles and they seem to me to be written in a spirit of gross boastfulness. They are written, if I may say so, in the style of 'How Bill Adams Won the Battle of Waterloo.' The writer has been so anxious to show how important he was, how invariably he was right, and how much more he could tell if only his mouth was not what he was pleased to call closed . . .

"And it seems to me, reviewing the whole subject and reviewing these articles, that it would be attaching far too much importance to the articles and to their author to take the step at the present time of forfeiting the pension which was conferred upon him nine years ago upon his retirement from the public service."

It was a masterful piece of humbug. Parliament was under no illusions about what had been going on between 1887 and 1889.

House of Commons, 21st April 1910—

Mr. John Redmond [Irish Parliamentary Party]—

"I say that all through those proceedings the Government of the day, from the head of the Government down to the least important Member of it, were up to their necks in this criminal prosecution, and nothing would delight me more than if it were possible for us to take the Vote, not on the pension of a miserable underling like Sir Robert Anderson, but on the conduct of those who were really responsible for the conspiracy, but we cannot do so. We have the opportunity on this Vote of condemning the Government of that day as a whole on the action of Sir Robert Anderson, and I do appeal to all Members of this House who believe with us that we were the victims in those days of a foul and criminal conspiracy . . ."

Jeremiah Macveagh spelled out the conspiracy—

"We had the Home Secretary, Mr. Matthews—now Lord Llandaff. We had Monro, Anderson, Scotland Yard, the Home Office, the Prisons Board,[191] and a vast army of well-paid spies and informers, all actively working in scouring the purlieus of the cities of America and Great Britain, as well as our convict prisons, to get evidence in support of The

---

[191]   From 1877 to 1887, prior to his becoming Assistant Commissioner of Police [CID], Robert Anderson was Secretary to the Prison Commissioners.

Times newspaper."

John Redmond pressed for a full inquiry, but Prime Minister Asquith, having come to the defence of Henry Matthews, [192] demurred—

"Unless the hon. and learned Gentleman can suggest that some useful purpose will be served by an inquiry, I do not myself at this moment propose to take the responsibility of embarking upon it."

Inevitable comparisons were made with Sir Charles Warren.

Mr. Macveagh— "What was the fate of a Commissioner of Police who wrote much less serious articles in 'Murray's Magazine'? He was censured and retired from office because he wrote an article on the administration of Scotland Yard. Anderson did infinitely worse than Warren; and yet Anderson was loaded with honours, while Warren was hounded from the public service."

Sir Robert Anderson retained his pension, just as he always knew he would. He was a survivor who knew exactly where all the bodies were buried.

In *The Times*, 12th April 1910, Anderson adopted a bullet-proof strategy—

"I have nothing to conceal in this matter," he wrote. " . . . if the Government will release me from the honourable obligations to reticence respecting the Secret Service work at Whitehall my defence will be full and complete."

Nobody was sufficiently foolhardy to risk picking up this particular gauntlet, thus exhuming a period of three years during which the bogus Jubilee plot, murder, suicide, forged letters, the Special Commission, CID complicity with *The Times* and the illegal employment of Scotland Yard officers in the United States finally culminated in the destruction of James Monro. And for good measure, during ten weeks of this tumultuous period "Jack the Ripper" had been stalking the streets of

---

[192]   Asquith: "I can say with some confidence that the Home Secretary had no knowledge of him [Anderson] being, or claiming to be, author or part author of The Times articles." [Hansard]. Wording taken from HO A49962/7, a briefing note prepared by Sir Charles Edward Troup, dated 8th April 1910.

London's East End.

Not surprisingly, perhaps, the conservative weekly magazine *The Spectator*, 23rd April 1910, felt inclined to give Sir Robert Anderson the benefit of the doubt. At worst his words had been ill-chosen—

"He has conveyed an impression, which we are certain was not the case, that the Government of the day were engaged in a dishonourable conspiracy to entrap the Nationalist Members, and show them guilty of offences in which they had no part."

This parliamentary squall soon blew itself out, and thus we shall probably never learn the full extent of Robert Anderson and James Monro's involvement in the writing of *The Times* articles, the publication of the forged Parnell letter and the wholly mythical Jubilee Plot.[193]

In "The Clan-na-Gael and the Murder of Dr. Cronin," published 1889, Chicago newspaperman John T. McEnnis wrote—

"The 'jubilee illumination' was declared to be series of dynamite outrages which the American Irish were preparing as a cynic and cruel protest against the general joy in Victoria's fifty years of sovereignty. It had absolutely no foundation in fact whatever. There was not one iota of reality to substantiate the fright, but the dove-cote at Scotland Yard was fluttered, and detectives absolutely worked over the whole of America and France to find a foundation for their blood-curdling romances. It is estimated that the scare, which was a scare pure and simple and nothing else, cost the English Government £14,000, or $70,000."

Sir Robert Anderson wrote—

"Men engaged in work of this kind do not indulge in hysterical emotion. But I remember as though it happened yesterday my visit to Monro on that eventful day, after the Queen had reached the Palace and the Abbey guests had scattered. The intense anxiety of many days was at an end, and we gripped each other by the hand without a word from either of us."[194]

---

[193] A fictitious Fenian plan inspired by the British government and "foiled" by James Monro which, by threatening to dynamite Queen Victoria at Westminster Abbey on Jubilee Day, June 1887, was designed to heap discredit upon the Irish Home Rule movement.
[194] *The Lighter Side of My Official Life.*

That the Jubilee plot was an invention is perhaps implicit in the fact that James Monro was not knighted for having spared the life of his Sovereign Lady Queen Victoria. To this day he remains the only Commissioner of the Metropolitan Police not to have received a knighthood.

As to the truth about Jack the Ripper, logic might suggest the last word on the subject should have rested with Sir Robert Anderson, head of the CID at the time of the Whitechapel murders; but the problem with this idea is that it begs the question of why in 1910, and also in later years, nobody believed a word he wrote.

Lloyds Weekly Newspaper, 17th April 1910—

"The Identity of Jack the Ripper.

"A curious controversy has arisen over the 'Ripper' murders.

"Sir Robert Anderson, ex-Assistant Commissioner of the Metropolitan Police, has declared that the assassin of the unfortunate Whitechapel and Spitalfields women was a Jew, and that the police could not get evidence because those of his race who knew of his guilt refused to give evidence.

"Yesterday Mr. George Kebble [*sic*], the well-known City solicitor, declared that this was inaccurate, and that the man arrested proved to be of Irish birth, was found guilty of the minor charge (his victim recovering), and was sentenced to ten years' imprisonment. Mr. Kebble added that he believed the man died in prison . . .

". . . 'I cannot understand him making that statement about a Jew,' he remarked, 'because he must remember the circumstances perfectly well. Moreover he must have had the knife with which the man attacked the woman, a very curious weapon, and if it is not in the criminal museum has probably got it still'."

The 61-year-old solicitor George Kebbell was recalling the 1895 case he had defended at Worship Street magistrates court—that of William Grant [Grainger], briefly suspected of being Jack the Ripper following an attack on Alice Graham in Butler's Street, Spitalfields. Found guilty at the Old Bailey of felonious wounding rather than attempted murder, Grant was sentenced to ten years' imprisonment at

Parkhurst prison on the Isle of Wight.

It wasn't long before others staked claims to their own patent solution to the identity of Jack the Ripper.

Cleveland Plain Dealer, 8th May 1910—

"Dr. Forbes Winslow, celebrated insanity expert, read Mr. Kebbell's communication and replied to it. He said Mr. Kebbell was quite right in saying Scotland Yard was mistaken about the identity of the murderer of Whitechapel, but that Mr. Kebbell didn't know what he was talking about.

"Scotland Yard, usually as silent as the tomb, has grown suddenly voluble. It could only repeat, what it had declared thirty years ago, that 'Jack the Ripper' was a Whitechapel Jew. He had died in a lunatic asylum. Dr. Winslow and Mr. Kebbell were a couple of busybodies."

Things got steadily more ridiculous—

"Mr. Kebbell came right back with the unqualified statement that Scotland Yard couldn't catch a cold, or words to that effect, and volunteered the further opinion that Dr. Winslow's claim that he knew [the identity of] Jack the Ripper was tommyrot.

"Dr. Winslow agreed with Mr. Kebbell that Scotland Yard couldn't follow the tracks of a cyclone through a cornfield, but if Mr. Kebbell thought that he (Dr. Winslow) was going to descend to the low level of Mr. Kebbell and indulge in a contest of abuse with a smart Aleck who had jumped to the ridiculously erroneous conclusion that 'Jack the Ripper' was a mad Irishman when he (Dr. Winslow) knew perfectly well he was a French Canadian, well—. Dr. Winslow became inarticulate.

"'Yah, yah!' retorted Mr. Kebbell, 'smarty yourself!'"

Since this exchange, levels of discourse in the world of internet Ripperology have not improved to any marked degree.

In the *Morning Advertiser*, 23rd April 1910, Edmund Reid, Local Inspector [CID], H Division, during the Whitechapel murders, stumbled over his faulty recollection of events whilst heaping scorn upon Major Griffiths' 1898 assertion that Jack the Ripper had committed suicide in the River Thames.

Writing from his home at Hampton-on-Sea in Kent, Reid asked—

"What should we do if it could be proved beyond all doubt that 'Jack the Ripper' was dead? We should have to fall back upon the big gooseberry or the sea serpent for stock.

"Some years ago the late Major Arthur Griffiths, in his book 'Mysteries of Crime and Police', endeavoured to prove that 'Jack's' body was found floating in the Thames seven weeks after the last Whitechapel murder in the last day of the year 1888. Considering there were nine murders said to have been committed by 'Jack the Ripper', I think it wonderful that the man's body should have been found in the Thames before the first of the murders was committed.

"I carried on a correspondence through the newspapers with a writer who signed himself 'Unofficial,' who tried to prove that 'Jack the Ripper,' Neill Cream and Klosowski, alias Chapman, were all the same individual. I pointed out that both Neill Cream and Klosowski were poisoners, and that to compare their work with 'Jack the Ripper' was like comparing the work of a watchmaker with that of a bricklayer. 'Unofficial' finished up by stating that he obtained his information from Major Griffiths' book, and expressed a wish to hear about what the Major, who was then alive, had to say about it. There was no response. Thus the matter ended.

"Now we have Sir Robert Anderson saying that 'Jack the Ripper' was a Jew. That I challenge him to prove; and, what is more, it was never suggested at the time of the murders . . . The number of descriptions that have been given of 'Jack the Ripper' are truly astonishing, but I challenge anyone to prove that there was a tittle of evidence against man, woman or child in connexion with the murders . . ."

The Dutch newspaper *De Gelderlander*, 29th April 1910, was understandably perplexed—

"Whom should one believe? Because of these conflicting stories, the mystery of Jack the Ripper remains unsolved."

In the *East London Observer*, 14th May 1910, Dr. Percy Clarke, assistant to H Division's Police Surgeon Dr. George Bagster Phillips at the time of the murders, thought that ". . . perhaps one man was responsible for three of them. I would not like to say he did the others."

Without specifying which three victims were by the same hand, Clarke then went on to speculate that the murderer was "one of the low type, of which you see thousands loafing around the street."

An *East London Observer* reporter said to Clarke— "Mr. George R. Sims states that the man committed suicide."

"That really is supposition," replied Clarke. "As far as I heard—and I think I heard most about the cases—there was never the slightest clue to anybody. The whole thing was theory."

Another policeman who took Sir Robert Anderson to task was Major Henry Smith, Acting Commissioner of the City of London police at the time of the Whitechapel murders. In Chapter Sixteen of "From Constable to Commissioner," [195] following a spirited but mostly unreliable account of his actions on the night of the double-event, he wrote—

"Since this chapter was written my attention has been drawn to an article in *Blackwood's Magazine*, of March this year - the sixth of a series by Sir Robert Anderson - entitled 'The Lighter Side of my Official Life.' In this article Sir Robert discourses on the Whitechapel, or Jack the Ripper, murders, and states emphatically that he, the criminal, 'was living in the immediate vicinity of the scenes of the murders, and that, if he was not living absolutely alone, his people knew of his guilt and refused to give him up to justice. The conclusion,' Sir Robert adds, 'we came to was that he and his people were low-class Jews, for it is a remarkable fact that people of that class in the East End will not give up one of their number to Gentile justice, and the result proved that our diagnosis was right on every point.'

"Sir Robert does not tell us how many of 'his people' sheltered the murderer, but whether they were two dozen in number, or two hundred, or two thousand, he accuses them of being accessories to these crimes before and after their committal.

"Surely Sir Robert cannot believe that while the Jews, as he asserts, were entering into this conspiracy to defeat the ends of justice, there was

---

[195]   Published in September 1910.

no one among them with sufficient knowledge of the criminal law to warn them of the risks they were running . . . a heavier indictment could not be framed against a class whose conduct contrasts most favourably with that of the Gentile population of the Metropolis."

Lloyd's Weekly News, 4th February 1912, ran another interview with retired Whitechapel detective Edmund Reid, whose message remained the same—

""I have been asked to tell the story of the 'Ripper' series many times, but to do so would necessitate the devotion of weeks of labour to the matter. But this I will say at once. I challenge anyone to produce a tittle of evidence of any kind against anyone. The earth has been raked over and the seas have been swept, to find this criminal 'Jack the Ripper,' always without success."

Reid did not mince his words—

"It still amuses me to read the writings of such men as Dr. Anderson, Dr. Forbes Winslow, Major Arthur Griffiths, and many others, all holding different theories, but all of them wrong. I have answered many of them in print, and would only add here that I was on the scene and ought to know."

In the following month, on 24th March 1912, the *People* newspaper began serialising "Scotland Yard and its Secrets" by Hargrave Lee Adam, a writer on criminal matters, in which the Whitechapel murderer was credited with an extra-canonical tally of seven victims.

The series was prefaced by Sir Robert Anderson—

"So again with the 'Whitechapel murders' of 1888," he wrote. "Despite the lucubrations of many an amateur 'Sherlock Holmes', there was no doubt whatever as to the identity of the criminal, and if our London 'detectives' possessed the powers, and might have recourse to the methods, of Foreign Police Forces, he would have been brought to justice."

Nowhere did Anderson mention his reportedly 'plausible' 1895 theory or his 1901 and 1910 positive assertions that the Ripper had been caged in an asylum.

In the 12th June 1912 installment, Adam stated—

"Sir Robert Anderson has assured the writer that the assassin was well known to the police, but unfortunately, in the absence of sufficient *legal* evidence to justify an arrest, they were unable to take him. It was a case of moral versus legal proof."

The following year, in "Police Work from Within, with Some Reflections upon Women, the Law and Lawyers," Adam repeated Sir Robert Anderson's earlier words, adding "that he states confidently that he was a low-class Jew, being shielded by his fraternity," and concluded his chapter on the Ripper murders with, "As to who the 'Ripper' was, and what became of him, I do not believe anybody knows who is able and willing to come forward and say." Nowhere was there a mention of Sir Robert Anderson's "Polish Jew caged in an asylum".

Hargrave Lee Adam was not always the most reliable of true-crime writers. In late 1912 he found himself and his publisher in court on a charge of libel against a Madame Steinheil, dubbed the Red Woman of Paris, who saw herself as some sort of modern-day Madame de Pompadour. She enjoyed affairs with many influential men, and was found *in flagrante de licto* with French President Félix Faure at the moment of his death from heart seizure.

Adam had accused Madame Steinheil of murdering her husband and mother, a charge on which in 1909 before the French Tribunal of Justice she had been acquitted.

The Times, 29th November 1912—

"The defendant author and publisher did not defend the action, and the publisher, after apologizing, agreed to pay £250 [$1250] and the costs of the action."[196]

At around this time Sir Melville Macnaghten's health was failing. In 1911, aged 58, he had taken a rest cure in the Swiss Alps, and later an ocean voyage to Australia, but his condition did not improve, and on 1st May 1913 he tendered his resignation as Assistant Commissioner [CID].

Washington [D.C.] *Post*, 4th June 1913—

---

[196] In November 1938 Madame Steinheil—by then Lady Abinger—sued author Guy Bertie Harris Logan for the very same libel, contained in his book "The World's Greatest Detective Stories."

"The fact that 'Jack the Ripper', the man who terrorized the East End of London by the murder of seven women during 1888, committed suicide, is now confirmed by Sir Melville Macnaghten, head of the criminal investigation department of Scotland Yard, who retired on Saturday after 24 years' service.

"Sir Melville says—

"It is one of the greatest regrets of my life that 'Jack the Ripper' committed suicide six months before I joined the force.

"That remarkable man was one of the most fascinating of criminals. Of course, he was a maniac, but I have a very clear idea as to who he was and how he committed suicide, but that, with other secrets, will never be revealed by me."

The *Frederick Post* [Maryland], 2nd June 1913, added that Macnaghten "will not write any reminiscences."[197]

The *Pittsburgh Press*, 6th July 1913—

"As no good purpose could be served by publicity, I destroyed before I left Scotland Yard every scrap of paper bearing on the case . . ."

This was wilfully misleading. The retired Assistant Commissioner CID had neither destroyed the 'draft' nor the official version of his 1894 'Macnaghten Report'.

Macnaghten concluded by saying—

"No one else will ever know who the criminal was—nor my reasons for keeping silent."

Further confusion lay ahead.

Unbeknownst to anyone else at the time, on 23rd September 1913 ex-Chief Inspector John George Littlechild, head of Section D [the secret political arm of the Metropolitan Police] at the time of the Whitechapel murders, replied to a letter from journalist George R. Sims.[198] It was clearly not their first correspondence on the subject.

It appears that Sims may have got hold of the name Druitt[199] and, perhaps seeking confirmation without wanting to reveal the extent or

---

[197] Macnaghten's reminiscences were published in October 1914.
[198] Littlechild letter to Sims, in the collection of author Stewart Evans.
[199] In January 1889 Druitt's suicide and inquest was reported in various newspapers.

possible source of his information, asked Littlechild if he had ever heard of a "Dr. D."

Littlechild replied—

"I never heard of a Dr. D. in connection with the Whitechapel murders but amongst the suspects, and to my mind a very likely one, was a Dr. T. (which sounds much like D.) He was an American quack named Tumblety and was at one time a frequent visitor to London and on these occasions constantly brought under the notice of police, there being a large dossier concerning him at Scotland Yard.

"Although a 'Sycopathia Sexualis'[200] subject he was not known as a 'Sadist' (which the murderer unquestionably was) but his feelings toward women were remarkable and bitter in the extreme, a fact on record. Tumblety was arrested at the time of the murders in connection with unnatural offences and charged at Marlborough Street, remanded on bail, jumped his bail, and got away to Boulogne. He shortly left Boulogne and was never heard of afterwards. It was believed he committed suicide but certain it is that from this time the 'Ripper' murders came to an end . . ."

Littlechild, who got half of his Tumblety information correct,[201] had either been told or had guessed that the original source of Sims' information was Major Griffiths' 1898 book "Mysteries of Police and Crime". But if, as suggested earlier, Sims was seeking to clarify that Griffiths' information had come from Macnaghten, he might now have been perplexed by Littlechild's closing remark—

"Now pardon me—it is finished. Except that I knew Major Griffiths for many years. He probably got his information from Anderson who only 'thought he knew'."

Why, of all people, Robert Anderson might have only 'thought he knew' is intriguing, but, irrespective of the original source, it appears that Littlechild did not hold Sims' information in any great store.[202]

---

[200]   "Psychopathia Sexualis", by Richard von Krafft-Ebbing, 1886, was one of the first books to study homosexuality/bisexuality.

[201]   Tumblety did not commit suicide. He died in St. Louis in 1903, aged 82.

[202]   Modern day Anderson devotees like to square the circle by suggesting that Littlechild

Sims appears to have been equally unimpressed with the idea of Tumblety as a Ripper suspect, for he clung to Macnaghten's drowned doctor right up until his last Dagonet article in 1917.

Sir Melville Macnaghten's amiable 1914 volume of reminiscences made no mention of a Polish Jew, a mad Russian or a drowned doctor, and the certitude of his earlier memoranda, the redacted contents of which he leaked to Major Griffiths and George R. Sims, had melted into circumspection.

Macnaghten wrote— ". . . the Whitechapel murderer, *in all probability*, put an end to himself soon after the Dorset Street affair in November 1888 . . ."

"There can be no doubt," Macnaghten continued, "that in the room at Millers Court the madman found ample scope for the opportunities he had all along been seeking, *and the probability is that*, after his awful glut on this occasion, his brain gave way altogether and he committed suicide; otherwise the murders would not have ceased" [author's italics].

Macnaghten next offered an indication as to when he first determined the probability of his scenario—

" . . . certain facts, pointing to this conclusion, were not in possession of the police till some years after I became a detective officer."[203]

Macnaghten had become hopelessly entangled in the logic of his narrative.

These "certain facts" could not have come to light prior to mid-February 1891. Had they, there would have been no reason for the Metropolitan Police to suspect James Sadler of being the Whitechapel murderer. Nor could these "certain facts" have come to light prior to January 1892, for at this time the Metropolitan Police had reportedly just ceased surveillance on a suspect, and yet another was serving twenty years in Portland prison. It had to be after May 1895 when these "certain facts" came to light, for the same reasoning applies to the investigation

---

actually meant Macnaghten.
[203]   1st June 1889.

of William Grant [Grainger] as the Whitechapel murderer, plus Robert Anderson's contention in the same month that the murderer's hideous career had been "cut short by committal to an asylum."

Yet the Macnaghten Report had been written in February 1894, fifteen months prior to these latter events.

Macnaghten was quick to foist blame for any confusion onto the press—

". . . the public were . . . quite ready to believe that any fresh murders, not at once elucidated, were by the same maniac's hand. Indeed, I remember three cases, two in 1889, and one in early 1891, which the Press ascribed to the so-called Jack the Ripper . . ."

Macnaghten concluded—

"I incline to the belief that the individual who held up London in terror resided with his own people; that he absented himself from home at certain times, and that he committed suicide on or about the 10th of November 1888, after he had knocked out a Commissioner of Police [Warren] and very nearly settled the hash of one of Her Majesty's principal Secretaries of State [Matthews]."

Sir Robert Anderson died in November 1918, James Monro in January 1920.

In 1920 Hargrave Lee Adam published "The Police Encyclopedia: Volume IV., in the preface of which he recycled the late Sir Robert Anderson's 1912 words.

Sir Melville Macnaghten died in May 1921, George R. Sims in September 1922 and John George Littlechild in January 1923.

Nine months later, on 23rd October 1923, *Empire News* reported— "In his book, *Things I Know*, published this week, Mr. William Le Queux claims to have revealed the actual identity of Jack the Ripper."

William Tufnell Le Queux [pronounced Le Q] was a prolific, hugely popular thriller writer who "had seen a manuscript in French written by Rasputin stating that Jack the Ripper was Alexander Pedachenko,[204] a

---

[204]   The name Pedachenko may have been inspired by Dr. Vladimir Panchenko who in 1911 was sentenced to fifteen years' imprisonment for murdering Vasily Buturlin with a lethal injection of diphtheritic toxin. *New York Times*, 19th February 1911.

Russian agent who committed the murders in order to confuse and ridicule Scotland Yard."

One bothersome detail about this piece of Ripperological malarkey is that, having been born in Pokrovskoye, a village one thousand miles east of Moscow, young Grigori Rasputin received little or no education, could barely read or write and certainly had no command of French— written or spoken. But this did not unduly perturb the ever-inventive William Le Queux—

"It [the manuscript] was in French, a language which the monk knew only slightly, and being typed, had evidently been dictated."

How considerate of Rasputin to have dictated his manuscript to a bilingual amanuensis, for William Le Queux, fluent in English, French, Italian and Spanish, had absolutely no understanding of Russian.

This elaborate story of international intrigue garnered little popular credence, but it certainly struck a nerve at Scotland Yard, which took the unprecedented step of dismantling parts of Le Queux's story in the *Star* newspaper.

Details from the *Star* were recounted in 1927 by J. Hall Richardson in his book "From the City to Fleet Street"—

"The next piece of nonsense in this story is that Pedachenko, 'the greatest and boldest of Russian criminal lunatics,' was encouraged by the Russian Government to go to London to commit that series of crimes in order to exhibit to the world certain defects of the English police system . . . Mr. Le Queux lets a large cat out of the bag when he reveals that the disclosure of the author of these atrocities originates with a 'Russian well known in London, named Nideroest, a spy in the Russian Police, who was a member of the Jubilee Street Club, the Anarchist centre in London.'

"The fact is that Johann Nideroest was not a Russian at all, but a Swiss. He was a member of the Russian and Lettish Socialist Club in the East End, but Chief-Inspector McCarthy gave evidence in 1909 that Nideroest was not an Anarchist, but had been selling newspapers information about bombs being made in Whitechapel, which the police found to be 'all nonsense'.

" . . . that Mr. Le Queux's theory rests on [Nideroest's] testimony, is sufficient for us to regard it as fiction, quite apart from the inherent internal improbabilities which we have mentioned."

Quite different Ripper revelations were soon to appear in the press. *Brighton and Hove Herald*, 6th December 1924—

"A 'Sherlock Holmes.'

"Death of Mr. Robert Sagar.

"A romantic career has ended by the death at Homeleigh, South Road, Preston,[205] of Mr. Robert Sagar, a former inspector of the City of London Police Force. Mr. Sagar was described as a 'born detective.' He had, indeed, the almost uncanny gifts of deduction associated with 'Sherlock Holmes,' and had remarkable success in the solution of criminal mysteries.

"Among the famous crimes in the investigation of which Mr. Sagar shared were the 'Jack the Ripper' murders. It was Mr. Sagar's view that the murders were committed by an insane man employed at Butcher's Row, Aldgate, who was subsequently placed by his friends in a private asylum."

There followed a hitherto unreported episode from Robert Sagar's career—

"On one occasion Mr. Sagar was sent with two other officers by the British Government to Spain to deal with a supposed plot to take the life of the present King of Spain,[206] who was then a child. The conspirators were arrested, and Mr. Sagar and his colleagues were honoured by having a group portrait of themselves hung in the Royal Palace at Madrid."

The *Auckland Star*, 21st February 1925, had a slightly different take on the story—

"Saved a King and Hunted 'Jack the Ripper.'

"In the vestibule of the Royal Palace at Madrid there hangs a photograph of a middle-aged Englishman. It is always pointed out to visitors, for a story attaches to it. The man in the photograph is Robert

---

[205] Preston in Sussex, not Preston in Lancashire.
[206] King Alfonso XIII reigned from 1886 to 1931.

Sagar, and the story tells of his acumen and cleverness in unravelling a plot to assassinate the infant King—for King Alfonso was born a King . . ."[207]

Here was an incident which warranted closer examination.

Until King Alfonso XIII [b. 1886] came of age on 17th May 1902 the Spanish throne was under the control of a Queen-Regent—Alphonso's mother, Maria Christina of Austria.

New York Times, 31st May 1901—

"Anarchist Plot To Kill Alfonso XIII?

"Paris, May 30. —A dispatch to the Patrie from Barcelona says: 'The police are keeping a vigilant watch on the frontier and at the ports in order to effect the capture of two Anarchists, a Spaniard and an Italian, who are believed to have landed at Marseilles and to be making their way to Madrid with the intention of attempting to assassinate the King. The plot was hatched in an Anarchist centre in North America. All vessels from Marseilles and Genoa are thoroughly searched.'"

King Alfonso XIII was enthroned on Saturday 17th May 1902.

The Times, 19th May 1902—

"Madrid, May 18.

"An arrest of suspected Anarchists which was made at 2 o'clock on Saturday morning seems to have been of a serious character. Six men in all were arrested, the principal one being Gabriel Lopez, the concierge of a well-known insurance office in the Carrera de San Jeronimo, who was found in possession of dynamite cartridges, which he admits having received from an Anarchist recently released from prison . . . Lopez declared after arrest that the packet of dynamite cartridges was given to him by another Anarchist, who told him to throw it at the moment when the Royal carriage was passing."

On another page The Times reported—

"Details of this plot against the King, if plot it be, have not yet been divulged; but we may reasonably believe that, as its development has thus been opportunely arrested, no further consequences are to be feared."

---

[207]   Alfonso XIII was born six months after the death of his father Alfonso XII.

Intrigued if these reports might be the basis of the Robert Sagar story, the Royal Archives in Madrid were contacted. They were exceedingly helpful yet knew nothing about Scotland Yard officers foiling a plot to kill the young King Alfonso XIII and even less about a commemorative portrait [or photograph] being hung in the Palacio Real, Madrid.

The Royal Archives were also asked about Melville Macnaghten who was made a 'Knight Commander of the White Military Order of Spain'—the "Orden del Mérito Militar con distintivo blanco"—but they could throw no light on the date or circumstances of his decoration.[208]

Newspaper archives provided other possible leads to the Sagar story.

On 31st May 1906 King Alfonso XIII married Princess Victoria Eugenie of Battenberg. After leaving the cathedral for the Palacio Real the wedding procession passed along Calle Mayor where, from a balcony, Spanish anarchist Mateu Morral threw a bomb disguised as a floral bouquet at the royal coach. The bomb missed its intended target, killing instead a number of soldiers, bystanders and horses.

Sagar was not in evidence on this occasion, but in the procession behind the royal coach were the Prince and Princess of Wales [later King George V and Queen Mary] with their Metropolitan Police bodyguard, Inspector John McCarthy.[209]

Later in the year at Cowes on the Isle of Wight King Alfonso XIII presented "Inspector [John] Walsh of Scotland Yard with a diamond and emerald scarf pin bearing the Royal monogram and surmounted by a gold crown studded with diamonds. His Majesty spoke in appreciation of the Inspector's service during the stay of the King and Queen at Cowes."[210]

King Alfonso XIII had become keen to reform the Spanish police through the establishment of a criminal investigation department in Barcelona based upon the Scotland Yard model. After talks between the

---

[208]   According to an Index to Foreign Awards and Honours in *The Peerage*, Melville Macnaghten is the only British person to have been presented with this award.

[209]   *Buffalo Courier*, 31st March 1907.

[210]   *The Times*, 22nd August 1906.

British consul general in Barcelona, the Spanish Ambassador to the Court of St. James—the dashingly-named Don Wenceslao Ramírez de Villa-Urrutia—and Metropolitan Police Commissioner Sir Edward Henry,[211] in March 1907 King Alfonso XIII offered the £1000 a year plus expenses position of Chief Superintendent of the Spanish CID to Inspector John McCarthy, who declined the offer due to his being a member of the British royal protection detail.[212]

The post was subsequently offered to newly-retired Chief Inspector Charles John Arrow, who had closed many a Whitechapel gambling den during his twenty-four- year career and in December 1903 received a personal commendation from Queen Alexandra for his investigation of a possible misappropriation of funds from a charity with which she was connected.[213] Arrow accepted the job, and on 21st July 1907 moved in with his wife and son to a luxury suite at Barcelona's Ranzini Hotel.

Like Robert Sagar, Charles Arrow had spiritual roots in 221B Baker Street.

Black & White: A Weekly Illustrated Record and Review, 27th July 1907— "A Twentieth-Century Sherlock Holmes.

"This country has lost one of its greatest detectives by the retirement of Chief Detective Inspector Arrow, who sailed a few days ago for Barcelona to take over control of the Spanish police in that city and reorganise the detective service. This appointment has been expressly made by King Alfonso, over whom the famous detective acted as guardian during his visit to England [June 1905] shortly before his marriage. Detective-Inspector Arrow has been associated with Scotland Yard for over a quarter of a century, and has been engaged in some of the most notorious cases of recent years. He was a master of subterfuge . . ."

---

[211] It is possible that Melville Macnaghten, Assistant Commissioner of Police [CID], was consulted during these proceedings, which perhaps earned him his June 1907 knighthood.

[212] PC McCarthy was a member of Littlechild's Section D and, according to the Macnaghten memorandum, "specially employed in Whitechapel at the time of the murders there."

[213] *ABC* [Madrid], 23rd July 1907.

Inspector Charles Arrow may well have been a master of subterfuge, but in the event his tenure in Spain was an unmitigated disaster. His arrival in Barcelona caused a great stir. Two thousand people gathered to protest his appointment, and a man was killed during the demonstration. Further hampered by the distrust of the local police and politicians, and the fact that he did not speak a word of Catalan, he was paid off by the Spanish authorities prior to the end of his contract.

"I had a very thrilling two and a half years in Barcelona," he said. "My hotel and my suite of offices were guarded day and night by machine gunners. My life was constantly threatened, sometimes by newspapers, and sometimes by word of mouth."[214]

In 1910 he returned to London, where he opened Arrow's Detective Agency—affiliated with the William J. Burns National Detective Agency Inc., New York—and eventually retired to No. 3 Wilbury Gardens, Hove, Sussex, where he died, aged 74, in May 1936.

Following an account in the New York *Daily Tribune*, 4th June 1906, of the attempted assassination of King Alphonso XIII there came an intriguing paragraph from William Melville. He resigned from Scotland Yard in November 1903 and to all intents and purposes retired, whereas in truth he had been secretly recruited to head MO3, a new counter-insurgency intelligence department at the War Office, a post he held at the time of this newspaper article—

"William Melville, former chief of the special police service in New Scotland Yard, who, during his tenure of that office was in the closest touch with the anarchist movement, informs the Daily Telegraph that seven years ago the London police frustrated an attempt to assassinate King Alphonso and his mother by the discovery of a plot against them in London, and the pursuit and capture of the plotters at Bordeaux, while they were on their way to San Sebastian to carry out the conspiracy."

Whether this 1899 incident was that referred to in the obituary of Inspector Robert Sagar remains as yet unknown.

On 25th November 1924 retired Chief Inspector Donald Swanson

---

[214] Singapore Free Press and Mercantile Advertiser, 8th September 1931.

died, aged 76, without offering any further public comment on the Whitechapel murders.[215]

In 1927 journalist J. Hall Richardson, following on from the Le Queux story, recorded that,[216] "the retired Sir Basil Thomson, Melville Macnaghten's immediate successor at Scotland Yard and later Director of Intelligence at the Home Office,[217] wrote in the *Radio Times*—

". . . the Jack the Ripper outrages are now believed by the police to have been the work of an insane Russian medical student whose body was found floating in the Thames immediately after the last of the outrages."

J. Hall Richardson continued—

"I venture to say that if any reliance is to be placed on this story it is because Sir Basil Thomson had access to the records of Scotland Yard. I do not think he would have obtained them first-hand from any officer who was engaged in the investigation of the Whitechapel murders, as no officer who had the personal experience remained in the office at the time that Sir Basil Thomson was occupying his special suite of room at Scotland House, a building which, by the way, did not form part of New Scotland Yard."[218]

Whilst the late Melville Macnaghten must have been tickled pink by this imaginative conflation of Michael Ostrog and Montague Druitt, there is no getting away from the fact that, forty-two years after the Whitechapel murders, Jack the Ripper remained a sensitive subject at Scotland Yard.

The mid-1920s signalled a lull in interest in the identity of Jack the Ripper. The murders had taken place almost forty years earlier. Queen

---

[215] Swanson obituary, Surrey Comet, 29th November 1924: "Viewing his work as decidedly a secret service, Mr. Swanson was opposed to public 'reminiscences' . . ."

[216] *From the City to Fleet Street.*

[217] After a career including the tracking down of Mata Hari, Sir Basil Thomson retired, a Knight Commander of the Bath, in 1921. In 1925, aged 64, he became a *cause célèbre* when he was arrested in Hyde Park with an 'actress' and known prostitute, the exotically-named Thelma de Lava, on charges of indecency, public impropriety and attempting to bribe a policeman. He was fined £5 and costs. See *The Times*, 6th February 1926.

[218] Scotland House, next to New Scotland Yard, was built between 1902 and 1906.

Victoria and King Edward VII had gone. The First World War intervened. Millions were slaughtered in a muddy and bloody family squabble. King George V was now on the throne. The future had arrived. Wireless, gramophones, dance bands, flappers, moving pictures, unemployment, strikes, fast cars and aeroplanes were the order of the day. Few bothered to recall five squalid Victorian murders, and those who could were now growing old, short on facts and busily polluting the historical gene pool with contradictory strands of urban folklore.

Doctor, Russian secret agent, foreigner, surgeon, Jew, seaman, maniac . . .

It sounds almost like a child's counting game.

The only thing upon which everybody could agree was the unforgettable name of Jack the Ripper.

10. CRIMSON CRIMES

The first three Jack the Ripper books appeared in late 1888.

The first, "The Curse Upon Mitre Square" by John Francis Brewer [pub. New York], was a Gothic penny dreadful [dime novel] of treachery, madness, murder and ghosts based around the murder of Catherine Eddowes.

"Leather Apron; Or, the Horrors of Whitechapel, London" by Samuel E. Hudson [pub. Philadelphia] tried to take an objective look at the victims, the police investigation and press coverage but got burdened by a vision of the Ripper as "an incarnate monster" scuttling around the alleyways and pest-ridden courts of a starkly-shadowed expressionist Whitechapel.

Hard on its heels came "The History of the Whitechapel Murders: A Full and Authentic Narrative of the Above Murders, With Sketches", by Richard K. Fox [pub. New York]. Fox was editor and proprietor of the *National Police Gazette*, a tabloid devoted to true crime, sport and tittilation, and in his book [at less than 40 pages it was more a pamphlet] he announced that Jack the Ripper was Nicholas Vassily, a theory advanced by *New York World* journalist John Paul Bocock.

However, Nicholas [Nicholaus] Wassilyi, Wassili, Vassily or Vasilev, known in Paris as the 'Sauveur des âmes perdues' (Saviour of Lost Souls) was the creation of Heinrich D'Altona,[219] Paris correspondent of the *New Yorker Staats-Zeitung,* the leading German-language newspaper in the United States.

According to his story, Vassily, from the Russian city of Tiraspol, had, in 1872, murdered a woman in the Faubourg St. Germain. Three days later another was murdered in the Quartier Mouffetard. Five more victims were found butchered in the Arrondissement des Pantheon between the Boulevards St. Michel and de l'Hopital. The murders were perpetrated in the same way as those in Whitechapel. Jewels and everything of value remained untouched.[220]

On 1st December 1888 the story appeared in the *Coburger Zeitung,* credited to a St. Petersburg newspaper—

"'Novosti', names Nikolai Vasilev as the murderer in Whitechapel. He was born in Tiraspol in 1847, studied at the University of Odessa, then became a fanatical anarchist and emigrated to Paris, where his monomania seems to have been that fallen women should suffer for their sins by death. He therefore murdered prostitutes in Paris in a similar way to those in Whitechapel. He was arrested and taken to a mental hospital for criminals. That happened sixteen years ago. Shortly before the first murders in Whitechapel, he was discharged as cured. Vasilev is supposed to have then gone to London. Since then he has disappeared and his friends believe that none other than their mad countryman was the murderer."

Two weeks earlier, in London, the *Star* had picked up the story and done some digging of its own—

"A story is being widely circulated that the Whitechapel murders were possibly committed by a certain Nicholas Wassili, who is said to have been placed in an insane asylum in 1872, after he had committed a series of crimes in Paris similar to those that have been lately committed

---

219   D'Altona, under his real name—Heinrich Grabow—was also a crime novelist. Born in Germany in 1842 to Johann J. Grabow and Maria Charlotte Dansky, Heinrich married Anna Sohia Ehlers and had 8 children. He died on 5th January 1895 in Gretna, Nebraska, USA.

220   *New York Sun,* 25th November 1888.

in the East-end of London. A certain amount of probability has been attached to this theory, in view of the fact that Wassili was, according to the reports, released from confinement last January. It is doubtful, however, whether such a man as Wassili ever existed. M. Macé,[221] a former Chef de la Sûreté, who is thoroughly posted in the criminal history of France, has said to an interviewer that no such person committed murders in Paris in 1872."

Reynold's Newspaper, 18th November 1888, agreed—

"The story which has been going the round of foreign papers, of a supposed Russian named Wassili being concerned in the [Whitechapel] crimes has now been shown to be a myth."

A present-day search by this author through the archives of the French newspaper *Le Temps* confirms that no such series of murders was reported during the 1870s.

But not to worry. Jack the Ripper still had plenty of mileage. Theories were becoming like London buses: if you happened to miss one, two or three others would be along in a moment.

On 24th April 1895 a story appeared in the *San Francisco Call* under the headline, "He Is Jack the Ripper. The Author of the Whitechapel Murders a London Physician. Confined in a Madhouse. The Story Told by an Englishman to William Greer Harrison."

Harrison was a member of the Bohemian Club, a private San Francisco hang-out, amongst whose members had been Harry Jackson Wells Dam, who in 1888 wrote about Leather Apron for the *Star* newspaper in London.

According to the newspaper story Dr. Howard, a "London physician of considerable prominence," told Harrison that Jack the Ripper was a medical man of high standing married to a "beautiful and amiable wife." She grew alarmed when he developed an unnatural pleasure for causing pain, and as one Whitechapel murder followed another her suspicions grew, for on the nights in question her husband was invariably away from home. She sought out some of his medical friends and asked for their

---

[221]   Gustave-Placide Macé, head of the sûreté from February 1879 to March 1884.

advice and assistance. They confronted her husband who, realising his truth, "begged to be removed from the world as a guilty and dangerous monster." He was committed to an asylum and within a month or two lost all semblance of sanity."

On the same day a representative of the Associated Press called upon William Greer Harrison to establish the accuracy of the story.[222] Harrison stated that "the dispatch was entirely correct in every particular so far as the matter reaching him through Dr. Howard was concerned. Dr. Howard is a well-known London physician who passed through San Francisco on a tour of the world several months ago and that while he was here [they] met at the Bohemian club and the latter told him the remarkable story and vouched for its authenticity."

Two days later, on 26th April 1895, the *Denver Evening Post* ran a story from the *St. Louis Star Sayings*—

"The *Star Sayings* prints the following editorial on a sample of the matter furnished by the Chicago organization styling itself the Associated Press to its clients—

"The Associated Press sent out from San Francisco yesterday a story about 'Jack the Ripper' which shows very clearly how that alleged news service comes by some of its information.

"'Dr. Howard, a London physician', is given as the authority. He tells that 'Jack the Ripper' was discovered to be an eminent London physician, whose wife found out his secret; that he was finally shown to be the guilty man; that he was confined in an asylum, and that he has become a raving maniac. No names, dates or details are given, the asylum is not located, the whole thing is a plain attempt to give airy nothingness a habitation and a name.

"The fact is that the whole tale was offered to the 'Star Sayings' over five months ago, as a letter from a New York syndicate. When the matter came by mail it was refused, because of its indefiniteness and general haziness of tone and treatment. Some few papers published it, and it has been floating about since."

---

[222] *Fort Wayne Weekly Gazette*, 2nd May 1895, and other newspapers.

This tallied with Harrison saying he had been told the story by Dr. Howard "several months" earlier.

The St. Louis newspaper was referencing a story which had appeared in *The Weekly Press* [NY], 21st November 1894, the *Ithaca Herald* [NY], 3rd December 1894, and the *Evening Star* [Washington DC], 15th December 1894.

The story's source was Curtis Brown, London correspondent of New York's *The Weekly Press*,[223] and it, too, featured the anxious wife of a London physician, certain her husband was Jack the Ripper, plus a narrator—a doctor—taking steps to have him examined by a panel of physicians.

"He was found to be totally unbalanced and then was placed in an asylum where he now remains."

It was essentially the same as the Dr. Howard version, except that its source had been Dr. Lyttelton Stewart Forbes Winslow M.R.C.P., psychiatrist and well-known London specialist on suicide and insanity.

The following day, 27th April 1895, the *San Francisco Call* published a footnote to its Ripper story—

"The Call's article in regard to the identity of London's Jack the Ripper was telegraphed to New York and thence to London and to all parts of Europe. A hint of this matter was published in an English paper a few months ago, but the full facts did not come out until published in the Call."

The earlier Forbes Winslow story was not mentioned, and thus far the English newspaper has not been identified.

The Dr. Howard story appeared again the following day, 28th April, in the *Chicago Sunday Times-Herald,* and on 5th May in the *Boston Post*, but not before having undergone major cosmetic surgery.

Dr. Howard remained the source, but spiritualist Robert James Lees was now responsible for tracking down the Ripper. Having convinced the police of his psychic abilities, Lees led them to a fashionable West

---

[223]   Albert Curtis Brown [b.1866], was an American journalist who came to London in 1888 to head the International Publishing Bureau, and in 1905 founded the Curtis Brown literary agency.

End mansion, home to a noted physician who had treated members of the Royal Family. The doctor was eventually put into a lunatic asylum under the name Thomas Mason, patient No. 124.

Neither version garnered any substantial press coverage. The story naming Forbes Winslow appeared in only three US newspapers, and that naming Robert James Lees in just two.[224]

Four months later Dr. Forbes Winslow arrived in New York to attend a medico-legal congress, by which time he had distanced himself from his earlier Ripper story.

New York Times, 1st September 1895—

"Jack the Ripper was a medical student of good family. He was a young man of slight build, with light hair and blue eyes. He studied very hard and his mind, being naturally weak, gave way. He became a religious enthusiast and attended early service every morning at St. Paul's.

"His religious fervor resulted in a homicidal mania towards the women of the street and impelled him to murder them. He lodged with a man I knew, and suspicion was first directed toward him by reason of the fact that he returned to his lodgings at unseasonable hours; that he had innumerable coats and hats stained with blood."

Forbes Winslow had evidence to back up his new theory.

"I have in my possession now a pair of Canadian moccasins stained with blood that the 'Ripper' wore while on his murderous expeditions. I notified the Scotland Yard authorities, but at that time they refused to cooperate with me. Subsequently the young man was placed in confinement and removed to a lunatic asylum, where he is today. Since his incarceration there has been no repetition of the horrible murders that he perpetrated.

"These facts are all known to the English authorities, and it is conceded that the man now in the asylum is 'Jack the Ripper'. It was deemed desirable, however, to hush the matter up. The details were too horrible to be made the matter of a public trial, and there was no doubt of the man's insanity."

---

[224]   The Lees story also appeared in the *People* newspaper [London], 19th May 1895

Quite how Forbes Winslow dreamed up this profile—or, indeed, that of his society doctor—is unknown, for six years earlier he had taken his Jack the Ripper suspicions to Scotland Yard regarding G. Wentworth Bell Smith, a 40-year-old Canadian lodging with the Callaghan family in Sun Street, Finsbury Park, who was in London to raise money for the Toronto Trust Society.

Chief Inspector Swanson wrote in his 23rd September 1889 report—

"He [Forbes Winslow] produced a pair of felt galoshed boots such as are in common use in Canada, and an old coat. The felt boots were motheaten, and the slough of the moth worm remained on one of them."

These, presumably, were the blood-stained Canadian moccasins which Forbes Winslow's young medical student 'Ripper' had worn whilst out on his murderous East End expeditions.

Forbes Winslow's theory was entirely without merit. However, firmly convinced he was correct, for many years afterwards he claimed that his actions had been responsible not for removing Jack the Ripper to an asylum but for causing him to flee the country.

There is little doubt that, despite being an acknowledged expert in his field, Forbes Winslow was a publicity-seeking fabulist; also that his original Ripper story, which originated in London, [225] provided the template for the Dr. Howard version, which in turn inspired the *Chicago Sunday Times-Herald* story featuring spiritualist Robert James Lees.

Theories were thin on the ground during the last half of the 1890s, but on 25th August 1901 the *Salt Lake Herald* redressed matters by claiming the identity of the Ripper had recently become known—

"Hunting Jack the Ripper.

"Thrilling Experiences of a Man Who Posed as Decoy in Woman's Garb.

"John T. Sullivan.

"The recent scare among Denver women because of the raids of the

---

[225] *The Weekly Press* claimed a scoop for its London correspondent. "Jack the Ripper Found At Last: Discovered by a 'Press' Correspondent in an Insane Asylum."

Capitol Hill thug reminds me of the reign of terror among the denizens of the Whitechapel district, London, during the months of September and November, 1888. I had been in London for some months playing at Henry Irving's Lyceum Theatre, and during the months mentioned was appearing as Joseph Surface, with Kate Vaughan, in 'The School for Scandal' . . .

It was decided by Sullivan's friends that whilst he dressed up as a woman to patrol the streets, alleys and yards of Whitechapel they would keep an eye on him.

". . . At 7 o'clock in the morning I was at the shop of Madame Auguste, a sister of the late Sir Augustus Harris. She was the best costumer in London, and had furnished me many dresses for the parts I had played. She entered into the plan enthusiastically, fixing me up with a hat, waist and skirt. C.H. Fox, a noted perruquier of King Street, Covent Garden, got up a wig for me at short notice. By 5 o'clock in the afternoon I was duly rigged out, and looked like a healthy country girl. I had a slit made on the right side of my skirt that opened on a leather holster, which was to hold a revolver, a hammerless Smith & Wesson, which I had brought from America."

Sullivan recounted his ten days down amongst the colourful denizens of Whitechapel—

"No murders were committed during the period of our sleuthing. Other murders followed close upon the conclusion of our vigil. My deduction was that the 'Ripper' knew of our movements, and I believe that to this day.

"As to the identity of 'Jack the Ripper', both the man and his habitat are known. But, mind you, it is only in the last three months that this fact has come out. At the time of which I write London was divided in its opinions. Some thought the work was that of a frenzied sailor - a butcher on one of the cattle transports, who had taken this form of revenge upon those poor outcasts for a fancied wrong. Others held that it was a physician who had suffered in the same way. The latter surmise was correct."

Here was yet another variation on an old and familiar theme—

"It was a physician, a reputable man in London - a perfect Jekyll and Hyde. He had developed a homicidal mania and had been confined in a private sanatorium in a suburb of London. How he escaped was a mystery, but Scotland Yard knows that man today. He is an exile from his country. He lives at Buenos Aires, in the Argentine Republic, and there being no law of extradition between that nation and England, he is entirely safe there. I have this on the best authority, although this is the first time the facts have been given to the public.

"'Jack the Ripper' has not been in evidence since Dr. E. left England. I need hardly say that he is under close surveillance in the Argentine capital, so that there will no repetition of his offense."

The story was complete hokum. All the incidents were chronologically wrong and the details of the murders hopelessly incorrect. Sullivan's professional memory had also slipped his grasp, for his one London performance as Joseph Surface in Sheridan's "The School For Scandal," playing opposite Kate Vaughan as Lady Teazle, did not open at the Globe Theatre, London, until 9th February 1889.[226]

John T. Sullivan died in New York, 19th June 1904.

Hokum often has a long shelf-life, and just under thirty years later Dr. E. would become Dr. S. in a story that would blossom into one of the most evergreen 'solutions' to the Jack the Ripper mystery.

The first full-length work of fiction about Jack the Ripper appeared in 1905 as a serial in the *Illustrated Police News*. Written by Guy Bertie Harris Logan, "The True History of Jack the Ripper" was based on information from the Macnaghten memorandum contained in Major Griffiths' 1898 "Mysteries of Police and Crime." Logan's suspect was the ingeniously-named Doctor Mortemer Slade, who, shortly after the Millers Court murder, drowned himself in the Thames.

At around this time a familiar face popped up with yet another theory, as reported in the *Nottingham Evening Post*, 12th April 1905—

"Dr. Forbes Winslow believes in the genuineness of the confession

---

[226]   In October 1888 Sullivan was at the Lyceum Theatre, London, in "A Parisian Romance," playing opposite Beatrice Cameron. Both plays were produced by Richard Mansfield.

of the man who has told the New York authorities that he committed the Whitechapel murders 15 years ago. The doctor thinks he is the original 'Jack the Ripper' and that he is not suffering from hallucinations.

"A statement has been made that the original 'Jack the Ripper' was captured and confined in a lunatic asylum in England, but Dr. Winslow is of opinion that the perpetrator of the crimes was never captured . . ."

In late January 1893 Jabez Balfour, Liberal MP for Burnley, Lancashire, fled to Argentina, having duped hundreds of investors in the Liberator Building Society. Following two exasperating years of legal wrangling he was finally bundled aboard a train and spirited out of the country by Inspector Frank Froest of Scotland Yard. [227] Under tight security he was returned to London where, at the Old Bailey, November 1895, he was sentenced to fourteen years penal servitude, of which he served ten-and-a-half years. Balfour—Prisoner V460—was released on 13th April 1906.

Shortly after Balfour's release from Parkhurst prison on the Isle of Wight his jail memoirs began a 26-week serialisation on the front page of the *Weekly Dispatch,* a newspaper owned by his friend Alfred Harmsworth, Lord Northcliffe.

Later in the year advertisements began to appear—

"Crimson Crimes.

"Do not fail to read the first of this series of powerful articles by Mr. Jabez Balfour, which will appear in next Sunday's Weekly Dispatch.

"They will reveal the inner facts of some of the greatest crimes of modern times, and will deal with many events that have caused a world-wide thrill of horror, including the terrible tragedies of Jack the Ripper, an endless subject of universal conjecture and discussion. Many of these revelations are the result of the Author's independent investigations; often of mysteries totally unconnected with the results themselves."

Despite promises of fresh revelations, Balfour's four Ripper articles delivered nothing that was new, being mostly a cut-and-paste assemblage

---

[227]   Sir Robert Anderson referenced the incident in *The Lighter Side of My Official Life* [1910].

of information culled from 1888 newspaper reports.

As to the identity of the Ripper, Balfour dismissed theories about South American cattlemen, a fellow-convict who had been pointed out to him at Parkhurst prison and a man confined as a criminal lunatic at Broadmoor Asylum.

Jabez Balfour had another suspect in mind, for he had spoken to a man who in 1900 had been living in Johannesburg and knew two men "who knew Jack the Ripper personally."

This unnamed Ripper "was a man of good education and considerable talent, who from his youth had been filled with a morbid passion for cruelty and for gloating over deeds of bloodshed and horror. He had been trained as a surgeon, and was possessed of considerable surgical knowledge and of even greater manual dexterity . . .

"Inflamed by reports of the horrors of vivisection on dumb animals, he had been filled and possessed with an uncontrollable longing to practise and pursue similar experiments on the human frame."

Jabez Balfour concluded—

"Jack the Ripper is living still in a remote British colony."

Needless to say, the idea of Jack the Anti-Vivisectionist did not ignite the public imagination.

"The Lodger" by Marie Belloc Lowndes was the first influential spin on events. Published in McClure's Magazine, 1911, and novelised in 1913, it told the story of Mr. and Mrs Bunting who suspect their lodger is none other than the mysterious killer known as "The Avenger".[228]

Melville Macnaghten found the book interesting, because it "set forth in vivid colours what the Whitechapel murderer's life might have been like while dwelling in London lodgings."[229]

The *People* newspaper, 26th December 1926, provided yet another familiar twist on the Ripper mystery. Australian journalist Leonard Matters, who would later become the Labour Party MP for Kennington, south London, proposed that Jack the Ripper was an eminent doctor

---

[228] Clearly based on Jack the Ripper, this popular novel was first filmed in 1927 by Alfred Hitchcock.

[229] *Days Of My Years*, 1914.

whose son had died from syphilis caught from an East End prostitute.

Guy Logan's first published book was "Masters of Crime", 1928. In a chapter on the Ripper he dropped his earlier [fictional] drowned doctor theory—and, by extension, that of Melville Macnaghten, Major Griffiths and George R. Sims—declaring that "nothing to establish this story was ever put forward, and I regard it as pure myth."

Logan was now suggesting that Jack the Ripper may have been an American who contracted syphilis from an East End prostitute, resulting in a murderous mania levelled against others of her profession.

This bore an uncanny resemblance to Leonard Matters' 1926 theory in the *People* newspaper. But of more interest about Logan's theory was his reference to someone who appears to have been based on Dr. Francis Tumblety.

"'I know,' he wrote, 'that one of Scotland Yard's best men, Inspector Andrews, was sent specially to America in December 1888 in search of the Whitechapel fiend on the strength of important information, the nature of which has never been disclosed. Nothing, however, came of it, and the Inspector's mission was a failure'."

Some present-day theorists like to imagine that Logan [aged 19 in 1888] had contacts at Scotland Yard from whom he might have gleaned this spurious piece of information about Tumblety. But a more likely explanation is that at some time or other he consulted a press cuttings library, for the *Pall Mall Gazette*, 31st December 1888, had reported—

"Inspector Andrews, of Scotland Yard, has arrived in New York from Montreal. It is generally believed that he has received orders from England to commence his search in this city for the Whitechapel murderer."

Leonard Matters elaborated on his earlier theory in "The Mystery of Jack the Ripper", published 1929, positing a pseudonymous Dr. Stanley, an eminent London surgeon who, after the murders, fled to Buenos Aires. On his deathbed he confessed to the Whitechapel murders, carried out as part of an East End quest to find the prostitute who had fatally infected his son with a particularly virulent strain of syphilis.

Barring a few incidental details this was a direct lift from John T.

Sullivan's 1901 *Salt Lake Herald* story of Dr. E., the physician who had also fled to Buenos Aires.

Following publication of Leonard Matters' book, a Dr. Thomas Dutton wrote to the *Daily Mail*, 14th May 1929—

"Sir, —Living in Whitechapel (Aldgate) about the time of the Jack the Ripper murders, I took great interest in them from a medical point of view.

"I did not draw the same conclusion as Mr. Leonard Matters, but believe they were committed by a ship's butcher.

"Having been a surgeon in the Mercantile Marine I have seen these butchers with even greater skill with the knife than many expert operating surgeons. After the murders, going home one night with a black bag in which was a masonic apron, I was accosted by two women who shouted 'Jack the Ripper.'

"Thomas Dutton, M.D., 25 New Cavendish Street, Harley Street, W.1."

More would be heard about Dr. Dutton in the mid-1930s.

Also in 1929 came *Scoundrels and Scallywags*, "the amazing diary of an ex-Chief Inspector of the C.I.D., Scotland Yard . . ."[230]

The 67-year-old Tom Divall had been a Local Inspector CID [H Division] at around the turn of the 20th Century. He retired in March 1913 and became a Jockey Club official. He died, aged 82, in a WWII air raid on the south coast of England.

Of Jack the Ripper he wrote—

"We have never found any trace of this man, or any connection of his, nor have we been able to ascertain definitely the end of him . . .

". . . The much lamented and late Assistant Commissioner of the CID, Sir Melville Macnaghten, received some information that the murderer had gone to America and died in a lunatic asylum there. This may be correct, for after this, nothing new was ever heard of a similar crime ever being committed."

If true, Tom Divall's story throws a huge spanner into the works

---

[230]   Ernest Benn Books advertising blurb, *The Times*, 9th August 1929.

regarding Macnaghten's favoured Ripper suspect, Montague John Druitt, dragged from the River Thames on the last day of December 1888.

By the late 1920s the story of Jack the Ripper had become a hopeless tangle of myth, rumour, lies, gossip, variations on a theme, invention, self-publicity and sheer opportunism. What the subject sorely needed was an authoritative figure—someone with a first-hand knowledge of events who could clear away the detritus of the past forty-plus years.

Chief Inspector Frederick George Abberline was the last surviving senior police officer engaged upon the Whitechapel murders investigation. Born 1843, in Blandford Forum, Dorset, Abberline joined the Metropolitan Police [N Division, Islington] in 1863. He moved to Y Division [Kentish Town] and then H Division [Whitechapel] where he was stationed from 1878 to November 1887. Whilst in Whitechapel he and his wife, Emma, lived at Commercial Street police station, and on his promotion to Scotland Yard moved into a terraced house at 41 Mayflower Road, Clapham. He retired from the Metropolitan Police in January 1892 on the occasion of his 49th birthday, his annual pension of £216. 13s 4d. taking effect from 8th February 1892.

Two days earlier, on 6th February 1892, Maria Garfield Gibbons [nee Cook] gave birth to a son—her fourth—Harold Charles. At this time she was living with her husband, Edward, their other children, Ernest, Sidney and Percy, and her 82-year-old mother, Charlotte, above a corn dealer's shop[231] at 137 Walmer Road, North Kensington [Notting Hill].

By the time of the 1901 census Maria had given birth to a fifth son, Stanley [b. 1894], and the family had moved to accommodation above retail premises at 111 Queen's Road, Battersea.

The 1901 Census for England, taken on the night of Sunday 31st March, recorded Maria, her husband and four sons—Ernest, Sidney, Percy and Stanley. Harold Charles, by this time nine-years-old, was not amongst their number.

Going from electoral records and street directories, at a date

---

[231]   Owned by brothers Francis Henry and William James Jennings.

between 1893 and 1894 Abberline and his wife moved three quarters of a mile north from 41 Mayflower Road into a nine-roomed house at 313 Clapham Road. They lived here until 1906 and were thus duly recorded in the 1901 Census.

Two entries in the 1901 Census confirm that Abberline was running a boarding house at 313 Clapham Road—

"John Philip Collins, Boarder, Single, age 30, Author and Newspaper Editor."

"Lawrence Alban Jones, Single, Boarder, 27, Consulting Engineer."

Also recorded in the census was "Mary Isabella Yates, Single, 18, General Servant (domestic), b. Hanover Square workhouse."

Most intriguing is the following entry—

"Harold Chas. Gibbons, Single, Visitor, 9, born Notting Hill."[232]

Frederick George Abberline and his wife, Emma, were somehow acquainted with Edward and Maria Gibbons.

In 1906 Abberline and his wife moved from London to Bournemouth, a resort town in Hampshire[233] on the south coast of England.

Their first Bournemouth address was a brand-new[234] detached house at No. 4 Methuen Road, recorded in ex-Chief Inspector Donald Swanson's personal address book as "Vintimilli."

The actual name of the house was *Vintimille,*[235] the French rendition of *Ventimiglia*, an Italian town on the Mediterranean coast a few miles from the French border. The choice of name is perhaps understandable, for a few years after leaving the Metropolitan Police in 1892 Abberline worked for the Pinkerton Detective Agency, under whose aegis he spent three seasons watching the gaming tables at Monte Carlo, about ten miles from Ventimiglia.

---

[232] Notting Hill was part of North Kensington.

[233] Bournemouth became part of Dorset in 1974.

[234] The house was built in 1905.

[235] For those of a conspiratorial turn of mind regarding Abberline's connection with the top-level Cleveland Street scandal, there is the story of Lascaris de Vintimille, Chevalier of the Order of Malta and one of Napoleon's secret agents, who underwent a long period of disgrace and exile after having blundered on a secret diplomatic mission.

The Abberline and Gibbons families appear in the 1911 Census, taken on Sunday 2nd April. By this time Maria Gibbons had died [age 49 in 1908], and Edward, together with three of his sons—Sidney, Percy and Stanley—was still living at 111 Queen's Road, Battersea.

Ernest, aged 28, and Harold Charles, aged 19, were not in evidence.

In 1907 Abberline and his wife moved from their four-bedroomed house at No. 4 Methuen Road into a ten-roomed house about five hundred yards away at 195 Holdenhurst Road.

Abberline named the house 'Estcourt',[236] which has led to much inventive speculation, the most popular interpretation being that Jack the Ripper "is caught".

The truth may be more prosaic, for during this time many of Bournemouth's roads and buildings—such as Methuen, Lowther, Wellington, Estcourt[237] and Malmesbury—were being named after prominent people and places from the Boer War.

The 1911 Census records Abberline and his wife at this new address. Mary Isabella Yates, the by-now 28-year-old "general Servant (domestic), b. Hanover Square workhouse," was not in evidence. However, another person from the 1901 Census was still living in the Abberline household—

"Harold Charles Gibbons, Visitor, 19, Single," who was now a "Shop Assistant to Grocer."

The 1911 Census also recorded Harold's eldest brother, Ernest, five miles from Bournemouth, boarding with the Short family at "Glenroy", Kingston Road, Poole, Dorset. He was employed as a pianist at the Picture Palace.[238]

In 1919 Harold Charles Gibbons, aged 27, returned to England aboard the *RMS Osterley* from Melbourne, Australia. He was listed on the passenger manifest as a "discharged soldier." He died on the Isle of Wight,

---

[236]   The previous occupant of 195 Holdenhurst Road was John Johnson, during whose occupancy the house was unnamed. The house-name "Estcourt" first appears in the 1911 Bournemouth Street Directory.

[237]   Estcourt House, Bournemouth, was an Invalid Home for Gentlemen.

[238]   In 1911 Amity Hall and the Poole Electric Theatre both showed cinematographs.

1st February 1965.

This is all that is so far known about Abberline's connections with the Gibbons family.

Adoption and fostering have always existed in the United Kingdom, in the sense of people taking other people's children into their homes and looking after them on a permanent or temporary basis. However, adoption, the permanent removal of a child into another family, had no legal basis in the United Kingdom until the 20th century and was done on an informal basis. The closest concept to adoption was "wardship," under which a guardian was given effective custody of a child by the Chancery Court, but this was little used and did not give the guardian parental rights. Fostering, where a child lives temporarily with another family, began to be regulated from the middle of the 19th century onwards, following a series of "baby farming" scandals. By the end of the 19th century, some poor law authorities and voluntary organizations were calling it "boarding out" and using it as an official alternative to putting neglected children in the workhouse or an orphanage.[239]

Abberline died from bronchitis and heart disease, aged 86, on 10th December 1929.[240] Witness to the death was 50-year-old Bella Harding who, in the absence of any information to the contrary, we must assume to have been a family friend or professional nurse. His estate was valued at £317. 4s. 10d. Harold Charles Gibbons was not mentioned in the will. Everything went to his wife Emma, who died intestate on 15th March 1930, aged 85. In September 1930 her estate was probated. It totalled £66 6s. 3d.

During the twenty-six years between his March 1903 *Pall Mall Gazette* interview in London and his death in Bournemouth, the detective most closely associated with the Whitechapel murders fell off the social radar. From available records this keen gardener and rose-grower does not appear to have been a member of any of the town's horticultural societies. He is not to be found as a member of any of its social clubs;

---

[239] "History of Adoption and Fostering in the United Kingdom," Jenny Keating.

[240] Abberline's death certificate gives his cause of death as "(1/a) Bronchitis and (b) mitrial valvular disease of the heart)." There was no post mortem.

nor in Bournemouth's many masonic lodges, such as Horsa, Hengist, Rowena, Boscombe and Malmesbury. Whereas many other retired policemen of the period unfailingly had an apocryphal Jack the Ripper anecdote tucked up their sleeves with which to enliven an otherwise humdrum after-luncheon talk, Abberline never uttered a single word on the subject.

Except—allegedly—on one occasion.

In the *Evening News,* 26th June 1976, author, critic and editor Nigel Morland, age 71, [241] recounted a visit he paid to Abberline in Bournemouth—

"I visited Abberline when he was living in retirement in Dorset. In spite of my efforts he was very cagey and said he had no intention of discussing the case in detail. He was sick of the whole business. But when I mentioned two friends of mine—Edgar Wallace and Henry Battley, who became Chief Inspector of the fingerprint bureau—he relented a little. The case, he said, was tightly shut. 'I've given my word to keep my mouth permanently closed about it.'

"But he allegedly let slip some revealing comments.

"'There was a lot of material never entered in any records,' he said. 'Hearsay stuff, word-of-mouth information and orders in 1888-9 to forget all about the affair.'

"'Then neither you nor anyone else knows who the Ripper was?' [I said] as I was ushered firmly out of the house.

"'I know,' he said, 'and my superiors know certain facts.' He was not going to give the details to me or anyone else. But he added, and I remember distinctly his exact words—

"'It wasn't a butcher, Yid or foreign skipper, as he was supposed to be . . . you'd have to look for him not at the bottom of London society at the time, but a long way up. That's all I will ever say. Goodbye.' And the door was firmly closed."

This should be taken with a large pinch of salt, for the words did not originate with Abberline but from an anonymous piece of doggerel

---

[241]   Died 3rd April 1986.

which Sir Melville Macnaghten used in his 1914 memoirs to preface a chapter on Jack the Ripper—

"I'm not a butcher, I'm not a Yid, Nor yet a foreign Skipper, But I'm your own light-hearted friend, Yours truly, Jack the Ripper."

There is nothing to substantiate Nigel Morland's story.

During the period 1906/7-1929 when Abberline was living in Bournemouth, Nigel Morland [born Carl Van Biene, London, 1905] grew up, attended school and in 1919 travelled to China, where he worked as a journalist on the *Shanghai Mercury,* the *China Press* and *Shanghai Sports.* During 1923 and 1924 he published three stories in Shanghai as Nigel Van Biene.[242] He next moved to Hollywood, where he "ghosted show business memoirs, wrote for *Movie Day* and Hearst newspapers."[243]

Morland told Abberline he was a friend of thriller writer Edgar Wallace, who died in Beverly Hills on 10th February 1932. By the late 1930s Morland was telling the press he had been Edgar Wallace's secretary.

Here we find ourselves skating on factually thin ice.

The Times, 11th February 1932—

"His [Edgar Wallace's] secretary of many years, Mr. Robert Curtis, and Mr. Walter Huston, the actor, were with him when he died."

Robert Curtis first met Edgar Wallace in 1913. In 1919, having three years earlier contracted malaria during military service in Egypt and been invalided out of the army, Curtis was permanently employed as private secretary to Wallace at four pounds a week. Following Wallace's death Curtis completed some of his unfinished manuscripts and reworked a number of plays and film scripts into novels. He died on 20th August 1936.

In the early summer of 1921 Edgar Wallace married his only other secretary, Ethel Violet King.

---

[242] "The Sibilant Whisper," "Ragged Tales," and "Miscellanea." The last named stories [both under 80 pages] were published by Lettercraft, 73a Szechuan Road, Shanghai.
[243] *The Times*, 12th April 1986.

The prolific Nigel Morland[244] told many tall tales about his early days[245] and became something of a legend in his own lunchtime. His June 1976 Abberline story appears to have been cut from whole cloth simply to secure a seat aboard the then voguish but wholly bogus "Royal Ripper" bandwagon—which in the following month, with the publication of Stephen Knight's "Jack the Ripper: The Final Solution", was to become standing-room only.

---

[244]   Nigel Morland wrote in excess of 70 books, edited various magazines, ran a Mystery Book Club and, together with author John Creasey, founded the Crime Writers' Association.
[245]   Nigel Morland told "Edgar Wallace Mystery Magazine" editor Keith Chapman that in the 1930s he ghosted for author Leslie Charteris on the book "Follow the Saint". However, the book was a collection of three Charteris novellas previously published in "The Thriller," "Black Mask" and "Detective Fiction" magazines. The jury is still out on Morland's claim.

11. THE INCIDENT AT MARBLE ARCH

Pall Mall Gazette, 4th October 1888—

"There is some sense, though not much importance, in the suggestion that the Whitechapel murders afford the practitioners of occult science (or religion) an unexampled opportunity to prove and advertise the genuineness of their pretensions. If spiritualists, clairvoyants, and thought-readers all lie low and say nuffin' we may at least conclude that, whatever spirits may be at their séances, public spirit is notably absent . . ."

The Jack the Ripper mystery was tailor-made for the burgeoning spiritualist movement, of which Arthur Conan Doyle was a leading proponent.

The *Pall Mall Gazette,* 4th October 1888, threw down the gauntlet—

"Interviews with Carlyle and Shakespeare may be all very interesting, but a short conversation with one of the six spirits so recently sent to their long abode, 'unhousel'd, disappointed, unanel'd', would for practical purposes be worth more than a volume of trans-Stygian Carlylese. Clairvoyants, even if the mere local influence be insufficient to unseal their spiritual eyes, might set to work upon 'Jack the Ripper's letter' and determine whether it be genuine or a hoax. Why does the Society for Psychical Research stand ingloriously idle?"[246]

Jack the Ripper quickly attracted an esoteric following.

Daily News, 8th October 1888—

"An extraordinary statement bearing upon the Whitechapel tragedies was made to the Cardiff [south Wales] police last night by a respectable looking elderly woman, who stated that she was a spiritualist, and in company with five other persons held a séance on Saturday night. They summoned the spirit of Elizabeth Stride, and after some delay the spirit came, and in answer to questions stated that her murderer was a middle aged man, whose name she mentioned, and who resided at a given number in Commercial road or street, Whitechapel, and who belonged to a gang of twelve."

Evening News, 8th October 1888—

"Yesterday, a Bolton [Lancashire] spiritualist held a séance with the special object of discovering the Whitechapel murderer. The medium was successful, as the spirits revealed a vision of a man having the appearance of a farmer, but dressed like a navvy with a strap wound his waist and peculiar pockets. He had a dark moustache and scars behind his ears, besides other marks. He will commit one more murder and be caught red-handed."

Mixed messages were coming across the ether.

At the Metropole Hotel in November 1888 thought-reader/mentalist Stuart Cumberland gave a demonstration of the value of his skills in the detection of crime to an audience including magistrate Curtis Bennett and Metropolitan Police Chief Constable Adolphus Frederick Williamson. In 1889 Cumberland, who ran his own one-penny newspaper,[247] wrote a shilling-shocker entitled "A Fatal Affinity." Loosely based on the Whitechapel murders, the killer was a member of the Brotherhood of Darkness.

Aberdeen Journal, 25th September 1889—

"Whitechapel ought to be very lively soon, for Mr. Stuart

---

[246]   *Pall Mall Gazette* editor W.T. Stead became a convert to spiritualism in 1892.

[247]   *Stuart Cumberland's Illustrated Mirror—A Reflector of People, Politics, Finance, the Drama, etc.*

Cumberland and Dr. Forbes Winslow have announced they intend spending a few nights in that locality for the purpose of capturing 'Jack the Ripper.' They are both very smart men, and each has his own theory as to the identity of the murderer. It is to be hoped that they will not end by capturing each other. The latest theory that the criminal is a woman in disguise is generally scouted, but then there is so little evidence and so many conjectures have been made that any hypothesis seems tenable."

Two days later a New Zealand newspaper[248] reported that Stuart Cumberland had experienced a premonition of the Mary Kelly murder.

A face had appeared to him in a dream—

"The first time this face appeared to me was when I was in Dundee last October [1888], soon after the perpetration of the sixth [sic] murder, and the next day I related the particulars of my dream to a representative of the *Dundee Advertiser*, who made, I believe, a note of them. A couple of weeks later I again saw the face, and I remarked to Dr. [James] Rubie, who was then editing the London *Evening News*, I believed that within a couple of days we should have another Whitechapel murder.

"'A couple of days,' remarked the doctor; 'why, that will make it Lord Mayor's Day, and on that day I am to lunch with you; and if Jack the Ripper goes to work, then I shall be detained at the office, and you won't have me to lunch.'

"Lord Mayor's Day came round, and I was at my Club waiting for Dr. Rubie; but the luncheon hour passed and he did not arrive. Presently there arrived a boy from the *Evening News* with a note. It was from my expected guest, and ran as follows—

"'Your prophecy has come true. Jack the Ripper has been at work again. I am therefore detained at the office and can't, I am sorry to say, lunch with you.'"

On 1st December 1888 the *Pall Mall Gazette* published "The Whitechapel Demon's Nationality: And Why He Committed the Murders." Written by "One Who Thinks He Knows," the article concluded that not only was Jack the Ripper a black magician, but that

---

[248]   *Star* [NZ] 27th September 1889.

he was also a Frenchman.

'One Who Thinks He Knows' referenced '*Le Dogme et Rituel de la Haute Magie*' by Alphonse Louis Constant [aka Eliphas Levi], an occult volume written in French which contained the "most elaborate directions for working magic spells of all kinds."

'One Who Thinks He Knows' elaborated—

"The second volume has a chapter on Necromancy, or black magic, which the author justly denounces as a profanation. Black magic employs the agencies of evil spirits and demons, instead of the beneficent spirits directed by the adepts of *la haute magie*. At the same time he gives the clearest and fullest details of the necessary steps for evocation by this means . . ."

Jack the Ripper first had to secure a shopping list of unsavoury items—amongst other things strips of skin from a suicide, candles made from human fat, the head of a black cat which had been fed forty days on human flesh, and nails from a murderer's gallows.

Also listed were the horns of a goat "which has been made the instrument of an infamous capital crime". This was a rather coy rendition of Eliphas Levi's original "les cornes d'un bouc *cum quo puella concubuerit*"— "the horns of a goat with whom a maiden had conjoined."

Last but by no means least on Jack's shopping list was "a preparation made from a certain portion of the body of a harlot."

This was presumably intended to suggest the uterus, as removed from Annie Chapman and Catherine Eddowes, but interestingly this ingredient had not been specified in Eliphas Levi's original recipe. It appears to have been included by "One Who Thinks He Knows" simply to lend satanic verisimilitude to Jack's activities.

'One Who Thinks He Knows' was named by W. T. Stead in 1896 as Robert Donston Stephenson [aka Dr. Roslyn D'Onston], who claimed to be a practitioner of magic. He was in the London Hospital, Whitechapel, as a neurasthenic patient[249] throughout the murders and tried to insinuate himself into the Ripper investigation by pestering the

---

[249]   Neurasthenia is similar to chronic fatigue syndrome.

press and police with letters written from his private hospital bed.

The late Melvin Harris described him "as the only man who can be taken seriously as the Ripper,"[250] but as this is an assertion heavily dependent upon one's interpretation of the word "seriously" Robert Donston Stephenson's black magical mumbo-jumbo need detain us no longer.

Necromancy is defined as the ritualistic conjuration of the spirits for the purpose of magically revealing the future or influencing the course of events, whilst spiritualism is defined as a belief that the spirits of the dead communicate with the living, usually through a medium. Both had their shamans, charlatans, bells and whistles, but in the late Victorian period spiritualism was generally considered the more genteel and socially acceptable of the two. How much nicer to investigate the unknown whilst enjoying a sponge finger and a cup of Earl Grey rather than having to dance naked around a ruined altar under a cold winter moon.

East London Observer, 10th August 1889—

"The letters which reach Superintendent Arnold at the Leman Street police station are both numerous and curious, and partake chiefly of the character rendered familiar to readers of newspapers during the time the murder scare was at its height in the autumn of last year. There are for instance no end of letters from Spiritualists and thought readers, who profess in some cases to have seen the spirits of one or other of the murdered women with whom they have entered into conversation as to the appearance of the murderer. The striking disparities evident, however, are sufficient on the face of them to condemn the letters and their writers as being absolutely useless for all practical purposes."

Spiritualist Robert James Lees [1849-1931] is a regular performer in the Ripper repertory company. Others have come and gone, but Lees has endured, making appearances in Stephen Knight's 1976 book "Jack the Ripper: The Final Solution", the 1979 movie "Murder by Decree",

---

[250]   Author of *Jack the Ripper the Bloody Truth*, 1987; *The Ripper File*, 1989; *The True Face of Jack the Ripper*, 1994.

the 1988 TV mini-series "Jack the Ripper", the 1990 graphic novel "From Hell" and its 2001 movie adaptation.

His story started in earnest on 23rd November 1929, when an article written by journalist Hugh Mogford[251] appeared in the *Leicester Illustrated Chronicle*—

"As a young man he [Robert James Lees] was a Government agent, and his psychic powers enabled him to unravel many important mysteries which defeated the brains of Scotland Yard.

"In fact he is one of the few people who know the identity of the notorious Jack the Ripper, whose terrible murders terrorised London during the last few years of the 19th century.

"He was sworn to secrecy, and on oath promised not to divulge the name, and as a Government servant refusing to give information which was badly wanted, he was banished to St Ives for five years."

Never mind that this last paragraph makes little sense. Forty-one years after the long forgotten 1895 *Chicago Sunday Times-Herald* story, Robert James Lees was once again centre-stage. Fleet Street beat a path to Lees' Leicester front door, but he and his daughter, Eva, refused to talk.

Robert James Lees died, aged 82, on 11th January 1931, and it is believed that Hugh Mogford wrote Lees' obituary which appeared the following day in the *Leicester Mercury*—

"A noted spiritualist, Mr. Robert James Lees, who claimed to be the only surviving person who knew the identity of Jack the Ripper, the notorious murderer, has died at his home in Leicester . . .

". . . Some months ago, he told a *Leicester Mercury* man that he offered his services to Scotland Yard, with a view to tracing the criminal.

"His visits to the Yard became so persistent, that at length, the authorities agreed to his co-operation.

"Mr. Lees made the astounding statement to the Leicester Mercury

---

[251] Born Devon 1883.

that he actually enabled the Yard to associate with the crime a man who died in a lunatic asylum.

"This story has never been revealed by any police authority, and it is commonly supposed that the mystery has never been cleared up."

Eva Lees was offered £500 by *Daily Express* crime reporter Cyril Morton to tell the story, but she allegedly refused. At about this time she was interviewed by a research officer from the Society for Psychical Research, Mrs Eve Brackenbury, described by Eric Robertson Dodds[252] as a "tough little sceptic." Mrs Brackenbury took the report of her interview[253] to Scotland Yard, where she was told that they had no knowledge of Robert James Lees or of a psychic assisting in the search for Jack the Ripper.

However, two months later, on 7th March 1931, the *Daily Express* announced that it was "to publish an astonishing document, which has long been kept a close secret, and which purports to describe how a clairvoyant solved the mystery of the 'Jack the Ripper' crimes and enabled the ferocious murderer to be identified and arrested—

"The recent death of Mr. Robert James Lees, the famous spiritualist and clairvoyant, who died in Leicester at the age of eighty-one, will revive and possibly answer the question, 'Who was Jack the Ripper?'

"No official solution has ever been offered for these outrages. Today they are almost forgotten . . ."

Robert James Lees, a government agent with psychic powers?

Three entries in Lees' personal diary[254] written just after the double-event of 30th September 1888 reveal the extent of his psychic involvement in unravelling the Ripper mystery—

"Tuesday 2nd October 1888: Offered services to Police to follow up East End murders—called a fool and lunatic. Got trace of man from spot near Berner Street."

"Wednesday 3rd October 1888: Went to City Police again—called

---

[252]   President of the Society for Psychical Research, 1961-1963.

[253]   Mrs Brackenbury published her report in the May 1931 edition of the *Journal of the Society for Psychical Research*.

[254]   Stansted Hall archive - The College For Psychic Science

a madman and fool."

"Thursday 4th October 1888: Went to Scotland Yard—same result, but they promised to write me."

Another unsubstantiated rumour which has hardened into historical fact is Lees having played a rôle in the apprehension of Dr. Thomas Gallagher and his New York Clan-Na-Gael confederates, arrested in London, 1883, for "devising and intending to depose the Queen from the Imperial Crown of Great Britain and Ireland" [viz. plotting to blow up the Palace of Westminster].

There is nothing to link Robert James Lees with the arrest of Dr. Gallagher by Inspector Littlechild. Contemporary newspaper reports and trial transcripts make it clear that his arrest had more to do with astute detective work, an informant named Joseph Lynch and a countrywide surveillance operation.

The only pointer to Lees possibly having provided his services to the police is contained in a scrappily-written note on plain paper dated 20th August 1894. And here it is worth noting that just six months earlier Melville Macnaghten had penned his memorandum naming three 'more likely' Jack the Ripper suspects.

The letter read as follows—

"Sir, I have been directed by Mr. Anderson Director of Criminal Investigation Dept (Scotland Yard) to call on you and thank you for your kind offer of assistance re anarchists and to say that he will avail of the offer to the fullest. With this object I am instructed to address the matter and would like to see you previous to next meeting night or say at your house at 7 pm on Saturday next subject of course to your convenience. If you can or other suitable arrangement if you would be good enough to drop me a line I will be delighted to attend to it."[255]

The note was signed "F. Powell".

This may have been Chief Inspector Francis Powell, a Special Branch officer working at the time under William Melville, who in 1912 was recruited into the pre-revolutionary Tsarist Okhrana [Department for

---

[255]   See http://www.rjlees.co.uk/documentary.htm

Defense of Public Security and Order] as head of its operations in England.[256]

The puzzling thing about this note is the apparent eagerness with which Robert Anderson now appeared ready to accept the assistance of a psychic whose October 1888 offer to help Scotland Yard catch Jack the Ripper had been roundly spurned.

Daily Express, 9th March 1931—

"The first part of the secret document which purports to describe how Mr. Robert James Lees, the famous clairvoyant, solved the mystery of 'Jack the Ripper' is published below. As stated on Saturday, the document was placed in the hands of the 'Daily Express' shortly after Mr. Lees' death by a friend who had been in his confidence. Mr. Lees dictated the document and left word that it should not be revealed until after his death."

The Lees story soon took on a new dimension—

"It is known that Mr. Lees was received more than once at Buckingham Palace by Queen Victoria, who was interested in his psychic powers. It is known that coincident with the end of this series of Whitechapel murders he was received once more at Buckingham Palace. The claim is now made that a pledge of secrecy—at which the police, medical men, and other high officials connived—was put on Mr. Lees."

Here it seems were the first green shoots of what would eventually mutate and blossom into the "Royal Ripper" theory.

"The Daily Express publishes this strange document with all reservations. In many ways it should be regarded as fantastic—and yet can anything be more fantastic than the facts which are already known?

"Miss Eva Lees, who is still living in the house in Fosse Road, Leicester, where Mr. Lees died, stated definitely that her father received a pension from the Privy Purse for many years. Envelopes from the Privy Purse and certain royal residences were produced as proof, although the letters were withheld on grounds of good taste."

---

[256]   HIA Okhrana archive 35/Vc/folder 1: Report no. 552, 24 April/7 May 1912, A.A. Krassilnikov, Head of Foreign Agency to S. P. Beleteskii, Director of Police, ff. 1-2.

A pledge of secrecy? Royal hush-money? Letters from Royal residences withheld on grounds of good taste? Who could not have wanted to read on?

However, the *Daily Express* articles were not based on a secret document dictated by Lees. They were a rehash of the 1895 *Chicago Sunday Times-Herald* story, both versions of which contained the following account—

" . . . Mr. Lees returned to England, where he made the acquaintance of Roland B. Shaw, a mining stockbroker of New York, and Fred C. Beckwith, of Broadhead, Wis., U.S.A., who was then the financial promoter of an American syndicate in London.

"These three gentlemen were dining one evening in the Criterion[257] when Mr. Lees turned to his two companions and suddenly exclaimed: 'Great God! Jack the Ripper has committed another murder.'

"Mr. Shaw looked at his watch and found it was eleven minutes to eight. At ten minutes past eight a policeman discovered the body of a woman in Crown Court, in the Whitechapel district, with her throat cut from ear to ear, and her body bearing all the marks of the Ripper's handiwork.

"Mr. Lees and his companions at once went to Scotland-yard. The news of the murder had not yet reached the inspector, but while Mr. Lees was relating his story a telegram arrived giving full details of the outrage."

The story was pure moonshine.

On 22nd May 1886, nine years before the *Chicago Sunday Times-Herald* story, a statement by Robert James Lees had appeared in the weekly spiritualist publication *Light*—

"During that month [November 1884] the question was introduced by a gentleman in a company where I was present, and a somewhat lively debate resulted. I advanced my theory, and offered to prove it, which was immediately accepted by a Mr. S., a gentleman of some scientific standing, who was also a Spiritualist. Another of the company, Mr. B.,

---

257   Criterion Restaurant, Piccadilly Circus, London.

wished to join us, the latter being an Atheist. An arrangement was made to sit a certain number of times, under conditions to which we all agreed, and at the termination of our investigation we were to compare notes. The sittings took place in the rooms of Mr. B., and commenced with table movements, but were, after the fourth sitting, principally devoted to the trance, I myself being the medium.

"Of the first three séances I have nothing particular to record except that I was perfectly satisfied. At the fourth the name of Samuel B. was given, and claimed to be an uncle of Mr. B., who laughed at the idea, as, he said, he never had an uncle of that name. Still, the correctness of the statement was maintained and additional details given by which to identify the spirit if Mr. B. would write home. Let me here say both these gentlemen were Americans. In answer to further inquiries, Mr. B. was told to re-open the workings of a certain mine which he had closed, as it contained valuable mineral, further details of which were promised at the next sitting . . ."

Thus were the two Americans, Mr. S. and Mr. B. from 1884, transformed into Mr. Roland B. Shaw and Mr. Fred C. Beckwith in 1895 and 1931.

Here is another episode from the *Daily Express* and *Chicago Sunday Times-Herald* versions——

"One day, while riding in an omnibus from Shepherd's Bush in company with his wife, he experienced a renewal of the strange sensations which had preceded his former clairvoyant condition. The omnibus ascended Notting Hill. It stopped at the top, and a man entered the interior of the vehicle. Mr. Lees at once experienced a singular sensation. Looking up he perceived that the new passenger was a man of medium size. He noticed that he was dressed in a dark suit of Scotch tweed, over which he wore a light overcoat. He had a soft felt hat on his head.

"Over a year had elapsed since Mr. Lees' clairvoyant vision, but the picture of the murderer had been indelibly impressed upon his mind. Leaning over to his wife he remarked earnestly, 'That is Jack the Ripper.' His wife laughed at this, and told him not to be foolish. 'I am not mistaken,' replied Mr. Lees, 'I feel it.' The omnibus traversed the entire length of the Edgware road, turning into Oxford street at the Marble Arch. At this point the man in the light overcoat got out.

"Mr. Lees determined to follow him. Bidding his wife continue on her journey in the direction of home, he followed the man down Park Lane . . ."

This story was also pure moonshine.

In *Light*, 22nd May 1886, Lees wrote—

"Let me give one case, which I received at this time, that did more than anything else to convince me that it was a spirit agency at work. I was returning home one night by 'bus, about 7.30, and had reached the Marble Arch, when a voice, speaking quite distinctly, told me to return to a certain hotel and see a Mr. R., who was stopping there. I returned, thinking this time I should find my spirit friend at fault, but was considerably astonished to find Mr. R. was there and occupying the room which had been mentioned."

Thus did Lees' 1886 story involving him alighting from a bus at Marble Arch following a psychic episode become fashioned into his pursuing Jack the Ripper down Park Lane.

In an article for *Psypioneer Journal*, December 2009, writer, researcher and historian Stephen Butt wrote—

"Many other details in the Chicago article indicate that the writer or writers had access to a source of personal information about Lees. American journalists would have seen the daily wires from London about the Ripper Murders and were as informed about them as their counterparts in London, but specific family details about Lees and of his work, and his address in the London suburbs also found their way into the spurious article."

Stephen Butt posed the questions—

"Who was the source in Chicago of so much personal family information about Lees? How did a copy of *Light* published in 1886 reach the Chicago journalists?" He offered two possible candidates: newspaper editor and fellow-spiritualist W.T. Stead, and Lees' eldest son, Norman Albert Lees.

This opens up myriad possibilities, for in a column entitled "London Gossip" in the New Zealand *Star*, 1st March 1893, Robert James Lees told his interviewer that he communicated directly with his children via a 1013-year-old Egyptian spirit, *Cushna*. "I have a son connected with the Associated Press in Chicago. There is constant communication going on between us, but we never use the cable."

Might there have been connections between Norman Lees, the Dr. Howard story sent from San Francisco by the Associated Press and its subsequent version featuring his father in the *Chicago Sunday Times-Herald*?

In 1895, the year the *Chicago Times* merged with the *Chicago Herald* to become the *Chicago Times-Herald*, the former newspaper's London correspondent was John Elbert Wilkie, who in 1887 co-wrote "The Chicago Police" with John J. Flinn[258], and in 1898 was appointed chief of the US Federal Secret Service, a job in which he soon established a reputation for "forgery, skulduggery and a masterly manipulation of the press."[259]

Tenuous connections abound in the story of Jack the Ripper. For instance, whilst working in London John Elbert Wilkie had been a close friend of Detective Sergeant Frank Froest, [260] one of the two Metropolitan Police officers named on the 1888 gross indecency indictment of alleged Ripper suspect Dr. Francis Tumblety.

Stephen Butt expanded upon W.T. Stead and Norman Lees—

"[The two men] had corresponded regularly for a number of years on spiritualist matters . . . Stead visited Chicago in 1891, and visited the Whitechapel Club – the society of Chicago journalists who had a specific interest in the Whitechapel Murders.

"A letter from Stead to Dr. Albert Shaw, the editor of the American edition of 'The Review of Reviews' in New York dated 27 July 1894 confirms that Norman had been with Stead in Chicago—

---

[258]   By turns, Associate Editor, *Chicago Daily News*, US Consul, Chemnitz, Germany, Managing Editor, *Chicago Mail* and *Chicago Times*, Chief Editorial writer, *Chicago Inter Ocean*, President, Press Club 1906-1907.

[259]   *New York Times*, 13th February 2005.

[260]   George Barton, *Adventures of the World's Greatest Detectives*, New York 1909.

"Norman Lees, the young English Police Reporter, who helped me in my Chicago Detective work, is leaving by the 'Etruria' with his brother for New York. He is returning to Chicago. He came round to ask me whether I thought you could get him a free pass to Chicago from New York. I told him that I doubted it in as much as we had to pay for our own tickets when we were in America, but that I would mention it to you."

Stephen Butt also noted—

"There is evidence in the Lees family papers of a rift between Norman and his father. He settled in New York where, after being involved in a society scandal, and, allegedly, setting fire to his family home, he was for some time incarcerated in an institution for the insane."

However, subsequent research suggests that Norman Lees may not have been an arsonist and was far from insane.

At a 1911 New York County Supreme Court hearing of a case which has no bearing on the subject at hand, Lees was cross-examined as a defense witness.

The following exchange has been condensed—

"When were you sent to Matteawan, Mr. Lees?

"Oh, just about four years ago . . . I had myself sent there."

"Preceding your having sent yourself there, some sort of charge was made against you, wasn't there?"

"No, sir; I made a charge against myself."

"Can you tell me what it was that you were indicted for at your request?"

"Yes. Arson."

"Now, Mr. Lees, will you please state the purpose of getting yourself committed to Matteawan; state all the circumstances."

"Allegations had been made against the Matteawan State Hospital people and I decided that it was possible, after investigating the subject, to get committed, investigate it from the inside and expose it, and I went in and did it; and for what I did, I was paid."

"Will you please state how long you stayed there?"

"About five and one-half months."

"As a matter of fact, did you commit arson?"

"No, sir."

New York Evening Telegram, 16th October 1911, reported that after leaving Matteawan, Norman Lees spent "more than $20,000 attacking the institution . . . to bring about the release of other inmates who he says are sane." Various newspapers observed that Norman Lees "was a man of no personal means", but failed to pinpoint the source of his funding.

However, one Matteawan inmate whose release Norman Lees was eager to secure was Harry K. Thaw, mentioned by retired Chief Inspector Littlechild in his 1913 letter to George R. Sims. Thaw, found guilty of the 1906 murder of architect Stanford White, was rich beyond the dreams of Croesus, and so it made perfect sense that many were suggesting him as the source of Lees' funding.[261]

Norman Lees denied the suggestion. He had known Thaw intimately during his five months at Matteawan, "But I am not associated with Thaw's agents. I will not deny that where we have information that would be mutually helpful we exchange it, which is natural."

Whilst peripherally interesting, none of the foregoing addresses the basic question of why anybody would go to such elaborate lengths to falsely credit Robert James Lees with having employed his psychic abilities to track down Jack the Ripper. What could such a story have possibly hoped to achieve? Also puzzling is that throughout his life Lees did not comment upon the story. If true, why not claim it as such? If false, why not disavow it?

One possible answer is that Lees felt silence might help foster the belief that he actually was a keeper of secrets. If true, it was an idea which sorely misfired, for between 1895 and 1929 Lees attracted little press interest. Aside from in 1923, at the age of seventy-four, having allegedly cured a 23-year-old Paignton, Devon, girl who had "been given up by doctors as a hopeless case of "dementia precox" or "precocious

---

[261]   Thaw escaped from Matteawan in 1913. He died in Florida, 1947, aged 76.

madness",[262] during those thirty-four years not one reporter appears to have called on Lees for an exclusive interview, or perhaps to seek clarification on any of the conflicting Ripper stories littering the early twentieth century.

The identity of the Dr. Howard cited as the source of the *San Francisco Call* and *Chicago Sunday Times-Herald* articles was never firmly established. However, in *The People* version, its author Joseph Hatton identified him as Dr. Benjamin Howard, an American doctor who had practised in London during the late 1800s.

On returning to London and being alerted to the article Dr. Benjamin Howard immediately took umbrage at *The People* in a letter dated 26th January 1896—

"In this publication my name is dishonourably associated with Jack the Ripper – and in such a way – as if true – renders me liable to shew cause to the British Medical Council why my name with three degrees attached should not be expunged from the Official Register. Unfortunately for the Parties of the other part – there is not a single item of this startling statement concerning me which has the slightest foundation in fact. Beyond what I may have read in the newspapers, I have never known anything about Jack the Ripper. I have never made any public statement about Jack the Ripper – and at the time of the alleged public statement by me I was thousands of miles distant from San Francisco where it was alleged that I made it."

Blithely ignoring the fact that the *Chicago Sunday Times-Herald* story had not named the source of the Lees story as Dr. *Benjamin* Howard, five days later Joseph Hatton replied to Dr. Howard who, it turned out, was an old acquaintance—

"Dear Dr. Howard,

"I took the 'Jack the Ripper' notes from a two-column report in the *Chicago Times*. It was published in such evident good faith that I never thought of doubting it. You will observe that I spoke of you not only with respect but with admiration. I hope at all events that the incident may

---

[262]   The *Daily Herald* [Adelaide, SA] 12 May 1923 described the incident as an exorcism.

lead to a renewal of our friendship. Tell me what you would like me to do and I shall be only too glad to comply with your wishes.

"I always remember you as an appreciative acquaintance of the dear son whom I lost and of whom you predicted great things.

"Won't you come and see me?

"Joseph Hatton."

Introducing Robert James Lees as "the gentleman to whom the unfortunates of the East End of London owe their present immunity from the attacks of a monster . . ." the *Chicago Sunday Times-Herald* further informed its readers—

"Mr. Lees is at present the proprietor of a novel institution for the higher education of the workingmen at Peckham, a suburb of London. Over 1,800 workmen attend his classes and he has invested a large sum of money in the enterprise which is now on a paying basis. Mr Lees is recognised today as one of the most advanced labor leaders in England and is an intimate friend of Keir Hardie, the leader of an independent labor party. He [Lees] at present resides at 26 The Gardens, Peckham Rye, London S.E."

This "novel institution" was the People's League. Central Hall on Peckham High Street, built in 1894[263], was its headquarters, and the "large sum of money" was a £10,000 [$50,000] donation from a Christian 'well-wisher', which enabled its construction. But in the following year Lees stated in a hearing at Lambeth Police Court, 18th April 1895, that a clergyman[264] had lent him the £10,000, on which he was currently paying interest, and that he [Lees] was earning his living as a magnetic masseur. Lees also stressed that he did not hold séances.[265]

It has been said that Robert James Lees accepted a "proportion of the reward" offered for the apprehension of Jack the Ripper, a reward to which the *Chicago Sunday Times-Herald* had put a figure—

"It must be borne in mind that this madman had for years baffled all

---

[263]   A service of dedication was held on Sunday 11th November 1894.

[264]   Reverend Frederick Payler Morgan-Payler, b. 24th June 1841, d. 6th February 1897. See *The Cornishman*, 14th November 1895.

[265]   *The Standard*, 19th April 1895.

the resources of the greatest police force in the world – that, rendered desperate at last, the British authorities had summoned to their assistance the most experienced detectives in France, Germany, Holland, Italy, Spain and America, that they had lavished immense sums in an endeavour to trace the fiend, that there was then pending an aggregate reward of £30,000 [$150,000] together with a life pension of £1,500 [$7,500] per annum, all to go to the man who should first deliver to justice the terrible 'Ripper'."

This fanciful idea doesn't fly. £30,000 was then a colossal sum of money. [266] Following the Mitre Square murder the Corporation of London offered a reward of £500, but it produced no results, and in the House of Commons, 12th November 1888, the Home Secretary pointed out that a reward of £10,000 offered following the 1882 Phoenix Park murders in Dublin had "proved ineffectual and produced no evidence of any value."

The *Chicago Sunday Times-Herald* also asserted that Robert James Lees was an intimate friend of [James] Keir Hardy, the Scottish socialist, labour leader and first Independent Labour candidate elected to Parliament.

Various biographies of Keir Hardie make no mention of Robert James Lees. The only connection between Hardie and spiritualism appears to be that, following the 1892 general election, he lived in the Chelsea house of Frank Smith, a founding member of the Independent Labour Party, salvationist and, later, a spiritualist.

Lees espoused Hardie's socialist principles, but on a political level the only connection between the two men appears to have been on 8th June 1894, when a William Sutcliffe wrote to the editor of *Reynolds Newspaper* complaining that Keir Hardie had improperly given the support of the National Independent Labour Party to Lees, who was standing as an Independent Labour candidate in Peckham.

William Sutcliffe claimed that Lees held a meeting at the House of

---

[266] For purposes of 1895 comparison, the £1,500 per year life pension was equal to the annual salary of the Commissioner of the Metropolitan Police.

Commons "with you in the course of yesterday afternoon with another member of his Association, and that you had promised him most cordially your assistance and also that of the National Independent Labour party for the purpose of getting him into Parliament."

The omnipresent William Sutcliffe then wrote disparagingly of Lees—

"I have only to say that he is a Spiritualist, preaches on religion on Peckham Rye, describes himself on his cards as being a 'psychopathic therapeutist'—that is, a sort of a faith healer by stroking or making passes. He has formed what is called the 'People's League', and it is believed that a certain person has given a donation of £8,000 towards the funds of this League."

There was a P.S. to the letter—

"I do not write in a spirit of hostility to Labour candidature, but I may mention as significant that at the meeting held last night Lees and his chairman refused to allow any opposition, and could not even put the resolution, so great was the opposition of the working men present."

Keir Hardie's reply was short, sharp and to the point—

"Dear Sir,

"Reply to your favour of the 8th inst., I find from the South London Press of this date that Mr. Lees did not make the statement which you impute to him. Further reply, therefore, is unnecessary.

"Yours faithfully, Keir Hardie, M.P."

At a meeting of the People's League, on 8th August 1894—twelve days prior to receipt of the letter from F. Powell accepting his offer of help "re anarchists"—Lees asked to be allowed to withdraw his name as Independent Labour candidate for Peckham as his work for the League required all his time. A motion to this effect was carried unanimously.[267]

And that appears to have been the extent of their political relationship.

It has been asserted that Robert James Lees fled London for Cornwall as a direct consequence of the article in the *Chicago Sunday*

---

[267] *Reynolds Newspaper*, 12th August 1894.

Times-Herald.

Writing in St. Ives on New Year's Day 1896 about events the previous year, Lees in his personal diary told a different story.

"I left London again on April 20th with Mrs. Lees and remained here until June 7th (seven weeks) . . ."

Although Lees' was absent from London on publication of the *Chicago Sunday Times-Herald* story, 28th April 1895, and in *The People* [London] on 19th May 1895, it is difficult to believe that he was not made aware of such a fantastic story by relatives or spiritualist colleagues.

Lees' health had not been good for quite some time.

"As usual I tried to do too much, the burden was to heavy, the strain too great, and 'man's inhumanity to man' too indescribable to be continued. Wearied with insomnia caused by overwork, and trying to tide over difficulties which constantly increased (not so much financial as those which arose from people who were trying to crush everything for their personal gain and profit).

"On February 6th [1895] I was attacked for the third time by the Influenza . . . I dragged along until the 18th when I became so ill that for several days it was doubtful which way it would turn . . ."

This was the earlier-mentioned epidemic which had laid many people low, including Chief Inspector Donald Swanson.

". . . on March 8th after much anxiety and persuasion I consented to leave London for a few days and come here (St. Ives, Cornwall). My few days lengthened into three weeks, during which time the malcontents used their best endeavours to ruin my work and reputation; and on March 29th I left St. Ives for London to answer their charges and try and resume my work, but before I reached my journey's end and I found I was by no means so strong as I imagined. Another three weeks of work, worry and declining health during which my influenza settled down in my left leg which I dragged behind me in a state of half-paralysis, before my friends could persuade me to come back to St. Ives . . ."

It was at this point in his diary that Robert James Lees offered a further clue to what had been going on—

". . . But let me faithfully record that all the disturbance in London was created by four men in the league—and these men who owed me considerable money which I had loaned them—and a number of others, many of whom for various reasons had been expelled membership."

At Lambeth Police Court on Thursday 18th April 1895 eight men had been summoned by Robert James Lees for having "unlawfully disturbed a certain meeting and congregation of persons there assembled for religious worship."

Lees had convened the meeting to address unspecified "malicious and unfounded charges made during his absence."

The eight defendants were members of the League, four of whom had not paid their subscriptions. Lees identified these men as G.F Morgan, George Bitten, Frederick Polkinghorne and George Maxted.

Not only was Lees ill. He was paying interest on a £10,000 loan. He was also owed "considerable money" loaned to four men in the People's League who, together with various expelled members, were bent on ruining his work and reputation for their personal gain.

Robert James Lees was being kicked whilst he was down in more ways than one; and so, all things considered, the article in the *People* newspaper, 19th May 1895, appeared at an interesting time.

There is another, possibly coincidental, aspect to the timing of the article, for it followed hard on the heels of an eclectic assortment of other Ripper stories.

On 7th May 1895 the *Pall Mall Gazette* ran the story of William Grant being investigated as the Ripper, together with Inspector Swanson's contradictory belief that the Whitechapel murders were "the work of a man who is now dead"; and in the May 1895 issue of the *Windsor Magazine* Major Arthur Griffiths told of Robert Anderson's "perfectly plausible theory" that "Jack the Ripper was a homicidal maniac, temporarily at large, whose hideous career was cut short by committal to an asylum."

Lees' diary continued—

"On 7th June [1895] we left St. Ives for the second time, thinking that the long stay was surely enough to set me up quite and my people in London were growing very impatient of my return. But again, before we reached home it was very apparent that the heavy air was disastrously telling on me. I was only able to preach once on Sunday and by Monday I was so bad that Sally and the Morgan Payler's begged me to come back at once and they would wind matters up and come after me. So it happened that I came away again on the 12th. And left the great work— as I thought of my life, to be closed up."

The People's League was no more. The 650-seat Central Hall closed its doors, to become by turns over the next century a cinema, refreshment rooms, a rock & roll venue and a nightclub.[268]

But even in St Ives, which is almost as far as you can escape from London without leaving England, Lees did not fully discover the rural idyll he might have imagined, and he closed his diary entry on this period in enigmatic fashion—

"Now I have had six months here, but I am scarcely able to say just where I stand. As a visitor I was welcomed and admired; as a resident, with my undoubted power of speech, and a financial position which no one knows anything about, I am regarded with very mixed feelings. I am a very unknown quantity and that troubles everyone."

A financial position which no one knew anything about? Lees, his wife and fourteen [14] children were neither begging for alms nor beating a path to St. Ives' workhouse door, so the question arises of how he managed to survive, or so quickly recover from, his financial debacles in London on his earnings as a magnetic masseur. And whilst there may have been a perfectly reasonable explanation for his good fortune, it is easy to see how such an ambiguous remark might later have been spun into implying a pension from the privy purse.

Lees and his family did not become isolated from their immediate friends in Cornwall. In June 1895 the Reverend Frederick Payler Morgan-Payler, who had funded the People's League with a £10,000 loan, his wife Julia and nineteen-year-old daughter Charlotte moved into

---

[268]   In the 1895 General Election, held just one month after the closure of the People's Party, there was no Independent Labour Party candidate for Peckham. The seat was held by the Conservative incumbent Frederick George Banbury, later 1st Baron Banbury of Southam, against the Liberal candidate Charles Clements.

"Turville", a house on Draycott Terrace, St. Ives.

Frederick Payler Morgan-Payler was paralysed. He had not walked since 1892. Whilst in London Robert Lees enjoyed little success in healing him and so had recommended St. Ives as a "capital health resort."

However, over the next eighteen months Frederick Payler's health steadily deteriorated until he became too weak to hold even a knife and fork.[269] He died at "Turville" on 6th February 1897 and was buried at Barnoon Cemetery, overlooking Porthmeor Beach, St. Ives.

Julia Morgan-Payler remained in St. Ives, assisting Lees with his ministry until 1900, the year her daughter, Charlotte Julia Rosa Morgan, married Vivian Claud Blyth.[270] In this year the Lees family moved to Plymouth and later into "Craigmore", a 17-room house in Ilfracombe, where Lees' wife Sarah died in 1912, and finally to Leicester where Robert Lees died in 1931. Julia Morgan-Payler died the following year. What happened regarding repayment of her late-husband's £10,000 loan to Lees is not known.

In 1931 the *Daily Express* wrote, "Mr. Lees was received more than once at Buckingham Palace by Queen Victoria who was interested in his psychic powers" and "at the age of nineteen he was summoned before the Queen, where he gave evidence of his powers as a clairvoyant . . ."

In the following year Arthur Findlay O.B.E., accountant, stockbroker and Essex magistrate, together with newspaper columnist Hannen Swaffer and journalist/medium Maurice Barbanell, founded the publication *Psychic News*.

A Royal connection with spiritualism and a psychic solution to the mystery of Jack the Ripper should have proved irresistible grist to the spiritualist mill, but nothing appeared in print of Lees' Royal connections until the 1947 publication of Arthur Findlay's two-volume history of Christianity, "The Curse of Ignorance", published by the Psychic Press and hailed by many reviewers as a masterpiece of its kind.

---

[269]   Inquest report, *The Cornishman*, 11th February 1897.
[270]   Prior to leaving St. Ives, Robert Lees and Julia Morgan-Payler were presented respectively with an engraved silver loving cup and a butter dish from the Fishermen of St. Ives. *The Cornishman*, 15th March 1900.

In Volume Two, having established that scientists were becoming ever more interested in psychic phenomena, Arthur Findlay wrote—

"A fact worthy of mention, and one which is quite unknown to historians, is the interest Queen Victoria took in Spiritualism . . . [her] deep interest began shortly after the death of her husband, the Prince Consort."

Queen Victoria's interest in spiritualism had hitherto been "quite unknown to historians." Here, it appeared, was an historical scoop.

Findlay next told of the mediumistic thirteen-year-old Robert James Lees who, whilst in a trance at home, received a communication from the late Albert, Prince Consort. The message was that Queen Victoria be told that they could make contact through Lees.

Hearing of this, Queen Victoria sent two members of her Court to Lees' home. They did not mention who they were, nor from whom they had come, but Lees had not long been in a trance before the Prince Consort spoke, greeting the two courtiers as his friends and calling them by their correct names.[271]

Arthur Findlay continued—

When her envoys returned to Windsor, Queen Victoria was satisfied that these communications could only have come from her late husband, and she was especially impressed by a letter the boy wrote whilst controlled by the Prince. This was of an intimate nature, and signed in a manner used only by the Prince in letters to the Queen when alive.

This was a phenomenon known as automatic writing, in which the spirit of the deceased takes over the hand of the medium in order to pen a message. In this instance, we are told, the message was packed with intimate details and signed with a pet name used only between Albert and Victoria.

Lady Elizabeth Longford in her biography of Queen Victoria[272]

---

[271]   Reginald Mountstephens Lester, in his 1957 book *Towards the Hereafter*, identified one of these courtiers, or envoys, as Arthur Bigge, later Lord Stamfordham, Private Secretary to Queen Victoria 1895 – 1901. Arthur Bigge was born in 1849, the same year as Lees, and was a boy of 13 at the time of Lees' first communications with the late Prince Albert.

[272]   *Victoria R.I.*, Weidenfeld and Nicolson, London, 1964. Elizabeth Longford's biography

contended that Albert did not use personal endearments. His private letters to Queen Victoria were invariably signed 'Albert' or 'A'.

Arthur Findlay had more revelations in store—

Queen Victoria then sent for Robert James Lees, asking if he would give her a sitting, which he did, and the Prince again spoke through the medium. The Queen then said to her late husband that she wanted Lees to become a permanent fixture at Court so that he would be available at all times, but the Prince objected, saying that he did not wish the boy to be his medium. Albert could speak to her equally well through the son of a gillie on the Balmoral estate. Queen Victoria immediately sent for the gillie, John Brown, who, it is widely rumoured, became the medium through whom she communicated with her late husband.

The John Brown revelation was not exactly breaking news.

Seventy-nine years earlier, in October 1868, *Tinsley's Magazine* published an article by theatrical manager and journalist Stephen Ryder Fisk[273] entitled "English Photographs by an American"—

"Soon after my arrival in England, at a table where all the company were gentlemen by rank and position, there were constant references to and jokes about "Mrs. Brown". Confounding her with Arthur Sketchley's heroine in 'Fun', I lost the point of all the witty sayings, and should have remained in blissful ignorance throughout the dinner had not my host kindly informed me that 'Mrs. Brown' was an English synonym for the Queen . . .

"I have been told that the Queen was not allowed to hold a review in Hyde Park because Lord Derby and the Duke of Cambridge objected to John Brown's presence; that the Prince of Wales took a special train for Osborne to remonstrate with his royal mother when the *Tomahawk's* Brown Study[274] was published; that the Queen was insane, and John

---

is widely acknowledged as the major reference work for those studying the life of Queen Victoria.

[273]   In England, Fisk became manager of the Royal English Opera Company and the St. James's Theatre.

[274]   "Brown Study", the notorious 1867 *Tomahawk* cartoon, depicts John Brown standing between an obedient British lion and the throne.

Brown was her keeper; that the Queen was a spiritualist, and John Brown was her medium—in a word, a hundred stories, each more absurd than the other, and all vouched for by men of considerable station and authority, who ought to have known better than to mystify a poor foreigner upon such a subject."[275]

Ten years later, in September 1878, the *Whitehall Review* asked "Is the Queen a Spiritualist?"

"It is rumoured in circles not likely to be victimised by an absolute canard that among the converts to Spiritualism must be numbered our gracious Sovereign. It is, we believe, a fact that one of Her Majesty's most confidential friends, the late Madame [Elizabeth] Van de Weyer, was a thorough Spiritualist, and held séances at New Lodge, in order to communicate with *quicquid fuit immortale* of her husband. If the Queen was, indeed, ever present at these séances, the idea at once suggests itself that her motive in taking part in a function of this sort would be something more than mere vain curiosity or a morbid search after excitement.

"Like her friend, the Queen has suffered a terrible bereavement, and we can well imagine that the hope of penetrating, if only for a second, behind the veil, and of learning the fate of the illustrious personage with whom her life was linked, may have drawn her unresistingly towards the medium and have converted the séance—associated as it is in most minds with absurdity and trickery—into a solemnity of rare significance."

Fearing the Queen might make spiritualism a fashionable trend amongst "pitiably weak people", the journal *Spirit World* noted with an almost audible sigh of relief that the author of the *Whitehall Review* article had avoided "asserting positively that Her Majesty has, even *sub rosa*, ranged herself on the side of the Spiritualists, or taken an active part in spiritual functions . . . Heaven save us from any but honest converts to our cause."

The *Saratoga* [NY] *Sentinel*, 16th January 1879, reprinted an article

---

[275]   *Tinsley's* editor, Edmund Yates, added, "Without attempting to defend the silly nonsense which was talked on this subject, we think our contributor has taken the matter more *au sérieux* than was intended."

written by Elisha T. Jones for *Independent Age*—

"It has been known for some time that Queen Victoria was in sympathy with modern Spiritualism . . . Some two months ago it was whispered among the knowing ones in Windsor, that Queen Victoria had had spirit manifestations in her home and that in her private reception chamber there was a cabinet[276] made of walnut veneered with mahogany, elegantly lined with silk by Michael De Pon, of Dryde Square.

"On the evening of the sixteenth a séance was held for materializations in this specially prepared chamber . . . Mme. Van der Weyer, the late bosom friend of the Queen appeared [and] was recognized by the Queen . . ."

Spirit World, January 1879, thought the story was hogwash—

"The American Journals publish, on the authority of Elisha T. Jones, a correspondent of the *Independent Age*, a minute account of a materialising séance with the Queen, at Windsor—the cabinet being made of 'walnut veneered with mahogany, elegantly lined with silk by Michael de Pon, of Dryde Square.' Who is Michael de Pon, and where is Dryde Square? The whole account is manifestly a hoax!"

Despite this royal spiritualist activity having generally been considered little more than idle society tittle-tattle, Arthur Findlay pressed on with his narrative—

"Robert James Lees became a highly respected journalist and author of several books, the best known being *Through the Mists*, a record of communications he received from the etheric world. Queen Victoria ordered six specially bound copies, which she presented to members of her family.

"Queen Victoria's relationship with Lees continued throughout her life-time, and shortly before she died she thanked him for all he had done for her.

---

[276] In the mid-1850s William Henry and Ira Erastas Davenport from Buffalo, New York, introduced the spirit cabinet. During a "séance" these cabinets screened the medium from the audience's view whilst they "manifested their spiritual phenomena." Ira Davenport later taught Harry Houdini many of his best routines. Today, Las Vegas illusionists use the same apparatus.

"From time to time she offered him honours, a comfortable annuity for his life-time, and gifts, all of which he refused. He would take nothing, he said, in return for his services."

According to Findlay the Queen never wrote directly to Lees. She always sent her messages by special courier, but she did keep a record of all that took place at her sittings with both John Brown and Robert James Lees.

After John Brown's death in 1883 Queen Victoria wrote a monograph about him. She wanted it published, but her Court Chaplain, Dr. Randall Davidson, and her Private Secretary, Sir Henry Ponsonby, firmly objected, the former threatening to resign his position. Moreover, Ponsonby allegedly seized and destroyed Brown's private diaries. Thus it was that the influence of two Court officials prevented the Queen from publicly attesting to the spiritual comfort she had received through the mediumship of her highland gillie.

The extremely well-informed Arthur Findlay was postulating a cover-up of the highest order, and one to which the Lees family was party.

Findlay closed by saying that Lees never spoke to anyone outside his own family about his times with Queen Victoria, or of her communications with her husband. Consequently only members of his family knew what was happening, and this they kept private.

But by 1947 Lees was dead and the late Sir Henry Ponsonby had long since destroyed John Brown's diaries. So from where or from whom had Arthur Findlay received his information?

In her biography of Queen Victoria, Lady Longford doubted Lees ever served as Queen Victoria's medium, but she did acknowledge rumours of royal séances—

"It was said and still is repeated that he [Ponsonby] had burned the records of Brown's spiritualist séances with Queen Victoria." She then told of a rumour that "these interesting skeletons" may not have been "cremated by Ponsonby after all, but were extant. And there may have been leaks."

According to *Psychic News*, wrote Lady Longford, Lionel Logue, the speech therapist who cured the stammer of King George VI, told

Hannen Swaffer, the well-known journalist, that he had read John Brown's diary at Windsor Castle.

Author J.H. Brennan, retelling the Lees story in his 2013 book "Whisperers: The Secret History of the Spirit World"[277], hitched a ride on the Royal cover-up wagon whilst putting a minor spin on events.

According to his account, George VI happened upon a surviving record of a John Brown séance. He mentioned this to his speech therapist, Lionel Logue, and eventually the story was leaked by the popular British journalist, Hannen Swaffer, who was also a Spiritualist. Brennan also wrote that Swaffer's press revelations failed to make an impression on the public mind, and less still on those historians and biographers dealing with the Victorian period.

This must be regarded as hokum, for there were no press revelations about Queen Victoria and John Brown from Hannen Swaffer, who up until his death in 1962 was hailed by London's *World's Press News* as "more abused, praised, hated and feared than any journalist living." Thriller writer Edgar Wallace used to enjoy poking fun at his belief in spiritualism, whilst H. G. Wells called him "the most dangerous man in London."

Maurice Barbanell of *Psychic News* mentioned nothing of John Brown's diary in his 1959 book "This Is Spiritualism". He wrote that Lionel Logue had contacted Hannen Swaffer to learn if it was possible to obtain evidence that his wife, Myrtle, who died in 1945, had survived in the after-life. Swaffer contacted the deep-trance medium Lilian Bailey, asking if she would come to his flat to give a sitting to "a man in great distress."

Without knowing Logue's identity Lilian Bailey announced, "I don't know why it is, and I scarcely like to tell you, but King George V is here. He asks me to thank you for what you did for his son."

Lady Elizabeth Longford—

"Though Mr. Logue shared Hannen Swaffer's spiritualist beliefs, neither the Royal Archives nor his [King George VI's] private papers contain any confirmation of this [diary] story and it is not in fact credited

---

[277]   Published by Overlook Duckworth, Peter Mayer Publishers, Inc.

by Mr. Logue's family."

So how had the world first received confirmation of a mediumistic relationship between Queen Victoria and John Brown? The story certainly hadn't been leaked by Lionel Logue or Hannen Swaffer to a popular British newspaper; nor had it appeared in even the most ardent of republican-minded American newspapers.

For the answer we must first go back to 6th November 1928 and a letter written to Robert James Lees by Sir Arthur Conan Doyle—

"Dear Mr. Lees,

"I was wondering whether the remarkable story of the late Queen and your psychic experiences could not be put on record—even if it were not publicly used. It seems to me, so far as I understand it, to be a point of great historical interest.

"The general outline as it reached me was that as a young Medium you got a message from Prince A. That you sent it. That two Court Officials came to investigate. That they got messages. That these messages indicated JB as having the same powers as you, and that from then onwards JB did act as medium.

"We are all growing older & it would be good to leave a clear record behind.

"Yours sincerely,

"A. Conan Doyle."[278]

Arthur Findlay wrote—

"Lees never spoke to anyone outside his own family about his times with Queen Victoria."

Doyle's discreet letter therefore tells us there had been a leak from within the Lees family. A rumour about his 19th Century séances with Queen Victoria and her mediumistic relationship with John Brown was circulating amongst the spiritualist set but was not at that time public knowledge. The letter also tells us that, no matter whether true or false, Conan Doyle wanted to believe the rumour.

However, the story remained nothing more than a rumour. Stephen

---

[278] See http://www.rjlees.co.uk/documentary.htm

Butt records that, "Lees received several letters from people wishing to use this story to advance Spiritualism . . . He never confirmed the story; he simply wrote to ask where the information had come from."

Arthur Findlay provided the answer to this question at the end of his section on Lees in "The Curse of Ignorance"—

"The foregoing information was given to the author by his daughter Eva Lees, with permission to incorporate it in this book, and this is the first occasion that all the facts have been made public."

Eva Lees being his source was reconfirmed on 4th June 1948 when Findlay wrote to the *Essex Chronicle* thanking them for their praiseworthy comments about "The Curse of Ignorance". In relating Queen Victoria's discovery that John Brown was a medium, he wrote, "I told how this primarily came about by her getting to know Robert James Lees, a medium in London, and the extraordinary events which followed this acquaintance."

Findlay added, "Everything I said was passed by my informant as correct, and I have now received, from Mr. Lees' daughter, a letter in which she says—

"I have now had time to read the incident in your book, recording my father's connection with Queen Victoria and the Prince Consort after his death. You may like to know that I approve of the way you have quoted what I told you, as nearly as possible as my father gave it to me."

Thus can 1947 be pinpointed as the year in which a detailed account of a mediumistic relationship between Queen Victoria and John Brown first entered the public domain; and we can name the source of the account as Lees' daughter Eva.

In preparation for her biography of Queen Victoria, Lady Elizabeth Longford tested one of Eva Lees' claims Findlay had recorded in "The Curse of Ignorance".

He had written that, "[Lees] wrote several books, of which the best known is *Through the Mists*, it being a record of the communications he believed he had received from the etheric world. Queen Victoria ordered six specially bound copies, which she presented to members of her family."

This latter statement was untrue.

The books, bound in crimson morocco with the royal cipher stamped in gold on the front cover, had not been commissioned by Royal command.[279] The volume shown to Elizabeth Longford by Eva Lees—allegedly a gift from Queen Victoria to her father—was one of a number of copies Lees had bound at his own expense, four of which he sent to members of the Royal household.

In 1931 the *Daily Express* had written—

"Miss Eva Lees, who is still living in the house in Fosse Road, Leicester, where Mr. Lees died, stated definitely that her father received a pension from the Privy Purse for many years. Envelopes from the Privy Purse and certain royal residences were produced as proof, although the letters were withheld on grounds of good taste."

The envelopes shown to the *Daily Express* by Eva Lees had not contained payments from the Privy Purse. Stephen Butt was able to reveal that they contained acknowledgements from the secretaries of the four Royal recipients of Lees' 1898 book—

The Duchess of York, acknowledged from Sandringham, 18th January 1899; Princess Henry of Battenburg, acknowledged from Osborne House, same date; the Princess of Wales, acknowledged by Miss Knollys from Sandringham, 15th January 1899; and Queen Victoria, acknowledged by the Queen's private secretary [by this time Sir Arthur Bigge], from the Privy Purse Office, 23rd January 1899.

Robert James Lees having received a Royal pension now looks decidedly implausible, especially as Arthur Findlay, as informed by Eva Lees, wrote—

"From time to time she [Queen Victoria] offered him [Lees] honours, a comfortable annuity for his life-time, and gifts, all of which he refused. He would take nothing, he said, in return for his services."

On 30th November 1948 P.S. Seward[280] wrote to the Home

---

[279]   Lady Elizabeth Longford noted that all books in the Royal Archives were bound in fine-grain calf, not coarse-grained morocco. Also, the cipher on the cover of Lees' book lacked the diamond point between each word of the Garter motto, *Honi soit qui mal y pense*.

[280]   Member of the Society for Psychical Research. Later President of the Association of

Secretary James Ede, enquiring about the Lees story. The Home Office replied on 29th December 1948—

". . . there is no reference in the records of the Department to the statement said to be left by a medium named Lees and that no such file as you mention appears to exist."

Shortly afterwards Dr. Donald James West, Research Officer to the Society for Psychical Research, interviewed Eva Lees, concluding in his report [281] that her stories "were so unlikely that he felt they were probably hysterical fantasies." Dr. West also noted "that in every curious story related by Miss Lees circumstances conspired ingeniously to make investigation impossible."

He followed up his interview with Eva Lees by writing to the Commissioner of the Metropolitan Police, Sir Harold Scott, regarding Robert Lees and the story of Jack the Ripper being tracked down by a psychic, receiving in reply much the same letter as Mrs Eve Brackenbury and Mr. P.S. Seward—

". . . there is no foundation for the newspaper stories that the murderer was known to the police, and traced through the aid of a medium. I am to add that there is no record of the person named James Lees [sic] to whom you refer in your letter."

Eva Lees died in 1968.

In 1981 the Reverend Allan Barham, a retired Church of England vicar living in Canterbury, Kent, published "Strange to Relate," an account of his years in psychic research, in which he maintained that John Brown was a spiritual medium through whom Queen Victoria communicated with Prince Albert.

What had been the source of his story?

The *Australian Women's Weekly*, 8th April 1981—

"His [Barham's] evidence is a tape recording he made before she died with Eva Lees, daughter of Robert Lees, a famous writer of psychic literature in England in Victoria's time . . . Eva remembered on rare

---

Psychical Research Societies and of the Ghost Club.
[281] *The Identity of Jack the Ripper: An Examination of an Alleged Psychic Solution.* Journal of the Society for Psychical Research, July-August 1949.

occasions a carriage drawing up outside their house and two gentlemen coming to fetch her father. 'We knew where he was going and what he was going for,' she said."

Though many questions remain unanswered, it appears from the evidence at hand that the *Chicago Sunday Times-Herald* and *Daily Express* stories about Lees tracking down the Ripper were completely bogus, based as they had been upon a story from Dr. Forbes Winslow and Lees' own earlier writings.

Whether, at the age of sixteen, Eva Lees had a hand in the 1895 *Chicago Sunday Times-Herald* story is unknown, but it now seems clear that she had not only perpetuated the story of her father's involvement with Jack the Ripper but also fabricated his involvement in Royal séances and the matter of payments for these services from the Privy Purse.

Most egregiously, perhaps, Eva Lees betrayed the spiritualist movement by using her father to falsely substantiate what had only been a rumoured mediumistic relationship between Queen Victoria and John Brown.

Why might Eva Lees have spread such elaborate untruths about her father?

Stephen Butt—

"The reason why Eva was active in writing about her father and talking to journalists at that time was because she was working towards the centenary of her father's birth. In 1948/9 most of the spiritualist press published brief articles about Lees based on a short biography she had sent them. Eva also republished some of her father's books that year as 'centenary editions.'"

So perhaps it was all a matter of commerce over integrity.

Reaction to the Lees story teetered on the non-existent.

Daily Express, 16th March 1931—

"I have read with interest the most extraordinary articles by the late Robert James Lees on the capture of Jack the Ripper . . ."

So began a letter from Robert Clifford Spicer, a uniformed constable aged twenty-two at the time of the Jack the Ripper murders.

". . . I had the pleasure of capturing him, and taking him to

Commercial Street police station, after he had committed two murders.

"On this particular night I had walked my beat backwards [in the opposite direction] and had come to Henage Street, off Brick Lane. About fifty yards on Henage Street is Henage Court. At the bottom of the court was a brick-built dustbin.

"Both Jack and a woman (Rosy) were sitting on this. She had 2s [two shillings] in her hand and she followed me when I took Jack on suspicion. He turned out to be a highly respected doctor and gave a Brixton address.

"His shirt cuffs still had blood on them. Jack had the proverbial bag with him (a brown one) . . .

"I took the man before the inspector, and said that I charged him on suspicion with being Jack the Ripper. There were about eight or nine inspectors in the station at the time – all taking part in the hunt for the criminal.

"Imagine how I felt when I got into trouble for making the arrest! The station inspector asked me what I meant by arresting a man who had proved to be a respectable doctor.

"'What is a respectable doctor doing with a notorious woman at a quarter to two in the morning?' I asked, but no one would listen to me. The man was released, and that, as far as I was concerned, was an end to the matter.

"Mr. Spicer is now sixty-four years of age. He left the police force five months after the suspect had been released, and he has worked until recently as the groundsman of a school sports ground.

"'I was so disappointed when the man was allowed to go that I no longer had my heart in police work,' he said. 'The case was taken out of my hands by the detective branch, but I am sure I would have been able to prove my suspicions if the matter had been left to me.'"

Spicer gave the impression he had resigned from the Metropolitan Police due to his intuition being questioned, whereas on 25th April 1889 he was dismissed for unknown reasons, but with his conduct rated "[3]"—Good.[282]

---

[282]   MEPO 4/339

Spicer's contradictory story is undoubtedly an invention. Its chronology puts the Henage Court arrest after Jack "had committed two murders" [between the 8th and 30th September 1888], but dates the doctor's release from police custody "the same morning" as having taken place in November 1888.

Here was yet another example of no two pieces of the Ripper puzzle fitting together.

12. THE BLACK JAPANNED BOX

"The Trial of George Chapman" by Hargrave Lee Adam, a volume in the "Notable British Trials" series from William Hodge & Co., was published in 1930.

Of interest is the introduction, in which the author set out a case for Chapman having been Jack the Ripper—

"Several prominent officials have from time to time asserted that they had established his identity. The late Sir Melville Macnaghten, the late Sir Robert Anderson, Sir Henry Smith, and many others of less importance have assured us regarding this. Sir Melville Macnaghten even went so far as to declare that he had once possessed documentary proof of the identity of the criminal, but that he had burnt the papers. An unprecedented thing, surely, for a police official to do!

"These declarations, as mere declarations without evidence to support them, are unsatisfactory. It is quite certain that nobody ever did know for certain who Jack-the-Ripper was.

"It is now proposed to present the case for supposing—one cannot put it in stronger terms—that George Chapman, or Severin Klosowski, was actually Jack-the-Ripper."

There followed a chronological table which paralleled the activities of Jack the Ripper and those of George Chapman.

"Chief Inspector Abberline, who had charge of the investigations

270

into the East End murders, thought that Chapman and Jack-the-Ripper were one and the same person . . . Both Inspector Abberline and Inspector Godley spent years in investigating the 'Ripper' murders. Abberline never wavered in his firm conviction that Chapman and Jack-the-Ripper were one and the same person. When Godley arrested Chapman, Abberline said to his confrere 'You've got Jack-the-Ripper at last!' . . ."

There is nothing to substantiate this apocryphal story.

"That Chapman's career coincides exactly with the movements and operations of Jack-the-Ripper must appeal strongly to all who endeavour to throw light upon the shadows of the latter's obscurity. The whole of Chapman's life cannot be made quite clear. At his trial the prosecution proved that he murdered Mrs. Spink, Bessie Taylor, and Maud Marsh; but as they made no effort to discover others no one can say, with confidence, how many murders he committed. A reasonable case for supposing that Chapman was Jack-the-Ripper has, at least, been furnished. At that the subject must be left, without material proof of the connection. Upon that strange period of Chapman's career, when he worked and lodged in Whitechapel, no new light can be shed, and the identity of Jack-the-Ripper will for ever remain a mystery."

The puzzling thing about Hargrave Lee Adam's interest in George Chapman as Jack the Ripper twenty-seven years after his 1903 execution was his neglect to have mentioned a word of his suspicions in a 1912 newspaper serial "Scotland Yard and its Secrets" and a subsequent book.

Perhaps after all this time the 63-year-old author felt the inclusion of Jack the Ripper might help sell an otherwise run-of-the-mill book.

Also in 1930 came "Detective Days"[283] by Frederick Porter Wensley, who joined the Metropolitan Police in 1888, was appointed to the CID in 1895, became Chief Constable in 1924 and retired in 1929.

Wensley had a refreshing take on his involvement with the Whitechapel murders investigation—

"Not that I had much to do with it," he wrote. "In common with

---

[283]   It was published in America, 1933, under the title *Forty Years of Scotland Yard*.

hundreds of others I was drafted there [from L Division, Lambeth], and we patrolled the streets—usually in pairs—without any tangible result. We did, however, rather anticipate a great commercial invention. To our clumsy regulation boots we nailed strips of rubber, usually bits of old bicycle tyres, and so ensured some measure of silence when walking.

"Officially, only five (with a possible sixth) murders were attributed to Jack the Ripper. There was, however, at least one other, strikingly similar in method, in which the murderer had a very narrow escape. This occurred something more than two years after the supposed last Ripper murder."

Frederick Porter Wensley did not subscribe to any particular Ripper theory. He concluded his Whitechapel involvement by briefly detailing the story of PC Ernest Thompson's 1891 discovery of Frances Coles in Swallow Gardens, after which he moved on to the rest of his career.

This most capable and respected police officer, who had been awarded the King's Police Medal in 1910 and finally rose to the rank of Chief Constable, died aged eighty-four on 4th December 1949.

The *Aberdeen Journal*, 5th December 1949, awarded Wensley the ultimate posthumous accolade—

"It is said he was the only living person who knew the identity of Jack the Ripper."

Gettysburg Times [Pennsylvania], 1st April 1933—

"The favorite haunt of mystery fans may now be investigated at first hand in a book by Arthur Fowler Neil—who should know Scotland Yard if anyone does. For years he was superintendent of the criminal investigations department and naturally his 'Man-Hunters of Scotland Yard' [284] deals with that phase of the organization's work.

"Those who like to exhume ancient sensations will be interested to know that Mr. Neil has a new solution for the Jack the Ripper murders in England and the United States."

Jack was now a transatlantic killer.

Arthur Fowler Neil joined the Metropolitan Police in May 1888. A

---

[284]   UK title: *Forty Years of Man-Hunting*.

Detective Sergeant, M Division [Southwark] in 1903, he testified at the Old Bailey to having searched the marriage registers at Somerset House looking for the wedding of George Chapman and Mary Isabella Spink; also of George Chapman and Bessie Taylor.

Brooklyn Daily Eagle, 2nd April 1933—

"Superintendent Neil begins his book with the question: 'Who was Jack the Ripper?' He admits he cannot prove it, but he is certain that Jack was none other than the Borough Poisoner, one Severino Klosowski alias George Chapman.

There followed nothing which Hargrave Lee Adam had not included in his earlier book, and so Neil could not provide anything to further endorse what appear to have been the solitary suspicions of Chief Inspector Abberline.

Secret documents, confessions and mysterious sealed packets had long been staple ingredients of Ripper lore, and in "Crime and the Supernatural," published in 1935, Edwin Thomas Woodhall, ex-policeman, secret service agent and royal bodyguard, saw no reason to meddle with a winning formula. His chapter on the Whitechapel murders opened with this intriguing paragraph—

"In a blacked japanned box somewhere in the archives of the British Home Office are confidential papers concerning the identity of the most mysterious and spectacular murders of the last hundred years Jack the Ripper."

All too soon the story became strangely familiar.

Woodhall claimed that Jack the Ripper, tracked down by clairvoyant Robert James Lees, proved to be a physician of high standing with a dual personality who lived in a select part of London's West End. Once his identity had been established all those in the know were sworn to secrecy and the matter hushed up.

Of the Lees story, which Woodhall lifted wholesale from the *Daily Express*, he wrote "I have no actual proof of its truth, but during my years at the Yard it was more than once recounted to me as I have related it, and I have not the slightest doubt that it is true, and that psychic science, even 45 years ago, was enabled to step in where police work had lamentably failed."

To a Canadian reviewer at the time the book sounded "like a story of Edgar Wallace", which is perhaps understandable. Woodhall, two-years-old at the time of the Ripper murders, did not join the Metropolitan Police until 1906.

13. CHRONICLES OF CRIME

On 8th November 1935 Dr. Thomas Dutton, who in 1929 stated his belief that Jack the Ripper was a ship's butcher, died a lonely and undignified death.

Nottingham Evening Post, Tuesday 12th November 1935—

"Doctor-Recluse's Death.

"Mysterious Life in Poor Home.

"Link with 'Jack the Ripper Days'.

"A brilliant doctor, and one-time Harley-street specialist, has been found dead, surrounded by signs of abject poverty.

"He was Dr. Thomas Dutton, 80, who, for years, had lived the life of a recluse in Uxbridge Road, Shepherd's Bush.

"His body lay for several days before discovery.

"The police are inquiring into the doctor's mysterious life in his poor home.

"Dr. Dutton, it is stated, practised in Whitechapel at the time of the Jack the Ripper crimes, on which he had many theories.

"He had many degrees, was a specialist in certain diseases, and wrote several medical books. He gained prominence when he bitterly opposed the panel system on the introduction of Health Insurance.

"When the police were summoned they found the house covered with cobwebs and dust, and the surgery appeared as if it had not been used for years.

"It is believed that the doctor had a sister living in Hastings and another relative at Hampstead."

The *Daily Express*, Tuesday 12th November, provided extra detail—

"West End Specialist Dies In Poverty. Police Visit Surgery.

"Detectives visited a surgery in Uxbridge Road, Shepherd's Bush, W., last night and took away documents belonging to seventy-nine-year-old Dr. Thomas Dutton, who was found dead beside his bed during the weekend.

"The doctor lived the life of a semi-recluse.

"He was a specialist in obesity, practising at New Cavendish Street, W., and was famed throughout the world as a dietician . . . Dr. Dutton rarely received patients.

"He used his New Cavendish Street consulting room every Tuesday and Friday, chiefly for writing articles on dietetics.

"Police inquiries last night were directed to the visit to the surgery by a woman living in the West End. The doctor gave prescriptions to her.

"When the coroner's officer called at the house in Shepherd's Bush he found the doctor's apartments in a state of great confusion.

"The furniture was covered in dust and cobwebs. The officer took away a number of articles, including a fully-loaded revolver. It was rusty and had obviously not been used for many years.

"When Dr. Dutton was a young man he inherited valuable estates, but realised them and went through a large fortune.

"When found dead Dr. Dutton had only £2 in his possession. No cheque book or bank pass book has been found. He was behind with his rent.

"Among thousands of papers in cupboards and strewn about the surgery and his bedroom were bookmakers' accounts for large amounts, letters and accounts with stockbrokers, and a number of old summonses.

"Dr. Dutton held many degrees, was a Fellow of the Hunterian Society[285] and a former vice-chairman of the Pure Food Society."

Daily Express, 13th November 1935, developed the story—

"A diary has been found that he kept faithfully for more than fifty years."

---

[285]   Founded in 1819 to honour the Scottish surgeon John Hunter (1728–1793).

The diary, which may have been part of the documentation taken away by the police, recounted Dutton's days as a keen racegoer and student of crime, and in its pages mentioned such royal, business, social and criminal luminaries as the Duke of Clarence [who, reportedly, was Dutton's friend], Sir Robert Perks, whose company built the Manchester Ship Canal,[286] Lady Vera Cathcart, the British peeress turned cause célèbre turned playwright, and Alma Rattenbury, who, in Bournemouth, March 1935, together with her 18 year-old chauffeur and lover, George Stoner, were charged with the brutal murder of her husband.

The *Daily Express* article concluded—

"No inquest is considered necessary, but the police are trying to trace a woman whose name appears in his prescription book as one of his few patients.

"It is thought she may be able to help the police in certain formal inquiries. She is not known at the address she gave to the doctor."

Could there have been another connection between Dr. Thomas Dutton and his surgery at Shepherd's Bush?

In the *American Journal of Nursing*, Volume 17, No. 4, January 1917, receipt was acknowledged of a new book, "Every Mother's Book and Young Wife's Guide", by Thomas Dutton, M.D., University of Durham."

Amongst his accreditations was "Member of the Royal College of Physicians, Edinburgh; and Honorary Physician, *Uxbridge Road Auto-Natal and Infant Consultations Clinic*."

Auto-natal has no medical definition, but the 1916 "Child Welfare Annual" contained the following entry—

"Uxbridge Road Infant Consultations & Ante-natal Clinic, Loftus Precinct, 290 Uxbridge Road. Hon. Medical Officer: Dr. Thomas Dutton, 25 New Cavendish Street, W."[287]

Dutton's surgery and home were at the same address.

---

[286] One of the Directors of the Manchester Ship Canal Company was James Monro's predecessor, once known as Britain's "Spymaster-General", Edward George Jenkinson.

[287] Loftus Precinct was a parade of shopfronts, each with a separate side entrance to the house immediately behind. 290 Uxbridge Road is on the corner of Loftus Road. Dutton's house is still there.

The *West London Observer*, 15th November 1935, reported that—

"The discovery was made by Mr. Willis, a sub-tenant of the doctor's house.

"Miss H. Dutton, of Cornwall Road, Westbourne Park, a sister of the doctor, called at the house as she had heard her brother was ill. Mr. Willis told her he had not seen the old man for several days, and on going to his rooms found him dead.

"Dr. J. Dockrill, of Uxbridge Road, was called in and found the man had been dead about 20 hours . . . death was due to heart disease [and] he saw his last patient at Shepherd's Bush on November 5th."

On Dr. Dutton's Death Certificate, registered 12th November 1935, in the column headed 'Signature, Description and Residence of Informant' was entered "B.A. Dutton, Sister, 57 Cornwall Road, Westbourne Park W. 11."

Dr. Dutton had two younger sisters—Helena [age 66] and Barbara Ada [age 68]—so it is possible that Helena was present at the discovery of her brother's body and Barbara Ada later supplied details to the Coroner and Registrar.

Aside from the police removing documents, Dr. Dutton's death appeared to be a relatively straightforward matter. And so far, aside from a reference to his early days in Whitechapel, there had been no mention of Jack the Ripper.

However, this all changed when the *Sunday Chronicle* managed to locate one of Dutton's few patients.

Sunday Chronicle, 17th November 1935—

"Secret Diary Revelations of Dead Doctor.

"He Knew Jack the Ripper.

"'Sunday Chronicle' Special Correspondent.

"I know Jack the Ripper. I know why he committed the Whitechapel Murders."

The secret diary trope was alive and well.

"This dramatic revelation in a secret diary of Dr. Thomas Dutton, the eighty-year-old specialist who was found dead at his house in Shepherd's Bush last week, was disclosed to me yesterday by a woman who for years had been one of his few patients.

"Miss Hermione Dudley, friend and patient of the doctor, told me the story of his 'passionate interest in crime' when I called on her at a Bayswater boarding house."

Hermione Dudley knew the doctor when she was quite a young girl. "He was then at the height of his fame—an excellent doctor, a brilliant specialist, and an authority on all manner of diseases. But it was as a criminologist that he revealed most of his outstanding genius."

Hermione Dudley had no doubts about Dr. Dutton's criminological skills. "By far the most interesting document he compiled was his *Chronicles of Crime*, three volumes of handwritten comments on all the chief crimes of the past sixty years."

How had this friend and patient of Dr. Dutton learned about the three-volume *Chronicles of Crime*?

Hermione Dudley explained—

"My father was one of the few men to whom he showed this document, and owing to my interest in it, Dr. Dutton gave it to me some time ago."

Hermione Dudley did not show this three-volume document to the *Sunday Chronicle* reporter—

"Miss Dudley described to me some of the remarkable entries in these crime diaries. In the first volume there are several pages devoted to the notorious Whitechapel murderer—the series of maniacal murders of women during the autumn of 1888."

"I am certain," continued Miss Dudley, "that the doctor assisted with the post mortems on the 'Jack the Ripper' victims. His diary makes this quite clear. Often, he told me, and he repeats it in his diary—that he knew the identity of 'Jack the Ripper'."

There should now have followed a startling revelation, but her story proved to have an all too familiar ring about it. And here it is worth recalling that in 1929 Dutton had written to the *Daily Mail* expressing his opinion that the murders were committed by a ship's butcher.

"He described him," Hermione Dudley continued, "as a middle aged doctor, a man whose mind had become embittered by the death of his son. The latter had suffered cruelly at the hands of a woman of the streets and the father believed this to be the cause of the brilliant son's death.

"For months after his son's death," Miss Dudley continued, "the father roamed the streets of the East End, where he had been told this particular woman was to be found.

"Dr. Dutton did his best to persuade his colleague that the nature of his son's death was best forgotten, but for a while this embittered man disappeared completely."

She added, "I understand from Dr. Dutton that in the course of a post mortem examination on a 'Ripper' victim he formed his own conclusion as to who committed the murder."

There is nothing on record to suggest that Dr. Dutton was involved in a post mortem on any of the 'Ripper' victims. All that is known about his career between 1885 and 1890 is that he was "London Consulting Physician to the Mont Doré Company (Limited), Newton Dale."[288]

The *Empire News*, 17th November 1935, took up the story of Dr. Dutton—

"The author . . . was for years the hon. Physician to a maternity and child welfare clinic in Uxbridge Road where he died, and his last book was called 'Every Mother's Book.'[289]

". . . He had died in abject poverty after being one of the best-known specialists of the day and numbering among his patients many of the most famous men and women of the past forty years."

"Such was the man who, as a young doctor, started out his career in the East End of London at a time when 'Jack the Ripper' was causing a thrill of horror to pass throughout the world.

"Like every other person in the district he had taken a keen interest in the efforts of the police and public in endeavouring to round up the murderer and had been quietly making inquiries among his women patients, many of whom were of the class who had been selected by the

---

[288] *Hospital Gazette and Students Journal*, 25th July 1885. The Mont Doré Company, based in France, built grandiose health spa hotels. The first, in Bournemouth, 1881, was sold in 1886 and re-opened as the Mont Doré Hotel, and today is Bournemouth's Town Hall.

[289] *Every Mother's Book and Young Wife's Guide*, pub. H. Kimpton 1915

'Ripper' for his victims. Dr. Dutton . . . had specialised in the study of women's diseases . . ."

There was no mention here of Dr. Dutton's diaries.

Gathering together all the various strands in these newspaper articles we have a doctor who specialised in the study of women's diseases; a doctor who, amongst his patients, boasted many of the most famous men and women of the past forty years; a doctor who had treated many of the class from whom Jack the Ripper had selected his victims; a doctor who was in Whitechapel at the time of the Ripper murders, and a doctor who was a friend of the Duke of Clarence.

Here was a recipe ripe for exploitation. But all the Allied Newspaper group [owners of the *Sunday Chronicle* and the *Empire News*] could manage was a tepid rehash of Leonard Matters' 1929 story about Dr. Stanley, which itself was a rehash from a turn-of-the-century American newspaper article written by John T. Sullivan.

Perhaps the conceit of this story lay in the fact that Dutton's Chronicles of Crime made their one and only appearance in the *Sunday Chronicle*.[290]

The story fizzled out, yet to this day there is still heated debate as to whether or not Dutton's diary and/or his three-volume *Chronicles of Crime* existed. If this seems incredible, it is well to remember that in the field of Ripper studies no story, myth or theory ever gets discarded; for, as we shall later see, almost a quarter of a century later Dr. Thomas Dutton's *Chronicles of Crime* reappeared, all dressed up in a brand new suit of clothes.

In 1936 Edwin T. Woodhall published "Secrets of Scotland Yard", which did not mention the Whitechapel murders. However, blithely ignoring the story of Dr. Dutton or his own earlier theory about the spiritualist Robert James Lees, in 1937 Woodhall returned to the fray, publishing "Jack the Ripper; or, When London Walked in Terror."

This loose assemblage of facts and imaginative fiction revealed Jack

---

[290]   In 1895 the Beaver Publishing Company of Toronto published a series of cheap books called *Chronicles of Crime and Criminals*. The first in the series covered the Whitechapel murders and the murder of Harriet Lane.

the Ripper to have been a Russian woman, Olga Tchkersoff, avenging the death of her sister for reasons which need not detain us.

In the following year, 1938, retired Chief Inspector Walter Dew, then aged 75, published his memoirs "I Caught Crippen" in which he devoted 25,000 words to his personal involvement as a young H Division detective constable during the Whitechapel murders investigation. How much of his involvement was actual has never been firmly established, but, personal anecdotes aside, for the first time in a long time readers were presented with a clear, concise and mainly factual account of the Whitechapel murders, of which he believed Millers Court to have been the last.

No Russians, West End physicians, drowned doctors or caged lunatics for Walter Dew—

"I was on the spot, actively engaged throughout the whole series of crimes. I ought to know something about it. Yet I have to confess I am as mystified now as I was then by the man's amazing elusiveness."

William Douglas Stewart was five years old at the time of the Whitechapel murders. By turns an advertising director, cartoonist, short story writer and theatrical scenic designer, he developed a keen interest in Jack the Ripper, took photographs of the extant murder locations and formulated a theory. In 1939 he published "Jack the Ripper: A New Theory", based on the old idea that "Jack" was "Jill", but this time a midwife[291] seeking revenge on those of her clientele who had exposed her to the police as an abortionist.

Plans to turn William Stewart's book into a movie were halted by the ambitions of Adolph Hitler, a set-back that was apparently no great loss to the British film industry, for in 1994 the late historian and author Philip Sugden dismissed William Stewart and his book in no uncertain terms—

"He was an uncaring fictioneer and his book is one of the worst ever written on the subject. Even inquest testimony is reported wrongly.

---

[291]   First suggested in a letter signed "J.O." to the Evening News, 16th October 1888.

Sometimes he invents witnesses as well as testimony."[292]

Thus on the eve of the Second World War, fifty-one years after Jack the Ripper's brief reign of terror in the East End, all the major players in the police investigation had died, nobody was in possession of any facts, and the subject had been appropriated by fraudsters, charlatans, liars and opportunists, leaving the public not in the least bit wiser about the murderer's identity.

Although it would be another twenty years before there was a revival of interest in the identity of Jack the Ripper, this unfortunate trend would persist.

---

[292]   *The Complete History of Jack the Ripper*, Carroll and Graf, 2002, p 11.

14. THE WAVE OF TERROR

1959 saw the publication of Donald McCormick's compellingly written but utterly worthless "The Identity of Jack the Ripper", in which he put a spin on William Le Queux's 1923 story of Dr. Alexander Pedachenko, sent to England by the Russian secret police to commit the Whitechapel murders in order to discredit the Metropolitan Police.

According to McCormick, Alexander Pedachenko, alias Vassily Konovalov, [whose personal history bore an uncanny resemblance to the fictional Nicholas Vassily or Vasilev, known in Paris as the 'Sauveur des âmes perdues' (Saviour of Lost Souls)], was apparently a Russian feldscher[293] suspected of having killed and mutilated a *grisette*[294] in Montmartre. He escaped arrest, came to London, and the rest, as they say, is history.

Donald McCormick further confounded matters by citing as his main source, not the manuscript dictated by Grigori Rasputin but the three-volume *Chronicles of Crime* allegedly penned by Dr. Thomas Dutton.

Donald McCormick had certainly done his homework, for in a letter dated 15th May 1995 in reply to questions from researchers about the elusive *Chronicles of Crime*, he wrote that as a journalist he had reported Dutton's death in the press, that between 1935 and 1938 he had run a news agency and was certain "my story" had been published in the *Sunday Chronicle*. He went on to narrow the dates— "I should say the

---

[293]   Russian feldsher, from German Feldscher, Feldscherer field surgeon, from Feld=field + Scherer=barber, surgeon.

[294]   Part-time prostitute

actual date was between September 1935 and December 1936.

McCormick's logic appeared to be that the *Chronicles of Crime* were a fact because he had originally reported their existence. He also wrote that "in some way Hermione Dudley has confirmed my story, but I cannot recollect any more details and, as I have told you, all my records are now gone."

But just like William Le Queux, McCormick remained light on his feet and unfailingly inventive. In a later edition of his book he wrote—

"He [Dutton] allowed me to take notes from them [the *Chronicles of Crime*] as long ago as 1932 . . . By a lucky chance my notes were safely tucked away, forgotten and then discovered after World War II."

Serendipitous indeed.

In repackaging William Le Queux's story Donald McCormick had forgotten [or simply wasn't aware] that in 1929 Dr. Thomas Dutton had placed on record his belief that Jack the Ripper was a ship's butcher. Also, if Donald McCormick was the *Sunday Chronicle's* "special correspondent", in 1935 there would have been no need for him to track down Hermione Dudley in order to detail "some of the remarkable entries in these crime diaries" when three years earlier he had read them for himself.

McCormick neatly countered Hermione Dudley's original account of the Ripper being "a middle-aged doctor whose mind had become embittered by the death of his son"—

"The story referred to the doctor's 'three volumes of handwritten comments on all the great crimes of the past sixty years', but the patient (Miss Hermione Dudley) did not reveal the name of the killer. Indeed it is doubtful whether she knew very much more than Dutton's claim to have established the identity of the 'Ripper', for her subsequent story (given in an interview) resembled very much the theory of Leonard Matters. Possibly she had read Mr. Matters' book and confused his version with that of Dutton."

This is an odd conclusion to draw, for, according to McCormick, Dr. Dutton first mentioned Pedachenko in his diary for 1924, five years before he wrote to the *Daily Mail* with his ship's butcher theory.

McCormick also tells us that Dutton later revealed in his diaries his Russian Ripper's motive for committing the Whitechapel murders—

"This surgeon, whose name was Konovalov, was said to have had a violent hatred of prostitutes due to a relative of his having suffered cruelly from contact with a woman of the streets. The description of Konovalov exactly fits that of Pedachenko . . ."

Here was yet another iteration of the 'revenge for a disease caught from a prostitute' theory first advanced in October 1888 by Colonel Francis Hughes-Hallett, and it is hard to believe that Hermione Dudley confused these decidedly Slavic names with that of the veddy British-sounding Dr. Stanley.

McCormick was redacting all references from the *Sunday Chronicle* story which flew in the face of his Pedachenko theory. All he wanted to salvage was the basic concept of the elusive Chronicles of Crime so that he could insert his own narrative upon its pages. As an instance, he neglected to mention that Hermione Dudley told the *Sunday Chronicle* that her "middle-aged doctor" had been a colleague of Dr. Dutton—

"Dr. Dutton did his best to persuade his colleague that the nature of his son's death was best forgotten, but for a while this embittered man disappeared completely."

So who was telling the truth about Dr. Dutton's diaries? Hermione Dudley in the *Sunday Chronicle* with her vague rendition of Leonard Matters 1929 theory, or Donald McCormick with his post-WWII spin on William Le Queux's 1924 theory?

The answer is probably neither.

Donald McCormick died in 1998. Thus we shall never learn the true extent, if any, of his involvement in the *Sunday Chronicle* story and of his earlier dealings with Dr. Dutton. And as for Hermione Dudley, it should not come as a big surprise to learn that every effort by some of the world's most tireless researchers in this field has failed to locate this mysterious woman.

She appears to have been an invention, a narrative device for dispensing the content of Dr. Dutton's non-existent *Chronicles of Crime* in what was nothing more than an opportunistic 400-word column-filler for the *Sunday Chronicle*.

McCormick's book was a cornucopia of wild invention, including a dialogue between Dr. Dutton and Inspector Abberline, the latter advancing the idea that Jack the Ripper may have been Jill the Ripper and Dutton replying that, if so, she must have been a midwife. To prop up this misleading narrative Donald McCormick had to fall on back on citing parts of William Stewart's equally worthless 1939 book "Jack the Ripper: A New Theory."

Make anything you want of Donald McCormick's book except the truth.

Of greater interest that year was "Farson's Guide to the British", two series of Associated-Rediffusion TV documentaries [1959–1960] which looked at Britain's struggle to find a post-WWII relevance. During the first series writer and reporter Daniel Farson appealed for information about Jack the Ripper, and the first two episodes of the second series, broadcast on November 5th and 12th 1959, entitled *The British As Murderers*, were subtitled *Jack the Ripper, Part 1: The Wave of Terror*, and *Jack the Ripper, Part 2: The Curious Incident at the Tombstone*.

This was the first time the Ripper had been discussed on a nation-wide scale, and the programmes revived interest in the subject by introducing to the world the hitherto publicly unknown Macnaghten Memorandum.

In his 1972 book *Jack the Ripper*, Dan Farson [great nephew of Bram Stoker, author of *Dracula*] explained the circumstances behind his earlier Jack the Ripper TV programmes—

"In 1959 I became part of the Ripper story. This happened by accident. I was staying with Lady Rose MacLaren in North Wales and mentioned the television programmes I was preparing on the Ripper.

"That's an extraordinary coincidence, she said, and explained that we were going to visit her mother-in-law, the Dowager Lady Aberconway, that same afternoon. A few hours later at Maenan Hall, I explained my interest to Christabel Aberconway and she was kind enough to give me her father's private notes which she had copied out soon after his death [1921]. At the time I hardly realised the discovery that lay in my hands, for her father, Sir Melville Macnaghten, had been in charge of the CID after the last Ripper murder and it had been his task to complete the file on the murderer. Because the official Scotland Yard files will not be open to the public until 1992, no one has known the name of the man whom the police suspected. Now, for the first time, this name lay in my hands.

"I finished my television programmes. At Lady Aberconway's request I gave the suspect's initials only: M.J.D. Since then my discovery has been the basis for various investigations and publications and the full name has been revealed."

In 1960 Colin Wilson, a novelist and philosopher who also wrote widely on true crime, published a series of articles in the London *Evening Standard* entitled "My Search for Jack the Ripper."

As a result he was invited to lunch by Dr. Thomas Stowell, a retired surgeon then aged 75, who related his own theory about the identity of Jack the Ripper. It was Queen Victoria's grandson—heir to the throne—the Duke of Clarence, who had died in 1892. Dr. Stowell had seen the private papers of Sir William Gull, Physician-in-Ordinary to Queen Victoria, "who had dropped mysterious hints about Clarence and Jack the Ripper, as well has mentioning that Clarence had syphilis, from which he died."[295]

Colin Wilson asked if he could write about this theory, but Stowell said no. "It might upset Her Majesty."

One problem with this story is that Sir William Gull died two years before Clarence, so Stowell could not have learned from the doctor's private papers about syphilis being the cause of the Duke's death.[296]

Two years later in a biography of Edward VII, French author Philippe Jullian wrote—

"Clarence was a great anxiety to his family . . . on one occasion the police discovered [him] in a *maison de recontre* of a particularly equivocal

[295] The Mammoth Encyclopedia of the Unsolved, Colin Wilson and Damon Wilson, 2000.
[296] The Duke of Clarence reportedly died of influenza.

nature during a raid . . . The young man's evil reputation soon spread. The rumour gained ground that he was Jack the Ripper (others attributed the crimes committed in Whitechapel to the Duke of Bedford)."

Ripper author Stewart Evans undertook a smart piece of detection and figured out how Dr. Stowell's Clarence story crossed the channel to gain credence as part of an authoritative biography.

Evans noted that in contributing to an introduction in "Jack the Ripper A Bibliography and Review of the Literature" by Alexander Kelly, 1973, Colin Wilson had related the 1960 Stowell story, adding—

"I told Sir Harold Nicolson[297] about it on the evening of the day I lunched with Stowell; it would be interesting to find out whether he recorded it in his journal."

Evans further noted that in the acknowledgments to his 1962 Edward VII biography Philippe Jullian had written, "In England it is to Sir Harold Nicolson, for allowing me to delve into his works and for telling me a number of hitherto unpublished anecdotes, that I am most indebted."

The shortest distance between two points is always a straight line.

In 1965, six years after Dan Farson's groundbreaking television documentary, the public finally learned the meaning of the initials M.J.D. when Tom Cullen, an American journalist living in London, published "Autumn of Terror", in which he set out a case for Melville Macnaghten's suspect of choice, Montague John Druitt.

Tom Cullen had managed to source Lady Aberconway's undated version of her father's memorandum, but was later trumped when author Robin Odell published "Jack the Ripper in Fact and Fiction" in which he argued for the Ripper being a Jewish *schochet* or slaughterman. Odell became the first author to examine the 1894 "Macnaghten Report" contained in the Scotland Yard files.

---

[297]   English diplomat, author, diarist and politician [1886 – 1968].

He explained to me the circumstances of his discovery—

"I had access to this document in, I think, 1965, when Joe Gaute,[298] using one of his contacts at Scotland Yard, brought home several box files containing Ripper material to be perused over the weekend and returned without fail on the Monday morning."

The discovery of the Macnaghten Report came too late for inclusion in the first edition of Robin's book, so first appeared in the subsequent 1967 *Mayflower* paperback edition.

Intelligently written and well researched, the books of Tom Cullen and Robin Odell are today still considered milestones in the study of the Whitechapel murders.

In the following year Colin Wilson let the Royal cat out of the bag whilst pouring cold water on the unnamed Stowell's theory.

Vancouver Sun, 30th January 1968—

"Wilson said Saturday in an interview a London brain surgeon told him in 1960 the notorious killer was the Duke of Clarence, grandson of Queen Victoria.

"Wilson said he has kept the new theory under wraps for seven years because the surgeon, whom Wilson refused to name, asked him not to make it public."

"Wilson, currently a writer in residence at Simon Fraser University in Burnaby, did not make clear why he was disclosing it at this time.

"He personally believes a man named John Montague Druitt was the Ripper.

"'I don't think the surgeon's report is true,' he added. 'I look upon it as a humorous anecdote.'"

"Nevertheless, Wilson had some evidence to offer in support of the theory.

"Wilson said the Duke was known to have figured in a scandal involving alleged activities in a brothel.

"And he said a 'medium' named Lees, with whom Queen Victoria consulted, once identified the Ripper as a member of the Royal Family."

---

[298] Joseph Hatchell Hogarth Gaute, crime historian, author and publisher.

Colin Wilson was peddling poppycock. Nothing could have been further from the truth. As has been shown, the 1895 and 1931 versions of the fictional Lees story both identified the Ripper as a West End doctor.

Two years later an article appeared in *The Criminologist*, a magazine edited by Nigel Morland, entitled "Jack the Ripper—A Solution?"

The author was the now eighty-five-year-old Doctor Thomas Stowell.

He named his suspect "S.", describing him as an "heir to power and wealth" which the press eagerly took to mean a member of the Royal Family, namely Queen Victoria's grandson Prince Albert Victor, Duke of Clarence and Avondale.

Stowell denied his suspect was the Duke of Clarence, but died, overwhelmed by press reaction to his article, the day before his letter to this effect appeared on 9th November 1970 in *The Times*—

"I have at no time associated His Royal Highness, the late Duke of Clarence, with the Whitechapel murderer or suggested that the murderer was of royal blood.

"It remains my opinion that he was a scion of a noble family.

"The particulars given in *The Times* of November 4 of the activities of His Royal Highness[299] in no way conflict with my views as to the identity of Jack the Ripper.

"Yours faithfully, a loyalist and a Royalist, Thomas E. A. Stowell."

Despite Stowell's protestations, the die was cast. Forget midwives, Russians, society physicians, insane Polish Jews and drowned doctors.

A new cast of characters was about to tread the boards in Ripperland.

---

[299]   *The Times* published details from Court Circulars showing where the Duke of Clarence had been on the various murder dates.

15. SECRET CEREMONY

On 13th July 1973 BBC Television broadcast the first episode of "Jack the Ripper", a six-part docudrama scripted by Elwyn Jones and John Lloyd in which the popular fictional TV detective duo of DCS Charlie Barlow and DCS John Watt[300] retrospectively investigated the Whitechapel murders.

The final episode on 17th August 1973 entitled "The Highest in the Land?" featured the story of Joseph "Hobo" Sickert—who claimed to be the illegitimate son of the artist Walter Sickert—which alleged that the Prime Minister, Lord Salisbury, conspired with Queen Victoria and various Freemasons, including senior Scotland Yard officers, to murder a number of women who had knowledge of an illegitimate Catholic heir to the British throne sired by Prince Albert Victor, Duke of Clarence and Avondale.

In July 1976 George G. Harrap & Co. published "Jack the Ripper: The Final Solution". Written by the late Stephen Knight, then a local north London journalist, the book was based on the testimony of Joseph Sickert and took over the story from the earlier TV episode.

Joseph Sickert's story ran thus—

In 1884 when Prince Eddy, later Duke of Clarence and Avondale,

---

[300]   From the BBC TV series *Softly, Softly*.

was about twenty, his mother, Princess Alexandra, concerned about his lack of worldliness and the stifling environment of his Court upbringing, asked Walter Sickert to introduce him into artistic circles. Eddy was taken to Sickert's studio at 15 Cleveland Street where the heir to the throne met Annie Elizabeth Crook, a shop girl who modelled for Sickert. She lived in the basement of No. 6 Cleveland Street, and worked in a tobacconist's shop a few doors along at No. 22. They fell in love, the girl becoming pregnant almost immediately, and the following year, 1885, gave birth to a daughter at the St. Marylebone Workhouse. The child, Alice Margaret underwent two baptisms—Anglican and Catholic. Because of Annie's Catholicism marriage to Eddy was constitutionally unthinkable, but so deep was their love that they went through a secret Catholic wedding ceremony at a St. Saviour's Chapel.

There were two witnesses to this wedding. One was Walter Sickert. The other was an Irish Catholic girl who had worked with Annie in the Cleveland Street shop and later been paid by Sickert to be the child's nanny. Her name was Mary Jane Kelly.

Queen Victoria soon learned of the wedding, and Lord Salisbury, the Prime Minister, took responsibility for clearing up the mess the Queen's grandson had got himself into.

In 1888 Salisbury staged a raid on Cleveland Street, whisking Eddy back to Court from Sickert's studio and dragging Annie from the basement of No. 6 to spend the next 156 days in Guy's Hospital. Mary Kelly managed to escape and made her way back to the East End. That should have been an end to the affair, but Kelly fell in with a group of prostitutes and an ambitious blackmail scheme was conceived.

Thus was Jack the Ripper born. He was not a lone avenger stalking the streets on a misguided moral crusade, but an unholy trinity of officially-sanctioned killers out to silence those who knew of Eddy's marriage to the Catholic girl.

The three men forming the composite identity of Jack the Ripper were Walter Sickert, a coachman named John Netley, and Sir William Gull, Physician in Ordinary to Queen Victoria.

While Netley drove, Sickert and Gull lured the members of the blackmail scheme into the coach where they were fed poisoned grapes. Once dead, their bodies were mutilated by Gull and dumped in quiet alleyways and backyards. Mary Kelly was the last to be found, and as she was the only one of the five victims to have her own room she was murdered indoors.

With the death of Mary Kelly silence about events in Cleveland Street was assured and Jack the Ripper vanished as mysteriously as he had first appeared on the streets of the East End.

During her time in Guy's Hospital Annie Elizabeth Crook underwent an operation at the hands of Sir William Gull to erase from her mind the events of Cleveland Street. The operation left her an epileptic. She was now a broken woman, both in body and spirit, yet the Freemasons, of which Gull was a member, thought it a wise precaution not to allow her to return to a normal life. She spent the rest of her days in prisons, workhouses and infirmaries, finally dying—hopelessly insane—in 1920.

Alice Margaret Crook, the daughter of Eddy and Annie, was brought up by Walter Sickert. In 1918 she married a man named Gorman, who proved to be impotent. She turned to Sickert, became his mistress and in 1925 bore him a son, Joseph, who, fifty years later, told his story to Stephen Knight.

Stephen Knight began his investigation of the Sickert story with this paragraph—

"Unlikely as Sickert's story was, it would have been irresponsible to dismiss it merely because it sounded absurd—it cried out to be investigated. To be fair, though, even absurd was an understatement. It sounded the most arrant, if entertaining nonsense ever spun about Jack the Ripper, with the possible exception of the suggestion that the murderer was an escaped gorilla."

Having thus nailed his disbelief firmly to the mast Stephen Knight set out, quite properly, to see if Annie Elizabeth Crook had actually existed. He had no luck in this direction, but Karen de Groot, a BBC researcher, made a discovery in the 1888 Rate Books for Cleveland Street.

Number 6: Elizabeth Cook (Basement).

Crook—Cook. It was close. According to Sickert her surname was often given as Cook. So far, so good. Next, the birth certificate of Alice Margaret Crook was examined—

When and Where Born: Eighteenth April 1885. Marylebone Workhouse.

Name, if any: Alice Margaret.

Sex: Girl.

Name and Surname of Father: Blank.

Name and Surname and Maiden Name of Mother: Annie Elizabeth Crook, confectionary assistant—from Cleveland Street.

Occupation of Father: Blank

Signature, Description and Residence of Informant: X. The mark of Annie Elizabeth Crook, Mother—6 Cleveland Street, Fitzroy Square.

From these two pieces of official information Stephen Knight reached a confident conclusion—

"The address book shows that the Elizabeth Cook of the Rate Book and Annie Elizabeth Crook were one and the same."

Stephen Knight's next stop was the Greater London Record Office where Mr. Alan Neate, the Record Keeper, was able to provide details of Annie Elizabeth Crook's life in various workhouses and infirmaries. From the time of her daughter's birth in 1885 to her death in 1920 the sad sequel to her "romance with Prince Eddy" was chronicled in detail.

He had her in his sights: Annie Elizabeth Crook, the woman whose involvement with Prince Eddy was at the centre of the Ripper murders. Here was the key to unlock and almost century-old mystery. This was the breakthrough Ripperologists had been searching for. The evidence in support of Sickert's story was overwhelming.

Or was it?

Frankly, it wasn't. In fact, the information contained in the Cleveland Street Rate Books and the documents from the Greater London Record Office ruled out any involvement on the part of Annie Elizabeth Crook with events in the context of Stephen Knight's book.

In 1976 Mr. Alan Neate of the Greater London Record Office was generous enough to supply me with the exact information he had given to Stephen Knight.[301] When I put this together with what I had gleaned from the Cleveland Street Rate Book, the 1885 St. Marylebone Electoral Register and the Kelly Street Directories 1883-1888 a different picture emerged of Annie Elizabeth Crook. It was no less harrowing than Stephen Knight's heavily wrought account of her demise, but it was the truth.

What follows is a summary of what I discovered about Annie Elizabeth Crook and her family, 1838-1925, with special reference to events described in "Jack the Ripper: The Final Solution."

Annie Elizabeth Crook's grandparents came from Berwick-on-Tweed. Her mother, Sarah Anne, was born 31st August 1838 at 22 Great Marylebone Road. Sarah Anne married William Crook at St. John's Church [location unknown] in 1863. Sarah Anne had two other daughters who appear in the documentation as Annie Greenwood [or Greenaud] and Mrs. Jackson.

Annie Elizabeth Crook was born on 10th October 1862 at the St. Marylebone Infirmary. There is no birth certificate on record under this name, date and place, so it is possible that, as she was born a year before her mother's marriage to William Crook, her birth was registered in her mother's maiden name. Records of Births in Workhouses held by the GLC only go back as far as 1866, so it has not been possible to discover her mother's maiden name.

August 19th 1880—

Sarah Anne Crook was brought by the police to the St. Marylebone Workhouse. She was ill, and a note on her admission form reads "To be seen again." At this time she was living with her husband at 44 Berwick Street, where they had been since September 1879. A statement taken from William Crook reads "When about 15 years of age I was apprenticed to a Mr. Charles Boddy, a cabinet maker of 55 Eagle (Street) off Red Lion Square under judicature premium £14. Bound for 7 years.

[301] Alan Neate later gave the same information to Donald Rumbelow. All my original 1976 documentation is on file at the Tower Hamlets Local History Library and Archive, 227 Bancroft Road, London E1 4DQ. Stock number L.8383, Class Number 341.

Served 4½ years." Sarah Anne was discharged to her husband.

May 13th 1882—

Sarah Anne and William Crook were destitute. The St. Pancras Relieving Officer gave them meat and bread to the value of 1/5d. Sarah Anne was "suffering from epilepsy." This suggests that Annie Elizabeth's epilepsy was inherited from her mother and not brought about by surgery at the hands of Sir William Gull. An order was made to admit Sarah Anne to the Workhouse but, as someone wrote across the Receiving Officer's Report, she "didn't come." The couple had been living at 24 Francis Street for three months. No mention was made of their daughter Annie.

April 18th 1885—

Alice Margaret Crook was born in the St. Marylebone Workhouse. In the Workhouse Creed Register Annie and Alice are listed as "Church of England." This documented fact knocks a sizeable hole in Stephen Knight's story. Why would Eddy and Annie go through a Catholic wedding ceremony when neither of them were of that religion?

Stephen Knight used the birth certificate as proof that Annie worked in the tobacconist shop at 22 Cleveland Street. The certificate reads: *Annie Elizabeth Crook, Confectionery Assistant—from Cleveland Street.* This has been interpreted as meaning that the confectionery shop was in Cleveland Street, whereas the correct interpretation is that her job was that of a confectionery assistant and that she herself came from Cleveland Street. But even assuming the former interpretation it is possible that she could have worked in any of the following establishments.

Kelly Street Directory, Cleveland Street, 1888—

22: Mrs Agnes Pooley, Confectioner

75: Charles William Davis, Confectioner

93: William Kearne, Tobacconist

113: Charles Manly, Tobacconist

116: Mrs Rebecca Jackson, Confectioner

In the events described, having Annie working in the shop at No. 22 was the most desirable. It was on the corner of Tottenham Street, only eight doors along from where she lived at No. 6 and almost opposite No.

15 where Walter Sickert had his studio.

Alice Margaret's birth certificate tells us that in 1885 Annie Elizabeth Crook was living at No. 6 Cleveland Street.

The Cleveland Street Rate Books tell us that in 1888 Elizabeth Cook was living in the basement of No. 6 Cleveland Street.

Same address, same person?

We are told that in 1888 Lord Salisbury staged a raid on Cleveland Street. A "fat man and a woman" went into the basement of No. 6 and dragged Annie Elizabeth off to Guy's Hospital whilst "two men in brown tweed" went into Sickert's studio at No. 15 and escorted Prince Eddy back to Court.

From 1885 to 1887 the ratepayer for No. 6 Cleveland Street was William Tubb. The address was a shop run by John Pugh—Hairdresser, and the 1885 Electoral Register shows James Hinton and Charles Horne also living at this address. At this time women did not have the vote, so the only record of Annie Elizabeth Crook's tenure would have been the landlord's rent book.

It has not been possible to discover where Annie Elizabeth Crook was living from late 1886 to early 1888, but one thing is certain: it wasn't at No. 6 Cleveland Street. In between these dates Nos. 4 to 14 were demolished and the row of shops with their upstairs rooms replaced by a red-brick block of flats, Cleveland Residences, which stands there today.

According to the Rate Books, Elizabeth Cook continued to live at No. 6 Cleveland Residences until 1893, so she could not have been the woman dragged off to Guy's Hospital.

The "two men in brown tweed" who took Prince Eddy from Sickert's studio at No. 15 Cleveland Street would have had a difficult job on their hands, for at this address in 1888 they would have encountered a collection of bemused nurses.

In 1886, two years before Salisbury's alleged raid, Nos. 15 and 17 were demolished to make way for the Middlesex Hospital Trained Nurses Institute at No. 17 Cleveland Street. During the same period Nos. 25 to 35 were demolished to make way for the Middlesex Hospital

Residential College and the adjoining Middlesex Hospital Training School on Union Street.

The Times, 29th September 1887—

"The new buildings, which form the eastern and north-eastern portions of the quadrangle enclosing the old gardens of the hospital, and abut upon Cleveland and Union Streets, are in the Elizabethan style of architecture, and are six storeys in height . . . the new buildings [will be] opened by the Lord Mayor on Monday next."

The British Medical Journal, 1st October 1887—

"A new building, facing Cleveland Street on one side, and on the other the garden of Middlesex Hospital, designed to accommodate thirty trained nurses for private nursing, is now nearly completed. The building consists of five floors and a basement."

The Sunday at Home, 21st July 1888—

". . . the Middlesex Hospital Trained Nurses' Institute is built upon the site of some old houses in Cleveland Street, and has been opened only a few months."

Clearly the Cleveland Street raids as described by Stephen Knight could not have taken place. The incident is a complete fabrication.

Three houses on the west side of Cleveland Street escaped demolition in 1886. These were Nos. 19, 21 and 23 [facing Tottenham Street], one of which, in 1889, the police took a keen interest.

In July 1889 a number of uniformed Post Office boys aged between 15 and 21 were discovered to have been earning extra money as rent boys at 19 Cleveland Street, a male brothel frequented by members of the aristocracy.

The Scotland Yard detective put in charge of the case was Inspector Frederick George Abberline, the Ripper inquiry having been handed over to Inspector Henry Moore in early 1889.[302]

Press coverage was minimal, and it wasn't until 16th November 1889, when Ernest Parke, editor of *The North London Press*, named Henry James Fitzroy, Earl of Euston, as having been involved in "an

---

[302]   On 22nd December 1890 Abberline was promoted to Chief Inspector.

indescribably loathsome scandal in Cleveland Street", that the story broke and the Establishment scurried for cover.[303]

Charles Hammond's brothel must have been a very discreet operation, for how such a notorious house—which backed onto the Middlesex Hospital gardens whilst co-existing on one side with the Trained Nurses Institute and on the other with the Residential College—managed for so long with all its aristocratic comings and goings to escape the attentions of the police and hospital authorities is little short of miraculous.

By 1894 Nos. 19, 21 and 23 had been demolished and the site redeveloped as part of the perimeter buildings of the Middlesex Hospital.[304]

Charles Booth, "Walk with PC French", 21st October 1898—

"Cleveland Street. The hospital has now taken all the west side between Mortimer and Union Streets. Used to be a notorious brothel here."

Many years later a curious legend sprang up about No. 19 Cleveland Street.

Daily Telegraph, 21st October 2000—

"If you wander up and down Cleveland Street in the fashionable Fitzrovia area of London, you will look in vain for Number 19. Officially, it no longer exists. This is because the house was once the venue for one of the most notorious sleaze stories in late-Victorian England and was quietly removed from the Land Register.

"The renumbered house is now divided into three flats, and Flat Two - where the bedrooms used to be - is owned by a German chef, Michael von Hruschka."

Sunday Times, 16th January 2005—

"Secret Britain: What you won't find in the Guidebooks.

"19 Cleveland Street, London W1: Sex and Sleaze in Victorian

---

[303] Recommended reading on this establishment cover-up, which may or may not have involved Prince Eddy, are *The Cleveland Street Scandal,* by H. Montgomery Hyde (W. H. Allen, 1976) and *The Cleveland Street Affair*, by Simpson, Chester and Leitch (Little, Brown, 1976)
[304] See 1894 Ordnance Survey Map.

Britain.

"This house, now renumbered and divided into flats, was the scene of the most notorious sex scandal of Victorian Britain."

Charles Hammond was the lessee of 19 Cleveland Street. In response to my inquiry the Land Registry replied that "we cannot find evidence that the property had ever been registered [prior to 1889] . . . the house was first registered when the Middlesex Hospital purchased it, but there are no details of who previously owned it."

The story of the house which had been demolished in 1894 hiding in plain sight in modern London wearing only a new street number as a fig-leaf may now be confidently discarded as the most imaginative yarn yet spun by an estate agent.[305]

Further proof that Cook and Crook were not one and the same can be found on Annie Elizabeth Crook's admission form to the Endell Street Workhouse, dated January 22nd 1889—

Together with her daughter she was brought to the Workhouse by PC 453D. She was destitute and had last been living at No. 9 Pitt Street, Tottenham Court Road.

At this time Elizabeth Cook was living at No. 6 Cleveland Residences.

April 29th 1894—

Annie Elizabeth Crook was in prison. Her daughter, Alice, was living at No. 42 New Compton Street. On this date an order was made by the Endell Street Workhouse to "send Girl (aged) 9—30th April/To Northaw."

Northaw is a village in Hertfordshire, fifteen miles north of London.

Miss Harriet Le Blanc, whose family had lived in Northaw House for about a hundred years, had interests in an institution in London. She and Mrs Kidston, Lord of the Manor of Northaw, had one of the latter's cottages (adjacent to the Two Brewers public house) converted for the use of destitute children. Every fortnight throughout the summer six children were brought from the London institution by train to Potters

---

[305]   Estate Agent. US = Realtor.

Bar station and then on to Northaw by pony and trap, for a holiday in the country. [306]

October 12th 1895—

Sarah Anne, Annie's mother, was admitted to the St. Pancras Workhouse, suffering "Hysteria, Alcohol." Her address was No. 11 Pancras Street. A daughter, Mrs Jackson, was living at No. 9 Phoenix Street, Charing Cross Road.

May 29th 1897—

Sarah Anne was brought to the Poland Street Workhouse by the police at 9.50 pm. She was suffering "Fits". She gave her daughter's name as Annie Greenwood (Greenwood crossed out and Crook inserted), No. 91 Sardinia Buildings (this address crossed out and 25 Ward Westminster Union inserted). She had no place of residence and gave her occupation as "Factory Hand." A note on the Relieving Officer's Report reads "Appl(icant) sent to Cleveland Street a few weeks back, but took her own discharge, not liking the food."

June 20th 1898—

Sarah Anne was admitted to the St. Pancras Infirmary. She stated that she was married at St. John's Church 35 years ago, and that her husband had been dead for 6½ years. Her occupation was "Market Porter."

August 26th 1902—

Alice Margaret was admitted to the St. Pancras, suffering from "Measles." She was living at No. 5 Pancras Street wither her mother and grandmother. She was recorded as "Deaf and Illegt." Under the heading Observations ins "Grandmother keeps them in food – Mrs Sarah A. Crook, No. 5 Pancras Street, rent 2/- per week. Amount now due 12/-. Number of rooms – 1. Weekly income of Applicant (Alice Margaret). Rent paid by a friend."

February 7th 1903—

Annie Elizabeth Crook was admitted to the St. Pancras Workhouse, suffering from "Epilepsy." Together with her mother and daughter she

---

[306] Information courtesy of Mr. Gerald Millington, Northaw.

had been living at No. 5 Pancras Street. Alice is noted to be "Stone Deaf" and Annie's occupation given as "Casual Hand – Cross & Blackwell." The following notes are recorded on the admission form—

"I was called to this case by police at 2.30 pm 7/2/03. Visited 3.00 am and issued medical order on Dr. Murphy, No. 52 Huntley Street. Dr. not at home – as the case appeared to be urgent I called Dr. Forbes, No. 2 Charlotte Street. He did not answer bell. I then called Dr. MacCarthy of Gower Street who sent his deputy Dr. Cortellie – 3.50 am."

October 11th 1905—

Alice Margaret was admitted to the Cleveland Street Infirmary. "Cause of distress: Deaf. Bad foot. Present address – none. Occupation – Charwoman."

November 22nd to 26th 1906—

Sarah Anne, Annie Elizabeth and Alice Margaret were all in the Poland Street Workhouse. Each had been admitted at a different time, but from the same address – No. 19 Portland Street.

December 4th 1906 to January 28th 1907—

All three women were once again together in the Poland Street Workhouse.

April 29th 1913—

Sarah Anne and Alice Margaret were admitted to the Endell Street Workhouse. "Occupations: Market Porteresses. Shortly after this Alice Margaret was recorded as working for "Deatons, Covent Garden."

November 18th 1916—

Sarah Anne Crook died in Caterham Mental Hospital.

July 14th 1918—

Alice Margaret Crook married William Gorman, aged 45, a fish curer living at No. 195 Drummond Street. The marriage took place at St. Aloysius's Chapel, St. Pancras, according to the "Rites and Ceremonies of the Roman Catholics" and was witnessed by Thomas Jackson and Alice Ellen. Alice Margaret gave her father's name as William Crook (deceased) – General Labourer. It would appear that Alice disguised her illegitimacy in the Marriage Register by entering details of her grandfather as those of her unknown father.

March 23rd 1920—

Annie Elizabeth Crook died in the Lunacy Ward of the Fulham Road Workhouse. The Report Book reads—

"Bodily condition – fair. L. Hemiplegia. Occupation – Packer. Religious Creed – C of E. Name and address of nearest relative or friend – Daughter, Mrs Gorman, 195 Drummond Street, Hampstead."

Her case notes read—

"Has spells of amentia. Is an epileptic. Admitted Hendon Infirmary 12.3.1913.

"20.2.20 - Confused – sometimes noisy and hilarious, at other times almost stuporous – has delusions she is being tortured – takes no interest in her surroundings.

"23.2.20 – Sudden attack of cardiac failure, which ended in death at 12.40 am."

Stephen Knight asserted that—

"The St. George's Club ran a hospital at 367 Fulham Road, where Annie Elizabeth Crook died. This new evidence indicates how the Freemasons in charge of the cover-up could have handled the incarceration of Annie Elizabeth."

In a letter accompanying the documents received from the GLC, Mr. Alan Neate wrote—

"Knight's statement that the St. George's Club ran a hospital at 367 Fulham Road in the period under review is quite untrue. At all times material to the present consideration, this was the address of the Fulham Road Workhouse maintained by the statutory Poor Law authority – the St. George's (Westminster) Board of Guardians up to 1913 and the City of Westminster Board of Guardians thereafter."

Regarding the certification of Annie Elizabeth Crook as a lunatic, Mr. Neate added—

"It ought to be stated quite categorically that she was not a certified lunatic at any time whilst in Poor Law institutions after 1903."

October 22nd 1925—

Alice Margaret Gorman gave birth to a son – Joseph William Charles Gorman (Sickert). Joseph's Catholicism came from his father,

William Gorman; not from his grandmother, Annie Elizabeth Crook.

So ends the documented history of the Crook family. They were no strangers to the workhouse, and there is not one shred of evidence to suggest that Annie Elizabeth Crook's mental and physical decline was due to anything other than natural misfortune.

Annie Elizabeth Crook was not Catholic—the crux of this elaborate Ripper story—and her epilepsy was more than probably inherited from her mother. We know she was not living in Cleveland Street in 1888 and that Walter Sickert's studio, if it ever did exist here, had earlier been demolished.

As for the notion that on a number of occasions during the autumn of 1888 the 72-year-old Sir William Withey Gull sallied forth for the East End in a drafty coach, mutilating the female members of a blackmailing gang of prostitutes, *The Times* of 30th January 1890 carried the following report—

"We regret to announce that Sir William Gull died at half-past 12 yesterday at his residence, 74, Brook-street, London, from paralysis. *Sir William was seized with a severe attack of paralysis just over two years ago* while staying at Urrard, Killiecrankie, and never sufficiently recovered to resume his practice" [author's italics].

In the light of the foregoing, events at the very heart of Stephen Knight's book could not have taken place.

Joseph Sickert later retracted his story. In the *Sunday Times,* 18th June 1978, he was quoted as saying, "It was a hoax; I made it all up" and, it was "a whopping fib."

Stephen Knight died from a brain tumour in 1985 at the tragically early age of 33, but history would demonstrate that you can't keep a good story down.

In 1990 author, biographer, artist, astrologer, theosophist and mystic Jean Overton Fuller in her book "Sickert and the Ripper Crimes" hypothesised that Walter Sickert was Jack the Ripper. This was based on claims made by Florence Pash, a fellow artist and friend of Walter Sickert, who told the author's mother, Violet Overton Fuller, the "royal baby story" in 1948.

Her book contains a wealth of information about Walter Sickert. It is only when she tries to reconcile what she was told by her mother with the various fictions of Stephen Knight and Joseph Sickert and begins to formulate some rather startling ideas of her own that you start to feel you've fallen down a Ripperological rabbit hole.

There is no doubt that Walter Sickert, aged 28 at the time of the Whitechapel murders, was fascinated by the phantasmagoric landscape created by Jack the Ripper. His 1908 oil painting "Jack the Ripper's Bedroom" is a chilling study of light, shade and half-glimpsed menace, but one painting twenty years after the event does not a murderer make. However, when put together with a secret marriage, a "royal baby" and a high-level cover-up the possibilities start to become endless.

Florence Pash had recounted the "royal baby story" as early as 1948. How might such rumours have come into circulation if not because of a secret marriage between Prince Eddy and Annie Elizabeth Crook?

Luckily there is no need to look very far afield.

16. THE MALTA STORY

In November 1891 Prince Albert Victor, having just been extricated from a scandalous affair with chorus girl Lydia Manton, who may have been pregnant at the time of her agonising death,[307] became engaged to his second cousin once removed, Princess Victoria Mary of Teck, known as "May." Her father, Prince Francis, Duke of Teck, belonged to a morganatic, cadet branch of the house of Württemberg. Her mother, Princess Mary Adelaide of Cambridge, was a male-line grand-daughter of King George III and a first cousin of Queen Victoria.

The Times, 7th December 1891—

"His Royal Highness the Duke of Clarence and Avondale arrived at the Castle [Windsor] on Saturday evening [5th December], and communicated to the Queen, as head of the Family, for Her Majesty's approval, his engagement to Her Highness the Princess Victoria Mary of Teck."

Five-and-a-half weeks later, on 14th January 1892, the Duke of Clarence and Avondale died of influenza at Sandringham, with Princess Victoria Mary of Teck at his bedside. This left his younger brother, Prince

---

[307]   Amidst rumours of murder, in October 1891 an inquest found that Lydia Manton committed "suicide whilst in a state of unsound mind" by drinking a large quantity of carbolic acid.

George, in line for the throne.

Having soon overcome her grief Queen Victoria came to regard Princess May as a suitable match for George, and the couple were encouraged to grow close during their shared period of mourning. A year after the Duke of Clarence's death Prince George proposed to Princess May.

Dark clouds began to gather.

The Advertiser [Adelaide, SA], 20th June 1893—

"There is a lot of ill-natured gossip current concerning the Royal engagement, which the flaneurs of the clubs protest has been crammed down the Duke of York's throat by his relations. All one can say is that H.R.H behaves as though he were the happiest of men. He has, indeed, hardly left the side of the beloved object since his engagement was announced. First of all, he and the Prince of Wales went to stay at the White Lodge, and now "the dear Tecks" are H.R.H.'s guests at Marlborough House. This, says the Tattler, signifies little. Precisely the same formulas were gone through when poor Prince Eddie became affianced to the young lady.

"Unquestionably recollections of the former engagement do take a little of the bloom off the betrothal. Even the most gushing scribes cannot go the length of pronouncing this *union de convenance* (as they did Prince Eddie's) 'a pure love match.' But Royalists, let the romantic remember, are not like our common selves. When settlements are satisfactory, and both the contracting parties healthy, mutual respect and liking are a promising basis whereon to marry."

Prince George and Princess May were married on 6th July 1893 in the Chapel Royal, St. James's Palace, London.

News Observer Chronicle [Raleigh, NC], 11th July 1893—

"The London correspondent of the New York Times[308] reports that there is current in London a suppressed passage from the life of Prince George, who has just married Princess May, to the effect that a few years ago he married by the Roman Catholic ritual the beautiful daughter of a

---

[308] Harold Frederic, who first broke the Leather Apron story.

navy officer stationed at Malta, who is even now in London. According to law the marriage is a nullity, but Prince George hoped that his elder brother [Prince Eddy], now dead, would marry and have children, in which case he could have had his marriage legalised. The death of his brother banished this hope, and George has been miserable ever since. The ways of Princes are different from those of plain folk."

The *Observer* [NZ], 7th October 1893, followed up—

"Contradictory rumours are still afloat respecting that Maltese beauty whom it is alleged in certain quarters the Duke of York married prior to his engagement to Princess May. One London paper states that the lady from Malta is now living at South Kensington, London, with her three children, and that she would have turned up at the York—Teck wedding wheeling a perambulator laden with infants but for the arrival of baby number three on the auspicious day. The Prince treats the whole thing as a joke."

The story refused to lie down. In the following year Prince George's Maltese bride was named.

The *Johnstown Daily Republican* [NY], 16th August 1894—

"A Startling and Romantic Story Which is Important if True.

"The Prince of Wales was quite right to make the denial; the morning newspapers were quite right to publish it. Permit me to quote the Prince's statement which was issued by his private secretary, Colonel Sir Francis Knollys. Then I wish to add a rider:

"London, Aug. 15. —A letter signed by Sir Francis Knollys, K.C.M.G., one of the grooms in waiting upon the Prince of Wales directs him to say that there is not a shadow of foundation for the report that the Duke of York was married previous to his union with Princess May of Teck. The letter adds that the report of a previous marriage was obviously invented to cause pain and annoyance to the young couple."[309]

"There is more than a 'shadow of proof' for the Duke's marriage— there is the record in the English church in Malta. The marriage took place four years ago, when Prince George was with the Mediterranean

---

[309] Sir Francis Knollys' full letter was published in The Times, 15th August 1894.

squadron . . . There would never have been a question of the legality of their marriage had not "Collars and Cuffs" [Prince Eddy] died . . . When he died suddenly, his brother, Prince George, was ordered to keep the engagement. In spite of all his resistance he was married to his brother's fiancée.

"[His first bride] was a Miss Tryon and the niece of one of England's most famous sailors—a man under whom the 'sailor Prince', this charming Duke of York, had learned his seamanship. When Admiral Tryon learned of the shame he had cast upon his name, he was half mad. The drink he took did not mollify him. The one thing he could do was kill himself, and he committed suicide by sinking the finest man-of-war in the English navy. He drowned hundreds of men, sank a million pound ironclad and went down laughing drunk on the bridge.[310]

The story was by-lined "Vance Thompson [who would later write a Leather Apron story] in the *New York Commercial Advertiser*."

Aside from veiled mutterings little was heard of this story until February 1911, when Edward Frederick Mylius, a Belgian-born British journalist, appeared in court on a charge of having libelled King George the Fifth.

The libel appeared in the *Liberator*, a monthly Republican leaflet printed in Paris and distributed in England by Mylius.

"Sanctified Bigamy"—

"During the year 1890, in the island of Malta, the man who is now King of England was united in lawful holy wedlock with the daughter of Sir Michael Culme-Seymour, an Admiral of the British Navy. Of this marriage offspring were born. At the time of that marriage the Duke of Clarence, the eldest brother of the present King, was Heir to the Throne. Subsequently the Duke of Clarence died, leaving the present King Heir to the Throne. It is now that we are offered the spectacle of the immorality of the Monarchy in all its sickening, beastly monstrosity. In

---

[310] On 22nd June 1893, HMS Victoria, commanded by Admiral George Tryon K.C.B., collided with HMS Camperdown and sank. "It's all my fault," were the last words Tryon spoke to his officers before going down with his ship.

order to obtain the woman of Royal blood for his pretended wife George Frederick fully abandoned his true wife, the daughter of Sir Michael Culme-Seymour, of the British Navy, and entered into a sham and shameful marriage with the daughter of the Duke of Teck in 1893."

The article went on to say that, if still alive, the daughter of Sir Michael Culme-Seymour was the rightful Queen of England and her children the only rightful heirs to the English Throne.

Sir Michael Culme-Seymour gave evidence in court. He and his family had not gone to Malta until 1893, when he replaced the late Admiral George Tryon as Commander in Chief of the Mediterranean Squadron. His daughter, Mary Elizabeth, who had married Captain Trevelyan Napier R.N.,[311] also gave evidence. Admiralty documents showed that between October 1888 and July 1893 Prince George had not held an appointment on any ship which went to Malta.

The marriage registers of Malta were produced. They held the records of every Roman Catholic, Protestant, Greek Church and civil service. Dr. Vincento Azopardi, Crown Advocate of Malta, showed the court that no woman by the name of Seymour, Culme or Culme-Seymour was married on the island between 1886 and 1903.

Edward Frederick Mylius was found guilty of libel and sentenced to twelve months imprisonment.

What is to be made of this story? After all, King George III was said to have married Hannah Lightfoot, a Quaker, and, whilst Prince of Wales, King George IV actually married Mrs Fitzherbert, a Roman Catholic who, it is rumoured, bore him two children.

Earlier the *New York World*, 10th September 1899, had written—

"If there has been any ecclesiastical union between the lady, who is now Mrs Napier, and the Duke of York it must be confessed that the Seymour family have acted with a discretion and tact and a savoir faire beyond all praise. For they have never presumed upon this affair, and that is probably why the Queen and the Government have simply

---

[311]   Mary Elizabeth Culme-Seymour married Commander Trevelyan Dacres Willes Napier at Portsmouth in September 1899.

overwhelmed Miss Seymour's father with every kind of honor and distinction . . . The natural inference is that his rapid promotion, as well as the marked favor which he has received from the Queen and the Prince of Wales, are due to the circumstance that by his discretion he has extricated the Duke of York and the royal family from an awkward predicament.

"For there is no doubt that had the British public positive knowledge of the Duke of York's secret union to Miss Seymour, public feeling would have been so strong as to prevent his marriage to the Princess, who consented to become his bride.

"Indeed, the marriage could hardly have become known without attention being called to the declaration said to have been made by the Duke while his elder brother was still alive.

"Before Miss Seymour would marry the Duke, he placed in Admiral Seymour's hands a paper reading—

I, George Frederick Ernest Albert of Wales, hereby renounce all my claim to the throne of England for myself and my heirs forever, and become a simple English gentleman, amenable to all such laws as are made for the citizens of Great Britain.

"This document might have an awkward look if brought to light: might even have political consequences. It is, therefore just as well, to keep Admiral Seymour good-natured."

Here it is useful to recall the spiritualist Robert James Lees, who allegedly received a £30,000 reward plus an annual pension of £1,500 from the Privy Purse in return for his silence.

The *New York World* continued—

"It is asserted that Miss Seymour has had an annuity of $10,000 a year settled upon her by the Crown in consideration of keeping her mouth shut."

How much of the foregoing is true is impossible to know for certain. But, just as with Jack the Ripper, stories like this have no need to be true in order for people to want to believe them. And here, years before Joseph Sickert and Stephen Knight came along, were all the basic ingredients of a Royal cover-up of epic proportions—a secret Catholic wedding ceremony, an illegitimate heir to the British throne and hush-money from the Crown.

Throw in Jack the Ripper, a spiritualist, an impressionist painter, a West End doctor and/or a lunatic asylum, a handful of freshly-picked freemasons, add a sprinkle of imagination and a few spurious facts, stir well, season to taste and there's no end to the variety of lip-smacking theories which can be whipped up to satisfy the public appetite.

A prime example is Frank Spiering's utterly worthless 1978 "Prince Jack", based upon the author's "discovery" in the library of the New York Academy of Medicine of a non-existent journal belonging to Sir William Gull, in which it was revealed that the Ripper was none other than Prince Eddy, later Duke of Clarence.

Joseph Sickert retracted his retraction in 1991. In a foreword to "The Ripper and the Royals" by Melvyn Fairclough, he wrote—

"Some years ago I agreed to cooperate with the journalist Stephen Knight by recounting to him my family history, which involved the story of the Ripper murders of 1888. I told him a good deal of what I had heard from my father, Walter Sickert. But during the course of our cooperation I began to realise that he was misinterpreting the material, and we quarrelled. I decided not to give him the whole story, and though his book Jack the Ripper: The Final Solution (1976) was broadly on the right lines it was not only wrong on many points but missed out on many vital details.

"It has always been a regret to me that the story has not been presented properly, and I am grateful to Melvyn Fairclough for agreeing to set the record straight. His book has my blessing. My sole purpose in cooperating with him here is to vindicate the reputation of my family— not only of my father, but of my mother and grandmother, and of my grandfather, the Duke of Clarence."

In "The Ripper and the Royals" Melvyn Fairclough skirted any cumbersome facts with alacrity, maintained the Prince Eddy/Annie Crook secret wedding and the blackmail scheme, threw in the purported diaries of Walter Sickert and Chief Inspector G.F. [sic] Abberline, gave details of a masonic conspiracy led by Lord Randolph Churchill, and posited that the Duke of Clarence had not died from influenza in 1892

313

but was confined at Balmoral until his death in 1933—this last a sort of modern-day spin on the Glamis Horror.

Whilst Melvyn Fairclough's rattling yarn might best be described as Stephen Knight on steroids,[312] the *pièce de résistance* in Ripperological monkeyshines came in 1992 with the arrival of a diary purporting to be that of Jack the Ripper. It was the most sublime conceit—sixty-three hand-written pages of rambling balderdash contained in the leather-bound remnants of a scrapbook or photograph album, with no direct references to its author but dangling just enough clues to identify him as Liverpool cotton merchant James Maybrick.

Maybrick died on 11th May 1889, aged 51, the victim of arsenic poisoning by his wife, Florence, having fortuitously survived just long enough to sign his diary "Jack the Ripper" and date it 3rd May 1889.

Forensic testing of the "diary" proved inconclusive, and tempers still run high as to whether it is genuine [unlikely in the extreme], a sophisticated modern fake [most probably], or a much earlier fake [the stay-out-of-jail position].

Maurice Chittenden in the *Sunday Times*, 19th September 1993, told of the matter being passed to SO1, Scotland Yard's serious crime branch, suggesting that it could be the biggest international publishing hoax since the Hitler diaries, and in the same edition veteran Ripper author Tom Cullen did not mince his words—

"It [the diary] seems to me to be a farrago of nonsense."

Money inevitably wins out over integrity, and "The Diary of Jack the Ripper" was finally published in 1993, "25 experts [having] examined the diary and found 'no substantial reason for rejecting it'"[313], and in the first week of publication it appeared at No. 6 in the *Sunday Times* list of best-selling hardbacks, bearing the strap-line "Liverpool businessman's private journal drops heavy whodunit hints."

In 1995 Stewart Evans and Paul Gainey published "The Lodger" [US, 1998, "Jack the Ripper: First American Serial Killer."], which set out a

---

[312]   Melvyn Fairclough has since disavowed his Royal conspiracy theory.

[313]   *The Times*, 9th September 1993.

case for Jack the Ripper being Dr. Francis Tumblety, an American quack whose specialty was a pimple-banishing ointment, arrested in London during November 1888 on four charges of "gross indecency with another male person," and four that he "unlawfully and indecently did make an indecent assault" against named men on specific dates in July, August, October and November 1888.

The impetus for evaluating Francis Tumblety's candidature as a Ripper suspect was Stewart Evans' 1993 purchase from the late antiquarian dealer Eric Barton of a letter written to journalist George R. Sims by ex-Chief Inspector John George Littlechild, head of the Special Department[314] until his retirement in 1893.

In the letter, dated 23rd September 1913, Littlechild wrote, ". . . amongst the [Ripper] suspects, and to my mind a very likely one, was a Dr. T . . . He was an American quack named Tumblety and was at one time a frequent visitor to London and on these occasions constantly brought under the notice of police, there being a large dossier concerning him at Scotland Yard . . ."

Little appeared about Tumblety's arrest in the British press. However, many stories of his being suspected in connection with the Whitechapel murders ran in the American press during late November and early December 1888, the story being that on 16th, 17th, 18th or 19th November [accounts vary] Tumblety was arrested in connection with the Whitechapel murders. Allegedly having no evidence with which to charge Tumblety, the police held him on four counts of gross indecency punishable under Section 11 of the Criminal Law Amendment Act 1885.

The American press had been woefully misinformed.

Tumblety's most recent gross indecency offence had been on Friday 2nd November. He was arrested on Wednesday 7th November and on Friday 16th November bailed on two sureties totaling £300 [$1500] to appear at the Old Bailey on Monday 19th November.

---

[314] "I am in charge of the Special Department, dealing with political crime . . ." J. G. Littlechild, Departmental Committee Upon Police Superannuation, 29th November 1889

Tumblety was fond of publishing pamphlets packed with bogus testimonials from various worthies which attested to his elevated sense of wonderfulness. In one of these pamphlets can be found the following reference to an undated letter listed amongst a number of others written in 1889—

"No later than November of last year Dr. Tumblety received a letter from Drexel, Morgan & Co., which contained the subjoined passage, quoted here to show the pleasant business relations existing between them.

"In accordance with your order of the 20th inst., we have forwarded you by this mail our sterling letter of credit for £263 1s. 6d., upon Messrs. Drexel, Morgan & Co., of New York.

"We are, etc.,

"J. P. Morgan & Co."

Those who support Tumblety's candidature for Ripperhood claim this letter is contained in his immodestly-titled 1889 pamphlet, "Dr. Francis Tumblety, A Sketch of the Life of the Gifted and World-Famed Physician." Thus was Tumblety's 'order' written on 20th November 1888, lending credence to the idea that prior to fleeing justice he was raising money to reimburse his two bondsmen who, according to the New York *World*, 2nd December 1888, "had only known the doctor for a few days previous to his arrest."

There are problems with this line of thinking. Firstly, the letter did not appear until 1893 in a pamphlet entitled "A Sketch of the Life of Dr. Francis Tumblety."

More mysteriously, the letter had allegedly been sent on behalf of "J.P. Morgan & Co." Anthony Joseph Drexel died in headline-grabbing style on 30th June 1893, but Drexel Morgan & Co. was not renamed J.P Morgan & Co. until 1st January 1895. Also, for purposes of clarity, in 1888 the London subsidiary of Drexel Morgan & Co. was J.S. Morgan & Co.

Tumblety's arrest and bail dates are documented in the Old Bailey Court Calendars for November and December 1888, so there is no doubt that between the 7th and 16th November he had been remanded

316

in custody, thus making him unavailable for the Millers Court murder on 9th November.

At no time was Tumblety arrested on suspicion of being Jack the Ripper.

However, on 16th November 1888 Sir George Compton Archibald Arthur, a 28-year-old baronet with an honorary Captaincy in the Hertfordshire Yeomanry Cavalry, went slumming in Whitechapel. Dressed in an astrakhan coat[315] and a slouch hat, he was spotted by two policemen approaching a well-known prostitute.

NewYork *World*, 18th November 1888—

"It occurred to two policemen that Sir George answered very much the popular description of Jack the Ripper. They watched him, and when they saw him talking with women they proceeded to collar him. He protested, expostulated and threatened them with the vengeance of royal wrath, but in vain. Finally, a chance was given to him to send to a fashionable West End Club to prove his identity, and he was released with profuse apologise for the mistake. The affair was kept out of the newspapers. But the Jolly young Baronet's friends at Brook's Club considered the joke too good to be kept quiet."

Tumblety later appropriated Sir George Arthur's story—right down to the slouch hat—to bolster own his candidature as a Ripper suspect. In an interview with the New York *World*, 29th January 1889, Tumblety was asked—

"What do you think of the London police?"

"I think their conduct in this Whitechapel affair is enough to show what they are. Why, they stuff themselves all day with potpies and beef and drink gallons of stale beer, keeping it up until they go to bed late at night, and then wake up the next morning heavy as lead. Why, all the English police have dyspepsia. They can't help it. Their heads are as thick as the London fogs. You can't drive an idea through their thick skulls with a hammer. I never saw such a stupid set. Look at their treatment of me. There was absolutely not one single scintilla of evidence against me. I

---

[315]   *Echo*, 26th November 1888. *Wrexham Advertiser*, 30th November 1888.

had simply been guilty of wearing a slouch hat, and for that I was charged with a series of the most horrible crimes ever recorded."

At the Old Bailey, 19th November 1888, a Grand Jury found sufficient evidence to warrant a trial on the charges of gross indecency.[316] On the following day Mr. Bodkin [Tumblety's defense counsel] applied to postpone the proceedings until the December Sessions. Mr. Muir [prosecuting for the Treasury] agreed to the request.[317] This ensured a continuance of Tumblety's bail, which he immediately jumped. Four days later, using the name Frank Townsend, he boarded the steamship *La Bretagne* at Le Havre bound for New York, where, as earlier discussed, he was not troubled by anyone from Scotland Yard in search of Jack the Ripper.

Special Branch had a resident port-watcher at Le Havre. Author Andrew Cook[318] maintains that in November 1888 this officer was Inspector William Melville who, five years later, took over from John George Littlechild as head of Special Branch, whereas author and journalist E. Thomas Wood[319] asserts that Melville—whose son James was born in Le Havre in 1885—returned to London in 1887. But irrespective of the Special Branch officer's identity, it beggars belief that such an imposing figure as Tumblety—he was described in the *New York Times* as "considerably over six feet in height, of graceful and powerful build, with strongly marked features, beautifully clear complexion, a sweeping mustache, and jet-black hair"—managed to evade security at every railway station and port on his journey from London, via Folkestone, Boulogne and Paris, to Le Havre.[320]

Brooklyn Citizen, November 23rd 1888—

"Police Superintendent Campbell received a cable dispatch

---

[316] Cases warranting a trial were marked 'true bills'; those rejected were marked 'ignoramus' (we are uninformed) or 'not found' and the case dropped.

[317] CRIM 6/17—Central Criminal Court Book, 1st April 1887 to 31st March 1891.

[318] *M: MI5's First Spymaster*, Tempus Publishing, 2004.

[319] *Wars on Terror*, 2002. M. Lit dissertation, European Studies, Cambridge University.

[320] Tumblety's alternate routes were [a] Dover, Calais, Paris, Le Havre, [b] Newhaven, Dieppe, Paris, Le Havre, [c] London, Southampton, Le Havre.

yesterday from Mr. [Robert] Anderson, the deputy chief of the London Police, asking him to make some inquiries about Francis Tumblety, who is under arrest in England on the charge of indecent assault."

Anderson made no mention in his cable of the Whitechapel murders.

London *Evening Post*, 10th December 1888—

"On the name of Francis Tumblety, who was out on bail, being called at the Old Bailey this morning to take his trial for a serious offence, it was intimated to the Recorder by the prosecuting counsel that the accused had left the country for the country's good. A fresh warrant was asked for and granted for his arrest."

Leaving Britain for the country's good was a noble gesture. You can almost see Tumblety on the prow of *La Bretagne* laughing up his sleeve.

"Tumblety was taken into custody on November 18 on suspicion of being the Whitechapel murderer, and, his lodgings being searched by the police, he was detained on the charge for which he should have taken his trial today."

Here again the press was giving an erroneous account of Tumblety's arrest details and dates.

The London *Evening Post* next offered an insight into how he had first come to the attention of the Metropolitan Police—

"A few years ago the pimple-banishing enterprise was moved to London, where the doctor for a time is said to have made money. It was his queer method of spending his money which first attracted the Scotland Yard detectives to him, and after a slight investigation he was arrested, the idea being that if he were not the Whitechapel fiend, he was a dangerous character, and not entitled to his liberty."

The *Evening Post* article then went some way to explaining Littlechild's remark in his 1913 letter to George R. Sims about "a large dossier concerning him at Scotland Yard . . ," at the same time providing what might be seen as a template for many popular misconceptions about Jack the Ripper—

"In various cities the doctor has been shadowed by the police. Detectives have followed him, watched his office, dogged his footsteps, noted his companions, and tried every way to find out the secret of his private life which he so jealously guarded, and not one of them has been successful. Who is he? What is his nationality? Where is his home, his family? Who are his friends, his associates? None of these questions has ever been answered."[321]

Not one jot of evidence links Dr. Francis Tumblety with the Whitechapel murders, but slender facts are beginning to emerge [which it would be premature to detail here] that his homosexual activities were at the politically thin end of the Cleveland Street wedge. Certainly on his return to America his candidacy for the mantle of Jack the Ripper was played to the hilt whilst the actual reason for his arrest in London was soft-pedalled, and Tumblety himself countered claims that he was any sort of euphemistic 'woman-hater', going so far as to recite to the New York *World* a mawkish poem allegedly dedicated to him by Mary, a Duchess with whom he had breakfasted in Torquay, Devon.

French political red tape could possibly have prevented Tumblety's arrest at Le Havre and extradition to England, but such a scenario would have come to the attention of the American press.[322] What appears to have happened is that, given the potential for an embarrassing scandal had his trial proceeded, Tumblety received a free pass, his bail was paid and he was given one of the most ingenious cover stories in history.

The London *Evening Post* which, in a number of 1888 and 1889 articles, named Tumblety as a suspect in the Whitechapel murders suggests that in his 1913 letter Littlechild did not reveal anything which George R. Sims, the most avid Ripperphile, had not already been aware of and subsequently dismissed in favour of the drowned doctor. It also appears that Littlechild, who by the very nature of his job at the time would have known the exact circumstances of Tumblety's flight from English justice, was—just like Melville Macnaghten with his drowned doctor—wilfully misleading George R. Sims.

---

[321]   This paragraph first appeared in the Washington DC *Evening Star*, 27th November 1888.

[322]   As was the case with two Irish-American Fenians—Frank Byrne in 1883 and Patrick Tynan in 1896.

Every good story deserves an extra spin around the block, and in 2002 US crime writer Patricia Cornwell published "Portrait of a Killer: Jack the Ripper—Case Closed", having spent a whopping seven-figure sum attempting to prove by dint of questionable scientific analysis, subjective artistic interpretation and the standing of logic on its head that Jack the Ripper was the artist Walter Sickert.

Some suspects just refuse to lie down.

The book was panned by art historians and Ripperologists alike, which made Patricia Cornwell feel she had somehow encroached upon a curiously British male preserve. Had she been a British male, she contended, her theory would have been accepted.

Whilst this is unlikely in the extreme, she did score a resounding bullseye in observing that Ripper students would sooner have the mystery than the solution.

Thus did Jack the Ripper step boldly into the 21st Century.

17. BLACKMAIL

On 19th September 1888 Inspector Frederick George Abberline of the Criminal Investigation Department, Scotland Yard, wrote a report on the *Murders in Whitechapel*. It began—

"With reference to the subject named in the margin, I beg to report that about 3.40 am Aug 31st Ult, as Charles Cross, Carman, of 22 Doveton Street, Cambridge Road, Bethnal Green was passing through Bucks Row Whitechapel (on his way to work) he noticed a woman lying on her back on the footway (against some gates leading into a stable yard) . . ."

The victim was Mary Ann 'Polly' Nichols, allegedly a 43-year-old 'unfortunate.' Her throat was cut and she had been mutilated in the genital area.

On this last day of August 1888, during which James Monro would pass the baton of Assistant Commissioner [CID] to Robert Anderson, Jack was not even a twinkle in his creator's eye, and by rights Polly Nichols should have been little more than a random statistic in the on-going violence of the East End.

But Polly Nichols soon assumed a special significance. Within hours of her murder she was dubbed the third victim of a lone perpetrator in a series of murders going back to April 1888.

London *Evening Post*, 1st September 1888—

"It has been suggested that a lunatic is at large in the East-end, but this theory does not bear examination. No lunatic was ever yet so methodically mad. What is more probable is that there exists in the East-end a gang of hellish ruffians who blackmail the wretched women of the streets and enforce their demands at the point of the knife. They must be tracked out. Every circumstance of this latest crime tends to force the conclusion that a number of people hold its terrible secret."

Polly Nichols was in fact the seventh victim of a knife attack/murder by an unknown perpetrator in the East End since the beginning of the year,[323] but her murder was specifically linked to that of Emma Smith, who died in hospital after being attacked in the early hours of 3rd April, and Martha Tabram who, just three weeks earlier than Nichols, on 7th August, suffered thirty-nine stab wounds.

According to the press, aside from the proximity of the three incidents the police were at first undecided as to their common denominator.

The *Echo*, 31st August 1888, quoted a "Criminal Investigation officer" as saying that Polly Nichols' injuries were such "that they could only have been inflicted by a madman," whilst the *Evening News* reported that the police were "pushing their inquiries in the neighbourhood as to the doings of certain gangs known to frequent these parts . . ."

The *Evening News* went further—

"It is believed that these gangs, who make their appearance during the early hours of the morning, are in the habit of blackmailing these poor unfortunate creatures, and when their demands are refused, violence follows, and in order to avoid their deeds being brought to light they put away their victims. They have been under the observation of the police for some time past, and it is believed that with the prospect of a reward and a free pardon, some of them might be persuaded to turn Queen's evidence, when some startling revelations might be expected."

Startling revelations? Other than pitiless violence, what might have

---

[323] Including the "Ripper victims" a total of thirty-seven women in the East End were attacked and/or murdered by beating, bludgeoning, strangling or stabbing and cutting between January and December 1888. Fourteen of these were domestic incidents.

been startling about the activities of a gang of thugs blackmailing prostitutes? The *Evening News* appeared to be telling less than it either knew or suspected.

At a meeting of St. Luke's Vestry, 31st December 1887, Mr. J.T. Pedder told of six watches being snatched in Featherstone Street, reporting that "there is a gang in the parish known as the 'Forty Thieves', who carry on their depredations at all hours of the day and night, yet never appear to be caught."

This sounded like "mugging", small beer compared with the blackmail and murder of prostitutes. At what else might the *Evening News* have been hinting?

The Victorians had an uncomfortable relationship with sex and sexuality. Certain loves could never speak their name. Polite society was a tangle of rampant hypocrisy, private vice and public virtue, and of sexual inequality which never forgave in women what it so readily condoned in men.

Until the 1885 publication of William Thomas Stead's crusading exposé of child prostitution and London's sex-trade [324] the average Victorian probably never suspected that a criminal network of sex-trafficking and a labyrinth of brothels and private torture chambers was in operation beneath the respectable veneer of the hub of Queen Victoria's British Empire. W.T. Stead's "infernal narrative" revealed that *virgo intacta* girls of eleven could be bought and sold for as little as £3, whilst in the sound-proofed opulence of West London villas aristocratic paedophiles could indulge in rape and exult in "the cries of an immature child."

Not only were children used and abused in this sordid trade. Stead wrote that "London's lust annually uses up many thousands of women, who are literally killed and made away with—living sacrifices slain in the service of vice."

Whilst untold horrors may have lurked behind the smartly-painted

---

[324]   W.T Stead. "The Maiden Tribute of Modern Babylon". Pall Mall Gazette, 6th to 12th July 1885. www.attackingthedevil.co.uk

doors of Kensington or Bloomsbury, for most people in Victorian London the visible tip of this sex-trade were street prostitutes. William Booth, founder of the Salvation Army, estimated that in 1880s London they numbered between 60,000 and 80,000.

Except for social reformists, this blatant street marketing of sex was not considered an outrage in the Victorian mind. Prostitution was legal[325]. The law reflected medical and religious thinking on men's sexual needs. The services of prostitutes were deemed preferable to men debasing "pure" women or, even worse, indulging in the evil and self-destructive practice of masturbation.

Prostitutes out-numbered beat constables six-to-one, and in the West End of London it was reported to be almost impossible for a smartly-dressed gentleman to stroll along Piccadilly, down the Haymarket, around Leicester Square or up Regent Street without being accosted, solicited or propositioned almost every step of the way by a parasol-twirling doxy. However, as the police were to discover to their dismay, not all women arrested on West End streets were prostitutes.

One major obstacle to the solving of the mystery of the Whitechapel murders is a stubborn belief amongst students of the subject that every single member of the Metropolitan Police was earnest, dogged and determined, incorruptible and wore a white hat.

In June 1887 Police Constable DR42 Bowden Endacott caused a scandal when he arrested a 24-year-old dressmaker, Elizabeth Cass, in Regent Street, accusing her of prostitution and testifying at her Magistrates Court appearance that he had witnessed her soliciting on three previous occasions.

Miss Cass's employer, Mrs. Bowman, testified that she was a respectable woman of perfect character and in a good job, but although Magistrate Robert Milnes Newton found Miss Cass not guilty he reportedly said that "he thought she was out for an improper purpose."

Mr. Newton told Miss Cass—

"Just take my advice: if you are a respectable girl, as you say you are,

---

[325]   It was the solicitation which was unlawful.

don't walk in Regent Street at night, for if you do you will either be fined or sent to prison after the caution I have given you."

Aghast at Newton's remarks, a coalition of Regent Street shopkeepers met at the Banqueting Room, St James's Hall—

". . . now a respected magistrate seems to constitute Regent Street a special preserve for prostitutes, telling a respectable girl she is liable to be locked up if she walks our street in the evening—as if the virtuous had no business to use our street at all after 9 o'clock."

The meeting went on to deplore the fact that "a large number of very well-known women, mostly foreign, were allowed indiscriminately to walk the streets at all hours of the day and night, and to molest passers-by."

Mr. Thrower, a Regent Street tradesman, agreed—

"It was a remarkable fact," he said, "that whenever the police interfered with anybody it was always somebody against whom they had only suspicion, and not any actual knowledge . . . It was a suspicious fact that women who had been on the streets for years were not interfered with, while women who, if they were bad characters at all, were newcomers to the place were taken up [to the police station]. It looked very much as though there was a system of blackmail imposed by the police."[326]

Miss Cass had been branded a common prostitute. Her mind was "quite unhinged", Mrs Bowman told Sir Charles Warren in a letter demanding an inquiry into the case. Questions were raised in parliament, and after the government was defeated in a "Motion that this House do now adjourn to debate on the subject of the circumstances connected with the Arrest of Miss Cass in Regent Street", Home Secretary Henry Matthews ordered Sir Charles Warren to undertake an inquiry[327].

PC Bowden Endacott, married eleven years with three children, and with twelve years' service in the Metropolitan Police, during which he had been awarded a number of commendations, was suspended from

---

[326]   The Times, 8th July 1887.
[327]   HO 144/472/X15239

duty without pay.

PC Endacott told Central News—

"I have had a large number of charges before Mr. Newton against loose women, and this is the first time that my evidence has been questioned . . . The majority of the women who are about Regent Street I know by sight well." He then added gratuitously, "I have been offered money by these women scores of times not to interfere with them, but I have never taken a single penny."[328]

Sir Charles Warren ordered immediate changes. From now on the police were not "to take upon themselves the responsibility of prosecuting any person without sufficient evidence to prove her guilt." They were to keep prostitutes moving along. If a complaint was made by a member of the public, the constable was to ask the complainant to accompany him to the police station to prefer charges. "Unless the request is complied with the constable is not to interfere in the matter."

The Miss Cass affair drew criticism of the police generally and PC Endacott personally.

Henry Pole, in a letter to the *Echo*, 14th July 1887, told a very different story about PC Endacott, whose perjured evidence had apparently resulted in an innocent young man being sentenced to six months' hard labour. "Let us tear the mask from this constable and hold him up to the world in his true character."

In the same edition T.S. Goodlake[329] characterized the police in less than flattering terms—

"Those who say that policemen, though blackguards, are preferable to the thieves and robbers whom they partly replace, should remember that we are allowed to defend ourselves against the latter, while any attempt to resent the ruffianism of our nocturnal tyrants ensures reckless perjury on their part, reckless subornation of perjury on the part of the Magistrate, and imprisonment without the option of a fine."

Sir James Stansfield, MP for Halifax, called PC Bowden Endacott a

---

328   *The Echo*, 8th July 1887. *Lloyd's Weekly London Newspaper*, 10th July 1888.
329   Thomas Surman Goodlake, son of the Rev. T.W. Goodlake, entered Marlborough College 1858. Called to the Bar 1878. 7 Stone Buildings, Lincoln's Inn, London W.C.

"wretched man".

Sir Charles Warren was "not prepared to say that I can see any grounds for accusing PC Endacott of wilful perjury. However, that is a matter on which I think the Public Prosecutors should decide".

Meanwhile the Lord Chancellor had commenced an inquiry into the conduct of Magistrate Newton, concluding that he had made a mistake in law in issuing a reprimand to a defendant "who had been found guilty but whom the Magistrate felt was undeserving of any sentence."

Newton was himself to receive a formal reprimand.

In the summer of 1887 Miss Elizabeth Cass married her fiancée, Thomas William Langley, by which time she and Mrs. Bowman had commenced a private prosecution. On 13th September 1887 a Grand Jury found a true bill for perjury against PC Endacott.

Bowden Endacott again made the newspapers in September 1888, this time for being struck off the Holborn voters' list for failing to pay his rates.[330]

The perjury case was heard at the Old Bailey in October and November 1887. On the second day the case against Endacott was withdrawn by the Solicitor General after the Judge, Mr. Justice Stephen, asked, "what is the evidence that what he [Endacott] said was not true? Simply the contradiction by the witness Cass . . ."

It was a case of her word against his, and "the conviction of Endacott would probably have been illegal, and it might have been a cruel punishment for what is now seen to be a mistake." Mr. Justice Stephen thus told the jury, "I must direct you under the circumstances to acquit the prisoner."

The Times, 2nd November 1887—

"As to Miss Cass's case . . . She has cleared her character of all the gross charges made against her . . ."

The Times, 3rd November 1887—

"Police Constable Endacott has been reinstated in his former position in the Metropolitan Police by Sir Charles Warren, with full pay."

---

[330]   US = City Taxes. *The Times*, 16th September 1887.

One final indignity awaited Miss Cass.

The clearing of her name and reputation had come at a high cost, and in the case file[331] is a letter from Mrs Bowman and Miss Cass [by this time Mrs. Langley] requesting payment for their legal expenses. To this is attached a note from Godfrey Lushington, Permanent Under-Secretary at the Home Office—

"I see no ground for giving compensation either to Miss Cass or Mad[ame] Bowman. My own belief is that Miss Cass did solicit & that Endacott made no mistake."

MP William Sproston Caine [Liberal, Barrow-in-Furness] took a close interest in the Miss Cass affair, saying that "no more scandalous and disgraceful episode in the history of the police in London had ever been brought before the House."

Whilst the Cass affair was rumbling on, Caine proceeded to open another can of worms, charging the police with levying blackmail "on women at whose wretched trade they winked" across the metropolis.

This was hardly breaking news. Two years earlier the *Pall Mall Gazette* had revealed that—

". . . police, generally, with some honourable exceptions, receive regular payment from abandoned women, besides insisting on having favours. The lewd women of London fully understand that unless they regularly bribe policemen they must quit London or otherwise be arrested and annoyed by trumped-up charges. The strongest Freemasonry among policemen exists in this direction. One keeper says: 'The police are our best friends. They keep things snug, and brothel-keepers are the policemen's best friends, because they pay them. I only keep a small house, but pay the police £3 weekly.'"

This was institutional corruption, a far cry from turning a blind eye to the activities of regular informants or the anonymous Yuletide arrivals at police stations across London of geese, turkeys and cases of good cheer.

House of Commons, 7th July 1887—

Mr. William Leatham Bright [Liberal, Stoke-upon-Trent] asked the

---

[331]   HO 144/472/X15239B

Home Secretary "whether on certain occasions it has been found necessary to remove police constables in considerable quantities from the West End to the East End of London, where the opportunities for the practice are less frequent?"

Henry Matthews replied that the "Chief Commissioner cannot ascertain that it has ever been found necessary to remove police constables in considerable quantities from the West End to the East End of London on this account, or that any charge of this nature has been proved except in isolated cases."

Mr. Peter Esslemont [Liberal, Aberdeen, E.] asked, "Is any notice to be taken of the statement made in the House by an hon. Member as regards 30 such cases?"

Henry Matthews replied, "There is question [tabled] on that subject." But it was a question which remained unasked.

On 8th July 1887 a letter from MP Henry Richard Farquharson[332] [Tory, Dorset Western] appeared in *The Times*—

"When, on Tuesday afternoon, the case of Miss Cass came before the House of Commons, I declined to support the Government, mainly because I had been, for a long while, convinced that the Metropolitan Police are in the habit of levying blackmail and of trumping up charges, which they support by perjury."

Farquharson went on detail a personally insulting incident which occurred at the American Exhibition at Earl's Court. It involved a number of policemen who collectively assumed "a threatening attitude" and who threatened to arrest him for drunkenness.

In the *Pall Mall Gazette*, 9th July 1887, Caine described the prevailing state of affairs on Clapham Common—

". . . I found that there were thirty-two women who got their miserable living after dark on Clapham Common . . . The great majority of these women informed me that they deliberately placed themselves under the patronage of the police by bribing them with sixpence or a

---

[332]   It was MP Henry Richard Farquharson who, in 1892, was identified as the source of the 1891 Jack the Ripper suicide story.

shilling a night."

By the end of the month Henry Matthews had initiated an inquiry. House of Commons, 29th July 1887—

"I am sure the hon. Member will feel that it will be better that I should not describe the steps which will be taken, as publicity would defeat any efforts to discover the truth."

On 3rd August 1887 *Judy or the Serio-Comic Journal* wrote—

"Sir Charles Warren insinuates that the charge against the police of levying blackmail has come upon him as a sort of surprise. This admission clearly proves he is not fit for his post. Either he is blind as a bat, or he has an unfortunate tendency to follow in the footsteps of Mr. Ananias."

In mid-September the inquiry was still proceeding.

Mr. Henry Matthews: "I am informed by the Commissioners of Police that they have failed to obtain as yet any information or any evidence to show whether there is any foundation for the allegations referred to."

Assistant Commissioner James Monro conducted the inquiry into W Division [Clapham]. It ran for over six months, and in February 1888 Sir Charles Warren reported the outcome—

"The result of this inquiry, which was reported to the Secretary of State, was that the grave charge brought against the police was found to be unsupported by a tittle of proof . . ."

Sir Charles Warren further stated—

"With reference to the general question I have to state that Mr. Matthews is glad to find that the result of the inquiry is that no evidence has been forthcoming against the police, and that the charges made against them have not in any manner been sustained."[333]

Though not surprised at the outcome of the inquiry, many people did not accept its conclusions. There were suggestions of a whitewash.

MP William Caine recounted a conversation with an "inspector of detective police," who "frankly admitted that the temptation to the police in districts resorted to by prostitutes was practically irresistible,

---

[333]   *The Times*, 6th February 1888

and he agreed with me in the difficulty, if not impossibility, in obtaining evidence against the police from a class of witnesses whose very daily bread depends on the forbearance of the police, and who can be driven into gaol or workhouse by the action of the police . . ."[334]

But if people believed the police could get away with anything, *Reynolds News*, 15th June 1888, was able to assure them that when it came to really serious infractions Metropolitan Police internal discipline could be swift and decisive—

". . . certain inspectors and Sergeants and several constables of the Hunter Street sub-division of the E division [Holborn] of the Metropolitan police were on Monday called before the Assistant-Commissioner of Police, Colonel Pearson, in reference to a 'draw' between certain members of the division for a watch and one or two canary birds, the property of one Police Constable Hackett. Three inspectors, three Sergeants, and 10 constables were peremptorily transferred to other divisions, and eight constables [including Hackett] were dismissed from the force."

The newspaper added as a footnote that " . . . for some time past a secret inquiry has been proceeding at the Home office before Mr. Curtis Bennett, the Westminster magistrate, into the conduct of certain officials at Scotland Yard, which promises to rival in public interest the revelations at the Board of Works inquiry."[335]

There was no further mention of Curtis Bennett's deliberations at Scotland Yard. His secret inquiry remained a secret.

Pall Mall Gazette, 7th July 1888—

"The power of the police over women in the streets is already ample, not merely for the purposes of maintaining order and for preventing indecency and molestation, but also for the purpose of levying blackmail upon unfortunates. I have been assured by a chaplain of one of Her Majesty's gaols, who perhaps has more opportunities of talking to these women than any other individual in the realm, that there is absolute

---

[334]   *The Times*, 8th February 1888
[335]   An 1888 Royal Commission to investigate allegations of graft and corruption at the Board of Works not only found them to be true, "but understated."

unanimity in the ranks that if they do not tip the police they get run in. From the highest to the lowest, he informs me, the universal testimony is that you must pay the constable, or you get into trouble . . ."

As late as November 1895 Harold Frederic in the *New York Times* was detailing the blackmailing activities of police in C Division [St. James's] and E Division [Holborn]—

"Some girl, who gets arrested, swears that she is being persecuted because she is unable to pay the half-crown or five shilling demanded as hush money; but no effort is ever made to test the truth of her story. The public does not need proof, because it firmly believes it already. Scotland Yard and the Magistrates do not want any proof either, because they would deem it their duty to disregard it in any case.

". . . there are two respects in which the metropolitan police anger Londoners very much. One is the systematic way in which they support on oath any police story whatever which may be set up in the witness box against a private citizen . . . I cannot recall more than one instance in which punishment of any sort was visited upon the offender. Scotland Yard stands stoutly by its men. What is worse, the metropolitan magistrates stand by them, too."

Despite police constables having allegedly been transferred from the West End to the East End, the *Evening News's* anticipated "startling revelations" and reports from overseas that the police were "trying to screen" the Whitechapel murderer, [336] there is no available evidence that the murders of Emma Smith, Martha Tabram and Polly Nichols were the work of policemen attempting to blackmail East End prostitutes.

However, police blackmail may have been a subject the Metropolitan Police was keen to avoid. This is evidenced by a theory of sublime unlikeliness which sprang out of nowhere to briefly engage the public imagination.

---

[336]   *Evening Post* [NZ], 18th September 1888.

18. THE MAD SNOB

Eastern Post, 7th April 1888—

"On Thursday the authorities of the London Hospital informed the coroner of the death in that institution of Emma Elizabeth Smith, aged 45, a widow, lately living at 18, George Street, Spitalfields. It appears that the deceased was out on Bank Holiday, and when returning home along Whitechapel Road early on Tuesday morning, she was set upon by some men and severely maltreated. The men made off, leaving the woman on the ground in a semi-conscious condition, and have not yet been apprehended. She was taken home, and subsequently conveyed to the hospital where she died."

The *Echo*, 10th August 1888—

"'No crime more brutal has ever been committed in the East-end,' said a Criminal Investigation officer, this morning, 'than the one at George Yard Buildings.' The murder to which allusion was made was that of the young woman [Martha Tabram] found in a block of model dwellings in Whitechapel Road, with thirty-nine stabs on her body, one over her heart . . ."

The *Star*, 31st August 1888—

"Such horrible work [the murder of Polly Nichols] could only be the deed of a maniac. The other murder, in which the woman received 30 stabs, must also have been the work of a maniac. This murder occurred on Bank Holiday. On the Bank Holiday preceding another woman was murdered in equally brutal but even more barbarous fashion by being stabbed with a stick. She died without being able to tell anything of her murderer. All this leads to the conclusion, that the police have now formed, that there is a maniac haunting Whitechapel, and that the three woman were all victims of his murderous frenzy."

The *Star*, 1st September 1888—

"The first murder [Emma Smith], which, strangely enough, did not rouse much interest, was committed in Osborn Street. The woman in that case was alive when discovered, but unconscious, and she died in the hospital without recovering her senses, consequently she was unable to whisper a word to put the police on the track of her fiendish assailant, and her murder has remained a mystery . . . The fact that these three tragedies have been committed within such a limited area, and are so strangely alike in their details, is forcing on all minds the conviction that they are the work of some cool, cunning man with a mania for murder."

Both *Star* reports contained blatant lies.

Emma Smith survived long enough to tell George Haslip, house surgeon at the London Hospital, that she had been attacked by a gang, one of whom was 'a youth of 19', who proceeded to take all the money she had 'and then committed the outrage.' A blunt instrument had ruptured her peritoneum, and she later died 'through peritonitis set up by the injuries.'[337]

Chief Inspector John West [H Division] wrote in an undated report—

"Deceased could not describe the men who had ill-used her but said there were three of them . . ."

The *Star's* version of events was steering minds away from the subject of blackmailing gangs, just as the *Echo* had done earlier in reporting the murders of Emma Smith and Martha Tabram—

"For ferocity the two cases are somewhat analogous, and some of the Scotland Yard experts in tracing criminals and fathoming crime

---

[337]   *The Times*, 9th April 1888

incline to the opinion that one man is responsible for the two crimes."[338]

Had it been recalled that Emma Smith was the victim of gang violence, Tabram and Nichols could not have been linked to her as the second and third victims of the same lone perpetrator.

If the three murders were linked, they were more likely to have all been the work of a gang. The only other alternative is that the murders were unconnected, which makes it even more strange that an attempt was being made to give them false context as part of a series.

On 1st September 1888, The *Evening News* reported that the lone madman theory was generally accepted "amongst the inhabitants of the district, the female portion of which is greatly alarmed."

Yet the newspaper did not itself subscribe to the idea—

"The more probable theory is that the murder has been committed by one or more of a gang of men, who are in the habit of frequenting the streets at late hours of the night and levying blackmail on women."

For the next twelve days the *Star* was at the forefront in promoting a very different theory.

On 1st September 1888 the newspaper asked—

"Have we a murderous maniac loose in East London? It looks as if we have. Nothing so appalling, so devilish, so inhuman—or, rather, non-human—as the three Whitechapel crimes has ever happened outside the pages of Poe or De Quincey.

"The unravelled mystery of 'The Whitechapel Murders' would make a page of detective romance as ghastly as 'The Murders in the Rue Morgue'. The hellish violence and malignity of the crime which we described yesterday resemble in almost every particular the two other deeds of darkness which preceded it . . ."

There again was the blatant lie. Was the *Star* reporting Metropolitan Police thinking, or creating its very own Frankenstein monster?

". . . Rational motive there appears to be none. The murderer must be a Man Monster, and when Sir Charles [Warren] has done quarrelling with his detective service he will perhaps help the citizens of East

---

[338]   *Echo*, 10th August 1888

London to catch him."

The die was cast. A monster was on the loose. News spread fast.

The *New York Times*, 1st September 1888—

"London, Aug. 31.

"The police have concluded that the same man did all three murders and that the most dangerous kind of a lunatic is at large."

The name of Leather Apron had not been mentioned in connection with the murders of Emma Smith and Martha Tabram. It made its debut in the *Sheffield and Rotherham Independent*,[339] 1st September 1888—

"The women in a position similar to that of the deceased allege that there is a man who goes by the name of 'Leather Apron' who has more than once attacked unfortunate and defenceless women. His dodge is, it is asserted, to get them into some house on the pretence of offering them money. He then takes what little they have and 'half kills' them in addition . . ."

On the same day the *Morning Advertiser* reported—

"The police are of the opinion that the deceased was murdered in a house, and afterwards carried to the spot where she was found . . ."

The *Echo* elaborated—

"The theory is that the woman was murdered in a house and killed whilst undressed, her clothes being then huddled on the body, which was afterwards conveyed out, to be deposited in the street. Though a 'High Rip' gang is suspected of the deed, most of the detectives who are investigating the case believe that it was the work of a maniac."

Two days later, 3rd September 1888, the *Echo* announced—

"For some reason the police have abandoned the theory that the deceased was murdered in a house and carried to the spot. They now believe she was killed at the place where she was discovered . . ."

The next chapter in the story of the man-monster loose on the streets of the East End also originated in the *New York Times,* when its London correspondent picked up and expanded upon cues earlier provided by the *Star* and the *Sheffield and Rotherham Independent.*

---

[339]   Sheffield and Rotherham are two industrial cities 170 miles north of London.

New York Times, 4th September 1888—

"London, Sept. 3.

"Whitechapel has a murder mystery which transcends anything known in the annals of the horrible. It is Poe's 'Murders of the Rue Morgue' and 'The Mystery of Marie Roget' rolled into one real story. It is nothing less than a midnight murderer, whose step is noiseless, whose strike is deadly, and whose cunning is so great that he leaves no trace whatever of his work and no clue to his identity. He has just slaughtered his third victim, and all the women in Whitechapel are terrified, while the stupidest detectives in the civilized world stand aghast and say they have no clue . . ."

Thus, on the basis of absolutely no supporting evidence whatsoever, was the mystery defined in the public mind—

Cunning monster outwits incompetent police force.

Who might this mysterious murderer have been?

" . . . This man is called 'Leather Apron' and nobody knows him by any other name. He is in character half way between Dickens's Quilp[340] and Poe's Baboon[341]. He has small, wicked black eyes and is half crazy. He is always hanging about the deep shadows that fill the intricate network of the courts, passages, and alleyways in Whitechapel. He does not walk, but always moves on a sharp, queer run and never makes any noise with his feet . . . One peculiar feature of the case is that none of the police or detectives appears to know him."

London's first brief introduction to the mysterious Leather Apron was a brief mention in the *Star* on 4th September 1888—

"With regard to the man who goes by the sobriquet of 'Leather Apron', he has not, it is stated, been seen in the neighborhood much for the past few nights, but this may mean nothing, as the women street wanderers declare that he is known as well in certain quarters of the West End as he is in Whitechapel."

The Times offered an insight into official thinking—

---

[340]   'I'm a little hunchy villain and a monster,' says Daniel Quilp in Charles Dickens's *The Old Curiosity Shop*, 1841.

[341]   *The Murders in the Rue Morgue*, Edgar Allan Poe, 1841. The culprit was an orangutan.

"Although the Whitechapel murders are without example, the police have also an unexampled number of data from which to draw their conclusions . . . "

None of this police data appears to have involved gang-related activity. A lone perpetrator remained the preferred hypothesis.

The Times continued—

". . . The most salient point is the maniacal frenzy with which the victims were slaughtered, and unless we accept, as a possible alternative, the theory that the assassin was actuated by revenge for some real or supposed injury suffered by him at the hands of unfortunate women, we are thrown back upon the belief that these murders were really committed by a madman . . ."

By the following day any lingering suspicions about a gang of blackmailing thugs had evaporated.

The *Star*, 5th September 1888—

"'Leather Apron' by himself is quite an unpleasant character. If, as many of the people suspect, he is the real author of the three murders which, in everybody's judgement, were done by the same person, he is a more ghoulish and devilish brute than can be found in all the pages of shocking fiction . . ."

According to the London correspondent of the *New York Times* "none of the police or detectives appears to know him," yet the remarkably well-informed *Star* was able to offer a detailed description—

"From all accounts he is five feet four or five inches in height and wears a dark, close-fitting cap. He is thickset, and has an unusually thick neck. His hair is black, and closely clipped, his age being about 38 or 40. He has a small, black moustache. The distinguishing feature of his costume is a leather apron, which he always wears, and from which he gets his nickname . . .

"His expression is sinister, and seems to be full of terror for the women who describe it. His eyes are small and glittering. His lips are usually parted in a grin which is not only not reassuring, but excessively repellent . . ."

The *Star* next added its *pièce de résistance*—

"His name nobody knows, but all are united in the belief that he is a Jew or of Jewish parentage, his face being of a marked Hebrew type."

Thus was Leather Apron endowed with a characteristic which made him the ideal suspect. Not only was he a violent, ghoulish and devilish brute, half-man and half-monster; he was also a Jew—which played straight into the hands of every stereotypical prejudice against the burgeoning Jewish population of the East End, blamed amongst a host of other things for driving the English out, rents up and wages down.

The cry soon became loud and clear—

". . . a gang of youths marched down Hanbury Street shouting, 'Down with the Jews!' 'It was a Jew who did it!' 'No Englishman did it!'"[342]

Meanwhile, on 5th September 1888, the *Echo* was busily throwing a spanner into the works of the Leather Apron story, claiming the *Star* had been well and truly gulled—

"An American journalist, anxious to distinguish himself in his paper, sent another scribe hailing from the other side of the Atlantic down into Whitechapel to interview the natives on the subject of the murder, and get their ideas. They gave him them, which were to the effect that they believed the murder had been committed by a 'wild looking man, wearing a leather apron', who had been seen about in Whitechapel lately, and was believed to be an escaped lunatic.

"Filled with this splendid idea, the young man made some 'beautiful copy', which his chief telegraphed off to New York forthwith, only to learn, a very little while afterwards, that his assistant had been thoroughly well hoaxed, and that the real murderer is, if not actually known to the police, believed to be within very easy reach of a warrant—and quite sane."

A variant on this story, by Vance Thompson, appeared ten years later in the August 1898 edition of *Lippincott's Magazine*—

Discussing the "bureau system" whereby newspapers farmed out police news to different agencies, Thompson wrote, " . . . I find it

---

[342] *Lloyd's Weekly London Newspaper*, 9 September 1888.

pleasant to look back upon an idiot who was reporting [on the Whitechapel murders] for one of the London papers in '88 and '89. The editor of the paper was an Irish member of Parliament."

This firmly established the newspaper as T.P. O'Connor's *Star*.

"The newspapers were aroused and . . . thereupon all the journalists who could "write a wee bit" were sent out to do the Whitechapel murders. And one of these reporters was an idiot with an eye-glass[343] . . . and the plump editor ordered him to go to Whitechapel and discover and describe 'Jack the Ripper.'

"The young reporter led his eye-glass down the stairs and found himself in Fleet Street. He did not know how to set about the business, so he strolled into Mitre Court, which is off Fleet Street, and there he found a tavern that is known as the Mitre.[344]

Here the young reporter met Henry Pottinger Stephens, librettist of "Billee Taylor", an 1880 comedy opera with music by Edward Solomon.

"What are you doing?" asked Stephens.

"The Whitechapel murders," said the reporter.

"Descriptive?"

"Yes, a general descriptive story."

"Why don't you read up on De Quincy?"

"What—Leathern Apron?"

"To be sure: it is excellent stuff," said Stephens.

"Then the young man . . . wrote up a description of the wicked man who had done to death the wicked women of Whitechapel. He used as his prototype the leathern-aproned Jew with the knife in his belt and the white face blurred with black eyebrows . . . Then the idiot went down and interviewed the periwinkle-men and apple-women of Mile-End Road. Of course they had seen Leathern-Apron slinking about the streets, with his knife whisking in his hand.

"The young man turned [the story] into the office. But there was

---

[343] Harry Dam sported pince-nez.

[344] The Mitre Tavern was demolished in 1829. The 1888 Post Office Street Directory lists the one public house in Mitre Court as The Clachan.

one odd end to it: the day after the story was printed the police began to look for Leathern-Apron. By some whimsical mischance they found a poor innocent Hebrew who answered the description: he was a butcher down in Besis Court, and he lay in jail for two weeks, and—well, 'Billee Taylor' was responsible for it."

However, on the day after the *Echo* story the *Star* had the last laugh. Not only was Leather Apron real; he had slipped through the fingers of the police.

The *Star*, Thursday 6th September 1888—

"The hunt for 'Leather Apron' began in earnest last evening. Constables 43 and 173, J Division, into whose hands 'Leather-Apron' fell on Sunday afternoon, were detailed to accompany Detective Enright, of the J Division, in a search through all the quarters where the crazy Jew was likely to be. They began at half-past ten in Church Street, in Shoreditch, rumour having located the suspected man there. They went through lodging-houses, into 'pubs', down side streets, threw their bull's-eyes into every shadow, and searched the quarter thoroughly, but without result . . .

". . . The clue furnished by the woman who denounced the man on Sunday is a very unfortunate one. Her offer to prove by two women that 'Leather Apron' was seen walking with the murdered woman in Baker's Row [west of Bucks Row] at two o'clock last Friday morning, is the most direct bit of evidence that yet has appeared . . ."

As regards this timing, it is worth noting that Emily Holland testified at Polly Nichols' inquest that at "About half-past two on Friday morning [she] saw deceased walking down Osborn Street, Whitechapel Road [which is 600 yards further east from Bakers Row]. She was alone, and very much the worse for drink" [author's brackets].

Given all these contradictory press reports it must have been difficult for an 1888 newspaper reader to decide whether Leather Apron was real or imaginary. Yet there were clues. A keen-eyed reader may have noticed that Leather Apron owed much of his alleged physical appearance to press coverage of a play starring actor-manager Richard

Mansfield which was shocking audiences at the Lyceum, Drury Lane.[345]

The Times, 6th August 1888—

'The Strange Case of Dr. Jekyll and Mr. Hyde.

"Mr. Hyde is a crouching, Quilp-like creature, a malignant Quasimodo, who hisses and snorts like a wild beast."

The Times, 8th August 1888, ran a display advertisement for *The Strange Case of Dr. Jekyll and Mr. Hyde*—

'Daily Chronicle: 'The apish, sneering, malignant and crouching Hyde . . .'

"Pall Mall Gazette: '. . . the abominable and apish Hyde.'

"Star: '. . . the odious monster, with brutality in every line, and look, and gesture.'"

Following the murder of Polly Nichols it did not take long for life to start imitating art. Having in the same edition dismissed the idea of a lone maniac in favour of the exploits of a gang, the *London Evening Post*, 1st September 1888, decided to hedge its bets—

"It seems pretty clear that Mr. Hyde has broken loose in Whitechapel. Can it be that Mr. Stevenson's ghoul has a prototype in actual life?"

Meanwhile, unbeknownst to anyone outside the Metropolitan Police, Leather Apron had become a person of interest.

He now also had a name.

In a report dated 7th September 1888, Inspector Helson, J Division [Bethnal Green], wrote—

'The inquiry has revealed the fact that a man named Jack [sic] Pizer, alias Leather Apron, has, for some considerable period been in the habit of ill-using prostitutes in this, and other parts of the Metropolis, and careful search has been, and is continued to be made, to find this man in order that his movements may be accounted for on the night in question, although at present there is no evidence against him."

At 6.00 am on Saturday, 8th September 1888, the hideously-

---

[345]   On 5th October 1888 the City of London Police received an anonymous letter claiming that Richard Mansfield was Jack the Ripper. CLRO Police Box 3·16 No. 155. London Metropolitan Archives.

mutilated body of Annie Chapman, a forty-seven year-old unfortunate, was discovered in the back yard of 29 Hanbury Street.

Star, 8th September 1888—

"The murder is certainly the fourth of a series by the same fiendish hand. The blood-crazy man or beast that haunts Whitechapel has done his latest work on the same line as its predecessors."

Discovered under a water tap in the yard was a leather apron.

The *Evening News*, 8th September 1888—

". . . One report has it that a leather apron and a long knife have been found near the place where the body lay, belonging, it is said, to a man whose name is unknown, but who is surnamed 'Leather Apron,' and evidently known in the district."

Here was a clue as big as the Rock of Gibraltar. Yet seven detectives and one Divisional Surgeon neglected to record its presence in their various reports and testimonies.[346]

Meanwhile the *Pall Mall Gazette*, 8th September 1888, was having none of it, reasoning that the real murderer may have been attempting to capitalize on the Leather Apron scare—

"The fact that the police have been freely talking for a week past about a man nicknamed Leather Apron may have led the criminal to leave a leather apron near his victim in order to mislead."[347]

On 9th September 1888, the *New York Sun* published a story filed by its London correspondent, Arthur Brisbane—

"The police are industriously looking for a certain individual, who is probably innocent. Since Friday's [sic] murder, one newspaper has been clamoring for the arrest of a so-called Leather Apron, who is minutely described, but who is probably a half mythical character, if not altogether the product of some heated imagination."

Appended to Arthur Brisbane's story was the description of Leather Apron as earlier published in the *Star*.

---

[346]   West, Abberline, Styles, Thick, Helson, Swanson, Chandler and Dr. George Bagster Phillips.

[347]   The leather apron proved to be the property of the son of Mrs Amelia Richardson, a widow who ran a packing-case business at 29 Hanbury Street.

There is a widely-held present-day belief that the 'new [tabloid] press' of the late Victorian period—the *Star* in particular—was staffed by hacks who could not be trusted when it came to the facts of the matter, had scant regard for journalistic integrity and sexed-up this grisly series of murders solely to boost circulation.

The *Star* eschewed gutter journalism; understandably when boasting such a stellar line-up of editorial staff. George Bernard Shaw was its leader-writer at two guineas a week, and many others—Ernest Parke, Robert Donald, Clement King Shorter and Thomas Marlowe— went on to achieve considerable reputations as newspaper editors.

Harry Jackson Wells Dam, Ph. B., alleged creator of the *Star's* Leather Apron story, was a playwright[348] and accomplished journalist whose 1887 series of articles in the *New York Times* on East Coast society watering holes won him wide acclaim. In 1890, aged 34, he became the *New York Herald*'s Paris correspondent.

Harold Frederic, London correspondent of the *New York Times* since 1885, was described as "the best of English correspondents."[349] The same age as Harry Dam, he was a student of bee-keeping and also the author of ten novels including *The Damnation of Theron Ware* [1896], considered to be a masterpiece of *fin-de-siècle* American fiction. On his UK tax returns, under the heading "Profession", he would write "paper-stainer." He died young, aged 42, in 1898.

In 1886 the precocious 21-year-old Arthur Brisbane became the New York *Sun's* London correspondent, taking over from the redoubtable T.P O'Connor, who was almost twice Brisbane's age and at that time preparing to launch his own newspaper, the *Star*.

Oliver Carlson, in his 1937 "Brisbane: A Candid Biography" wrote—

"When the gruesome murders by Jack-the-Ripper took place in London, it was Brisbane who pictured them in their most horrible details for the readers of the *Sun*. They thrilled and shivered at the word pictures

---

[348]   Harry Dam wrote the book [libretto] for *The Shop Girl*, a musical composed by the previously mentioned Ivan Caryll.
[349]   *Review of Reviews*, 1891

drawn of this dastardly fiend who ripped open the bodies of his unsuspecting female victims."

Portraying Brisbane as a purveyor of blood-soaked Gothic horror was wide of the mark. He certainly spared few details of the mutilations to Catherine Eddowes and Mary Kelly, but in the *Sun*, 10th November 1888, he did take care to explain his reasoning—

"A description of such butchery is unpleasant to write, but it is necessary to understand London's state of terror and to form an opinion as to this remarkable murderer."

Meanwhile the manhunt for Leather Apron continued, with *Lloyd's Weekly London Newspaper,* 9th September 1888, publishing a letter from a correspondent named 'Eye-Witness' detailing "an incident which [he/she?] witnessed on Sunday [2nd September] between half-past four and a quarter-past five pm."

'Eye-Witness' reported that, as he/she was about to turn into Albert Street, a woman rushed across the street by Cohen's Sugar Refinery, screaming "There goes Leather Apron, the Whitechapel murderer," to a policeman standing on a nearby corner. Two other constables arrived, and when the man was apprehended the woman again accused him of "being the man the police were looking for—Leather Apron. This she repeated about 20 times without receiving a single denial from the man."

The woman also said that she knew two women who saw the man pacing up and down Baker's Row with Polly Nichols about two hours before the murder took place [and an hour before the Emily Holland encounter in Osborn Street]. The man sneered at her accusations, saying that he didn't know what she was talking about, after which, "to crown it all, the policemen then let the man go."

Lloyd's Weekly Newspaper did not say when the letter from Eye Witness was received, but on the day after the incident was first mentioned in the *Star* the story was promoted via an advertisement in *The Times*.[350]

---

[350] *The Times*, 7th September 1888. 'Strange Story of a Ruffian called 'Leather Apron'.
Lloyd's News. 66 Columns. One penny.

Lloyd's continued—

"At first the police attached little importance to the story of 'Leather Apron', but after the appearance of the above letter the detectives showed their regret at the stupidity of the constable in failing to arrest him by eagerly searching different lodging-houses and casual wards for this 'Leather Apron'. A chase has now begun in earnest. He was last seen outside the Leigh Hoy[351] public-house in Spitalfields. In addition to being known as 'Leather Apron' he is also known as the 'Mad Snob'.[352]

"The police description of him is:—Aged 30 years; height, 5ft. 3in.; complexion dark, sallow; hair and moustache black; thick set; dressed in old and dirty clothing; and is of Jewish appearance . . ."

This description bore an uncanny resemblance to that of Leather Apron which had earlier appeared in the *Star*.

Lloyd's continued—

". . . The inquiries of our special representative led to the discovery that he is the son of a fairly well-to-do Russian Jew, but he is discarded by the Jewish fraternities as one who is a disgrace to their tribe."

Of more interest is the fact that there was no mention of the 2nd September Leather Apron incident involving two J Division constables in Inspector Helson's 7th September report.

Daily News, 10th September 1888—

"Detective Inspector Abberline of Scotland Yard . . . held a consultation with Detective Inspector Helson, J Division . . . and with Acting Superintendent West, in charge of the H Division. The result . . . was an agreement in the belief that the crimes were the work of one individual only, and that, notwithstanding many misleading statements and rumours - the majority of which in the excitement of the time had been printed as facts - the murders were committed where the bodies had been found, and that no 'gang' were the perpetrators."

During this period H Division and the CID at Scotland Yard were in

---

[351]   A "Leigh Hoy" was a type of fishing smack.

[352]   In the late 18th Century a 'snob' was a cobbler, or shoe-maker.

operational disarray. Superintendent Arnold and Local Inspector Reid were on annual leave, Monro had gone to the Home Office, Anderson was "in Switzerland," and Warren, who earlier in the year inaugurated a new system for the submission of divisional Special Reports which delayed their receipt by the CID, had not long returned from summer vacation.

Things soon went from bad to worse.

Star, 10th September 1888—

"To add to the list of clumsy follies which have made Sir Charles Warren's name stink in the nostrils of the people of London, the Chief Commissioner has lately transferred the whole of the East End detectives to the West and moved the West End men to the East. That is to say he has deprived the people of Whitechapel of the one guarantee they had for reposing confidence in their ordinary guardians - viz., that to the [? unreadable] skill of the detective was being added the local knowledge indispensable when the investigation of criminal or semi-criminal quarters is in question. Whitechapel, then, is practically defenceless."

If the *Star* was correct, this was an odd way to be running what was purportedly the hunt for a local maniac.

The *Daily News*, 10th September, denounced what it saw as the lynch mob mentality of Whitechapel—

"The public are looking for a monster, and in the legend of 'Leather Apron' the Whitechapel part of them seem to be inventing a monster to look for. This kind of invention ought to be discouraged in every possible way, or there may soon be murders from panic to add to murders from lust of blood. A touch would fire the whole district, in the mood which it is now. Leather Apron walks without making a noise, Leather Apron has piercing eyes and a strange smile, and finally Leather Apron looks like a Jew. The last is brutal as well as foolish, and it has already had its effect in a cry against Whitechapel Jews. Already, as our columns show today, the list of savage assaults in the neighbourhood has shown an alarming increase since the discovery [of Annie Chapman] on Saturday. Every man who can say a reasonable word ought to say it, or worse may follow than all we have already known."

On the same day Leather Apron became a reality when a 38-year-old Polish Jew—John Pizer, a boot finisher—was arrested at his stepmother's house.

A Press Association report published in *Freeman's Journal and Daily Commercial Advertiser*, 13th September 1888, quoted him as saying—

"On Monday morning Sergeant Thick came. I opened the door. He said I was wanted and I asked what for. He replied, 'You know what for; you will have to come with me.' I said, 'Very well; I will go with the greatest pleasure.' The officer said, You know you are 'Leather Apron,' or words to that effect. Up to that moment I did not know I was called by that name."

"Is John Pizer the much-talked-of 'Leather Apron'? asked the *Star*. John Pizer, John Pizer's step-mother, step-brother, step-sister and neighbors all say 'No'. Sergeant Thicke, who is an officer of high reputation, and who knows, perhaps, more of the East-end and its rough denizens than any other man in the force, says almost positively that Pizer is 'Leather Apron'."

John Pizer was taken to Leman Street police station, where he was kept for about two hours before being taken to Commercial Street police station.

The *Star*, 10th September 1888—

"At half-past twelve he was ushered into the main office of the station, half a dozen policemen guarding the doors. Piser sat down on the seat next the outside wall. He looked pale and rather dejected. No questions were asked him, the only ceremony being that a woman sitting in the corner behind the table was told to look sharp. She had been sitting there all the forenoon, doubtless for the purpose of identification. Then Pizer was taken into the inner office, the doors were closed, and the further ceremonies were known only to the detectives."

At nine o'clock the following morning "Pizer was still comfortably quartered in a room at Leman Street police station, and there he is likely to remain until the detectives have cleared up the strong suspicion there is against him. No one is allowed to see the prisoner but his brother this morning called at the police station and left both food and drink, which was afterwards given to the prisoner. Pizer asked to be allowed to see his brother, but was refused."[353]

At just before one o'clock in the afternoon "11 men passing by Leman Street police station were asked and consented to go into the station yard for a few minutes. Pizer was brought out, and put amongst them. A middle-aged man, with a face of negro cast, but not black, was then asked whether he could 'identify the man,' and unhesitatingly he picked out Pizer.

"'What,' said Pizer, 'you know me?'

"But an inspector raised a warning hand, and without anything else being said the men dispersed and Pizer was led back to his room."[354]

John Pizer had a slightly different recollection of this incident

"Between eleven and twelve o'clock yesterday a man came to Leman Street police-station. One of the authorities asked me if I had any objection to go out to see if I could be identified. I at once went into the station yard. There were several men there. One of them I know to be a boot finisher. He is a stout, stalwart man, of negro caste. He came towards me, and without saying a word he deliberately placed his hand on my shoulder.

"I promptly replied, 'I don't know you; you are mistaken.'"[355]

The "middle-aged man, with a face of negro cast, but not black" was a 63-year-old immigrant, Emanuel Delbast Violenia [Violena], also described in the press as "half-Spaniard and half-Bulgarian."[356]

The Times, 12th September 1888—

"Early last Saturday morning [8th September], walking alone along Hanbury Street, he noticed a man and woman quarreling in a very excited manner. Violenia distinctly heard the man threaten to kill the woman by sticking a knife into her. They passed on, and Violenia went to his lodging."

---

[353]   *Star*, 11th September 1888.

[354]   Ibid.

[355]   *Star*, 12th September 1888

[356]   At Oxford, June 1889, Emanuel Delbast Violena was sentenced to fourteen months' imprisonment on charges of indecent assault against four young girls.

The police thought it prudent to take Violenia to the Whitechapel mortuary to see if he could identify Annie Chapman as the woman he had witnessed in Pizer's company.

The Times, 12th September 1888—

"The result is not announced, but it is believed that he was unable to identify her. Subsequently, cross-examination so discredited Violenia's evidence that it was wholly distrusted by the police, and Pizer was set at liberty."

Other newspapers were critical about Violenia's identification of John Pizer as Leather Apron.

The *Penny Illustrated Press,* 15th September 1888—

'The conduct of the man who professed to identify Pizer has caused much indignation, it having kept several experienced officers from prosecuting inquiries in other directions. His statement, clear enough at first, utterly failed to stand the test even of ordinary questioning."

From this it appears that the police considered Pizer's identification and arrest an unnecessary and time-wasting diversion.

"The police, however, attach far more importance to the arrest which has been made at Gravesend . . ."[357]

On the morning of Pizer's arrest, Inspector Abberline made a sixty-mile round trip by train to Gravesend, Kent, to bring back to London 53-year-old William Henry Piggott, whom the local police had arrested and various newspapers reported as "answering the description of Leather Apron."

But it was all to no avail. Nothing was found to connect him with the murders and, following an examination by divisional surgeon Dr. George Bagster Phillips, Piggott was pronounced insane and removed to the infirmary, where he was treated for *delirium tremens* and later released.[358]

---

[357]   *Star*, 10th September 1888.

[358]   Three years later, on 27th July 1891, William Henry Piggott pleaded guilty at the Old Bailey to stealing £10. He also pleaded guilty to a charge of bigamy, having married Lavinia Wing whilst still legally married to Elizabeth Alice Smith. Piggott was sentenced to three days' imprisonment.

Earlier on the day of the Pizer identification parade a *Star* reporter spoke with the arresting officer, Sergeant William Thick, "a stout-built, keen, but pleasant-faced man, with thick, drooping, yellowish moustache, dressed in a light check suit."

The *Star,* 11th September 1888—

"The Sergeant who, by the rough characters among whom his profession takes him, is better known as Johnny Upright, had just been deep in consultation in the station yard with a crowd of detectives, when our representative had the good fortune to get an introduction.

"'Of course, you've come about the Whitechapel murder,' he said, when a *Star* card was handed to him. 'Now, you know as well as I do that I cannot tell you anything.'

"Our representative urged that he might be able to say something without damaging the public interest, and with a little questioning a few facts were obtained.

"The sergeant emphatically denied that, as the neighbors had said, 'Leather Apron' had for the last six weeks been going about his business in an ordinary manner. 'He's been in hiding safe enough, and it's my opinion his friends have been screening him. He has not been in lodging houses; he is too well known there and the people who frequent them would have been ready to lynch him. Why the other day a woman told me plainly that if she saw him she would kill him, and I could do what I liked with her afterwards. No,' keen Johnny Upright continued, 'Leather Apron has not been into a lodging-house since the Sunday the woman denounced him in Whitechapel, and the police were bamboozled into letting him go.'"

This appears to have been the incident reported in the *Star* and in the letter from 'Eye-Witness' published in *Lloyd's Weekly London Newspaper*.

A variation on the incident given by Pizer himself was reported in the *Echo* on 12th September—

"On Sunday week last, while I was walking through Church Street, two women accosted me. I did not know them. One of them accused me of committing the crime in Bucks Row. The other, the elder of the two, however, said, 'You are not the man, are you?' I said, 'I know nothing about it.' At that moment a stalwart and strong-looking man came up. Addressing me, he exclaimed, 'Mate, come and stand me half-a-pint.' I, however, refused, and walked away."

On the same day, Pizer's brother, Gabriel, who maintained that John had never been known to him as Leather Apron, gave yet another version—

"[John Pizer] had related to him an incident which he says occurred in Spitalfields on Sunday week and which seems to have contributed greatly to his alarm. Some women had pointed him out as 'Leather Apron', and the attention of a policeman was called to him. The officer refused to take him in charge, and Piser [sic] was pursued by a howling crowd that had collected, which seems to have frightened him considerably."

No policemen had been bamboozled in John Pizer's version of the incident; nor had 'Eye-Witness' noticed Gabriel Pizer's 'howling crowd'.

If, despite some alarming incongruities, these accounts are essentially the same, they tally with the *Star* report about Constables 143J [Gorden] and 173J [Murphy], accompanied by Detective-Sergeant Enright, commencing a belated search for Leather Apron at 10.30 pm on Wednesday 5th September in Church Street, Shoreditch.

Pizer said he was accosted in Church Street, which the police understood to be a thoroughfare in Shoreditch. Yet the location of this street is misleading. The three policemen were flashing their bullseye lanterns in the wrong district.

Church Street, Spitalfields, disappeared in 1879, subsumed as the eastern section of Hanbury Street. A sugar refinery stood at No. 157, on the corner of Deal Street, which led north into Albert Street. Up until 1st August 1871 the refinery was run by the partnership of Thomas Burns Dakin and James Bryant Jr. After the partnership was dissolved the refinery remained under the sole ownership of Thomas Burns Dakin, whose name is recorded in the 1882, 1884 and 1888 Post Office Street Directories. A search through available records has not revealed the name Cohen in connection with the refinery, but it should perhaps be noted that a large London sugar refiner of the time was Cowan & Sons, located at Barnes, West London, which sounds very similar.

That the alleged incident actually took place in Hanbury Street is lent added weight by *Lloyd's* report that Leather Apron "was last seen outside the Leigh Hoy public house in Spitalfields." The Leigh Hoy was in Hanbury Street, at the corner of Queen Street, a few doors east from Thomas Dakin's sugar refinery.

On 10th September 1888 the *Echo* published a Press Association interview with Pizer's stepmother and sister-in-law—

". . . They further state that Pizer is unable to do much work on account of his ill-health, and that he is by no means a strong person, as, some time ago, he was seriously injured in a vital part. About six weeks ago he left a convalescent home, of which he had been an inmate on account of a carbuncle on his neck . . ." and on the following day the *Echo* reported—

"It appears that a man answering the description of 'Leather Apron' was recently an in-patient of the Jewish Convalescent Home at Norwood, recovering from a very severe carbuncle in the neck. The man stated that he had previously been treated at the Paddington Infirmary."[359]

The Times, 10th September 1888, was not completely sold on the concept of a lone maniac—

"The case of Emma Smith, who died from the effects of a barbarous assault in the early morning of Easter Tuesday last, is different, and possibly it ought to be entirely dissociated from the murders of last month. Smith lived long enough to describe the outrage . . . If this murder is to be classed with the three recent ones, then the theory that they were the work of a gang of blackmailers is more than tenable . . ."

Somebody had at last spotted a disconnect between the first three murders.

However, the police, as *The Times* reported on the same day,

---

[359] Pizer was released from the Paddington Infirmary in June 1888, having been treated for a ruptured carbuncular boil. Admission to the Norwood convalescent home was by a governor's or subscriber's recommendation or on payment of ten shillings per week. Free admission required the patient to first go to the Duke's Place Synagogue to be examined by a practitioner appointed by the Jewish ruling council.

continued to believe "that the murder has been committed by the same person who perpetrated the three previous ones in the district, and that only one person is concerned in it."

The lone perpetrator scenario still reigned supreme; but at the same time, if the following story is to be believed, the Metropolitan Police was busily washing its hands of Leather Apron.

Echo, 11th September 1888—

"It is stated that the many absurd rumours about the man 'Leather Apron' have been enquired into and found to be utterly void of truth. A high authority at Scotland Yard, asked what truth there is in the ensuing account of the personage, said: 'just as much as there is in the career of Leatherstocking; only I prefer Fenimore Cooper's literary style'. . ."

The *Echo* continued with its account of the personage—

"The man suspected - rightly or wrongly - of being him is a person of weak physique, and but a short time ago underwent a very painful operation, when a large carbuncle was extracted from the back of his neck. Since then, until within quite recently, he has been an inmate of a convalescent home, and at the present time his physical powers are less than those of any woman."

What chance did a regular newspaper reader stand of getting at the truth? The Metropolitan Police was sending mixed signals. J Division [Bethnal Green] was searching for a man in whom Scotland Yard held little store.

Meanwhile, Pizer, who had been arrested as the mysterious Leather Apron, established his whereabouts at the times of the murders of Polly Nichols and Annie Chapman[360] and was released from custody the following evening at 9:30 pm. The police announced that they did not believe Leather Apron to be the guilty man. They also pointed out disingenuously that it was the public and the press who had accused him and not themselves.[361]

Leather Apron was supposed to have been responsible for four

---

[360]   Chief Inspector Swanson, summary report, 19 October 1888
[361]   *Star*, 11 September 1888.

murders. Yet, during his exoneration at Annie Chapman's inquest, Leather Apron suspect Pizer was asked only about his whereabouts at the time of the murders of Polly Nichols and Annie Chapman. No reference was made to the murders of Emma Smith and Martha Tabram, both purportedly committed by the same "lone maniac."

On 19th September 1888 Inspector Frederick George Abberline submitted a report on the murders of Polly Nichols and Annie Chapman.[362]

Regarding Leather Apron, he wrote—

"In the course of our inquiries amongst the numerous women of the same class as the deceased it was ascertained that a feeling of terror existed against a man known as Leather Apron who it appeared [has] for a considerable time past been levying blackmail and ill-using them if his demands were not complied with although there was no evidence to connect him with the murders. It was however thought desirable to find him and interrogate him as to his movements on the night in question, and with that view searching inquiries were made at all common lodging houses in various parts of the Metropolis, but through the publicity given in the 'Star' and other newspapers the man was made acquainted with the fact that he was being sought for and it was not until the 10 inst. that he was discovered when it was found that he had been concealed by his relatives."

Thus, according to Abberline, the hunt for Leather Apron had been underway *before* the *Star* published its 5th September story which had made John Pizer go into hiding. In turn, the *Star* reported that the police had not begun their hunt for Leather Apron 'in earnest' *until* that day— once, it can be assumed, *Lloyd's Weekly Newspaper* had apprised them of the letter from 'Eye Witness'.

Somebody was not telling the truth.

In his 1924 book "Some Piquant People", ex-*Star* journalist Lincoln Springfield reminisced about Leather Apron—

---

[362]   MEPO 3/140, ff. 242 - 256

"At all events, [Harry] Dam[363] had arrived hastily and quietly from the States, had joined us on the Star, and had, like the rest of us, been put upon the job of solving the mystery of the Whitechapel murders. But Dam, a free-born American, was not, as were the rest of us, cowed by the English libel laws, and he created a sensation by developing a theory of the authorship of these grisly crimes. They were, he proceeded to demonstrate, the work of a miscreant known as 'Leather Apron', and so known in consequence of the attire he wore at his everyday trade of tanning, or slipper-making, or whatever it was. Day after day Dam gave the public all the thrills it wanted along these lines. But unfortunately there actually was in existence a man known to the nobility and gentry of the Mile End Road as 'Leather Apron', and he was an honest, hard-working fellow, as innocent of the series of Whitechapel murders, or any one of them, as you or I."

T.P. O'Connor, a Member of Parliament who in 1888 was owner of the *Star*, agreed. In his 1929 *Memoirs of an Old Parliamentarian* he wrote—

"In the search for 'Jack the Ripper' there came into prominence a man of the East End who was universally known as 'Leather Apron', and there were allusions to him in the Star which almost pointed to him as the assassin. The poor man was quite innocent . . ."

Both anecdotes ended with Pizer attempting to sue the *Star* for libel. This had been noted by the press at the time, and various American newspapers had reported that Pizer was about to sue not only the *Star*, but also the *Daily Telegraph* and an unnamed New York newspaper, presumably the *New York Times*.

On the morning of 12th September 1888, Pizer told the Press Association—

"The Star has published a portrait intended to represent me, but it has no more resemblance to me than it has to the man in the moon. I have been told that I shall be wanted at the inquest this afternoon. I am quite ready to go and to make a full statement as to my whereabouts. I shall see if I cannot legally proceed against those who have made

---

[363]   Harry Jackson Wells Dam, born San Francisco, USA, 1856, died Havana, Cuba, 1906.

statements about me."[364]

Lincoln Springfield wrote that before any lawyers could get involved, Leather Apron was paid off with "£10 in gold, and left behind him, in consideration thereof, a stamped receipt for the amount in full settlement of any claims he might have against the paper in respect of the deplorable theory of the ingenious but misguided Harry Dam."

T. P. O'Connor had a different recollection of the incident—

"Leather Apron made a demand for a hundred pounds for his assent to abandon all legal proceedings. [Ernest] Parke insisted on fifty pounds. When the man still dissented, Parke made a counter-proposition that he would tell Leather Apron where to get another fifty pounds which would make up the hundred pounds he claimed. Leather Apron assented; and Parke then revealed to him the fact that another paper had made insinuations against him as direct as those of the Star, and that he could certainly get fifty pounds from them. The bargain was made, and by this bit of information and by our gift of fifty pounds we were kept out of an action which might have cost us thousands of pounds."

These accounts, although different in detail, tally with a story which appeared in the *Birmingham Daily Post,* 27th September 1888—

"A London correspondent telegraphs: —The widely circulated statement that 'Leather Apron' is suing the Star and the Daily Telegraph for libel is incorrect. Pizer's suit against the former journal has been compromised . . ."

It next appeared that Pizer's libel actions were even more wide-ranging.

The *Birmingham Daily Post* continued—

". . . and though he is promoting actions against several journals, including the Evening News, the Echo, and the Weekly Dispatch, the [Daily] Telegraph is not one of them. The Pall Mall Gazette has also settled with Pizer, whose misfortunes promise to turn out profitable."

A week later, the details of Pizer's libel actions underwent developments.

---

[364]   *Star,* 12 September 1888.

The *Birmingham Daily Post,* 2nd October 1888—

"The man Pizer, better known as 'Leather Apron', who was arrested in connection with the fourth of the Whitechapel murders, is determined to carry his case to the law court against the two London evening papers which, he alleges, pointedly referred to him as being the murderer. The matter is in the hands of an energetic solicitor, and damages, I learn, are fixed at £5,000."

Lincoln Springfield's assertion that "Dam, a free-born American, was not, as were the rest of us, cowed by the English libel laws", thus allowing him to create "a sensation by developing a theory of the authorship of these grisly crimes", holds no water.

Article 8 of 'The Law of Libel in its Relation to the Press', together with the 'Law of Libel Amendment Act 1888',[365] held the following people "liable for a libel in a newspaper or journal"—

"The proprietor, the publisher, the editor, the printer, the author, and any person who utters, gives, sells, or lends a copy of the newspaper or journal. Each or all of such persons may be proceeded against . . ."

Harry Dam being an American citizen was no defence.

Here we need to briefly examine the legal grounds upon which John Pizer might have pursued a case of libel, for neither the *Star* nor any other newspaper had uttered a libel. Until the police arrested John Pizer at his stepmother's house on the morning of 10th September, his name had not been mentioned in the press, let alone associated with the person of Leather Apron. It was the Metropolitan Police who conflated the man with the myth.

Libel was described in *Parmiter v. Coupland* [1840] as "a publication without justification or lawful excuse which is calculated to injure the reputation of another by exposing him to hatred, contempt or ridicule." It was also held that to constitute an offence a libel must be falsely and maliciously published.

Neither malice, once called the *animus injuriandi*, nor falsity obtained in the reporting of John Pizer. Following his arrest, the press

---

[365]   Hugh Fraser M.A., LL.M., Reeves & Turner, London 1889.

had simply detailed the many contradictions of the police investigation.

John Pizer was finally exonerated on 12th September 1888, the second day of the Annie Chapman inquest, when Coroner Wynne Baxter allowed him a public platform [the witness box] to establish his innocence.

Earlier that same day he had once again denied to the press that he was known as Leather Apron. The Press Association reported him as not acknowledging the name; nor to having recently worn a leather apron. [366]

An *Echo* reporter asked him— "'Were you not surprised when he [Sergeant Thick] said you were known as 'Leather Apron'? 'Yes,' replied Pizer, sticking firmly to his statement made the previous day. 'I was not aware that I was known by that name. None of my neighbours have ever called me by it.'"

However, later that afternoon at the inquest—

Coroner Wynne Baxter— "Are you known by the nickname of 'Leather Apron'?"

John Pizer—"Yes, sir."[367]

Why Pizer changed his story is puzzling. A possible answer is that he *was* known as Leather Apron and realised that continuing to deny it under oath[368] might have led to charges of perjury. If true, it begs the question of why, earlier, Pizer, his family and their Mulberry Street neighbours had all denied it so strenuously.

But if Pizer had *never* been known as Leather Apron, what purpose might have been served by his lying under oath?

Could John Pizer have come to a deal with the police and agreed to play the mythical Leather Apron? His admission would certainly have forestalled any charges being brought against the police in connection with his wrongful arrest on suspicion of murder based upon mistaken identity. But whilst this may have been a handy expedient for the police, what could have been in it for John Pizer? What was the *quid pro quo*?

---

[366]   *Star*, 12th September 1888.

[367]   *Daily Telegraph*, 13th September 1888.

[368]   *Irish Times*, 13th September 1888— "Pizer produced his own Bible, put his hat on his head, and swore 'by Jehovah.'"

The *Star* had libelled the innocent Leather Apron, dubbing him a "lunatic" and a "murderer." As long as Pizer denied being known as Leather Apron no libel could attach to him. But if Pizer changed his story, he and Leather Apron would become as one and thus able to pursue a libel case against the *Star*.

However, libel requires a person to be uniquely recognizable and identifiable as the object of a libellous 'publication'. In order to pursue a case against the *Star* or any other newspaper, John Pizer first had to prove that a libel against Leather Apron was an incontrovertible libel against himself. No lawyer worth his brief would have accepted Pizer's word on the matter, so what was needed was third-party confirmation from an impeccable source that he, and he alone, was known as Leather Apron.

The *Star*, 6th September 1888—

"Mike —, the grocer in George's Yard . . . knows 'Leather Apron' very well, and has known him for six years. He says that the man is unquestionably mad and that anybody who met him face to face would know it."

The 1888 Post Office Street Directory lists "Michael Fitzgerald, chandler's shop, George Yard." If they were one and the same, Michael Fitzgerald was not called upon to officially identify John Pizer as Leather Apron.

Timothy Donovan, deputy lodging house keeper at 35 Dorset Street, where Annie Chapman last stayed, claimed to know Leather Apron. A while ago he had ejected him from the lodging house "for offering violence to a woman who was staying there." But Donovan, who was summoned on two separate days to the inquest, was not asked to identify John Pizer, and he himself expressed surprise that the police had not asked him to go to Leman Street police station to identify the suspect, as he would have had no difficulty "in deciding whether [he was] Leather Apron."[369]

Also not asked to identify John Pizer as Leather Apron were the women, the policemen, the stalwart man or any members of the

---

[369]   *Morning Advertiser*, 12th September 1888

'howling crowd' present at the 2nd September incident in Hanbury Street.

However, the matter of establishing Leather Apron's true identity was in hand.

Daily News, 13th September 1888—

"John Pizer— 'Pardon me; I wish to vindicate my character to the world at large.'

"Coroner Wynne Baxter—'Yes; you are called here partly to give you the opportunity of doing so.'

"Coroner Wynne Baxter [having heard Pizer's testimony]— 'It is only fair to say that I believe the witness's statement is completely corroborated.'

"John Pizer [bowing several times]—'Thank you, sir. I am quite satisfied, and I hope you are. Mr. [Sergeant] Thicke [sic], that has my case in hand, has known me for upwards of eighteen years.'

"The Coroner— 'I don't think you need to say any more.'

"John Pizer— 'Thank you, sir; so long as you believe that I have clean hands.'"

With his innocence now established, incontrovertible evidence sworn on oath that John Pizer was alone known as Leather Apron would be delivered by the next witness.

Daily News, 13th September 1888—

"Detective-Sergeant Thick deposed that on Monday morning he apprehended the last witness [Pizer] at 22 Mulberry Street.

"Coroner Wynne Baxter— 'When people in the neighbourhood speak of 'Leather Apron', do they mean Pizer?'

"Detective Sergeant Thick— 'They do, sir.'"

On the same day the *Morning Advertiser* gave a fuller account of Thick's response to the Coroner's question—

"Knowing the rumours in circulation concerning 'Leather Apron', I arrested Piser [sic] at 22 Mulberry Street on Monday morning. I have known him for many years under the nickname of 'Leather Apron.' When people in the neighbourhood speak of 'Leather Apron' they referred to Piser."

On the sole testimony of Detective Sergeant Thick, Pizer and Leather Apron were officially conjoined and thus empowered to pursue a case for libel.

Thus was John Pizer's *quid pro quo* delivered.

Not surprisingly the *Star* called Pizer's arrest a "police blunder"—

"The detectives searched with unusual diligence, but could find positively nothing against him. And this is not surprising considering that he is not 'Leather Apron,' at least not the 'Leather Apron' who has been the terror and blackmailer of the women of Whitechapel."[370]

The *Star* was suggesting there might be another 'Leather Apron', an idea which flew in the face of Sergeant Thick's sworn inquest testimony but was more likely a shrewd move to mitigate possible legal action. The last thing the *Star* or the Metropolitan Police wanted was John Pizer / Leather Apron spilling the beans in a court of law.

It is instructive to compare and contrast the mythical Leather Apron of the *Star* and *New York Times* with the reality of John Pizer. And we can immediately dismiss as flummery any references to De Quincey, Dickens, Poe and Jekyll & Hyde.

Was Leather Apron a journalistic myth?

The myth said Leather Apron was Jewish.

John Pizer was Jewish.

The myth said Leather Apron was a slipper-maker.

John Pizer was a shoemaker, or boot-finisher.

The myth said Leather Apron was aged 38 to 40.

John Pizer was 38.

The myth said Leather Apron was five feet four or five inches in height and had a small, black moustache.

John Pizer was described as being of medium height, with florid complexion, and wearing a moustache with side whiskers.

The myth said Leather Apron was as well known in the West End of London as he was in Whitechapel.

John Pizer had lived in Peter Street, Soho, in London's West End.

---

[370]   *Star*, 12th September 1888.

According to Lincoln Springfield, *Star* journalist Harry Dam had conjured Leather Apron from his imagination. Yet six days later the police arrested John Pizer, a man who in almost every basic detail fitted the profile of this mythical personage.

This went far beyond coincidence or serendipity, and in a court of law the *Star* would have been hard-pressed to convince a judge that in its reporting of Leather Apron it had been writing about anyone other than John Pizer.

Was Leather Apron a real person?

John Pizer claimed Sergeant Thick had known him for "upwards of eighteen years"—almost the entirety of Thick's Metropolitan Police career.[371]

Sergeant Thick testified under oath that the name Leather Apron referred to nobody other than John Pizer.

John Pizer told the Coroner he had gone to 22 Mulberry Street "shortly before eleven pm" on Thursday 6th September, not leaving the house until he was arrested "at nine am" on the morning of Monday 10th September.

Inspector Abberline reported that through publicity given in the *Star* and other newspapers Leather Apron learned he was being sought and "it was not until the 10th inst. that he [Pizer] was discovered when it was found that he had been concealed by his relatives."

John Pizer had strung along with this idea at his inquest appearance.

Daily News, 13th September 1888—

"Coroner— 'How long did you remain indoors?'

"Pizer— 'Til I was arrested by Sergeant Thick on Monday last at 9.00 am. I had never left the house from Thursday night.'

"Coroner— 'Why were you remaining indoors?'

"Pizer— 'Because my brother advised me.'

"Coroner— 'You were the subject of suspicion?'

"Pizer— 'I was the subject of false suspicion.'

---

[371] John Pizer, born 1850. Sergeant Thick first joined H Division 1868. Transferred to B Division 4th January 1872. Returned to H Division 18th September 1872. Transferred to P Division 8th July 1878. Returned to H Division 9th May 1886.

"Coroner— 'It was not the best advice that could be given to you.'

"Pizer— 'I had proofs that I should have been torn to pieces.'"

Torn to pieces by whom? A howling mob of people who knew him to be Leather Apron? This idea doesn't fly. Everyone who knew John Pizer denied that he was Leather Apron or had ever been known by that name.

Star, 11th September 1888—

"The Sergeant [Thick] modestly disclaimed any great deal of credit in making the capture. 'I've known him for years,' he said. 'I didn't take him on the strength of any published descriptions of him . . .'"

This was an interesting remark. Thick allegedly knew that Leather Apron was John Pizer, yet exactly a week earlier, on 4th September 1888, Harold Frederic had written of Leather Apron in the *New York Times*—

"One peculiar feature of the case is that none of the police or detectives appears to know him, he having always kept out of their sight . . ."

Sergeant Thick continued in the *Star*, 11th September 1888—

". . . It was not, however, till the early hours of this [Monday] morning I was told where I could put my hands on him.'"

Thick, who in the following year was accused of being Jack the Ripper,[372] had allegedly known John Pizer for years. It therefore beggars belief that this seasoned policeman had not thought to call at the house of Pizer's stepmother [who had been recorded at 22 Mulberry Street since the 1871 Census] until two days after the murder of Annie Chapman.

Furthermore, Inspector Abberline's remarks had been disingenuous, for John Pizer, the London-born son of a Polish Jew, had returned to his stepmother's home for the very best of reasons.

Sunset on Thursday 6th September 1888 marked the start of Rosh

---

372   HO. A49301/193. 14 October 1889. Mr. T.H. Haslewood wrote to Scotland Yard that 'Sergt. T. Thicke [sic]' should be watched 'and his whereabouts ascertained upon other dates when certain women have met their end . . .' An earlier letter from Mr. Haslewood was dismissed as 'plainly rubbish'.

Hashanah, Jewish New Year.[373] Prayers and festive meals would continue in the Pizer household at 22 Mulberry Street until sunset on Saturday 8th September.

This makes it even more difficult to believe it had not occurred to Sergeant Thick that John Pizer might have been with his family during this most important Jewish festival.

The prevailing logic of the Leather Apron scenario is bewildering.

According to the police a lone maniac known as Leather Apron was wanted in connection with four murders. John Pizer was uniquely known as Leather Apron, but proved to have alibis for the murders of Polly Nichols and Annie Chapman, and Emma Smith had died the day after being attacked by a gang. This left Martha Tabram as Leather Apron's only possible victim, yet John Pizer was not asked to account for himself concerning her murder.

In examining the twelve-day life-cycle of Leather Apron, which witnessed the creation, manifestation, arrest and exoneration of a 'lone maniac', it is impossible to square the components of the Abberline/Thick/Pizer/Eye-Witness circle with those of the Dam/Springfield/O'Connor circle and arrive at a conclusion other than that Leather Apron was a carefully-managed deception created in a full knowledge of John Pizer. The only way the story could have played out is [a] if the *Star* had somehow been bamboozled into running the Leather Apron story, or [b] if there had been complicity between the *Star,* Pizer and members of the police.

But to what possible end?

Therein lies the real mystery. We simply do not know, although it is possible to draw some conclusions based on the scant information at our disposal.

Leather Apron appears to have originally been conceived to give shape and form to the mythical 'lone maniac' said to be responsible for the murders of Emma Smith, Martha Tabram and Polly Nichols. Annie Chapman's murder, which appears to have had no connection to those

---

[373]   1888 = Jewish Year 5649.

which had gone before, brought Leather Apron's alleged reign of terror to an abrupt halt. He had to be taken out of the equation as a viable suspect, for had the hunt continued the arrival of the "Dear Boss" letter would have pitted two lone maniacs against one another for the kudos of having murdered Annie Chapman.

Thus in a four-day whirlwind of activity was John Pizer identified, arrested, questioned, kept overnight in a police station, placed in a line-up, declared innocent, released from custody, validated as Leather Apron and publicly exonerated.

On the day of John Pizer's appearance at the Chapman inquest a letter from Dr. Lyttelton Stewart Forbes Winslow appeared in the press. It was to be the first of his many theories about the nature and identity of the Whitechapel murderer.

The Times, 12th September 1888—

". . . That the murderer of the three victims in Whitechapel is one and the same person I have no doubt . . .

". . . I think that the murderer is not of the same class of which 'Leather Apron' belongs, but is of the upper class of society, and I still think that my opinion given to the authorities is the correct one—viz., that the murders have been committed by a lunatic lately discharged from some asylum, or by one who has escaped. If the former, doubtless one who, though suffering from the effects of homicidal mania is apparently sane on the surface, and consequently has been liberated . . ."

Winslow's theory would soon morph into the popular notion of the society doctor.

Following John Pizer's exoneration the hunt for Leather Apron fizzled out. The police made a few desultory inquiries but put no real effort into discovering whether another person known as Leather Apron may have been responsible for the four murders.[374]

---

[374] On 12th September 1888, the day of Pizer's exoneration, Jacob Isenschmidt, who suffered bouts of madness and had been telling women in Holloway, north London, that 'I am Leather Apron', was arrested and confined as a lunatic in the Infirmary Asylum at Bow, where Sergeant Thick went to examine his clothes for bloodstains. Still in the asylum at the time of the 'double-event', Isenschmidt was dropped as a suspect.

This lack of continued interest in Leather Apron by the police is telling, for, a week after John Pizer's exoneration, it appeared that the lone maniac may have still been at large, as evidenced by a report in the *Echo*, 19th September 1888, involving an Annie Chapman inquest witness—

"Passing through Spitalfields with John Richardson, a curious incident occurred. A rough, demented-looking fellow came from a group, grinning, and, with clenched fist, muttered some threat to John Richardson.

"In answer to the question 'Who is he? What does he mean?' Richardson then replied: 'That is a man who they say is mad. A great many of the women and people round our house think that he is the most likely man that they know of to commit a murder. In fact many of them say that he is the real Leather Apron.' When asked to go back to inquire what the man meant, Richardson said, 'You had better not, for he would be most likely to spring upon you and knock you down at once, without a word. I shall not stop to speak to him, for he is very dangerous; and a great many of the women think that he is the murderer."

By the following week the story of the lone maniac known as Leather Apron was but a fading memory. Annie Chapman's five-day inquest closed on 26th September 1888 with a long summing-up by Coroner Wynne Baxter, during which he regaled the jury with the following story—

"It has been suggested that the criminal is a lunatic with morbid feelings. This may or may not be the case; but the object of the murderer appears palpably shown by the facts, and it is not necessary to assume lunacy, for it is clear that there is a market for the object of the murder [removal of the uterus].

"To show you this, I must mention a fact which at the same time proves the assistance which publicity and the newspaper press afford in the detection of crime. Within a few hours of the issue of the morning papers containing a report of the medical evidence given at the last sitting of the Court [19th September], I received a communication from an officer of one of our great medical schools, that they had information which might or might not have a distinct bearing on our inquiry.

"I attended at the first opportunity, and was told by the sub-curator of the Pathological Museum that some months ago an American had called on him, and asked him to procure a number of specimens of the organ that was missing in the deceased. He stated his willingness to give £20 for each, and explained that his object was to issue an actual specimen with each copy of a publication on which he was then engaged. Although he was told that his wish was impossible to be complied with, he still urged his request. He desired them preserved, not in spirits of wine, the usual medium, but in glycerine, in order to preserve them in a flaccid condition, and he wished them sent to America direct. It is known that this request was repeated to another institution of a similar character . . . I need hardly say that I at once communicated my information to the Detective Department at Scotland Yard. Of course I do not know what use has been made of it, but I believe that publicity may possibly further elucidate this fact, and, therefore, I have not withheld from you my knowledge."

Here was a Coroner wilfully introducing hearsay into the facts surrounding the murder of a woman under his jurisdiction.

The right-wing magazine *The Spectator*, 29th September 1888, which only a week earlier had criticised Wynne Baxter for coercing Dr. Phillips into revealing that Annie Chapman's killer had removed her uterus, now declared the Coroner to be "the first to offer a reasonable explanation of the murders"—

"The theory looks probable, and if correct, should limit and direct the search, the miscreant being clearly a foreign medical student, or more probably attendant of a dissecting-room, known to be dark— possibly half-caste—over forty, not tall, of shabby-genteel appearance, and dressed in a deerstalker hat and a dark coat. He would be almost certain to describe himself at his lodgings as a student of medicine. If this is the history of these crimes, they are by far the most devilish committed in this country during this generation, and it will be a disgrace to our civilisation if the criminal escapes."

"Foreign," "dark," "possibly half-caste." The message from the highbrow *Spectator* was no different from the lowbrow cry of the Hanbury Street mob—the Whitechapel murders could not possibly be the work of an Englishman.

The New York *Sun*, 5th October 1888, reported the findings of the *British Medical Journal*—

"The Coroner's theory that the assassin's work was carried out under the impulse of a pseudo-scientific mania has been exploded by the first attempt at serious investigation. It is true that a foreign physician inquired a year ago as to the possibility of securing certain parts of the body for the purpose of scientific investigation: but no large sum was offered, and the physician in question is of the highest respectability and came exceedingly well accredited."

In other quarters Coroner Wynne Baxter's theory was met with derision.

Henry Labouchere wrote in *Truth*—

"Of all the ludicrous theories of the murders, the theory of the coroner is assuredly the most grotesque. I am glad to see that the medical opinion of Sir Risdon Bennett[375] coincides with this conclusion, to which my purely lay mind instantaneously sprung up when I read the astounding summing-up. I don't know whether there is any way of getting rid of a Comic Coroner. But if any machinery does exist for the purpose, it ought, without a moment's delay, to be put in force."

East London Advertiser, 6th October 1888—

"There was, indeed, something intrinsically absurd about parts of Mr. Baxter's theory. It was, for instance, incredible that any medical book should be issued with portions of the human body attached in bags, or in some other manner. Booksellers do not sell books in this fashion."

One other correspondent was most definitely in agreement.

Jack the Ripper's 'Dear Boss' letter, dated 25th September but not mailed until the day after the close of Annie Chapman's inquest, carried the P.S.—

---

[375]   Variously – President of the College of Physicians, Senior and Consulting Physician and Governor of St. Thomas's Hospital, and a leading member of the General Medical Council.

"They say I'm a doctor now. <u>ha ha</u>."

By rights Coroner Wynne Baxter should have been led away in leather restraints for ice-water treatment at Colney Hatch asylum, but instead was permitted to later preside over the inquest of Elizabeth Stride, another "Jack the Ripper" victim, at which he surpassed himself in his mismanagement of the proceedings.

John Pizer shuffled off into history to the sound of his own footsteps, with no further press reports about his pending libel actions against those newspapers which had not previously—or allegedly—settled out of court.

However, in the following month he did appear before a magistrate. *Lloyds Weekly Newspaper*, 14th October 1888—

"At the Thames Police Court yesterday, John Pizer, who claimed for himself over the fourth Whitechapel murder that he was 'Leather Apron' and who was arrested on suspicion of being concerned in the Hanbury street murder, but afterwards released, summoned Emily Patzwold for assaulting him . . ."

Here was an interesting turn of events.

". . . Pizer stated that on the morning of the 27th ult., he went out to get some cheese for his breakfast, when he met the defendant, who made use of an insulting expression and called him 'Leather Apron.' He took no notice and walked on. When he returned she struck him three blows in the face, and his hat was knocked off. While he was picking it up she again struck him. Some neighbours came to the witness's assistance and got him away . . .

"Mr. [Franklin] Lushington fined the woman 10 shillings with 2 shillings costs."

In July 1897, at 22 Mulberry Street, John Pizer died, aged 47, from gastroenteritis, and was buried at the Plashet Jewish Cemetery, Manor Park, London.

Three years later, on October 17th 1900, a curious story appeared in the *Daily Express* plus many local and overseas newspapers—

"Not Jack the Ripper.

"A man named Julius Lipman[376] has just died in the East End of drink, neglect and starvation. He was a cobbler by trade, and was known as 'Leather Apron.' He fell under the suspicion of being Jack the Ripper, and although he completely proved his innocence the stigma never quite left him, and his business dwindled away.

"Lipman was peculiarly unfortunate in the matter. 'Leather Apron' as a possible Jack the Ripper was invented by an imaginative journalist on a sensational paper. He did not suspect for a moment that there was a real man in the district known by that name."

Not for the last time, the *Daily Express* had got hold of the wrong end of the stick.

If a whiff of collusion between the *Star* newspaper, Pizer and members of the Metropolitan Police seems unthinkable, consider also that at this time there may have been a hint of darker deeds in the air—deeds which T.P. O'Connor considered a step too far.

On 8th September 1888, the day of Annie Chapman's murder, a cryptic message appeared in the "People's Post Box" column of the *Star*—

"Mothers-In-Law—The editor of the Star is a bold man, but he shrinks from the task 'Jack' would impose on him."

Could Jack the Ripper, soon to become the bogeyman *sine pari*, have already been in the pipeline just under three weeks prior to the arrival of the iconic "Dear Boss" letter and "Saucy Jacky" postcard at Central News? Had T. P. O'Connor's reluctance to help promote 'Jack' perhaps been the reason why the *Star* pointedly refused to publish facsimiles of the Ripper correspondence, chastised the *Daily Telegraph* for having done so and dismissed the whole thing as a practical joke by "one of those foolish but bad people who delight in an unholy notoriety"?[377]

On the day of Annie Chapman's murder it appears to have been a matter of no small importance to the police that everyone believed all four women had been victims of the same lone maniac.

---

376   1881 Census: Julius Lippman, born Birmingham, 1861. Slipper maker.
377   *Star*, 4th October 1888

But not everyone bought into this premise.

Earlier, *Reynolds News,* 2nd September 1888, suggested that the idea of a lone maniac was being employed by the police as an umbrella solution to three murders which could not otherwise be comfortably explained—

"Some imaginative detective has invented a 'theory' that the murderer of the woman [Nichols] is a madman with a monomania for murdering outcasts, by the brutallest means. This ingenious officer should be promoted. At one stroke, all the blunders and incapacity of the force are accounted for, and its place in the respect of the disappointed public is recovered. It has a double value. During the last few months, half a dozen, more or less, barbarous murders have been committed. Why may they not all be the work of the same mysterious hand . .?"

However, as time would prove, not all the murders were necessarily by the same "same mysterious hand."

19. RINGS ON HER FINGERS

Annie Chapman was originally the fourth victim of Leather Apron. But by 25th September 1888, the date on the "Dear Boss" letter, she had become the first victim of Jack the Ripper—

"Grand work the last job was. I gave the lady no time to squeal."

Some argue that "last job" [previous job] does not necessarily mean "first job", that Annie Chapman was the second victim of Jack the Ripper and Polly Nichols his first.

So, was Annie Chapman the Ripper's first or second victim?

On 25th October 1888 Robert Anderson wrote [with Sir Charles Warren's authorisation] to Dr. Thomas Bond [police surgeon, 'A' Division, Westminster], enclosing copies of the medical evidence from the inquests of Polly Nichols, Annie Chapman, Elizabeth Stride and Catherine Eddowes.

"In dealing with the Whitechapel murders the difficulties of conducting the enquiry are largely increased by reason of our having no reliable opinion for our guidance as to the amount of surgical skill and anatomical knowledge probably possessed by the murderer or murderers.

"He [Warren] feels that your eminence as an expert in such cases— and it is entirely in that capacity that the present case is referred to you, will make your opinion especially valuable."

Anderson's letter tells us that, despite publication of the Jack the Ripper correspondence and the ensuing scare, the police were uncertain if they were dealing with what today we would call a serial killer, or if the four murders were unconnected, the work of a number of perpetrators. The letter also tells us that the medical opinion expressed at the various inquests had been insufficient for Bond to gauge the levels of surgical skill and anatomical knowledge involved.

Here is a short precis of what Dr. Bond would have read—

Polly Nichols: No suggestion of surgical skill involved.

Annie Chapman: The Coroner asked if the way in which the viscera were extracted showed some anatomical knowledge. Dr. Phillips agreed.

Catherine Eddowes: The Coroner asked if the murderer must have had a good deal of knowledge as to the position of the abdominal organs and the way to remove them. Dr. Brown agreed. The Coroner also asked if the removal of the kidney would have required a good deal of knowledge as to its position. Dr. Brown agreed. Finally the Coroner asked if such knowledge was likely to be possessed by someone used to cutting up animals. Doctor Brown replied, "Yes."

Elizabeth Stride: No suggestion of surgical skill involved.

Bond replied on 10th November 1888, having the previous day performed a post-mortem examination of the Millers Court victim—

"All five murders were no doubt committed by the same hand."

Thus was the canonical list [a better word might be Rippertoire] of five victims originally cast in stone, with Annie Chapman now officially the murderer's second victim.

But it appears Bond had not been given the full inquest transcripts, for he wrote— "In the four murders of which I have seen the notes only I cannot form a very definite opinion as to the time that had elapsed between the murder and the discovering of the body.

"In one case, that of Berner Street, the discovery appears to have been made immediately after the deed—In Buck's Row, Hanbury Street, and Mitre Square *three or four hours only could have elapsed* [author's italics].

Dr. Bond's comment placed a squib under Jack the Ripper's unique signature of his victims being discovered just minutes after their dispatch.

He went on to contradict the inquest testimonies of Doctors Phillips and Brown—

"In each case the mutilation was inflicted by a person who had no scientific nor anatomical knowledge. In my opinion he does not even possess the technical knowledge of a butcher or horse slaughterer or any person accustomed to cut up dead animals."

In closing, Dr. Bond offered a profile of the murderer—

"The murderer must have been a man of physical strength and of great coolness and daring. There is no evidence that he had an accomplice. He must in my opinion be a man subject to periodical attacks of Homicidal and erotic mania. The character of the mutilations indicate that the man may be in a condition sexually, that may be called satyriasis. It is of course possible that the Homicidal impulse may have developed from a revengeful or brooding condition of the mind, or that Religious Mania may have been the original disease, but I do not think either hypothesis is likely. The murderer in external appearance is quite likely to be a quiet inoffensive looking man probably middle-aged and neatly and respectably dressed. I think he must be in the habit of wearing a cloak or overcoat or he could hardly have escaped notice in the streets if the blood on his hands or clothes were visible.

"Assuming the murderer to be such a person as I have just described he would probably be solitary and eccentric in his habits, also he is most likely to be a man without regular occupation, but with some small income or pension. He is possibly living among respectable persons who have some knowledge of his character and habits and who may have grounds for suspicion that he is not quite right in his mind at times. Such persons would probably be unwilling to communicate suspicions to the Police for fear of trouble or notoriety, whereas if there were a prospect of reward it might overcome their scruples."

Whilst Dr. Bond felt there was no evidence to suggest the murderer had an accomplice, on the same day as his reply to Anderson an irreconcilable police notice appeared in various newspapers—

"Murder. Pardon. — Whereas on November 8 or 9, in Miller-court, Dorset Street, Spitalfields, Mary Janet Kelly was murdered by some person or persons unknown: the Secretary of State will advise the grant of Her Majesty's gracious pardon to any accomplice, not being a person who contrived or actually committed the murder, who shall give such information and evidence as shall lead to the discovery and conviction of the person or persons who committed the murder.

"Charles Warren, Commissioner of Police of the Metropolis. Metropolitan Police Office, 4 Whitehall Place, S.W., Nov. 10, 1888."

Notwithstanding the subsequent murders of Alice McKenzie [1889] and Frances Coles [1891], by 23rd February 1894, the date on the Macnaghten Memorandum, Jack the Ripper's tally remained just '5 victims—& 5 victims only'. And of these '5 victims only,' Mary Jane Kelly had been the last—as endorsed by Sir Robert Anderson in his 1910 memoirs—

"The last and most horrible of that maniac's crimes was committed in a house in Miller's Court on the 9th of November."[378]

This made Polly Nichols and Annie Chapman the first and second victims of Jack the Ripper. Yet on another page Sir Robert Anderson suggested otherwise—

"The *second* of the crimes known as the Whitechapel murders was committed the night before I took office [31st August], and the *third* occurred the night of the day on which I left London [8th September]," thus making Martha Tabram the first in a series of six victims.[379] [author's brackets and italics].

What was to be believed?

In his 1914 memoirs[380] Sir Melville Leslie Macnaghten cleared the ground by detailing the early Whitechapel murders—

"The attention of Londoners was first called to the horrors of life (and death) in the East End by the murder of one, Emma Smith, who was found horribly outraged in Osborne Street in the early morning of 3rd April 1888. She died in the London Hospital, and there is no doubt that her death was caused by some young hooligans who escaped arrest.

---

[378] The Lighter Side of my Official Life, 1910, p. 137.
[379] Ibid, p. 135.
[380] *Days of my Years*, pp. 57-58.

"On 7th August the body of Martha Tabram was discovered lying on the stairs of a house in George Yard. Her death was due to a number of wounds in the chest and abdomen, and it was alleged that a bayonet had been the weapon used upon her. The evening before she had been seen in the company of two soldiers and a female friend. Her throat was not cut, and nothing in the shape of mutilations was attempted . . .

"The first real 'Whitechapel murder' . . . took place on 31st August, when Mary Ann Nichols was found in Bucks Row . . . This was succeeded nine days afterwards by the murder of Annie Chapman."

If Sir Melville Macnaghten is to be believed, logic dictates that Emma Smith, Martha Tabram and Polly Nichols were murdered by different persons. Yet in 1888 these three murders were being promulgated by the Metropolitan Police as the work of a single 'lone maniac'.

Unknown details remain, but of one thing we can be certain: something of a sensitive nature must have been going on at the time to make the wholly false premise of a lone maniac stalking the streets of the East End more palatable to the public than the truth.

The game-changer in the Whitechapel murders was Annie Chapman, the victim who passed the serial-killing baton from Leather Apron to Jack the Ripper. At first glance there was nothing special about her murder, except perhaps for the fact that the circumstances which resulted in her being out on the streets in the early hours of 8th September 1888 were an almost exact word-for-word replay of those involving Polly Nichols a week earlier on the morning of 31st August.

Of Polly Nichols, Inspector Abberline wrote—

"When she informed the Deputy of the lodging house that she had no money to pay her lodgings she requested that her bed might be kept for her and left stating that she would soon get the money—at this time she was drunk."[381]

And of Annie Chapman, Inspector Abberline wrote—

"She was last seen alive at 2 am on the morning of the murder, but

---

[381]   19th September 1888 report. MEPO 3/140 ff. 242-256

not having the money to pay her lodging left the house remarking she would go and get it—at the time she appeared the worse for drink."[382]

No lodging-house keeper was called to give evidence at the inquest of Polly Nichols. But at Annie Chapman's inquest Timothy Donovan, the deputy of her lodging house at 35 Dorset Street and the man who allegedly ejected the mythical Leather Apron from the premises, added a further detail—

"'Never mind, Tim', [Annie Chapman had told him] 'I shall soon be back. Don't let the bed.'"

The odds on such identical circumstances occurring in the preludes to two murders are as astronomical as their coincidence is unbelievable.

There was, however, one major difference between the two victims. Whilst Polly Nichols lacked fourpence for a single bed for the night,[383] Annie Chapman was accustomed to more spacious accommodation.

Daily Telegraph, 11th September 1888—

"Coroner— 'How much was it [her bed]?'

"Timothy Donovan— 'Eightpence for the night. The bed she occupied, No. 29, was the one that she usually occupied.' And in answer to a question from the jury, Donovan said that 'the beds were double at 8d per night, and as a rule deceased occupied one of them by herself.'"

Here was a 47-year-old Spitalfields unfortunate who could regularly afford twice the usual nightly rate for a lodging-house bed. Business must have been brisk.

Inquest witness Eliza Cooper stated that Annie Chapman wore "three rings on the middle finger of the left hand. They were all brass."

The Coroner asked witness Edward Stanley— "Was she wearing rings when you saw her?"

Stanley replied— "Yes, I believe two. I could not say on which finger, but they were on one of her fingers.

---

[382]   Ibid.

[383]   *Pall Mall Gazette*, 1st September 1888. 'Women from that place were fetched, and they identified the deceased as 'Polly,' who had shared a room with three women in the place on the usual terms of such houses - nightly payment of 4d. each, each woman having a separate bed.'

Coroner— "What sort of rings were they—what was the metal?"

Stanley— "Brass, I should think by the look of them."

Inquest witness William Stevens had spoken to Annie Chapman just hours before her murder.

Coroner— "Had she got any rings on her fingers?"

Stevens— "Yes."

All this interest in her personal jewellery was because the rings had been wrenched from her finger and were missing, for at the post mortem Dr. George Bagster Phillips noted that her ring finger bore "distinct markings of a ring or rings—probably the latter."

Inspector Abberline reported—

"The deceased was in the habit of wearing two brass rings (a wedding and a keeper) these were missing when the body was found and the finger bore marks of their having been removed by force. Special inquiries have been made at all places where they may be offered for pledge or for sale by a person believing them to be gold, but nothing has resulted therefrom."[384]

In his final summing-up Coroner Wynne Baxter said—"On her wedding finger she was wearing two or three rings, which appear to have been palpably of base metal, as the witnesses are all clear about their material and value . . . when we find an easily accomplished theft of some paltry brass rings and such an operation, after, at least, a quarter of an hour's work, and by a skilled person, we are driven to the deduction that the mutilation was the object, and the theft of the rings was only a thin-veiled blind, an attempt to prevent the real intention being discovered."

The theft of the rings being a thin-veiled blind to disguise the murderer's real intention is a real stretch. A more reasonable explanation for the taking of what everyone appeared to agree were worthless brass rings is that for the perpetrator they held some sort of personal attachment.

Annie Chapman had not been a recent lodger at 35 Dorset Street, last having stayed there on Sunday 2nd September in an eightpenny bed

---

[384]   Ibid.

with Edward Stanley, a man known as 'the pensioner'. Her subsequent movements in the days leading up to her murder are shrouded in mystery.

In the early hours of 8th September 1888, Timothy Donovan asked Annie Chapman where she had been since Monday. "She replied that she had been in the infirmary, but did not say which."

Amelia Palmer told the inquest—

"On the Tuesday afternoon [4th September] I saw Chapman again near to Spitalfields Church. She said she felt no better, and she should go into the casual ward for a day or two."

Morning Advertiser, 10th September 1888—

"Timothy Donovan, deputy at the lodging house, 35 Dorset Street, stated that after the deceased left on Monday last he found two large bottles in the room, one containing medicine, and labelled as follows: 'St. Bartholomew's Hospital. Take two tablespoonfuls three times a day.' The other bottle contained a milky lotion, and was labelled 'St. Bartholomew's Hospital. The lotion. Poison.' This confirmed her statement that she had been under medical treatment."[385]

On the same day the *Manchester Guardian* reported—

"The authorities of St. Bartholomew's Hospital, where the woman spent some time, have been communicated with, but they have not been able to afford any information of a useful character."

Fellow-lodger William Stevens told Inspector Chandler—

"I know that on Friday 7th inst the day before the murder she came into the lodging house and said she had been to the hospital, and intended going to the infirmary the next day. I saw that she had a bottle of medicine, a bottle of lotion and a box with two pills. . ."

From this it appears that Annie Chapman had been undergoing medical treatment prior to and following Edward Stanley's visit on the weekend of 1st September; and the *Star,* 8th September 1888, reported fellow-lodger Frederick [William?] Stevens as saying that Chapman had told him she had been "in the casual ward of the Whitechapel Infirmary

---

[385]   St. Bartholomew's did not supply medicine bottles free of charge. Patients brought their own, or purchased one from an itinerant bottle-seller outside the hospital.

from Wednesday night [5th] till Friday morning [7th]."

However, Annie Chapman's name does not appear in the Admissions & Discharge Book of the Whitechapel Workhouse Infirmary during the period 1888-1889.[386]

Edward Stanley, known as 'the pensioner', was variously described as about 47 years old, five feet six to eight in height, and decidedly superior to the ordinary run of those who frequented the lodging houses of Spitalfields.

Timothy Donovan said that Edward Stanley had "a dark moustache and short beard;" that "sometimes he was dressed like a dock labourer, and at other times he had a gentlemanly appearance," and on the fourth day of Annie Chapman's inquest Donovan identified Edward Stanley in court, insisting that on the Saturday before Chapman's death he had come to the lodging house and stayed until Monday. Edward Stanley had paid for one night, and Annie Chapman afterwards came down and paid for the other.[387]

Eliza Cooper, a hawker, agreed—

"On the previous Saturday [Chapman] brought Mr. Stanley into the house where I lodged in Dorset Street . . . Mr. Stanley gave her two shillings, and paid for her bed for two nights."

All of which Edward Stanley denied. He had an alibi for the date in question. Between Monday 6th August and Saturday 1st September he had been in Gosport, Hampshire, although he did not offer a reason why. Consequently, he had not seen Annie Chapman until the afternoon of Sunday 2nd September, "between one and three in the afternoon."

This was good enough for Coroner Wynne Baxter who, without any further ado, readily accepted Edward Stanley's story, remarking that "Probably the deputy has made a mistake."

Thus were two eye-witness accounts [Timothy Donovan and Eliza Cooper] of Edward Stanley's presence at the lodging house on Saturday 1st September 1888 summarily discounted.

---

[386] Philip Sugden, *The Complete History of Jack the Ripper*, 1994. GLRO, StBG/Wh/123/20.
[387] *Daily Telegraph*, 20th September 1888

Inspector Abberline was the police officer who confirmed Stanley's Gosport alibi and also gave the reason for his being there. In a report dated 19th September 1888 he wrote—

"She [Annie Chapman] had occasionally been visited by a man named Edward Stanley, a labourer who resides at 1 Osborn Place, Whitechapel. With that exception she was not known to be acquainted with any particular man. Stanley has been found and interrogated and from his statement it has been clearly established that on the night of 30th ult. [August] he was on duty with the 2nd Brigade Southern Division Hants [Hampshire] Militia at Fort Elson, Gosport . . ."[388]

This neatly established Stanley's alibi for the murder of Polly Nichols.

Inspector Abberline also established Stanley's alibi for the morning of Annie Chapman's murder—

". . . during the night of 7th inst. he was in bed at his lodgings from midnight until 7 am, an hour after the body was discovered."[389]

This particular alibi was neither asked for nor offered at the inquest. Nor was it reported in the press. Yet it proved to be an alibi which Charles Argent, the owner of Edward Stanley's men-only lodging house, was reluctant to confirm or deny. Asked by the *Echo* on 15th September 1888 where Stanley had slept on the night of Friday 7th September, Charles Argent replied—

"That I cannot say. We have not him booked, but then that is nothing. No, I cannot say where he slept then. Perhaps a man who sleeps in the same room may recollect, but it is quite uncertain."

This was the most cautious of responses, especially considering that four days later Inspector Abberline would include Stanley's "in bed at his lodgings" alibi in his official Metropolitan Police report.

Charles Argent also told the *Echo* that Edward Stanley, whom he had known for twelve years, "belongs to the militia—somewhere near Barnet" and "worked at Roberts' cooperage, Bancroft Place,

---

[388] MEPO 3/140 ff. 242-256
[389] Ibid.

Whitechapel[390] . . . He was absent at his militia duties from July, and came in again here on the 2nd of this month, and has lived here since then . . . I may say that he went by the name of Wand here . . . He never kept his accoutrements here, and I have never seen him with a knife or, for that matter, in uniform."

Edward Stanley told the inquest— "I am a bricklayer's labourer."

Other details given by Charles Argent conflicted with Abberline's report which established that Stanley was in the Hampshire militia at Gosport, eighty miles south-west of London, and not Barnet, nine miles north of London, on the borders of Middlesex and Hertfordshire. From this it might be argued that either Charles Argent or the *Echo* had got their facts muddled.

Possibly. But there was a major flaw in Inspector Abberline's investigation of Edward Stanley, who appears to have been the key to Annie Chapman's murder. But, as we shall later learn, the Metropolitan Police was keeping this information strictly to itself.

---

[390]   50 Bancroft Road—*1888 Post Office Street Directory*. "Messrs. Henry Roberts & Co. of the Crown Works, Bancroft Road, Bethnal Green, London E1, was a brewery plant production company—*The Brewing Industry, English Heritage*.

20. MURDER, MYSTERY AND MADNESS

The *Servia*, the first Cunard transatlantic liner to be fitted with incandescent electric lighting, arrived at New York from Liverpool on Sunday 30th September 1888, the day of Jack the Ripper's double event. Amongst its first-class passengers was the diminutive Hadji Hossein Ghooly Khan Motamed-el-Var, the newly-appointed Envoy Extraordinary and Persian Minister Plenipotentiary to the United States, who would be staying at the Windsor Hotel.

On the quay the liveried coachman from the Brevoort House was awaiting the disembarkation of someone very different—a British Army officer and Tory Member of Parliament for the Kentish constituency of Rochester. He was 50-year-old Colonel Francis Charles Hughes-Hallett, described in the monthly magazine *Time* as resembling William Thackeray's 'Lady-Killing Military Snob.' [391]

Together with his trunks and cases, Colonel Hughes-Hallett was whisked from the bustle of Pier 42 on West Street to the quiet tree-lined elegance of Fifth Avenue, where, on stepping from his coach into the lobby, he might have agreed with the Reverend G. W. Weldon that "after tossing wearily for many days and nights on a very treacherous ocean, the peaceful repose and pleasant surroundings of the Brevoort House are

---

[391]   From Thackeray's *The Book of Snobs*, 1848

like entering Paradise."

This was Hughes-Hallett's first visit to America. The UK parliament, in summer recess since 13th August, would reconvene on 6th November, and he wanted to use the intervening weeks seeing as much of the country as possible. A trip to Mexico to evaluate the silver mines of Sonora was on his itinerary, as was a duck-hunting expedition in the company of his recent new friend, Colonel William F. Cody, popularly known as Buffalo Bill.[392]

On the morning of Thursday 4th October, Hughes-Hallet travelled to Niagara, returning on Saturday 6th to the Brevoort House, where he was met by a journalist from the *New York World*.

Hughes-Hallett had a lot to tell. He was still smarting from a year-old scandal involving an improper sexual relationship and financial arrangement with Beatrice Eugénie Selwyn, a step-daughter from his first marriage. At the time there had been talk of the couple eloping. Also, as co-director of the *Genoa Waterworks Company*, he was awaiting a decision from London's Chancery Court concerning alleged fraudulent claims in the company's initial share allocation prospectus.[393]

Not everyone was excited about Hughes-Hallett's arrival in New York—

"That gallant ornament of the British army, Colonel Hughes-Hallett, is registered at the Brevoort. It is unusual for New York to be honoured with the presence of a more pronounced blackguard . . ."[394]

Hughes-Hallett had a reputation to salvage. The British press, most noticeably the *Pall Mall Gazette*, had been merciless, and this interview, away from his native soil, was his first real opportunity to set the record straight and reveal 'the political conspiracy to disgrace him.'

On Sunday 7th October 1888 his account of events ran to almost

---

[392]   The two men met in London 1887 when Buffalo Bill performed his Wild West Show for Queen Victoria during her Jubilee celebrations. Colonel Francis Charles Hughes-Hallett and Lord Ronald Gower rode in the Deadwood Stage as it was attacked by Sioux Indians.
[393]   *The Times*, 8th August 1888. In July 1888 *The Statist* financial journal warned investors against buying stock in companies associated with Hughes-Hallett. The West Indian Gold Mine and The Genoa Waterworks were to be particularly avoided.
[394]   *New Ulm Review*, Minnesota, 10th October 1888.

two full columns on page eleven of the *New York World*. The article revealed that "he had retained his commission in the army, his resignation never having been requested by the Queen, who thoroughly understands the real facts of the case."

Hughes-Hallett obviously enjoyed the trust and confidence of friends in the highest places.

He also had another story to tell the *New York World*, a story of murder, mystery and madness which had nothing to do with his financial and marital improprieties. This story appeared in the same edition on page three. It also appeared in differing forms in the *Atlanta Constitution*, the *Boston Daily Globe* and the *St. Louis Republic* on Sunday 7th October 1888. On the following day, the *Reno Evening Gazette* published a 400-word column-filler version.

The four main newspaper reports differed in style and degree of sub-editing. *The New York World, Boston Daily Globe* and *St. Louis Republic* each credited the story to one of its own reporters, suggesting to its readers an exclusive rather than a syndicated story. By contrast, the *Atlanta Constitution* article featured a by-line—John Paul Bocock— confirming the story's source as the *New York World*.[395]

Colonel Hughes-Hallett's story concerned the Whitechapel murders.

"So intense is the feeling among all classes in London in regard to the bloody horrors, committed with impunity in Whitechapel, that it is not surprising to hear of so prominent a member of parliament and social luminary as Colonel F. C. Hughes-Hallett, of Her Majesty's service, turning detective with the deliberate intention, if possible, of meeting and apprehending the murderous monomaniac."

Hughes-Hallett's story commenced—

"Just after the second of these crimes had been committed, I determined to make an effort to get at the secret of their commission.

"You may remember that the second of the mutilated bodies

---

[395]   John Paul Bocock, joined the *New York World* in 1888, aged 32, having previously been an editor on the *New York Times*, the *New York Press* and *The Daily News*.

discovered in Whitechapel was that of Martha Turner,[396] a hawker, who was found on the first floor landing of the George's Yard buildings in Commercial Street, Spitalfields. The similarity of mutilation, the identity of the district and of the woman's occupation with those of the first victim, convinced me that I had to deal with a case of homicidal mania.

"I chose a bright, moonlight night for my expedition to Whitechapel. I had already a theory of my own about the kind of man the assassin would turn out to be. I had more upon my mind, and I have seen since no reason to change it, that the perpetrator of these atrocities is a West End man, a gentleman, a person of wealth and culture perhaps, but certainly of intellectual qualities, finesse and keen discrimination."

Pocketing a revolver and hailing a cab, Colonel Hughes-Hallett set out for Whitechapel dressed in 'a plain, quiet pair of trousers, a rough coat and a pot hat.' He took 'plenty of money, but no jewelry of any kind.' A lack of jewellery was understandable, but why he might have needed plenty of money was not explained.

"As we drove along St. James's Park I passed a very dear old friend and fellow clubman[397] and looked him straight in the eye. He didn't know me, for being an amateur actor as well as a detective, I had 'made up' my face and completed the disguise effectually . . ."

Besides being an army officer and Member of Parliament, Hughes-Hallett was also a gifted actor, popular in garrison shows, able to recite Shakespeare at the drop of a hat. Together with his 'famous poodle dog', he was also a popular act with children.[398]

Freemasons Magazine and Masonic Mirror, 5th September 1868—

"Royal Artillery Theatrical Club, Woolwich.

"On Wednesday, the 26th ult., a performance was given in the R.A. Recreation Rooms by the officers of the above club . . . The performance

---

[396] The name by which Martha Tabram was originally identified.

[397] Hughes-Hallet was a member of the United Services, Junior United Service and Carlton clubs, from which he would later be accorded the rare privilege of withdrawing his memberships. *New York Daily Graphic*, 20th April 1889.

[398] *Putney and Wandsworth Borough News*, 14th February 1885

commenced with *Used Up*, Bro. F.C. Hughes-Hallett sustaining the principal part of "Sir Charles Coldstream.'"

The character of Sir Charles Coldstream in Dion Boucicault's two-act comedy "Used Up" was described by *The Gentleman's Magazine* as that of a "languid English dandy, elegant of aspect and manner, superfine of dress and sublimely calm of speech." This was surely a rôle made in heaven for the future Colonel Hughes-Hallett.

On 11th October 1887, the *Brooklyn Daily Eagle* reprinted a piece from the *New York Graphic* regarding his acting skills—

"It is said that Colonel Hughes-Hallett has been known to perform frequently in private theatricals in London. No atrocity that he may be guilty of should surprise the public under the circumstances."

Although detection was not a talent listed upon his *curriculum vitae,* he obviously considered himself better suited to the task than the Metropolitan Police.

Hughes-Hallett's story continued—

"Just here I may say I would gladly give up my seat in parliament to become the head of the criminal investigation department in London, which never needed a head worse than now. Our police officers and detectives are subordinated to the same authority where they should be separate and independent. A detective is born, not made by uniform, clubs, orders and a star on his breast. A detective may be a gentleman and should be a man of brains, culture and literary acquaintance. A policeman need only be obedient, strong and brave. He may be, and after all, is densely stupid."

Having thus taken a fashionable swipe at Sir Charles Warren, Hughes-Hallett continued his journey to Whitechapel, where a "thrill of terror pervaded the neighbourhood." So palpable was the terror that he witnessed a prostitute faint in a shriek of fear at the unexpected sight of her own misshapen shadow cast by gaslight.

"I had not been out on my expedition more than three quarters of an hour and I was now at the door of the house where the latest disemboweled and murdered woman had been found. There was not a soul in sight save a policeman a block away, watching the doorway as if he expected to see the fiend come out, hoofs, horns and all. I crossed the street to him, and after a great deal of persuasion he described the appearance of the latest victim, where she was found a few hours before, bleeding like an abattoir, and sliced to suit the murderer's purpose with anatomical accuracy."

Hughes-Hallett's nocturnal adventure came to naught. There was no dramatic finale: no wild chase through the dingy courts and alleyways of Whitechapel, no breathless 'Drat! I almost had the blighter cornered.' He seemed content to just stand in quiet communion for a few moments in what appears to have been Hanbury Street while a policeman recited the grim details of the latest murder, after which he presumably returned home to 108 Cromwell Road, South Kensington. [399]

Apart from its sheer unlikeliness, Hughes-Hallett's story falls to pieces for two fundamental reasons—

No door to a house featured in the 7th August murder of Martha Tabram. Nor had she been disembowelled. Since Hughes-Hallett had arrived in New York on the day of the double event, his "latest disemboweled and murdered woman" could only have been Annie Chapman, found in the backyard of 29 Hanbury Street. His reference to what can only have been her murder [in September] appearing in a story allegedly having taken place in August, 'just after the commission of the second atrocity,' was an anachronism.

Stripped of its melodramatic trappings the story is little more than that of a West End clubman dressing down for an evening's slumming in the East End. But this was no ordinary tale of Lord Snobby having a good time with bad girls on a Saturday night. His destination was specific—in the course of his narrative he mentioned Hanbury Street three times—he travelled alone, in disguise, and carried a revolver.

Hughes-Hallett believed that "the perpetrator of these atrocities is a West End man, a gentleman, a person of wealth and culture perhaps, but certainly of intellectual qualities, finesse and keen discrimination." He believed the murderer to be "an army doctor retired, perhaps, or a

---

[399]   Post Office Street Directory, 1888

medical student, or a gentleman who has read medicine as amusement, or as a part of a liberal education. He is a man of the world, a gentleman, a club man, perhaps, who pursues his customary action during the day, and at night sallies out with his knife and dagger to feast a homicidal mania bred in him by disease, most likely contracted from some of the unfortunate women to whom he confines his horrible revenge."

He went on to discuss the perpetrator's psychopathy—

"By the organs he has cut out and carried away [not a feature of Martha Tabram or Polly Nichols' murder], he proves himself a sexual pervert, that is the victim of a brain bias superinduced by the disease alluded to, and driving him to frenzy at stated intervals."

Regarding where the perpetrator could be located—

"But it is not in Whitechapel that he must be found. It is where he lives; at his home, his club, his lodgings. When the mania is on him he will be too cunning to be caught, It is when he returns to his normal frame of mind and to his normal life as a man of the world that he may betray himself, by tell-tale blood on his clothes, by the possession of his knife, or razor, or cleaver, by those portions of his victims' bodies which he has carried away—the treasures of his madness."

Despite the specificity of detail in Hughes-Hallett's profile of the murderer, with its nod to the mental ravages of syphilis and the newly popular idea of the Jekyll-and-Hyde dual personality, it remained unclear whether he had a particular person in mind or was simply blessed with a vivid imagination.

Interestingly, Hughes-Hallett's schizophrenic syphilitic revenge scenario would form the future basis of a number of "solutions" to the Ripper mystery.

There was no press comment on his Whitechapel adventure, but later in the month it transpired that in other respects he had been playing with fire.

United Service Gazette [exact date unknown]—[400]

"It has been reported in the public Press, apparently on the authority

---

[400]   Story carried by the *Poverty Bay Herald* [NZ], 31st December 1888.

of Colonel Hughes-Hallett, that Her Most Gracious Majesty the Queen has vindicated this officer from any blame in the recent scandal with which he was connected by not requesting his resignation. Being somewhat sceptical as to the truth of the statement, which is obviously of very grave importance, we communicated with Sir Henry Ponsonby [Private Secretary to Queen Victoria] on the subject, and have received the following reply:

"Balmoral, October 25 1888.

"Sir, —As all recommendations respecting public affairs can only be made to the Queen by the Secretary of State, I can give you no information in reply to your enquiry, as I have no knowledge of what may have taken place. But it appears to me that the statement you enclose is obviously untrue. —I have the honour to be, sir, your obedient servant, Henry F. Ponsonby."

The *Pall Mall Gazette* had pre-empted Ponsonby's letter. Five days earlier, on 20th October 1888, it remarked in no uncertain terms that Hughes-Hallett's statement in the *New York World* was "an infamous attempt to traduce Her Majesty."

Hughes-Hallett was not asked to comment.

On 27th October 1888, the *New York Times* announced that Colonel Hughes-Hallett, Buffalo Bill and others were to sail up Long Island Sound to Fenwick Hall on a duck-shooting expedition.

Situated at the mouth of the Connecticut River, Fenwick Hall was a luxury hotel owned by Edward S Stokes, a New York politician who had spent four years in Sing Sing for the 1872 murder of his business partner 'Jubilee Jim' Fisk. The party would later be joined by Lord Charles Beresford, Lord Clifford and Lord Mandeville, and travel to Buffalo Bill's ranch in North Platte, Nebraska, through northern Mexico, over the Sierra Madre mountains and into California, where they would be entertained by Senator George Hearst, father of newspaper tycoon William Randolph Hearst.

It is clear from this itinerary that Hughes-Hallett had no intention of returning to Britain in time for the re-opening of Parliament on 6th November 1888.

Two weeks later he was still in New York when the latest news arrived from London.

New York Times, 10th November 1888—

"London, Nov. 9. — At 11 o'clock this morning the body of a woman cut into pieces was discovered in a house on Dorset Street, Spitalfields. The police are endeavoring to track the murderer with the aid of bloodhounds. The appearance of the body was frightful, and the mutilation was even greater than in the previous cases . . ."

St. Paul Globe [Minnesota], 12th November 1888—

"Portrait of a London Swell.

"New York World.

"A very tall, slender man in evening clothes strode across Madison square a night or two ago with a big cape over his shoulders, a slender, silver-headed cane in one hand and a cigar in his mouth. He was evidently a swell, and quite as evidently not a New York swell. His black doeskin trousers were ever so much tighter than such garments are worn by well-dressed men in New York. The next morning the tall, distinguished-looking man's costume presented even a more marked contrast to that of the well-dressed men he met on Fifth avenue. His trousers were still tight, almost skin-tight; his bluish-black Prince Albert coat rolled low and was buttoned tightly over a military chest; his vest was cut out low and showed a large black cravat spreading over his shirt front, the cravat being of a pattern very popular here some years ago as a 'linen protector,' but seldom seen now; his high white collar gaped half an inch in front; his boots were pointed patent leather gaiters. He was Col. Hughes-Hallet, and he knows thoroughly how fashionable men dress in London."

Auburn Bulletin [NY], 19th November 1888—

"Buffalo Bill will make a hunting expedition through Northern Mexico the latter part of this month as the host of Lord Clifford, Lord Mandeville and six other Englishmen."

Early the following month New York City received a surprise visitor in whom Colonel Hughes-Hallett should have had more than a passing interest.

New York World [Evening Edition], 3rd December 1888—

"Dr. Francis Twomblety, the eccentric American physician who was arrested in London suspected of the Whitechapel murders, arrived on the French steamship La Bretagne yesterday. He was shadowed to a boarding house in West Tenth Street by two of Inspector Byrnes's detectives . . . The London police are anxiously searching for samples of his handwriting to compare with that of "Jack the Ripper".

As yet it remains uncertain whether Colonel Hughes-Hallett and Dr. Francis Tumblety were in New York City at the same time.

Later the same month Hughes-Hallett's prolonged absence from England became a topic of discussion.

New York Times, 8th December 1888—

"Other by-elections are rumored to be impending, and among the vacancies is said to be one for Rochester, from which some mysterious new developments threaten to drive Colonel Hughes-Hallett."

These mysterious new developments were not revealed.

Except for sporadic gusts of righteous indignation, most notably from the office of the Archbishop of Canterbury[401], the storm over the Beatrice Selwyn scandal had blown itself out long ago. The Tory Party had no wish to lose Hughes-Hallett. In July 1888 it had lent him constituency support in the persons of Aretas Akers-Douglas and Walter Hume Long, respectively political secretaries to the Treasury and Local Government Board. So was it possible that Queen Victoria had not been amused by his "infamous attempt to traduce" her, as reported in the *New York World*?

The timing of Buffalo Bill's hunting expedition to Northern Mexico fits with a much later report that Hughes-Hallett had gone 'to Mexico to inspect a mine in which he was interested, and there fell seriously ill.'

Two years earlier, on 13th April 1886, Hughes-Hallett, together with five others directors, had registered the *Sonora Silver Mining Company* with capital of £365,000 [$1,825,000]. The mine was located

---

[401]   Lambeth Palace asked Hughes-Hallet to return an "inadvertently sent" garden party invitation.

near Soyopa, north-west Mexico, on the Rio Yaqui. The investment sounded promising, but by 12th May 1888 *The Statist*, a financial journal, was issuing a warning to investors—

"Some of the directors in this Sonora venture [Charles G.H. Teniswood M.A., LL.M and Colonel William Wallington Knollys] figured on the Board of the notorious London and Leeds Bank [liquidated in 1886 with assets of just £1. 6s. 9d.], and others have been mixed up with a great many miscellaneous companies, which have perhaps put money into the pockets of the promoters, but which have not been profitable to shareholders." [author's brackets]

On 15th December 1888, a week after the "mysterious new developments" threatening Hughes-Hallett's Rochester candidacy, the *New York World* reported that news had been received in London that he was "very ill of fever." On 13th January 1889, the *New York Herald* revealed that he was "suffering from partial paralysis, the result of rheumatic fever." The newspaper added: "All hopes of his complete recovery are abandoned."

Evening Star [Washington DC], 8th February 1889—

"Colonel Hughes-Hallett . . . lies paralyzed in both legs and can hardly raise his hands. His financial collapse is as complete as his physical . . . A parliamentary vacancy is thus created at Rochester . . ."

Hughes-Hallet finally tendered his resignation "on account of physical infirmities", "caused by fever and gout." It was later reported that, in a letter sent from São Miguel in the Azores to his Rochester constituency office, he wrote that rheumatic fever and gout had left him in a crippled condition, and that if he was ever to regain the use of his limbs a month at least must first elapse.

Hughes-Hallett's condition appeared grave. Given that ill health was not simply a ruse for his staying away from England until any political dust had settled, what might have caused this sudden onset of fever, gout and a "stroke of paralysis" which would later spread to "both legs and hands"?

Whilst it is impossible to accurately diagnose his condition at such a remove, it is worth noting that for many years gout and rheumatism had been euphemisms for the symptoms of syphilis, for which there was no effective treatment until the 1910 introduction of the arsenic-based 'Compound 606', branded as Salvarsan—which had serious side-effects—and the 1940s arrival of penicillin. In the 1880s mercury treatment killed more people than it cured, so could this have been the reason for Hughes-Hallett's journey to the Azores?

Syphilis, Victor Cornil, 1882—

"There exist observations on cerebral syphilis in which the symptoms have approached very nearly to general paralysis."

A System of Physiologic Therapeutics, 1902—

"San Miguel, the largest island of the group, possesses thermal springs in the Las Furnas valley, which are employed with considerable success in chronic rheumatic affections, syphilis, and diseases of the skin."

Journal of Cutaneous Diseases including Syphilis, 1913—

"Sulphur water internally and as baths acts brilliantly in syphilitic patients who also suffer from rheumatism or gout."

Health benefits aside, the amenities on São Miguel were far removed from those of New York's Brevoort House.

Watkins Express [NY], 20th October 1887—

"These springs are undoubtedly among the best of the world's medicinal waters, but under Portuguese enterprise are practically of no value. The bath houses are fair, but the hotel accommodations are simply disgusting, filth and dirt being prominent in food, beds, and rooms."

A System of Physiologic Therapeutics, 1902—

"Dr. H. Canfield said that a patient should not be sent there alone for a lengthy stay, 'unless he is full of resources for his own enjoyment and pleasure'; also that . . . 'people dependent upon luxuries would fare badly'."

Hughes-Hallett's journey to São Miguel could not have been a spur of the moment decision or a simple stop-off on the voyage home to Britain, for at the time there was no direct steamship service between the United States and the Azores.[402]

---

[402]   *Watkins Express* [NY], 20th October 1887. NB—The Anchor Line and the Compagnie

Medical and Surgical Reporter, 28th April 1883—

"The only steam service to the Azores is by way of England and France, and then by taking a Brazilian steamer to San Miguel, or by going overland to Lisbon and taking the small mail steamer, which makes the round trip, to all the islands, twice every month."

Alternatively, Hughes-Hallett could have taken a sailing packet from Boston to the Azores. These three-masted clippers called at Horta on the island of Fayal [Faial] and, dependent on weather conditions, made the voyage in around sixteen to twenty-five days. But this would not have been his journey's end. Next would have come an almost 200-mile island-hop to São Miguel.

One thing is certain. No matter which way Hughes-Hallett chose to travel, his trip to the Azores—where he would have enjoyed a far greater degree of anonymity than in more fashionable European spa towns— was a most determined venture.

On 6th April 1889, the *Hackney Express and Shoreditch Observer* reported that he was no longer in America, and that "a fortnight ago" he was staying in the Azores. This suggests he had arrived at São Miguel at some time in March. But on 10th April 1889 the *New York Evening Post* told a different story whilst adopting a more conspiratorial view of these electoral matters—

"There is a curious instance of electioneering sharp practice at Rochester. Colonel Hughes-Hallett really resigned weeks ago, but the Tories, being unprepared with a good candidate, kept his resignation back and, when ready, produced it, post-dating it Azores, March 26th. The trick was too clever, for they have miscalculated Colonel Hughes-Hallett's movements. He has not yet reached the Azores."

The *New York Evening Post* had been right to smell a rat. Almost three

---

Générale Transatlantique tried to start a direct New York to the Azores service in the early 1880s, but were forestalled by a rival Boston shipping line whose service proved to be short-lived. The Anchor Line finally started a winter service in October 1889, but it wasn't until the mid-to-late 1890s that the Empresa Insulana de Navegaçao and the Linha de Vapores shipping lines began regular year-round passenger services between New York, the Azores and Portugal.

weeks earlier, on 22 March 1889, the Washington DC *Evening Star* had reported Hughes-Hallett's parliamentary resignation, and on the following day, three days prior to his 'post-dated' letter from the Azores, a successor, having undergone the constituency selection process, was announced.

The Times, 23rd March 1889—

"Rochester. —In view of the next election, Colonel and Alderman Horatio David Davies, J.P., of Strode Park, Herne, Kent, has been selected as the Conservative and Unionist candidate."

It appeared that Colonel Hughes-Hallett's Rochester seat had been vacated. Yet, despite this announcement, the Tory party continued to fudge the matter of his resignation.

The Times, 26th March 1889—

"Representation of Rochester.

"Mr. P. O'Brien asked the Chancellor of the Exchequer whether he had yet received an application for the stewardship of the Chiltern Hundreds from the member for Rochester, Colonel Hughes-Hallett; and, if so, had it been granted."

The Chancellor of the Exchequer, George Goschen, replied, "No application has been received."

A Member of Parliament cannot simply resign his seat. An appointment by the Chancellor of the Exchequer to the Chiltern Hundreds or to the Manor of Northstead is required. This places an MP in a nominal 'office of profit under the Crown', which automatically disqualifies him from sitting in the Commons. Only via this process can an MP resign.

This fact had not gone unnoticed.

The Times, 27th March 1889—

"Colonel Hughes-Hallett.

"Mr. P. O'Brien asked the First Lord of the Treasury whether any communication, written or oral, direct or indirect, had reached the Patronage Secretary from the Hon. Member for Rochester conveying his intention or desire to vacate his seat; and whether the Government would take any and what action in the matter to relieve the Rochester

Division from practical disenfranchisement."

William Henry Smith, First Lord of the Treasury and Leader of the House of Commons, was eloquently evasive—

"The hon. Gentleman asks whether communications have passed between my hon. friend the Secretary to the Treasury and the hon. Member for Rochester with regard to his seat. I venture, with great respect to the House, to say that it would be most improper and unusual to ask that private communications unconnected with the discharge of his official duties which may pass between my hon. Friend or anyone holding his position either side of the House, should be communicated to the House."

More obfuscation followed—

"I have reason to believe that the hon. Member for Rochester, who has been absent from the House during the present Session, has been disabled by severe and protracted illness, and steps will be taken to ascertain whether there is any reasonable hope that he will be able to return to the House or whether he wishes to vacate his seat."

From W H Smith's statement it appeared that as late as 27th March 1889 Hughes-Hallett had not vacated his seat and might yet return as MP for Rochester.

Matters remained confused.

The Times, 1st April 1889—

"Rochester. —Although certain formalities have yet to be carried out before the seat at Rochester is declared vacant, and which may be delayed for another four of five weeks, the campaign has virtually begun . . . Alderman Horatio Davies, who has been selected by the Conservatives, is regarded as a strong candidate, and there is no doubt the contest, which will in all probability take place as soon as Mr. Davies has completed his house-house visitation, will be one of the keenest on record."

The Times, 8th April 1889—

"Rochester—A letter from Colonel Hughes-Hallett, tendering his resignation on account of physical infirmities, was published in the constituency on Saturday [6th April], and it is expected that the writ will be moved without delay . . ."

This was his purported letter from the Azores, dated 26th March 1889.

". . . The Conservatives wound up an arduous week with a great meeting at Strood, at which Mr. Alderman Davies, the Conservative candidate, was supported by Mr. Darling, M.P., and Mr. Hayes Fisher, M.P., and the usual resolutions were unanimously passed."

The Times, 9th April 1889—

"Monday, April 8—New Writ.

"On the motion of Mr. Akers-Douglas a writ was ordered to issue for the election of a member for Rochester in the room of Colonel Hughes-Hallett, who has accepted the Chiltern Hundreds."

W.T. Stead later wrote—

". . . a fatal want of pence and failing health compelled Colonel Hughes-Hallett to accept the Chiltern Hundreds. Even then his resignation was again and again postponed out of deference to the wishes of the Unionist Whips and the Unionist wire-pullers, who urged him not to retire until they had his successor ready."[403]

On 24 April 1889, the *True Witness and Catholic Chronicle* [Montreal], was in agreement with the *New York Evening Post*:

"When all was ready [for the Rochester election] the Colonel's letter of resignation was suddenly announced, dated Azores, March 26, before it is said he could have reached the islands whither he has gone for his health."

From the above—plus reports in *The Times* and answers given in the House of Commons—it appears that, just as the *New York Evening Post* had reported, Hughes-Hallett resigned several weeks before 6th April 1889, the day his 'official' resignation was published, which, according to the British Parliamentary Library, was also the day of his appointment as a Steward of the Chiltern Hundreds.

On 25th May 1889 his presence in the Azores was reported by the

---

[403] *The Discrowned King of Ireland,* 1891

Town and Country Journal [NSW, Australia]—

"Colonel Hughes-Hallett is at the Azores, where he is taking the sulphur baths to get over a severe attack of rheumatism in the legs."

On balance it appears that Hughes-Hallett returned from America to Britain at some time in March to settle his resignation with the Tory Whips before starting out in early April—just prior to the Rochester by-election—for the sulphur springs of São Miguel. This in turn suggests that the 'letter from the Azores' dated 26th March was concocted in London in prior knowledge of his future travel plans.

Horatio David Davies, J.P., was an almost carbon-copy Tory candidate—the same age as Hughes-Hallett, a City of London Alderman, retired army Lieutenant-Colonel and member of the Carlton Club. Perhaps the Tory whips thought the Rochester electorate might not notice the difference. However, on 16th April 1889, Rochester, at the time considered a safe Tory stronghold, fell to the Gladstonian Liberal candidate Edward Knatchbull-Hugessen by a slim majority of seventy-five votes.

The Times, 1st May 1889—

"Mr. Knatchbull-Hugessen took the oath and his seat as member for Rochester, in the room of Colonel Hughes-Hallett, resigned."

By June 1889 Colonel Hughes-Hallett had returned from the Azores to England, where he would soon tender another resignation.

* * * * * * *

Here we return to London, September 1888, and Edward Stanley.

Inspector Frederick George Abberline had written in a Metropolitan Police report dated 19th September that "Stanley has been found and interrogated and from his statement it has been clearly established that on the night of 30th ult. [August] he was on duty with the 2nd Brigade Southern Division Hants Militia at Fort Elson, Gosport . . ."

The Hants Militia's correct title was "2nd Brigade, Southern Division, Royal Artillery."

Here is what is known of the Brigade's 1888 activities—

"The brigade assembled for twenty-seven days' training on August 6 at Fort Elson, Gosport . . . the strength being 13 officers and 160 non-commissioned officers and men, and it was inspected by Colonel H. Maxwell Robertson, Royal Artillery, commanding Auxiliary Artillery, Southern District, on August 29 and 30.

"On August 31 1888 the following brigade order was issued—

"The Officer commanding cannot allow the brigade to be dismissed without recording his opinion of the excellent manner in which the men turned out both days for inspection, earning the emphatic approbation of the Inspecting Officer.

"The men themselves turned out clean, smart and soldier-like, their uniforms and accoutrements were well put on, the folding of the great coats and the fitting of the valises being exceptionally good. The kits and the barrack rooms were in excellent order, and the Commanding Officer fully appreciates the zeal, energy, and esprit de corps which has animated the Officers and non-commissioned officers, so as to produce such satisfactory results.

"On September 1st 1888 the men were dismissed to their homes."[404]

These dates matched Edward Stanley's inquest testimony, immediately ruling him out as a possible suspect in the murders of Martha Tabram and Polly Nichols. But it is here we encounter problems with Inspector Abberline's 19th September report, for, going from all currently available information, Edward Stanley was ineligible to volunteer with the 2nd Brigade, Southern Division, Royal Artillery.

On 17th September 1888, the *Evening Standard* reported him as being "a man of 47 years of age."

Edward Stanley was too old to have been in the Militia Reserve.

War Office Army Circulars, 1st January 1878—

---

[404]   Records of the Infantry Militia Battalions of the County of Southampton, from A.D. 1757 to 1894, and Records of the Artillery Militia Regiments of the County of Southampton, from A.D. 1853 to 1894. Lieut. Colonel George Hope Lloyd Verney and Lieut. Colonel J. Mouat F. Hunt. Published by Longmans, Green and Co., 1894

"Militia Reserve.

"A man may not be enlisted or re-enlisted for the Militia Reserve after 34 years of age."

This restriction was still in place in 1899—

"Service in the militia reserve cannot be extended beyond the age of 34."

The 'general' or 'regular' Militia was recruited from volunteers willing to enlist for six years "with leave to extend their service for further periods of four years . . . The limit of age for all services is between 18 and 35 years . . .

". . . No soldier of the militia is allowed to continue to serve if he has passed his 45th year, but men who have served no less than 3 years in the army or army reserve, without having earned a pension, are allowed to enter the militia within 3 years of the day of their discharge, if they are under 45 years of age."

Thus could the 47-year-old Edward Stanley have entered the 'general' or 'regular' militia as late as the age of 44, having been discharged from the army or army reserve aged 41.

However, from all accounts he had been a long-time resident of Middlesex, much of which in 1888 became the County of London.

Charles Argent, proprietor of his lodging house at 1 Osborn Place, said, "I have known Ted Stanley for about twelve years. During that time he has mainly lodged here."

Militia Regulations, War Office, 15 July 1853—

"Volunteers must, at the time of their engagement, be resident within the county in the Militia of which they engage to serve, or in the county immediately adjoining thereto."

Hampshire did not and still does not adjoin Middlesex.

Up until 1888 recruitment in the 2nd Brigade, Southern Division, Royal Artillery was restricted to men from Hampshire, an arrangement which by early the following year had become a problem.

"1889: In January of this year, it being found impossible to keep the 1889 brigade up to its proper strength by the enlistment only of recruits from the county of Hampshire, the authorities sanctioned recruiting in the two other counties forming the Southern Division, viz. Dorsetshire and Wiltshire."[405]

Had Edward Stanley originally been a resident of Hampshire but later moved to Middlesex, *Militia Regulations, War Office* 1853 stipulated—

"Volunteers who, after enrollment, desire to change their place of residence, may do so upon notifying their wish to the Adjutant of the regiment in which they are enrolled . . . in every case of a volunteer removing any considerable distance beyond the border of the county, he should be transferred to the Militia regiment of the county in which he resides."

On 15th September 1888, Charles Argent told the *Echo* that Edward Stanley belonged "to the militia—somewhere near Barnet", which is on the Middlesex-Hertfordshire border, 10 miles north of Central London.

If Edward Stanley had moved from Hampshire and was now a member of the Middlesex Militia, *War Office Regulations for the Volunteer Force*, 18th April 1878, further stipulated—

"No member of a Volunteer Corps will be enrolled in another Corps until he has legally ceased to be a Member of the former Corps."

On the basis of these regulations, in 1888 Edward Stanley was eligible to join one of the various Middlesex militias, which were based at Hounslow, 10 miles west of Central London, but could not at the same time have been a volunteer with the Hampshire militia.

On 11th September, the first day of the Annie Chapman inquest, Timothy Donovan, the lodging-house deputy, said that Chapman ". . . used to come and stay at the lodging-house on Saturdays with a man - a pensioner - of soldierly appearance, whose name I do not know."

John Evans stated that "[Annie Chapman] associated with a man, a pensioner, every Saturday, and this individual called on Saturday [8th September] at 2.30 pm and inquired for the deceased. He had heard something about her death, and came to see if it was true. I do not know his name or address."

---

[405]   Ibid.

On the second day of the inquest [12th September], Amelia Palmer stated that "[Annie] Chapman told me that she was with some other man, Ted Stanley, on Saturday, Sept. 1. Stanley is a very respectable man."

On day three of the inquest [13th September] the foreman of the jury asked if Inspector Chandler [H Division] was "going to produce the man Stanley?"

Inspector Chandler: "We have not been able to find him as yet."

Foreman: "He is a very important witness. There is evidence that he has associated with the woman week after week. It is important that he should be found."

Inspector Chandler: "There is nobody that can give us the least idea where he is. The parties were requested to communicate with the police if he came back. Every inquiry has been made, but nobody seems to know anything about him."

The Coroner: "I should think if that pensioner knows his own business he will come forward himself."

The Times, 15th September 1888—

"All inquiries have failed to elicit anything as to the whereabouts of the missing pensioner who is wanted in connexion with the recent murder."

The police could not have been looking very hard, for the *Echo*, 15th September, reported lodging house keeper Charles Argent as saying that Edward Stanley "came in again here on the 2nd of this month, and has lived here since then."

Pall Mall Gazette, 15th September 1888—

"The pensioner, Edward Stanley, whose name has been constantly mentioned in conjunction with that of the murdered woman, Annie Chapman, attended at the Commercial Street police station last night and made a statement . . ."

On the same day, the *Echo* reported—

". . . In view of his relations with the deceased woman, Edward Stanley felt considerable diffidence in coming forward, but after the expressions of opinion by the coroner at the inquest on Thursday he placed himself in indirect communication with the police. It was by

arrangement that he subsequently proceeded to Commercial Street
Police station . . ."

"Indirect communication"? "By arrangement"? Arrangement with
whom?

How could Edward Stanley have provided Coroner Wynne Baxter
with such accurate dates [6 August – 1 September] regarding his time at
Gosport, thus alluding to a militia artillery brigade to which he could
not have belonged?

Conversely, how could Inspector Abberline have "clearly established"
that Edward Stanley *had* been on duty with the 2nd Brigade, Southern
Division, Royal Artillery at Fort Elson, Gosport?

In seeking an answer to these questions we encounter yet another
of the strange coincidences which permeate the mystery of the
Whitechapel murders.

Since 13th July 1885 the officer commanding the 2nd Brigade,
Southern Division, Royal Artillery, had been Colonel Francis Charles
Hughes-Hallett—

"The brigade assembled for twenty-seven days' training on August 6
at Fort Elson, Gosport, under the command of Colonel Hughes-
Hallett . . . On September 1, 1888 the men were dismissed to their
homes."[406]

Since it is now clear that Edward Stanley could not have been on
duty with the Hampshire militia, it becomes conceivable that the witness
who attended Annie Chapman's inquest may, in fact, have been Colonel
Hughes-Hallett—the man who would later tell the *New York World* that
"being an amateur actor as well as a detective, I had 'made up' my face
and completed the disguise effectually."

Edward Stanley, aged 47 at the time, was described as "a tall elderly
working man superior to the usual denizens of Spitalfields lodging-
houses—sometimes he was dressed like a dock labourer; at other times
he had a gentlemanly appearance." According to his death certificate,
Colonel Hughes-Hallett was aged 48 in 1888, although his birth date is

---

[406]   Ibid.

recorded as 1838, making him 50 at the time.

Both men appear to have been approximately the same height. Hughes-Hallett was reported as being of 'middle height', whilst, according to the *Daily Telegraph* of 11 September 1888, Timothy Donovan described Edward Stanley as between "five feet six or five feet eight inches in height."

As for styling himself Edward Stanley whilst slumming in Whitechapel, Colonel Hughes-Hallett may have appropriated the name of one of his fellow Tory MPs—the 62-year-old honourable member for the Bridgewater Division of Somersetshire and fellow member of the Carlton club—Edward James Stanley.

The dual-identity witness scenario, usually the stuff of ingeniously-plotted Agatha Christie novels, is not as preposterous as it might first appear.

Hughes-Hallett would not have been easily recognisable outside Parliament, the Army, his club or constituency. There were no half-tone photographs in British newspapers at the time: everyone's portrait—be they a music-hall star, sportsman, bishop or politician—was either a pen sketch or a caricature, so it is unlikely that the inquest witnesses and reporters at the Working Lads' Institute, Whitechapel Road, might have recognised Stanley as the MP for Rochester in Kent.

Daily Telegraph, 20th September 1888—

"Coroner Wynne Baxter— 'Did ever you see that man (pointing to Stanley) before?'

"Timothy Donovan— 'Yes.'

"Coroner Wynne Baxter— 'Was it he who used to come with the deceased on Saturday and stay till Monday?'

"Timothy Donovan— 'Yes.'

"Coroner Wynne Baxter— 'What have you got to say to that, Mr. Stanley?'

"Edward Stanley— 'You can cross it all out, sir . . . It is all wrong. I went to Gosport on Aug. 6 and remained there until Sept. 1.'"

And without bothering to ask Edward Stanley why he had been in Gosport for almost a month or, indeed, if there was anyone who could confirm his alibi, Coroner Wynne Baxter immediately gave him the benefit of the doubt, remarking that, "Probably the deputy has made a mistake."

The person identifiable by Timothy Donovan as the mysterious "Edward Stanley" had to attend the inquest, else suspicion attached to him for possible involvement in the murder of Annie Chapman, which in turn would have undermined the prevailing belief that she had been the fourth victim of the Whitechapel murderer.

If true, this scenario carries with it serious implications, for Hughes-Hallett could not have succeeded in brazening out such a performance without assistance from the police.

It is a known fact that Colonel Hughes-Hallett was in Gosport with the 2nd Brigade, Southern Division, Royal Artillery. If Edward Stanley was also in the 2nd Brigade, as his commanding officer Colonel Hughes-Hallet would have been the ideal person to vouch for him, yet Abberline did not reveal by what means he had verified the Gosport alibi. But as we now know that Edward Stanley could not have served in Gosport under Hughes-Hallett, it begs the question of why Inspector Abberline falsified his 19th September report by providing the former with the latter's alibi.

But if Edward Stanley and Hughes-Hallett were one and the same person, the Gosport alibi was essentially sound. Inspector Abberline's falsification was in attributing it to Hughes-Hallett's Whitechapel alter ego, which might help explain why "Edward Stanley" put himself in "indirect communication" with the police before going "by arrangement" to Commercial Street police station.

Harder to understand is the alibi of Edward Stanley for the night of 7/8 September, which was not called into evidence at the inquest. Inspector Abberline recorded in his 19th September report that Stanley was in bed at his lodgings at 1 Osborn Place from midnight to 7 am - an hour after the body was discovered.

Lodging-house proprietor Charles Argent told the Echo on 15th September that Edward Stanley came "on the 2nd of this month, and has lived here since," yet two days earlier Inspector Chandler told the

Coroner—There is nobody that can give us the least idea where he is . . . Every inquiry has been made, but nobody seems to know anything about him." The police had obviously not thought to call at Charles Argent's men-only lodging house at No. 1 Osborn Place, situated just three hundred yards from the scene of Annie Chapman's murder at 29 Hanbury Street.

This was probably just as well, for it is unlikely that Edward Stanley/Hughes-Hallet had stayed at this address for two weeks.

Assuming Inspector Abberline had not simply accepted the word of 'Edward Stanley' for his whereabouts on the morning of Annie Chapman's murder, the detective leading the murder investigation must have found someone to confirm his alibi, the most obvious person being Charles Argent.[407]

Pursuing its own line of inquiry, the *Echo*, 15th September 1888, had asked the lodging house keeper about Edward Stanley's sleeping arrangements.

"But how do you account for the fact, Mr. Argent, that he slept at 35 Dorset Street, with Annie Chapman?"

"Ah, that I cannot tell,' answered Mr. Argent. 'You see, as soon as he comes here he engages a bed right off for a week. He may be a night out, and we should not notice it."

The *Echo* pressed him further.

"Now tell me, Mr. Argent,' asked the reporter, 'where Ted Stanley slept on Friday night. Did he sleep here?"

"'That I cannot say,' replied Mr. Argent. 'We have not him booked, but then that is nothing. No, I cannot say where he slept then. Perhaps a man who sleeps in the same room may recollect, but it is quite uncertain.'"

Such obfuscation would have been wholly unnecessary had the alibi recorded in Inspector Abberline's report been true.[408]

---

[407]   Argent's late father is recorded in the 1861 census as running the lodging house at Nos. 1&2 Osborn Place.

[408]   An Edward Stanley, Lab[ourer], aged 40, born St. Luke's [Finsbury, London], is recorded in the 1881 UK Census at 12A Thrawl Street. This person also appears at a

The consequence of it ever becoming known that Colonel Hughes-Hallett, Tory MP for Rochester, had been in a relationship with a Whitechapel prostitute whose murder was later attributed to Jack the Ripper would have caused a scandal even greater than that the previous year with Beatrice Selwyn. Such a revelation would have caused immense damage to him and his family, his regiment [whose Honorary Colonel was Henry Wellesley, 3rd Duke of Wellington], the Tory government and, last but by no means least, the Metropolitan Police, who, having washed their hands of the lone maniac "Leather Apron", currently had four unsolved murders on their hands.

Colonel Hughes-Hallett wasted no time in putting as much distance as possible between himself and London. Four days after "Edward Stanley's" appearance at Annie Chapman's inquest he sailed from Liverpool aboard the Cunard steamship *Servia*, bound for New York.

Two days later, on Tuesday 25th September, with the *Servia* having cleared Queenstown, County Cork, and now steaming into the North Atlantic, someone in London sat down to write a letter. It would be received by the Central News Agency on Thursday 27th September, the day following the close of Annie Chapman's inquest.

Written in red ink, the luridly jocular 'Dear Boss' letter provided a timely solution to Annie Chapman's murder—

"Grand work the last job was. I gave the lady no time to squeal . . ."

It also held the promise of more murders to come:

"Keep this letter back till I do a bit more work, then give it out straight . . ."

It was signed—

"Yours truly, Jack the Ripper."

Central News at first treated the letter as a joke. Yet two days later, on Saturday 29th September, it was forwarded to Chief Constable Frederick Adolphus Williamson at Scotland Yard. What prompted Central News to finally attach importance to the letter is not known.

different address in the 1851 Census as the son of John Stanley, a Bricklayer's labourer; and at yet another address in the 1861 Census as an errand boy, aged 20, the son of Bridget Stanley [a widow]. He does not appear in the 1871 Census. [author's brackets].

Had they thrown it in the waste-basket, the world would have never heard of Jack the Ripper and the Whitechapel murders would now be of scant interest.

On Sunday 30th September, the day of the double event and Colonel Hughes-Hallett's arrival in New York, the Metropolitan Police prepared the text of a printed handbill to be distributed throughout the Whitechapel district—

"POLICE NOTICE.

"To the Occupier.

"On the mornings of Friday, 31st August, Saturday, 8th, and Sunday, 30th Sept., 1888, women were murdered in or near Whitechapel, supposed by some one [sic] residing in the immediate neighbourhood. Should you know of any person to whom suspicion is attached, you are earnestly requested to communicate at once with the nearest Police Station.

"Metropolitan Police Office, 30th Sept., 1888."

The handbill implied that Polly Nichols and Annie Chapman were the first two victims of a perpetrator other than the recently-exonerated 'Leather Apron'. Also, the exclusion of Emma Smith and Martha Tabram implied that they had been murdered by an entirely different person [or persons]. Taken literally, the handbill was telling the public that the police were now looking for two, perhaps even three murderers. Yet the Metropolitan Police wasted no time in obeying Jack's injunction to "Keep this letter back till I do a bit more work, then give it out straight . . ." The following morning, Monday 1st October, Jack's 'Dear Boss' letter was published in the *Daily Telegraph*.

Later that morning a postcard was received at the Central News Agency—

"I was not codding dear old Boss when I gave you the tip. You'll hear about saucy Jacky's work tomorrow. Double event this time. Number one squealed a bit. Couldn't finish straight off. Had not time to get ears for police. Thanks for keeping back last letter till I got to work again. — Jack the Ripper."

The Dear Boss letter "solved" the murder of Annie Chapman, and the Saucy Jacky postcard "solved" the murders of Elizabeth Stride and Catherine Eddowes.

Jack the Ripper was nothing if not obliging.

"Leather Apron" was instantly forgotten. Annie Chapman became the second victim of "Jack the Ripper", a murderer who—with a *nom de guerre* beyond the wildest dreams of the most shameless publicity agent—would engage the imagination of the world in history's longest-running murder-mystery franchise.

Over breakfast at the Brevoort House on Monday 1st October 1888, Hughes-Hallett may have read in the *New York Times* about the double event—

"Two More Murdered Women Found—One Night's Work of the Mysterious Assassin Who Has Baffled the London Police Thus Far."

And of the Mitre Square murder in particular—

". . . the body of the unfortunate woman had been disemboweled, the throat cut, and the nose severed. The heart and lungs had been thrown aside, and the entrails were twisted into the gaping wound around the neck . . . Pending the report of the doctors it is not known whether or not a portion of the viscera was taken away . . ."

If ever there was an Annie Chapman look-alike murder which confirmed Hughes-Hallett's assertion that the perpetrator "will, no doubt, return to the same locality with each recurring frenzy to glut his revenge," this was surely it. Yet he made no reference to this escalation of events in his interview with the *New York World* on 7th October. Nor, evidently, did journalist John Paul Bocock solicit his opinion on the matter.

Colonel Hughes-Hallett's Whitechapel adventure centred solely around the murder of Annie Chapman.

* * * * * * *

On 17th June 1889 the 2nd Brigade, Southern Division, Royal Artillery, once again assembled at Fort Elson, Gosport, "for twenty-seven days' training, Colonel Hughes-Hallett commanding, the strength being fourteen officers and 242 non-commissioned officers and men."[409]

Four days later Colonel Hughes-Hallett resigned—

"June 21 1889—

"Colonel F. C. Hughes-Hallett, having tendered his resignation, desires the following order to be published —

'In resigning, through ill-health, the command of the 2nd Brigade Southern Division Royal Artillery, the Officer commanding tenders his thanks to the officers and non-commissioned officers, for their strenuous and zealous support, and to the men for their steadiness, attention to drill, and general good conduct.

'In bidding the brigade farewell the Officer commanding begs to express his wishes to all, and his earnest hope that the brigade will continue to bear that good name for smartness and efficiency which he has reason to believe it bears now.'"[410]

Hart's Army List, 1889—

"20th July 1889. Lieut. Col. & Hon. Col. F.C. Hughes-Hallett res[igned] his Comm[ission], also is perm[itted] to retain his rank and to wear the prescribed uniform on retirement (Gaz[etted] 19th July)." [author's brackets].

Colonel Francis Charles Hughes-Hallett's self-immolation was now complete, his political and military careers at an end. Socially and financially ruined, by October 1889 he had moved from 108 Cromwell Road, his mail being re-directed to Messrs. Berkeley and Calcott, solicitors, 52 Lincoln's-Inn Fields.[411]

W. T. Stead's a *fatal want of pence* characterized Hughes-Hallett's latter years. Desperate for money, he had fallen easy prey to loan-sharks. On 5th November 1889 *The Times* reported his appearance in court, he 'and others' having in February 1888 taken out a loan of £400 from the *Southern Counties Deposit Bank*—in reality a firm of money-lenders described by Henry Labouchere in *Truth* magazine as a 'notorious usury-

---

[409]   Ibid.
[410]   Ibid.
[411]   *The Times*, 11th October 1889.

shop.' Hughes-Hallett claimed to have been 'fraudulently' induced to sign a promissory note for £648, the difference being interest, but by the time of the court hearing the total sum owed had swollen to £1,260, the final total 'being made up of further interest at the rate of 216 per cent.'

In 1892 Hughes-Hallett pressed an unsuccessful libel action against John Passmore Edwards, the Liberal candidate he had defeated in the 1885 Rochester election, who was now proprietor of the *Weekly Times and Echo*. The newspaper had suggested that Hughes-Hallett and another disgraced MP, Sir Charles Dilke, would make ideal parliamentary colleagues for the constituency of Sodom and Gomorrah. During this trial it was revealed that Hughes-Hallett was £1,700 overdrawn at Cox's Bank.

The following year, in a Philadelphia court, Hughes-Hallett filed an ante-nuptial claim against his wife, the wealthy American socialite Emilie Page Von Schaumberg, once popularly known as the Belle of Philadelphia. They had first met during the 1881 winter season at Nice on the Côte d'Azur and, despite rival attentions for Emilie's affections from a Russian Prince and a Portuguese Marquis, the dashing Colonel finally won her heart. Their nuptials delayed by the death of his mother in late 1881, they finally married at the British Embassy in Paris on 30th March 1882.

In the absence of her father, Emilie was given away by Levi Parsons Morgan, the United States Minister to France. Colonel Hughes-Hallett's best man was Colonel Henry Brackenbury, R.A., British military attaché in Paris [1881-82], who in January 1886 was appointed as the first Director of Military Intelligence. The ceremony was conducted by the Rev. Francis J. C. Moran, chaplain to the embassy and formerly vicar of St. Stephen's, Twickenham, following which a lavish party was thrown at the Hotel des Deux Mondes on the Avenue de l'Opera.[412]"

On 16th October 1887 the *Brooklyn Daily Eagle* reported Mrs Hughes-Hallett's English solicitor as saying that "the lady's entire fortune was settled upon herself prior to her marriage at her intended husband's own request, therefore estopping him from using it even if he so desired",

---

[412]   St. Louis Globe Democrat, 28th April 1882

so Colonel Hughes-Hallett's ante-nuptial claim was finally dismissed, the court ordering him to pay all costs.[413]

Mrs Hughes-Hallett was never less than gracious in support of her husband, a man variously described as a 'fortune-hunter' and 'opportunist' who always had an eye on her substantial wealth. Indeed, it is conceivable that his scandalous affair with Beatrice Selwyn had been calculated to induce Emilie to divorce him, in which event he would have received a handsome settlement. Yet Emilie appears to have realised that it wasn't in her husband's financial interests to elope with his step-daughter, nor to ever file for divorce himself [fleetingly rumoured in 1890], and so set out to take revenge on her errant Colonel.

Mrs Hughes-Hallett punished her husband's 1887 affair in the most exquisite manner. She forgave him. As the dutiful wife, she stood staunchly at his side, "endeavouring to live down the scandal which by weakness in an unfortunate moment her husband [had] brought upon himself."[414]

Fort Worth Daily Gazette, 19th October 1887—

"The wife of Colonel Hughes-Hallett has appealed to the Conservatives asking them not to be too hard on the old man. She claims that as the wife his amours hurt her first and worse, and if she is willing to condone his faults, common, ordinary, work-a-day constituencies should submit without a whimper. She volunteers to visit personally every voter who feels himself aggrieved and by the balm of her presence soothe him to tranquility . . ."

Although it was she who would leave him on 1st August 1890, allegedly 'without reasonable cause',[415] she steadfastly refused to grant him a divorce. Fully determined never to allow him to receive a penny

---

[413]   Pennsylvania State Reports, Vol. 152, 1893

[414]   Victoria [BC] Daily Colonist, 13th October 1887

[415]   Colonel Hughes-Hallett had accused his wife of having an affair with his financial agent John Arthur Chandor. It was a complex business involving charges of fraud and libel at a trial at the Old Bailey, 18th November 1889. He later rescinded his accusations of an affair. More details are contained in a 44-page pamphlet published by the "Private Vigilance Society" entitled *"Concerning the Man John Arthur Chandor, Alias Count Chandor, alias Captain Chandor, alias Montagu Chandor, alias Captain Carlton, &c.,"* 189[?].

of her fortune, she made certain they remained shackled until death they did part.

Never had a woman's scorn been visited upon a man with such fury.

On 2nd December 1896 Hughes-Hallett presided over a shareholder's meeting of *Ella (Transvaal) Gold Mining*, a company of which he was chairman, at Winchester House, Old Broad Street, London. The meeting sought increased shareholder investment. Although a further shareholder meeting was held in 1897, a few years later the Ella gold field failed.[416] On 26th September 1898, Hughes-Hallett chaired a meeting at Mullen's Hotel, Ironmonger Lane, London, to appoint a liquidator and voluntarily wind-up *West Kalgurli Gold Mines Limited*. "By reason of its liabilities" the company could no longer continue in business.[417] Thus far, the fate of the *Sonora Silver Mining Company* is not known.

By 1899 Hughes-Hallett was living at 'The Nest,' The Grove, Ealing, West London.[418] In 1901, by then desperately broke, he made one final attempt to realise money from his 1882 ante-nuptial agreement.

Pittsburgh Press, 9th August 1901—

"Englishman Wants to Dispose of His Regular Income for Cash.

"Philadelphia, August 9. —One of the most peculiar requests ever received by a mayor of this city was contained in a letter from a London solicitor who represents Lieut. Col. Francis Charles Hughes-Hallet, late member of the English parliament and an officer in the English army, and opened by the mayor's secretary yesterday . . .

"The letter says there was an ante-nuptial agreement between the colonel and his wife which provided that he should, if he survive her, receive a certain interest for life in securities that were named.

". . . the colonel and his wife have been separated for many years, but that his life interest in the securities still remains, and the mayor is besought to find some purchaser for this interest, which, it is said, will

---

[416] *Gold Mines of the World: Concise and Practical Advice for Investors,* J.H. Curle, 1899.

[417] Kalgurli [Kalgoorlie], Western Australia, boomed in the 1880s gold rush.

[418] In Henry Smetham's 1899 *History of Strood,* F.C. Hughes-Hallet appears at this address in the List of Subscribers.

approximate $5,974 [£1,262] annually . . . Col. Hallett is 63 years of age, but [says] that he is a good insurable risk of the first claim class."

It is not known whether Mayor Samuel Howell Ashbridge ever found a buyer. However, in the event Hughes-Hallett proved not to be such a good risk, for he did not outlive his wife. Just under two years later, on 22nd June 1903, at 39 Norland Square, Kensington, West London, Colonel Francis Charles Hughes-Hallett died, aged sixty-three, from 'Heart Disease and Cystitis'.[419]

His death went almost unremarked in the world's obituary columns. *Manitoba Free Press,* 1st August 1903—

"Death Hardly Noticed.

"End of Career of M.P., Once Most Popular Man in London.

"Colonel Hughes-Hallett was fifteen years ago a member of parliament for Rochester, a chairman of many mining and other companies, a heavy and generally unsuccessful speculator, an amateur actor of no small ability, and a glib and ready speaker . . . A year or two later Colonel Hughes-Hallett went to Mexico to inspect a mine in which he was interested, and there fell seriously ill. During his absence his seat in parliament was declared vacant.

"That was the beginning of the end, though for fifteen years he lingered on, a ruined, broken man. He might be seen tottering along the West End streets, shabbily dressed, with death written on his shrunken cheeks . . .

"Colonel Hughes-Hallet leaves a widow, an American lady who now resides at Dinard, France, where she entertains visiting members of New York society."

His passing did nothing to disrupt his widow's glittering social life on the other side of the English Channel. *Daily Mail,* London, 28th August 1903—

"The season at Dinard is now in full swing, and Mrs. Hughes-Hallett, who is the leading hostess of the place, has been as usual giving a series of pleasant entertainments at her charming villa, Monplaisir. This week

---

[419]   Details from Death Certificate. Born in 1838, he was 65 years old.

Mrs. Hughes-Hallett is giving a bal poudré,[420] and there is a ball, too, at the New Club, while when the weather is fine picnics and outdoor entertainments are the order of the day."

It is not known if the former Emilie Page Von Schaumberg ever danced on her husband's grave, but one can almost see the twinkling lights of *Monplaisir* and hear the sounds of music and laughter drifting across Dinard harbour.[421]

Francis Charles Hughes-Hallett's personal estate, which by his death had dwindled to £393 18s. 4d, passed to Frank Victor Hughes-Hallett, his eldest son from his first marriage. Also an army officer, he later wrote a number of sporting mysteries under the pseudonym Raymond Carew.[422]

Mrs Emilie Hughes-Hallett, the 'Queen of Dinard', died at *Monplaisir* on 1st February 1923.[423]

* * * * * * *

What might have precipitated Colonel Francis Charles Hughes-Hallett's flight to America fifteen days after the murder of Annie Chapman, a flight which resulted in his political, professional, social and financial destruction?

From various reports we know it is unlikely to have been his previous year's sexual and financial scandal. This had blown itself out, with any political debris soon swept up by government heavy-hitters

---

[420]   A powdered wig ball.

[421]   *Montplaisir* is now Dinard's "Marie" [Town Hall], 47 Boulevard Féart, at the corner of Rue Dumont.

[422]   *T.P.'s Weekly*, 3rd April 1914— "Raymond Carew in 'The Loose Box' (Everett, 6s.) has written a novel of sport and country life with a background of horror and mystery. It is as gruesome as a vampire story, and one feels that much more needs to be explained before we can believe the story of the distinguished surgeon's wife, and what became of her. It is not fair to give away the motive upon which the interest hangs. One can, however, appreciate the manner in which the ball is kept rolling amid an atmosphere of hunting and country life. And if one feels that a good many more details would have been welcome concerning lunacy and its strange freaks, one had to follow up the scent to the end."

[423]   *The Times*, 2nd February 1923. Mrs. Emilie Hughes-Hallett was 90-years-old.

keen to forgive his mortal sins in order to secure the Tory seat for Rochester.

On 9th December 1889 the *Chicago Tribune* reported that when Hughes-Hallett left Britain for America "a security debt of £4,000 was about to become due." The newspaper further stated that in letters received by Hughes-Hallet from his financial agent [John Arthur Chandor] whilst in America it was suggested that it would be unwise for him to return to England "as bankruptcy proceedings would be entered against him and he would be plunged into costly and tedious litigation."

But after Hughes-Hallett returned from America in 1889 he was not declared bankrupt. The matter appears to have had more to do with the November 1889 Old Bailey trial of Clara Bloomfield-Moore, at which John Arthur Chandor and Mrs Hughes-Hallett appeared as material witnesses.

Colonel Hughes-Hallett was running from something big— something which may have been connected to the murder of Annie Chapman and the bizarre tale of his hunt for the murderer which appeared in the *New York World*.

Not for him the diminutive Jewish slipper-maker—the Quilp-like, half-man, half-monster known as Leather Apron—once so heavily promoted by the *Star* and the Metropolitan Police before being abruptly dropped as a suspect. Colonel Hughes-Hallett's Whitechapel murderer was unmistakably a toff—

". . . a West End man, a gentleman, a person of wealth and culture . . . a man of the world, a club man . . . a medical student, or a gentleman who has read medicine as amusement, or as a part of a liberal education . . . a man of intellectual qualities, finesse and keen discrimination."

It has been argued that this was a character sketch of Dr. Francis Tumblety, the alleged Ripper suspect who arrived in New York amidst a blaze of publicity at about the same time Hughes-Hallett was leaving the city for Mexico.

This, however, is a hasty conclusion to draw, for there was one other person who more closely fitted this description.

It is not known if Hughes-Hallett ever 'read medicine as amusement or as part of a liberal education' at either Brighton College or the Royal Military Academy, Woolwich.[424] Yet during his early parliamentary years he had been a champion of the Brigade Surgeons of India,[425] a correspondent to the British Medical Journal, and had also put his political weight behind achieving proper rank and status for Army Medical Staff.[426]

And at one time Hughes-Hallett certainly had been ". . . a West End man, a gentleman, a person of wealth and culture . . . a man of the world, a club man . . . a man of intellectual qualities, finesse and keen discrimination."

All in all, it is not unreasonable to suggest that Colonel Francis Charles Hughes-Hallett may have been describing himself.

But what of his Whitechapel murderer's motive—the "homicidal mania bred in him by disease, most likely contracted from some of the unfortunate women to whom he confines his horrible revenge"?

There is a measure of circumstantial evidence to suggest that Hughes-Hallett may have been suffering the physical and mental torments of syphilis. But how might such a dashing military figure have contracted such a disease?

National Police Gazette [US], 15th October 1887—

"Hughes-Hallett, M.P.

"Two years ago an unpleasant scandal took place at one of the newly constituted clubs in Pall Mall.[427] Taking advantage of the fact that lady guests were admitted, he ventured to bring to supper there one of the

---

[424] *Brighton College Register* 1847-1863— "Hughes-Hallett (Francis Charles), 12 (1850), son of Charles Hughes-Hallett, Esq., of the Madras Civil Service." *Hart's Army List*, 1886— "Entered the Royal Artillery (1859), saw considerable service in Gibraltar and Ireland, and was appointed to the Royal Horse Artillery. Colonel Hughes-Hallett was ordered out to Sindh and Beloochistan (1868), whence he returned invalided (1870). Commanded the 2nd Brigade North Irish Division Royal Artillery (1875). Exchanged into the 2nd Brigade Southern Division Royal Artillery (1885), a command he holds at the present time (1886)."

[425] *House of Commons*, 11th March 1887. *British Medical Journal*, 19th March 1887.

[426] *British Medical Journal*, 19th March 1887.

[427] The "newly constituted" club may have been the *Imperial and American* at No. 4 Hanover Square [about half a mile north of Pall Mall], which held its inaugural dinner in July 1885.

frail sisterhood. In consequence of this outrageous insult towards the other ladies present in the club at the time, he was requested to leave the premises at once, and subsequently to resign."

The 'frail sisterhood' was a nineteenth century euphemism for prostitutes.

21. THE WRITING ON THE WALL

In the early hours of Sunday 30th September 1888 Metropolitan Police Commissioner Sir Charles Warren was roused from his Pimlico bed[428] with the news that two murders had taken place: the first in Berner Street, Whitechapel; the second in Mitre Square, within the one square-mile of the City of London.

He hastened to Commercial Street and Leman Street police stations for briefings on the situation before going to Goulston Street, Whitechapel, where earlier that morning, in the entrance to a block of flats, PC Alfred Long 245A had found something of interest.

Echo, 1st October 1888—

"The police have made an important discovery, which they are of opinion affords a clue to the direction in which the murderer made his escape. Yesterday afternoon a portion of apron was found in Goldstein [sic] Street, and when the body of the woman found in Mitre Square was searched, it was discovered that she was wearing the upper portion of the apron to which the piece found belonged. It is therefore concluded that the murderer made his way into Whitechapel."

---

[428]   *New York Times*, 1st October 1888— "As soon as the news was received at Police Headquarters a messenger was dispatched for Sir Charles Warren, Chief Commissioner of Police, who was called out of bed and at once visited the scene of the murders."

The *Star*, 2nd October 1888, added— "That he [dropped the bloodstained rag] in Goulston Street does not occasion any surprise. The police have never doubted that this midnight murderer lived in the midst of the community he has been terrorising."

The last murder, that of Annie Chapman, had been on 8th September 1888, it's memory kept alive by Coroner Wynne Baxter's time-wasting inquest which closed just four days prior to the double-event. Yet the East End rumour mill was instantly at the ready with countless tales of arrests, further attacks and mysterious strangers which over the next century would provide the visual cliches for a raft of movie posters and the covers of tawdry paperbacks—

A woman professed to have seen a man of suspicious appearance standing in a side street. He stepped back into the darkness of a doorway as she approached. Seeing a flashing blade in his hand, she ran screaming in terror down the street.

Another woman met a man in a public house. Generally morose and taciturn, he put a sovereign[429] on the counter and ordered her a drink. Obviously charmed by this gesture, and not in the least bit apprehensive, she left the pub with him, only to be seized by the hair in a nearby street where, alarmed by her terrified screams, he hurried away and was lost in the gloom.

These incidents were reported on 2nd October 1888, the *Echo* insisting hand- on-heart that they were not the "imaginative escapades of hysterical women. They are actual incidents - incidents of the past night, gleaned by an Echo reporter in conversation with many persons in the neighbourhood of Aldgate at an early hour this morning."

Later in the same edition the *Echo* was able to scotch a particular rumour—

"One Of Many Canards.

"Among the many discredited rumours current in the neighbourhood is the assertion that Sir Charles Warren on visiting the yard on Sunday morning last discovered some writing on the wall in

---

[429]   In an 1888 pub a Sovereign [£1] would have bought 120 glasses of gin.

chalk, which gave expression to very objectionable sentiments of a religious character, and which was supposed to have been the handiwork of the murderer. This was alleged to have given such great offence that Sir Charles, fearing a disturbance in the neighbourhood, directed the writing to be washed out. Investigation, however, has proved, so far as can be judged, the absolute fallacy of the story. A careful examination of the brickwork in the yard this morning has revealed beyond dispute the fact that there has been no effacement of chalk marks on the walls, certainly within recent date."

The *Echo* was the only newspaper to run this story.

Everyone was soon convinced that the piece of bloodstained apron proved beyond doubt that after leaving Mitre Square the murderer had made his way back into Whitechapel.

On Wednesday 3rd October 1888 Sir John Whittaker Ellis, a former Lord Mayor of London and currently Tory MP for Kingston-on-Thames, wrote to Henry Matthews—

"My dear Matthews,

"There is no doubt but that the Whitechapel murderer remains in the neighbourhood. Draw a cordon of half a mile round the centre and search every house. This would surely unearth him. It is a strong thing to do, but I should think such occasion never before arose."

Ellis then offered his considered opinion as to the nationality and profession of the murderer—

"I should say he is an American Slaughterman, an occupation largely followed in South America."

Ellis's letter was forwarded to Sir Charles Warren, who thought a dragnet was a fine idea. However, fearful of a bloody and possibly deadly local uprising he sent a cautious two-page response to Henry Matthews' private secretary—

"Dear Mr. Ruggles Brise,

"I return Sir W. Ellis letter.

"I am quite prepared to take the responsibility of adopting the most drastic or arbitrary measures that the Sec of State can name which would further the securing of the murderer however illegal they may be, provided H.M. Gov will support me. But I must observe that the Sec of State cannot authorise me to do an illegal action and that the full responsibility will always rest with me over the Police Constables for anything done. All I want to ensure is that the Government will indemnify us for our actions which must necessarily be adapted to the circumstances of the case – the exact course of which cannot always be seen . . .

"I think I may say without hesitation that those houses could not be searched illegally without violent resistance and bloodshed and the certainty of one or more Police Officers being killed, and the question is whether it is worthwhile losing the lives of several of the community and risking serious riot in order to search for one murderer whose whereabouts are not known. . ."

Daily News, 4th October 1888—

"Yesterday the large force of police and detectives drafted into Whitechapel made a house-to-house visitation and left a handbill."

On the same day the inquest opened on the Mitre Square victim who, two days earlier, had been identified by John Kelly, her common law husband, as Catherine Eddowes.

On the following day Henry Matthews replied to Sir Charles Warren—

"R.B. has forwarded me your letter of the 4th Oct. with Sir J. Ellis' letter – the suggestion in which is open to your observations & is too sweeping.

"I thought my own suggestion of last Wed. more practical – take all houses in a given area which appear suspicious upon the best enquiry your detectives can make. Search all those, which the owners of persons in charge will allow you to search. Where leave is refused, apply to a magistrate for a search warrant, on the ground that it is probable or possible the murderer may be there. If search warrants are refused, you can only keep the houses under observation."[430]

Henry Matthews also wrote to his Principal Private Secretary,

---

[430]   HO 144/221/A49301C.

Evelyn Ruggles-Brise—

"I agree with Sir C.W. that he cannot act on Sir J. Ellis' suggestion and search houses illegally, with all the fearful consequences that might follow from resistance . . . A house to house search (of suspicious places) with the consent of the landlord, or under warrant, would be helpful— and it would give some satisfaction to the public. If it resulted in nothing (as it probably would) there would be some sort of ground for offering a reward."

From this it would appear that Henry Matthews later sanctioned the house-to-house search partly to appease public opinion.

Matthews closed the part of his letter dated 6th October by remarking that "Anderson was to return today."

A few days later the *Echo* story of the chalked message resurfaced.

Pall Mall Gazette, 8th October 1888—

"The East End Murders.

"A Strange Story About Jack-the-Ripper.

"The following extraordinary story has been sent to us by the Central News. We publish it with all reserve, and without at present attaching to it any special importance.

"The Central News Agency says 'A startling fact has just come to light. After killing Katherine Eddowes in Mitre Square, the murderer, it is now known, walked to Goulston Street, where he threw away the piece of the deceased woman's apron upon which he had wiped his hands and knife. Within a few feet of this spot he had written upon the wall, 'The Jews shall not be blamed for nothing.'

"Most unfortunately one of the police officers gave orders for this writing to be immediately sponged out, probably with a view of stifling the morbid curiosity which it would certainly have aroused. But in so doing a very important link was destroyed, for had the writing been photographed a certain clue would have been in the hands of the authorities. The witnesses who saw the writing, however, state that it was similar in character to the letters sent to the Central News and signed 'Jack the Ripper,' and though it would have been far better to have clearly demonstrated this by photography, there is now every reason to believe that the writer of the letter and postcard sent to the Central News (facsimiles of which are now to be seen outside every police-station) is the actual murderer. The police, consequently, are very anxious that any citizen who can identify the handwriting should without delay communicate with the authorities . . ."

The police thought the author of the Ripper correspondence was the murderer and that the chalked message bore a resemblance to his handwriting.

Ergo! Jack the Ripper dropped the piece of bloodstained apron and chalked the message in Goulston Street whilst making his way back into Whitechapel.

The *Star* of the same day was sceptical about the chalked message—

"The Central News Agency, which first gave publicity to the original 'Jack the Ripper' letter and postcard now resuscitates the rumor - which has already been dismissed as false - that on a wall, within a few yards of the spot where the blood-stained part of an apron was found, were written the words, 'The Jews shall not be blamed for nothing.'"

Over the next few days the rumour gathered strength.

Pall Mall Gazette, 11th October 1888—

"A very strange, startling rumour as to the manner in which Sir Charles Warren performs the duty of Chief Detective of Scotland-yard is current this morning in the City. Those who repeat it assert that it will be verified at the inquest which is now proceeding and a report of which will be continued in succeeding editions. The rumour in question is to the effect that rather than face the danger of allowing a crowd to assemble in a public thoroughfare Sir Charles Warren deliberately destroyed a clue - the only clue which the City Police believed to afford any guidance as to the identity of the assassin."

Other rumours started to circulate. On the following day a number of American newspapers reported that—"The Pall Mall Gazette charges that the words 'I have murdered four and will murder sixteen more before I surrender myself to the police,' written by the supposed Whitechapel murderer upon a shutter of a house adjoining the one in the yard of which the body of one of his victims was found, were erased by order of Sir Charles Warren, chief of the London police force, before the authorities had the opportunity to photograph them."

At the second day of the Catherine Eddowes inquest Metropolitan Police Constable Alfred Long 245A, who had discovered the bloodstained piece of apron and chalked message in Goulston Street, gave evidence, stating that the chalked message read—

"The Jews are the men that will not be blamed for nothing."

Henry Crawford, the City of London solicitor representing the London Corporation, said—"As to the writing on the wall, have you not put a 'not' in the wrong place? Were not the words, 'The Jews are not the men that will be blamed for nothing'?"

PC Alfred Long stood his ground—

"I believe the words were as I have stated."

At this point the Coroner intervened—

"Was not the word 'Jews' spelt 'Juwes'?"

"It may have been."

The Coroner pressed home his point—

"Yet you did not tell us that in the first place. Did you make an entry of the words at the time?

"Yes, in my pocket book."

"Is it possible that you have put the 'not' in the wrong place?" suggested the Coroner.

"It is possible, but I do not think that I have."

Following supplementary questions from the Coroner, the Jury Foreman asked PC Long—

"Where is the pocket-book in which you made the entry of the writing?"

Unaccountably, PC Alfred Long had not thought it necessary to bring his pocket book to the inquest of a putative Jack the Ripper victim.

"At Westminster,"[431] he replied.

Whilst PC Alfred Long's pocket book was fetched from King Street

---

[431] PC Alfred Long was transferred to Whitechapel from A Division [Whitehall], based at 22 King Street, Westminster. He discovered the apron piece and chalked message during the first night of his new beat in Goulston Street, on which he was unaccompanied.

police station, the next witness was called to give evidence. He was 45-year-old City of London Detective Constable Daniel Halse, who rendered the chalked message as "The Juwes are not the men who will be blamed for nothing" and described it as being in "three lines of writing in a good schoolboy's round hand. The size of the capital letters would be about ¾ [of an inch], and the other letters were in proportion. The writing was on the black bricks, which formed a kind of dado, the bricks above being white."[432]

This was not high-visibility graffiti.

PC Long returned to the witness box with his pocket book.

Mr. Crawford: "What is the entry?"

PC Long: "The words are, 'The Jews are the men that will not be blamed for nothing.'"

Confusion reigned. The spelling and grammar contradicted the testimony of DC Halse, a fact not lost on the Coroner—

"Both here and in your inspector's report the word 'Jews' is spelt correctly?"

"Yes," agreed PC Long, "but the inspector remarked that the word was spelt 'Juwes.'"

"Why did you write 'Jews' then?"

"I made my entry before the inspector made the remark."

"But why did the inspector write 'Jews'?

"I cannot say."

"At all events, there is a discrepancy?"

"It would seem so," agreed PC Long.

And so, PC Long having testified that the chalked message "was rubbed out in my presence at half-past five," the subject was dropped.[433]

Neither DC Halse or PC Long, both of whom were present in Goulston Street at the time of the incident, was asked who ordered the erasure.

On the same day a reporter from *The Irish Times* visited Scotland

---

[432]   *Daily Telegraph*, 12th October 1888.

[433]   In his 6th November 1888 written report on the incident PC Long spelled the operative word "Juews."

Yard—

"Our representative saw Sir Charles Warren's private secretary, who, on returning from the Chief Commissioner's room, stated, 'Sir Charles Warren was in Goulston Street shortly after the murders, and if he had wished to make any communication to the Press on the subject he would have done so then.'

"In reply to a further question as to whether he was to understand from this that Sir Charles Warren preferred to say nothing about the allegation, our representative was informed that such was the case."

Sir Charles Warren had obviously noted the chalked message during his visit to Goulston Street. But whereas DC Halse had testified to it being composed on three lines, Warren in his 6th November 1888 report tendered a five-line rendition—

"The Juwes are
The men that
Will not
be Blamed
for nothing."[434]

Warren also noted in his report that Acting Chief Rabbi Hermann Adler had written to him concerning another spelling variant— 'Juewes.'

Adler had written—

"I was deeply pained by the statements that appeared in several papers today, the 'Standard', 'Daily News', etc., that in the Yiddish dialect the word Jews is spelled 'Juewes'. This is not a fact. The equivalent in the Judao-German (Yiddish) jargon is 'Yidden.' I do not know of any dialect or language in which 'Jews' is spelled 'Juewes.'"[435]

Refusing to wait until there was sufficient light to have the minuscule chalked message photographed for fear that if left in place "the house was likely to be wrecked," Sir Charles Warren had ordered it erased.

Between them, the City of London and Metropolitan Police officers

---

[434]   HO A49301C/8C. Home Office Date Received stamp 6th November 1888.
[435]   Letter cited by Chaim Bermant, Point *of Arrival / A Study of London's East End*, Eyre Methuen, London, 1975.

who reported the chalked message [now popularly known as the GSG—Goulston Street Graffiti] offered a combination of seven variations on its spelling, grammar, capitalization and linage.[436] Also there was no overall consensus as to the precise location of the chalked message within the entrance to the block of flats.

Whilst a Central News telegram [to the press] of 12th October 1888 remained circumspect, telling of a "highly-placed officer in the Metropolitan Police Force," who though full of good humane intentions in not wanting to inflame anti-Jewish sentiment "was guilty, to say the least, of a very grave error of judgment," the *Pall Mall Gazette* of the same day did not mince its words—

"The case against the Chief Commissioner is overwhelming. Strange, almost incredible though it appears, this excellent Major-General, whose first thought is ever how to repress disorder, and to whom the detection of crime is but a secondary consideration, actually persisted in destroying this clue, in face of the protests of the city police and of the suggestion of one of his own men . . . He was destroying evidence that might have been of priceless value . . . and so perished the only clue which the murderer has left us by which he might be identified."

The much-maligned *Star*, 12th October 1888, exercised due diligence in its reporting of the spelling of the chalked message—

"A News Agency says: - The police authorities attach a great deal of importance to the spelling of the word 'Jews' in the writing on the wall. The language of the Jews in the East-end is a hybrid dialect, known as Yiddish, and their mode of spelling the word Jews would be 'Juwes.'

"This is absolutely incorrect. A representative of the Star called at the Jewish Chronicle office, and was informed by the editor, and by a responsible member of the staff whose father is a Polish Jew, that the Yiddish word for Jew is Yiddin, the word 'Yiddish' meaning, of course, the language of the Yiddins. Much indignation is felt amongst the Jews at these repeated and unjustifiable attempts to fasten the responsibility for the dastardly crimes on them."

---

[436]   The operative word was rendered as Juwes, Jewes, Jeuws and Juews.

However, the die was cast as to the murderer being Jewish when a number of newspapers reported that "the police consider [the spelling of Juwes] a strong indication that the crime was committed by one of the numerous foreigners by whom the East end is infested."[437]

The ultimate responsibility for eradicating the chalked message rested with Commissioner Sir Charles Warren. He shouldered all the criticism, yet was not the police officer who originally felt it should be removed.

Report by Superintendent [H Division] Thomas Arnold, 6th November 1888[438]—

"I beg to report that on the morning of 30th Sept. last my attention was called to some writing on the wall of the entrance to some dwellings No. 108 Goulston Street, Whitechapel which consisted of the following words 'The Juews are not [deleted] the men that will not be blamed for nothing', and knowing that in consequence of a suspicion having fallen upon a Jew named 'John Pizer' alias 'Leather Apron' having committed a murder in Hanbury Street a short time previously a strong feeling existed against the Jews generally, and as the Building upon which the writing was found was situated in the midst of a locality inhabited principally by that Sect. I was apprehensive that if the writing were left it would be the means of causing a riot and therefore considered it desirable that it should be removed having in view the fact that it was in such a position that it would have been rubbed by the shoulders of persons passing in & out of the Building. Had only a portion of the writing been removed the context would have remained. An Inspector was present by my directions with a sponge for the purpose of removing the writing when Commissioner arrived on the scene."

Superintendent Arnold was an experienced police officer who had recently given evidence before a House of Commons Select Committee on *Emigration and Immigration (Foreigners)* about the number of foreign Jews coming to the East End of London.

---

[437]   *Echo*, 13th October 1888.
[438]   HO. A49301C/8c

The Times, 30th July 1888—

"His [Arnold's] testimony was confirmatory of that of the previous witnesses as to the increasing numbers of foreign immigrants, and as to the manner in which they had driven English workmen from that quarter of the East End."[439]

On the same day the Commissioner was being pilloried in the *Pall Mall Gazette*, a letter arrived at the Foreign Office from Vienna regarding a mysterious informant's offer to identify the Whitechapel murderer.

The public did not discover if the erasure story was true or merely a rumour, for the only available documents specifically referencing the incident were Chief Inspector Swanson and Commissioner Warren's internal reports, received at the Home Office on 6th November 1888.

The press had learned of the two murders fairly quickly. As earlier mentioned, a reporter from *Lloyds Weekly Newspaper* arrived in Mitre Square soon after the double-event, but as far as is known none were in Goulston Street that morning. So of interest is who might have told Central News about the chalked message; also, how Sir Charles Warren came to be roused from his bed.

On being advised of the chalked message Superintendent Arnold felt it prudent to have it eradicated, but would not take responsibility for destroying what may have been vital evidence. He may therefore have contacted his immediate superior, Lieutenant Colonel Bolton James Alfred Monsell, Chief Constable of No. 1 Eastern District[440]. And if Monsell had felt similarly uneasy about sanctioning the erasure of the message, his immediate superior would have been the Assistant Commissioner [CID] at Scotland Yard.

However, Assistant Commissioner [CID] James Monro had resigned and was now ensconced at the Home Office, whilst his replacement, Robert Anderson, was clearing his throat in Switzerland. In their

---

[439] The Special Commission noted that in the 12 months between July 1887 and June 1888 5,558 Jewish (foreign) immigrants had arrived by ship and moved into Whitechapel and Spitalfields.

[440] Comprising G – Finsbury, H – Whitechapel, K – Stepney, N – Islington, and Thames Divisions.

absence the ailing Chief Constable Frederick Adolphus Williamson had day-to-day charge of the CID, with Senior Assistant Commissioner Alexander Carmichael Bruce in temporary overall command under Sir Charles Warren.[441]

Thus was Warren's visit to Whitechapel a direct consequence of this broken link in the hierarchical chain at Scotland Yard. Had circumstances been normal the chalked message incident would have been handled at Assistant Commissioner [CID] level.

It is interesting to note that the three police reports relating to the discovery of Goulston Street graffiti on 30th September——Warren, Arnold and Long——were all written over a month later, on 6th November.

As to who might have told Central News about the erasure of the chalked message, the absence of newspaper reporters in Goulston Street on the morning of the double-event suggests that the story—perhaps leaked in order to deal a further blow to Sir Charles Warren's steadily dwindling credibility—came from a source within the police.

---

[441] *Star*, 14th September 1888— "Mr. Bruce, Assistant Commissioner, and Colonel Monsell, Chief Constable, paid a private visit to the Whitechapel district without notifying the local officials of their intention to do so. They visited the scene of the Buck's Row murder as well as Hanbury Street, and made many inquiries. They spent nearly a quarter of an hour at No. 29, Hanbury Street, and minutely inspected the house and the yard in which were found the mutilated body of Mrs. Chapman."

22. THE MYSTERIOUS INSPECTOR SOYLE

The Dear Boss letter and subsequent Saucy Jacky postcard did not come from the killer. That much is crystal clear; and had this correspondence not been splashed across London on crown-size posters the resultant terror and hysteria over the name Jack the Ripper would not have taken place.

In later years a number of writers, journalists and police officers disavowed "Jack the Ripper."

In 1891 journalist Arthur Brisbane wrote, "'Jack the Ripper,' though illiterate, wrote a hand marvellously like that of the refined Mr. Moore.[442] Mr. Moore was no criminal, but he was 'Jack the Ripper'. This fact was not mentioned in London, as public feeling would not have endured being imposed upon to that extent nor have accepted business enterprise as an excuse."

In 1910 Sir Robert Anderson thought Jack "the creation of an enterprising London journalist . . . I am almost tempted to disclose the identity of . . . the pressman who wrote the letter . . .but no public benefit would result . . ."

In a 1913 letter to George R. Sims, ex-Chief Inspector John George Littlechild recycled the gist of Arthur Brisbane's earlier story—"With

---

[442] John Moore, manager of Central News.

regard to the term 'Jack the Ripper' it was generally believed at the Yard that Tom Bullen [Bulling] of the Central News was the originator but it is probable Moore, who was his chief, was the inventor."

It is difficult to believe that this revelation came as breaking news to the seasoned journalist, poet, dramatist, novelist and Ripperphile George R. Sims. He was a friend of Melville Macnaghten who, in the following year, wrote, "I have always thought I could discern the stained forefinger of the journalist —indeed, a year later, I had shrewd suspicions as to the actual author!"

In his 1935 book "Life and Death at The Old Bailey" Robert Thurston Hopkins, a prolific author of topographical and biographical works—who was just four years old at the time of the Whitechapel murders—subsequently came to believe the journalistic hoax story.

Hopkins wrote— "The Criminal Investigation Department looked upon [the Ripper] letter as a 'clue' and possibly a message from the actual murderer . . . It was perhaps a fortunate thing that the handwriting of this famous letter was not identified, for it would have led to the arrest of a harmless Fleet Street journalist."

On the basis of these opinions, if the handwriting of the chalked message had matched that of the Dear Boss letter, then on the morning of the double-event John Moore of Central News must have been busily running around the streets of the City of London and Whitechapel.

However, in his 6th November 1888 report, Chief Inspector Donald Swanson wrote— "To those police officers who saw the chalk writing, the handwriting of the now notorious letters to a newspaper agency bears no resemblance at all."

It seems that nobody had been under any illusions about "Jack the Ripper" being a 'journalistic' hoax. Nobody, that is, except Sir Charles Warren, stranded atop Scotland Yard and saddled with sole responsibility for dealing with the running sore of the Whitechapel murders, a mystery which he was singularly ill-equipped to tackle.

This is not to disparage Sir Charles Warren. He did not lack courage. Nor cunning and guile. He also had a ruthless streak. In August 1882 he was sent by the Admiralty to Egypt on a secret expedition to discover the fate of Professor William Henry Palmer, who had travelled there to secure a plentiful supply of camels plus Bedouin support for the Suez Canal. Warren set out into the desert, finding that Palmer and his party had been robbed and murdered. In taking hostages and appropriating their camels he succeeded in capturing eight of the guilty parties, who were brought to trial, convicted and hanged. Warren also brought back to England the remains of Professor Palmer, who was interred in Westminster Abbey.

Who actually penned the "Dear Boss" letter—John Moore or Thomas Bulling of Central News, or, as one author[443] nominated in an effort to pin its creation on the *Star* newspaper,[444] journalist Frederick Best[445]—is a moot point. Of far more interest is who originally conceived the darkly jocular persona of Jack the Ripper, which was designed to tip Sir Charles Warren's Metropolitan Police into a no-win situation.

"Dear Boss" is dated 25th September 1888 [a Tuesday], but its author did not feel an immediate urge to mail it to Central News. Annie Chapman's inquest finally came to a close the following day. Coroner Wynne Baxter regaled the proceedings with his nonsensical story of a medical man in search of organs to include with "a publication on which he was then engaged," which prompted Jack the Ripper to add the postscript, "They say I'm a doctor now - ha ha."

The letter was mailed to Central News on Thursday 27th September 1888.

On Saturday 29th September 1888 "Dear Boss" was forwarded to Chief Constable Frederick Adolphus Williamson at Scotland Yard, where it was received the same day.

Attached was a covering letter on headed Central News stationery—

---

[443]   Andrew Cook, *Jack the Ripper*, Amberley Publishing, 2009.

[444]   The "Dear Boss" letter first appeared in the morning edition of *The Daily Telegraph*.

[445]   According to an article written by Nigel Morland for the book *Crime and Detection*, 1966, in 1931 a journalist named Best [no first name] admitted writing the Ripper letters to "keep the business alive."

"The Editor presents his compliments to Mr. Williamson & begs to inform him the enclosed was sent the Central News two days ago, & was treated as a joke."

Chief Constable Williamson's reaction on receipt of the "Dear Boss" letter is not known, but he must have wondered why, if Central News had sat on the letter for two days, considering it a joke, they finally decided to forward it. Was he meant to share the joke or take the letter seriously?

The crowing rhetoric contained just enough to perhaps make the seasoned Chief Constable Williamson take it seriously. "Grand work the last job was. I gave the lady no time to squeal." Jack was confessing to the murder of Annie Chapman and promising to strike again. "You will soon hear of me with my funny little games . . . I want to get to work right away if I get a chance."

By the date on the letter it had been almost three weeks since the murder of Annie Chapman and there were an estimated 1200 prostitutes in the Whitechapel district.[446] If Jack was down on whores, what had been preventing him from getting back to work right away? Certainly not a lack of opportunity. Nor was a targeted police manhunt curtailing his ambitions, for until the arrival of "Dear Boss" he was a wholly unknown quantity.

In his *Sunday Referee* column, 7th October 1888, journalist George R. Sims mused on the source of the letter—

"How many among you, my dear readers, would have hit upon the idea of "the Central News" as a receptacle for your confidence? You might have sent your joke to the Telegraph, the Times, any morning or any evening paper, but I will lay long odds that it would never have occurred to communicate with a Press agency."

Launching "Dear Boss" via Central News ensured that by 1st October 1888 everyone who read a newspaper, at home or as far away as Texas and Kansas, was aware of the name Jack the Ripper.

Sims concluded—

---

[446]   MEPO 3/141, ff. 158-9.

". . . It is an idea which might occur to a Pressman perhaps; and even then it would probably only occur to someone connected with the editorial department of a newspaper, someone who knew what the Central News was, and the place it filled in the business of news supply. This proceeding on Jack's part betrays an inner knowledge of the newspaper world which is certainly surprising.

"Everything therefore points to the fact that the jokist is professionally connected with the Press."

Four days later, in his weekly magazine *Truth*, Henry Labouchere hinted at a possible cross-pollination between matters criminal and political—

"On the doctrine of possibilities, it is long odds against the murderer having written the 'Jack the Ripper' letters . . . But there is a coincidence in respect to these letters to which attention has not been drawn. The handwriting is remarkably like that of the forgeries which the *Times* published, and which they ascribed to Mr. Parnell and to Mr. Egan. I do not go so far as to suggest that the *Times* forger is the Whitechapel murderer, although this, of course, is possible; but it may be that the forger takes pride in his work, and wished to keep his hand in."

Labouchere's condemnation of *The Times'* letters as forgeries at this stage is intriguing, for it wasn't until four months later, at a Special Commission hearing in February 1889 that they were publicly exposed as such.

Sir Charles Warren's disastrous decision to publish "Dear Boss" and "Saucy Jacky" on posters effectively placed him at the head of a police force in blind pursuit of a phantom of his own creation.

"Dear Boss" could never have succeeded without Sir Charles Warren having received tacit support for believing the correspondence to be from the killer and that plastering it across London in an attempt to identify the handwriting was a fine idea. Even had the letter actually been from the killer, such a move was a calculated risk. Also to be considered was public reaction, not to mention the costs of printing and distributing the posters to the 198 police stations[447] within the 690-square-mile Metropolitan Police area.

On Wednesday 3rd October 1888 Home Secretary Henry Matthews "had a long conference" with Sir Charles Warren and James Monro. Two old adversaries had been brought back together in a common cause, and one of the topics on the agenda was the matter of rewards, about which Monro approved and Warren "did not disapprove."[448]

Another topic on the agenda is detailed in a letter[449] Sir Charles Warren wrote on the same day to Sir James Fraser, Commissioner of the City of London Police, who narrowly missed the "double-event" having the following day returned from two months' leave in Scotland.

"3rd October 1888.

"I have seen Mr. Matthews today and he is anxious to know whether it can be known that the torn bib of the woman murdered in Mitre Square cannot have been taken to Goulston Street by any person except the murderer. In order to do this it is necessary [to discover] if there is any proof that at the time the corpse was found the bib was found with a piece wanting, that the piece was not lying about the yard at the time the corpse was found and taken to Goulston Street by some of the lookers on as a hoax, and that the piece found in Goulston Street is without doubt a portion of that which was worn by the woman."

Even to this day the answer to Warren's first two questions remains 'no.'

The body was discovered at 1.44 am and removed from Mitre Square at 3.00 am for conveyance to Golden Lane mortuary, about a mile distant, where City police officer Daniel Halse was the first to notice the apron had been cut.

Halse testified—

"I heard that a woman had been found murdered in Mitre Square. We ran to the spot, and I at once gave instructions for the neighbourhood

---

[447]   1888 London Post Office Directory.

[448]   Henry Matthews letter to Evelyn Ruggles-Brise, 6th October 1888.

[449]   MEPO 48/1. Private Letter Book, Metropolitan Police.

to be searched and every man stopped and examined. I myself went by way of Middlesex Street into Wentworth Street, where I stopped two men, who, however, gave a satisfactory account of themselves. I came through Goulston Street about twenty minutes past two, and then returned to Mitre Square, subsequently going to the mortuary. I saw the deceased, and noticed that a portion of her apron was missing."

This puts his discovery at somewhere around 3.15 to 3.30 am, by which time PC Long of the Metropolitan Police had shown commendable perspicacity by discovering the missing piece of apron in Goulston Street at 2.55 am, twenty to thirty five minutes before Daniel Halse noticed it was missing.

Warren's final question to Sir James Fraser was answered the following day at Catherine Eddowes' inquest—

Inspector Collard [City of London Police]: "A piece of cloth was found in Goulston Street, corresponding with the apron worn by the deceased."

[Coroner to Dr. Gordon Brown]: "Was your attention called to the portion of the apron that was found in Goulston Street?

[Dr. Gordon Brown]: "Yes. I fitted that portion which was spotted with blood to the remaining portion, which was still attached by the strings to the body."

What prompted Home Secretary Henry Matthews to question what he had heard about the Mitre Square scenario is not documented, but his questions, coupled with Warren's inability to provide satisfactory answers, cast doubt upon the popular idea that the murderer, having cut away the piece of apron for the purpose of wiping his blade and/or carrying away Eddowes' missing organs, deposited it in Goulston Street together with an enigmatic chalked message.

Apart from supporting a widely-held but erroneous belief that the Mitre Square murderer was a Jew returning to Whitechapel the chalked message and piece of apron were worthless as evidence, other than for use as a stick with which to beat Sir Charles Warren.

It is not unreasonable to suggest that also on the agenda of this 3rd October conference was the matter of reproducing the Jack the Ripper correspondence on posters, with James Monro consulting as to its probable/possible efficacy and Henry Matthews deciding the pros and cons of such an action. For even had the letter and postcard actually been written by the killer, the chance of someone identifying the handwriting had to be carefully weighed against any possible public unrest over the spectre of a multiple murderer stalking the streets.

The posters started going up on 5th October, so somebody at the Home Office conference that day must have taken the decision to risk public unrest in the vain hope of identifying the handwriting. As to who might have taken the decision, in the light of the on-going mise-en-scène in Whitechapel the most likely scenario is that, although the decision was out of his hands, Monro thought it a worthwhile risk, with Henry Matthews agreeing to sanction the exercise but only if Sir Charles Warren was in accord with Monro. Thus would the ultimate decision rest with Sir Charles Warren and further add to his list of poor judgment calls.

Warren's letter to Fraser tells us that in respect of the Mitre Square murder there had been little cooperation between the City of London and Metropolitan police forces, which given Warren's erasure of the chalked message is perhaps not surprising. The letter also tells us that Warren, having been at the crime scene just hours after the murder, had done nothing to establish any of the known facts and was hopelessly unprepared for the Home Secretary's questions.

At around this time Sir Charles Warren was visited by a reporter from the Montreal daily newspaper *La Presse*. The interview appeared in the edition of 8th October 1888—

"I had barely entered his room—a large but very simple apartment, having as its entire furnishing three armchairs, a small bookcase and a large work desk— when Sir Charles came over to me, shook my hand as the English are accustomed to do, and immediately began conversing about the business of the moment.

"Well, sir," said he, "I am going to question you first. Do you think that the murderer comes from a lower level of society?"

"From what I have read in the English papers, I would undoubtedly think that you have here a case of a murderer belonging to the ruling class of society, as you say in England. Don't you think that I am correct?"

"I am completely of your opinion. And my own private information allows me to practically assert it. You see, the Whitechapel district is not only inhabited by the poor. There are those from all classes in this district. There are beggars and bishops, noblemen, members of both the House of Commons and the House of Lords."

Sir Charles then stopped and continued, smiling: "It could be a bishop - or a Prime Minister. I really have reason to think that it must be someone who came from a good family but who is today an outcast."

"No doubt you now possess some weighty clues and we are maybe on the brink of an arrest. And that arrest may lead to a great scandal . . ."

Sir Charles Warren: "Perhaps... we are currently following several lines of inquiry and I believe that the public will have its curiosity satisfied."

On the following day, 9th October 1888, Warren once again wrote to Sir James Fraser—

"My dear Fraser,

"In order to prevent our working doubly over the same ground I have to suggest that our CID should be in more constant communication with yours about the W[hitechapel] murders.

"Could you send an officer to Ch[ief] Insp[ector] Swanson here every morning to consult or may I send an officer every morning to consult with your officers.

"We are inundated with suggestions and names of suspects.

"Truly Yours,

"C. W."[450]

On the same day Sir Charles Warren wrote to the Home Secretary—

". . . during the last three or four days I have been coming to the

---

[450]   MEPO 1/48. In a report dated 27th October, City of London Police Inspector James McWilliam wrote, "This department is co-operating with the Metropolitan Police in the matter, and Chief Inspector Swanson and I meet daily and confer on the subject." HO. A493018b

conclusion that useful results would be produced by the offer of a pardon to accomplices. Among the variety of theories there is the possibility that the murderer is someone who during the daytime is sane, but who at certain periods is overtaken in his mind; and I think it possible in that case that his relatives or neighbours may possibly be aware of his peculiarities and may have gradually unwittingly slid into the roles of accomplices . . ."

Warren may have been keeping abreast of the newspapers, for on the same day the *New York World* published "A Startling Theory", asking if the Whitechapel murderer was "Dr. Jekyll and Mr. Hyde in Real Life?"

Warren next delivered a sudden about-turn in his reasoning, suggesting that Jack the Ripper may not be a lone operator—

". . . On the other hand if it is the work of a gang in which only one actually commits the murder, the free pardon to the accomplice may make the difference of information being obtained . . ."

Sir Charles Warren continued—

". . . As a striking commentary on this matter I have today received a letter from a person asserting himself to be an accomplice and asking for a free pardon; and I am commencing a communication with him through an advertisement in a journal. This letter is probably a hoax, for we have received scores of hoaxing letters, but on the other hand it may be a bona fide letter and if [text missing] would be to the discovery of the murderer by omitting to offer the pardon; and I cannot see what harm can be done in this or any further case by offering a pardon."

By this time Robert Anderson had returned from Switzerland to London—

"I spent the day of my return to town, and half the following night, in reinvestigating the whole case, and next day I had a long conference on the subject with the Secretary of State and the Chief Commissioner of Police. 'We hold you responsible to find the murderer,' was Mr. Matthews' greeting to me. My answer was to decline the responsibility. 'I hold myself responsible,' I said, 'to take all legitimate means to find him.'"

Noble sentiments, yet here was Sir Charles Warren not knowing which way the Whitechapel winds were blowing. He didn't know if he was looking for a lone maniac, a killer with an accomplice or a gang, a bishop or the Prime Minister. His investigation was floundering, and for good reason.

The Press Association later reported[451]—

"Since Mr. Monro's transference to the Home Office matters have become worse. Sir Charles complains that, whereas he has been saddled with all the responsibility, he has had no freedom of action, and in consequence his position has become daily more unbearable. Although Mr. Monro has been no longer in evidence at Whitehall Place, he has to all intents and purposes retained control of the Criminal Investigation Department.

"Latterly, in spite of the remonstrances of Sir Charles Warren, the control of the Criminal Investigation Department has been withdrawn more and more from Whitehall Place. Every morning for the last few weeks there has been a protracted conference at the Home Office between Mr. Monro, Mr. Anderson, and the principal detective inspectors, and the information furnished to the Commissioner in regard to these conferences has been, he stated, of the scantiest character."

The Commissioner of the Metropolitan Police was being left out in the cold, with no clue as to the status of the investigation.

"Dear Boss" had an ineluctable winning air about it. The phrasing, the dark jocularity, the Americanism thrown in for good measure, and, above all, the name Jack the Ripper—a marketing man's dream—were pitch-perfect. The letter was not from a knuckle-dragging down-on-whores East End malefactor—Gentile or Jewish—nor some high-minded moral crusader of a more outwardly respectable stripe. "Dear Boss" and the persona of Jack the Ripper were conceived by someone who had carefully thought the whole thing through and prepared the ground for its success before committing pen to paper.

"Dear Boss" having been conceived by a journalist is unlikely.

---

[451]   Daily News, 13th November 1888.

No journalist taking a unilateral decision to write "Dear Boss" in order to whip up a circulation-boosting panic could ever have hoped to score such a resounding bullseye, especially as the letter's ultimate success rested with someone in authority at Scotland Yard taking it seriously and bestowing upon it the official imprimatur of the Metropolitan Police. No journalist could have been certain of such an eventuality, for in the wake of the Leather Apron lone maniac fiasco there was every chance that Sir Charles Warren might simply dismiss the letter as a time-wasting hoax and toss it into his wastepaper basket.

If not a journalist, who else?

One possible clue to the inspiration for the Jack the Ripper letter and the involvement of the Central News Agency is provided by the retired Chief Inspector John George Littlechild.

In his 1913 letter to journalist George R. Sims he wrote—

"It was a smart piece of journalistic work. No journalist of my time got such privileges from Scotland Yard as Bullen. Mr. James Munro [sic] when Assistant Commissioner, and afterwards Commissioner, relied on his integrity."

Although this line of thinking may be too extreme for some, it does have a certain merit, for there was a small group of people who met regularly at the Home Office who stood to directly benefit from exploiting the Whitechapel murders as a means to undermine Sir Charles Warren and bring about his resignation once the time was right—

Home Secretary Henry Matthews would stave off repeated demands in the press for his own resignation and remain in office for a further four years. His work at the Home Office on *The Times* case at the Special Commission complete, James Monro would make a triumphal return to Whitehall Place as Commissioner of the Metropolitan Police. Monro-appointee Robert Anderson would permanently retain his initially *pro tem* position as Assistant Commissioner [CID], and in the following year Melville Macnaghten—another Monro-appointee and one who was resident in London throughout the Whitechapel murders—would assume the post of Assistant Chief Constable.

The Metropolitan Police as a whole was also a beneficiary. Henry Matthews had been in regular communication with James Monro regarding the reorganisation of the detective staff, and two months after Monro took over the Commissionership it was announced that the CID was to receive the augmentation of manpower it had long been denied under Warren.

Glasgow Herald, 1st February 1889—

"The need for such a step has long been felt . . . Last year, however, the inability of the Department to meet such exceptional strains as that occasioned by the Whitechapel outrages without seriously interfering with its ordinary duties brought the question into greater prominence."

Subsequent events tell us that the disastrous decision to publish the Ripper letter and postcard dashed any hope of apprehending the murderer, for the posters unleashed a blizzard of mail from a rich assortment of pranksters. People leapt onto the Ripper bandwagon— some to make mischief; and others, perchance, to earn a little extra money.[452]

On 12th October 1888 builder George Lusk, Chairman of the Whitechapel Vigilance Committee, formed to augment police activity in the area, received a letter couched in traditional Ripperese—

"I write you a letter in black ink, as I have no more of the right stuff. I think you are all asleep in Scotland Yard with your bloodhounds, as I will show you to-morrow night (Saturday). I am going to do a double event, but not in Whitechapel. Got rather too warm there. Had to shift. No more till you hear me again. 'Jack the Ripper'."[453]

The letter bore a Kilburn [north London] postmark, and the handwriting was reportedly similar to the original Jack the Ripper correspondence. How the writer confused an East End builder with Scotland Yard remains a puzzle.

Earlier in October, Lusk had told the police about a mysterious stranger who was prowling around his premises "with the object, it is

---

[452]   For an excellent illustrated study and discussion of this correspondence see Stewart Evans and Keith Skinner's *Letters From Hell*, Sutton Publishing, 2001.
[453]   The letter was published in *The Times*, 15th October 1888.

believed, of striking through Mr. Lusk at the Vigilance Committee."[454]

Shortly after the arrival of the letter Lusk received a postcard, again written in Ripperese—

"Say Boss - You seem rare frightened, guess I'd like to give you fits, but can't stop time enough to let you box of toys[455] play copper games with me, but hope to see you when I don't hurry too much. Bye-bye, Boss."

Lusk does not appear to have linked the correspondence with his mysterious prowler, at first thinking them the work of a practical joker. However, on receipt of his third communication in four days he began to take things seriously.

Shortly after 5.00 pm on the evening of Tuesday 16th October 1888 Lusk received via Parcels' Post a small paper-wrapped package bearing an indistinct postmark. Inside was a cardboard box about three-and-a-half inches square containing a meaty substance which gave off an offensive odour. Also in the box was a letter written in a dramatic hand—

"From Hell - Mr. Lusk. - Sir, I send you half the kidne I took from one woman. Prasarved it for you. Tother piece I fried and ate it was very nise. I may send you the bloody knife that took it out, if you only wate a whil longer.

"Signed Catch me when you can Mishter Lusk."

With no thought for the offensive odour permeating his house Lusk put the package and letter in his desk and did no more about it until the following evening when, at a meeting of the Whitechapel Vigilance Committee, it was agreed to investigate the matter. Accordingly, the following morning the treasurer, the secretary and two other members of the Vigilance Committee went to Lusk's house to inspect the parcel.

Nobody could identify the odoriferous meaty substance. It was therefore decided to call upon Dr. Frederick Wiles, a surgeon in the Mile

---

[454] *The Times*, 8th October 1888.
[455] According to Partridge's 1937 *Dictionary of Slang and Unconventional English*, "Box of toys" was late 19th Century rhyming slang for "noise," which makes little sense in the context of the Lusk letter. "Box of toys" intended rhyme may have been "boys."

End Road, in whose absence his assistant, Dr. Reed, examined the contents of the box. It looked to him like half a human kidney sliced longitudinally. He thought it best to have it examined by Dr. Thomas Openshaw, Curator of the Pathology Museum at the London Hospital, who determined by use of a microscope that the kidney had been taken from a full-grown human being, and that it was part of a left kidney.

A sinister picture was taking shape.

Catherine Eddowes inquest, 4th October 1888—

Mr. Crawford: "I understand that you found certain portions of the body removed?"

Doctor Frederick Gordon Brown: "Yes. The uterus was cut away with the exception of a small portion, and the left kidney was also cut out. Both these organs were absent and have not been found."

Could George Lusk have been the recipient of the missing kidney from the Mitre Square murderer, a murderer who in his accompanying letter had abandoned his carefully-crafted trade name?

Joseph Aarons, treasurer of the Whitechapel Vigilance Committee, said in a press statement—

"[After seeing Dr. Openshaw] It was then agreed that we should take the parcel and the letter to the Leman Street Police-station, where we saw Inspector Abberline. Afterwards some of us went to Scotland-yard, where we were told that we had done quite right in putting the matter into Mr. Abberline's hands."

However, before doing their bounden duty as citizens and members of a committee pledged to uphold the safety of Whitechapel, George Lusk and his colleagues made a detour, paying a visit to 12 Whitefriars Street—just off Fleet Street, where the *Evening News* had its offices—taking with them what might prove to be vital pieces of evidence in the murder of Catherine Eddowes.

Evening News, 19th October 1888—

"Mr. George Lusk, builder, of 1, 2 and 3, Alderney Road, Globe Road, Mile End, E., who is chairman of the Whitechapel Vigilance Committee, called at our office yesterday afternoon, accompanied by Mr. Harris, of 83, Whitehorse-lane, Mile End, secretary to the Committee;

Mr. Aarons, treasurer, and Messrs. Lawton, Reeves, G. Lusk and Dr. F. S. Reed. They brought with them a small cardboard box containing half a human kidney, which had been delivered by Parcel Post at Mr. George Lusk's residence on Tuesday evening . . ."

"We need only add that the contents of the box and the letters were shown to us by Mr. Lusk, who allowed one of our staff to copy the letters. Mr. Lusk and his friends then left our office, en route for Scotland Yard."

Press Association report, *Daily News*, 19th October 1888—

"Yesterday two members of the committee took the parcel to Scotland Yard, but the police authorities there referred them to the detectives at Leman Street."

Chief Inspector Swanson, 6th November 1888 report—

"The kidney was at once handed over to the City Police, and the result of the combined medical opinion they have taken upon it is, that it is the kidney of a human adult, not charged with a fluid, as it would have been in the case of a body handed in for purposes of dissection[456], but rather as it would be in a case where it was taken from the body not so destined. In other words similar kidneys might & could be obtained from any dead person upon whom a post mortem had been made from any cause by students or dissecting room porter."

Inspector James McWilliam [City Police] report, 27th October 1888—

"The kidney was forwarded to this office & the letter to Scotland Yard. Chief Inspector Swanson having lent me the letter on the 20th Inst. I had it photographed & returned it to him on the 24th. The kidney has been examined by Dr. Gordon-Brown who is of opinion that it is human . . . It might turn out after all, to be the act of a Medical Student who would have no difficulty in obtaining the organ in question."

The *Evening News*, 20th October 1888, reported that the police thought the matter a hoax, but in the next breath announced— "The idea of its being a practical joke is not generally endorsed . . . A small

---

[456]   Bodies sent to hospitals for dissection were charged with formalin, a preserving fluid. The kidney received by Lusk had been preserved in spirits.

portion only of the renal artery adheres to the kidney, and it will be remembered that in the Mitre Square victim a large portion of the renal artery adhered to the body.[457] This leads the police to attach more importance to the matter than they otherwise would."

The *Star*, 20th October 1888, wasn't buying it—

"Whitechapel.

"Easy to Hoax the Police —The Kidney Story.

"As a motive for the disgusting hoax of the kidney, it is suggested that the person who sent it to its recipient desired to keep up the excitement about the crimes. We are now informed that the information of the receipt of the parcel was sold at a high figure, so that the hoax does not appear so stupid as it seemed at first."

The *Star* was implying the *Evening News* had paid generously for its fleeting scoop, so perhaps the kidney and letter had been a publicity stunt or fund-raising exercise by the overstretched and cash-strapped[458] Whitechapel Vigilance Committee.

We shall never know for certain, but on the following day—and this may have been sheer coincidence—*Lloyds Weekly Newspaper* reported that George Lusk had announced his resignation as Chairman of the Whitechapel Vigilance Committee, citing his reason as the need for absolute rest "which he felt to be necessary after the worry and anxiety and horror he has experienced during the past few days." Mr. Aaron, the treasurer, and Mr. Harris, the secretary, also announced their intention to resign "on account of the lack of moral and material support they have experienced during their philanthropic efforts to benefit their fellow citizens."

Whilst all this malarkey had been playing out, plain clothes officers of the Metropolitan Police were hard at work in Whitechapel, continuing the hunt for Jack the Ripper, the success of which Home Secretary Henry Matthews did not hold out much hope.

Star, 17th October 1888—

---

[457]   There is no medical evidence to support this.
[458]   See *East London Observer,* 13th October 1888.

"The police are making a house to house visit amongst the Jews at the East-end. They demand admission to every room, look underneath the beds, and peer into the smallest cupboards. They ask for the production of knives, and examine them. In some cases they have been refused admittance until proof was produced of authority."

On 18th October 1888 Sir Charles Warren attempted to paint a smile on the face of the tiger, assuring readers of *The Times* that the Metropolitan Police had been mindful of East End sensitivities—

"Sir Charles Warren wishes to say that the marked desire evinced by the inhabitants of the Whitechapel district to aid the police in the pursuit of the author of the recent crimes has enabled him to direct that, subject to the consent of occupiers, a thorough house-to-house search should be made within a defined area. With few exceptions, the inhabitants of all classes and creeds have freely fallen in with the proposal, and have materially assisted the officers engaged in carrying it out."

The London *Evening Post*, 18th October 1888, was not impressed—

"It really is very touching to read that 'Sir Charles Warren feels that some acknowledgment is due on all sides for the cordial co-operation of the inhabitants, and he is much gratified that the police officers have carried out so delicate a duty . . . with the marked goodwill of all those with whom they have come to contact' . . . There is a sort of 'bless you, my children' ring about the notification."

The house-to-house enquiry was an ambitious undertaking. Given that right from the start Home Secretary Henry Matthews had not been optimistic about it flushing out Jack the Ripper, perhaps it served another purpose which justified the cost and manpower.

Chief Inspector Swanson, 19th October 1888 report—

"Leaflets were printed & distributed in H Division asking the occupiers of houses to give information to police of any suspicious persons lodging in their houses . . .

"80,000 pamphlets to occupier were issued and a house-to-house enquiry made not only involved the result of enquiries from the occupiers but also a search by police & with a few exceptions—but not such as to convey suspicion—covered the area[459] bounded by City Police boundary on the one hand, Lamb Street, Commercial Street, Great Eastern Railway and Buxton Street, then by Albert Street, Dunk Street, Chicksand Street & Great Garden Street to Whitechapel Road and then to the City boundary, under this head also Common Lodging Houses were visited & over 2000 lodgers were examined . . ."[460]

This small overcrowded area was fast becoming predominantly Jewish. Effective policing was difficult when the locals spoke little or no English and the police spoke nothing else.[461] Which makes the decision to distribute 80,000 leaflets printed exclusively in English appear somewhat limited in scope.

Chief Inspector Swanson also reported on enquiries by the Thames Police into sailors on ships in the London Docks; also an "extended enquiry as to Asiatics present in London." About eighty people were detained at various police stations and enquiries made into the movements of upwards of three hundred people "respecting whom communications were received by police & such enquiries are being continued." Seventy six butchers and slaughterers were visited; enquiries were made into the alleged presence in London of Greek Gipsies, "and three of the persons calling themselves Cowboys who belonged to the American Exhibition[462] were traced and satisfactorily accounted for themselves."

It had been a busy eleven days—

"Up to date although the number of letters daily is considerably lessened, the other enquiries respecting alleged suspicious persons

---

[459]   H Division covered 1.25 sq. miles. The search area was approximately 0.2 sq. miles

[460]   *Reynolds News*, 14th October 1888. "Police Sergeant 32H said the registered lodging houses in the district were 127 in number—common lodging houses accommodating about 6000 persons. They were all visited once a week on average. He doubted if a single registered lodging house would be found without thieves and prostitutes amongst its lodgers."

[461]   It wasn't until 1904 that the Home Office agreed to create a cadre of Yiddish-speaking police constables. MEPO 2/733

[462]   The American Exhibition ran in London from May to October 1887. Swanson's reference was to Mexican Joe's Wild West Show which ran in London and Europe during 1888. Mexican Joe [Colonel Joe Shelley] was Buffalo Bill's arch show-business rival.

continues as numerous. There are now 994 Dockets besides police reports."

Further details about this enormous undertaking were supplied by Detective Inspector Soyle of the CID who was breaking his journey west at the Continental Hotel, Philadelphia.[463]

Philadelphia Times, 25th November 1888—

"Interesting Chat With a Famous Scotland Yard Detective.

"After the second murder, for some reason never clear to me, the mind of the executive became permeated with the idea that the criminal was a dweller in one of the miserable holes scattered all over the poorer districts of London, where a night's lodging may be had for fourpence or sixpence."

He next imparted some specific information regarding police tactics—

"Two hundred and fifty detectives from the manufacturing and rural districts were brought up to town and one was placed as a spy in every common lodging [house] in London.

"Being countrymen, professedly come up to town in search of work, these men excited no suspicion among the lodgers. Many arrests were made through information furnished by the officers relating to suspicious lodgers, but nothing came of any one of them.

Inspector Soyle next referenced a far more wide-ranging house-to-house search than that described in Chief Inspector Swanson's report—

"Meanwhile every inspector in charge of a police district was ordered to detail men to personally visit every householder who let apartments, furnished or unfurnished, in his division, and inquire as to the character and habits of their tenants, requesting them also to promptly inform the police if they noticed any marked peculiarity in the behavior of any new lodger who might come along. In the event of

---

[463] Although details of their police careers are almost an exact match, "Soyle" may not have been Superintendent John Shore of Scotland Yard. "Soyle" arrived in New York aboard the SS *Elbe* on 21st November and was heading west, "where his eldest son is engaged in farming." Shore's arrival in America was noted in early December. *The Times*, 16th November 1888, reported Superintendent Shore to be on sick leave.

another murder of the same nature taking place, they were instructed to notify the police if any lodgers had been out of doors at the time. In short, the Police Department did its best to induce every householder in London who let lodgings to constitute him or herself for the time being a detective, at least as regarded these mysterious crimes. Of course, it was impossible to do such a work as this thoroughly in a city like London, with its millions of inhabitants spread over such a large area."

Regarding enquiries by the Thames Police into sailors on ships in the London Docks, Detective Inspector Soyle said—

"Then somebody at the Yard struck the theory that the murderer was a sailor, who made short voyages to the continent, to the North of England or elsewhere. Some color was given to this idea by the fact that the butcherings took place at the end of the week, when these coasting, freight and passenger steamers crowd the Thames from London bridge to away down below the Tower. Forthwith, by arrangement with the owners, over a hundred officers were directed to permanent duty on board these boats. The police shipped as handy men and when they were not seasick talked the murder over among their mates and stayed on board keeping night watches when the steamers lay in the river and closely scrutinized the sailors, firemen and coal-passers when they came on board to sleep after their customary runs ashore. Numbers of arrests were made from these ships, but all to no purpose."

Asked about the "Dear Boss" letter, Soyle said, "The Jack the Ripper letters are simply the work of some stupid and brutal joker. Their phrasing should make that evident to the meanest capacity.

"Throughout all this time more than 14,000 policemen[464] have been patrolling the streets with their eyes wide open and their minds dominated by one idea, that of catching the Whitechapel fiend. Hundreds of innocent people have been arrested on suspicion only to be

---

[464]   In 1888 the total number of officers in the Metropolitan Police area was 14,081. Of these 1,621 were specially employed and paid for by the Government, public companies and private individuals, making the actual number of police available for duty properly so called in London 12,460, giving an average of one officer for every 439 inhabitants. *Pall Mall Gazette*, 8th October 1888.

discharged in a few hours on satisfying the authorities of their respectability. Hardly a night passes but some drunken fool rolls into one or other of the district station houses and wants to give himself up as the Whitechapel murderer. Of course all these people's antecedents have to be looked up and the extra work entailed on the force from this and the other causes I have mentioned has been simply prodigious."

Regarding overseas inquiries—

"If we have sent one officer abroad on clues which were apparently promising during the past four months we have sent fifty, and the service, always courteously and ably rendered by your police in response to cablegrams, has run out and proved worthless at least a dozen clues."

Seven days after this interview Dr. Francis Tumblety would arrive in New York City.

The *Daily Telegraph*, 18th October 1888, credited the police with a measure of success regarding the house-house search—

"It was reported yesterday that the police authorities have information tending to show that the East-end murderer is a foreigner who was known as having lived within a radius of a few hundred yards from the scene of the Berner Street tragedy. The place where he now lodges is asserted to be within official cognisance. If the man be the real culprit, he lived some time ago with a woman, by whom he has been accused. Her statements, it is said, are now being investigated. In the meantime the suspected assassin is closely watched."

Once again the Metropolitan Police was backing the wrong horse, for their close surveillance did nothing to stop "Jack the Ripper" from striking again three weeks later in Millers Court, Dorset Street.

Much time, expense and manpower had been expended by the Metropolitan Police on what was either a fool's errand or possibly an unofficial head count of Jews, assorted foreigners and potential anarchists conducted under the pretext of a murder hunt. Or perhaps this large police presence—further augmented between December 1888 and March 1889—was connected with Melville Macnaghten reportedly having linked Jack the Ripper with the leader of a plot to assassinate Balfour.

Washington [DC] *Post*, 8th January 1889—

"Balfour's Body Guard.

"London, Jan. 7—The number of policemen detailed to protect Mr. Balfour has been increased, in consequence of a report that the Invincibles are planning to murder him."

Over a month later the threat remained.

Wisconsin State Register, 23rd February 1889—

"A Scotland Yard Scare.

"The Irish Invincibles Said To Be Plotting for Assassination.

"London, Feb 21—The Scotland Yard officials have received information leading to a general belief in police circles that the Invincibles are engaged in perfecting the details of a most desperate plot to murder several of the high officers of the government. So circumstantial are the stories poured into the ears of the police officials that even Lord Salisbury is impressed with a belief in their truth, and notwithstanding his persistent refusal to be guarded by the officers of law, he was yesterday placed under the protection of the police, the men assigned to the duty of protecting him keeping him constantly in sight. Balfour's personal safety has for some time past been a special charge of the police, and it is likely in view of this latter scare that several other members of the cabinet will avail themselves of such protection as Scotland Yard may be able to afford them against the real or supposititious assassins lying in wait for them."

There is no way to gauge the accuracy of these newspaper reports, so any idea of an Irish-inspired plot to assassinate Arthur Balfour must be treated with as much caution as the bogus 1887 Jubilee plot.

Owen McGee, author of "Irish Republican Brotherhood", wrote in the popular magazine *History Ireland*—

"Foreign Office papers (FO 5/2044) indicate that . . . John Walsh was secretly funded to come back from America as an agent provocateur in November 1887. Walsh launched a bogus plot to assassinate Chief Secretary Balfour that, if men could be implicated and then exposed, would boost the retrospective claim of the Tory government that the Land League was behind the Phoenix Park murders.

"Although these bogus plots had no significant consequences, they show the extent to which British intelligence was prepared to play with fire in order to further its aim of dividing and conquering Irish nationalist public opinion."

In fairness it should be pointed out that in correspondence with this author Mr. McGee warned that— "the lines between revolutionary organisations and police services are often impossible to draw . . . Furthermore, whatever answers you produce may lead readers to either misinterpret the picture you attempted to present . . . or lead readers to believe you are obsessed with conspiracy theories and are perhaps some crazy ideologue."

Sir Robert Anderson felt the house-to-house search had been worthwhile in respect to the hunt for Jack the Ripper. In his 1910 memoirs he wrote—

"During my absence abroad[465] the Police had made a house-to-house search for him [Jack the Ripper], investigating the case of every man in the district whose circumstances were such that he could go and come and get rid of his blood-stains in secret. And the conclusion we came to was that he and his people were certain low-class Polish Jews; for it is a remarkable fact that people of that class in the East End will not give up one of their number to Gentile justice . . . In saying that he was a Polish Jew I am merely stating a definitely ascertained fact."

If Anderson's Polish Jew was Macnaghten's "Kosminski, a Polish Jew," who in turn was Aaron Kosminski, the Polish Jew who on 7th February 1891—a week prior to the murder of Frances Coles—was admitted to Colney Hatch Lunatic Asylum, it is interesting to note that at no time was he recorded as living within the immediate house-to-house search area as delineated by Chief Inspector Swanson in his 19th October report.

Meanwhile, letters from "Jack the Ripper" continued to pour in to Scotland Yard—

---

[465]   His father, Matthew Anderson, died on 11th October 1888, the funeral taking place in Dublin on 14th October 1888. We may therefore assume that around this time Robert Anderson was once again away from London.

"October 19 1888. Wouster [Worcester].

"Dear boss iff you are the boss you have not got the right man 100 miles off scent bloodhounds no use will not catch me have been in Wouster a week have spotted 3 out will visit them again shortly don't know much about this part off too Brum [Birmingham] to-day

"Post this on me way, hope I shall have luck there The Atmosphere was to hot at Whitechapel had to clear off smelt a rat saw last victim buried I felt rather down hearted over my knife which I lost coming here must get one to night. I shall kill 15 at Brum call and settle 3 I have spotted at Wouster Shall then finish up at Hull before going to Poland.

"Silly looking in low lodging houses for me do not visit them description posed at Ploise [sic] stations nothing like me look out for Octer 27th at Brum will give them ripper."

There was nothing unique about the studied illiteracy of this letter. Many in a similar vein arrived each week. What makes this particular example of interest is the manner in which the writer signed himself—

"Jack a Poland Jew.

"Better known as Jack the Ripper."

Appended was a dramatic reddish-brown flourish captioned "A drop of Strides Blood."[466]

This letter was the first suggestion of Jack the Ripper being a Polish Jew.

Official correspondence at around this time confirms that events on a wider scale were playing out.

On 23rd October 1888 Sir Charles Warren informed the Home Office that he had "directed the necessary enquiries to be made and had ascertained the particulars as to the number of trains which will arrive at Euston daily with passengers from America, and the hours of their arrival; and as two Police Constables must be present at each examination of luggage, I find it will be necessary to have three reliefs, thus requiring an augmentation of six Police Constables. I have therefore to ask for authority for this increase . . ."

---

[466] MEPO 3/142 p. 252.

Later he discussed the costs of "the proposed Police arrangements for the examination in London of the luggage of passengers arriving from America via Liverpool . . ." He also stressed that the police examination was quite distinct from the Customs examination.

This heightened interest in transatlantic passengers is hard to reconcile with the hunt for a local "Ripper" in Whitechapel, but makes perfect sense if the alleged plot to kill Balfour was being masterminded from New York or Chicago.

On 25th October 1888, in response to Godfrey Lushington, Permanent Under-Secretary at the Home Office, asking about the extent of prostitution in the East End, Sir Charles Warren forwarded the requisite information, closing his letter with a remark which directly contradicts Sir Robert Anderson's later contention that the house-to-house search suggested the Ripper "and his people were certain low-class Polish Jews."

Sir Charles Warren wrote—

"I do not think there is any reason whatever for supposing that the murderer of Whitechapel is one of the ordinary denizens of that place."[467]

How Warren reached this conclusion is uncertain, but may have had its roots in a diplomatic incident which took place during October and November 1888, details of which do not appear to have crossed the desk of Chief Inspector Swanson [designated to be Warren's "eyes and ears" in the Whitechapel murders case] and most certainly did not come to the attention of the press and public.

---

[467]   MEPO 3/141 ff. 158-63.

23. TALES FROM THE VIENNA WOODS

Matters began on Monday 8th October 1888 when a letter arrived at the British embassy in Vienna "stating that the writer would undertake within fourteen days to deliver up the man who had committed the recent murders of women in London."

Sir Alexander Paget G.C.B., H.M. Ambassador at Vienna, forwarded the letter to Prime Minister, Lord Salisbury, in an encrypted communication flagged "Secret" dated 10th October 1888.[468]

"Without attaching undue importance to this communic[atio]n, I thought that in a case of such mystery and horror no possible clue was to be neglected."

Consul-General Gustavus Nathan first arranged for the informant to call on him, "and was so impressed with what he said that he suggested I should see him myself this morning. I have accordingly done so in Mr. Nathan's presence, & I have closely cross questioned him, his answers being given in a perfectly straightforward & ready manner, & with an air of good faith."

Polish-born, but now an Austrian subject, the informant was "well-

---

[468]   Most of the following correspondence is taken from HO 144/221/A49301.
Transcripts may be found in Stewart Evans and Keith Skinner's invaluable reference work,
"The Ultimate Jack the Ripper Companion," first published in the UK by Robinson, 2000.

dressed & of very respectable appearance." He was one of the Chiefs of the Internationalist Society. [469] He had a colleague in Paris, without whom it was impossible for him to act. "The rules of the Society are absolute Secrecy, so much so, that the members are frequently not known to one another, and no one can act without the order of his superior or chief . . ."

The Ambassador continued—

"The man who has committed the murders was formerly a member of the Society, but he was dismissed in consequence of having denounced some of the party, who were innocent, as being connected with the Moss affair in New York; in which city, he, the present murderer, murdered his mistress and her child . . .[470]

"I asked him if he knew the murderer personally; he replied that he did, & when I showed him the portraits published in the *Daily Telegraph* of Saturday last the 6th October, he said that they did not bear the slightest resemblance to him."

The Ambassador also showed the informer facsimiles of the letters signed 'Jack the Ripper' from the *Daily Telegraph* of 4th October.

"He said that he did not believe that the murderer could write; at all events he was quite sure he could not have written these letters, tho. they might have been written by his accomplice (Helper) for accomplice he undoubtedly had."

"I asked the informer what motive he and his party had for denouncing the murderer. He said to avenge themselves for his having betrayed the party. They wanted to get rid of him once and for all.

"[The informer] then produced a cyphered letter from the head of the party in London and decyphered it before me by means of a piece of cardboard with holes in it which he placed in different positions over the paper.

---

[469]   The Internationalist Society was an amorphous, many-headed socialist/anarchist movement—in structure not unlike today's Al Qaeda—dedicated to a classless world society.

[470]   Inquiries with various true-crime historians have failed to unearth anything about the Moss affair in New York.

"The part of the letter referring to this business runs in translation (the original being in German) as follows:

"'There is no doubt that No. 49E(I)? (E the informer said meant Irish) is <u>identical with the murderer and</u> that he has a helper unknown to the party. All orders strictly observed to prevent escape, escape impossible. Highest time (hochste Zeit) to put an end to it.'"

By this time Sir Alexander Paget was on the edge of his seat.

"I asked what the orders referred to meant and by whom they were issued. He replied that they were to prevent the murderer escaping and that <u>he</u> (the informer) <u>and his Paris colleague had given them</u>. 'Highest time to act' means that by delay the murderer may possibly escape to France."

"The informer then in answer to my enquiry said that in order to effect capture he must go himself to London, <u>taking his Paris colleague with him</u> . . ."

He required 2000 florins for travel and expenses. "He is ready to give written engagement to refund <u>the money should capture not be accomplished</u>, but this of course must be taken for <u>what it is worth</u>.

"I reminded him that a large reward had been offered.[471] Why, I asked, could he not direct his party in London to deliver up the culprit without he and his Paris colleague going over . . ."

It was a smart question.

". . . He said the rules of the Society were such that it was impossible for action to be taken without presence of the two chiefs. He could not <u>even divulge to me his name without his colleague's sanction</u>."

An all-expenses-paid trip for two to London appeared to be the order of the day, and the 65-year-old Sir Alexander Berkeley Paget, previously HM Ambassador at Copenhagen and Rome, did not sound the type of man to be easily fooled.

Temple Bar: A London Magazine, 1888—

"[Paget] looks every inch an Ambassador. Tall, square-shouldered

---

[471]   On 5th October 1888 in the pages of "Police Gazette" the City of London Police had offered £500 [approximately 6000 Austrian florins] for information leading to the arrest and prosecution of Catherine Eddowes' murderer.

and handsome, he has a thoroughly English face—the clean-shaved chin and upper lip with the whiskers of English faces in the old time. Careful and tasteful in his dress, jovial in manner, a capital host, a good talker, a keen sportsman, bold rider, and active lawn-tennis player, he is the perfect impersonation of the popular English gentleman . . . He is a kind-hearted man, a little quick of temper, plain-spoken and not used to dissembling; but he has the shrewdness which comes from long official experience and from a fund of native humour. He has no disposition for intrigue; but he detects an intrigue, if not in its first stage at least in its second; and he plays it with a quiet block as a good as a cricketer does a "twister." Unendowed with the brilliant imagination which invents grand "coups" in diplomacy or ingenious expedients . . . he is a prudent adviser . . ."

Paget ran a background check on his informant—

"I have caused Mr. Nathan to make enquiries of the police here respecting the informer, & they say that they know him to be a socialist, that he denounced a plot to assassinate the Emperor <u>in 1883</u> but that the attempt was <u>not made</u>, & they <u>therefore have not much trust in him</u> . . .

"It is of course possible that the whole story may be a trumped up one from beginning to end, but I am bound to say that it <u>does not give that impression</u> & that I am <u>inclined to place some trust in it</u>. The man's manner, his appearance, the readiness with which he replied to all my enquiries tended to give me this impression, though of course I may be mistaken.

"I must say that at first I was inclined to be extremely sceptical on account of his not being willing to act without himself going over, but having already heard something of the workings of these secret societies & listening to what he now said, it has occurred to me as quite possible that he may be unable to act from here & without the cooperation of his colleague."

Sir Alexander Paget continued to swallow the bait.

"He lays the greatest stress on gaining time, & I have promised him a reply by Friday evening or Saturday morning next by which time I hope to be furnished with Y. L's [Your Lordship's] instructions by telegraph.

Should I be required to send him, I beg to be informed to whom I am to give a letter in London, & on whom I am to draw the money (2000 florins) without which he will not go."

The despatch was forwarded from the Foreign Office to Robert Anderson, who by this time had returned from Switzerland. In a report to Sir Charles Warren dated 12th October 1888 he wrote—

"After giving this matter my most earnest & careful attention, I cannot recommend compliance with the informant's proposal.

"The answer I should send to Sir A. Paget would be to the effect that the Government cannot authorise compliance with the informant's terms, unless he gives <u>the name of the murderer</u> with <u>definite details</u> which can be tested, or in some other way gives tangible proof of capacity & <u>bona fides</u> . . .

"I have arrived at this conclusion not merely from considering the story on its merits—& it seems to be so utterly incredible & I infer that the Austrian Police do not regard the informant as trustworthy—but further, I dread the trouble & mischief which such a man, if an imposter, might cause should he come to London on the proposed terms."

Despite Anderson's caution, this international intrigue scenario which pointed a finger at an illiterate Irishman with an accomplice appealed to Sir Charles Warren. Not for him the slipper-making Leather Apron or the various lunatics who had been arrested on suspicion. In a memo to Charles Murdoch, Assistant Under-Secretary at the Home Office, 13th October 1888, he wrote—

"As Mr. Matthews is aware I have for some time past inclined to the idea that the murders may possibly be done by a secret society, as the only logical solution of the question, but I would not understand this being done by a Socialist because the last murders were obviously done by someone desiring to bring discredit on the Jews and Socialists or Jewish Socialists . . .

"I propose that Mr. Anderson's views should be telegraphed to Sir A. Paget as a suggestion, but specially giving him freedom to use his own discretion in the matter. If from our straining in the matter we miss the opportunity of capturing the murderer it would be unfortunate."

It is not known how Sir Charles Warren squared these Viennese events with his decision to erase the chalked message in Goulston Street and splash the "Jack the Ripper" correspondence across London in an effort to identify the handwriting of someone who it now seemed was unable to put pen to paper.

Godfrey Lushington, Permanent Under Secretary at the Home Office, in a memo dated 13th October 1888, agreed with Robert Anderson—

"To my mind the whole story is incredible . . .

"I think a telegram should be sent to the Ambassador that no further attention need be given to the informant unless he states the name of the murderer with definite details which can be tested showing that these are reasonable grounds of suspicion . . .

"[If the matter is left to the Ambassador's discretion, it is pretty clear he will send the man over—which I think would be a most regrettable step.

"I cannot at all agree with the Commissioner's idea that the only logical solution of the question is that the murders may possibly have been done by a Secret Society. He also says that he cannot understand this having been done by a Socialist, because the last murders were evidently done by someone desiring to bring discredit on the Jews and Socialists or Jewish Socialists. It seems to me on the contrary that the last murder was done by a Jew who boasted of it]."

Ambassador Paget continued to be enthralled by his Viennese informant.

"Home Office, 16 Oct 88. Letter received from Foreign Office—

"Secret and pressing.

"With reference to your letter of 14th instant, I am directed by the Marquis of Salisbury to transmit to you herewith, to be laid before the Secretary of State for the Home Department, the substance of a telegram received from Her Majesty's Ambassador at Vienna respecting the Whitechapel murders."

"Your most obedient humble servant, P. W. Currie."[472]

Attached was Ambassador Paget's "Secret" telegram—

"Have seen informant who does not know murderer's residence but states he was employed formerly in San Francisco as a butcher. A further letter has been received by him saying he is being watched by two of the smartest men in the Society. He is confident that he will be able to inform the Police of murderer's whereabouts within 24 hours after he arrives in London. Informant cannot go without having 2000 florins, or act without being himself in London in company with his superior, the head man from Paris."

These "two of the smartest men in the Society" must have been fairly inept if Paget's informer was aware they had him under surveillance.

Sir Alexander Paget continued—

"I believe in his bona fides so much that I advance the money on my personal responsibility, while telling him that on the arrest of the culprit and proof of his crime, he, informant can claim offered reward out of which must be deducted the 2000 florins for repayment to me. I mention his name in a letter which I give him to Sir Charles Warren, but he will not present it until he appears to denounce criminal and get necessary aid from police. He has stipulated that his name is never to be divulged or the Society will not effect arrest. He departs this day and he stipulates in addition that neither himself nor those of the Society at present watching the criminal are in any way to be interfered with by police, which has been promised by me. It is my opinion that he should be permitted to work unwatched even by the detectives."

Three weeks later the Whitechapel murderer had a name.

In a letter to the Home Office dated 5th November 1888, Sir Julian Pauncefote, Permanent Under-Secretary of State at the Foreign Office, wrote—

---

[472]   Sir Philip Henry Wodehouse Currie, in 1888 Assistant Permanent Under Secretary of State at the Foreign Office. Amongst many other achievements, Currie reformed the F.O. cypher department and was also responsible for employing in 1889 the first female typist, Mrs Sophia Fulcher. She and her later colleagues were given the official title of "Lady Typewriters."

". . . I am directed by the Marquess of Salisbury to transmit to you herewith the substance of a further telegram from Her Majesty's Ambassador at Vienna giving details respecting the identity of the supposed perpetrator of the Whitechapel murders."

Letter from Sir Alexander Paget to Sir Charles Warren, 4th November 1888—

"Copy. Mr. Phipps delivered this memorandum personally to Mr. Matthews, who authorised him to telegraph to Sir A Paget guaranteeing the expenses of Jonas' journey to London (if he be without means of his own). Mr. Phipps also stated that he would remain in town to meet Jonas and take him to see Sir C. Warren."

Home Office, 5th Nov. 88. From Sir A. Paget. Vienna. Nov 4/88—

"Mr. Phipps stated that he had given Sir C. Warren a copy of this. ELP. Following for Sir C. Warren and Mr. Phipps—

"Have just seen informant [here a note in the margin reads "The informant's name is Jonas ELP"][473] who returned here on Friday evening, but was unwell yesterday. His object in returning to Vienna is to procure further funds, but from his friends and not from myself; when he has this money, he purposes starting once more for London on Tuesday or Wednesday, and is convinced he will catch the murderer . . .

"When in San Francisco the Whitechapel murderer's name was Johann Stammer; when in London John Kelly,[474] medium height, broad shoulders, aged between 35 and 38, strongly marked features and extremely brilliant large white teeth. Has a stab wound beneath the left eye and walks like a sailor, having been a ship's cook for three years."

The informant reached Paris, but by 7th November 1888 had returned to Vienna where he was enquiring about the extra £100 he required before going to England. Sir Alexander Paget wanted to know if he was authorised to advance the money.

Home Office, 7th November 1888—

---

[473] ELP were the initials of Edward Leigh Pemberton, Legal Assistant Under-Secretary at the Home Office.
[474] Coincidentally the name of the common-law husband of "Ripper" victim Catherine Eddowes.

"It is said that he [the informant] sent from Paris to the Commissioner the name and description of the man he accuses of these murders. Ask Commissioner."

Warren had heard from the informant. A week beforehand, on 29th/30th October 1888, he wrote[475] to Sir Edmund Constantine Henry Phipps, First Secretary at the British Embassy, Vienna, who was in London, staying at Brook's Club, St. James's—

"Dear Mr. Phipps,

"On consideration it would be impolitic for Police to write to Mr. Kasimir Jonas. It is difficult to say what mischief he might do with any letter from Scotland Yard.

"I think the only plan is for him to come here & see me & submit to cross examination as to whether he is a true man or no.

"Would you like to write to him.

"Truly yours, Charles Warren."

There was a PS—

"His address is Kasimir Jonas, Hotel Bellevue, 39 Avenue de l'Opéra, Paris."

File Minute "Pressing & Secret", 7th November 1888—

"To Commissioner of Police for observations—in the first instance. In another record about this man [Kasimir Jonas] it is said that he sent from Paris to the Commissioner the name and description of the man he accuses of these murders? Ask Commissioner: at same time whether he has been able to make any use of the particulars, & whether he attached any importance to them, CM."[476]

Accordingly, Godfrey Lushington asked the question in a letter to the Commissioner sent the same day— "GL Wrote 7. Nov. 88."

On 9th November 1888 at Millers Court, Dorset Street, Spitalfields, "Jack the Ripper" claimed the fifth and final member of his Rippertoire.

On 27th December 1888 a letter was sent from Scotland Yard to G.R. Moran, Superintendent of Registry at the Home Office—

---

[475]   Metropolitan Police Private Letter Book. MEPO 1/48.
[476]   Charles Murdoch, Assistant Under-Secretary, Home Office.

"I return the Confidential papers which you were good enough to lend yesterday for Mr. Monro.

"Yours truly, M.M."[477]

Kasimir Jonas did not receive his extra £100. Nor did he reach London. But this did not prevent Sir Alexander Paget from persisting in his belief that Jonas had valuable information to impart. In a cypher cable to London dated 29th December 1888 he wrote—

"Informer states that there are at present in Brussels from 15 to 20 terrorists, mostly leaders, who may shortly be expected in London. One was here on Monday on his way to St Petersburgh. He is a chemist and prepares explosives &c. He returns soon to London but whether by Vienna informer is ignorant [sic]. This man is acquainted with Kelly & can identify him. Informer does not know where these Terrorists will live in London, but if on the spot could soon discover. He will furnish some names in writing tomorrow. He says that a large number of dynamite outrages are contemplated in London but details can only be given personally to authorities."

There next followed a bargain offer—

"He is ready to come to London for 1500 florins [£125.00] & remain there until favourable results respecting murder of which he is certain. He pressed for decision saying no time is to be lost."

If accepted, this latest offer would have involved HM Government in a total expenditure of 4700 Austrian florins [£392.00 or $1960.00].

On 2nd January 1889 James Monro finally drove a stake through the heart of the matter, writing to Godfrey Lushington at the Home Office—

"With reference to Sir A. Paget's telegram of the 29th inst. giving particulars of further information offered by his informant who recently undertook to discover the Whitechapel Murderer, I have to acquaint you for the information of the Secretary of State, that I attach no importance to this person's statement, and I do not recommend any further

---

[477]   If these initials seem familiar it should be noted that Melville Macnaghten did not join the Metropolitan Police until 1st June 1889.

expenditure upon him."

On 20th March Godfrey Lushington wrote to Sir Reginald Welby, Permanent Secretary at the Treasury, detailing the circumstances of the situation—

"Acting on the recommendation of the then Commissioner of Metropolitan Police and influenced also by Sir A. Paget's strong belief in the bona fides of the informant, the Secretary of State expressed to the Foreign Office the opinion that it should be left to his Excellency's discretion as to whether the man's terms should be agreed to.

"The sum demanded was paid; and Jonas appears to have proceeded to Paris for the purpose, as he explained, of connecting with and obtaining the cooperation of a colleague in the International Society, of which they and the alleged murderer were alike members. He presently returned to Vienna: but declined to proceed to London with a view to carrying out what he had undertaken unless a further sum of £100 was given to him.

"Hereupon Mr. Matthews again consulted the Commissioner of Police [by this time James Monro] and on his recommendation wrote to the Foreign Office explaining his opinion that no more money should be spent on Jonas, whose alleged information he regarded of no importance."

Lushington closed by asking if he would "move the Lords Commissioners of the Treasury to sanction the repayment of the £165 already expended by Sir A. Paget."

The Treasury did not reply.

Five days later, Lushington wrote in a file note—

"I have seen Mr. Mowatt[478] on this. He says the Treasury would decline to pay this Bill, but that it is inexpedient for a letter to be written stating the reasons."

Lushington continued—

"I have always been of the opinion that this would have to be paid out of Met. Pol. Funds.

---

[478]   Francis Mowatt C.B., Assistant Secretary to the Treasury.

"So Pay accordingly.

"Inform ruling.

"Withdraw our letter to Treasury."

By the end of March 1889 Sir Alexander Paget was still wondering if he would ever be reimbursed the £165 he had advanced in good faith to the unknown informant who professed to be able to identify the Whitechapel murderer.

Whether or not Sir Charles Warren actually received the name and description of the Whitechapel murderer from Kasimir Jonas is uncertain. All we know is that in the House of Commons,12th November 1888, Henry Matthews announced his acceptance of Warren's resignation.

This affair was being dealt with at the highest diplomatic levels, including the Prime Minister. If, as seems apparent, Kasimir Jonas was being taken seriously, how was Anderson's low-class Polish Jew or Macnaghten's drowned doctor involved in these intrigues?

Whilst the identity and motives of the Viennese informer remain a mystery, of possible interest in this G.K. Chesterton-esque intrigue is the fact that Sir Edward Jenkinson, dismissed in 1887 as Britain's "Spymaster-General" by Home Secretary Henry Matthews and supplanted by James Monro, was in Vienna during October 1888.[479]

---

[479] Jenkinson letter to Earl Spencer, 18th October 1888. Althorp Papers KS 252.

24. JACK AND THE GRAPESTALK

Jack the Ripper's defining moment was the double-event in the early hours of Sunday 30th September 1888 when he allegedly claimed two victims a mile apart and within forty minutes of each other.

The first victim, Elizabeth Stride, was discovered at 1.00 am in Dutfields Yard, Berner Street, within the jurisdiction of the Metropolitan Police. She died from a cut throat, with no further mutilation. The second, Catherine Eddowes, was discovered at 1.44 am in Mitre Square, within the jurisdiction of the City of London Police. She had been mutilated in an horrific manner not dissimilar to that of Annie Chapman, found on 8th September in the backyard of 29 Hanbury Street.

The following week Thomas Catling, Editor of *Lloyd's Weekly Newspaper* wrote—

". . . intelligence of the two murders reached Lloyd's office [in Salisbury Square, off Fleet Street] simultaneously, from two entirely different sources, at ten minutes past two on Sunday morning. Confirmatory evidence was received five minutes later, but as particulars were wanting of the Aldgate tragedy, it was necessary to despatch a reporter to Mitre Square. He returned in time for us to have an account written, composed, stereotyped, and printing by four o'clock."

Thomas Catling was the reporter who went to Mitre Square. In a later column of personal reminiscences[480] he wrote—

"Hurrying to Bishopsgate [police] station I was fortunate enough to meet Major Henry Smith . . . With the facts he kindly gave me, supplemented by others derived from a visit to Mitre Square, and an interview with my friend, Dr. Gordon Brown, the police surgeon, whom I found busy making the post-mortem at the mortuary, I was enabled to get Lloyd's out with a detailed story of the murders long before any other paper."

In his 1911 autobiography "My Life's Pilgrimage," Thomas Catling offered a further detail about his visit to Bishopsgate police station on the morning of the murders—

"In response to my inquiry [Major Henry Smith] said he feared both murders must be put down as the act of the unknown 'Ripper'."

It is uncertain whether at this early hour of Sunday morning Major Smith had been apprised of the Jack the Ripper letter, but of greater importance is his apparent belief, less than two hours after the murders, that both were the work of the same person.

On 30th September 1888 Lloyd's also reported that—

". . . reasons exist for believing that the assassin was disturbed, and thus his savage intention unfulfilled."

It is hard to understand how the police reached this conclusion so soon after the murders.

Daily News, 1st October 1888—

"It is announced by the police that in all probability the wretch was disturbed in his work, and made off in the direction of the City with the ghoulish thirst for blood still blazing within him; that he beguiled another hapless victim into a dark secluded spot, and then again fell to his butchery."

Aside from the physical and temporal proximity of the two murders there was no evidence to support this scenario. None, that is, until the late morning of 1st October 1888, when a postcard bearing a "London E." postmark dated "Oc 1 88" arrived at Central News—

---

[480]   *Lloyds Weekly Newspaper*, 27th November 1892.

"I was not codding dear old Boss when I gave you the tip, you'll hear about Saucy Jacky's work tomorrow double event this time number one squealed a bit couldn't finish straight off. had not the time to get ears for police. thanks for keeping last letter back till I got to work again. Jack the Ripper."

Saucy Jacky obligingly confirmed earlier police suspicions. Both murders were by the same hand, the work of someone styling himself Jack the Ripper, and in writing that he "couldn't finish straight off" with "number one" lent credence to the earlier notion as reported by Lloyd's Weekly Newspaper that the murderer "was disturbed, and thus his savage intention unfulfilled."

The postcard reads as if written and posted on Sunday 30th September 1888 ["you'll hear about Saucy Jacky's work *tomorrow*"], before anyone except Central News and the Metropolitan Police knew about the name Jack the Ripper, yet is postmarked [Monday] 1st October 1888, by which time "Dear Boss" had appeared in the *Daily Telegraph*. So the question is whether the writer of the postcard was displaying any foreknowledge of Dear Boss or simply taking advantage of the name Jack the Ripper going public.

There were eight postal districts in London. The main Eastern Central district boasted twelve deliveries per day, nine of which were hourly. Districts within three miles had eleven deliveries a day, and the suburbs six. A postcard mailed at 8.00 am in central London could reach another destination in central London within two to three hours. And if posted on a Sunday—

"Letters posted in the pillar-boxes within the town limits, and in some of the nearer suburbs, on Sundays, are collected early on Monday morning in time for the general day mails, and for the first London district delivery."[481]

This makes the question of whether the postcard was mailed on Sunday or Monday impossible to answer, as in either case it would have been postmarked 1st October 1888.

---

[481]   Charles Dickens (Jr.), *Dickens's Dictionary of London*, 1879.

However, other questions arise regarding the Saucy Jacky postcard.

The press carried differing accounts of how the body of Elizabeth Stride was discovered, and so for a measured account of events and details we can do no better than the definitive version from the summing-up of Coroner Wynne Baxter—

"At 1 o'clock the body was found by the manager of the [International Workingmen's Education] Club. He had been out all day, and returned at the time. He was in a two-wheeled barrow drawn by a pony, and as he entered the gateway his pony shied at some object on his right. There was no lamp in the yard, and having just come out of the street it was too dark to see what the object was and he passed on further down the yard. He returned on foot, and on searching found the body of deceased with her throat cut."

Wynne Baxter then added gratuitously—

"If he had not actually disturbed the wretch in the very act, at least he must have been close on his heels; possibly the man was alarmed by the sound of the approaching cart, for the death had only just taken place."

The first medical man on the scene in Dutfields Yard was Dr. Frederick William Blackwell, a physician and surgeon residing at 100 Commercial Road. He testified on day two of the Elizabeth Stride inquest—

"On Sunday morning last, at ten minutes past one o'clock, I was called to Berner Street by a policeman. My assistant, Mr. Johnston, went back with the constable, and I followed immediately I was dressed. I consulted my watch on my arrival, and it was 1.16 a.m."

Coroner Wynne Baxter— "Did you form any opinion as to how long the deceased had been dead?"

Doctor Blackwell— "From twenty minutes to half an hour when I arrived. The clothes were not wet with rain. She would have bled to death comparatively slowly on account of vessels on one side only of the neck being cut and the artery not completely severed."

Not only had Elizabeth Stride died four to fourteen minutes before 1.00 am, the time at which her body was discovered; she also "bled to death comparatively slowly," making the time of her attack even earlier.

If she died at 12.56 am, having taken, say, ten minutes to bleed to death, this would place the time of her attack at around 12.46 am, leaving the murderer ample time to inflict further injury before her discovery at 1.00 am. Yet in his summing-up Coroner Wynne Baxter told the inquest jury that at 1.00 am the murderer must have been disturbed in the very act, thus explaining his lack of opportunity to mutilate her body.

Taking Dr. Blackwell's timing literally, the period between 12.46 and 1.00 is of interest.

Star, 1st October 1888—

"Information which may be important was given to the Leman Street police late yesterday afternoon by an Hungarian concerning this murder. This foreigner was well dressed, and had the appearance of being in the theatrical line. He could not speak a word of English, but came to the police-station accompanied by a friend, who acted as an interpreter. He gave his name and address, but the police have not disclosed them . . ."

The man's name was Israel Schwartz.

Chief Inspector Donald Swanson, 19th October 1888 report—

"12.45 am, 30th Israel Schwartz of 22 Helen [sic – Ellen] Street, Backchurch Lane stated that at that hour on turning into Berner Street from Commercial Road & had got as far as the gateway where the murder was committed he saw a man stop & speak to a woman, who was standing in the gateway. The man tried to pull the woman into the street, but he turned her around and threw her down on the footway & the woman screamed three times, but not very loudly. On crossing to the opposite side of the street, he saw a second man standing lighting his pipe. The man who threw the woman down called out apparently to the man on the opposite side of the road 'Lipski' & then Schwartz walked away, but finding he was followed by the second man he ran as far as the railway arch but the man did not follow so far. Upon being taken to the mortuary Schwartz identified the body as that of the woman he had seen & he thus describes the first man who threw the woman down: - age about 30 ht. 5ft. 5 in. comp. Fair hair dark, small brown moustache, full face, broad shouldered, dress, dark jacket & trousers black cap with peak, had nothing in his hands . . ."

Star, 1st October 1888—

". . . A Star man, however, got wind of his [Schwartz's] call, and ran him to earth in Backchurch Lane. The reporter's Hungarian was quite as imperfect as the foreigner's English, but an interpreter was at hand, and the man's story was retold just as he had given it to the police. It is, in fact, to the effect that he saw the whole thing.

"It seems that he had gone out for the day, and his wife had expected to move, during his absence, from their lodgings in Berner Street to others in Backchurch Lane.

"When he came homewards about a quarter before one he first walked down Berner Street to see if his wife had moved.

"As he turned the corner from Commercial-road he noticed some distance in front of him a man walking as if partially intoxicated. He walked on behind him, and presently he noticed a woman standing in the entrance to the alley way where the body was afterwards found.

"The half-tipsy man halted and spoke to her. The Hungarian saw him put his hand on her shoulder and push her back into the passage, but, feeling rather timid of getting mixed up in quarrels, he crossed to the other side of the street.

"Before he had gone many yards, however, he heard the sound of a quarrel, and turned back to learn what was the matter, but just as he stepped from the kerb a second man came out of the doorway of the public-house a few doors off, and shouting out some sort of warning to the man who was with the woman, rushed forward as if to attack the intruder.

"The Hungarian states positively that he saw a knife in this second man's hand, but he waited to see no more. He fled incontinently to his new lodgings.

"He described the man with the woman as about 30 years of age, rather stoutly built, and wearing a brown moustache. He was dressed respectably in dark clothes and felt hat. The man who came at him with a knife he also describes, but not in detail. He says he was taller than the other, but not so stout, and that his moustaches were red. Both men seem to belong to the same grade of society.

"The police have arrested one man answering the description the Hungarian furnishes. This prisoner has not been charged, but is held for inquiries to be made. The truth of the man's statement is not wholly accepted."

Despite some differences in detail—for instance a pipe had turned into a knife—the two stories were essentially the same. Israel Schwartz had seen Elizabeth Stride being attacked at 12.45 am, which was an almost perfect fit with the medical evidence of Dr. Blackwell.

Ten minutes earlier than the Schwartz incident PC 452H Smith had seen a man talking with a woman wearing a red rose in Berner Street. His description of the man he saw differed from that given by Schwartz.

Chief Inspector Donald Swanson, 19th October 1888 report—

" . . . If Schwartz is to be believed, *and the police report of his statement casts no doubt upon it*,[482] it follows if they are describing different men and that the man Schwartz saw and described is the more probable of the two to be the murderer, for a quarter of an hour afterwards the body is found murdered . . ."

Chief Inspector Swanson next tried to reconcile the Schwartz incident with the prevailing belief that at 1.00 am the murderer had been interrupted—

". . . At the same time account must be taken of the fact that the throat only of the victim was cut in this instance which measured by time, considering meeting (if with a man other than Schwartz saw) the time for agreement & the murderous action would I think be a question of so many minutes, five at least, ten at most, so that I respectfully submit it is not clearly proved that the man Schwartz saw is the murderer."

At this point in Chief Inspector's Swanson's report a note appeared in the margin—

["This is rather confused: if the man whom the PC saw is not the same as the man whom Schwartz saw at 12.45 then it is clearly more probable that the man whom Schwartz saw was the murderer, because Schwartz saw his man a quarter of an hour later than the PC.

---

[482] Schwartz's statement was taken by Inspector Abberline at Leman Street police station.

["But I understand the Inspector to suggest that Schwartz's man need not have been the murderer. True, only fifteen minutes elapsed between 12.45 when Schwartz saw the man & 1.0 when the woman was found murdered on the same spot. But the suggestion is that Schwartz's man may have left her, she being a prostitute then accosted or was accosted by another man, & there was time enough for this to take place & for this other man to murder her before 1.0[clock].

"The Police apparently do not suspect the 2nd man whom Schwartz saw on the other side of the street & who followed Schwartz."]

This Alice in Wonderland scenario being advanced by Chief Inspector Donald Swanson in support of the murder being *mutilandum interruptus* and thus part of a double-event was painting Elizabeth Stride as the most unfortunate unfortunate in East End history.

There followed more from Chief Inspector Donald Swanson in support of the double-event—

"Before concluding in dealing with the descriptions of these two men [seen by PC Smith and Schwartz] I venture to insert here for the purpose of comparison with these two descriptions, the description of a man seen with a woman in Church Passage close to Mitre Square at 1.35 am 30th by two men coming out of a club close by:- age 30 ht. 5ft 7 or 8 in. comp. fair, fair moustache, medium build, dress pepper and salt colour loose jacket, grey cloth cap with peak of same colour, reddish handkerchief tied in a knot, round neck, appearance of a sailor. In this case I understand from City Police that Mr. Lewin [sic – Lawende] one of the men identified the clothes only of the murdered woman Eddowes, which is a serious drawback to the value of the description of the man. Ten minutes afterwards the body is found horribly mutilated & it is therefore reasonable to believe that the man he saw was the murderer, but for the purposes of comparison, this description is much nearer to that given by Schwartz than to that given by the P.C."

The suggestion was that the man seen by Lawende in Church Passage bore a resemblance to the man seen by Schwartz in Berner Street.

Ergo! Two murders, one perpetrator. A double-event.

Unfortunately, what Swanson neglected to mention was that in order to make his 1.00 am *mutilandum interruptus* scenario work he had postulated that Elizabeth Stride was murdered by someone other than the man seen by Schwartz.

There was a measure of independent support for Israel Schwartz's story.

Echo, 1st October 1888—

"A Man Pursued – Said To Be The Murderer.

"In the course of conversation (says the journalist) the secretary [of the IWEC at 40 Berner Street] mentioned the fact that the murderer had no doubt been disturbed in his work, as about a quarter to one o'clock on Sunday morning he was seen—or, at least, a man whom the public prefer to regard as the murderer—being chased by another man along Fairclough Street, which runs across Berner Street close to the Club, and which is intersected on the right by Providence-street, Brunswick-street, and Christian Street, and on the left by Batty Street and Grove Street, the [two latter?] [run?] up into Commercial-road. The man pursued escaped, however, and the secretary of the Club cannot remember the name of the man who gave chase, but he is not a member of their body."

This also fitted the medical evidence of Dr. Blackwell. If it was the same incident as that described by Israel Schwartz, the 1.00 am *mutilandum interruptus* scenario with the Ripper's "ghoulish thirst for blood still blazing within him" was looking shaky, yet still formed part of Coroner Wynne Baxter's summing-up. Perhaps not surprisingly Israel Schwartz was not subpoenaed to give evidence at the Elizabeth Stride inquest.

Star, 2nd October 1888—

"In the matter of the Hungarian who said he saw a struggle between a man and a woman in the passage where the Stride body was afterwards found, the Leman Street police have reason to doubt the truth of the story. They arrested one man on the description thus obtained, and a second on that furnished from another source, but they are not likely to act further on the same information without additional facts."

Israel Schwartz's evidence didn't stand a chance. Odd, then, that on 19th October 1888, the same day as Chief Inspector Swanson's report, the following notice should appear in the *Police Gazette*—

"Apprehensions Sought. Murder. Metropolitan Police District.

"At 12.45 a.m., 30th, with same woman, in Berner Street - A man, age about 30, height 5 ft. 5 in., complexion fair, hair dark, small brown moustache, full face, broad shoulders; dress, dark jacket and trousers, black cap with peak."

It was a word-for-word transcript of Israel Schwartz's description of the man he had seen attacking Elizabeth Stride at 12.45 am, the man whom Chief Inspector Swanson had discounted in favour of her being killed *mutilandum interruptus* at 1.00 am by another person.

In a 1st November 1888 report Inspector Abberline wrote—

"I beg to report that since a jew named Lipski was hanged for the murder of a jewess in 1887 the name has very frequently been used by persons as mere ejaculation by way of endeavouring to insult the jew to whom it has been addressed and as Schwartz has a strong jewish appearance I am of opinion it was addressed to him as he stopped to look at the man he saw ill-using the deceased woman.

"I questioned Israel Schwartz very closely at the time he made the statement as to whom the man addressed when he called out Lipski, but he was unable to say."[483]

Four days later, on 5th November 1888, Robert Anderson drafted a letter to the Home Office regarding the name "Lipski." It was a distillation of Abberline's earlier report. Of real interest is Anderson's opening statement—

"Draft letter to H.O.

"With ref. to yr letter &c. I have to state that the opinion arrived at in this Dept. *upon the evidence of Schwartz at the inquest in Eliz. Stride's case* is that the name Lipski which he alleges was used by a man whom he saw assaulting the woman in Berner St. on the night of the murder, was not addressed to the supposed accomplice but to Schwartz himself. It appears that since the Lipski case, it has come to be used as an epithet in addressing or speaking of Jews [Author's italics].

---

[483] Inspector Abberline did not capitalise the words jew, jewess or jewish.

"With regard to the latter portion of yr letter I have to state that [copy passage in the report as written in blue]."

Anderson's draft letter had been prepared for Sir Charles Warren who, on 7th November 1888, sent a two-page report to the Home Secretary—

"With reference to your letter of the 29th ulto. I have to acquaint you, for the information of the Secretary of State, that the opinion arrived at *upon the evidence given by Schwartz at the inquest in Elizabeth Stride's case . . .*" [Author's italics].

Anderson misinformed Warren, who in turn misinformed Home Secretary Henry Matthews, that Israel Schwartz had appeared as a witness at the Elizabeth Stride inquest.

The inquest was widely covered in the press, most comprehensively by *The Times*. Over the five days of hearings the newspaper devoted almost thirteen full columns to the proceedings, and nowhere in its coverage, nor in that of any other newspaper, is the name of Israel Schwartz to be found.

It has been suggested that the evidence of Israel Schwartz may have been given *in camera* [literally, *in private*, or *in chambers*] and thus not reported by the press, but this is unlikely. To do so would have required the Coroner to announce that such a procedure was to follow [on the grounds, for example, that the evidence of the witness might hinder police inquiries] before excluding the press and public, leaving only the police, the jury, the witness and a translator in the courtroom.

No such *in camera* procedure was reported in the press.

Israel Schwartz's evidence appears to have been disavowed in order to lend weight to the *mutilandum interruptus* nature of Stride's murder and promote the double-event scenario as initially asserted by the police and endorsed by the serendipitous arrival of Jack the Ripper's 'Saucy Jacky' postcard.

Other evidence in the Berner Street murder which gave the lie to the double-event scenario was also disavowed.

Evening News, 4th October 1888—

"We are enabled to present our readers this morning in the columns

483

of the Evening News with the most startling information that has yet been made public in relation to the Whitechapel murderer, and the first real clue that has been obtained to his identity. The chain of evidence in our possession has been pieced together by two gentlemen connected with the business of private inquiries, who, starting on the track of the assassin without any pet "theory" to substantiate, and contenting themselves with ascertaining and connecting a series of the simplest facts, have succeeded in arriving at a result of the utmost importance.

"There are no suppositions or probabilities in the story we have to tell; we put forward nothing but simple facts, each substantiated by the evidence of credible witnesses. What they go to establish is that the perpetrator of the Berner Street crime was seen and spoken to whilst in the company of his victim, within forty minutes of the commission of the crime and only passed from the sight of a witness ten minutes before the murder and within ten yards of the scene of the awful deed.

"We proceed to give hereunder the story of the two detectives, Messrs. Grand and J.H. Batchelor, of 283 Strand: When they began their quest, almost from the first place at which they sought evidence from No. 44 Berner street, the second house from the spot at which the body was found. This is the residence of a man named Matthew Packer, who carries on a small business as a greengrocer and fruiterer. His shop is an insignificant place, with a half window in front, and most of his dealings are carried on through the lower part of the window case, in which his fruit is exposed for sale.

"On the 29th ult., about 11.45 pm., a man and woman came to his shop window, and asked for some fruit. The man was middle aged, perhaps 35 years; about five feet seven inches in height; was stout, square built; wore a wideawake hat and dark clothes; had the appearance of a clerk; had a rough voice and a quick, sharp way of talking.

"The woman was middle aged, wore a dark dress and jacket, and had a white flower in her bosom. It was a dark night and the only light was afforded by an oil lamp which Packer had burning inside his window, but he obtained a sufficiently clear view of the faces of the two people as they stood talking close in front of the window, and his attention was particularly caught by the white flower which the woman wore, and which showed out distinctly against the dark material of her jacket. The importance attached to this flower will be seen afterwards.

"The man asked his companion whether she would have black or white grapes; she replied 'black'.

"'Well, what's the price of the black grapes, old man?' he inquired.

"'The black are sixpence and the white fourpence,' replied Packer.

"'Well then, old man, give us half a pound of the black,' said the man. Packer served him with the grapes, which he handed to the woman. They then crossed the road and stood on the pavement almost directly opposite to the shop for a long time more than half an hour. It will be remembered that the night was very wet, and Packer naturally noticed the peculiarity of the couple's standing so long in the rain. He observed to his wife, 'What fools those people are to be standing in the rain like that.'

"At last the couple moved from their position, and Packer saw them cross the road again and come over to the club, standing for a moment in front of it as though listening to the music inside. Then he lost sight of them. It was then ten or fifteen minutes past twelve o'clock, Packer, who was about to close his shop, noting the time by the fact that the public houses had been closed.

"With a view of testing the accuracy and honesty of Packer's testimony, the detectives obtained an order to view the body of the woman murdered in Mitre Square, and took Packer to see it, leaving him under the impression that they were taking him to see the Berner street victim. On seeing the body he at once declared that it was not the woman for whom the grapes had been bought, and not a bit like her."

Star, 4th October 1888—

"The police most emphatically deny the truth of the story that has been published as to the discovery of a shopkeeper who had talked with the murderer and his Berner Street victim, had sold them grapes, and had seen them at the entrance to the fatal alley ten minutes before the deed was done. The fact is, that the alleged informant contradicts himself, and there is no evidence that there were any grapes in the possession of the woman."

Despite official denial, the story galvanised the Metropolitan Police.

Report of Inspector Henry Moore, 4th October 1888—

"Referring to attached Extract from 2nd. Edition, 'Evening News', of this date.

"I beg to report that as soon as above came under my notice I at once (in the absence of Inspr. Abberline at C.O.) directed P.S. White, 'H', to see Mr. Packer, the shopkeeper referred to, and take him to the mortuary with a view to the identification of the woman Elizabeth Stride; who it is stated was with a man who purchased grapes at his shop on the night of 29th Ins.

"The P.S. returned at noon and acquainted me as in report attached; in consequence of which Telegram No. 1 was forwarded to Chief Inspector Swanson and the P.S. sent to C.O. to fully explain the facts. Telegram No. 2 was received at 12.55 pm from Assistant Commissioner [Alexander Carmichael Bruce] re same subject; in reply to which Telegram No. 3 was forwarded" [Author's brackets].

The nature of Telegrams Nos. 1, 2 and 3 are unknown.

The P.S. was 34-year-old Police Sergeant Stephen White, H Division. In a report also dated 4th October 1888 he wrote—

"On 4th Inst. I was directed by Inspr. Moore to make further inquiry & if necessary see Packer and take him to the mortuary."

Further inquiry?

On Sunday 30th September, the day of the murder, "Acting under the instructions of Inspector Abberline," White made enquiries at every house in Berner Street. He had been given a book in which to note any information he obtained. At about 9.00 am—eight hours after the discovery of Stride and eight hours before Israel Schwartz would tell his story—Sergeant White called on Matthew Packer at 44 Berner Street—

"I asked him what time he closed his shop on the previous night. He replied half-past twelve, in consequence of the rain it was no good for me to keep open. I asked him if he saw anything of a man or woman going into Dutfields Yard, or saw anyone standing about the street about the time he was closing his shop. He replied, 'No I saw no one standing about neither did I see anyone go up the yard. I never saw anything suspicious or heard the slightest noise, and know nothing about the murder until I heard of it in the morning.'

"I also saw Mrs. Packer, Sarah Harrison and Harry Douglas residing in the same house but none of them could give the slightest information regarding the matter.'"

A few days later an *Evening News* reporter visited Matthew Packer.

Evening News, 4th October 1888—

"Well, Mr. Packer, I suppose the police came at once to ask you and your wife what you knew about the affair, as soon as ever the body was discovered.

"The police? No. They haven't asked me a word about it yet. A young man in plain clothes came in here on Monday and asked if he might look at the yard at the back of our house, so as to see if anybody had climbed over. My missus lent him some steps [a stepladder]. But he didn't put any questions to us about the man and the woman.

"I am afraid you don't quite understand my question, Mr. Packer. Do you actually mean to say that no detective or policeman came to inquire whether you had sold grapes to any one that night? Now, please be very careful in your answer, for this may prove a serious business for the London police.

"'I've only got one answer,' said the man, 'because it's the truth. Except a gentleman who is a private detective, no detective or policeman has ever asked me a single question nor come near my shop to find out if I knew anything about the grapes the murdered woman had been eating before her throat was cut.'"

Somebody was not telling the truth.

On October 4th when Sergeant White arrived at 44 Berner Street in order to take Matthew Packer to the mortuary, Mrs Rose Packer told him her husband had already gone there with two detectives.

Sergeant White's report continued—

"I then went towards the mortuary [St George's in the East, Cannon Street Road] when I met Packer with a man. I asked where he had been. He said, 'This detective asked me to go to see if I could identify the woman.' Shortly afterwards they were joined by another man. I asked the men what they were doing with Packer and they both said they were detectives. [When] I asked for their authority one of the men produced a card from a pocket book, but would not allow me to touch it. They then said they were private detectives. They then induced Packer to go away with them. About 4.00 pm I saw Packer at his shop and while talking to him the men drove up in a Hansom Cab, and after going into the shop they induced Packer to enter the Cab, stating that they would take him to Scotland Yard to see Sir Charles Warren.

"From inquiry I have made there is no doubt that these are the two men referred to in attached Newspaper cutting, who examined the drain in Dutfields Yard on 2nd Inst. One of the men had a letter in his hand addressed to Le Grand & Co., Strand."

Why P.S. White didn't pull rank and tell the two PIs that Warren would be wasting his time is a mystery. After all, he allegedly had Packer's 30th September statement in the book issued to him especially for the purpose, which said the fruiterer saw nobody and heard nothing, and that the *Evening News* story was a fabrication.

A possible explanation is that Packer's story was not a fabrication and that the two detectives were from Scotland Yard and outranked White.

A two-page statement made by Packer, dated 4th October 1888 and initialed ACB [Alexander Carmichael Bruce, Senior Assistant Commissioner], suggests that the fruiterer was taken to Scotland Yard[484]—

"Matthew Packer keeps a shop in Berner St. has a few grapes in window, black & white.

"On Sat night about 11 pm a young man from 25—30—about 5.7, with long black coat buttoned up—soft felt hat, kind of Yankee hat rather broad shoulders—rather quick in speaking, rough voice. I sold him ½ pound black grapes 3d. A woman came up with him from Back Church end (the lower end of street) She was dressed in black frock & jacket, fir

---

[484]   MEPO 3/140/221/A49301C, ff. 216-216

round bottom of jacket & black crepe bonnet, she was playing with a flower like a geranium white outside and red inside. I identify the woman at the St. George's mortuary as the one I saw that night.

"They passed by as though they were going up Com[mercial] Road, but – instead of going up they crossed to the other side of the road to the Board School, & were there for about ½ an hour till I shd. say 11.30 talking to one another. I then shut up my shutters.

"Before they passed over opposite my shop, they waited near to the club for a few minutes apparently listening to the music.

"I saw no more of them after I shut up my shutters.

"I put the man down as a young clerk.

"He had a frock coat on – no gloves.

"He was about 1½ inch or 2 or 3 inches – a little higher than she was.

"ACB. 4. 10. 88."

Chief Inspector Swanson did not mention this meeting at Scotland Yard. In his 19th October 1888 report Matthew Packer's involvement with the two PIs "acting conjointly with the Vigilance Committee and the press" ended with his being taken to identify Stride at the mortuary. It is an odd omission, for the section of Swanson's report dealing with Packer contains word-for-word extracts from the statement initialed by Alexander Carmichael Bruce.

Swanson's massaging of the facts concluded with a dismissal of Packer—

"Packer who is an elderly man, has unfortunately made different statements so that apart from the fact of the hour at which he saw the woman (and she was seen afterwards by the P.C. and Schwartz as stated) any statement he made would be rendered almost valueless as evidence."

Evening News, 8th October 1888—

"The only notice taken by our contemporaries on that day was a denial of the truth of our information, made ostensibly on the authority of the police. On Friday, no public admission of the value of the clue was given, but on Saturday, after mature consideration, the Daily Telegraph gave out that Packer, whom our informants had discovered, and the worth of whose testimony they recognised, had been summoned by Sir Charles Warren, at Scotland Yard, and questioned as to the appearance of the man."

It takes a brave or foolhardy man to try to hoodwink the police. But, as with Schwartz's evidence, there was independent support for Packer's grape story.

Irish Times, 1st October 1888—

"A reporter who has seen the corpse states that . . . in her right hand were tightly clasped some grapes . . .

". . . A young Russian Pole, named M. Kozebrodski, born in Warsaw, and who spoke the English language imperfectly, gave the following information: - 'The officers did not touch the body, but sent for a doctor. A doctor came, and an inspector arrived just afterwards. While the doctor was examining the body I noticed that she had some grapes in her right hand . . .'"

Evening News, 1st October 1888—

"[Louis] Diemschutz [who discovered Elizabeth Stride's body at 1.00 am] being then asked to describe the body as well as he could, said: 'Her hands were tightly clenched, and when they were opened by the doctor I saw immediately that one had been holding sweetmeats and the other grapes'" [Author's brackets].

Asked by the Coroner if he had noticed the deceased's hands, Diemschutz replied, "I did not notice what position her hands were in." Neither Wynne Baxter nor Louis Diemschutz made any reference to grapes.

Fifty years later further corroboration of Matthew Packer's grape story arrived from an unexpected source.

"I Caught Crippen," Walter Dew, Blackie & Son, 1938—

"The Berners [sic] Street murder yielded a clue which, for a time, raised the hopes of us all. Our inquiries brought to light the important fact that a few minutes or at any rate a very short time before her death Elizabeth Stride, or "Long Liz", as she was known to her intimates, had actually been seen in the company of a man.

"This evidence was supplied by a man who kept a small fruit shop in Berners Street. His story was that in the early hours of that Sunday morning he had sold the couple some grapes.

"The real value of the fruit vendor's information lay in the fact that he swore he had seen the woman's companion before and would recognize him if he saw him again.

"Unfortunately his story was backed by a description of the man which could only be described as vague. It might have applied equally to thousands of men.

"Then came dramatic corroboration of his story. In the little Berners Street court, quite close to the spot where the body was found, detectives searching every inch of the ground came upon a number of grape skins and stones."[485]

Matthew Packer's 4th October 1888 grape-selling story in the *Evening News* obviously ruffled a few official feathers, for on the following day Drs. Phillips and Blackwell were recalled to the inquest.

Dr. George Bagster Phillips was first onto the witness stand.

The Times, 6th October 1888—

"I have also carefully examined the two handkerchiefs, and have not found any blood on them. I believe the stains on the larger one were fruit stains . . ."

Without elaborating on the nature of the fruit stains, Dr. Phillips said—

". . . I am convinced that the deceased had not swallowed either skin or seed of a grape within many hours of her death."

Asked by a juror if he had seen any grapes in the yard, Dr. Blackwell replied— "No, I did not."

The *Daily Telegraph*, 6th October 1888, reported one final exchange between Coroner Wynne Baxter and Dr. Blackwell—

"Did you hear any person say that they had seen grapes there?"

Dr. Blackwell— "I did not."

Earlier, on the actual day of the inquest, the *Star* reported—

---

[485] As earlier mentioned, it's caveat emptor with Walter Dew, as the extent of his involvement, if any, in the Whitechapel murders investigation has not yet been firmly established.

"The grape story is effectually disposed of by the statement of the authorities at Leman Street to a Star reporter. In the first place the police have no evidence that any grapes were found on the site of the Berner Street murder, and, moreover, Dr. Phillips' post mortem disclosed no trace of grapes or grape-stones in Elizabeth Stride's stomach."

Matthew Packer's story was dead in the water.

Evening News, 1st November 1888—

"The police authorities do not attach any importance to the statement attributed to Matthew Packer, the fruiterer, who says he sold grapes to the deceased woman Stride on the night of the murder."

Someone did not want the inquest jury to hear what Israel Schwartz and Matthew Packer had to say, for had their statements been admitted into evidence the 1.00 am *mutilandum interruptus* story, the confirmatory Saucy Jacky postcard and the whole notion of the double-event would have been exposed as an elaborate fiction.

25. THE WOMAN FROM ROTHERHITHE

At 1.00 am on Sunday 30th September—the time that Louis Diemschutz discovered the body of Elizabeth Stride in Dutfields Yard— a woman was being released from Bishopsgate Police Station in the City of London, having at 8.30 pm on Saturday been arrested in Aldgate for drunkenness. She gave her name to Sergeant James Byfield as Mary Ann Kelly, her address as 6 Fashion Street, Spitalfields, and said she had been 'hopping'.486

On the second day of the inquest, 11th October 1888, George Henry Hutt, Police Constable 968, the City Gaoler of Bishopsgate Police Station, told the inquest—

"I visited her several times until 5 to one on Sunday. I found deceased was sober, brought from the cell into the office and . . . discharged. I pushed open the swing door leading to the passage and said 'This way Misses'. She passed along the passage to the outer door. I said to her please pull it to - she said 'All right Good Night Old Cock' she pulled the door within half a foot and turned to the left leading towards Houndsditch."

Further questioned by City solicitor Mr. Henry Crawford, PC Hutt

---

486 Hop-picking. Partridges Dictionary of Slang lists a hop-picker as a "A harlot: low (?orig. c.): from ca 1880."

said that when bringing her out of the cell "she asked what time it was – I replied 'Too late for you to get any more drink.' She said, 'Well what time is it?' I said, 'Just on one,' and 'I shall get a Damned fine hiding when I get home.' I said, 'And serve you right you have no right to get drunk.' I noticed she was wearing an apron. I believe the one produced [in court] was the one she was wearing when she left the Station. It would take 8 minutes ordinary walking to get to Mitre Square."

Forty-four minutes later City Police Constable 881, Edward Watkins, found the mutilated body of a woman in the south-east corner of Mitre Square. He sent George James Morris, night watchman of Kearley and Tonge's warehouse, for assistance whilst he remained by the body until the arrival of City PC Holland, Dr. Sequira [2.00 am], Inspector Collard [2.03 am] and Dr. Gordon Brown, surgeon to the City Police Force [approximately 2.18 am].

Inspector Edward Collard testified at the inquest that "Sergeant Jones picked up on left side of deceased 3 small black buttons generally used for women's boots, [a] small metal button, [a] common metal thimble, [and] a small mustard tin containing 2 pawn tickets which were handed to me" [Author's brackets].

Echo, 1st October 1888—

"The two pawn-tickets found in the mustard box a few feet away from the Mitre Square victim have so far been of very little value to the police in prosecuting their inquiries. By an official at the headquarters of the City Force in Old Jewry, this morning, a reporter was informed that it was generally considered the tickets would not be of material assistance . . . the articles to which they related might have been pawned either by a woman for the man whose name appeared upon one, or by the man for the woman whose name appeared on the other. Should such be the case, it is very improbable that the pawnbroker's assistant by whom they were issued would be able to identify any person in connection with them."

Old Jewry was dispensing faulty information. Neither of the pawn tickets was in the name of a man.

Pall Mall Gazette, 1st October 1888—

"The names given on the tickets were Emily Burrell and Jane Kelly, and the addresses Dorset Street and White's Row, Whitechapel, both being fictitious."

The two pawn tickets, one for a man's flannel shirt pledged for 9d on 31st August 1888, and the other for a pair of men's boots pledged for 2s 6d on Friday 28th September 1888, were issued by the same pawnbroker—Joseph Jones, 31 Church Street, Spitalfields.

The unidentified woman was removed from Mitre Square at 3.00 am and taken to Golden Lane mortuary.

Official police descriptions of the deceased varied in the press.

The *Evening Standard*, 1st October 1888, reported "Tattoo marks on right forearm, 'T.C.,'" whilst the *Evening News* of the same day reported, "The deceased had T.C. on left forearm . . ." *The Times* and the *People* made no mention of a tattoo.

Evening Standard, 1st October 1888—

"Yesterday afternoon Sergeant Outram [City of London Police] accompanied two women and a man from a lodging-house in Spitalfields to the mortuary, one of the former stating her belief that the victim was a Mrs. Kelly. After carefully scrutinising the features for some time, however, they were unable to give a decided opinion on the matter. It may be mentioned that the tattoo marks on the arm are slightly obscured from view unless the arm is almost fully exposed; and further, that the nose and face are hacked about to such an extent as to render recognition almost impossible."

Star, 2nd October 1888—

"A woman from Rotherhithe accompanied by her son-in-law and another man, called at the Bishopsgate Street Police station yesterday to get permission to see the body.

"She had read a description of the murdered woman and feared it was her sister. Her attention had been particularly attracted by the statement that the letters 'T. C.' were tattooed upon the left forearm in blue ink. The woman said she had for many years lost sight of her sister, who was living she understood, with a man named Kelly, in a street leading from Bishopsgate. This sister had had 'T. C.' tattooed upon her arm by her husband, whose initials they were. Kelly was the name, it will be remembered, which figured on one of the pawn tickets supposed to belong to the deceased.

"The party were taken to the mortuary, and recognised the body as that of the relation they were in search of. The woman said she knew it from the forehead (the only part of the face that was recognisable) as well as from the marks on the arms, and also from some peculiarity of the body. There seemed to be no doubt of the identification, and an officer went with the visitors to make inquiries at the place where the missing woman was said to have lived.

"The door of the house was opened by the woman herself. Her sister nearly fainted at the sight. The officer brought the news back to the police station, where his story was barely credited, so positive had the woman been in her identification. This is the only occasion thus far that any one has thought they recognised the body, and the authorities are very doubtful if it is ever to be identified."

The *Echo* of the same date named the tattooed sister-in-law as Cunningham, and her address as a lodging house in Dorset Street, Spitalfields.

Daily Telegraph, 3rd October 1888

"It appears that Detective-Sergeant Outram, of the City Police, came to the mortuary in Golden-lane, with a party of six women and a man. Some of the former had, it is said, described the clothing of the deceased so accurately that they were allowed to confirm their belief by viewing it at the Bishopsgate Street Police-station. Subsequently they were taken to the chief office in Old Jewry, and thence conducted to the mortuary. Here two of the women positively identified the deceased as an associate, but they did not know her by name. She does not seem to have borne a nickname. They were ignorant of her family connections or her antecedents, and did not know whether she had lived with a man."

The dead woman remained unidentified at the mortuary throughout Sunday, Monday and most of Tuesday 2nd October, on which evening between 9.00 and 10.00 o'clock "a labouring man, giving the name of John Kelly, 55 Flower and Dean-street—a common lodging-house—entered the Bishopsgate Street police station and stated that he believed that the woman who had been murdered in Mitre Square was his 'wife'."[487] Her name was Catherine Eddowes. He last saw her on the afternoon of Saturday 29th September.

John Kelly's stories were many and various.

Here is part of his evidence from Catherine Eddowes' Inquest, together with sections of a February 1891 report into "The Homeless Poor of London."

[Coroner]— "Where did you sleep?"

[John Kelly]— "On Monday, Tuesday, and Wednesday we were down at the hop-picking, and came back to London on Thursday. We had been unfortunate at the hop-picking, and had no money. On Thursday night we both slept in the [Shoe Lane, City of London] casual ward . . ."

[John Kelly]— "On the Friday I earned 6d at a job, and I said, 'Here, Kate, you take 4d and go to the lodging-house and I will go to Mile End,' but she said, 'No, you go and have a bed and I will go to the casual ward,' and she went. I saw her again on Saturday morning early."

Kelly wanted to spend the sixpence on food, telling Eddowes that 'Fred' [lodging house deputy, Frederick Wilkinson] would not turn them away if they could not pay.

[Coroner]— "At what time did you quit one another on Friday?"

[John Kelly]— "I cannot tell, but I think it would be about three or four in the afternoon."

[Coroner]— "What did she leave you for?"

[John Kelly]— "To go to Mile End."

[Coroner]— "What for?"

[John Kelly]— "To get a night's shelter in the casual ward."

"The doors of the casual ward are usually opened in winter at about five, and in summer about six o'clock, and at most of these places, some time before the appointed hour, the casuals will be seen collected at the door waiting for admission.

"Admitted within the doors, each applicant for relief is in turn questioned as to his name, his age, occupation, where he slept the previous night and where he

---

[487]   *Pall Mall Gazette*, 3rd October 1888.

is going on departure. The particulars are recorded, and any further questions bearing on the fact of destitution may, if the superintendent thinks fit, be asked. Next the casual undergoes the ordeal of a search, and any money or other property found upon him is taken away.

"*Articles other than money are restored to the casual on his departure; money may by order of the guardians be retained, but is in practice usually returned. If however the casual has as much as fourpence, admission is refused. When the search is completed the applicant is conducted to the bath. Here he strips, and his clothes are taken away to be 'baked' for the purpose of disinfecting them and destroying vermin. They are returned to him the following morning; in the meantime a clean night-shirt is given him.*"

[Coroner]— "When did you see her next morning?"

[John Kelly]— "About eight o'clock. I was surprised to see her so early . . ."

[Juryman]— "Is not eight o'clock a very early hour to be discharged from a casual ward?"

[John Kelly]— "I do not know."

[Juryman]— "There are some tasks - picking oakum - before you can be discharged."

[John Kelly]— "I know it was very early."

"*On each day of his detention (Sundays excepted) the casual, unless in case of illness, does a task of work, which consists, in the case of men, of picking not more than four pounds of unbeaten or eight pounds of beaten oakum, or breaking not more than 13 cwt.*[488] *of stones, while women usually pick two pounds of oakum, or else are employed in washing or scrubbing. The task of work is in no case an excessive one, and may usually be finished early in the afternoon, though the casual frequently dawdles over his work and makes it last on till five or six o'clock.*"

In 1871 The Pauper Inmates Discharge and Regulation Act (34 and 35 Vic., cap. 108) provided that— "a casual pauper, who is defined to be a destitute wayfarer or wanderer, applying for relief, should not be entitled to discharge himself before 11 o'clock on the morning following

---

[488]   One hundredweight [cwt.] = 112 pounds.

his admission, nor before performing the task of work prescribed for him"

The Casual Poor Act 1882 amended the 1871 Act, stating that— "A casual pauper shall not be entitled to discharge himself from a casual ward before nine o'clock in the morning of the second day following his admission."

If Eddowes had stayed at the Mile End Casual Ward on the night of Friday 28th September, she would not have been discharged until 9.00 am on Sunday 30th September, thus missing her appointment with fate in Mitre Square.

John Kelly had a ready explanation.

The Times, 5th October 1888, reported him telling the Coroner that— "there had been some bother at the casual ward, and that that was why she had been turned out so soon. He did not know the regulations of the casual ward at Mile-end, and whether she could discharge herself when she liked."

A week after Eddowes' funeral an apocryphal story appeared in the *East London Observer*, 13th October 1888—

"A reporter gleaned some curious information from the Casual Ward Superintendent of Mile End, regarding Kate Eddowes, the Mitre Square victim. She was formerly well-known in the casual wards there, but had disappeared for a considerable time until the Friday preceding her murder. Asking the woman where she had been in the interval, the superintendent was met with the reply that she had been in the country 'hopping.' 'But,' added the woman, 'I have come back to earn the reward offered for the apprehension of the Whitechapel murderer. I think I know him.

"'Mind he doesn't murder you too,' replied the superintendent jocularly.

"'Oh, no fear of that,' was the remark made by Kate Eddowes as she left.

"Within four-and-twenty hours afterward she was a mutilated corpse."

This was just so much moonshine. Compare and contrast this story to an alleged exchange between John Kelly and Eddowes, reported in the *Echo*, 3rd October 1888—

"I didn't want her to go that night, somehow. I was a bit afraid because of the Hanbury Street affair. However, she said she'd go, because she could get some help there, and the last words I said to her as she went out of the door were, 'Don't be late, Kate, because of the knife!'

"'What did that mean?' [asked the reporter].

"Well, that's how we talk about the man who's done all these murders, Sir. She turned round just before she went out and said, 'Don't you trouble, Jack; I won't be late, and I shall be all right.' Then she left the house, and I saw her next in the mortuary."

The *Star*, 3rd October 1888, reported a similar exchange—

"She told me she had made up her mind to go to her daughter's in Bermondsey. I begged her to be back early, for we had been talking about the Whitechapel murders, and I said I did not want to have that knife get at her. 'Don't you fear for me,' said she, 'I'll take care of myself, and I shan't fall into his hands.' With that she went out. I went with her to the street corner below, and I never laid eyes on her again till I saw her down at the mortuary last night."

Catherine Eddowes had no need to stay at the casual ward on Friday night. Not only had Kelly told her that their credit was good with Wilkinson, the lodging house deputy; she had also pawned Kelly's boots on the Friday night for 2/6d, providing more than sufficient money for their regular bed.

[John Kelly]— "I think it was on Saturday morning that we pawned the boots."

[Mr. Crawford]— "Is it not the fact that the pawning took place on the Friday night?"

[John Kelly]— "I do not know. It was either Friday night or Saturday morning. I am all muddled up."

The tickets were produced, and were dated the 28th, Friday.

An inquest juryman picked up on this discrepancy.

The Evening News, 4th October 1888, reporting him saying that "if the pawning took place on the Friday it rather upset the theory that the deceased had to go to the casual ward on the Friday night because they had not money for a lodging."

[Mr. Crawford]— "Seeing the date on the tickets, cannot you recollect when the pawning took place?"

[John Kelly]— "I cannot say, I am so muddled up. It was either Friday or Saturday."

[Coroner]— "Had you been drinking when the pawning took place?"

[John Kelly]— "Yes."

And there the whole matter was dropped, with nobody asking how, if John Kelly and Eddowes had been flat broke, he had been drinking before the pawning took place.

Star, 1st October 1888—

"The articles pledged at Jones's, the pawnbroker, in Church Street, have been taken away by Detective-Inspector McWilliam, who has charge of the case. The pawnbroker states that the articles must have been pledged by a woman, as it is against the rule to receive goods from a man pledged in a woman's name."

Here we encounter yet a further flaw in John Kelly's story—

If on Friday 28th September Catherine Eddowes set off at "about three or four in the afternoon" to reach the Mile End Casual Ward, how could she have pawned Kelly's boots in Church Street, Whitechapel, that same night?

Only a woman could have pawned John Kelly's boots. But the question remains as to whether it was Catherine Eddowes.

Mr. Crawford— "She pawned the boots, did she not?"

Kelly— "Yes; and I stood at the door in my bare feet."

This begs the question of whether Kelly attended the inquest barefoot or in the meantime had earned sufficient money to buy a replacement pair of boots.

Some modern theorists have suggested that the pawning actually took place on Saturday morning, and that the pawnbroker [a] mistakenly entered the wrong date or [b] back-dated the ticket by a day in order to earn more interest.

This idea does not work, for the simple reason that each pawn ticket carried a unique number. Tickets were issued in strict sequential order, with details of the transaction entered into the pawnbroker's Pledge Book. Also, by law, pawnbrokers charged fixed rates of interest. On redemption of the boots [at any time within one calendar month from the date of the pledge] Joseph Jones would have levied a penny in interest, plus a half-penny fee for the pawn ticket. Pawnbrokers made the most profit from short-term pledges so, even if possible, back-dating the pawn ticket by a single day would not have earned Joseph Jones any extra interest until after 28th October.

Also, had Kelly's boots fetched a good price if not redeemed, the pawnbroker would not have had the legal right to sell them until twelve months and seven days after the date of the pledge.

For anyone thinking that Joseph Jones of 31 Church Street may have been a shady character in the world of Whitechapel pawnbroking it is worth noting that between 1880 and 1889 he and his son made a number of expert witness appearances at the Old Bailey, one on 19th November 1888 together with Sergeant Patrick Enright [J Division] in a case of theft.

Joseph Jones was not summoned to appear at the inquest. This is interesting, for the pawnbroker appears to have been taken to the mortuary to identify the dead woman.

The Times, 2nd October 1888—

"The tickets had been made out in two names—Emily Birrell and Anne Kelly —and the articles had been pawned for 1s. and 6d. [sic] respectively with Mr. Jones, of Church-street, Spitalfields, who, however, cannot identify the woman as having made the pledges."

Catherine Eddowes' whereabouts on the night before her death are crucial to our understanding of the double-event; as is the question of who pawned the boots and how the pawn ticket later found its way into Eddowes' mustard tin.

The Times of 5th October 1888 reported John Kelly telling the inquest that he and Eddowes parted company in Houndsditch[489] at 2.00

---

[489]   Kelly told the *Echo*, 3rd October 1888, that he and Eddowes parted company at the Flower and Dean Street lodging house.

pm on Saturday afternoon. She was going to try to locate her daughter, Annie, in Bermondsey, "and get a little money from her, so that she need not walk the streets." Eddowes promised to be back by 4.00 pm and no later. She did not return.

We know from the later testimony of Eddowes' daughter, Annie Phillips, that the last time she had seen her mother was two years and one month earlier. She had lived in Bermondsey "about two years ago" but, on moving, her new address was purposely withheld from Eddowes to prevent her applying for money.

What Annie Phillips did not tell the inquest about was an incident reported in the *Daily News*, 4th October 1888—

"Last night Eliza Gold, or Frost, the sister [of the deceased], who lives at 6 Thrawl Street, Spitalfields, made the following statement . . . 'Her name was Catherine Eddowes . . . She had two or three children . . .'"

"'It's rather strange – one of them, the girl that's married [Annie Phillips] came to me last week and asked me if I had seen anything of her mother. She said it was a very long time since she had seen her; but it was a long time since I had, too, and I told her so.'"

John Kelly heard on Saturday that Eddowes had been locked up at Bishopsgate police station because of a "drop of drink."

Daily Telegraph, 5th October 1888—

Coroner— "Did you make any inquiry after her?"

John Kelly— "I heard she had been locked up at Bishopsgate Street on Saturday afternoon. An old woman who works in the lane[490] told me she saw her in the hands of the police."

Coroner— "Did you make any inquiry into the truth of this?"

John Kelly— "I made no further inquiries. I knew that she would be out on Sunday morning, being in the City."

Frederick Wilkinson, the lodging house deputy, told the inquest that when Kelly came in to pay for his single bed on Saturday night between 7.30 and 8.00 pm he told him he heard Eddowes had been locked up.

---

490   Possibly Petticoat Lane [Middlesex Street].

However, according to the inquest evidence of the City Police, Catherine Eddowes was not arrested until "about half-past 8 o'clock" . . . [and] "brought to Bishopsgate police station at 8.45 pm."

John Kelly also failed to make any enquiries about Eddowes after she had not returned on Sunday, Monday and Tuesday morning.

When interviewed in the *Star*, 3rd October 1888, his story had undergone a sea change—

"I was out in the market all day, but did no good. When she did not come home at night I didn't worry, for I thought her daughter might have asked her to stay over Sunday with her. So on Sunday morning I wandered round in the crowds that had been gathered by the talk about the two fresh murders. I stood and looked at the very spot where my poor old gal had laid with her body all cut to pieces and I never knew it. I never thought of her in connection with it, for I thought she was safe at her daughter's. Yesterday morning I began to be worried a bit, but I did not guess the truth until after I had come back from another bad day in the market. I came in here and asked for Kate, she had not been in. I sat down on that bench by the table and carelessly picked up a *Star* paper. I read down the page a bit, and my eye caught the name of Burrill.

"It looked familiar, but I didn't think where I had seen it until I came to the word 'pawn-ticket.' Then it came over me all at once. The tin box, the two pawn-tickets, the one for that flannel shirt, and the other for my boots. But could Kate have lost them? I read a little further. The woman had the letters 'T. C.' in India ink, on her arm. Man, you could have knocked me down with a feather. It was my Kate, and no other. I don't know how I braced up to go to the police, but I did. They took me down to see the body, and I knew it was her."

John Kelly made no mention of Eddowes being arrested for drunkenness.

Also, the story of the pawn ticket in the name of Birrell had appeared in the *Star* on Monday 1st October and that of the tattoo in the *Star* on Tuesday 2nd October. The two pieces of information did not appear conjointly. So the question arises of why he had not gone to the police a day earlier.

As we know that Eddowes did not visit her daughter, and was later arrested for drunkenness, also of interest is where and how she got the money.

John Kelly told the inquest he did not know that she ever went out for immoral purposes; he had never allowed her to do so. But he also said that Eddowes had gone to find her daughter to "get a little money from her, so that she need not walk the streets."

Coroner— "What do you mean by 'walking the streets?'"

John Kelly— "I mean that if we had no money to pay for our lodgings we would have to walk about all night."

City solicitor Henry Crawford— "You were asked before if she walked the streets, and you said she did not."

John Kelly replied— "Sometimes we were without money to pay for our lodging, and we were at the time I speak of."

Make of this remark what you will.

Inconsistencies also abounded in John Kelly's account of their hop-picking adventures in Kent, which lodging house deputy Frederick Williamson told the inquest began in late August/early September.

The Times, 5th October 1888—

"He believed the last time the deceased and Kelly slept together at the lodging house was five or six weeks ago; before they went hopping."

John Kelly told the inquest that he and Eddowes had just "returned from hopping at a place which he was understood to call Hunton," adding that it was about two miles from Coxheath in Kent.

Hunton was also two miles east of Yalding and six miles south-west of Maidstone.

Echo, 5th September 1888—

"Bad Luck For Hop-Pickers.

"The unfortunate people who have gone hop-picking this year seem to have had a decided poor time of it. Many who went to the gardens in hope are walking back in despair, having got nothing to do. One lad who, with three others, last week, walked to Maidstone informs us that he found the 'home-dwellers' were able to accomplish all the work there was to do, and his opinion is that Maidstone is the best place for hops this year; but outsiders could get nothing to do. He went to Yalding, and there discovered that, for the most part, the hops were not considered worth picking. After trying many quarters for work, he started to walk back to London, having earned nothing during his stay in the hop district. His experience seems to be that of a great many more."

John Kelly, *Star*, 3rd October 1888—

"We went hopping together mostly every year. We went down this year as usual. We didn't get on any too well, and started to hoof it home. We came along in company with another man and woman who had worked in the same fields, but who parted with us to go to Chatham when we turned off towards Maidstone. The woman said to Kate, 'I have got a pawn ticket for a flannel shirt. I wish you'd take it, since you're going up to town. It is only in for 9d., and it may fit your old man.' So Kate took it and we trudged along. It was in at Jones's, Church-street, in the name of Emily Burrell. She put the ticket back in our box and we moved on."

Eddowes accepting a pawn ticket for a flannel shirt which may or may not have fitted Kelly, and which, with interest and the pawn ticket fee, would have cost her 10½d to find out, does not make a great deal of sense, fiscal or otherwise.

Although allegedly broke, having turned off towards Maidstone Eddowes and Kelly stopped in town to make two purchases.

Kent and Sussex Courier, 12th October 1888—

"While in Maidstone Kelly purchased a pair of boots from Mr. Arthur Pash, of High Street, and the murdered woman bought a jacket at Mr. Edmett's pawnbroker's shop nearby. One of Mr. Edmett's assistants distinctly remembers selling the jacket to a woman answering the description of Eddowes. It was this garment that the woman wore at the time of her death,[491] and Kelly has identified it. A pawn-ticket for 2s. 6d. was also found in her possession, for the pair of boots which Kelly

---

[491]   When found, Eddowes was wearing a "Black cloth jacket trimmed around the collar and cuffs with imitation fur and around the pockets in black silk braid and fur. Large metal buttons."

bought at Mr. Pash's shop."[492]

"Steven's Directory of Maidstone, 1885"—

"Pash, Arthur, 'London Boot Stores,' boot and shoe manufacturer, 5 High Street Maidstone."

An article on the cost of living in the magazine "The Nineteenth Century," March 1888, lists the price of a pair of men's boots at 10s 6d [half a guinea].

Mr. Edmett's pawnbroking shop was in Rose Yard, accessed through a narrow alleyway situated immediately between his up-market outfitters and Arthur Pash's boot shop.

"1889 Maidstone Directory"—

"Edmett, G. & Co.'s Successors, hosiers, tailors & outfitters, 3&4 High Street, & pawnbrokers, 1&2 Rose Yard, High Street."

Having made their purchases, Eddowes and Kelly next walked the thirty-seven miles from Maidstone to London, spending the night of Thursday 27th October in the casual ward at Shoe Lane.[493]

In the *Echo*, 31st August 1888, a writer described a walk from Trafalgar Square to the hop fields of Kent—

"Taking the route by Gravesend and Chatham, *on the third day* I reached East Farleigh, about two miles from Maidstone."

Eddowes and Kelly made the walk from Maidstone to London along country lanes and unmetalled roads in a single day, with him wearing new boots and also not being in the best of health.

Evening News, 10th October 1888—

"Kelly is not a strong man, as he suffers from an affection of the kidneys and a bad cough. These ailments have prevented him from doing much hard work, and he has earned his living by doing odd jobs about

---

[492]   "When the hop-pickers were finally paid-off, they would go into the nearest town to buy new clothing, etc. Their discarded garments, boots and shoes would be left in the roadway outside the shops. About 50 years ago it was not unusual for three or four cartloads to be cleared away after a Saturday's shopping in Maidstone." J. W. Bridge, *Kent Hop Tokens* (Archaeologia Cantiana, Vol. LXVI) 1953.

[493]   In an interview with the *Star*, 3rd October 1888, Kelly omitted the Shoe Lane detail, saying "We did not have money enough to keep us going till we got to town, but we did get there and came straight to this house"— 55 Flower and Dean Street.

Spitalfields Market and running errands for the Jews."

Catherine Eddowes was buried on Monday 8th October 1888 in an unmarked grave at Manor Park Cemetery.

Lloyds Weekly Newspaper, 14th October 1888, reported that "Mr. G.C. Hawkes, a vestryman of St. Luke's, undertook the responsibility of carrying out the funeral at his own expense,[494] and the City authorities, to whom the burial ground belongs, remitted the usual fees." The newspaper also reported "a vast crowd following in procession. The funeral cortége consisted of a hearse, a mourning coach containing relatives and friends of the deceased, and a brougham conveying members of the press . . . The mourners were the four sisters of the murdered woman, Harriet Jones, Emma Eddowes, Eliza Gold and Elizabeth Fisher; her two nieces, Emma and Harriet Jones, and John Kelly, the man with whom she had lived."

Eddowes' daughter, Annie Phillips, who at the inquest "was dressed entirely in black, with much crepe on her hat" and who drew "many an inquiring glance,"[495] did not attend her mother's funeral.

Questioned about her father's pension by City Solicitor Henry Crawford, Annie Phillips said— "She was not sure that her father was a pensioner of the 18th Royal Irish. It might have been the Connaught Rangers."

Henry Crawford then told the inquest that there was a pensioner of the 18th Royal Irish named Conway, but he was not the Conway who was wanted.

Detective Sergeant John Mitchell [City Police] testified "that he had made every effort, acting under instructions, to find the father and the brothers of the last witness [Annie Phillips], but without success. He had found a pensioner named Thomas Conway belonging to the 18th Royal Irish, but he was not identified as the Thomas Conway in question."

The following witness, Detective Baxter Hunt [City Police], stated— "acting under instructions he had discovered the pensioner

---

[494] George Cornelius Hawkes, 41A Banner Street, St Luke's, London EC, also paid the funeral expenses of Elizabeth Stride.
[495] *Star*, 11th October 1888.

Conway belonging to the 18th Royal Irish. He had confronted the man with two of the deceased's sisters, who had failed to recognise him as the man who used to live with the deceased. [He] had made every effort to trace the Thomas Conway and the brothers referred to, but without result."

It is unclear whether the two City detectives were referring to the same or to different pensioners with the 18th Royal Irish, However, the latter confrontation must have taken place before 6th October, the day on which Annie Phillips was located[496] for, when questioned by a juryman, Detective Hunt said—"the reason the daughter had not seen the man Conway, whom [he] had traced, was that she had not at the time been discovered."

In his final summing up on 11th October the Coroner said— "There was nothing to suggest that either Conway or Kelly had anything to do with the murder, both of them seeming to be totally inoffensive men."

It was an interesting remark, for at this time Thomas Conway, late of the 18th Royal Irish, or possibly the Connaught Rangers, had yet to be located by the police and was an unknown quantity.

Thomas Conway finally spared the police the further bother of searching for him. He presented himself at Old Jewry on the afternoon of Monday 15th October, four days after the close of the inquest and one week after Catherine Eddowes' funeral.

The Times, 16th October 1888—

"The City Police have succeeded in discovering Thomas Conway, who some years ago lived with Catherine Eddowes, the woman murdered in Mitre Square. Up to yesterday the efforts of the detectives had been at fault, owing, as was suggested by the City Solicitor at the inquest, to the fact that Conway had drawn his pension from the 18th Royal Irish Regiment under a false name, that of Thomas Quinn . . ."

There is no record of the City Solicitor having suggested any such thing.

". . . Apparently he had not read the papers, for he was ignorant till

---

[496]   *Evening News*, 6th October 1888.

the last few days that he was being sought for. Then, however, he learned that the City detectives were inquiring for him, and yesterday afternoon he and his two sons went to the detective offices of the City Police in Old Jewry and explained who they were. Conway was at once taken to see Mrs. Annie Phillips, Eddowes' daughter, who recognized him as her father."

Born around 1837 in County Mayo, Ireland, Thomas Conway joined the 1st Battalion 18th Irish regiment in October 1857 as Private No. 350, spending just over two years in India before being invalided out due to serious illness. He was finally discharged from the army in October 1861.[497]

Throughout the nineteenth century invalidity pensions were granted either to soldiers suffering from a sickness or injury caused directly by their military service, or to men with a minimum of fourteen years' service discharged for medical reasons not attributable to the exigencies of their duty.

Pension rates for invalids incurred as a direct result of military service varied from 8d to 2s per day for privates and up to 3s per day for sergeants, contingent upon the nature and extent of their disability. Conway, having completed only just over two years' service, would have been at the lower end of the scale.

Pensions were paid by a 'Staff Officer of Pensioners'. Large cities such as Glasgow, Liverpool and Manchester had two. London had eleven. Men queued up at designated places to receive their pension, usually paid quarterly in advance.

Annie Phillips, aged 23, told the inquest under oath that her father was a pensioner who had drawn a pension only "since [she] was eight years old" [1873], twelve years after his discharge from the army.

Whatever the truth, how Thomas Conway managed to collect a pension in the name of Thomas Quinn is not known.

Thomas Conway died on 31st July 1908 [aged 71] at St Olave's

---

[497]   *The Victims of Jack the Ripper*, Neal Stubbings Shelden, Inklings Press 2007.

Workhouse, Bermondsey, from senility and dementia.[498]

Chief Inspector Donald Swanson agreed with the Coroner about John Kelly's innocence. In his 6th November 1888 report he wrote—

"[Eddowes] was living in adultery with a man named John Kelly, respecting whom enquiry was at once made by Metropolitan and City Police, the result of which was to show clearly that he was not the murderer."

The last word on Catherine Eddowes and John Kelly came from Major Henry Smith, Acting Commissioner of the City of London police at the time of the double-event, in an article for *Blackwoods Magazine*, May 1906—

"More About the Streets of London.

"Lieutenant-Colonel Sir Henry Smith, KCB.

"Ex-Commissioner City of London Police.

"The Ashford hop fields furnished the Whitechapel murder with one of his victims. The night of September 29, 1888, was a glorious one. It was light as day when shortly after midnight Catherine Eddowes left the police station in Bishopsgate, and not three-quarters of an hour afterwards was cut to pieces. This woman was the wife of a soldier, whom she left to drink heavily, and, that, as I afterwards discovered, was not her only failing. She and her 'husband' had made some money 'hopping,' and had got through it all in a week's time. On the afternoon of the 29th she pawned a pair of boots to get something for supper; but, instead of doing so, got drunk on the proceeds and was locked up—a typical case altogether of everyday life in the 'Far East.' When sober enough to take care of herself she was released, the 'reserve man' in charge of the cells advising her to go straight home and face the 'hiding' which she said she was sure to get from her 'old man.' His advice she did not follow, for instead of walking away northwards in the direction of 'Flower and Dean Street,' one of the very worst streets in that notorious locality, he noticed that she turned to the left, and to the left again up Houndsditch, which would lead her to Mitre Square, where she met her

---

[498]   Ibid.

fate, presumably in the endeavour to replace by other means the money she had squandered. A ghastly sight she was by the light of the harvest moon as she lay in the corner of the Square, and one not easily forgotten. Her 'husband'—bad as he was, he was good for her—I found fairly intelligent, and with a certain amount of confidence in and chivalrous feeling for the miserable being with whom he lived. God knows how his confidence was abused.

"'She drank a bit, sir,' he admitted, 'but I am sure she would never do anything wrong.'

"'I don't want, I assure you,' I said, 'at such a time to hurt your feelings, but what was she doing about Aldgate and Mitre Square at that hour?'

"'Well, sir, you see,' he replied, 'this is how it was: she had a daughter, very comfortable, living in Bermondsey; and whenever we were hard up she would go across to her, and she never came back without something.'

"This story I was disinclined to believe, seeing that he could not, or would not, tell me where the daughter lived; but after a great deal of trouble, having discovered the woman in question, I found she had not seen her mother for years. How the money was got when times were hard does not call for an explanation from me. That explanation 'the streets of London' will afford."[499]

---

[499] There was no harvest moon on the night of the double event, 30th September. In 1888 the closest full moon to the autumn equinox [22nd September] was on 19th September.

26. THE QUATUOR CORONATI

Evening News, Tuesday 9th October 1888—

"Detectives Reinforced from Dublin.

"The correspondent of the Irish Times states that a number of Irish constables have been withdrawn from Dublin for special duty in connection with the Whitechapel murders."

The 11th October 1888 edition of the *Irish Times* dismissed the Whitechapel angle—

"From London Correspondence.

"It has been denied that any officers of the Irish police have been sent here on a special mission, and Superintendent Mallon's presence in London is explained by the statement that he is on holiday.

"The contradiction, I am assured, is at once correct and inaccurate. It is not the case that any representative of the Irish police force has been sent here in connection with the Whitechapel tragedies, but it is the case that three members of the detective department are now in London in connection with the new international organisation, of which the Home Office has been for some weeks in receipt of private information, which has caused a communication with the Irish Executive. The result of this communication has been the despatch of three experts to London, where it is known the conspiracy proposes to establish one of its headquarters, with a branch in Dublin."

Whether this activity had anything to do with the Arthur Balfour assassination rumours doing the rounds, or perhaps Sir Alexander Paget's Viennese informer who alleged he was a leading member of the Internationalist Society, is unknown. What is certain, however, is that Superintendent John Mallon, Head of Detectives at Dublin Castle, was not in London on holiday.

Mallon had been subpoenaed to appear as a witness at the Special Commission, a task he refused because it would "destroy his influence with the army of informers he had at his beck and call." Following a lively exchange with Attorney General, Sir Richard Webster and Sir Henry James, both representing *The Times*, and Sir David Harrel, Chief Commissioner of Police in Dublin, John Mallon returned to Dublin.[500]

Catherine Eddowes and Elizabeth Stride were soon forgotten amidst interest in the standing-room-only Special Commission. For the press it was back to business as usual, and aside from stories about mostly foreigners being arrested on suspicion of the Whitechapel murders and then released without charge newspaper readers might have been forgiven for believing the whole thing had been little but a bad dream.

On 23rd October 1888, the day after the opening of the Special Commission, Elizabeth Stride's inquest closed with a verdict of "Wilful murder against some person or persons unknown."

A few days later a lengthy article written by Sir Charles Warren appeared in *Murray's Magazine*, a monthly publication priced at a shilling. Containing a wide range of conservative-minded articles on social, political and cultural topics plus literary criticism and reviews, it was squarely aimed at the educated middle class. A shilling [twelve pennies] was a lot of money for the not-so-well-educated, and so on 25th October 1888 the halfpenny *Star* newspaper, unable to resist an opportunity to take a swipe at the Commissioner of Police, published— ". . . a large number of extracts from Sir Charles Warren's article on 'The Police of the Metropolis' in the November number of *Murray's Magazine*."

---

[500]   For a full account of this meeting see: Irish Conspiracies: Recollections of John Mallon (the great Irish detective) and other Reminiscences, Frederick Moir Bussy, 1910.

Sir Charles Warren rebutted the idea of the police as a military force whilst condemning successive governments for failing to tackle the sinister influences of the political mob. It was an admixture of police history, statistics and duties, all wrapped up in an naive wish that if the population of London would only behave itself the job of the police would become that much easier—

"There are over 12,000 police in London . . . and it is probable that these might readily be reduced to 10,000 if the inhabitants would do their duty as citizens and uphold the law."

The *Star* was merciless—

"A more extraordinary document never found its way into print; and, on the other hand, a more complete vindication of everything that has been said in these columns about Sir Charles Warren's management of the force, it would be impossible to imagine. It would be charitable to suppose that when he penned this remarkable addition to the literature of Colney Hatch [asylum], Sir Charles Warren was laboring under some unusual excitement. But that, unfortunately, is impossible . . . It is bad enough to have one amateur maniac at large, but we begin to lose touch of solid ground when we find Scotland Yard in possession of the victim of an equally dangerous and uncomfortable form of hallucination."

Warren dismissed the CID as "a drop in the ocean for all the myriads of common-place offences which might develop readily into serious crime if not looked after by the uniform police and by citizens," making no reference to his failure to elucidate the Whitechapel murders. This was probably just as well, for just under two weeks later on 9th November 1888 in Millers Court, Dorset Street, Spitalfields, "Jack the Ripper" claimed his fifth and final victim, Mary Jane Kelly.

It is generally agreed that Sir Charles Warren did not resign because of this fifth and final Jack the Ripper murder. Rather, he resigned on the previous day, 8th November, as a result of his unauthorised article in *Murray's Magazine*.

This idea has little merit.

In a letter to Henry Matthews dated 8th November 1888 Sir Charles

Warren argued that he was not aware he was constrained by an 1879 Home Office rule which forbade police officers from publishing without permission works which related to their duties.

He wrote—

"I desire to say that I entirely decline to accept these instructions with regard to the Commissioner of Police, and I have again to place my resignation in the hands of Her Majesty's Government."

Sir Charles Warren was throwing down the gauntlet. Henry Matthews could either accept that he was unaware of a Home Office ruling with which he disagreed, or he could take a stand and demand his resignation.

Henry Matthews made his decision, and during a debate on the evening of the same day he told the House of Commons—

"In 1879 the then Home Secretary issued a Rule by which officers attached to the Department were precluded from publishing works relating to the Department without permission, and a copy was sent to the then Commissioner of Police. The present Commissioner, however, informs me that he was not aware of the existence of this Rule. I have accordingly drawn his attention to it, and have requested him to comply with it in future."

"... and have requested him to comply with it in future."

The *Echo*, 9th November 1888—

"Mr. Matthews, last night, announced that he had rapped Sir Charles Warren's knuckles."

Thus on the morning of the Millers Court murder there was no hint of Sir Charles Warren's resignation.

Charles Augustus Vansittart Conybeare [Liberal, Camborne, Cornwall] [501], House of Commons, 9th November 1888, asked the Home Secretary—

"Whether he has seen by the evening papers that another terrible murder has been committed . . . and whether he does not think it is time to replace Sir Charles Warren by some other officer who will investigate

---

[501]   Charles Conybeare was imprisoned in 1889 under the Irish Coercion Act.

these crimes?"

"Order, order!" cried the Speaker of the House. "The honourable Member must give notice in writing [of the question] at the Table in the ordinary way."

Hansard reported Robert Gent-Davis [Conservative, Lambeth, Kennington][502] as stating—

"At the request of the Home Secretary, he would postpone until Monday asking a question and initiating a discussion on the retirement of Mr. Monro from the office of Assistant Commissioner of Police."

The weekend passed.

Charles Conybeare, House of Commons, 12th November 1888, "wished to know whether it was true, as reported in the newspapers that afternoon, that Sir Charles Warren had tendered his resignation, and that it had been accepted?"

Home Secretary Henry Matthews neatly back-dated the event to Warren's letter of 8th November. —

". . . With regard to the final question of the honourable Member, I have to say that Sir Charles Warren did, on the 8th instant, tender his resignation to Her Majesty's Government, and that it has been accepted."

Since the 1976 publication of Stephen Knight's "Jack the Ripper: The Final Solution" there has been much Ripperological interest in the Whitechapel murders possibly having been a Masonic conspiracy. The focus of this interest has been Sir Charles Warren who, in January 1886 [six weeks before his appointment as Commissioner of the Metropolitan Police], was installed as the first Worshipful Master of the Quatuor Coronati [The Four Crowned Ones (or Martyrs)] Lodge, which took its name from a 14th Century Masonic document, the Regius Poem.[503]

Whilst most students of the subject [myself included] reject the idea of a Masonic conspiracy, there is no getting away from the fact that

---

[502] In late November 1888 Robert Gent-Davis was sent to prison for contempt of court when he failed to pay into Court a large sum of money in trust which he had appropriated for his own use.

[503] Also known as the Halliwell MS, the Regius Poem contains the legend of the Four Crowned Martyrs beheaded by the Roman emperor Diocletian.

November 9th is the Feast Day of the Quatuor Coronati, a red-letter day on the Masonic calendar; but of more significance is that this date was also Lord Mayor's Day, [504] on which the City of London hosts "The Presentation of the Lord Mayor at The Royal Courts of Justice" with a colourful pageant through the streets of London.

The generally accepted Mary Jane Kelly murder scenario can be written on the back of a napkin—

A twenty-five-year-old girl estranged from her live-in paramour gets down on her luck and resorts to her previous life as a prostitute. One night, desperate for money, she ventures out onto the Whitechapel streets and meets Jack the Ripper. Next morning her mutilated body is discovered in her squalid Spitalfields room.

Aside from her age and the fact that she had her own room, her immediate circumstances on the morning of her murder were identical to those of Polly Nichols, Annie Chapman and Catherine Eddowes.

The scene of the murder was Millers Court—six tiny houses accessed via a narrow arched entrance between numbers 26 and 27 Dorset Street, Spitalfields, dubbed in 1901 by the *Daily Mail* as "the worst street in London."

Daily Mail journalist Frederick Arthur McKenzie wrote—

"Here we have a place which boasts of an attempt at murder on an average once a month, of a murder in every house, and one house at least, a murder in every room. Policemen go down it as rule in pairs. Hunger walks prowling in its alleyways, and the criminals of to-morrow are being bred there to-day... The lodging-houses of Dorset Street and of the district around are the head centres of the shifting criminal population of London. Of course, the aristocrats of crime — the forger, the counterfeiter, and the like do not come here. In Dorset Street we find more largely the common thief, the pickpocket, the area meak, the man who robs with violence, and the unconvicted murderer. The police have a theory, it seems, that it is better to let these people congregate together in one mass where they can be easily be found than to scatter

---

[504] Lord Mayor's Day was held on 9th November from 1751 to 1959.

them abroad. And Dorset Street certainly serves the purpose of a police trap."

"The worst street in London" was not a newly-won appellation. In 1898 Inspector W. Miller of E Division [Holborn] talked to philanthropist and social researcher Charles Booth about his time on J Division [Bethnal Green] from 1891 to 1895—

"As to prostitution Bethnal Green was remembered for its absence. There was nothing like the degradation of the Whitechapel and Spitalfields area in this respect. The lowest of all prostitutes are found in Spitalfields, on the benches, around the church, sleeping in the common lodging houses of Dorset Street. Women have often found their way there by degree from the streets of the West End. Dorset Street is in his opinion the worst street in respect of poverty, misery, vice - in the whole of London - a cesspool into which had sunk the foulest and most degraded. Dorset Street might be stirred but its filth would always sink again on the same spot."

Whitechapel Board of Works Annual Report, Summer Quarter 1878—

"[Millers] court contains six houses, and is about 50 feet long, 5 feet 6 inches wide at the north end, and 7 feet 10 inches wide at the south end, and is approached by a covered entrance 26 feet 4 inches long and 2 feet 10 inches wide. At the north [far] end of the court there are three public privies, and at the south end there is a public dust-bin [trash can] . . ."

The houses in Millers Court—one room up, one room down—were occupied by two or more families. The rooms measured 12 x 12 x 8ft and were designated as Nos. 1-12.

The murder took place in Room 13, attached to the rear of 26 Dorset Street. Originally a scullery or out-house with its own entrance, it had been partitioned off from the main body of the house to form a 12ft by 10ft living space furnished with a double bed, a chair and two tables at a weekly rent of 4s 6d., something of a bargain at twopence less per week than a double bed in a common lodging house.

The murder was discovered at 10.45 am by Thomas Bowyer, sent by his employer, landlord John McCarthy, to collect the rent for Room

13 which was 29 shillings [amounts vary] in arrears. Bowyer knocked, received no answer, peered through a broken window, glimpsed the horror within, informed his employer, and together [accounts vary] reported their findings to Inspector Beck at Commercial Street police station.

The Times, 7th November 1888—

"On Friday, from the hour of 10 a.m. until the Lord Mayor's Procession has returned to the Guildhall, and for such longer period as may be found necessary, the following streets and approaches thereto will be closed to all wheeled traffic . . ."

The Times and the *Daily Telegraph* reported that sixty streets would be closed in central London, including Victoria Embankment, Fleet Street, Scotland Yard and parts of the Strand.

From 10.00 am until mid-afternoon the East End was virtually inaccessible by wheeled traffic from the West End, Whitehall or Fleet Street.

It is worth pausing here to recall that the last "Jack the Ripper" murders had taken place at the end of September. Memories were short. By early November people were not perched on the edge of their seats in anticipation of an encore.

Nevertheless, without any effort to first investigate the facts of what Bowyer had glimpsed through a broken window, Inspector Beck, Sergeant Betham and "forty constables who had been held in readiness in anticipation of a possible Socialist disturbance attending the Lord Mayor's Show, at once proceeded to the scene of the murder, running to the house as quickly as they could. By this time the news had spread so rapidly that over a thousand persons were gathered in the street, and these were rapidly cleared away from the court and the side of Dorset street adjoining immediately while the Inspector made his way into Millers Court."[505]

Star, 9th November 1888—

"Cordons of police are drawn up at all the entrances to Dorset-

---

[505]   *Daily News*, 9th November 1888.

street, and no one is allowed to enter it. A *Star* man went to Commercial Street police station to learn some further particulars, but was politely but firmly referred to Scotland Yard . . . there seems little doubt that the murderer is the man who has given Whitechapel a regular succession of horrors."

The door to Room 13 was locked and the key missing. At 11.15 am Doctor George Bagster Phillips arrived, and looking "through the lower of the broken panes" satisfied himself "that the mutilated corpse lying on the bed was not in need of any immediate attention from me."

Local news stringers quickly arrived on the scene.

The *Daily News*, 9th November 1888—

"Medical assistance was immediately summoned, and a description of the discovery telegraphed to all the metropolitan police stations in the terse sentence: 'The woman is simply cut to pieces.' Within a very short time half a dozen cabs arrived in Dorset Street from Whitehall, conveying detectives from the Criminal Investigation Department, among them Inspectors Abberline and Reid . . ."

Inspector Abberline told the inquest—

"I arrived at Millers Court about 11.30 on Friday morning."

The *Daily News* continued—

". . . Never before had so many men been dispatched to the scene of a murder from Whitehall . . . and quite a small army of plain clothes constables was located in Dorset Street within an astonishingly short space of time."

Inspector Reid was H Division's Local Inspector CID, so it is unlikely he had arrived from Scotland Yard. Also, because of the Lord Mayor's Day road closures, it would have been impossible for Inspector Abberline and his fellow detectives to have arrived from Scotland Yard so speedily.

On 14th November 1888 Arthur Brisbane, the New York *Sun's* *London* correspondent, went to Scotland Yard.

New York *Sun*, 26th November 1888—

"Notes from Whitechapel.

"London, November 14th—Though extremely busy, Dr. Anderson,

the head for the hour of the Metropolitan Police, has been kind enough, on knowing that I was a representative of the Sun, to give me a few minutes of his just now priceless time."

The *Sun* reporter actually wanted an interview with Superintendent Arnold, to see what measures had been taken to secure the arrest of the Whitechapel murderer, but Robert Anderson was keen to keep Arnold at arm's length.

"He told me that he would rather that I should not see Mr. Arnold, as it was almost impossible to realize the amount of work he had on hand just now, but that he would himself answer as best he could to my inquiries."

Anderson told Arthur Brisbane that no stone was being left unturned in the Whitechapel murders investigation.

"To give you an instance of the care we have taken not to neglect any source of information, we have a special staff which does nothing but read the thousands of letters which are reaching us from all parts with the certain clue to the murderer or the positively only way to outwit him."

Robert Anderson was next asked why the bloodhounds had not been employed.

Anderson replied—

"At 11 o'clock the last murder was discovered, and we knew of it here in Scotland Yard a few minutes later. The officer who had wired us the event asked us also to send the bloodhounds. I personally object to the service of these animals in a thickly populated city like this, though I believe it would be extremely valuable in the case of a rural murder. However, as Superintendent Arnold was just then with me, I asked him what he thought, and he begged me not to send the hounds: that it would only lead to mischief."

The Times, 10th November 1888—

"Inspector Beck, H Division, who was in charge of the station at the time, accompanied Bowyer back [to Millers Court], and on finding that a murder had been committed, at once sent for assistance. Dr. Phillips, the divisional surgeon of police, and Superintendent Arnold were also sent for . . . On the arrival of Superintendent Arnold he caused a telegram to be sent direct to Sir Charles Warren informing him what had happened."

This is interesting, as news of the murder was not received by Sir Charles Warren at Scotland Yard until an hour-and-a-half later in a telegram sent on the orders of Superintendent Arnold.

Memo from Sir Charles Warren to Godfrey Lushington, Permanent Under-Secretary at the Home Office—

"Mutilated dead body of woman reported to be found this morning inside room of house in Dorset Street, Spitalfields. Information just received (12.30) 9.11.88"[506]

Warren immediately informed Charles Beilby Stuart-Wortley, Parliamentary Under Secretary of State at the Home Office, repeating the scant information sent to Lushington and further advising him that— "The matter has been placed in the hands of Mr. Anderson, Assistant Commissioner."[507]

From 11.30 am the police in Millers Court kicked their heels for two hours.

Inspector Abberline told the inquest— "I had an intimation from Inspector Beck that the bloodhounds had been sent for, and the reply had been received that they were on the way. Dr. Phillips was unwilling to force the door, as it would be very much better to test the dogs, if they were coming."

According to Robert Anderson, Arnold, having miraculously arrived at Scotland Yard just after the telegram he had ordered arrived from Whitechapel, had "begged me not to send the hounds: that it would only lead to mischief." With many of the central London streets closed from 10.00 am for the Lord Mayor's parade, how Arnold reached Scotland Yard by just after 11 o'clock, had a conversation with Anderson and returned to Millers Court by 1.30 pm is anyone's guess.

Inspector Frederick George Abberline—

---

[506] HO144/221/A49301F f3.
[507] Ibid. ff 4 & 5.

"We remained until about 1.30 pm, when Superintendent Arnold arrived, and he informed me that the order in regard to the dogs had been countermanded, and he gave orders for the door to be forced."

Somebody was not telling the truth.

Regarding the bloodhounds—

Daily Telegraph, 13th November 1888—

"About a fortnight ago this gentleman received a telegram from Leman Street Police station, asking him to bring the dog to assist in discovering the perpetrators of a burglary in Commercial-street. The police then admitted that subsequently to the burglary they had been all over the premises, and Mr. Taunton pointed out to them that it was absurd to expect that the bloodhounds could accomplish anything under such conditions . . . The owner of the dogs, on learning these facts, telegraphed peremptorily insisting that Barnaby should be returned to him at once . . .

"From these circumstances it will be seen that there has been no trained bloodhound in the metropolis at any time during the past fortnight."

Superintendent Arnold had been begging Anderson not to send non-existent dogs to Millers Court.

Landlord John McCarthy had a different take on the story. He told Central News—"The Inspector [Abberline] waited a little while, and then sent a telegram to Sir Charles Warren to bring the bloodhounds, so as to trace the murderer, if possible."[508]

The Times, 10th November 1888—

"Mr. Arnold, having [returned at 1.30 pm] satisfied himself that the woman was dead, ordered one of the windows to be entirely removed. A horrible and sickening sight then presented itself . . . [Whilst the body was being examined] a photographer, who, in the meantime, had been sent for, arrived and took photographs of the body, the organs, the room, and its contents. Superintendent Arnold then had the door of the room forced."

---

508   *Western Mail; The Times*, 10th November 1888.

If *The Times'* story is accurate, it begs the question of why the door had to be forced when police and doctors already had access to the room.

Having been alerted to the murder by Sir Charles Warren at around 12.30 pm, Robert Anderson, Assistant Commissioner [CID], drove "up in a cab at around ten minutes to two, and he remained for some time."[509]

He, too, made good time from Scotland Yard.

"The Gospel and its Ministry," Robert Anderson, [originally published 1876, updated and reprinted 1893]—

"The sight of a room thus [blood] stained will not easily fade from my memory. It was the scene of the last and most fiendish of the crimes known as the "Whitechapel murders" in London. Blood was on the furniture, blood was on the floor, blood was on the walls, blood was everywhere. Did this speak to me of life? Yes, but of life gone, of life destroyed, and, therefore, of that which is the very antithesis of life. Every bloodstain in that horrid room spoke of death."

Robert Anderson did not stay very long in Millers Court. He left to seek out the nearest telephone, as borne out by a memo from Ernie Sacheverell Wilberforce Johnson [Private Secretary to Mr. Charles Beilby Stuart-Wortley], 9th November 1888—

"Dear Mr. Wortley,

"Anderson says through the telephone that the murder was committed at Spitalfields which is in the Metropolitan Police district. It is believed that the murdered woman is a prostitute named Kelly. The Police Surgeon was while Anderson spoke still examining the body."[510]

Also in Millers Court was Dr. Frederick Gordon Brown, who performed the post-mortem on "Jack the Ripper" victim Catherine Eddowes.

Scotland Yard was being kept informed of events—

"Body is believed to be that of a prostitute [next words scribbled out]. Much mutilated. Dr. Bond is at present engaged in making his examination – but his report has not yet been received. Full report

---

[509]   *Daily Telegraph*, 10th November 1888
[510]   HO 144/221/A49301C ff 78 & 79.

cannot be furnished until medical officers have completed enquiry."[511]

For the eight months prior to 30th October 1888 the tenants of Room 13 had been 30-year-old Joseph Barnett, a Billingsgate fish porter, and his 25-year-old common-law inamorata Mary Jane Kelly, born Limerick, Ireland, who enjoyed the pretension of styling herself Marie Jeanette Kelly.

Barnett told the inquest— "I separated from her on Oct. 30 . . . Because she had a woman of bad character there, whom she took in out of compassion, and I objected to it. That was the only reason. I left her on the Tuesday between five and six pm."

Landlord, John McCarthy, confirmed the incident— "A short time ago they had a row and the windows were broken."

At the inquest Inspector Abberline added— "An impression has gone abroad that the murderer took away the key of the room. Barnett informs me that it has been missing some time, and since it has been lost they have put their hand through the broken window, and moved back the catch. It is quite easy."

Here was even less reason to break down the door. Serendipitously the window got broken before the key went missing. Had it been the other way around Barnett would have had to deliberately break the window in order to gain access to the room.

On the day of the inquest the *Star* was able to report that "The key of the woman's door has been found, so her murderer did not carry it away with him, as was at first supposed."

Another doctor summoned to Millers Court that afternoon was Dr. John Rees Gabe of Mecklenburgh Square. He was Surgeon to the S.P.C.C., the Society for the Prevention of Cruelty to Children.[512]

What might a pediatrician have been doing in Millers Court?

In an interview with the *Star*, 10th November 1888, Joseph Barnett reportedly said—

"Kelly had a little boy, aged about six or seven years, living with her."

---

[511]   HO 144/221/A49301F f2.
[512]   Located at 7 Harpur Street, Bloomsbury, London.

He was neither asked nor made any mention of this in his 12th November inquest testimony.

Reynolds News, 11th November 1888—

"Further inquiries show that Kelly had no son. The boy who lived with her belonged to a woman with whom she was very friendly, and who stayed with her on several occasions. It is stated that it was the presence of this woman which caused the quarrel between Kelly and the man Barnett, with who she had until recently lived." She had been in the house when Joe Barnett called, and amongst some dirty laundry she left with Kelly was a little boy's shirt.

The *Illustrated Police News*, 17th November 1888, ran a piece which had previously appeared in *The Times* seven days earlier. This suggests it was an agency story—

"Another account says that she had a little boy, aged about six or seven years, living with her, and latterly she had been in narrow straits, so much so that she is reported to have stated to a companion that she would make away with herself, as she could not bear to see her boy starving . . . Soon after they [Kelly and the companion] parted a man who is described as respectably dressed came up and spoke to the murdered woman Kelly, and offered her some money. The man then accompanied the woman home to her lodgings, and the little boy was removed from the room and taken to a neighbour's house. Nothing more was seen of the woman until Friday morning, when, it is stated, the little boy was sent back into the house, and subsequently dispatched on an errand by the man who was in the house with his mother."

The *Galveston Daily News*, 11th December 1888, reported that—

"The little boy was removed from the room and taken to a neighbour's house. The little boy has been found and corroborates this, but says he cannot remember the man's face."

Stories about a young boy living in Mary Kelly's room were many and varied, but although the generally accepted version of her murder precludes the presence of a child there appears to be little doubt that he was the reason for the presence of Dr. John Rees Gabe.

Illustrated Police News, 17th November 1888—

"Dr. J. R. Gabe, of Mecklenburgh Square, saw the body, but, in reply to a question put to him, he declined to give any details. He merely said that he had never, in all his life, seen such a horrible sight as the murdered woman presents."

"It must have been the work of a full half hour," he told a reporter from the *New York Herald* on 9th November 1888.

There was also confusion about the time of Mary Kelly's death.

Dr. Thomas Bond, 10th November 1888 police report——[513]

"In the Dorset Street case the body was lying on the bed at the time of my visit, 2 o'clock, quite naked and mutilated as in the annexed report.

"Rigor Mortis had set in, but increased during the progress of the examination. From this it is difficult to say with any degree of certainty the exact time that had elapsed since death as the period varies from 6 to 12 hours before rigidity sets in. The body was comparatively cold at 2 o'clock and the remains of a recently taken meal were found in the stomach and scattered about over the intestines. It is, therefore, pretty certain that the woman must have been dead about 12 hours and the partly digested food would indicate: that death took place about 3 or 4 hours after the food was taken, so one or two o'clock in the morning would be the probable time of the murder."

Dr. Bond's findings were not introduced at the inquest. Aside from a witness testifying to having heard a cry of "oh, murder" between 3.30 and 3.45 am and another to having heard a scream and a cry of "murder" at around 4.00 am [times vary in both accounts], no attempt was made to establish Kelly's time of death, one of the four fundamental requirements of an inquest—identity of deceased, place of death, time of death and manner of death.

This was understandable, for inquest witness Caroline Maxwell threw the whole matter into disarray.

Coroner Macdonald warned her— "You must be very careful about your evidence, because it is different to other people's. You say you saw her [Mary Kelly] standing at the corner of the entry to the court?"

---

[513]   HO 144/221/A49301C ff 220 – 223.

"Yes," replied Mrs Maxwell, "on Friday morning, from eight to half-past eight. I fix the time by my husband's finishing work. When I came out of the lodging-house she was opposite."

Caroline Maxwell had spoken to Mary Kelly on the morning of Friday 9th November, six hours after Dr. Bond determined she had died.

Many students of the subject believe that Mrs Maxwell got the day wrong, but this is unlikely, for she had first given a statement the police on 9th November, the day of the murder.

"Statement of Caroline Maxwell, 14 Dorset Street Spitalfields, the wife of Henry Maxwell, a lodging house deputy. I have known deceased woman during the past 4 ['or 5' — deleted] months, she was known as Mary Jane and that since Joe Barnett left her she has obtained her living as an unfortunate. I was on speaking terms with her although I had not seen her for 3 weeks until Friday morning 9th [a marginal note reads 'at about half past 8 o'clock.'] instant, she was then standing at the corner of Millers Court in Dorset Street."

There was more.

"I then passed on, and went to Bishopsgate on an errand [to buy milk], and returned to Dorset Street about 9 am. I then noticed deceased standing outside Ringers[514] public house, she was talking to a man, age I think about 30, height about 5 ft 5 in, stout, dressed as a Market Porter, I was some distance away and am doubtful whether I could identify him. The deceased wore a dark dress black velvet body, and coloured wrapper round her neck" [author's brackets].

Although the Bishopsgate shopkeeper confirmed Mrs. Maxwell's purchase of milk on that particular morning, Kelly's landlord and Dr. Phillips dismissed her sighting of Mary Kelly.

The Times, 12th November 1888—

"It is the opinion of Mr. McCarthy, the landlord of 26 Dorset Street, that the woman was murdered at a much earlier hour than 8 o'clock, and that Mrs. Maxwell and the other person must have been mistaken."

---

[514]   The Britannia public house was on the corner of Commercial Street and Dorset Street. The publican's name was Matilda Ringer.

And the professional opinion—

"Against these statements is the opinion of Dr. George Bagster Phillips, the divisional surgeon of the H Division, that when he was called to the deceased (at a quarter to 11) she had been dead some five or six hours."

This suggests that Mary Kelly's death took place somewhere between 4.45 and 5.55 am, three or four hours after Dr. Bond's estimation.

However, there is a misleading discrepancy in *The Times'* reporting of Dr. Phillips, who testified at the inquest that he arrived at Millers Court at 11.15 am.

"Having ascertained that probably it was advisable that no entrance should be made into the room at that time, I remained until about 1.30 pm, when the door was broken open by McCarthy.

"On the door being opened it knocked against a table which was close to the left-hand side of the bedstead, and the bedstead was close against the wooden partition. The mutilated remains of a woman were lying two-thirds over, towards the edge of the bedstead, nearest the door. Deceased had only an under-linen garment upon her, and by subsequent examination I am sure the body had been removed, after the injury which caused death, from that side of the bedstead which was nearest to the wooden partition previously mentioned. The large quantity of blood under the bedstead, the saturated condition of the palliasse, pillow, and sheet at the top corner of the bedstead nearest to the partition leads me to the conclusion that the severance of the right carotid artery, which was the immediate cause of death, was inflicted while the deceased was lying at the right side of the bedstead and her head and neck in the top right-hand corner."

Thus, by his own admission, Dr. Phillips could not have examined the body in Room 13 until 1.30 pm,[515] and so, if, as he said, "she had been dead some five or six hours" at the time of his examination this put the time of death somewhere between 7.30 and 8.30 am, six or seven

---

[515] Inspector Beck testified that Dr. Phillips was the first to enter the room.

hours after Dr. Bond's estimation.

"The other person" mentioned by landlord John McCarthy as having seen Kelly at an early hour on the morning of 9th November was Maurice Lewis, a tailor living in Dorset Street.

The *Star*, 10th November 1888—

"A tailor named Lewis says he saw Kelly come out [of Millers Court] about eight o'clock yesterday morning and go back."

Other newspaper reports state that Lewis saw her in the Horn of Plenty[516] pub between 10.00 and 11.00 pm, 8th November 1888, drinking with some women. One he recognised as 'Julia' [possibly Julia Venturney, a 47-year-old charwoman, resident at No. 1 Millers Court] and a man named 'Dan'.[517] Lewis said Kelly left with a respectably dressed man.

At 10.00 am the following morning, Lewis claimed to have seen Mary Kelly drinking with some people in The Britannia, but was uncertain if a man was with them.

Caroline Maxwell told the inquest—

"Returning [from buying milk] I saw her outside the Britannia public-house, talking to a man."

Coroner— "This would be about what time?"

"Between eight and nine o'clock. I was absent about half-an-hour. It was about a quarter to nine."

Coroner— "What description can you give of this man?"

"I could not give you any, as they were at some distance."

Inspector Abberline— "The distance is about sixteen yards."

"I am sure it was the deceased. I am willing to swear it."

Coroner—"You are sworn now. Was he a tall man?"

"No. He was a little taller than me and stout."

Inspector Abberline— "On consideration I should say the distance was twenty-five yards."

Coroner— "What clothes had the man?"

---

[516] Corner of Dorset Street and Crispin Street.

[517] Joseph Barnett told the *Star*, 10th November 1888 that his brother [Daniel] had met her on the Thursday evening.

"Dark clothes; he seemed to have a plaid coat on. I could not say what sort of hat he had.

Coroner— "What sort of dress had the deceased?"

"A dark skirt, a velvet body, a maroon shawl, and no hat."

The *Herts and Cambs Reporter and Royston Crow*, 16th November 1888, named the man as Joseph Barnet.

Mrs Caroline Maxwell was unwavering in her testimony.

It should have been possible for the Coroner to quickly settle the matter: that the victim identified as Mary Jane Kelly had died prior to the time Mrs. Maxwell claimed to have seen here. But no medical evidence was introduced in support of this argument and the subject was dropped.

As to the identification of the victim, the face had been so slashed and hacked that it was barely recognisable as that of a human being.

Joseph Barnett made the identification. He told the inquest—

"I have lived with the deceased one year and eight months. Her name was Marie Jeanette Kelly with the French spelling as described to me. Kelly was her maiden name. I have seen the body, and I identify it by the ear and eyes, which are all that I can recognise; but I am positive it is the same woman I knew."

What Barnett did not tell the inquest were the unsatisfactory circumstances of his identification—

The *Star*, 10th November 1888, reported Barnett as saying that he "had been taken by the police down to Dorset Street, and had been kept there for two hours and a half. He saw the body by peeping through the window."

Another person identified Kelly. In an untimed and undated report by Superintendent Arnold[518] he wrote—

"I have just received information that Mrs Smith[519], wife of the Superintendent of the Wash houses in Castle Alley, has identified deceased as a person who occasionally attended the wash houses for the

---

[518]   HO144/221/A49301 I

[519]   Sarah Frances Smith, wife of the Bath House attendant Richard Smith, gave inquest testimony at the Alice McKenzie murder.

purpose of washing her clothing and was known by the name of Kelly, but whether that is her right name, or where she has resided, or any of her associates, nothing is yet known."

The Coroner closed the inquest by addressing the jury—

"The question is whether you will adjourn for further evidence. My own opinion is that it is very unnecessary for two courts to deal with these cases, and go through the same evidence time after time, which only causes expense and trouble. If the coroner's jury can come to a decision as to the cause of death, then that is all that they have to do . . . I do not want to take it out of your hands. It is for you to say whether at an adjournment you will hear minutiae of the evidence, or whether you will think it is a matter to be dealt with in the police-courts later on, and that, this woman having met with her death by the carotid artery having been cut, you will be satisfied to return a verdict to that effect . . . It is for you to say whether you will close the inquiry to-day; if not, we shall adjourn for a week or fortnight, to hear the evidence that you may desire."

The Foreman considered that the jury had quite sufficient evidence before them upon which to give a verdict.

Coroner— "And what is the verdict?"

"Wilful murder against some person or persons unknown."

St. James Gazette, 13th November 1888—

"Some surprise was created among those present at the inquest in the Shoreditch Town Hall by the abrupt termination of the inquiry, as it was well known that further evidence was available.

"The coroner himself distinctly told the jury that he was only going to take the preliminary portion of Dr. G.R. Phillips' evidence, the remainder of which would be more fully given at the adjourned inquiry. No question was put to Dr. Phillips as to the mutilated portions of the body, and the coroner did not think fit to ask the doctor whether any portions of the body were missing . . .

"The examination of the body by Dr. Phillips on Saturday lasted upwards of six and a half hours [times vary]. Notwithstanding reports to the contrary, it is till confidently asserted that some portions of the body of the deceased woman are missing.[520]

Morning Advertiser, 10th November 1888—

"The photographer who had been called in to photograph the room and the body removed his camera from the premises at half-past four, and shortly afterwards a detective officer carried from the house a pail with which he left in a four-wheel cab. The pail was covered with a newspaper, and it was stated that it contained portions of the woman's body. It was taken to the house of Dr. Phillips, 2 Spital Square."

The Times, 12th November 1888—

"As early as half past 7 on Saturday morning [10th November], Dr. Phillips, assisted by Dr. Bond (Westminster), Dr. Gordon Brown (City), Dr. Duke (Spitalfields) and his (Dr. Phillips') assistant, made an exhaustive post-mortem examination of the body at the mortuary adjoining Whitechapel Church.

"It is known that after Dr. Phillips 'fitted' the cut portions of the body into their proper places *no portion was missing*" [author's italics].

The Times, 13th November 1888—

"Notwithstanding reports to the contrary, it is still confidently asserted that some portions of the body of the deceased woman are missing."

The Observer, 18th November 1888, was more specific—

"Though the coroner prevented most of the medical evidence from coming out, it is believed that much of it will be of a curious nature. According to one report published on Friday it seems that the assassin cut the woman's heart out and carried it away . . ."

The only known possible source for this assertion is a leak from Dr. Thomas Bond's 10th November internal report to Robert Anderson [which was not made public], in which he wrote—

"The Pericardium was open below & the Heart absent."

Whether Bond meant the heart was absent from the body or absent from the room is a debate which has rumbled on inconclusively for years. We shall probably never learn the answer, unless, of course, like many

---

[520]   This press agency report also appeared in *The Times* of the same day.

other artifacts anonymously returned to Scotland Yard, the shrivelled organ arrives in a bubble pack postmarked "Croydon," south London.

There were rumblings of discontent about the inquest.

Daily Telegraph, 14th November 1888—

"It is in the power of the Attorney-General to apply to the High Court of Justice to hold a new inquest, if he is satisfied that there has been rejection of evidence, irregularity of proceedings, or insufficiency of inquiry. This course is improbable, as it is stated that Mr. Phillips, the divisional surgeon of police, with whom the coroner consulted in private, has had a commission from the Home Office for some time, and he does not consider himself a 'free agent'; but it is pointed out that by hurriedly closing the inquest the opportunity has been lost of putting on record statements made on oath, and when the memory of witnesses is fresh. It is not improbable that a long interval may elapse before a prisoner is charged at the police-court."

The matter of George Bagster Phillips not being a free agent and the nature of his commission from the Home Office are unknown, but he appears to have been treading a fine line between Whitechapel and Whitehall.

Daily Telegraph, 10th November 1888—

"During the course of last evening [the day of the Kelly murder] Dr. G. B. Phillips visited the House of Commons, where he had a conference with the Under Secretary for the Home Office, Mr. Stuart-Wortley."

Echo, 10th November 1888—

"Cabinet Council Today.

"A Cabinet Council was held at noon today at the Foreign Office. The Duke of Rutland and Lord Cranbrook were the first Members to arrive. All the members of the Cabinet were present at today's meeting, with the exception of Lord Ashbourne and Lord Knutsford. The Cabinet did not break up until a quarter to three o'clock. Mr. Ritchie, Lord Cadogan, Mr. Henry Matthews and the Lord Chancellor were the first to leave."

Cabinet Councils are convened on a fairly regular basis, [521] so perhaps we should not read any special significance into this gathering of Privy Councillors.

Or perhaps in this instance we should . . .

Echo, the same day—

"Dr. G.B. Phillips, the divisional surgeon of the H Division, whose reticence is justified by an assurance he gave of secrecy, has copious notes of the result of the post-mortem examination, and with nearly every conclusion at which he has arrived, Dr. Thomas Bond, of Westminster, a well-known expert on crimes of violence, agrees.

"Dr. Phillips has only vaguely indicated to the local police the result of his investigations, but a report on the question has, it has been asserted, been jointly made by him and Dr. Bond, and submitted to Sir Charles Warren."

The Metropolitan Police maintained its silence, careful not to discourage the press and public from believing this murder to have been the work of Jack the Ripper.

Jack the Ripper, or the Whitechapel Murderer, has always been spoken of in the singular. For instance, Sir Robert Anderson wrote in his 1910 memoirs— "The last and most horrible of that maniac's crimes was committed in a house in Miller's Court on the 9th of November," and Sir Melville Macnaghten in his 1914 memoirs stated that—" . . . in the room at Millers Court the madman found ample scope for the opportunities he had all along been seeking . . ."

However, it seemed that the perpetrator was not a lone operator.

On the day of the inquest a notice appeared in *The Times*—

"Murder. — Pardon. —Whereas on November 8 or 9, in Miller-court, Dorset-street, Spitalfields, Mary Janet Kelly was murdered by some person or persons unknown: the Secretary of State will advise the grant of Her Majesty's gracious pardon to any accomplice, not being a person who contrived or actually committed the murder, who shall give such information and evidence as shall lead to the discovery and

---

[521]   Thirty-one were recorded in *The Times* during 1888.

conviction of the person or persons who committed the murder.

"Charles Warren, the Commissioner of Police of the Metropolis.

"Metropolitan Police Office, 4 Whitehall-place, S.W.,

"Nov. 10, 1888"

In his 10th November report to Anderson, Dr. Bond wrote— "There is no evidence that he [the murderer] had an accomplice," whilst Dr. Phillips thought otherwise.

Echo, 12th November 1888—

"It is asserted that the Home Secretary's offer of a pardon to any accomplice was mainly at the instigation of Dr. G. B. Phillips, the Divisional Surgeon of the H Division, who pointed out to the authorities at the Home Office the desirability of such a step being taken."

As Dr. Phillips was unlikely to have plucked such a conclusion out of thin air, there must have been evidence which he alone noticed and only revealed at a House of Commons meeting on the evening of 9th November, which on the following day led to a Cabinet decision to issue a reward to an accomplice.

How might an accomplice have been deployed, if not in the murder itself?

Sarah Lewis, inquest witness—

"I live at 24 Great Pearl Street, and am a laundress. I know Mrs. Keyler, in Millers Court, and went to her house at 2 Millers Court, at 2.30 am on Friday. It is the first house. I noticed the time by the Spitalfields' Church clock. When I went into the court, opposite the lodging-house, I saw a man with a wideawake [hat]. There was no one talking to him [in her 9th November statement the words "talking to a female" had been deleted]. He was a stout-looking man, and not very tall. The hat was black. I did not take any notice of his clothes. The man was looking up the court; he seemed to be waiting or looking for some one."

Here was a man who could have been the murderer's accomplice or look-out, a man whose presence opposite Millers Court required investigation.

The inquest closed at around 4.30 pm.

At 6.00 pm the same day a man walked into Commercial Street

police station to make a statement. He had been in Dorset Street, standing opposite Millers Court at the time Sarah Lewis returned home on the morning of the murder.

His name was George Hutchinson.

27. THE WOMAN WHO NEVER WAS

"Metropolitan Police, Criminal Investigation Department, Scotland Yard.

"12th November 1888.

"Subject: Whitechapel Murder.

"Reference to Papers 52983.[522]

"I beg to report that an inquest was held this day at the Shoreditch Town Hall before Dr. Macdonald M.P., Coroner, on the body of Marie Jeneatte [sic] Kelly, found murdered at No. 13 Room, Millers Court, Dorset Street, Spitalfields. A number of witnesses were called who clearly established the identity of deceased. The Coroner remarked that in his opinion it was unnecessary to adjourn the inquiry and the jury returned a verdict of wilful murder against some person or persons unknown."

Inspector Abberline dispensed with the murder and inquest of Mary Jane Kelly in just eighty-two words before moving on to more urgent matters—

"An important statement has been made by George Hutchinson

---

[522] The file reference 52983 appears on various reports, yet has never been clarified. It does not appear amongst available MEPO files, but does appear in various Special Branch ledger indexes.

which I forward herewith. I have interrogated him this evening and I am of the opinion his statement is true. He informed me that he had occasionally given the deceased a few shillings and that he had known her about 3 years. Also that he was surprised to see a man so well dressed in her company which caused him to watch them. He can identify the man and arrangement was at once made for two officers to accompany him round the district for a few hours tonight with a view of finding the man if possible.

"Hutchinson is at present in no regular employment, and he has promised to go with an officer tomorrow at 11.30 am to the Shoreditch mortuary to identify the deceased.

"Several arrests have been made on suspicion of being connected with the recent murder, but the various persons detained have been able to satisfactorily account for their movements and were released.

"F.G. Abberline Inspr.

"T. Arnold Supt."

The statement of George Hutchinson—

"Metropolitan Police, Commercial Street, H Division, 12th November 1888.

"At 6pm 12th George Hutchinson of the Victoria Home Commercial Street came to this station and made the following statement.

"About 2:00 a.m. on the 9th I was coming by Thrawl Street, Commercial Street and just before I got to Flower and Dean Street I met the murdered woman Kelly and she said to me: 'Hutchinson, will you lend me sixpence?' I said: 'I can't. I have spent all my money going down to Romford.' She said: 'Good morning, I must go and find some money.'

"She went away to Thrawl Street. A man coming in the opposite direction to Kelly (i.e. from Aldgate) tapped her on the shoulder and said something to her. They both burst out laughing. I heard her say: 'All right' to him and the man said: 'You will be alright for what I have told you.' He then placed his right hand around her shoulder. He also had a kind of small parcel in his left hand with a kind of strap around it. I stood against the lamp of the Queen's Head Public House and watched him.

They both came past me and the man hung his head down with his hat over his eyes. I stooped down and looked him in the face. He looked at me stern.

"They both went into Dorset Street. I followed them. They both stood on the corner of the court for about three minutes. He said something to her. She said: 'All right, my dear. Come along. You will be comfortable.' He then placed his arm on her shoulder and she gave him a kiss. She said she had lost her handkerchief. He then pulled out his handkerchief, a red one, and gave it to her. They both went up the court together. I went to the court to see if I could see them, but I could not. I stood there for about three quarters of an hour to see if they came out. They did not, so I went away."

There followed a description of the man seen by Hutchinson

"Age about thirty four or thirty five; height five feet six inches; complexion pale; dark eyes and eyelashes; slight moustache curled up at each end and hair dark; very surly looking; dress – long dark coat; collar and cuffs trimmed with astrakhan and a dark jacket underneath; light waistcoat; dark trousers; dark felt hat turned down in the middle; button boots and gaiters with white buttons: wore a very thick gold chain with linen collar; black tie with horseshoe pin; respectable appearance; walked very sharp; Jewish appearance. Can be identified."

The statement was signed by George Hutchinson and four policemen—

Sergeant E. Badham, Inspector E. Ellisdon, Superintendent T. Arnold and Inspector F.G. Abberline.

The Times, 13th November 1888—

"The police yesterday evening received an important piece of information. A man, apparently of the labouring class, with a military appearance, who knew the deceased, stated that on the morning of the 9th inst. he saw her in Commercial Street, Spitalfields (near where the murder was committed), in company with a man of respectable appearance. He was about 5 ft. 6 in. in height, and 34 or 35 years of age, with dark complexion and dark moustache turned up at the ends. He was wearing a long, dark coat, trimmed with astrakhan, a white collar with a black necktie, in which was affixed a horse-shoe pin. He wore a pair of dark gaiters with light buttons, over button boots, and displayed from his waistcoat a massive gold chain. His appearance contrasted so markedly with that of the woman that few people could have failed to remark them at that hour of the morning.

"This description, which confirms that given by others of the person seen in company with the deceased on the morning she was killed, is much fuller in detail than that hitherto in the possession of the police."

Echo, 13th November 1888—

"From latest inquiries it appears that a very reduced importance seems to be now - in the light of later investigation - attached to a statement made by a person last night that he saw a man with the deceased on the night of the murder. Of course, such a statement should have been made at the inquest, where the evidence, taken on oath, could have been compared with the supposed description of the murderer given by the witnesses.

"Why, ask the authorities, did not the informant come forward before? As many as fifty-three persons have, in all, made statements as to 'suspicious men,' each of whom was thought to be Mary Janet Kelly's assassin. The most remarkable thing in regard to the latest statement is, *that no one else can be found to say that a man of that description given was seen with the deceased*, while, of course, there is the direct testimony of the witnesses at the inquest, that the person seen with the deceased at midnight was of quite a different appearance [author's italics].

The Times, 14th November 1888—

"The following statement was made yesterday evening by George Hutchinson, a labourer."

There followed a variation on Hutchinson's original police statement, the main difference being that the man he saw was no longer of a "Jewish appearance." He now "looked like a foreigner."

The Times article concluded thus—

"The description of the murderer given by Hutchinson agrees in every particular with that already furnished by the police and published yesterday morning."

Evening News, 14th November 1888, sub-head—
"Another Statement Confirming One Made On Monday."
Los Angeles Herald, 14th November 1888—
"Two person have been found who saw the man who accompanied the last victim to her room on the night she was murdered. Their descriptions of the man tally in every respect."

This was hardly surprising, for the description "already furnished by the police and published yesterday morning" was from George Hutchinson's original police statement.

The police were using George Hutchinson to corroborate himself.

But his story was short-lived.

Star, 15th November 1888

"Another story now discredited is that of the man Hutchinson, who said that on Friday morning last he saw Kelly with a dark-complexioned, middle-aged, foreign-looking, bushy-eyebrowed gentleman, with the dark moustache turned up at the ends, who wore the soft felt hat, the long dark coat, trimmed with astrakhan, the black necktie, with horseshoe pin, and the button boots, and displayed a massive gold watch-chain, with large seal and a red stone attached."

Evening Star [Washington DC], 14th November 1888—

"Unless the story told by the man Hutchinson is made out of whole cloth - a question which it ought not to take a competent detective two hours to settle - there is now a shadow of hope of capturing the miscreant who has been committing so much butchery."

The newspaper story ended on a cryptic note—

"But, in the meantime, it would be just as well to keep a sharp eye upon Hutchinson himself. He may be a convenient person to have about at a critical stage of the investigation which is soon to follow. The man popularly known as 'Jack the Ripper' is full of devices, and it would not be surprising if it were found necessary later to put Hutchinson in his turn on the defensive."

George Hutchinson walked off into the sunset, his task complete, never to be seen or heard from again. The man Sarah Lewis had seen standing opposite Millers Court at 2.30 am was not an accomplice or a look-out. The reason for his presence in Dorset Street had now been fully explained.

Attention turned briefly to another possible murder suspect.

Mary Ann Cox, a Millers Court resident and inquest witness, gave a statement to the police on 9th November as to having seen Mary Kelly at about 11.45 pm the previous night. She was going into her room with a man Cox described as "about 36 years old, about 5ft 5in high, complexion fresh and I believe he had blotches on his face, small side whiskers, and a thick carroty moustache, dressed in shabby dark clothes, dark overcoat and black felt hat."

Evening News, 16th November 1888—

"Mr. Galloway, a clerk employed in the City and living at Stepney, has made the following statement: 'As I was going down the Whitechapel Road in the early hours of Wednesday morning, on my way home, I saw a man coming in the opposite direction, about fifty yards away. We both crossed the road simultaneously, and came face to face. The man had a very frightened appearance, and glared at me as he passed. I was very much struck with his appearance, especially as he corresponded, in almost every particular, with the man described by Mary Ann Cox. He was short, stout, about 35 to 40 years of age. His moustache, not a particular heavy one, was of a carroty colour, and his face was blotchy through drink and dissipation. He wore a long, dirty, brown overcoat, and altogether presented a most villainous appearance.

"'I determined to follow him, and just before reaching the coffee-stall past the church he again crossed the road. On nearing George-yard he crossed over and entered a small court. He reappeared in a couple of minutes, crossed Whitechapel Road for the sixth time, and proceeded up Commercial Street. Up to this time he had walked along briskly, but directly he got into Commercial Street he slackened speed and accosted the first woman whom he met alone, but was repulsed.

"'On approaching Thrawl Street a policeman on point duty suddenly appeared. The man was evidently startled, and for a moment it looked as though he would turn back or cross the road. He recovered himself, however, and went on. I then informed the constable of what I had seen, and pointed out the man's extraordinary resemblance to the individual described by Cox. The constable declined to arrest the man, saying that he was looking for a man of a very different appearance.'"

Evening News, 17th November 1888—

"The police state that the man who aroused the suspicion of Mr. Galloway by frequently crossing and recrossing the road, is a respectable citizen, and that he was, as a matter of fact, acting in concert with them in his 'mysterious movements.' "The streets of Whitechapel presented their normal appearance last night."

Jack the Ripper's reign of terror was at an end.

On Monday 19th November 1888 a polished oak and elm coffin with metal fittings was interred at St Patrick's Catholic Cemetery, Leytonstone, six miles east of Whitechapel. On a brass plate were inscribed the words: 'Marie Jeanette Kelly, died 9th November 1888, aged 25 years,' and upon the coffin were two crowns of artificial flowers and a cross made up of heartsease, a variety of wild pansy also known as "Jack-jump-up-and-kiss-me."

There was a colossal outpouring of grief amongst the people of the East End, as evidenced by this account of the funeral from the *St Peter Port Star* [Guernsey], 22nd November 1888—

"The bell of St. Leonard's began tolling at noon, and the signal appeared to draw all the residents in the neighbourhood together. There was an enormous preponderance of women in the crowd, scarcely any had any covering to their heads, and their tattered dresses indicated too surely that they belonged to the very class to which the murdered women belonged.

"The wreaths upon the coffin bore cards inscribed with remembrances from friends using certain public houses in common with the deceased. As the coffin appeared, borne on the shoulders of four men, at the principal gate of the church, the crowd appeared to be moved greatly. Round the open car in which it was to be placed men and women struggled desperately to touch the coffin. Women, with faces streaming with tears, cried out 'God forgive her!' and every man's head was bared in a token of sympathy."

The history of this Limerick girl brought as a child to Wales, later married a collier, was subsequently widowed, moved to Cardiff, travelled to London, worked in a Knightsbridge brothel, made several journeys to France in grand style, slowly gravitated to the East End where she lived with a number of men, led a loose life, found redemption in the arms of a market porter, slipped back into her old ways and died at the hands of Jack the Ripper has resisted every effort by genealogists, local historians, parish archivists and the most tireless and tenacious researchers in the business to confirm any of its details.

Yet Ripperologists still cling to a hopelessly romantic vision of Mary Kelly, some placing flowers at her grave, on which was once a small marble slab bearing the opening line from a poem by Goethe—

"None but the lonely heart can know my sadness."

Jack the Ripper and Mary Jeanette Kelly were made for each other—he the ultimate destroyer of life, she the ultimate Victorian fallen woman. Blood, sex and violent death—the formula was pitch-perfect. Two years earlier Krafft-Ebing had published his "Psychopathia Sexualis" and in the light of this new sexual self-awareness people tingled with a delicious frisson, lapping up each gory detail of the murder as they filled in the missing details for themselves within the privacy of their own imaginations. It is not hard to understand where Bram Stoker got his inspiration for the sexual motifs in his 1897 "Dracula."

Who was Mary Kelly?

Joseph Barnett— "She said she was born in Limerick, and went when very young to Wales."

Elizabeth Phoenix— "She stated first that she was Welsh, and that her parents, who had discarded her, still resided at Cardiff . . . On other occasions, however, she declared that she was Irish."

John McCarthy— "Her mother lives in Ireland, but in what county I do not know. Deceased used to receive letters from her occasionally."

The press made inquiries in Ireland.

Limerick Chronicle, 10th November 1888—

"A rumour prevailed in Limerick today that the murdered woman was in some way connected with the city, where it is said her parents at one time resided; but this may be found to be one of those vague reports which are so freely circulated on occasions such as this. However, we are informed that the police in this city have been communicated with, and that inquiries are now being instigated to ascertain the truth or otherwise of the rumour in question."

Morning Advertiser, 12th November 1888—

"A Limerick telegram states that inquiries made in that city had failed to identify the latest Whitechapel victim as a native of that town. The Limerick police were reported to have been communicated with by the London police regarding Kelly's antecedents, but the report was unfounded."

If this last report is accurate the Metropolitan Police had not wasted its time looking for Mary Kelly's antecedents in Limerick.

The press also explored the alleged Welsh connection.

Star, 12th November 1888—

"It appears from inquiries made at Carmarthen and Swansea, that after leaving the former place for the latter, Kelly, who was then only 17 years of age, entered the service of a Mrs. Rees, who stands committed to the next assizes on a charge of procuring abortion, and who is the daughter of a medical man formerly resident at Carmarthen."[523]

Cambrian Daily Leader, 12th November 1888—

"It is stated in the Western Mail that the murdered woman Kelly was at one time a servant with Mrs. Rees in Trafalgar Terrace, Swansea. We are asked to say that this is not true."

Western Mail, 12th November—

"Our reporter made inquiries at Cardiff Police station, in order to discover if the unfortunate woman was known to the police. He was informed by Mr. [Walter] Hemingway, the head constable, that he had no recollection of anyone answering the description of the victim, and that so far as he was aware, the woman had not come under the notice

---

[523] On December 19th 1888, together with Louisa Wilson, Mrs Mary Jane Florence Rees was charged with the wilful murder of Maude Neville Williams at Cardiff on 20th July 1888 by using instruments upon her with intent to procure an abortion at a lodging house kept by Wilson. She was found guilty and sentenced to ten years' penal servitude.

of the police."

Despite an anecdotal story surfacing about a Mary Kelly having been born at Llanelli, Carmarthenshire, the daughter of a marine store dealer,[524] inquiries proved fruitless.

The *Western Mail*, 13th November 1888, summed it up—

"So far the attempts made to identify the poor girl in Wales have not been very successful, which is not surprising looking to the contradictory character of the information secured in London."

The Times, 14th November 1888—

"The funeral of the murdered woman Kelly will not take place until after the arrival from Wales of some of her relatives and friends, who are expected to reach London this evening. If they be unable to provide the necessary funeral expenses, Mr. H. Wilton, of 119 High-street, Shoreditch, has guaranteed that the unfortunate woman shall not be buried in a pauper's grave."

It is not recorded whether these friends and relatives ever reached London, but it was undertaker Henry Wilton who alone bore the cost of the funeral.

Unlike the earlier "victims of Jack the Ripper" Mary Jane Kelly resisted, and over a century later continues to resist, all attempts to positively identify her.

Cooler minds believe her history reads more like a carefully-crafted back-story bearing faint traces of an Elizabeth Gaskell novel, and that when it comes to identifying The Woman Who Never Was we have to reconsider who might have died in Room 13, Millers Court.

Options are few—

It was a young woman of another name who, for unknown reasons, was masquerading as a fictional Mary Jane Kelly from Limerick.

It was someone else entirely, mutilated beyond recognition in order

---

[524] A marine store dealer was a dealer in scrap materials—an occupation commonly, though not exclusively, practised by itinerant gypsies. A great number of them were little more than receivers of stolen property. Between 1870 and 1890 *The Times* reported almost 200 court cases involving marine store dealers, some operating Fagin-like schemes which encouraged children to steal lead from their school roofs.

to be passed off as the person known as Mary Jane Kelly from Limerick.

Here we must return to Mrs. Maxwell at the inquest.

The Coroner could not dismiss her story of having seen Kelly between 8.00 and 8.45 am because no medical evidence was presented to conclusively establish that she had died earlier.

The failure of the inquest to use Dr. Bond's post-mortem notes or to press Dr. Phillips in the witness box for an accurate time of death was negligent, especially as prior to the inquest, whilst not under oath, Phillips had expressed his opinion on the matter to *The Times*.[525] It was an opinion which differed considerably from that of Doctor Bond.

Following Dr. Phillips inquest testimony, "the jury had no questions to ask at this stage, and it was understood that more detailed evidence of the medical examination would be given at a further hearing."[526] But by the end of the inquest an hour or so later the Coroner deemed a further hearing unnecessary, the jury concurred and the proceedings closed with the matter of Kelly's time of death unresolved.

There is no valid reason to believe that Mrs. Caroline Maxwell lied or was mistaken, so as far as the official evidence is concerned this time-of-death omission allows for the possibility that "Mary Kelly" may have been murdered and mutilated *after* being seen by Mrs Maxwell.

This brings us to the second option—

"Mary Kelly" may have lain dead in Room 13 at the same time as "Mary Kelly" was seen alive. However, in order to pass off the corpse as "Mary Kelly," the woman who had been assuming the fictional identity of the 25-year-old "Mary Kelly" from Limerick would herself have had to disappear.

Whilst any attempt to further expand upon this scenario would be condemned as groundless speculation, I cannot close this chapter without first recording that during the course of my researches I have been introduced to some very interesting people from our secret world who, off the record, told me a lot of interesting things, one going so far

---

[525]   *The Times*, 12th November 1888.

[526]   *The Times*, 13th November 1888.

as to assure me that the clandestine truth about the period 1887 to 1891 is far more involved than the history books would have us believe.

I will have to accept her word for that.

Others who had given the subject more than a moment's consideration were of the opinion that Millers Court bore the hallmarks of a Special Branch operation rather than a CID investigation. It is an idea which certainly explains the paucity of MEPO documentation on the case.

"Secrets get recorded," one of my contacts explained. "If things turn sour, you need to know the whole truth in order to construct a plausible lie. The 'Jack the Ripper' paperwork, for want of a more accurate designation—which must have been substantial—can't all have gone missing, been pulped, destroyed by the Luftwaffe, got misfiled or appropriated by collectors." He indicated my printed lists of holdings at the National Archives and London Metropolitan archives. "Look at what did manage to survive."

I had to concede the point. The surviving paperwork is just sufficient to give vague shape and form to the official version of events in which a person known as Jack the Ripper murdered five east end prostitutes, enjoying a last hurrah in Millers Court.

So where was I to look in search of more information?

Unsurprisingly, I did not receive an answer, except for an enigmatic, "Not where you might expect to find it."

28. THE MAN WHO NEVER WAS

We have now come full circle.

Over a century and a quarter has passed since the Whitechapel murders first seized the attention of the world. We are not a step nearer to an understanding, yet, as I write, three more speculative Jack the Ripper theories have surfaced, all paying homage to the authorised version of events.

Two are books, the other a British TV documentary. The first, based on specious DNA analysis of a shawl, places the Polish Jew, Aaron Kosminski, at the scene of Catherine Eddowes' murder in Mitre Square. The second posits that Jack the Ripper was Michael Maybrick, brother of James Maybrick of Diary fame.

The TV documentary postulates that Charles Cross, who first happened upon the body of Polly Nichols, was her killer, and concludes, by dint of equal parts convoluted logic and wishful thinking, that he must have also murdered the other four 'canonical' victims and thus was Jack the Ripper.

One theorist has taken the money and run. Another maintains a snooty silence about his suspect, whilst the other is doomed for all eternity to defend his untenable position via Socratic exchanges on the internet with Ripperologists determined to either return the mystery to its default settings—so everything can start afresh—or promote their own suspects, amongst whom Francis Tumblety, Aaron Kosminski, Robert D'Onston Stephenson—and even Prince Albert Victor, Duke of Clarence and Avondale—remain perennial favourites.

The hunt for Jack the Ripper is a decidedly no-win competition.

As an historical discipline Ripperology has zero credibility. Its adherents are viewed by the public and press as little more than trainspotters indulging in a hobby which operates on its own unique set of historical methodologies—

Anything which cannot be shown to be false must be true, and anything which cannot be shown to be true might still be true, depending on who said it or to what it refers. Press reports, medical opinions and public clocks are unfailingly accurate when promoting theories but hopelessly inaccurate if disputing them, and truth dripped like freshwater pearls from the lips of the policemen involved in the Whitechapel murders investigation.

There have been calls for Ripperology to shrug off its dilettante/hobbyist status and aspire to more academic heights. This noble idea is doomed to failure, for the Ripper industry is not about to allow it to happen. Ripperology doesn't want the mystery solved; it just wants to argue about it. This is why most academics and historians refuse to go anywhere near it. They will tell you that the subject has more to do with a belief in superstition and legend than history, whilst also pointing out that Jack the Ripper's historicity [defined as the actuality of a person existing in a certain place and time] has yet to be established, which is something of a major setback to any attempt at identification.

Students of the Whitechapel murders have no such misgivings. They are hamstrung by a belief that someone known as Jack the Ripper not only skulked around the East End, but was what today we would call a serial killer, a term first coined in the 1970s and the qualification for which is a minimum of three victims—one at a time over a relatively short period. Five victims are not divisible by two, so this eliminates more than one serial killer, but not the possibility of two killers with unequal tallies being in operation or five discrete murders taking place which were first subsumed under the rubric of 'Leather Apron' and then, once that idea proved unsupportable, 'Jack the Ripper.'

This is not a new idea. As previously referenced, on 2nd September 1888 *Reynolds News* suggested that the idea of a lone maniac was being employed by the police as an umbrella solution to three murders which could not otherwise be comfortably explained. Five murders carried out by a single unknown perpetrator would certainly have looked better on a political briefing note than five separate unsolved murders. However, this idea does postulate five murderers gleefully rubbing their hands together, unable to believe their luck at having their handiwork ascribed to the mysterious Jack the Ripper. If word had got out, it would have heralded an open-day on murder in the East End of London.

Many insist that Jack the Ripper must have existed because top officers of the Metropolitan Police offered various ideas about his identity. This argument poses its own problems. If the accepted Ripper story is true, these policemen must at one time or another have sat around a table to discuss the Nineteenth Century's greatest murder mystery. Yet we have been left with nothing even remotely approaching a consensus. Sir Robert Anderson's "definitely ascertained fact" that Jack the Ripper was a Polish Jew, Abberline's hunch that he was the poisoner George Chapman, and Sir Melville Macnaghten's insistence that he was a young doctor who drowned himself after Millers Court cannot all have been right, and what has not yet been explained, except by way of excuses about advancing years, misremembering, forgetfulness and conflation, is why, if any one of these senior policemen was right, the others could have been so dismally wrong.

Were the canonical victims prostitutes?

We cannot be certain. In various police reports they were identified as such, but none of the women had a record for solicitation [prostitution itself was legal] and the various divisional constabularies did not recognise or know any of them by name,[527] so it may have been an assumption based on the fact that, aside from Elizabeth Stride, all the victims allegedly found themselves in precisely the same predicament

---

[527] Walter Dew claimed to know Mary Kelly by sight.

prior to their deaths—out on the streets in the early morning hours in desperate need of a few pence with which to secure a bed in a common lodging house. Even the person known as Mary Jane Kelly, who boasted her own room and a more than generous line of credit from her slum landlord, allegedly experienced a sudden 2.00 am urge to venture out onto Commercial Street to borrow sixpence.

In its acceptance of the authorised version of events Ripperology cleaves to an unshakable belief in the integrity of the police in its handling of the Whitechapel murders. Chief Inspector Abberline has been immortalised on film and TV and with a blue plaque on his house in Bournemouth and a black granite headstone on his nearby grave. Chief Inspector Swanson has been recently honoured with a stone memorial outside the Police Station at Thurso in his native Scotland. As his only real contribution to the Ripper mystery was to have allegedly scribbled the name "Kosminski" in the endpaper of his personal copy of "The Lighter Side of My Official Life," it can now only be a matter of time before Ripperology builds an ornate shrine to the memory of Sir Robert Anderson.

"If you tell a lie big enough and keep repeating it, people will eventually come to believe it," said master propagandist Joseph Goebbels, who for once in his miserable life was actually telling the truth.

And the truth we have been left with is that Jack the Ripper— psychopath, schizophrenic, sexual sadist, gentile, Jew, lunatic, society doctor, crazed midwife, impressionist painter, Russian secret agent, politician, Portuguese sailor, the Elephant Man, philanthropist, convicted murderer, heir to the British throne and darkly jocular letter writer—murdered five, maybe seven or perhaps as many as nine prostitutes, outwitted two London police forces and set the benchmark for all subsequent serial killers.

Anyone who does not subscribe to this pick-and-mix assortment or who questions the integrity of the authorities during the Whitechapel murders is branded by the hardcore Ripper community as a conspiracy theorist. This is mildly amusing, for the irony is that the real conspirators, whether unwittingly or not, are those who, with no supporting evidence whatsoever, unquestioningly defend the status quo.

Even Scotland Yard has played a rôle in keeping the eternal flame of Jack the Ripper burning bright.

BBC News, 20th November 2006—

"An e-fit showing what detectives believe serial killer Jack the Ripper looked like has been revealed.

"Head of analysis for Scotland Yard's Violent Crime Command Laura Richards, who has studied serial killer Fred West and Soham murderer Ian Huntley, revisited the case using modern police techniques. She brought together a team of experts, including pathologists, historians and a geographical profiler, to find out if the case could ever be solved. The result has been the most accurate physical, geographical and psychological portrait of the Ripper ever put together."

"Ms. Richards said the 118-year-old evidence shows the Ripper was between the ages of 25 and 35, between 5ft 5ins and 5ft 7ins tall. He was also of stocky build. Investigators have even been able to pinpoint his address.

"Metropolitan Police Commander John Grieve, who has worked with the team of experts, believes the killer would have been caught if officers at the time had this new information."

Were it not so risible this remark would be a model of understatement.

The Scotland Yard investigation was the subject of a 2006 Channel Five TV documentary—actually more a loose assemblage of historical and visual Ripper cliches—in which the resultant e-fit of a swarthy, heavily-moustached Jack looked more like Freddie Mercury from Queen than Melville Macnaghten's Ripper candidate, the rather delicate-looking Montague John Druitt, or the blue-blooded Duke of Clarence. However, the most interesting revelation was that forensic tests on a shawl, which in 2014 would be used by author Russell Edwards to mitochondrially link Aaron Kosminski and Catherine Eddowes, failed to reveal any human DNA.

There is no hard evidence in the Whitechapel murders; just a mass of irreconcilable witness statements and police, medical and newspaper reports. Like some maddening Maurits Escher drawing, the mystery of the Whitechapel murders can be viewed from any number of angles and still appear to make sense whilst reason and logic fight a losing battle reminding us it is nothing but a trompe-l'œil.

An illusionist produces a tiger from an empty cage and we stare transfixed, wildly applauding, desperately trying to make sense of something which makes no sense, putting out of our minds the fact that the most dazzling showman is nothing but a conspirator with an army of unseen assistants behind the scenery, under the stage and, quite possibly, in the seat beside you.

Before becoming Chief of the US Federal Secret Service, the previously mentioned John Elbert Wilkie was a journalist and amateur magician. In 1890, writing under the name of Fred S. Ellmore [read *Fred Sell More*], Wilkie wrote a completely bogus eye-witness account for the *Chicago Tribune* about the Indian Rope Trick. So widely-believed was his article that it resisted all later attempts by the newspaper to retract it as a hoax.

And so it is with Jack the Ripper.

He is as much a part of our inherited DNA as belief in any deity passed down over generations, his actuality unquestioningly accepted as an article of faith. For reasons best known to themselves, people want to believe in Jack.

All Ripper theories try to make sense of themselves by carefully picking and choosing from other theories. In 1976 Stephen Knight retained the doctor trope, eschewed the crazed midwife and Russian secret agent and postulated that Jack's victims—five members of the frail sisterhood involved in a royal blackmail scheme—were picked off one-by-one over a ten week period by agents of the Crown.

Any scenario which links the five victims in a group initiative makes little sense. East End women were street smart. Once is happenstance and twice may be coincidence, but by the time Polly Nichols and Annie Chapman had been murdered by the mysterious Leather Apron/Jack the Ripper it is not unreasonable to suggest that had Catherine Eddowes been party to the group initiative she might have sensed the approaching swish of the Grim Reaper and considered it imprudent to return from the hop fields of Kent to the East End of London.

Mary Kelly had no such fears. Her fate is a matter of official police record. Venturing out onto the rain-slicked streets of early morning Spitalfields to borrow sixpence she made the acquaintance of a man flamboyantly attired in an Astrakhan-trimmed coat and dripping with bling who was depicted in an *Illustrated Police News* drawing as a racial parody of the rich Jew. If the royal blackmail angle was actually true, then this inconspicuously-dressed character, careless enough to allow his minutely-detailed description to be given to the police and press, must have been the undercover agent assigned by the Crown to silence her.

Rather like a children's book with third-cut pages of heads, bodies and legs which allow an almost infinite assemblage of humorous caricatures or fantastic creatures, mixing and matching facts to build up an accurate picture of Jack the Ripper is an impossibility. Nothing connects with anything else in the Whitechapel murders. Montague Druitt, a cricket-playing barrister, cannot be squared with the description of Astrakhan Man. The "good schoolboy's round hand" of the Goulston Street graffito cannot be reconciled with Aaron Kosminski, the insane Polish Jew. The man seen by Mrs. Long talking to Annie Chapman "appeared to be a little taller than deceased," whereas Annie Chapman was five feet tall and Francis Tumblety over six feet tall.

Like the mythical personage of Jack the Ripper itself, the theories as to his identity and motivation are just so much hokum. From Francis Tumblety [the first to be named in the press as a Whitechapel murders suspect] to the weird and wacky theories of Dr. Forbes Winslow, countless contradictory reminiscences by retired policemen, the elaborate fantasies of William Le Queux and Donald McCormick, Stephen Knight's royal theory and its many derivatives involving Impressionist painters, and Jack the Ripper's "Diary" are all products of vivid imaginations—one in the interests of political expedience, the others for a fast buck from a gullible public and fifteen minutes of fame. Even more erudite accounts in the Ripper canon—some of which have contributed much to our understanding, and others less so—fall down for one fundamental reason: an unquestioning belief that someone known as Jack the Ripper actually existed.

Dr. Thomas Bond believed it.

In November 1888 he attempted to profile the Whitechapel murderer. " . . . He must in my opinion be a man subject to periodical attacks of Homicidal and erotic mania. The character of the mutilations indicate that the man may be in a condition sexually, that may be called satyriasis . . ."

The late Philip Sugden believed it.

Sugden was a most meticulous historian, yet did not bat an eyelid at the fact that "there was no single police view on the subject," or that no police theory "seems to have been based upon tangible evidence linking a suspect to the crimes." However, this did not prevent him from declaring that, whilst he could not "find a convincing case against [any known suspect]," George Chapman [Severin Klosowski] was "the most likely of the known suspects to have been Jack the Ripper."

Professor David Canter believed it.

Director of the International Centre for Investigative Psychology at The University of Huddersfield, author of "Criminal Shadows - Inside the Mind of the Serial Killer", "Mapping Murder: The Secrets of Geographical Profiling", "Forensic Psychology: A very short introduction" and "Forensic Psychology for Dummies," he has stated that Jack the Ripper felt himself at odds with society, was withdrawn and difficult to relate to, and may have been James Maybrick, alleged author of the alleged Ripper diary.

The FBI believed it.

A 1988 profile concluded that the Ripper had an absent father and was raised by a domineering mother given to drink. His pent-up desires and emotions were expressed by lighting fires and torturing small animals. By perpetrating these acts he discovered increased areas of dominance, power and control, and learned how to continue violent destructive acts without detection or punishment.

When it comes to identifying Jack the Ripper, all this retro-analysis is about as useful as the two aforementioned spiritualists who after the murder of Elizabeth Stride tuned into the ether, only to receive differing descriptions of the perpetrator.

It is impossible to profile or psychoanalyse someone who did not exist.

Clinical psychologist Jared DeFife, PhD[528]—

"Fictional characters, however, are ideal targets for psychologists to diagnose with mental illnesses or personality defects. Diagnosing fictional characters allows the public to learn about mental illnesses, and offers opportunities for psychologists to feel smart and get public recognition."

James Bond and Sherlock Holmes have undergone this treatment. Sigmund Freud analysed Oedipus, a character from Greek drama, thus introducing the world to the Oedipal Complex, but whilst all the interpretations of their various motives, passions and behavioral traits may well be valid the characters themselves remain stubbornly fictional. Ultimately, all you can glean are insights into the minds of Ian Fleming, Sir Arthur Conan Doyle and Sigmund Freud.

". . . The only thing to be revealed in the investigation of Jack the Ripper is ourselves . . ."

From the moment of his world debut on 1st October 1888 Jack became the new bogeyman, beguiling a world who believed he was real because two police forces were searching for him. But for the first six years of his existence he was little more than a nameless concept thought of by those not simply content to believe he was a Jew as an embodiment of the dark side of the human psyche, a Mr. Hyde lurking behind the mild-mannered façade of Dr. Jekyll, a dark spirit able to manifest itself in flesh and blood through some mysterious transmutation. Heady stuff in the nascent world of psychiatry and psychoanalysis.

Whilst no amount of analysis will ever make Jack the Ripper come true, an idea worth pursuing—one which is beyond the scope of this particular book—is the nature and identity of the person/people who

---

[528]   Adjunct Assistant Professor in the Department of Psychiatry and Behavioral Sciences at Emory University School of Medicine, Atlanta.

dreamed up and masterminded such a pitch-perfect creation.

However, this phantasmagoric character was not entirely successful. Some people had been harbouring suspicions about Jack the Ripper or, more specifically, his non-existence, and just prior to the UK General Election in March 1894 the *Sun* newspaper decided the time was right to call his bluff.

Sun, 16th February 1894—

"It has already been stated more than once that the principal features in the career of the infamous criminal, Jack the Ripper, have been known to The Sun for many weeks, and that they were previously withheld from publication to permit of the most searching and patient inquiry in every direction. When the net of evidence began to close round one man - when it had been established beyond all reasonable doubt that the perpetrator of the Whitechapel murders was under the lock and key of the law - two representatives of The Sun went to Broadmoor Criminal Lunatic Asylum in order to come face to face with that inscrutable criminal."

Suddenly the non-existent Jack the Ripper was flesh and blood. He was alive. He had been caught, incarcerated and was now receiving visitors. He had not committed suicide, as in the 1891 story from MP Henry Farquharson, nor been sentenced to twenty years in Portland prison.

Sun, 19th February 1894—

" . . . we shall send to the police, when they ask for it, all the material at our disposal . . . We understand that the attention of the highest police authorities has been called to our statements, and we confidently look forward to our story being subjected to the closest and most searching investigation."

A *Sun* reader wrote—

"Surely some action by the Home Office is necessary. What have the Police authorities to say? It reflects no credit on Scotland Yard that the detection of this infamous scoundrel should be left to the enterprise of The Sun. If Scotland Yard still entertains a doubt, let Mr. Asquith appoint a committee of experts to examine into and sift the mass of evidence which you have gathered with so much labour."

The *Sun* story was elaborate fiction.

Editor T.P. O'Connor, a political bruiser, was unscrupulously using the unnamed Thomas Hayne Cutbush, incarcerated at Broadmoor in April 1891 for jabbing girls in the buttocks, as a stalking horse to trigger an inquiry into the Whitechapel murders, an inquiry which would have exposed the deception of Jack the Ripper and embarrassed the Tory party, during whose watch the Whitechapel murders had taken place.

On paper it was a clever ploy. If an inquiry ensued Scotland Yard would have had to demonstrate that the non-existent Jack the Ripper was not Thomas Hayne Cutbush, and in order to do that would have to further show that the non-existent Jack the Ripper was or might have been somebody else: somebody about whom nobody could agree. Consensus might have led to a demand for evidence, whereas uncertainty reinforced the idea that Jack the Ripper may have conveniently died or been incarcerated before his identity was suspected, or perhaps been too shrewd for the police, avoided arrest and was possibly still at large.

What T.P. O'Connor had not anticipated was the *Morning Leader* running a spoiler story. His ploy ultimately failed but, unbeknownst to him, it had struck a nerve at Scotland Yard.

Just four days after the *Sun's* final Ripper article Chief Constable Melville Macnaghten signed and dated a memorandum which acknowledged Thomas Hayne Cutbush as the Broadmoor inmate and ticked all the right boxes with respect to its three "more likely" suspects—one dead, a second in an asylum, and a third whose whereabouts were as yet unaccountable.

The hurriedly-written and ill-thought-through Macnaghten Memorandum was a knee-jerk reaction to the *Sun* story. Riddled with errors, it is impossible to imagine what possessed him to write it. Had an inquiry ensued it would not have withstood a moment's scrutiny, especially as one of its three "more likely suspects," the as then unaccounted for Michael Ostrog, would eight months later clear himself of any possible complicity.

However, the exercise had not been a complete waste of time.

In the following year Chief Inspector Swanson was quoted as saying that the murders "were the work of a man who is now dead," and Major Arthur Griffiths, writing in *Windsor Magazine* under the name Alfred Aylmer, reported that Robert Anderson had "a perfectly plausible theory that Jack the Ripper was a homicidal maniac, temporarily at large, whose hideous career was cut short by committal to an asylum."

At a later date Melville Macnaghten reworked his memorandum, stressing his belief in the guilt of the drowned doctor whilst feeling inclined to exonerate his other two "more likely" suspects, and Major Griffiths proved a reliable conduit for leaking this information into the public domain.

In his November 1898 book "Mysteries of Crime and Police," he wrote—

". . . the police, after the last murder, had brought their investigations to the point of strongly suspecting several persons, all of them known to be homicidal maniacs, and against three of these they held very plausible and reasonable grounds of suspicion."

Major Griffiths next recounted details of the suspects from the Macnaghten memorandum, albeit with the names redacted, stressing that suspicion was strongest in the case of the drowned doctor "in the prime of life, believed to be insane or on the borderland of insanity" who was found in the Thames on the last day of 1888.

Jack the Ripper had been dead for ten years, which didn't speak volumes about Robert Anderson's plausible theory about the homicidal maniac committed to an asylum.

Almost from the start journalist George R. Sims had cast a mordant eye over the Whitechapel murders and all the attendant hoopla, but following the second edition of Major Griffiths' book in January 1899, his tone changed and he began to champion the drowned doctor as Jack the Ripper.

George R. Sims believed it.

Having read Major Griffiths' book Sims probably sought confirmation of these new facts from his friend Melville Macnaghten who, perhaps over a bottle of decent claret at one of his Monday night Corinthian dinners, neither confirmed nor denied that the suspect who drowned in the Thames was a doctor—a wholly bogus "fact" which Sims perpetuated right up until his final Dagonet article in 1917.

Melville Macnaghten regularly fed information to Sims. As late as 11th February 1907 he wrote in a letter ". . . It may also save you the trouble of research if I give you the times & places of Jack the Ripper's pleasantries." There followed the locations, dates and names of the five canonical victims,[529] which Sims included in a *Lloyds Weekly News* article on 22nd September 1907.

Of Melville Macnaghten's other two suspects, both of whom he had been inclined to exonerate, there is no evidence to suggest that "Kosminski, a Polish Jew" was the Whitechapel murderer. However, Sir Robert Anderson was a man who enjoyed telling people he was right, and there is little doubt that in 1910 he lifted the Polish Jew from the memorandum, thus neatly side-stepping any possible consensus with Macnaghten, and without naming him announced to the world as a "definitely ascertained fact" that he was Jack the Ripper.

Understandably perhaps, in later years Macnaghten's third "more likely" suspect, Michael Ostrog, the man with an iron-clad alibi and £10 compensation from the Police fund to prove it, was a no-show in the Ripper stakes.

Were it not for T.P. O'Connor we would not today be in possession of the names Montague John Druitt, Aaron Kosminski and Michael Ostrog, three innocent men—one conveniently dead, one incarcerated in an asylum, and one whose whereabouts were uncertain—plucked from the records in response to the *Sun's* bluff that the non-existent Jack the Ripper was Thomas Hayne Cutbush.

It is an article of faith that someone known as Jack the Ripper murdered five prostitutes between 31st August and 9th November 1888, but, as has been shown, there is scant evidence to support this idea but much to refute it. From the Leather Apron debacle, the Edward Stanley

---

[529]   Borowitz Collection, Kent State University.

alibis, the Ripper correspondence, the selective use of witness statements in the Berner Street murder to lend credence to the idea of a double-event, the erasure of the chalked message in Goulston Street, the rushed inquest which neglected to establish the Millers Court victim's time of death, to the flight from justice of Dr. Francis Tumblety and the antics of Scotland Yard detectives in North America—in all these instances differing measures of official jiggery pokery can be discerned.

If any of the Jack the Ripper "suspects" named by a policeman was guilty there would be no good reason for us not to know which it was; no reason for the Whitechapel murders to remain a mystery and the void of our unknowing force-fed with over a hundred years of patent poppycock involving a Polish Jew, a drowned doctor, various Freemasons, an heir to the throne, a Liverpool cotton merchant, an Impressionist painter and an American quack.

It might appear to follow that if none of these "suspects" was guilty then Jack the Ripper must have been someone else and that there is a very good reason why we have not been told his identity. Like a game of Snakes and Ladders such an idea sends us right back to square one, at the same time tying in neatly with a hoary old rumour that on their first day in office each new Commissioner of Police of the Metropolis learns the identity of Jack the Ripper.

Asked about this rumour, Commissioner Sir Bernard Hogan-Howe replied—

"A fabulous rumour! But I'm afraid untrue."[530]

Any quest to identify Jack the Ripper will ultimately lead to insanity. It is a wild goose chase. Jack's name is not to be found within the pages of a Special Branch ledger held in a government depository, nor in a private archive to protect the scion of a noble family. His name is unrecorded, just like that of his predecessor Leather Apron.

Occam's Razor,[531] a 14th Century problem-solving principle also

---

[530]   Author's personal correspondence.
[531]   William of Ockham (c. 1287–1347), an English Franciscan friar, philosopher and theologian.

known as the law of parsimony, broadly states that among competing hypotheses the one with the fewest assumptions should be selected—

Jack was a myth.

This heretical but elegantly simple hypothesis explains everything.

Once the myth had served its purpose, Jack could not be arrested, officially declared dead or otherwise identified. Jack could only vanish into the mists of time as mysteriously as he had first appeared.

Which is exactly what happened.

Five dead bodies are the only facts in the Whitechapel murders.

Everything else we have been told, or think we know, about Jack the Ripper has been a lie or, as Emperor Napoléon Bonaparte shrewdly observed, "est un ensemble de mensonges convenues"—a set of lies agreed upon.

Jack the Ripper did not exist.

Perhaps now we can apply ourselves to the task of discovering the truth behind the Whitechapel murders.

THE BEGINNING.

Index

Abberline, Frederick George, Inspector -
17, 19, 51, 114, 148, 149, 150, 157,
227, 228, 229, 230, 231, 232, 233, 270,
271, 273, 287, 300, 313, 322, 347, 351,
356, 364, 365, 366, 378, 380, 383, 384,
401, 402, 406, 408, 409, 449, 482, 486,
521, 523, 524, 526, 531, 539, 540, 541,
553, 554

Aberconway, Christabel - 128, 288

Adam, Hargrave Lee – 200, 201, 205,
270, 271, 273

Anderson, Sir Robert [see also Curious]
- 11, 16, 17, 19, 20, 23, 24, 25, 27, 28,
29, 35, 39, 42, 60, 61, 62, 67, 68, 69,
71, 72, 73, 75, 78, 83, 84, 85, 87, 88,
96, 97, 99, 100, 106, 108 fn, 137, 141,
145, 146, 154, 155, 156, 157, 158-159
Order of St. Anne, 161, 162, 164, 165,
166-168 Albert Gate; 169, 170-171 New
York Times; 172, 173, 174, 175, 176,
177, 178, 181, 185, 186, 187, 188, 189,
190, 191, 192, 193, 194, 195, 196, 198,
199, 200, 201, 203, 205, 241, 242, 254,
270, 319, 322, 348, 374, 375, 376, 377,
426, 433, 435, 444, 445, 446, 458, 460,
465, 466, 472, 482, 483, 521, 522, 523,
524, 525, 534, 536, 537, 553, 554, 562,
563

Andrews, Walter Simon, Inspector - 54,
55, 56, 59, 62, 63, 64, 65, 66, 67, 68,
69, 70, 71, 72, 75, 78, 80, 85, 88, 98,
225

Arnold, Thomas, Superintendent – 16,
238, 348, 432, 433, 434, 522, 523, 524,
532, 540, 541

Arrow, Charles John – 210, 211

Autonomie Club - 126

Aylmer, Alfred - 137, 562

Balfour, Arthur - 8, 91, 142, 143, 456,
457, 460, 514

Balfour, Jabez - 223-224

Barnardo Dr. - 3

Barnett, Joseph - 526, 527, 529, 531 fn,
532, 546

Barnett, Roland Gideon Israel - 54, 55,
56, 59, 60, 61, 71

Barton, Thomas - 53, 67, 73, 74, 75, 76,
77, 78, 84

Baxter, Wynne Edwin [Coroner] - 8, 14,
360, 362, 368, 369, 370, 371, 380, 382,
406, 407, 408, 423, 437, 476, 477, 481,
490, 491

Beach, Thomas Billis [see Le Caron]

Bell, Edward [aka Ivory] - 160, 162, 163,
164

Bourdin, Martial - 126-127

Brisbane, Arthur - 10, 344, 345, 346,
435, 521, 522

Bradford, Edward Ridley Colbourne Sir -
46, 93, 94, 105, 106, 107, 111, 114,
130, 132, 146

Brennan, J.H. - 262

Brown, John – 258, 259, 261, 262, 263,
264, 266, 267

Browne, Douglas Gordon - 8, 141-142

Bruce, Alexander Carmichael – 19, 40,
42, 434, 486, 488, 489

Bullen, Tom [Central News] - 11, 436,
446

Byrnes, Thomas Superintendent - 37, 55,
161, 394

Camp, Elizabeth – 144 fn, 153

Carroll, Lewis – 3

Casement, Roger Sir – 71

Cass, Elizabeth – 325, 326, 327, 328,
329, 330

Catling, Thomas – 30 fn, 473, 474
Chapman, Annie – 14, 27, 28, 30, 130, 238, 345, 349, 352, 356, 357, 361, 362, 366, 367, 368, 369, 370, 372, 373, 375, 376, 378, 379, 380, 381, 382, 383, 384, 385, 391, 405, 406, 407, 409, 410, 411, 412, 413, 419, 420, 424, 435 fn, 438, 439, 474, 519, 557, 558,
Chapman, George – 146, 148, 149, 150, 270, 271, 273
Churchill, Winston - 103 fn, 169, 185, 190, 192
Churchill, Randolph – 313
Clarke, Percy Dr. – 198, 199
Coles, Frances - 110, 111, 112, 118, 129, 132, 180, 272, 377, 458
Cook, Andrew - 318
Copeland, Meyrick Shaw – 162
Cornwell, Patricia – 321
Cox, Henry, Inspector - 151-152
Cream, Thomas Neill Dr. - 98, 198
Crook, Alice Margaret – 294, 295, 297, 298, 302, 303
Crook, Annie Elizabeth – 293, 294, 295, 296, 297, 298, 301, 304, 305, 306
Cullen, Tom - 289
Cumberland, Stuart – 235, 236
Cunliffe, Owen Frederick - 169, 170, 172
Curious [Robert Anderson], 83, 87, 88
Cutbush, Charles Henry - 16, 129
Cutbush, Thomas Hayne - 117, 118, 121, 123, 129, 130, 132, 134, 137, 153, 561, 563
Dagonet [see Sims]
Dam, Harry – 341 fn, 345, 358, 359, 364
Davis, Richard Harding - 39
Davitt, Michael - 53 fn, 71, 86
Dear Boss letter - 30, 367, 370, 372, 374, 410, 411, 435, 436, 437, 438, 439, 445, 446, 455, 475
Dear Boss letter [Montreal] - 64
Deeming, Frederick Bailey – 116
Dew, Walter – 282, 490, 491 fn, 553 fn

Digby, Kenelm – 146 fn, 163,
Divall, Tom – 226
Doyle, Arthur Conan – 117, 234, 263, 264
Druitt, Montague John - 109, 115 fn, 130, 131, 132, 138, 142, 148, 157, 202, 212, 227, 289, 290, 555, 557, 563
Dutton, Thomas Dr. – 226, 275-281, 284, 285, 286, 287
Eddowes, Catherine – 16, 112, 116, 129, 181, 183, 214, 237, 346, 374, 375, 412, 425, 426, 428, 441, 449, 473, 480, 497, 499-511, 514, 518, 525, 551, 555, 556,
Egan, Patrick – 79
Endacott, Bowden – 325, 326, 327, 328, 329
Evans, Stewart – 289, 314
Ex-Attaché [see Cunliffe-Owen]
Fairclough, Melvin – 313, 314
Farquharson, Henry Richard - 115, 131, 330, 560
Farson, Dan - 128, 287, 289
Federal Bureau of Investigation - 5, 558
Field Club - 48, 52
Findlay, Arthur – 256, 257, 258, 260, 261, 263, 264, 265
Flanagan, John Woulfe – 186, 187, 188
Frederic, Harold – 308 fn,
Froest, Frank – 223, 246
Fuller, Jean Overton - 306
Gladstone, William - 96, 121
Gonne, Maud - 164
Goremykin, Ivan Logginovitch - 158, 159, 164
Gosselin, Nicholas Sir - 25, 85 fn
Graham, Alice – 135, 196
Grant, William [aka Grainger] - 136, 137, 181, 197, 205, 255
Grasett, Henry James – 60 fn, 61, 62, 63 fn
Greaves, Edwin Tracey - 32-33
Greenberg, Leopold - 153
Griffiths, Arthur Major - 138 fn, 139, 140, 141, 150, 155, 157, 158, 197, 198,

200, 203, 204, 222, 225, 254, 562

Harcourt, William Vernon Sir - 24, 45, 155, 189

Hardie, Keir – 250, 251, 252

Heidelberg, Charles - 161

Hoare, William Robert - 86

Jack's Alive [game] - 101

Jarvis, Frederick Inspector - 53, 57, 62, 63, 67, 72-78, 80-100, 159 fn

Jenkinson, Edward Sir – 25, 26, 46, 163, 277 fn, 472

Johnson, Emma Matilda – 144 fn

Johnson, Ernie Sacheverell Wilberforce - 525

Jonas, Kasimir – 469, 470, 472

Jubilee plot – 22, 23, 86, 188, 194, 195, 196, 457

Kebbell, George – 196, 197

Kelly, John – 425, 496, 497, 498, 499, 500, 501, 502, 503, 504, 505, 506, 507, 508, 509, 511, 512

Kelly, Mary Jane – 129, 130, 236, 292, 294, 346, 376, 377, 515, 518, 525, 526, 527, 528, 529, 530, 531, 532, 533, 536, 539, 540, 542, 543, 544, 545, 546, 547, 548, 549, 553 fn, 554

Kirby, Joseph T. 53, 54, 67

Knight Stephen 1-2, 233, 238, 293, 294-297, 299, 304-306, 312, 313, 314, 517, 556, 557

Kosminski, Aaron - 6, 108, 130, 132, 134, 135, 137, 138, 157, 171, 177-180, 181, 182, 183, 184, 458, 551, 554, 555, 557, 558, 563

Labouchere, Henry - 48, 50, 81, 82, 83, 84, 87, 88, 89, 90, 91, 92, 93, 94, 95, 96, 97, 99, 100, 120, 370, 413, 439

Langhorn, [Laughon] John - 64, 66

Larkins, Edward Knight - 108 fn

Lawende, Joseph - 112, 113, 183, 480

Le Caron, Henri - 28, 69, 70, 71, 72, 86, 100, 163, 186, 191 fn

Le Grand, Charles - 117, 488

Le Queux, William – 205, 206, 207, 212, 284, 285, 286, 557

Lees, Eva – 240, 264, 265, 266, 267

Lees, Norman – 246, 247, 248

Lees, Robert James – 218, 219, 220, 238, 239, 240, 241, 242, 243, 244, 245, 246, 247, 249, 250-260, 261, 263, 264, 265, 267

Linden, R.J. Captain [Pinkertons] - 75, 76, 77

Littlechild, John George, Chief Inspector - 11, 126, 162, 203, 203, 205, 241, 248, 315, 318, 319, 320, 435, 446

Littlejohn, David – 190

Logan, Guy Bertie Harris – 201 fn, 2222, 225

Logue, Lionel – 263, 263

Longford, Lady Elizabeth – 257, 261, 262, 264, 265

Lucy, Henry W. - 68 fn, 109, 143

Lushington, Godfrey - 31, 60, 61, 91, 329, 460, 466, 469, 470, 471, 523

McCormick, Donald – 284-287, 557

M'Corquodale & Co. Limited - 31

Maclean, James Mackenzie - 114

Macnaghten, Melville Leslie Sir - 8, 11, 38, 39, 40, 72, 106, 128-134

Memorandum, 135, 137, 138, 140, 141, 142, 145, 148, 149, 150, 155, 157, 171, 177, 178, 180, 181, 183, 189, 201, 202, 203, 204, 205, 209, 210 fn, 212, 222, 224, 225, 226, 227, 232, 241, 270, 287, 288, 289, 290, 320, 377, 378, 436, 446, 456, 458, 470 fn, 472, 536, 553, 555, 561, 562, 563

Manton, Lydia - 307

Matters, Leonard - 224, 225, 226, 281, 285, 286

Matthews, Henry - 12, 16, 17, 18, 19, 21, 22, 23, 25, 26, 28, 29, 38, 41, 42, 43, 44, 45, 46, 50, 61, 70, 71, 72, 73, 82, 84, 95, 97, 99, 155, 163, 189, 193, 194, 205, 326, 330, 331, 424, 425, 426, 440, 441, 442, 444, 446, 447, 451, 452, 465, 468, 471, 472, 483, 515, 516, 517, 535

Maybrick, James – 314, 551

McKenzie, Alice – 39, 132, 180, 377, 532 fn

Melville, William - 126, 160, 211, 241, 318

Millen, Francis General - 67, 85, 86, 87, 187

Monro, Christopher - 101-102

Monro, James - 8, 16, 17, 18, 19, 21, 22, 23, 25, 26, 28, 35- 41, 42-51, 65, 85, 90, 92, 93, 94, 95, 97, 99, 100, 101, 102, 103, 104, 105, 106, 132, 141, 142, 146, 163, 177, 178, 180, 182, 185, 186, 189, 190, 191, 192, 193, 194, 195, 196, 205, 322, 331, 348, 433, 440, 442, 445, 446, 447, 470, 471, 472, 517

Moore, Henry Inspector - 300, 486

Moore, John [Central News] - 11, 436, 437

Moore-Anderson, Arthur Ponsonby – 165, 174, 175

Morland, Nigel – 231, 232, 233, 291

Morning Leader [Ripper story] - 117, 122-123

Moser, Maurice - 89

Murdoch, Charles - 61, 465, 469 fn

Murray, Alex Dr. - 9

Murray's Magazine - 17 fn, 35, 194, 514, 515

Mylius, Edward Frederick – 310, 311

Neil, Arthur Fowler – 272, 273

Neill, Stephen Bishop – 49, 50, 51,

Nicholas II Tsar - 158, 160, 164, 165

Nichols, Polly – 16, 27, 129, 323, 324, 333, 334, 336, 342, 343, 346, 355, 356, 366, 373, 374, 375, 377, 378, 379, 383, 391, 402, 411, 518, 551, 556

North Country Vicar - 140-141

O'Connor, Thomas Power - 109, 119, 120 fn, 121, 124, 125, 126, 561, 563

O'Keefe, Arthur – 187

O'Shea, William Henry Captain - 95, 96

Odell, Robin - 128, 290

Ostrog, Michael - 130, 132, 133, 134, 138, 212, 561, 563

Packer, Matthew – 484, 485, 486, 487,

488, 489, 490, 491, 492

Parke, Ernest - 125, 126, 300, 345, 358

Parnell, Charles Stewart - 8, 21, 52, 53, 57, 63, 66, 67, 74, 76, 77, 78, 80, 89, 93, 95, 96, 120, 186, 187, 439

Parnell Special Commission - 27, 69, 79

Parnellism and Crime [The Times articles] - 21, 142, 186, 187, 188, 192

Pearson, Richard Lyons Otway Lieut. Col. - 17, 26, 42, 43 death of, 44, 45, 332

Pigott, Richard – 80, 81, 186, 187

Pinkerton Detective Agency - 57, 67, 74, 76, 89, 228

Pinkerton, Robert - 57, 88-89

Pinkerton, William - 8, 57, 58, 89

Pizer, John – 343, 349, 350-368, 371, 372

Police Convalescent Home - 182

Porter, Bernard - 12

Powers, Michael Detective – 55

Prince Albert Victor [Prince Eddy] – 48, 291, 292, 293, 295, 298, 300 fn, 306, 307, 309, 310, 313, 555

Prince George – 307, 308, 309, 310, 311

Protocols of the Elders of Zion - 159

Queen Victoria - 1, 6, 23, 36, 46, 86, 143, 158, 160, 171, 195, 196, 213, spiritualism 242, 256, 257, 258, 260, 261, 262, 263, 264, 265, 266, 267; 288, 290, 291, 292, 293, 294, 307, 308, 324, 394

Race, William Nixon - 123, 124, 125

Rachkovsky, Pyotr Ivanovich - 158, 159, 164

Reade, Charles - 166, 167, 168

Reid, Edmund - 16, 138, 197, 200, 348, 521

Richardson, J. Hall – 206, 212

Ripper Legacy The - 102

Ritchie, Charles - 145, 146 fn, 535

Rumbelow, Donald - 154 fn, 296 fn

Ruggles-Brise, Evelyn John - 43 fn, 78, 426, 440 fn

Sadler, James Thomas - 111, 112, 113, 135, 136, 180, 183, 204

Sagar, Robert, Inspector - 150, 151, 152, 207-211

Salisbury Lord - 21, 46, 48, 49, 50, 81, 92, 143, 160, 187, 292, 293, 298, 299, 457, 461, 466

Satterfield, John 'Jack' - 12, 25 fn, 39

Saucy Jacky postcard - 31, 372, 411, 412, 435, 439, 475, 476, 483, 492

Schwartz, Israel – 477, 478, 479, 480, 481, 482, 483, 486

Shaw, James - 37

Sheridan, Patrick Joseph - 53, 54, 67, 80-90, 91, 92, 95, 99

Shore, John Superintendent - 57, 58, 62, 63, 67, 75, 76, 78, 80, 82, 88, 97, 98, 99

Sickert, Joseph – 292, 293, 313

Sickert, Walter – 292, 293, 294, 298, 299, 305, 306, 312, 313

Sims, George Robert - 11, 140, 141, 149, 150, 156, 157, 187, 199, 202, 203, 204, 205, 225, 248, 315, 319, 325, 436, 436, 438, 446, 562, 563

Spencer, Earl - 24, 25, 472 fn

Spicer, Robert Clifford – 267, 268

Spiering, Frank – 313

Springfield, Lincoln – 356, 358, 359, 364, 366

Star [Cutbush story] - 117-121, 560-561

Stephenson, Robert Donston – 237, 238, 552

Stewart, William - 282

Stowell, Thomas - 288-291

Stride, Elizabeth – 117, 129, 235, 371, 374, 375, 412, 459, 473, 476, 479, 480, 481, 482, 483, 486, 489, 490, 492, 493, 508 fn, 514, 553, 559

Stuart-Wortley, Charles Beilby - 17, 523, 525, 535

Sugden, Philip – 282, 283 fn

Sullivan, John T. – 220, 221, 222

Swaffer, Hannen – 256, 262, 263

Swanson, Donald Sutherland - 20, 35, 110, 111, 122 fn, 136, influenza 137;

marginalia 175-184; 212fn, 220, 228, 253, 254, 433, 436, 443, 450, 452, 453, 454, 458, 460, 477, 479, 480, 481, 482, 486, 489, 511, 554, 562

Teefy, Robert Baldwin – 59

Thick, William – 344 fn, 349, 352, 360, 362, 363, 364, 365, 366, 367 fn

Thomson, Basil Sir - 128, 142, 212

Thomson, James - 67, 85, 87

Tumblety, Francis Dr. - 36, 37, 54, 55, 56, 58 fn, 63, 65, 67, 68, 70, 73, 78, 84, 87, 203 fn, 204, 225, 246, 315-320, 394, 419, 456, 552, 557, 564

Tynan, Patrick - 160, 161, 163, 164, 320 fn

Ustinov, Peter – 6

Vassily, Nicholas – 214, 215, 216

Veteran Diplomat [see Cunliffe-Owen]

Violena, Emanuel Delbast - 350

Vincent, Howard - 13

Warren, Charles Sir - 7, 13, 16, 17, 18, 19, 20, 22, 24, 26-27, 29, 31, 33, 34-35 resignation, 38, 39 fn, 46, 51, 186, 194, 205, 326, 328, 331, 336, 348, 374, 377, 389, 422-425, 427, 428, 430, 432, 433, 434, 436, 437, 439-447, 452, 459, 460, 465, 466, 467, 468, 469, 472, 483, 488, 490, 514, 515, 516, 517, 523, 524, 525, 536, 537

Waters, Samuel – 71

Wensley, Frederick Porter – 271, 272

Wieder, Ignatius – 98

Wilkie, John Elbert – 246, 556

Williams, Montagu - 107, 108, 109, 112

Williamson, Adolphus Frederick, Chief Constable - 16, 19, 20, 40 death of; 51, 235, 410, 434, 437, 438,

Wilson, Colin – 288-291

Winslow, Forbes – 197, 200, 218, 219, 220, 222, 223, 236, 267, 367, 557

Witte, Sergei – 159

Wood, E. Thomas - 318

Wood, Malcolm - 25, 35

Woodhall, Edwin Thomas – 273, 274, 281

CPSIA information can be obtained
at www.ICGtesting.com
Printed in the USA
LVOW03s0740050816

499079LV00031B/92/P